D1608125

WITHDRAWN

Lynching and Vigilantism in the United States

Recent Titles in
Bibliographies and Indexes in American History

Lynching and Vigilantism in the United States

An Annotated Bibliography

Compiled by
NORTON H. MOSES

Bibliographies and Indexes in American History,
Number 34

GREENWOOD PRESS
Westport, Connecticut • London

Library of Congress Cataloging-in-Publication Data

Lynching and vigilantism in the United States : an annotated
 bibliography / compiled by Norton H. Moses.
          p.   cm. — (Bibliographies and indexes in American history,
    ISSN 0742–6828 ; no. 34)
     Includes bibliographical references and index.
     ISBN 0–313–30177–8 (alk. paper)
       1. Lynching—United States—Bibliography.   2. Vigilantes—United
    States—Bibliography.   I. Moses, Norton H., 1935–   . II. Series.
    Z5703.5.U5L95   1997
    [HV6457]
    016.3641'34—dc21   96–44068

British Library Cataloguing in Publication Data is available.

Library of Congress Catalog Card Number: 96–44068
ISBN: 0–313–30177–8
ISSN: 0742–6828

First published in 1997

Greenwood Press, 88 Post Road West, Westport, CT 06881
An imprint of Greenwood Publishing Group, Inc.

Printed in the United States of America

The paper used in this book complies with the
Permanent Paper Standard issued by the National
Information Standards Organization (Z39.48–1984).

10 9 8 7 6 5 4 3 2 1

With love and thanks

to a great human being,

my wife

Jeanette

Contents

Preface

The extremes of human behavior can be fascinating, a relief from the banal. Perhaps that is one reason lynchings, whether performed by vigilantes purporting to uphold law and order or by transient mobs with various goals, pull our interest into their deadly history. Or we may pursue their study for scholarly purposes. For several years, my interest in lynchings has driven me along a fascinating and scholarly road. The result is this bibliography.

I have tried to produce an accurate book which will guide others along this path. I hope it is free of errors. Some article titles may appear at first glance to be wrong, as in the case of entry number 23, but my policy has been to list the title exactly as it appears in the journal--except in the case of titles that are all capitals in the periodical, which I have changed to capitals and lower case.

I have actually read most of the works listed, including the novels. However, in the desire not to remove a possibly valuable item from the record, I have in some cases included an entry for a book or article I could not find or did not peruse. Item 3498 by Nannie Burroughs is an example.

I end Chapter III with the year 1881 and begin Chapter IV with 1882 because no statistics were kept on lynchings until the latter year. Then, the Chicago Tribune began keeping a record of lynchings on a year-to-year basis. Though the accuracy of the list has been questioned, it formed the statistical basis for many later studies of lynching.

Chapter VI, Frontier West, through 1890, ends with that year because it has become a commonplace of historical studies about the United States that the frontier ceased to exist at that time.

To the extent that my product is good, I owe a debt and much gratitude to library staffs at the following institutions: Montana State University-Billings (formerly Eastern Montana College), University of Oregon, University of Washington, University of Montana, Montana State University-Bozeman, Parmly Billings Library, Rocky Mountain College,

University of Chicago, Harvard University, Boston College, Emory University, University of Wyoming, University of California at Davis, and the Library of Congress. I went to all of those to do research.

Eastern Montana College gave me a sabbatical for part of the 1990-1991 academic year. I am thankful for that paid period of research time, some of which helped produce this bibliography.

A work such as this would be almost impossible to complete without the use of interlibrary loan facilities, and I am thankful for the cooperation of staffs at numerous libraries. Most particularly, the inter-library loan personnel at MSU-Billings, led by Ms. Pam Strait, were always extremely helpful, cooperative, dedicated, and, not least, friendly.

I also thank Mrs. Jeanne Grant of Columbia, Missouri, for her gracious kindness in allowing me to visit her home over the course of several days in 1993 to examine the lynching material collected by her late husband Donald L. Grant.

And much appreciation goes to Dr. Phil Roberts, History Department, University of Wyoming, for his help during two visits and for mailing some material to me.

My two editors at Greenwood Publishing Group--Cynthia Harris, Executive Editor, Reference Books, and Jane Lerner, Production Editor--deserve my sincere thanks. The suggestions they made after careful and detailed perusal of drafts I sent to them have helped create a much better book.

My largest debt, however, is to my wife, Dr. Jeanette Bieber-Moses. Without her encouragement, good humor, knowledge, excellent computer skills, and willingness to devote unnumbered hours to helping me, I could not have finished this book until some years from now. Therefore, with love and heartfelt appreciation to a great human being, I dedicate this book to her.

Introduction

Lynching and vigilantism had certain commonalities, which is why they are paired in this bibliography. Coming into existence in what is now the United States in the 1760s and 1770s, both involved the punishment of real or alleged miscreants by nongovernmental groups. Though vigilante groups often lynched their victims, only a minority of lynchings were done by them.

Vigilantes did not always engage in lynching. Because of that, and other reasons to be mentioned shortly, vigilantism had unique characteristics which are not applicable to all lynch mobs. Before dealing with those characteristics, it seems appropriate to try to define lynching and vigilantism.

In the United States, lynching first meant one thing, later another. Originally, and now less infamously, it was understood as nonlethal corporal punishment by extralegal groups.[1] But a change in dominant activity, from corporal punishment to murder, took place in the mid-1800s so that lynching came to mean, according to one source, an "open public murder . . . conceived and carried out more or less spontaneously by a mob."[2] If one were to speak now of a lynching, virtually all listeners would think reference was being made to a violent death, not mere corporal punishment.

The definition just given, however, satisfies neither all cases nor all people, a problem which will be addressed shortly.

Aside from the aforementioned change of activity (from corporal to lethal punishment), the other reason for the shift of meaning may have been the limitation of the term "lynching" in newspapers and periodicals to cases of murder by a mob. For example, starting with 1882, the <u>Chicago Tribune</u> began to keep lynching statistics, and they dealt only with cases of death.

Because of the two different meanings, it will be convenient here to refer to "nonlethal lynching" (or "corporal lynching") and "lethal lynching" (or "murderous lynching"), but those terms are not generally found in the literature.

The early development of murderous lynching fell between

approximately 1830 and 1860.[3] One historical condition responsible for that change was that slavery abolitionists caused an extreme reaction among their opponents, a reaction which produced fear and violence against them and against the slaves presumed to be influenced by them. Later, emancipation of the slaves was influential on the increase in lethality because the removal of slavery as a system of control over blacks caused white Southerners to resort to other forms of control; and since blacks were no longer valuable property, the new controls could more economically include killing.[4]

Because some lethal lynchings were accompanied by gross tortures and some were not, it seems appropriate to add a third category, "barbarous lynching" (or "sadistic lynching") to the two suggested earlier. Barbarous lynching was almost always fatal and can thus be considered a subcategory of murderous lynching.

Barbarous lynchings did not constitute a significant portion of murderous lynchings until the late 1800s and early 1900s. An examination of the lynchings mentioned in a highly detailed history of Ku Klux Klan violence after the Civil War reveals very few killings which were barbarous.[5] Perhaps the lesson to be drawn from that lack of sadistic lynchings during one of the most violent periods in American history is two-fold: (1) the sheer magnitude of the violence was deemed sufficient to accomplish the objects of the lynchers, and (2) the widespread resort to lethal lynchings was novel enough to satisfy most lynchers, and those with more sadistic appetites could not yet give free rein to their desires because there was not yet enough legitimation of the third type of lynching--but that was to come.

This second point is underscored by a comparison of lynch burnings in the United States for the 21 years from 1884 through 1904 and for the ten years from 1918 through 1927. During the earlier, longer period, 24 men and women were burned by lynch mobs.[6] During the later, shorter period, 43 people were roasted alive.[7] Thus, of the 3,019 people murderously lynched during 1884-1904, fewer than one percent were burned,[8] while during 1918-1927 almost ten percent of the 441 victims died in flames.[9]

Something must account for this large variance. As already suggested, the more brutal method may have received greater legitimation from earlier instances of it. Once done, it may have been easier to do again.[10] Another suggested cause is that public sentiment was becoming "inured to such things."[11] But is that just another way of talking about legitimation?

Two other possible causes are the effect of World War I and the boredom of lynch mobs with the more "humane" forms of lethal lynching. Regarding the first of these, it has been suggested that "the lust for blood and cruelty which the war did not wholly satiate doubtless stimulated the increase of burnings, mutilations, and other forms of mob sadism."[12] Yet the same author who puts forth that idea then turns around and denigrates it.[13]

Yet, can one say that lynch mobs were searching for new thrills? To do so would seem to suggest that those who engaged in such barbarities as burning people alive had participated earlier in some less brutal lynching the repetition of which would no longer give satisfaction. Except for some of the work on vigilante groups, no study has been done which posits sequential participation by the same individuals in a series of lynchings, and vigilantes seem not to have progressed to greater and greater barbarities. In some small Southern areas where many lynchings took place over a brief span of years[14] such earlier participation may have occurred--but we have no adequate records on individuals involved. In other cases, shocking horrors were perpetrated in places where no lynching had taken place for many years. In Sherman, Texas, for example, the mob fought off and drove away both the Texas Rangers and the state militia; killed its victim by burning and dynamiting the courthouse; dragged, hanged, and burned the body of the victim; and then torched a large part of the black sections of town--yet Sherman had not had a prior lynching for over forty years.[15]

One way to handle the new-thrills problem is to suggest that people participated vicariously in earlier lynchings and that when they later participated physically they were primed for baser acts. Thus, here again legitimation may have been at work. Children and adults in the "lynch belt" may have been warped over the years by hearing stories and lectures.[16] This may have preconditioned them to be brutal. There's the story of the little boy who said he had seen a man hanged and he did so want to see one burned.[17]

There are two further causes to advance for the increasing sadism of lynch mobs. One is that mob members may have obtained some sort of sexual excitement and gratification from the brutality.[18] The other is that mob members could gain a greater feeling of participation if the mob leaders drew out the suffering of the victim over a lengthy time, or more mob members could actually take part if there was an extended period of torture.

A lynching should be distinguished from the sort of mob murder which occurs during an unstructured riot situation, which raises the problem of defining lynching.

Not everyone agrees on which murders may be properly character- ized as lynchings. For instance, the beating and subsequent traffic death of Michael Griffith in the Howard Beach section of New York in 1986 has been cited as a killing for which "lynching" may not have been the proper term but to which that word will be attached "throughout history."[19]

Although numerous efforts were made in the past to create a single, all-inclusive definition of murderous lynching,[20] some recent scholarship has recognized the diversity of lynching situations, methods, goals, victims, and participants. One of the best recent studies sees lynch mobs as four different types: private mobs, terrorist mobs, posses, and mass mobs.[21] This seems to be a reasonable classification. With the sometimes differing activities and motivations of these four types, the problem of definition is made more stark.

Did a lynching have to be perpetrated by a mob? Usually, yes. But the Emmett Till murder (1955), while often considered a lynching,[22] was not a lynching as conventionally understood because it was not "communally organized"[23] and did not involve a mob (if only two people killed him-- because in most states two people are not numerous enough to constitute a mob).[24] In another instance of the use of "lynching" in a nontraditional way, a black prisoner was killed by a white guard on a prison bus.[25]

Perhaps no single definition can reasonably distinguish every murder which should be considered a lynching from those which should not, nor can one meaning take account of cases which are misclassified because of ignorance, varying interpretations, or ulterior agendas--such as the effort to load a case with emotional baggage, as when Supreme Court nominee Clarence Thomas spoke of being subjected to a "high tech lynching."[26]

Nevertheless, I offer the following definition as one that works reasonably well: a lethal lynching was a deliberate murder by a mob having a common purpose and targeting one or more previously specified individuals. The individual might be specified by name or only as an unnamed person falling into a limited category.

Notice that the definition of lethal lynching contains nothing about the instrumentality of the murder. Some people incorrectly assume that a lynching had to occur by hanging. Actually, the murder could take any form, including beating, shooting, and burning alive.

The term "vigilantism" has fewer definitional problems and little change in meaning. It is the creation and enforcement of law by organized, extralegal groups in the supposed absence of adequate law enforcement. Even that, however, will not satisfy all cases or every person. To advance a political or racial agenda and assign connotative meaning, rather than denotative meaning, people may choose to use "vigilante" or "vigilantism" when no group is involved or when no "law" is being created or enforced.

With at least working definitions established, the characteristics which distinguish vigilantism from many lynch mobs can be noted. A vigilante movement involved an organized group. It typically lasted much longer than a lynch mob. So-called vigilante "justice" was often dispensed in a semi-judicial fashion, as after a sort of trial in which the accused might have counsel and a chance to present a defense.[27] For their actions, vigilantes had justifications, such as the right of the people to rule, which arguably could withstand critical inquiry, and which many lynch mobs could not hide behind.

Turning to origins, there is less agreement about the beginning of lynching than vigilantism. One theory is that lynching originated in Virginia among patriots wanting to punish and discourage crime and collaboration with the British during the American Revolution.[28] But there are other theses about lynching's origins.[29]

Vigilantism began in what is now the United States in 1767 in South Carolina, where back-country people suffered from widespread depredations by outlaws.[30]

There have been at least 326 vigilante movements in American history.[31] They killed at least 729 people.[32] Names applied to them included vigilance committee, regulators, slickers, stranglers, committees of safety,[33] bald knobbers,[34] and white caps.[35] Some vigilante organizations were constructive, creating better communities, while others were destructive.[36] Vigilantism often occurred in frontier areas and targeted criminals.

No one will ever know how many people have been killed by lynching in the U.S.--especially when the definition of lynching has been unclear and the word is liable to misappropriation in the service of a cause. But another reason is that no collecting of yearly, national statistics occurred before 1882. From that year until 1952, which has been hailed as the first lynchless year of the twentieth century, almost 5,000 people were lynched in the U.S.[37] Most of the victims were blacks. Most lynchings occurred in the South. But almost every state has had at least one lynching. Those which have not are all in New England.[38]

American blacks have seldom committed lynchings, but some cases exist.[39]

By far the greatest number of lynchings occurred before World War II--and even before World War I. As the twentieth century progressed, there were fewer and fewer lynchings. Only a few have occurred since 1952.

This bibliography includes published works--books, articles, and government documents--as well as two types of unpublished material--theses and dissertations. Almost no attempt has been made to cite newspaper articles. Also omitted, with a few exceptions, are biographies and autobiographies, on the grounds that the portions of such books devoted to lynching and vigilantism are small. Manuscript collections are usually not cited here.

Recognizing that bibliographies are seldom complete,[40] I invite readers and researchers to send to me citations to items not herein included.

Norton H. Moses
History Department
Montana State University-Billings
Billings, MT 59101

Endnotes

[1]James Elbert Cutler, Lynch-Law: An Investigation into the History of Lynching in the United States (New York: Longmans, Green & Co., 1905), pp. 76-84.

[2]Richard Hofstadter and Michael Wallace, eds., American Violence: A Documentary History (New York: Vintage Books, 1971), p. 20.

[3]See numerous examples in Cutler, Lynch-Law, pp. 90-91, 100-01, 103, 117, 118, 119, 122-23, 124, 125, 126-27, 128-29, 132, 135.

[4]Ibid., pp. 124, 135.

[5]Allen W. Trelease, White Terror, the Ku Klux Klan Conspiracy and Southern Reconstruction (New York: Harper & Row, 1971), passim. See also Edward Raymond Turner, "The Habit of Torture," The Nation, Vol. 108, No. 2809 (May 3, 1919), p. 688.

[6]White, Rope & Faggot, p. 34, citing Cutler, Lynch-Law, n.p. [pp. 191-92]. In another place Cutler says twenty-five people were burned alive during 1891-1904; James Elbert Cutler, "The Practice of Lynching in the United States," The South Atlantic Quarterly, Vol. 6, No. 2 (April 1907), p. 134.

[7]White, Rope & Faggot, pp. 21-22. White says on p. 21 that forty-two were burned alive, but if one adds the state-by-state figures he gives on pp. 21-22, the total is forty-three.

[8]The figure 3,019 is derived from Jessie P. Guzman and W. Hardin Hughes, "Lynching--Crime," Negro Year Book: A Review of Events Affecting Negro Life 1941-1946, ed. by Jessie Parkhurst Guzman (Tuskegee, AL: Tuskegee Institute, 1947), p. 307.

[9]The figure 441 is derived from Guzman and Hughes, Negro Year Book . . . 1941-1946, p. 307. White, Rope & Faggot, p. 20, gives 454 as the total number of lynch victims during this period. By including sixteen cases of bodies burned after death and eight cases of "victims . . . beaten to death or cut to pieces," White (p. 21) lists sixty-six persons killed with great brutality; I have not included the sixteen cases (because of the difference between how a person is killed and what is done to the body after death) nor the eight cases (because of lack of detail on which to base an assessment).

[10]On legitimation of violence see Ted Robert Gurr, Why Men Rebel (Princeton: Princeton Univ. Press, 1970), pp. 168-77; Richard Maxwell Brown, Strain of Violence: Historical Studies of American Violence and Vigilantism (New York: Oxford Univ. Press, 1975), chapter 3 passim, and pp. 36, 238, 287; Edward C. Banfield, The Unheavenly City: The Nature and Future of Our Urban Crisis (Boston: Little, Brown, 1970), pp. 196-200.

[11]White, Rope & Faggot, p. 20.

[12]Ibid., p. 19. See also Frank Tannenbaum, Darker Phases of the South (New York: G. P. Putnam's Sons, 1924), pp. 13-16.

[13]White, Rope & Faggot, pp. 19-20; see also p. 38. See also Frank Shay, Judge Lynch: His First Hundred Years (New York: Ives Washburn, 1938; reprint ed., Montclair, NJ: Patterson Smith Pub. Corp., 1969), p. 95.

[14]Ralph Ginzburg, ed., 100 Years of Lynchings (New York: Lancer Books, p. 93 (eight lynchings in a Louisiana parish in five years). See also Cutler, Lynch-Law, pp. 190-91 (more lynchings in Decatur County, Georgia, than any other Georgia county, and ten lynchings in Dallas County, Alabama.

[15]Arthur F. Raper, The Tragedy of Lynching (Chapel Hill: Univ. of North Carolina Press, 1933), p. 354.

[16]O. B. Flower, "The Burning of Negroes in the South: A Protest and a Warning," The Arena, Vol. 7, No. 4 (April 1893), pp. 631, 639-40; White, Rope & Faggot, pp. 3-5.

[17]"Lynching," The Nation, Vol. 69, No. 1798 (Dec. 14, 1899), p. 440.

[18]Hadley Cantril, The Psychology of Social Movements (New York: John Wiley & Sons, 1941), pp. 115-16.

[19]J. Clay Smith, Jr., "The 'Lynching' at Howard Beach: An Annotated Bibliographic Index," National Black Law Journal, Vol. 12, No. 1 (Spring 1990), p. 29.

[20]W. Fitzhugh Brundage, Lynching in the New South: Georgia and Virginia, 1880-1930 (Urbana: Univ. of Illinois Press, 1993), pp. 17, 308 n.1; Guzman & Hughes, "Lynching--Crime," Negro Year Book 1941-46, p. 302. See Jessie Daniel Ames, The Changing Character of Lynching: Review of Lynching, 1931-1941, With a Discussion of Recent Developments in This Field (Atlanta: Commission on Interracial Cooperation, 1942), pp. 29-30, for a definition which "in effect could be made to convert into a lynching the death of every Negro at the hands of white persons."

[21]Brundage, Lynching in the New South, pp. 18-47.

[22]Simeon Booker, "30 Years Ago: How Emmett Till's Lynching Launched Civil Rights Drive," Jet, Vol. 68 (June 17, 1985), pp. 12-15, 18; Stephen J. Whitfield, A Death in the Delta: The Story of Emmett Till (New York: Free Press, 1988), p. 100, quoting Medger Evers' widow about the Till case.

[23]Ibid., pp. 57, 131.

[24]James Harmon Chadbourn, "Analysis of Anti-Lynching Laws Now Existing in the States," in "The Pro and Con Feature: Congress Considers the Costigan-Wagner Anti-Lynching Bill," Congressional Digest, Vol. 14, No. 6-7 (June-July 1935), pp. 168. The best compilation of Southern lynchings required that "a group of three or more persons must have participated in the killing"; Stewart E. Tolnay and E. M. Beck, A Festival of Violence: An Analysis of Southern Lynchings, 1882-1930 (Urbana: Univ. of Illinois Press, 1995), p. 260.

[25]Edward Bunker, "The Lynching of Vinson Harris," The Nation, Vol. 242, No. 19 (May 17, 1986), pp. 681, 697-99.

[26]Nell Irvin Painter, "Who Was Lynched?" The Nation, Vol. 253,

No. 16 (Nov. 11, 1991), p. 577; C. Thomas Preston, Jr., "Characterizing the Issue: Metaphor and Contemporary Impromptu Discussions of Gender," Argumentation and Advocacy: The Journal of the American Forensic Association, Vol. 28, No. 4 (Spring 1992), p. 187.

[27]Richard Maxwell Brown, "The American Vigilante Tradition," in The History of Violence in America: Historical and Comparative Perspectives, ed. by Hugh Davis Graham and Ted Robert Gurr (New York: Praeger, 1969), pp. 166, 170, 172-73.

[28]Alexander Brown, "Lynch Law," The Green Bag, Vol. 5, No. 3 (March 1893), p. 116; Cutler, Lynch-Law, pp. 24-40; Howell Colston Featherstone, "The Origin and History of Lynch Law," The Green Bag, Vol. 12, No. 3 (March 1900), pp. 150-58; "The Lynch Law Tree," The Green Bag, Vol. 4, No. 12 (Dec. 1892), pp. 561-62; Albert Matthews, "Lynch Law," The Nation, Vol. 75, No. 1953 (Dec. 4, 1902), pp. 439-41; Albert Matthews, "Lynch Law Once More," The Nation, Vol. 76, No. 1961 (Jan. 29, 1903), p. 91; Albert Matthews, "The Term Lynch Law," Modern Philology, Vol. 2, No. 2 (Oct. 1904), pp. 173-95 (1-23); Thomas Walker Page, "The Real Judge Lynch," The Atlantic Monthly, Vol. 88, No. 530 (Dec. 1901), pp. 731-43; William Romaine Tyree, "The Origin of Lynching," The Green Bag, Vol. 25, No. 9 (Sep. 1913), pp. 393-94.

[29]E. W., "Lynch-Law," The Spectator, Vol. 62, No. 3172 (April 13, 1889), p. 511; Featherstone, "The Origin and History of Lynch Law," pp. 151-53; Albert Matthews, "Origin of the Term Lynch Law," Publications of the Colonial Society of Massachusetts, Vol. 27 (Dec. 1929), pp. 256-71; Albert Matthews, "The Term Lynch Law," pp. 181-86 (9-14); No author, no title, The Central Law Journal, Vol. 6, No. 17 (April 26, 1878), p. 340; "Origin and Statistics Concerning Lynch Law," The American Lawyer, Vol. 5, No. 5 (May 1897), p. 215. See also Alfred Percy, Origin of the Lynch Law (Madison Heights, VA: Percy Press, 1959).

[30]Richard Maxwell Brown, Strain of Violence: Historical Studies of American Violence and Vigilantism (New York: Oxford Univ. Press, 1975), pp. 96, 98.

[31]Ibid., pp. 96, 101.

[32]Ibid., p. 102.

[33]Ibid., p. 97.

[34]A. M. Haswell, "The Story of the Bald Knobbers," The Missouri Historical Review, Vol. 18, No. 1 (Oct. 1923), pp. 27-35.

[35]Robert W. Larson, "The White Caps of New Mexico: A Study of Ethnic Militancy in the Southwest," Pacific Historical Review, Vol. 44, No. 2 (May 1975), pp. 171-85; Madeleine M. Noble, "The White Caps of Harrison and Crawford County, Indiana: A Study in the Violence Enforcement of Morality," Ph.D. diss., Univ. of Michigan, 1973.

[36]Brown, Strain of Violence, pp. 118-23.

[37]Although some sources give a definite number, such as 4,730 ("Lynching," in 1952 Negro Yearbook: A Review of Events Affecting Negro

Life, pp. 277-79, ed. by Jesse Parkhurst Guzman (New York: William H. Wise, 1952), in Allen D. Grimshaw, ed., Racial Violence in the United States (Chicago: Aldine Pub. Co., 1969), pp. 56-59), other sources dispute the number (see infra, endnotes 58 & 59).

[38]See Robert L. Zangrando, The NAACP Crusade Against Lynching, 1909-1950 (Philadelphia: Temple Univ. Press, 1980), p. 5, for a state-by-state tally of lynchings, 1882-1968. States not listed as having any lynchings are Alaska, Connecticut, Hawaii, Massachusetts, New Hampshire, and Rhode Island. Sources in this bibliography, however, deal with lynchings in Alaska and Hawaii.

[39]For examples, see Raper, The Tragedy of Lynching, p. 37; "The Lynching Spirit Again," The Voice of the Negro, Vol. 2, No. 11 (Nov. 1905), p. 750; Brundage, Lynching in the New South, 29-30, 45, 178-79, 347 n.75; Tolnay and Beck, A Festival of Violence, pp. 269, 271-72. Reportedly, a mob of blacks lynched a white man in Elkhorn, WV; see [No author; no title; in section "Editorial Notes"], The Independent, Vol. 46, No. 2384 (Aug. 9, 1894), p. 12 (1024). See report of 17-year-old white male "killed by a mob of Negroes" in Clarksville, TN: "Lynching," The Crisis, Vol. 8, No. 6 (Oct. 1914), pp. 279-81. See E. M. Beck & Stewart E. Tolnay, "When Race Didn't Matter: Black and White Mob Violence Against Their Own Color," in Under Sentence of Death: Lynching in the South, W. Fitzhugh Brundage, ed. (Chapel Hill: Univ. of North Carolina Press, forthcoming).

[40]Richard Newman, Black Access: A Bibliography of Afro-American Bibliographies (Westport, CT: Greenwood Press, 1984), p. xx.

I

General Works

1. Aguirre, Adalberto, Jr., and Baker, David V. RACE, RACISM AND THE DEATH PENALTY IN THE UNITED STATES. Berrien Spring, MI: Vande Vere Publishing, 1991. See Chap. 4, "The Socio-Cultural Dimension of the Death Penalty: Lynching as a Social Control Mechanism" (pp. 43-72). "Lynching" is given as "Lynchings" on contents page.

2. "American Vigilantes." SOCIETY, Vol. 13, No. 3 (March/April 1976): 26-52. Symposium. Most of the articles are from Vigilante Politics by Rosenbaum and Sederberg.

3. Andrews, Champe S. "Private Societies and the Enforcement of the Criminal Law." THE FORUM, Vol. 36 (Oct. 1904): 280-88. Does not deal with vigilantism as usually conceived. Mainly about large-city organizations which supplement police activities re particular types of crime.

4. "AN APPEAL TO THE CONSCIENCE OF THE CIVILIZED WORLD." RECORD OF LYNCHING. New York: National Association for the Advancement of Colored People, 1920.

5. Ayers, Edward L. VENGEANCE AND JUSTICE: CRIME AND PUNISHMENT IN THE NINETEENTH-CENTURY AMERICAN SOUTH. New York: Oxford Univ. Press, 1984. Has some material on lynch mobs.

6. Bardolph, Richard, ed. THE CIVIL RIGHTS RECORD: BLACK AMERICANS AND THE LAW, 1849-1970. New York: Crowell, 1970. See "lynching" in index.

7. Barr, Alwyn. BLACK TEXANS: A HISTORY OF NEGROES IN TEXAS, 1528-1971. Austin: Jenkins Pub. Co., 1973. Limited attention to

lynching (pp. 84-85, 136-40).

8.   Baughman, Laurence Alan. SOUTHERN RAPE COMPLEX: HUN-DRED YEAR PSYCHOSIS. Atlanta: Pendulum Books, 1966. See pp. 94, 105-06, 108-10, 159-61, 166, 169-82.

9.   Berkeley-Hill, Owen A. R. "The 'Color Question' from a Psychoanalytic Standpoint." THE PSYCHOANALYTIC REVIEW, Vol. 11, No. 3 (July 1924): 246-53.   Includes white male sexual jealousy of black males as the cause of black lynching.

10. Blalock, H. M., Jr. "Percent Black and Lynchings Revisited." SOCIAL FORCES, Vol. 67, No. 3 (March 1989): 631-33.   Comment on Tolnay, Beck, and Massey, ibid., 605-23.

11. Blauner, Robert. RACIAL OPPRESSION IN AMERICA. New York: Harper & Row, 1972.

12. Branch, Elijah Clarence. JUDGE LYNCH'S COURT IN AMERICA; THE NUMBER OF NEGRO CONVICTS IN PRISON IN AMERICA, AND OTHER INJUSTICE DONE TO THE NEGRO IN AMERICA. Houston: Elijah Clarence Branch, 1913.

13. Brawley, Benjamin Griffith. A SOCIAL HISTORY OF THE AMERI-CAN NEGRO, BEING A HISTORY OF THE NEGRO PROBLEM IN THE UNITED STATES, INCLUDING A HISTORY AND STUDY OF THE REPUBLIC OF LIBERIA. New York: Macmillan, 1921. Reprint ed.: Collier Books; New York: Macmillan, 1970.   See "Lynching" in index.

14. Brown, Richard Maxwell. "The American Vigilante Tradition." In VIOLENCE IN AMERICA, HISTORICAL AND COMPARATIVE PERSPECTIVES, Vol. 1, pp. 121-80. Ed. by Hugh Davis Graham and Ted R. Gurr. 2 vols.; Washington, DC: USGPO, 1969. Reprint: The History of Violence in America: Historical and Comparative Perspectives, pp. 154-226. Ed. by Hugh David Graham and Ted Robert Gurr. New York: Praeger, 1969.

15. Brown, Richard Maxwell. "The History of Vigilantism in America." In VIGILANTE POLITICS, pp. 79-109. Ed. by H. Jon Rosenbaum and Peter C. Sederberg. Philadelphia: Univ. of Pennsylvania Press, 1976.

16. Brown, Richard Maxwell. "Legal and Behavioral Perspectives on American Vigilantism." In PERSPECTIVES IN AMERICAN HISTORY, Vol. 5 (1971): 95-144.   Ed. by Donald Fleming and Bernard Bailyn. Cambridge: Charles Warren Center for Studies in American History,

Harvard University, 1971.

17. Brown, Richard Maxwell. STRAIN OF VIOLENCE: HISTORICAL STUDIES OF AMERICAN VIOLENCE AND VIGILANTISM. New York: Oxford Univ. Press, 1975.

18. Brown, Richard Maxwell. "Violence and Vigilantism in American History." In AMERICAN LAW AND THE CONSTITUTIONAL ORDER: HISTORICAL PERSPECTIVES, pp. 173-90. Ed. by Lawrence M. Friedman and Harry N. Scheiber. Cambridge: Harvard Univ. Press, 1978.

19. Brownmiller, Susan. AGAINST OUR WILL: MEN, WOMEN AND RAPE. New York: Simon and Schuster, 1975.   See "Lynching" in index.

20. Brundage, W. Fitzhugh, ed.   UNDER SENTENCE OF DEATH: LYNCHING IN THE SOUTH. Chapel Hill: Univ. of North Carolina Press, 1997 [forthcoming].   This is tentative title.   A collection of essays by several noted scholars.

21. Buckser, Andrew S.   "Lynching as Ritual in the American South." BERKELEY JOURNAL OF SOCIOLOGY: A CRITICAL REVIEW, Vol. 37 (1992): 11-28.

22. Burrows, William E.   VIGILANTE!   New York: Harcourt Brace Jovanovich, 1976.   History of American vigilantism and lynching. Chapter 8: Hennessy murder, 1890, and lynching of Italians in New Orleans, 1891.

23. Burrows, William E.   "The Vigilante rides again."   HARVARD MAGAZINE, Vol. 78 (Dec. 1975): 36-41.   Background of vigilantism, especially in San Francisco and Montana. Resurgence in 1960s and '70s.

24. Butcher, Jerry Lee.   "A Narrative History of Selected Aspects of Violence in the New South, 1877-1920." Ph.D. diss., Univ. of Missouri, 1977.   See Diss. Ab. Intl., Vol. 39, No. 2 (Aug. 1978): 1054A.   Includes lynching.

25. Bye, Raymond T.   CAPITAL PUNISHMENT IN THE UNITED STATES. Philadelphia: Committee on Philanthropic Labor of Philadelphia Yearly Meeting of Friends, 1919.   This was a Ph.D. diss., Univ. of Pennsylvania. See Chapter IV, "Lynching" (pp. 62-73).

26. Cantril, Hadley. THE PSYCHOLOGY OF SOCIAL MOVEMENTS. New York: John Wiley and Sons, 1941.   See Chapter 4, "The Lynching Mob" (pp. 78-122).

27. Carby, Hazel V. "'On the Threshold of Woman's Era': Lynching, Empire, and Sexuality in Black Feminist Theory." In "RACE," WRITING, AND DIFFERENCE, pp. 301-16. Ed. by Henry Louis Gates, Jr. Chicago: Univ. of Chicago Press, 1986. Originally published in Critical Inquiry, Vol. 12, No. 1 (Autumn 1985): 262-77. Considers the work of three African-American women in the 1890s, including Ida B. Wells on race, gender, and patriarchal power.

28. Carter, Hodding. WHERE MAIN STREET MEETS THE RIVER. New York: Rinehart, 1953. See Chap. 18, "Just What Is a Lynching?" (pp. 228-44). Problems about which murders should be classified as lynchings, and with proposed federal anti-lynching laws.

29. Cash, W. J. THE MIND OF THE SOUTH. New York: Knopf, 1941. See "Lynching" and "Violence" in index.

30. Cassity, Michael J., ed. CHAINS OF FEAR: AMERICAN RACE RELATIONS SINCE RECONSTRUCTION. Westport, CT: Greenwood Press, 1984. See "Lynching," "Violence," and "Whitecapping" in index.

31. Cassity, Michael J., ed. LEGACY OF FEAR: AMERICAN RACE RELATIONS TO 1900. Westport, CT: Greenwood Press, 1985. See "Lynching" and "Violence" in index. Pages 238-44 duplicate pp. 154-60 in Chains of Fear.

32. Caughey, John W. THEIR MAJESTIES THE MOB. Chicago: Univ. of Chicago Press, 1960.

33. Caughey, John W. "Their Majesties the Mob: Vigilantes Past and Present." PACIFIC HISTORICAL REVIEW, Vol. 26, No. 3 (Aug. 1957): 217-34.

34. Chapman, David L. "Lynching in Texas." M.A. thesis, Texas Tech Univ., 1973.

35. "Children of the Slaves." THE SPECTATOR [London], Vol. 125, No. 4822 (Nov. 27, 1920): 703-05. Lynching in the U.S.

36. Clayton, Bruce. "The Proto-Dorian Convention: W. J. Cash and the Race Question." In RACE, CLASS, AND POLITICS IN SOUTHERN HISTORY: ESSAYS IN HONOR OF ROBERT F. DURDEN, pp. 260-88. Ed. by Jeffrey J. Crow, Paul D. Escott, and Charles L. Flynn, Jr. Baton Rouge: Louisiana State Univ. Press, 1989. The Proto-Dorian Convention was the "bonding of the highest and lowest white classes" to keep blacks in a second-class status (p. 260). See pp. 263, 285-86 for lynching.

37. Clayton, Bruce. THE SAVAGE IDEAL: INTOLERANCE AND INTELLECTUAL LEADERSHIP IN THE SOUTH, 1890-1914. The Johns Hopkins University Studies in Historical and Political Science, Ninetieth Series. Baltimore: Johns Hopkins Univ. Press, 1972. The Savage Ideal was suppression of dissent and variety (p. 2). See "Lynchings" in index.

38. Cohen, William. AT FREEDOM'S EDGE: BLACK MOBILITY AND THE SOUTHERN WHITE QUEST FOR RACIAL CONTROL 1861-1915. Baton Rouge: Louisiana State Univ. Press, 1991.

39. Coker, Francis W. "Lynching." In ENCYCLOPAEDIA OF THE SOCIAL SCIENCES, Vol. 9, pp. 639-43. Edited by Edwin R. A. Seligman and Alvin Johnson. 15 vols. in 8; New York: Macmillan, 1930-35.

40. Congdon, Charles T. "Private Vengeance." THE NORTH AMERICAN REVIEW, Vol. 139, No. 332 (July 1884): 67-77. Deals with revenge; has brief references to lynch law and vigilantism.

41. Corzine, Jay; Creech, James; Corzine, Lin. "Black Concentration and Lynchings in the South: Testing Blalock's Power-threat Hypothesis." SOCIAL FORCES, Vol. 61, No. 3 (March 1983): 774-96.

42. Corzine, Jay; Huff-Corzine, Lin; and Creech, James C. "The Tenant Labor Market and Lynching in the South: A Test of Split Labor Market Theory." SOCIOLOGICAL INQUIRY, Vol. 58, No. 3 (Summer 1988): 261-78. Abstract: "We conclude that racial violence linked to economic competition between working-class whites and blacks was limited to that part of the South dominated by the plantation system."

43. Cox, Oliver Cromwell. CASTE, CLASS, & RACE: A STUDY IN SOCIAL DYNAMICS. Garden City, NY: Doubleday, 1948. See "Lynching" in index and especially pp. 548-64.

44. Creech, James C.; Corzine, Jay; Huff-Corzine, Lin. "Theory Testing and Lynching: Another Look at the Power Threat Hypothesis." SOCIAL FORCES, Vol. 67, No. 3 (March 1989): 626-30.

45. Cross, Samuel Creed. THE NEGRO AND THE SUNNY SOUTH. Martinsburg, WV: S. C. Cross, 1899. Chapter XI, "Persecution of the Negro" (pp. 78-90), includes lynching.

46. Culberson, William C. VIGILANTISM: POLITICAL HISTORY OF PRIVATE POWER IN AMERICA. Contributions in Criminology and Penology Number 28. New York and Westport, CT: Greenwood Press, 1990.

47. Cutler, J[ames] E[lbert]. "Capital Punishment and Lynching." THE ANNALS OF THE AMERICAN ACADEMY OF POLITICAL AND SOCIAL SCIENCE, Vol. 29, No. 3 (May 1907): 182-85 [622-25].   Argues that lynchings are more likely to occur if the death penalty is not available to satisfy the popular desire for justice.

48. Cutler, James E. LYNCH LAW: AN INVESTIGATION INTO THE HISTORY OF LYNCHING IN THE UNITED STATES. New York: Longmans, Green & Co., 1905.   Longtime standard work.

49. Cutler, James E. PROPOSED REMEDIES FOR LYNCHING. New Haven, 1904. From "Proposed Remedies for Lynching," The Yale Review, Vol. 13, [No. 2] (Aug. 1904): 194-212. Proposed remedies: public opinion and various laws. Gives details on the few people indicted and/or imprisoned for lynching.

50. Cutler, James Elbert. "The Practice of Lynching in the United States." THE SOUTH ATLANTIC QUARTERLY, Vol. 6, No. 2 (April 1907): 125-134.   Numbers 1 and 2 of this volume incorrectly state they are in Vol. 5.

51. "Cutler's Lynch Law." THE NATION, Vol. 81, No. 2090 (July 20, 1905): 57-58.   Mainly a review of his book. Page 57: "The [lynching] affair was simply a variant of the English sportsman's inspiration, 'What a beautiful day! Let's go out and kill something.'"

52. Dahlke, H. Otto. "Comment on Hart's 'Some Cultural-Lag Problems Which Social Science Has Solved.'" AMERICAN SOCIOLOGICAL REVIEW, Vol. 16, No. 4 (Aug. 1951): 551-53.   Especially critical of Hornell Hart's statements about lynching.

53. Dahlke, H. Otto. "Comment on Hart's Rejoinder." AMERICAN SOCIOLOGICAL REVIEW, Vol. 16, No. 6 (Dec. 1951): 841-42.   See Hart, Hornell.

54. Davie, Maurice R. NEGROES IN AMERICAN SOCIETY. New York: McGraw-Hill, 1949.   See Chapter 16: "Lynchings and Race Riots," and index, same headings and "Violence."

55. Davis, Angela Y. WOMEN, RACE & CLASS. New York: Random House, 1981.   See Chapter 11, "Rape, Racism and the Myth of the Black Rapist" (pp. 172-201). Includes successive rationalizations for post-bellum lynching of blacks. Includes anti-lynching leadership of black women, followed much later by white women.

56. Davis, John P. THE AMERICAN NEGRO REFERENCE BOOK.

Englewood Cliffs, NJ: Prentice-Hall, [1966].   See index for lynching.

57. Davison, Charles Clement. "Race Friction in the South Since 1865." Doctor of Theology diss., Southern Baptist Theological Seminary, 1922. Chapter III includes some material on lynching.

58. Day, Beth. SEXUAL LIFE BETWEEN BLACKS AND WHITES: THE ROOTS OF RACISM. New York: World Publishing, 1972.   See "Lynchings" in index.

59. Doob, Leonard W. SOCIAL PSYCHOLOGY: AN ANALYSIS OF HUMAN BEHAVIOR. New York: Henry Holt and Co., 1952.   See pp. 286-92 for lynching. Much of it is quoted from Southern Commission on the Study of Lynching, Lynchings and What They Mean.

60. Dowd, Jerome. THE NEGRO IN AMERICAN LIFE. New York: The Century Co., 1926.   See Chapter 16 for lynching and Chapter 17 for "Other Outrages upon Negroes."

61. Dumond, Dwight Lowell. ANTI-SLAVERY: THE CRUSADE FOR FREEDOM IN AMERICA.   Ann Arbor: Univ. of Michigan Press, 1961. See chapter on "Lynch Law."

62. Dvorak, James Patrick, Jr. "Louis I. Jaffe: A Southern Liberal's Critique of Lynching." M.A. thesis, Univ. of Virginia, 1991.

63. Dyrda, Cynthia Ann. "Lynching as a Social Effect of Modernization in the Early Twentieth Century America." Honors thesis, Pennsylvania State Univ., 1983.

64. Estes, Mary Elizabeth.   "An Historical Survey of Lynchings in Oklahoma and Texas." M.A. thesis, Univ. of Oklahoma, 1942.

65. Evans, Maurice S. BLACK AND WHITE IN THE SOUTHERN STATES: A STUDY OF THE RACE PROBLEM IN THE UNITED STATES FROM A SOUTH AFRICAN POINT OF VIEW. London and New York: Longmans, Green and Co., 1915. See index: "Lynchings."

66. Faris, John. "On 'Race, Sex, and Violence.'" AMERICAN JOURNAL OF SOCIOLOGY, Vol. 81, No. 3 (Nov. 1975): 634-35.   See Schulman, Gary I., in this chapter.

67. Finkelman, Paul, ed. LYNCHING, RACIAL VIOLENCE, AND LAW. New York: Garland, 1992. Vol. 9 of RACE, LAW, AND AMERICAN HISTORY, 1700-1990. THE AFRICAN-AMERICAN EXPERIENCE: AN

ELEVEN-VOLUME ANTHOLOGY OF SCHOLARLY ARTICLES. Reprints of 16 articles.

68. Fisher, William H. THE INVISIBLE EMPIRE: A BIBLIOGRAPHY OF THE KU KLUX KLAN. Metuchen, NJ: Scarecrow Press, 1980. The KKK is sometimes considered a vigilante organization.

69. Fligstein, Neil. GOING NORTH: MIGRATION OF BLACKS AND WHITES FROM THE SOUTH, 1900-1950. New York: Academic Press, 1981. See "Lynchings" in index.

70. Foner, Philip S. MARK TWAIN: SOCIAL CRITIC. New York: International Publishers, 1958. See "Lynching of Negroes" (pp. 218-21) for Twain's opposition to lynching and his unfulfilled plan to write a book on lynching.

71. Fredrickson, George M. THE BLACK IMAGE IN THE WHITE MIND: THE DEBATE ON AFRO-AMERICAN CHARACTER AND DESTINY, 1817-1914. New York: Harper and Row, 1972, ©1971. See "Lynching" in index. Chapter 9 is "The Negro as Beast: Southern Negrophobia at the Turn of the Century."

72. Friedman, Lawrence J.. THE WHITE SAVAGE: RACIAL FANTA-SIES IN THE POSTBELLUM SOUTH. Englewood Cliffs, NJ: Prentice-Hall, 1970. See "Lynching of Negroes" in index and "(see also specific individuals)."

73. Fritz, Christian G. "Popular Sovereignty, Vigilantism, and the Constitutional Right of Revolution." PACIFIC HISTORICAL REVIEW, Vol. 63, No. 1 (Feb. 1994): 39-66.

74. Fry, Gladys-Marie. NIGHT RIDERS IN BLACK FOLK HISTORY. Athens: Univ. of Georgia Press, 1991. See Chapter 3 on ante-bellum patrols, and Chapter 4 and Chapter 5 on Reconstruction KKK.

75. Gauba, Kanhaya Lal. UNCLE SHAM: BEING THE STRANGE TALE OF A CIVILIZATION RUN AMOK. 3d ed.; Lahore, India: Times Pub. Co., 1929. Attack on U.S. culture as reply to Katherine Mayo's attack on Indian culture in Mother India. Chapters IV and V include lynching.

76. George, John Palmer. "'With friends like that . . .': The role of the white upper class in the etiology of Southern racism, 1790-1975." Ph.D. diss., Mississippi State Univ., 1990. See Diss. Ab. Intl., Vol. 52, No. 7 (Jan. 1992): 2714A.

77. Giddings, Paula. WHEN AND WHERE I ENTER: THE IMPACT OF BLACK WOMEN ON RACE AND SEX IN AMERICA. New York: Morrow, 1984.   See "Lynching" in index. Page 79n.: "Between 1840 and 1860 there were three hundred recorded victims hanged or burned by mobs. Of that figure only 10 percent were Black."

78. Ginzburg, Ralph, ed. 100 YEARS OF LYNCHINGS. New York: Lancer Books, 1962.   Reprint: Baltimore: Black Classic Press, 1988.   See pp. 253-70 for state-by-state partial list of blacks lynched since 1859.

79. Goldbeck, J. Helen, ed. A SURVEY OF THE BLACKS' RESPONSE TO LYNCHING. Las Vegas, NM: New Mexico Highlands Univ. Media Materials Center, 1973.

80. Goode, Stephen. VIOLENCE IN AMERICA. New York: J. Messner, 1984.   Includes lynching and vigilantism.

81. Grant, Donald L. THE WAY IT WAS IN THE SOUTH: THE BLACK EXPERIENCE IN GEORGIA. New York: Birch Lane Press, Carol Publishing Group, 1993.   See "Antilynching," "Lynching," and "Whitecapping" in index.

82. [Green, Fletcher Melvin.] G., F. M. "Lynching and Lynch Law." ENCYCLOPEDIA BRITANNICA (Chicago, 1963), Vol. 14, pp. 526-27.

83. Greenberg, Jack. RACE RELATIONS AND AMERICAN LAW. New York: Columbia Univ. Press, 1959.   See pp. 320-22. See "Statutes Forbidding Lynchings" (pp. 394-96).

84. Griffin, Farah Jasmine. "Who Set You Flowin'? Migration, Urbanization, and African-American Culture." Ph.D. diss., Yale Univ., 1992. See Diss. Ab. Intl., Vol. 53, No. 12, Part I (June 1993): 4373A.

85. Grimshaw, Allen D. "Lawlessness and Violence in America and Their Special Manifestations in Changing Negro-White Relationships." THE JOURNAL OF NEGRO HISTORY, Vol. 44, No. 1 (Jan. 1959): 52-72.

86. Grossman, James R. "Black Labor Is the Best Labor: Southern White Reactions to the Great Migration." In BLACK EXODUS: THE GREAT MIGRATION FROM THE AMERICAN SOUTH, pp. 51-71.   Ed. by Alferdteen Harrison. Jackson: University Press of Mississippi, 1992.

87. Harper, Suzanne. "Lynching and the Intersection of Class, Gender, and Racial Oppression." M.A. thesis, Univ. of Texas, 1990.

88. Hart, Albert Bushnell. THE SOUTHERN SOUTH. New York and London: D. Appleton and Co., 1910.   See Chapter XV, "Lynching" (pp. 205-17), and pp. 361-65.

89. Hart, Hornell. "Has Social Science Solved Any Cultural-Lag Problems? A Rejoinder to H. Otto Dahlke."   AMERICAN SOCIOLOGICAL REVIEW, Vol. 16, No. 6 (Dec. 1951): 840-41.   Includes lynching.

90. Hart, Hornell. "Some Cultural-Lag Problems Which Social Science Has Solved." AMERICAN SOCIOLOGICAL REVIEW, Vol. 16, No. 2 (April 1951): 223-27.   Includes lynching decline as indication that society can develop methods to reduce "some of the menaces created by modern civilization" (p. 223). See also Dahlke, H. Otto.

91. Heard, Eliza (pseudonym). "In the Name of Southern Womanhood." In SOUTHERN RAPE COMPLEX: HUNDRED YEAR PSYCHOSIS, pp. 169-82.   Laurence Alan Baughman.   Atlanta: Pendulum Books, 1966. Originally published in New South (Nov.-Dec. 1962).

92. "History of Lynchings in America." SEPIA, Vol. 7, No. 11 (Nov. 1959): 51-53.   First of two parts. Largely black perspective. "Story by George Daniels." Concluded in "History of Lynchings in America." SEPIA, Vol. 7, No. 12 (Dec. 1959): 60-62 (Groveland Four case, Florida, 1949-1951).

93. Hodes, Martha. "Sex across the Color Line: White Women and Black Men in the Nineteenth Century American South." Ph.D. diss., Princeton Univ., 1991.   See Diss. Ab. Intl., Vol. 52, No. 4 (Oct. 1991): 1489A.

94. Hoot, John W. "Lynch Law: the Practice of Illegal Popular Co-ercion." Ph.D. diss., Univ. of Pennsylvania, 1935.

95. Hoskins, Richard Kelly. VIGILANTES OF CHRISTENDOM: THE STORY OF THE PHINEAS PRIESTHOOD. Lynchburg, VA: Virginia Pub. Co., 1990.   Fundamentalist Christian, white racist examination of some historical events. Includes statements about the future and a sort of call to battle. Pages 361-64 deal with lynchings. Negatively analyzed in Klanwatch Intelligence Report [Montgomery, AL], No. 83 (Aug. 1996): 1-5.

96. Hovland, Carl Iver, and Sears, Robert R. "Minor Studies of Aggression: VI. Correlation of Lynchings with Economic Indices." THE JOURNAL OF PSYCHOLOGY, Vol. 9 [No. 2] (April 1940): 301-10.

97. Hunton, George K. "Lynching and Mob Violence." THE SIGN, Vol. 16, No. 3 (Oct. 1936): 139-40.   General.

98. Johnson, Charles S. GROWING UP IN THE BLACK BELT: NEGRO YOUTH IN THE RURAL SOUTH. Washington, DC: American Council on Education, 1941.   See "Lynching" in index (pp. 316-18, interesting information).

99. Johnson, Charles S. THE NEGRO IN AMERICAN CIVILIZATION: A STUDY OF NEGRO LIFE AND RACE RELATIONS IN THE LIGHT OF SOCIAL RESEARCH. New York: Henry Holt and Co., 1930.   See "Lynching" in index.

100. Johnson, Charles S., et al., eds. STATISTICAL ATLAS OF SOUTHERN COUNTIES.   Chapel Hill: Univ. of North Carolina Press, 1941. Includes Tuskegee Institute's data on lynching, 1900-1931, used to compile map.   See Table 29, "Distribution of Counties According to Type and Lynching Rate (Number per 100,000 Population)," p. 32, and accompanying text, pp. 31-32.   In the County Tables for each state, see VI. B. Lynchings. For sources and methods of computing lynching data, see pp. 297-98; source was county map in Lynchings and What They Mean--General Findings of the Southern Commission on the Study of Lynching (Atlanta, 1931).

101. Johnson, Guy B. "Patterns of Race Conflict." In RACE RELATIONS AND THE RACE PROBLEM: A DEFINITION AND AN ANALYSIS, Chapter V, pp. 125-51.   Ed. by Edgar T. Thompson.   Durham: Duke Univ. Press, 1939.   Includes violence during Reconstruction, and lynching.

102. Jordan, Philip D. "Lincoln and Mob Rule." In FRONTIER LAW & ORDER: TEN ESSAYS, pp. 38-42. Philip D. Jordan. Lincoln: Univ. of Nebraska Press, 1970.   Originally published as "Lincoln's Views on Mob Action," Lincoln Herald, Vol. 70, No. 2 (Summer 1968): 73-76.

103. Kastler, Norman M. "The Abatement of Lynching of Negroes in the United States." M.A. thesis, Univ. of Wisconsin, 1928.

104. Kirven, Lamar L. "A Century of Warfare, Black Texans." Ph.D. diss., Indiana Univ., 1974.   See Diss. Ab. Intl., Vol. 35, No. 10 (April 1975): 6640A-6641A.

105. Kotecha, Kanti C., and Walker, James L.   "Vigilantism and the American Police." In VIGILANTE POLITICS, pp. 158-72. Ed. by H. Jon Rosenbaum and Peter C. Sederberg.   Philadelphia: Univ. of Pennsylvania Press, 1976.   A somewhat more detailed, longer version of "Police Vigilantes," Society, Vol. 13, No. 3 (March/April 1976): 48-52.

106. Kovel, Joel. WHITE RACISM: A PSYCHOHISTORY. New York: Columbia Univ. Press, 1984.   Index lists "Lynching" only on p. 67.

107. Kremer, Gary R., and Holland, Antonio F. MISSOURI'S BLACK HERITAGE, REVISED EDITION. Rev. ed.; Columbia, MO: Univ. of Missouri Press, 1993. See "Lynchings" in index.

108. Kreml, William P. "The Vigilante Personality." In VIGILANTE POLITICS, pp. 45-63. Ed. by H. Jon Rosenbaum and Peter C. Sederberg. Philadelphia: Univ. of Pennsylvania Press, 1976.

109. Lang, Kurt, and Lang, Gladys Engel. COLLECTIVE DYNAMICS. New York: Thomas Y. Crowell, 1961. See "Lynchings" in index.

110. Langford, B. J. A CONFLAGRATION OF SOULS. Plano, TX: B. J. Langford, 1977. Provides details of about 63 cases of men and women burned alive in the U.S. from 1900 onward.

111. LaPiere, Richard T. COLLECTIVE BEHAVIOR. New York: McGraw-Hill, 1938. See "The Lynching of Negroes," pp. 538-40, and "Extralegal 'Justice,'" pp. 540-42.

112. Lay, Howard D. "Governmental Liability Resulting From Mob Violence." JOURNAL OF THE MISSOURI BAR, Vol. 26, No. 8 (Aug. 1970): 406-18.

113. Leach, Eugene E. "Mastering the Crowd: Collective Behavior and Mass Society in American Social Thought, 1917-1939." AMERICAN STUDIES, Vol. 27, No. 1 (Spring 1986): 99-114.

114. Leach, Eugene E. "'Mental Epidemics': Crowd Psychology and American Culture, 1890-1940." AMERICAN STUDIES, Vol. 33, No. 1 (Spring 1992): 5-29. Brief references to lynching (p. 17) in broader context of crowd behavior.

115. Liska, Allen E. "A Critical Examination of Macro Perspectives on Crime Control." ANNUAL REVIEW OF SOCIOLOGY, Vol. 13 (1987): 67-88. See p. 79 for paragraph on lynching and references to articles.

116. Liska, Allen E. "Introduction to the Study of Social Control." In SOCIAL THREAT AND SOCIAL CONTROL, pp. 1-29. Ed. by Allen E. Liska. Albany: State University of New York Press, 1992.

117. Loescher, Frank S. THE PROTESTANT CHURCH AND THE NEGRO: A PATTERN OF SEGREGATION. New York: Association Press, 1948. See "Lynching" and "Mob violence" in index.

118. Loescher, Frank S. "The Protestant Church and the Negro: Recent

Pronouncements." SOCIAL FORCES, Vol. 26, No. 2 (Dec. 1947): 197-201. Includes lynching.

119. Lucas, Marion B. A HISTORY OF BLACKS IN KENTUCKY. 2 vols.; n.p.: Kentucky Historical Society, 1992. See I, 187-95; II, 46-48, 79-92.

120. "Lynch Law in General." THE AMERICAN MONTHLY REVIEW OF REVIEWS, Vol. 28, No. 3 (Sept. 1903): 266. A paragraph on causes, diminution, and remedies.

121. "Lynching." In 1952 NEGRO YEAR BOOK, pp. 275-79. Ed. by Jessie Parkhurst Guzman. 11th ed.; New York: Wm. H. Wise & Co., 1952.

122. "Lynching." In RACE RIOTS IN BLACK AND WHITE, pp. 31-38. Ed. by J. Paul Mitchell. A Spectrum Book. Englewood Cliffs, NJ: Prentice-Hall, 1970. Includes "Fred Alexander Dies at Stake." Victim was black man burned at Leavenworth, KS. From The Denver Republican, Jan. 16, 1901.

123. Madison, Arnold. VIGILANTISM IN AMERICA. New York: Seabury Press, 1973.

124. Maier, Pauline. "Popular Uprisings and Civil Authority in Eighteenth-Century America." WILLIAM AND MARY QUARTERLY, Third Series, Vol. 27, No. 1 (Jan. 1970): 3-35. Includes the "role of the mob as an extralegal arm of the community's interest" (p. 5).

125. Mangum, Charles S., Jr. THE LEGAL STATUS OF THE NEGRO. Chapel Hill: Univ. of North Carolina Press, 1940. See Chapter XI, "Mob Domination and Violence" (pp. 274-307), on lynching and law relating thereto.

126. Manheim, Jarol B., and Wallace, Melanie, eds. POLITICAL VIOLENCE IN THE UNITED STATES 1875-1974: A BIBLIOGRAPHY. New York: Garland Publishing, 1975. Includes "The Violent Response: Vigilantism, Lynching, Police Violence," pp. 78-95. Contains many errors, incomplete entries, and entries which are not about violence in the U.S.

127. Martin, Everett Dean. "Some Mechanisms Which Distinguish the Crowd from Other Forms of Social Behavior." THE JOURNAL OF ABNORMAL PSYCHOLOGY AND SOCIAL PSYCHOLOGY, Vol. 18, No. 3 (Oct.-Dec. 1923): 187-203. Brief references to lynching (pp. 188, 190, 194); see especially p. 198.

128. McDougall, William. THE GROUP MIND: A SKETCH OF THE PRINCIPLES OF COLLECTIVE PSYCHOLOGY WITH SOME ATTEMPT TO APPLY THEM TO THE INTERPRETATION OF NATIONAL LIFE AND CHARACTER. 2d ed.; New York: G. P. Putnam's Sons, 1920. See pp. 67-68 for Southern lynch mobs.

129. McKinney, T. T. ALL WHITE AMERICA. A CANDID DISCUSSION OF RACE MIXTURE AND RACE PREJUDICE IN THE UNITED STATES. Boston: Meader Pub. Co., 1937. See Chapter V, "Rape Fiend and Lynching Fiend--Twin Monsters" (pp. 77-96).

130. McPherson, James M., et al. BLACKS IN AMERICA, BIBLIOGRAPHICAL ESSAYS. Garden City, NY: Doubleday & Co., 1971. See pp. 140 ff., "Racial Violence: Lynching and Riots."

131. Meier, Norman C., Mennenga, G. H., and Stoltz, H. J. "An Experimental Approach to Study of Mob Behavior." THE JOURNAL OF ABNORMAL AND SOCIAL PSYCHOLOGY, Vol. 36, No. 4 (Oct. 1941): 506-24. An attempt to generate information about responses and motives in lynching situations.

132. Mintz, Alexander. "A Re-examination of Correlations Between Lynchings and Economic Indices." THE JOURNAL OF ABNORMAL AND SOCIAL PSYCHOLOGY, Vol. 41, No. 2 (April 1946): 154-60. Another look at data used by Hovland and Sears.

133. Moore, John Bassett. A DIGEST OF INTERNATIONAL LAW. 8 vols.; Washington, DC: Government Printing Office, 1906. See Vol. 6, pp. 837-52 for lynching.

134. Myers, Martha A. "The New South's 'New' Black Criminal: Rape and Punishment in Georgia, 1870-1940." In ETHNICITY, RACE, AND CRIME: PERSPECTIVES ACROSS TIME AND PLACE, pp. 145-66. Ed. by Darnell F. Hawkins. Albany: State University of New York Press, 1995. "Examines the relationship between criminal penalties for sexual assault and lynchings on the pretext of sexual assault" (p. 147).

135. Myrdal, Gunnar. AN AMERICAN DILEMMA: THE NEGRO PROBLEM AND MODERN DEMOCRACY. New York: Harper & Brothers, 1944. See "lynching" in index.

136. The National Board of the National Sharecroppers Fund. END THE SHAME OF LYNCHING. New York: National Board of the National Sharecroppers Fund, n.d. In "Lynching" folder, Schomburg Collection, New York Public Library.

137. Nearing, Scott. BLACK AMERICA. New York: Vanguard Press, 1929. See lynching photos, pp. 189-95. See Chapter 19, "Lynch Law" (pp. 197-212).

138. Newton, Michael, and Newton, Judy Ann. THE KU KLUX KLAN: AN ENCYCLOPEDIA. New York: Garland Publishing, 1991. "Lynching" entry, pp. 363-64. Some errors. "Vigilantes" and "Vigilantes, Inc." entries, p. 504.

139. Newton, Michael, and Newton, Judy Ann. RACIAL & RELIGIOUS VIOLENCE IN AMERICA: A CHRONOLOGY. New York: Garland, 1991. See "Lynchings" (pp. 688-705) in index.

140. Newton, Michael, and Newton, Judy Ann, eds. TERRORISM IN THE UNITED STATES AND EUROPE, 1800-1959: AN ANNOTATED BIBLIOGRAPHY. New York: Garland, 1988. Includes sections on "Lynching" and "Racial Violence." Has many errors, incomplete entries, items which have nothing to do with terrorism or violence, and many annotations which misstate the subject of the item.

141. Nolen, Claude H. THE NEGRO'S IMAGE IN THE SOUTH: THE ANATOMY OF WHITE SUPREMACY. Lexington: Univ. of Kentucky Press, 1967. See "Lynching" and "Mob violence" in index.

142. Notch, Frank K. (pseud.) KING MOB: A STUDY OF THE PRESENT-DAY MIND. New York: Harcourt, Brace and Co., 1930. Does not deal directly with lynching.

143. O'Brien, Kenneth Paul. "The Savage and the Child in Historical Perspective; Images of Blacks in Southern White Thought, 1830-1915." Ph.D. diss., Northwestern Univ., 1974. See Diss. Ab. Intl., Vol. 35, No. 6 (Dec. 1974): 3651A.

144. Olds, Madelin Joan. "The Rape Complex in the Postbellum South." Ph.D. diss., Carnegie-Mellon Univ., 1989. See Diss. Ab. Intl., Vol. 50, No. 5 (Nov. 1989): 1407A-1408A.

145. Olzak, Susan. "Analysis of Events in the Study of Collective Action." ANNUAL REVIEW OF SOCIOLOGY, Vol. 15 (1989): 119-41. Has little directly about lynching.

146. Painter, Nell Irvin. "'Social Equality,' Miscegenation, Labor, and Power." In THE EVOLUTION OF SOUTHERN CULTURE, pp. 47-67. Numan V. Bartley. Athens: Univ. of Georgia Press, 1988. Includes lynchings as "symbolic rapes" for the maintenance of white supremacy, which

was rooted in "the creation and maintenance of a powerless working class" (p. 63). Ends with some reasons for lynching's decline.

147. Peters, William. THE SOUTHERN TEMPER. Garden City, NY: Doubleday, 1959. See pp. 33-35 for female participation in lynching and in anti-lynching activities.

148. Ploski, Harry A., and Marr, Warren, II, eds. THE NEGRO ALMANAC: A REFERENCE WORK ON THE AFRO AMERICAN. Third ed. (1976 Bicentennial Edition); New York: Bellwether Co., 1976. See "Lynching," pp. 275-78.

149. Polk, William Tannahill. SOUTHERN ACCENT: FROM UNCLE REMUS TO OAK RIDGE. New York: Morrow, 1953. See pp. 158-61 for lynching and vigilantism.

150. Potholm, Christian P. "Comparative Vigilantism: The United States and South Africa." In VIGILANTE POLITICS, pp. 175-93. Ed. by J. Jon Rosenbaum and Peter C. Sederberg. Philadelphia: Univ. of Pennsylvania Press, 1976.

151. Powdermaker, Hortense. AFTER FREEDOM: A CULTURAL STUDY IN THE DEEP SOUTH. New York: The Viking Press, 1939. See "Lynching" in index [pp. 2, 52-55].

152. Raper, Arthur F. "Lynching and Racial Exploitation." In JUDGE LYNCH: HIS FIRST HUNDRED YEARS, pp. v-xxix. Frank Shay. Montclair, NJ: Patterson Smith Pub. Corp., 1969. See Taylor, Alva W.

153. Reed, John Shelton. "Comment on Tolnay, Beck, and Massey." SOCIAL FORCES, Vol. 67, No. 3 (March 1989): 624-25.

154. Reed, John Shelton. "A Note on the Control of Lynching." THE PUBLIC OPINION QUARTERLY, Vol. 33, No. 2 (Summer 1969): 268-71. Asserts that if the number of lynchings increased in one year, the number declined the following year (perhaps because better-class whites deplored negative publicity and used their influence accordingly); and after a down year "a greater proportion of attempted lynchings succeed" (perhaps because "lynchings diverted plebian aggression" away from better-class whites).

155. Reed, John Shelton. "Percent Black and Lynching: A Test of Blalock's Theory." SOCIAL FORCES, Vol. 50, No. 3 (March 1972): 356-60.

156. Reed, John Shelton. "Reply to Tufte." THE PUBLIC OPINION QUARTERLY, Vol. 33, No. 4 (Winter 1969-70): 625-26.

157. Reed, John Shelton; Doss, Gail E.; and Hurlbert, Jeanne S. "Too Good to be False: An Essay in the Folklore of Social Science." SOCIO-LOGICAL INQUIRY, Vol. 57, No. 1 (Winter 1987): 1-11.   On the doubts about Hovland and Sears' alleged correlation between lynchings and cotton-price fluctuations not being as well known as the original idea.

158. Reimers, David M. WHITE PROTESTANTISM AND THE NEGRO. New York: Oxford Univ. Press, 1965.   See "Lynching" in index.

159. Resnikoff, Philip. "A Psychoanalytic Study of Lynching." THE PSYCHOANALYTIC REVIEW, Vol. 20, No. 4 (Oct. 1933): 421-27. Includes idea that fatal lynching of blacks occurred mostly after the Civil War because freedmen, unlike former slaves, had sexual freedom, thus increasing white fears of black sexual threat (pp. 424-25).

160. Reuter, Edward Byron, and Masuoka, Jitsuichi. THE AMERICAN RACE PROBLEM. 3d ed.; New York: Thomas Y. Crowell Co., 1970.   See pp. 340-61 for lynchings.

161. Rolph, Daniel Nelson. "'To Shoot, Burn, and Hang': Folk-History from a Kentucky Mountain Family and Community." Ph.D. diss., Univ. of Pennsylvania, 1992.   See Diss. Ab. Intl., Vol. 53, No. 5 (Nov. 1992): 1627A. Includes lynchings.

162. Rosenbaum, H. Jon, and Sederberg, Peter C. "Establishment Violence." SOCIETY, Vol. 13, No. 3 (March/April 1976): 27-29.   Part of symposium on American Vigilantes.

163. Rosenbaum, H. Jon, and Sederberg, Peter C. VIGILANTE POLI-TICS. Philadelphia: Univ. of Pennsylvania Press, 1976.

164. Rosenbaum, H. Jon, and Sederberg, Peter C. "Vigilantism: An Analysis of Establishment Violence." COMPARATIVE POLITICS, Vol. 6, No. 4 (July 1974): 541-70.   There are slight differences between this article and the one of same title in Vigilante Politics, pp. 3-29.

165. Ross, John Raymond. "At the Bar of Judge Lynch: Lynching and Lynch Mobs in America." Ph.D. diss., Texas Tech Univ., 1983.   See Diss. Ab. Intl., Vol. 44, No. 3 (Sept. 1983): 845A.

166. Santoro, Victor. VIGILANTE HANDBOOK. Cornville, AZ: Desert Publications, 1981.   Focuses "on who present-day vigilantes are, why they are, how they go about it, and how successful they are" (p. 1). This is partly a "how-to" manual.

167. Schomburg Clipping File, The. A collection of clippings, pamphlets, and other items about blacks. In the New York Public Library Schomburg Center for Research in Black Culture. Arranged in 6950 subject headings. An index is published on microfiche: available from Chadwyck-Healey, Inc., 623 Martense Ave., Teaneck, NJ 07666. See also New York. Public Library. Dictionary Catalog of the Schomburg Collection of Negro Literature & History. 9 vols.; Boston: G. K. Hall, 1962.

168. Schrieke, B. ALIEN AMERICANS: A STUDY OF RACE RELA-TIONS. New York: Viking Press, 1936.   See pp. 135-39 for lynching.

169. Schulman, Gary I. "Race, Sex, and Violence: A Laboratory Test of the Sexual Threat of the Black Male Hypothesis." AMERICAN JOURNAL OF SOCIOLOGY, Vol. 79, No. 5 (March 1974): 1260-77.   Concludes that white males may see black males as sexually threatening and thus engage in violent racism against them.

170. Schulman, Gary I. "Reply to Yee and Faris." AMERICAN JOUR-NAL OF SOCIOLOGY, Vol. 81, No. 3 (Nov. 1975): 635-41.   Defends research procedures in "Race, Sex, and Violence." See Yee and Faris (separately) in this bibliography.

171. Sederberg, Peter C., and Rosenbaum, H. Jon. "Vigilante Politics: Concluding Observations." In VIGILANTE POLITICS, pp. 261-73. Ed. by H. Jon Rosenbaum and Peter C. Sederberg. Philadelphia: Univ. of Pennsylvania Press, 1976.

172. Shapiro, Herbert. WHITE VIOLENCE AND BLACK RESPONSE: FROM RECONSTRUCTION TO MONTGOMERY. Amherst: Univ. of Massachusetts Press, 1988.   See Chapter 2 and "Lynchings" in index.

173. Shay, Frank. JUDGE LYNCH: HIS FIRST HUNDRED YEARS. Montclair, NJ: Patterson Smith Pub. Corp., 1969; originally published, New York: Ives Washburn, Inc., 1938.   This 1969 edition includes Arthur F. Raper, "Lynching and Racial Exploitation."

174. Skaggs, William H. THE SOUTHERN OLIGARCHY: AN APPEAL IN BEHALF OF THE SILENT MASSES OF OUR COUNTRY AGAINST THE DESPOTIC RULE OF THE FEW. New York: Devin-Adair Co., 1924.   See Chapter XV, "Most Appalling Record of Crimes in the World" (pp. 291-309); Chapter XVI, "Lynch Law and the Ku Klux Klan" (pp. 310-40).

175. Sommerville, Diane Miller. "The Rape Myth in the Old South Reconsidered." JOURNAL OF SOUTHERN HISTORY, Vol. 61, No. 3

(Aug. 1995): 481-518. Though numerous cases of black-on-white rape occurred, antebellum white Southerners did not worry much about its race aspect. But after the War it "galvanized scores of lynch mobs" (p. 485).

176. Southern Regional Council. RACE IN THE NEWS: USAGE IN SOUTHERN NEWSPAPERS. Atlanta: Southern Regional Council, 1949.

177. Stanford, P. Thomas. THE TRAGEDY OF THE NEGRO IN AMERICA. Second ed. (Editor's Edition); North Cambridge, MA: n.p., 1897; reprint edition; Freeport, New York: Books for Libraries Press, 1971. See Chapter VIII, "Lynchings" (pp. 133-68), and pp. xviii, 132, 248-49.

178. Steelman, John R. "A Study of Mob Action in the South." Ph.D. diss., Univ. of North Carolina, 1928.

179. Stettner, Edward. "Vigilantism and Political Theory." In VIGILANTE POLITICS, pp. 64-75. Ed. by H. Jon Rosenbaum and Peter C. Sederberg. Philadelphia: Univ. of Pennsylvania Press, 1976.

180. Sutherland, Edwin H. CRIMINOLOGY. Philadelphia: Lippincott, 1924. See Chapter XI, "'Popular Justice'" (pp. 238-52), for lynching.

181. Thomas, William Hannibal. THE AMERICAN NEGRO: WHAT HE WAS, WHAT HE IS, AND WHAT HE MAY BECOME; A CRITICAL AND PRACTICAL DISCUSSION. New York: Macmillan, 1901. For lynching (and a proposal for emasculation) see pp. 224-36.

182. Tolnay, Stewart E., and Beck, E. M. "Toward a Threat Model of Southern Black Lynchings." In SOCIAL THREAT AND SOCIAL CONTROL, pp. 33-52. Ed. by Allen E. Liska. Albany: State Univ. of New York Press, 1992.

183. Tolnay, Stewart E.; Beck, E. M.; and Massey, James L. "Black Lynchings: The Power Threat Hypothesis Revisited." SOCIAL FORCES, Vol. 67, No. 3 (March 1989): 605-23.

184. Tolnay, Stewart E.; Beck, E. M.; and Massey, James L. "The Power Threat Hypothesis and Black Lynching: 'Wither' the Evidence?" SOCIAL FORCES, Vol. 67, No. 3 (March 1989): 634-40.

185. Toppin, Edgar A. "The Negro in America: 1901-1956." CURRENT HISTORY, Vol. 57, No. 339 (Nov. 1969): 269-74, 307.

186. Tufte, Edward R. "A Note of Caution in Using Variables That Have Common Elements." THE PUBLIC OPINION QUARTERLY, Vol. 33, No.

4 (Winter 1969-70): 622-24.   Analysis of John Shelton Reed's data and methodology in "A Note on the Control of Lynching," ibid., Vol. 33 (1969), pp. 268-71.

187. U.S. Bureau of the Census. HISTORICAL STATISTICS OF THE UNITED STATES, COLONIAL TIMES TO 1970. Bicentennial Edition. 2 volumes; Washington, DC: USGPO, 1975.   Supt. of Doc. #: C3.134/2:H62/789-970/pt.1 [and pt.2].   Part 1, p. 422, has lynching statistics; Part 1, p. 412, has explanatory text.

188. U.S. Library of Congress. Division of Bibliography. LIST OF REFERENCES ON LYNCH LAW. [Washington, DC], July 9, 1921. A copy is available from Library of Congress, Collections of the Manuscript Division.

189. U.S. Library of Congress. Division of Bibliography. LYNCHING AND LYNCH LAW: A LIST OF RECENT REFERENCES. Ann Duncan Brown, comp. Washington, DC: [Library of Congress], 1940. Supt. of Doc. #: LC2.2:L99.   16 pages.   On second page title is given as A LIST OF RECENT REFERENCES ON LYNCHING AND LYNCH LAW.

190. Van Deusen, John G. THE BLACK MAN IN WHITE AMERICA. Washington, DC: Associated Publishers, 1938. See Chapter XI, "The Mob."

191. Van Deusen, John G. THE BLACK MAN IN WHITE AMERICA. Revised ed.; Washington, DC: Associated Publishers, 1944. See "Lynching" in index.

192. "Vigilance Committees." CHAMBERS'S JOURNAL [London], Vol. 11 (4th Series), No. 525 (Jan. 17, 1874): 36-38.   General; not limited to two committees; United States.

193. THE VIGILANTE MANUAL, A HANDBOOK OF SOCIAL ORDER.   STANDARDS, INFORMATION AND SUGGESTIONS USEFUL TO THE VIGILANTE. New York, 1917.   See National Union Catalog, Pre-1956, Vol. 637, p. 195.

194. Walker, Samuel E.   POPULAR JUSTICE: A HISTORY OF AMERICAN CRIMINAL JUSTICE. New York: Oxford Univ. Press, 1980. See "Lynching" and "Vigilantism" in index.

195. Wallace, Michele. BLACK MACHO AND THE MYTH OF THE SUPERWOMAN. New York: Dial Press, 1979.   See pages 15-16, 23, 25-27, 120.

196. Whipple, Leon. "Why We Lynch." THE SURVEY, Vol. 63, No. 1 (Oct. 1, 1929): 43-44. Review of Rope & Faggot by Walter White.

197. White, Anthony G. THE RISE OF VIGILANTISM IN URBAN AREAS: A SELECTED BIBLIOGRAPHY. Monticello, IL: Council of Planning Librarians, 1976.

198. White, Walter. ROPE & FAGGOT: A BIOGRAPHY OF JUDGE LYNCH. New York: Knopf, 1929. Well-known standard work.

199. Wiegman, Robyn. "The Anatomy of Lynching." JOURNAL OF THE HISTORY OF SEXUALITY, Vol. 3, No. 3 (Jan. 1993): 445-67.

200. Williams, Charles H. THE RACE PROBLEM: THE NINETEENTH CENTURY BARBARISMS AND INJUSTICE OF TWO GREAT NATIONS, SPAIN AND THE UNITED STATES. 1898. Six pages. See National Union Catalog, Pre-1956, Vol. 664, p. 580.

201. Williams, Cortez Howard. "The Black Experience: An Investigation of the Plight of Blacks in the United States and Latin America from the Fifteenth to the Nineteenth Century." Ph.D. diss., Univ. of New Mexico, 1976. See Diss. Ab. Intl., Vol. 37, No. 5 (Nov. 1976): 3078A-3079A. Compares U.S. and Latin American slavery. Has material on slave rebellions and post-slavery lynchings. Examines why lynching ended.

202. Williams, Daniel T., ed. EIGHT NEGRO BIBLIOGRAPHIES. New York: Kraus Reprint Co., 1970. Number 7 is "The Lynching Records at Tuskegee Institute." Contains introduction (pp. [1]-5); "Lynching By States and Race, 1882-1968" (pp. 6-7); "Lynchings, Whites and Negroes, 1882-1968 (pp. 8-11); "Causes of Lynchings Classified, 1882-1968 (pp. 12-15); and a 24-page list of articles and books.

203. Williamson, Joel. THE CRUCIBLE OF RACE: BLACK-WHITE RELATIONS IN THE AMERICAN SOUTH SINCE EMANCIPATION. New York: Oxford Univ. Press, 1984. See "lynching" in index. Abridgement is A Rage for Order: Black-White Relations in the American South Since Emancipation.

204. Woodward, C. Vann. THE STRANGE CAREER OF JIM CROW. 3d ed.; New York: Oxford Univ. Press, 1974. See "Lynching" in index; brief references only.

205. Woolf, Patricia. "Science Needs Vigilance Not Vigilantes." JAMA: THE JOURNAL OF THE AMERICAN MEDICAL ASSOCIATION, Vol. 260, No. 13 (Oct. 7, 1988): 1939-40. Research fraud.

206. Work, Monroe N., ed. A BIBLIOGRAPHY OF THE NEGRO IN AFRICA AND AMERICA. New York: H. W. Wilson Co., 1928.   For lynching see pp. 550-59.

207. Work, Monroe N., ed. NEGRO YEAR BOOK: AN ANNUAL ENCYCLOPEDIA OF THE NEGRO. Tuskegee Institute, AL: Negro Year Book Co. Editions were published for 1912, 1913, 1914-15, 1916-17, 1918-19, 1921-22, 1925-26. Later years also, but edited by other people.

208. Wright, Barry Morgan. "Lynching in the South." Honors thesis, Harvard Univ., 1971.

209. Wright, Bobby E. THE PSYCHOPATHIC RACIAL PERSONAL-ITY AND OTHER ESSAYS. Chicago: Third World Press, 1984.   Author was a black psychologist. See "Black Suicide: Lynching By Any Other Name Is Still Lynching" (pp. 16-22), which does not deal with lynching per se but argues that Whites are programming Blacks mentally for self-destruction ("mentacide" [sic]). Also: "Black Suicide (Lynching By Any Other Name Is Still Lynching)", Black Books Bulletin, Vol. 7, No. 2 (1981): 15-17 [title given here is what appears on p. 15, but contents page has it as "Black Suicide--Lynching By Any Other Name Is Still Lynching"].

210. Yee, William. "Comment on Schulman's Article." AMERICAN JOURNAL OF SOCIOLOGY, Vol. 81, No. 3 (Nov. 1975): 629-34.   See Schulman, Gary I., in this bibliography.

211. Young, Donald. AMERICAN MINORITY PEOPLES, A STUDY IN RACIAL AND CULTURAL CONFLICTS IN THE UNITED STATES. New York: Harper & Brothers, 1932.   In Chapter VII see "Lynch Law" section (pp. 248-61). See also pp. 48, 348, 589.

212. Young, Erle Fiske. "The Relation of Lynching to the Size of Political Areas: A Note on the Sociology of Popular Justice." SOCIOLOGY AND SOCIAL RESEARCH, Vol. 12, No. 4 (March-April 1928): 348-53.

II

Origins to Civil War

213. Adams, George R. "The Carolina Regulators: A Note on Changing Interpretations." NORTH CAROLINA HISTORICAL REVIEW, Vol. 49, No. 4 (Oct. 1972): 345-52.

214. Adler, Nathan. "An American Tradition." NEW MASSES, Vol. 10, No. 10 (March 6, 1934): 16, 18. New York Negro revolt of 1741. Some people were burned alive. See Orozco in Chapter IX in this bibliography.

215. "American Lynching.--The Desperadoes of the South-West." HOWITT'S JOURNAL OF LITERATURE AND POPULAR PROGRESS [London], Vol. 3, No. 59 (Feb. 12, 1848): 109-10. No states or territories named; forest environment. Information from a periodical named Harbinger; consists largely of quotations from The Desperadoes of the South-West (see Summerfield, Charles, in this bibliography).

216. Andrews, H. "Mediaeval Lynch Laws in Modern Use." NOTES AND QUERIES [London], Ninth Series, Vol. 1, No. 6 (Feb. 5, 1898): 116.

217. "Arkansas. Terrible Application of Lynch Law." NILES' NATIONAL REGISTER, Fifth Series, Vol. 11, No. 1 [Vol. 61] (Sept. 4, 1841): 3. One report says citizen group drowned 27 counterfeiters at one time in Mississippi River. Different report says 50 to 75 were either drowned or shot.

218. Attebery, Eleanor. "The Bloody Neutral Ground in Harrison County." THE HISTORY TEACHERS' BULLETIN (Univ. of Texas Bulletin No. 2746), Vol. 14, No. 1 (Dec. 1927): 74-79. Regulator-Moderator war in east Texas.

219. Bardaglio, Peter W. "Rape and the Law in the Old South: 'Calculated to excite indignation in every heart.'" THE JOURNAL OF SOUTHERN

HISTORY, Vol. 60, No. 4 (Nov. 1994): 749-72.   Some antebellum cases of blacks raping white women and brief references to lynching.

220. Barde, Alexandre.   THE VIGILANTE COMMITTEES OF THE ATTAKAPAS.   Annotated and edited by David C. Edmonds and Dennis Gibson.   Trans. by Henrietta Guilbeau Rogers.   Acadiana Press, 1981. Originally published as Histoire des Comites de Vigilance aux Attakapas (St. Jean-Baptiste, LA, 1861).

221. Barde, Alexandre.   "The Vigilante Committee of Vermilion Parish." ATTAKAPAS GAZETTE, Vol. 10, No. 1 (Spring 1975): 84-97.   Activities in 1859-60.

222. Bassett, John S.   "The Regulators of North Carolina (1765-1771)."   In ANNUAL REPORT OF THE AMERICAN HISTORICAL ASSOCIA-TION FOR THE YEAR 1894, pp. 141-212. Washington, DC: Government Printing Office, 1895.   This is U.S. Congress, House of Reps., Mis. Doc. No. 91, 53d Cong., 3d Sess.   Serial Set 3343.

223. Berlin, Ira.   SLAVES WITHOUT MASTERS: THE FREE NEGRO IN THE ANTEBELLUM SOUTH.   New York: Pantheon Books, 1974. See "vigilantism, white" in index.

224. Black, J. Dickson.   "Murder on Cane Hill."   OLD WEST [Iola, WI], Vol. 17, No. 2, Whole No. 66 (Winter 1980): 39-41.   Arkansas vigilantes called Cane Hill 36 lynched John Richmond, James Barnes, and Jackson Turner, July, 1839.   William Bailey was lynched in December.

225. Borome, Joseph A.   "The Vigilant Committee of Philadelphia."   THE PENNSYLVANIA MAGAZINE OF HISTORY AND BIOGRAPHY, Vol. 92, No. 3 (July 1968): 320-51.   Group to protect blacks from slave catchers and kidnappers, 1830s-1840s, with successor group formed in 1852.

226. Boston.   Committee of Vigilance.   See several entries in National Union Catalog, Pre-1956, Vol. 68, p. 196, for items relating to fugitive slaves, 1850s.

227. Bradley, A. G.   "Judge Lynch, the Originator of Lynch-Law."   CHAM-BERS'S JOURNAL [Edinburgh], Seventh Series, Vol. 5, No. 227 (April 3, 1915): 281-84.   Charles Lynch, Virginia, 1780. Also gives account of lethal lynching, around 1890, of son of a former Confederate general.

228. Bragg, James W.   "Captain Slick, Arbiter of Early Alabama Morals." THE ALABAMA REVIEW, Vol. 11, No. 2 (April 1958): 125-34. Vigilan-tism and riot, 1830s.

229. Brothers, Thomas, ed. THE UNITED STATES OF NORTH AMERICA AS THEY ARE; NOT AS THEY ARE GENERALLY DESCRIBED: BEING A CURE FOR RADICALISM. London: Longman, Orme, Brown, Green and Longmans, 1840. See Appendix X, pp. 509-15, "A Few Cases of Lynch-Law Outrages."

230. Brown, Richard Maxwell. "Back Country Rebellions and the Homestead Ethic in America, 1740-1977. In TRADITION, CONFLICT, AND MODERNIZATION: PERSPECTIVE ON THE AMERICAN REVOLUTION, pp. 73-99. Ed. by Richard Maxwell Brown and Don E. Fehrenbacher. New York: Academic Press, 1977.

231. Brown, Richard Maxwell. THE SOUTH CAROLINA REGU-LATORS. Cambridge: Belknap Press of Harvard Univ. Press, 1963.

232. Brumbaugh, Alice L. "The Regulator Movement in Illinois." M.A. thesis, Univ. of Illinois, 1927.

233. [Chambers, William.] W. C. "American Jottings. Eccentricities in Criminal Jurisprudence--Lynch Law." CHAMBER'S JOURNAL OF POPULAR LITERATURE SCIENCE AND ARTS [London], Vol. 3, No. 59 (Feb. 17, 1855): 101-04.

234. Channing, Steven A. CRISIS OF FEAR: SECESSION IN SOUTH CAROLINA. New York: Simon and Schuster, 1970. See Chapter 1 for vigilantism and violence after the Harpers Ferry raid.

235. Clayton, E. G. "Mediaeval Lynch Laws in Modern Use." NOTES AND QUERIES [London], Ninth Series, Vol. 1, No. 15 (April 9, 1898): 298.

236. Cohee. "Lynch Law." HARPER'S NEW MONTHLY MAGAZINE, Vol. 18, No. 108 (May 1859): 794-98. Origin of term and of activity.

237. Coleman, J. Winston, Jr. RETRIBUTION AT THE COURT-HOUSE: AN ACCOUNT OF THE MOB ACTION IN LEXINGTON, KENTUCKY, IN JULY 10TH, 1858, AND THE EVENTS LEADING UP TO IT. Lexington: Winburn Press, 1957. Short booklet. William Barker, white, was hanged on same day he murdered city marshal.

238. Crenshaw, Ollinger. "The Psychological Background of the Election of 1860 in the South." THE NORTH CAROLINA HISTORICAL REVIEW, Vol. 19, No. 3 (July 1942): 260-79. Vigilance committees were formed to combat real or suspected violence from slaves and abolitionists.

239. Cutler, J. Elbert. "Lynching and Colonel Lynch." THE NATION, Vol.

76, No. 1977 (May 21, 1903): 415.   Advances evidence for Colonel Charles Lynch as the source for "Lynch" law.

240. Daniels, William M. A CORRECT ACCOUNT OF THE MURDER OF GENERALS JOSEPH AND HYRUM SMITH, AT CARTHAGE, ON THE 27TH DAY OF JUNE, 1844. In MURDER OF AN AMERICAN PROPHET: EVENTS AND PREJUDICES SURROUNDING THE KILLING OF JOSEPH AND HYRUM SMITH, CARTHAGE, ILLINOIS, JUNE 27, 1844, MATERIALS FOR ANALYSIS, pp. 160-84. Ed. by Keith Huntress. San Francisco: Chandler Pub. Co., [1963?].

241. Darby, John F.   PERSONAL RECOLLECTIONS OF MANY PROMINENT PEOPLE WHOM I HAVE KNOWN, AND OF EVENTS-- ESPECIALLY THOSE RELATING TO THE HISTORY OF ST. LOUIS-- DURING THE FIRST HALF OF THE PRESENT CENTURY. St. Louis: G. I. Jones and Co., 1880.   See pp. 237-42 for lynching of black man named McIntosh, 1836.

242. Dew, Charles B. "Black Ironworkers and the Slave Insurrection Panic of 1856." THE JOURNAL OF SOUTHERN HISTORY, Vol. 41, No. 3 (Aug. 1975): 321-28.   Includes lynchings in Texas, Tennessee, and Kentucky (pp. 322, 330, 331, 332, 337).

243. Dresser, Amos. THE NARRATIVE OF AMOS DRESSER, WITH STONE'S LETTERS FROM NATCHEZ. New York: American Anti- Slavery Society, 1836.   About a student given a whipping by a vigilance committee in Nashville in 1835 for possession of anti-slavery publications.

244. Dyer, Thomas G.   "A Most Unexampled Exhibition of Madness and Brutality':   Judge Lynch in Saline County, Missouri, 1859.   Part 1." MISSOURI HISTORICAL REVIEW, Vol. 89, No. 3 (April 1995): 269-89. Four separate lynchings of slaves in three days.

245. Dyer, Thomas G.   "A Most Unexampled Exhibition of Madness and Brutality':   Judge Lynch in Saline County, Missouri, 1859.   Part 2." MISSOURI HISTORICAL REVIEW, Vol. 89, No. 4 (July 1995): 367-83.

246. E., W. "Lynch-Law," THE SPECTATOR [London], Vol. 62, No. 3172 (April 13, 1889): 511.   Letter. Origin of term was in Galway, Ireland, in late 1400s or early 1500s.

247. Eaton, Clement. "Mob Violence in the Old South." THE MISSIS- SIPPI VALLEY HISTORICAL REVIEW, Vol. 29, No. 3 (Dec. 1942): 351- 70.   Includes anti-abolitionist and anti-insurrection vigilance committees and lynchings.

248. Edward, Brother C. "The Regulators: North Carolina taxpayers take arms against the governing elite." AMERICAN HISTORY ILLUS-TRATED, Vol. 18, No. 2 (April 1983): 42-48.   Backwoods protest culminating in Battle of Alamance, May, 1771.

249. Ekirch, A. Roger. "The North Carolina Regulators on Liberty and Corruption, 1766-1771." In PERSPECTIVES IN AMERICAN HISTORY, Vol. 11 (1977-1978), pp. 199-256. Ed. by Donald Fleming. Cambridge: Charles Warren Center for Studies in American History, Harvard Univ., 1978.

250. Ekirch, A. Roger. "'Poor Carolina': Society and Politics in North Carolina, 1729-1771." Ph.D. diss., Johns Hopkins Univ., 1979. See Diss. Ab. Intl., Vol. 39, No. 9 (March 1979): 5678a-5679A. Abstract: "Closes with the Regulator riots."

251. Ellsworth, Paul D. "Mobocracy and the Rule of Law: American Press Reaction to the Murder of Joseph Smith." BRIGHAM YOUNG UNIVER-SITY STUDIES, Vol. 20, No. 1 (Fall 1979): 71-82.

252. Featherstone, Howell Colston. "The Origin and History of Lynch Law." THE GREEN BAG, Vol. 12, No. 3 (March 1900): 150-58.

"A Few Cases of Lynch-Law Outrages." See Brothers, Thomas.

253. Fischer, David Hackett. ALBION'S SEED: FOUR BRITISH FOLKWAYS IN AMERICA. New York: Oxford Univ. Press, 1989. See especially pp. 766-67 for origins of regulators and vigilantes.

254. Fitzgerald, William S. "Did Nathan Bedford Forrest Really Rescue John Able?" TENNESSEE HISTORICAL QUARTERLY, Vol. 39, No. 1 (Spring 1980): 16-26. A near-lynching in 1857 in Memphis was thwarted, but Forrest had virtually no role in the episode.

255. Fleek, Sherman L. "Exodus Triggered By Assassins." WILD WEST [Leesburg, VA], Vol. 1, No. 3 (Oct. 1988): 26-33.   Joseph and Hyrum Smith were murdered at Carthage, IL, 1844.

256. Freehling, William W. THE ROAD TO DISUNION: SECESSION-ISTS AT BAY, 1776-1854. New York: Oxford Univ. Press, 1990. See Chapter 6, "Democrats as Lynchers."

257. "Gallows Ends East Texas Reign of Terror." FRONTIER TIMES [Bandera, TX], Vol. 7, No. 2 (Nov. 1929): 79-82.   Regulators and Moderators, 1840s.

258. Garrison, William Lloyd. THE NEW "REIGN OF TERROR" IN THE SLAVEHOLDING STATES, FOR 1859-60. New York: American Anti-Slavery Society, 1860. Reprinted as The New "Reign of Terror" in the Slaveholding States (New York: Arno Press and The New York Times, 1969). Compilation of newspaper stories, letters, etc., including many about vigilance committees and lynch law (corporal and lethal).

259. Gayler, George R. "Governor Ford and the Death of Joseph and Hyrum Smith." JOURNAL OF THE ILLINOIS STATE HISTORICAL SOCIETY, Vol. 50, No. 4 (Winter 1957): 391-411.

260. Griffin, H. L. "The Vigilance Committees of Attakapas Country; or Early Louisiana Justice." PROCEEDINGS OF THE MISSISSIPPI VALLEY HISTORICAL ASSOCIATION FOR THE YEAR 1914-15, Vol. 8 (1914-15), pp. 146-59. Deals with 1859.

261. Harr, John L. "Law and Lawlessness in the Lower Mississippi Valley, 1815-1860." THE NORTHWEST MISSOURI STATE COLLEGE STUDIES, Vol. 19, No. 1 (June 1, 1955): 51-70. Vigilantes, regulators, lynch law.

262. Harris, W. Stuart. "Rowdyism, Public Drunkenness, and Bloody Encounters in Early Perry County." THE ALABAMA REVIEW, Vol. 33, No. 1 (Jan. 1980): 15-24. Includes vigilantes. See p. 21 for a mob burning a black slave to death, 1827.

263. Henderson, Archibald. "The Origin of the Regulation in North Carolina." THE AMERICAN HISTORICAL REVIEW, Vol. 21, No. 2 (Jan. 1916): 320-32.

264. Hermann, Janet S. "The McIntosh Affair." BULLETIN OF THE MISSOURI HISTORICAL SOCIETY, Vol. 26, No. 2 (Jan. 1970): 123-43. Lynch burning of free black man named Francis McIntosh, April 1836, in St. Louis, and its aftermath.

265. Historiador. "A Remarkable Lynch-Law Case." THE LAW [Chicago], Vol. 1, No. 3 (Nov. 1889): 67-70. After much lawlessness in Ogle County, IL, including murder and the burning of the new court house, regulators tried and executed two men by firing squad in 1841.

266. Hogan, Mervin B. FREEMASONRY AND THE LYNCHING AT CARTHAGE JAIL. Salt Lake City; M. B. Hogan, 1981. Joseph and Hyrum Smith, 1844.

267. Hooker, Richard J., ed. THE CAROLINA BACKCOUNTRY ON

THE EVE OF THE REVOLUTION: THE JOURNAL AND OTHER WRITINGS OF CHARLES WOODMASON, ANGLICAN ITINERANT. Chapel Hill: Univ. of North Carolina Press, 1953. See Part Three: "The South Carolina Regulator Movement."

268. Hord, William T. "Breaking Up a Party of Arkansas River Gamblers." PUBLICATIONS OF THE ARKANSAS HISTORICAL ASSOCIATION, Vol. 4 (1917): 312-25. Ad hoc group engaged in vigilantism. No date, but pre-1849. Author listed as Heard on contents page, but as Hord on p. 312.

269. Hoyt, William D., Jr., ed. "Civilian Defense in Baltimore, 1814-1815: Minutes of the Committee of Vigilance and Safety." MARYLAND HISTORICAL MAGAZINE, Vol. 39, No. 3 (Sept. 1944): 199-224.

270. Huntress, Keith, ed. MURDER OF AN AMERICAN PROPHET: EVENTS AND PREJUDICES SURROUNDING THE KILLING OF JOSEPH AND HYRUM SMITH; CARTHAGE, ILLINOIS, JUNE 27, 1844. MATERIALS FOR ANALYSIS. San Francisco: Chandler Pub. Co., [1963?].

271. Ibredix. "Colonel Teadriver, the Regulator." DE BOW'S SOUTHERN AND WESTERN REVIEW, Vol. 10 (Old Series), No. 2 (Feb. 1851): 166-75. Brazoria County, TX, 1830s.

272. "Illinois. More Lynching." NILES' NATIONAL REGISTER, Fifth Series, Vol. 11, No. 1 [Vol. 61] (Sept. 4, 1841): 3. Corporal lynching.

273. January, Alan F. "The South Carolina Association: An Agency for Race Control in Antebellum Charleston." THE SOUTH CAROLINA HISTORICAL MAGAZINE, Vol. 78, No. 3 (July 1977): 191-201. It was a vigilance committee that began in 1823.

274. Johnson, Elmer Douglas. "The War of the Regulation: Its Place in History." M.A. thesis, Univ. of North Carolina at Chapel Hill, 1942. North Carolina Regulators, 1760s and 1770s.

275. Jolley, Clifton Holt. "The Martyrdom of Joseph Smith: An Archetypal Study." UTAH HISTORICAL QUARTERLY, Vol. 44, No. 4 (Fall 1976): 329-50.

276. Jones, Robert Huhn. "Three Days of Violence. The Regulators of the Rock River Valley." JOURNAL OF THE ILLINOIS STATE HISTORICAL SOCIETY, Vol. 59, No. 2 (Summer 1966): 131-42. Deals with 1841.

277. Jones, William Lawless. "Mob Violence Against Abolitionists in the

South." THE NEGRO HISTORY BULLETIN, Vol. 7, No. 6 (March 1944): 134-42.   Includes vigilance committees and lynching (both corporal and lethal).

278. Jordan, Philip D. "The Derringer and the Ace of Spades: Reflections on Middle Border Law and Order." LOUISIANA STUDIES, Vol. 6, No. 4 (Winter 1967): 315-31. Includes lynching. Deals with "territories and states bordering the Mississippi River" during mid-1800s from about 1830.

279. Junkins, Enda. "Slave Plots, Insurrections, and Acts of Violence in the State of Texas, 1828-1865." M.A. thesis, Baylor Univ., 1969.

280. Kay, Marvin L. M. "The North Carolina Regulation, 1766-1776: A Class Conflict." In THE AMERICAN REVOLUTION: EXPLORATIONS IN THE HISTORY OF AMERICAN RADICALISM, pp. 71-123. Ed. by Alfred M. Young. DeKalb: Northern Illinois Univ. Press, 1976.

281. Kay, Marvin Lawrence Michael. "The Institutional Background to the Regulation in Colonial North Carolina." Ph.D. diss., Univ. of Minnesota, 1962.   See Diss. Ab., Vol. 24, No. 11 (May 1964): 4653-54.

282. Kimball, Stanley B. "The Mormons in Illinois, 1838-1846: A Special Introduction." Ed. by Douglas L. Wilson and Rodney O. Davis. JOURNAL OF THE ILLINOIS STATE HISTORICAL SOCIETY, Vol. 64, No. 1 (Spring 1971): 5-21.   Includes Smith murders at Carthage, 1844.

283. Klein, Rachel N. "Ordering the Backcountry: The South Carolina Regulation." WILLIAM AND MARY QUARTERLY, Vol. 38, Third Series, No. 4 (Oct. 1981): 661-80.

284. Lack, Paul D. "Slavery and Vigilantism in Austin, Texas, 1840-1860." SOUTHWESTERN HISTORICAL QUARTERLY, Vol. 85, No. 1 (July 1981): 1-20.   See pp. 10-11, 13, 17-18 for minor violence, and p. 19 for major violence away from Austin.

285. Lawson, Elizabeth. "'Such a Gentlemanly Mob.'" LABOR DE- FENDER, Vol. 11, No. 4 (May 1937): 16.   Lovejoy's martyrdom at Alton, Illinois, 1837.

286. Ledbetter, Bill. "Slave Unrest and White Panic: The Impact of Black Republicanism In Ante-Bellum Texas." TEXANA, Vol. 10, No. 4 (1972): 335-50.   Includes vigilance committees and numerous lynchings (both corporal and deadly).

287. Little, Craig B., and Sheffield, Christopher P. "Frontiers and Criminal

Justice: English Private Prosecution Societies and American Vigilantism in the Eighteenth and Nineteenth Centuries." AMERICAN SOCIOLOGICAL REVIEW, Vol. 48, No. 6 (Dec. 1983): 796-808.   Similarities and differences in English and American systems for extralegal "justice." Both were responses to social-control problems on types of frontiers.

288. Love, John Warren. "The Regulator-Moderator Movement in Shelby County, Texas." M.A. thesis, Univ. of Texas, 1936.

289. Lundwall, N. B. THE FATE OF THE PERSECUTORS OF THE PROPHET JOSEPH SMITH; BEING A COMPILATION OF HISTORICAL DATA ON THE PERSONAL TESTIMONY OF JOSEPH SMITH, HIS GREATNESS, HIS PERSECUTIONS AND PROSECUTIONS, CONSPIRACIES AGAINST HIS LIFE, HIS IMPRISONMENTS, HIS MARTYRDOM, HIS FUNERAL AND BURIAL, THE TRIAL OF HIS MURDERERS, THE SORROW AND MOURNING OF HIS FOLLOWERS, THE FATE OF THOSE WHO PERSECUTED AND KILLED HIM, AND THE ATTITUDE OF HIS FOLLOWERS WHO ALSO ENDURED AND PASSED THROUGH MANY OF THESE EXPERIENCES. Salt Lake City: Bookcraft, 1952.

290. "Lynch Law." THE BRITISH AND FOREIGN REVIEW [London], Vol. XIV, No. 27 (1843): 28-44.

291. "Lynch-Law." CHAMBERS'S JOURNAL [Edinburgh], Seventh Series, Vol. 6, No. 262 (Dec. 4, 1915): 15-16. Response to A. G. Bradley's article. Gives Galway, Ireland, 1493, version of origin of term but says "there is little doubt that the verb 'to lynch' and the phrase 'lynch law' come from across the Atlantic" [i.e., from the U.S.].

"Lynch Law." See Cohee.

292. "Lynch law." NILES' NATIONAL REGISTER, Fifth Series, Vol. 13, No. 12 [Vol. 63] (Nov. 19, 1842): 192.   George Lore was recently lynched by hanging, Barbour County, Alabama.

293. "Lynch Law in Missouri." ONCE A WEEK, Vol. 9 (July 4, 1863): 47-51.   Author initials at end of article are W. C. M., but internal evidence indicates author was a Mr. Scudder. Lynching of horse thief named Tom Meyers by Regulators in about 1832.

294. "The Lynch Law Tree." THE GREEN BAG, Vol. 4, No. 12 (Dec. 1892): 561-62.   Attributes the origin of the terms "lynch law," etc., to Colonel Charles Lynch, a Revolutionary patriot, who, in about 1780, with others, gave 39 lashes to active loyalists 20 miles south of Lynchburg. From

the Philadelphia Times.

295. "The Lynch Law Tree."   REPORT OF THE THIRTEENTH ANNUAL SESSION OF THE GEORGIA BAR ASSOCIATION HELD AT WARM SPRINGS, GA., ON TUESDAY, JUNE 30, AND WEDNESDAY, JULY 1, 1896. Atlanta: Franklin Printing, 1897.   This is sometimes listed with Henry R. Goetchius as author (e.g., Index to Legal Periodicals, Vol. 2), but he was just the reader of this article which is virtually identical to that originally published in The Green Bag, Vol. 4, No. 12 (Dec. 1892): 561-62.

296. "Lynch Trial in California." HOUSEHOLD WORDS [London], Vol. 3, No. 78 (Sept. 20, 1851): 611-12.   Thirty-nine lashes each for three gold thieves; extreme court-like trial process; April 1851.

297. "Lynch's Law." SOUTHERN LITERARY MESSENGER, Vol. II, No. 6 (May 1836): 389.   Origin of term and life of Charles Lynch.

298. M. "Lynch Law." NOTES AND QUERIES [London], Tenth Series, Vol. 11, No. 284 (June 5, 1909): 445.   Origin of the term.

299. M. "Lynch Law." NOTES AND QUERIES [London], Tenth Series, Vol. 12, No. 290 (July 17, 1909): 52.   Origin of the term.

300. M. "Lynch Law." NOTES AND QUERIES [London], Tenth Series, Vol. 12, No. 296 (Aug. 28, 1909): 174.   Origin of the term.

301. M.   "Lynch Law."   NOTES AND QUERIES [London], Eleventh Series, Vol. 1, No. 3 (Jan. 15, 1910): 55-56. Origin of the term.

302. M.   "Lynch Law."   NOTES AND QUERIES [London], Eleventh Series, Vol. 1, No. 14 (April 2, 1910): 273.   Origin of the term.

303. M., W. P. "Mediaeval Lynch Laws in Modern Use." NOTES AND QUERIES [London], Ninth Series, Vol. 1, No. 6 (Feb. 5, 1898): 116.

304. Manders, Eric, and Snook, George A. "Shays' Regulators, 1786-1787." MILITARY COLLECTOR & HISTORIAN, Vol. 15, No. 3 (Fall 1963): 83, 85.   Part of longer section on "Military Dress."

305. Marryat, Capt. [Frederick].   A DIARY IN AMERICA, WITH REMARKS ON ITS INSTITUTIONS. 3 vols.; London: Longman, Orme, Brown, Green and Longmans, 1839.   See III, 226-52, "Lynch Law." See pp. 238-40 for black man burned alive in St. Louis, 1836.

306. Marsh, Eudocia Baldwin. "Mormons in Hancock County: A Reminiscence." Ed. by Douglas L. Wilson and Rodney O. Davis. JOURNAL OF THE ILLINOIS STATE HISTORICAL SOCIETY, Vol. 64, No. 1 (Spring 1971): 22-65. Includes Smith murder at Carthage.

307. Marten, James. TEXAS DIVIDED: LOYALTY AND DISSENT IN THE LONE STAR STATE, 1856-1874. Lexington: The Univ. Press of Kentucky, 1990. See Chapter 1, "Southern Vigilantism and the Sectional Conflict," and "violence" in index.

308. Martineau, Harriet. RETROSPECT OF WESTERN TRAVEL. 2 vols.; London: Saunders and Otley, 1838. See II, 30-31, for burning of black man named Mackintosh [St. Louis, 1836]. [In the 3-vol. edition (London: Saunders and Otley, 1838), this lynching is in II, 206-09.]

309. Matthews, Albert. "Lynch Law." THE NATION, Vol. 75, No. 1953 (Dec. 4, 1902): 439-41. Origin of the words "lynching," "lynch," etc.

310. Matthews, Albert. "Lynch Law." NOTES AND QUERIES [London], Tenth Series, Vol. 11, No. 287 (June 26, 1909): 515-16. Origin of the term. Further notes with same title and on same topic in this journal: [London], Tenth Series, Vol. 12, No. 294 (Aug. 14, 1909): 133-35; [London], Tenth Series, Vol. 12, No. 312 (Dec. 18, 1909): 495-96; [London], Eleventh Series, Vol. 1, No. 10 (March 5, 1910): 194-95.

311. Matthews, Albert. "Lynch Law Once More." THE NATION, Vol. 76, No. 1961 (Jan. 29, 1903): 91. Origin and early use of term "lynch law."

312. Matthews, Albert. "Not a New Crime." THE NATION, Vol. 77, No. 1988 (Aug. 6, 1903): 113. Letter. Black rape of white women existed long before slavery was abolished. Says lynching of Negroes started in 1835.

313. Matthews, Albert. "Origin of the Term Lynch Law." PUBLICATIONS OF THE COLONIAL SOCIETY OF MASSACHUSETTS, Vol. 27 (Dec. 1929): 256-71.

314. Matthews, Albert. "The Term Lynch Law." MODERN PHILOLOGY, Vol. 2, No. 2 (Oct. 1904): 173-95 (1-23).

315. Matthews, Albert. THE TERM LYNCH LAW. Chicago: Univ. of Chicago Press, 1904. Reprinted from preceding item.

316. Matthews, John Hobson. "Mediaeval Lynch Laws in Modern Use." NOTES AND QUERIES [London], Ninth Series, Vol. 1, No. 2 (Jan. 8, 1898): 37.

317. McCrady, Edward. "Lynch Law and South Carolina." THE NATION, Vol. 76, No. 1959 (Jan. 15, 1903): 52-53.   Origins and early uses of "lynch law" and "regulation."

318. McLoughlin, William G. "The Choctaw Slave Burning: A Crisis in Mission Work Among the Indians." JOURNAL OF THE WEST, Vol. 13, No. 1 (Jan. 1974): 113-27.   Black woman named Lucy was burned to death by mob, Dec., 1858 or Jan., 1859, in Indian Territory.

319. Middleton, John W.   HISTORY OF THE REGULATORS & MODERATORS AND THE SHELBY COUNTY WAR IN 1841 AND 1842, IN THE REPUBLIC OF TEXAS . . .   Fort Worth: Loving Pub. Co., 1883.

320. Middleton, John W. "The Regulators and Moderators." FRONTIER TIMES [Bandera, TX], Vol. 6, No. 1 (Oct. 1928): 451 [sic; should be 17]-36. Reprint of History of the Regulators & . . .

321. Miles, Edwin A. "The Mississippi Slave Insurrection Scare of 1835." THE JOURNAL OF NEGRO HISTORY, Vol. 42, No. 1 (Jan. 1957): 48-60. Includes lethal and corporal lynchings.

322. Moore, John Hebron. "Local and State Governments of Antebellum Mississippi." THE JOURNAL OF MISSISSIPPI HISTORY, Vol. 44, No. 2 (May 1982): 104-34.   See pp. 119-22 for vigilance committees (distinguished from lynch mobs, p. 121).

"More Lynching." See "Illinois. More Lynching."

323. Morgan, Forrest. "Lynch Law." NOTES AND QUERIES [London], Vol. 12, No. 290 (July 17, 1909): 52.   Origin of the term.

324. Mott, M. H. HISTORY OF THE REGULATORS OF NORTHERN INDIANA. Indianapolis: Indianapolis Journal Co., 1859.

325. Mounger, Dwyn M. "Lynching in Mississippi, 1830-1930." M.A. thesis, Mississippi State Univ., 1961.

326. Mount, C. B. "Mediaeval Lynch Laws in Modern Use." NOTES AND QUERIES [London], Ninth Series, Vol. 1, No. 2 (Jan. 8, 1898): 37.

327. Nash, Gary B. "The Transformation of Urban Politics, 1700-1765." THE JOURNAL OF AMERICAN HISTORY, Vol. 40, No. 3 (Dec. 1973): 605-32.   Includes mob activities and violence (pp. 620-23). Calls Paxton episode an "exercise in vigilante government" (p. 626).

328. Nicolosi, Anthony S. "The Rise and Fall of the New Jersey Vigilant Societies." NEW JERSEY HISTORY, Vol. 86, No. 1 (Spring 1968): 29-53. Various organizations, 1700s-1900s.

329. [No author. No title.] NILES' WEEKLY REGISTER, Fourth Series, Vol. 13, No. 5 [Vol. XLIX, Whole No. 1,254 (Oct. 3, 1835): 65.   References to activities of Judge Lynch and Judge Hang. See pp. 74, 76-77 for brief items on corporal lynchings.

330. [No author. No title.] THE CENTRAL LAW JOURNAL, Vol. 6, No. 17 (April 26, 1878): 340.   Ascribes origin of lynch law to incident in North Carolina during Revolutionary War.

331. Norton, Wesley. "The Methodist Episcopal Church and the Civil Disturbances in North Texas in 1859 and 1860." THE SOUTHWESTERN HISTORICAL QUARTERLY, Vol. 68, No. 3 (Jan. 1965): 317-41. Includes lynching of a Methodist preacher (p. 334).

NOTES AND QUERIES. This journal ran items on "Mediaeval Lynch Laws in Modern Use" and the origin of the term "lynch law." See S., N. S.; Mount, C. B.; Matthews, John Hobson; Peacock, Edward; M., W. P.; Andrews, H.; Clayton, E. G.; Seymour, T.; Udal, J. S.; Oliver, Andrew; Reid, A. G.; M.; Matthews, Albert; and Morgan, Forrest.

332. Oaks, Dallin H., and Hill, Marvin S. CARTHAGE CONSPIRACY: THE TRIAL OF THE ACCUSED ASSASSINS OF JOSEPH SMITH. Urbana: Univ. of Illinois Press, 1975.   He was murdered in Illinois in 1844.

333. O'Byrne, Cathal. "Galway of the Tribes and the Origin of 'Lynch Law.'" THE CATHOLIC WORLD, Vol. 139, No. 831 (June 1934): 295-304.

334. Oliver, Andrew. "Mediaeval Lynch Laws in Modern Use." NOTES AND QUERIES [London], Ninth Series, Vol. 2, No. 29 (July 16, 1898): 57. Very brief.

335. "Origin and Statistics Concerning Lynch Law." THE AMERICAN LAWYER, Vol. 5, No. 5 (May 1897): 215.

336. "The Origin of Lynch Law." THE NATIONAL CORPORATION REPORTER, Vol. 37, No. 24 (Jan. 28, 1909): 756-57.   Reversal of a conviction (in Minnesota case detailed here) on "trivial grounds" causes loss of respect for law and courts and causes future lynchings.

337. P. P. [Initials at end of article.] "Uses and Abuses of Lynch Law." THE AMERICAN WHIG REVIEW, Vol. 11, No. 28 (Vol. 5, No. 5, New

Series) (May 1850): 459-76.

338. P. P. [Initials at end of article.] "Uses and Abuses of Lynch Law. Article Second." THE AMERICAN WHIG REVIEW, Vol. 12, No. 35 (Vol. 6, No. 5, New Series) (Nov. 1850): 494-501.

339. P. P. [Initials at end of article.] "Uses and Abuses of Lynch Law. No. III." THE AMERICAN WHIG REVIEW, Vol. 13, No. 75 (Vol. 7, No. 3, New Series) (March 1851): 213-20.

340. Page, Thomas W. "Democracy and Lawlessness." UNIVERSITY CHRONICLE [Univ. of California, Berkeley], Vol. II, No. 1 (Feb. 1899): 120-37. Includes origin of lynching and how it has perpetuated lynching.

341. Page, Thomas Walker. "The Real Judge Lynch." THE ATLANTIC MONTHLY, Vol. 88, No. 530, (Dec. 1901): 731-43. History of Charles Lynch of Virginia and the origin of lynching.

342. Palmer, Bryan. "Discordant Music: Charivaris and Whitecapping in Nineteenth-Century North America." LABOUR [Canada], Vol. 3 (1978): 5-62.

343. Patch, Buel W. "Lynching and Kidnaping [sic]." EDITORIAL RESEARCH REPORTS, Vol. 2, No. 23 (1933): [421]-439. Deals mostly with lynching (1700s-1900s).

344. Peacock, Edward. "Mediaeval Lynch Laws in Modern Use." NOTES AND QUERIES [London], Ninth Series, Vol. 1, No. 2 (Jan. 8, 1898): 37-38.

345. Percy, Alfred. ORIGIN OF THE LYNCH LAW, 1780. Madison Heights, VA: Percy Press, 1959.   Argues that Howell Featherstone and Thomas Walker Page "are basically right" (p. 5) about the origin.

346. Percy, Alfred. VIRGINIA'S UNSUNG VICTORY IN THE REVOLUTION. Madison Heights, VA: Percy Press, 1964.   See pp. 26-47 on origin of lynch law.

347. Powell, William S. THE WAR OF THE REGULATION AND THE BATTLE OF ALAMANCE, MAY 16, 1771. Raleigh: State Dept. of Archives and History, 1965.   Originally published in 1949.

348. Powell, William S.; Huhta, James K.; and Farnham, Thomas J., eds. THE REGULATORS IN NORTH CAROLINA: A DOCUMENTARY HISTORY, 1759-1776. Raleigh: State Dept. of Archives and History, 1971.

349. "Recollections of a Retired Lawyer. Recollection II. Lynch's Law." SOUTHERN LITERARY MESSENGER, Vol. 5, No. 3 (March 1839): 218-21.   Examples of lynchings as whippings. Flogging of old black man led to his successful suit for damages, fines, and imprisonment for his assaulters.

350. Rees, Gary Lee. "The Birth of a Legend: John A. Murrell's Connection with the 1835 Mississippi Insurrection Hysteria." M.A. thesis, Univ. of Southern Mississippi, 1981.

351. Reid, A. G. "Mediaeval Lynch Laws in Modern Use." NOTES AND QUERIES [London], Ninth Series, Vol. 2, No. 39 (Sept. 24, 1898): 253.

352. Reid, John Phillip. "In a Defensive Rage: The Uses of the Mob, the Justification in Law, and the Coming of the American Revolution." NEW YORK UNIVERSITY LAW REVIEW, Vol. 49, No. 6 (Dec. 1974): 1043-91. Boston whigs considered freedom paramount and the mobs and local institutions which supported freedom as legally legitimate.   [Relates indirectly to vigilantism.]

353. Riddell, William Renwick.   "Judicial Execution By Burning at the Stake in New York." AMERICAN BAR ASSOCIATION JOURNAL, Vol. 15, No. 6 (June 1929): 373-76.   Executions in 1712 may have been of doubtful legality. Last sentence: "Judge Lynch may still condemn to death at the stake, [but] the more regular Courts have neither the power nor the inclination to do so."

354. Robbins, Peggy. "History's Slighter Side: History's Injustice to Charles Lynch." AMERICAN HISTORY ILLUSTRATED, Vol. 16, No. 5 (Aug. 1981): 6.   Briefly argues that Lynch's court in Virginia was "legal and proper in every way except that it was not in the capital" and that his infamy as the "first lyncher" ignores his reputation for mercy and his post-Revolution exoneration for any wrongful acts.

355. Robinson, Richard R. "Racism as an Aspect of the Violent History of the State of Texas in the 1830s and 1840s." M.A. thesis, Kean College of New Jersey, 1979.

356. Rose, James A. "The Regulators and Flatheads in Southern Illinois. ILLINOIS STATE HISTORICAL SOCIETY TRANSACTIONS FOR 1906. Vol. 11 (1906): 108-21.

357. Ross, Chevies Marguerite. "Watt Moorman, the Regulator Chief." FRONTIER TIMES [Bandera, TX], Vol. 11, No. 9 [sic; should be No. 10] (July 1934): 419-23. East Texas, 1840s.

358. Ross, Malcolm. "All Manner Of Men." NEGRO DIGEST, Vol. 6, No. 8 (June 1948): 83-94.   America's first lynching wave, New York, 1741. Also: Elijah Lovejoy [lynched at Alton, IL, 1837]. From Malcolm Ross, <u>All Manner of Men</u> (New York: Reynal and Hitchcock, 1948), pp. 1-17 (with parts of pp. 1-2, 8, 12-13 omitted from the article).

359. S., N. S. "Mediaeval Lynch Laws in Modern Use." NOTES AND QUERIES [London], Eighth Series, Volume 12, No. 311 (Dec. 11, 1897): 465.

360. Safire, William. "Vigilante." THE NEW YORK TIMES MAGAZINE, Vol. 134, No. 46, 316 (Feb. 10, 1985): 9-10.   Origin and use of term. Prefers "vigilante-ism" to "vigilantism."

361. Sanders, J[ohn] B[arnette]. HANGINGS IN SHELBY COUNTY, TEXAS. Center, TX: J. B. Sanders, 1966.   Legal hangings and lynchings, 1844, 1888, 1892, 1906, 1920, 1928.

362. Seymour, T. "Mediaeval Lynch Laws in Modern Use." NOTES AND QUERIES [London], Ninth Series, Vol. 1, No. 24 (June 11, 1898): 477-78.

363. "Slavery and the Abolitionists." NILES' WEEKLY REGISTER, Fourth Series, Vol. 13, No. 5 [Vol. 44, Whole No. 1,254] (Oct. 3, 1835): 72-80.   See p. 74 for gallows erected in Boston with inscription "judge Lynch's law" in protest against Garrison and his guest Mr. Thompson. See p. 74 for free black lynched in Mobile (corporal or lethal?). See pp. 76-77: four whites from Ohio went to Virginia to induce slaves to run away; locals lynched two of them (39 lashes each).

364. Smyrl, Frank H. "Unionism, Abolitionism, and Vigilantism in Texas, 1856-1865." M.A. thesis, Univ. of Texas, 1961.

365. Summerfield, Charles [pseud. of Alfred W. Arrington].   THE DESPERADOES OF THE SOUTH-WEST: CONTAINING AN ACCOUNT OF THE CANE HILL MURDERERS, TOGETHER WITH THE LIVES OF SEVERAL OF THE MOST NOTORIOUS REGULATORS AND MODERATORS OF THAT REGION. New York: W. H. Graham, 1847.   The Cane Hill Murders occurred in Arkansas in 1839. See "American Lynching.--The Desperadoes of the South-West" in this bibliography.

366. Summerfield, Charles [pseud. of Alfred W. Arrington]. ILLUSTRATED LIVES AND ADVENTURES OF THE DESPERADOES OF THE NEW WORLD; CONTAINING AN ACCOUNT OF THE DIFFERENT MODES OF LYNCHING; THE CANE HILL MURDERS; THE

VICTIMS; THE EXECUTION; THE JUSTIFICATION, ETC., ETC.; AS WELL AS THE LIVES OF THE PRINCIPAL DUELLISTS AND THE DUELLING.   TOGETHER WITH THE LIVES OF THE MOST NOTORIOUS REGULATORS AND MODERATORS IN THE KNOWN WORLD. Philadelphia: T. B. Peterson, [1849?].   The Cane Hill murders occurred in Arkansas, 1839.

367. Synhorst, Curtis H.   "Antebellum Vigilantes: The Slicker War in Missouri." GATEWAY HERITAGE, Vol. 3, No. 1 (Summer 1982): 34-48. Violence in 1830s and '40s for many different reasons.

368. Tabscott, Robert W.   "Elijah Parish Lovejoy: Portrait of a Radical." GATEWAY HERITAGE,   Vol. 8, No. 3 (Winter 1987-1988): 32-39. Lynched at Alton, IL, 1837.

369. "A tale of terror!" NILES' WEEKLY REGISTER, Fourth Series, Vol. 14, No. 14 [Vol. 50, Whole No. 1,289] (June 4, 1836): 234.   [McIntosh] was burned alive in St. Louis.   Brief.

"Terrible Application of Lynch Law." See "Arkansas.   Terrible . . ." in this bibliography.

370. [Thomas, William.] Defensor. THE ENEMIES OF THE CONSTI-TUTION DISCOVERED, OR, AN INQUIRY INTO THE ORIGIN AND TENDENCY OF POPULAR VIOLENCE.   CONTAINING A COM-PLETE AND CIRCUMSTANTIAL ACCOUNT OF THE UNLAWFUL PROCEEDINGS AT THE CITY OF UTICA,   OCTOBER 21ST, 1835; THE DISPERSION OF THE STATE ANTI-SLAVERY CONVENTION BY THE AGITATORS, THE DESTRUCTION OF A DEMOCRATIC PRESS, AND OF THE CAUSES   WHICH LED THERETO, TO-GETHER WITH A CONCISE TREATISE ON THE PRACTICE OF THE COURT OF HIS HONOR JUDGE LYNCH.   ACCOMPANIED WITH NUMEROUS HIGHLY INTERESTING AND IMPORTANT DOCU-MENTS. New York: Leavitt, Lord & Co.; Utica: G. Tracy, 1835. Judge Lynch part is on pp. 48-53.   Alleges that some community leaders secretly abet mob violence (riots).   Does not deal with corporal or lethal lynching.

371. Tyree, William Romaine.   "The Origin of Lynching." THE GREEN BAG, Vol. 25, No. 9 (Sept. 1913): 393-94.

372. Udal, J. S.   "Mediaeval Lynch Laws in Modern Use." NOTES AND QUERIES [London], Ninth Series, Vol. 2, No. 29 (July 16, 1898): 56-57.

"Uses and Abuses of Lynch Law." See P. P.

373. "The Vigilance Committee: Richmond during the War of 1812." THE VIRGINIA MAGAZINE OF HISTORY AND BIOGRAPHY, Vol. 7, No. 3 (Jan. 1900): 225-41.   Continued by "Richmond During the War of 1812," ibid., Vol. 7, No. 4 (April 1900): 406-18.

374. Vincent, J. W. "The 'Slicker War' and Its Consequences." MISSOURI HISTORICAL REVIEW, Vol. 7, No. 3 (April 1913): 138-45.   Vigilante conflict with criminals in Missouri.

375. Walker, James Loy. "The Regulator Movement: Sectional Controversy in North Carolina." Masters thesis, Louisiana State Univ., Baton Rouge, 1962.

376. Wallace, Charles.   A CONFESSION OF THE AWFUL AND BLOODY TRANSACTIONS IN THE LIFE OF CHARLES WALLACE, THE FIEND-LIKE MURDERER OF MISS MARY ROGERS, THE BEAUTIFUL CIGAR-GIRL OF BROADWAY, NEW YORK, WHOSE FATE HAS FOR SEVERAL YEARS PAST BEEN WRAPT IN THE MOST PROFOUND MYSTERY: TOGETHER WITH AN AUTHENTIC STATEMENT OF THE MANY BURGLARIES AND MURDERS OF WALLACE, AND THE NOTORIOUS AND DARING THIEF, SNELL-ING: AND AN ACCOUNT OF THE MURDER AND ROBBERY OF MR. PARKS, OF NEWPORT, KENTUCKY, ALSO PERPETRATED BY WALLACE; A THRILLING NARRATIVE OF HIS INTERCOURSE WITH THE BROWN MURDERESS, EMELINE MORERE, WHO, AT HIS INSTIGATION, ASSASSINATED HER MASTER AND MISTRESS, AND THEIR FOUR HELPLESS CHILDREN, WITH AN AXE.   FOR WHICH ATROCIOUS ACT THEY WERE BURNED ALIVE BY A MOB OF INFURIATED LYNCHERS, ON THE BANKS OF THE MISSISSIPPI, ON THE 11TH DAY OF AUGUST 1850.   FROM HIS OWN MEMO-RANDA, GIVEN AT THE BURNING STAKE, TO THE REV. HENRY TRACY. New Orleans: E. E. Barclay, & Co., 1851.   The double lynching is on pp. 30-31, with an illustration of it on p. [32].

377. "The War of the Regulation--Its Causes and Its Effects." In COLO-NIAL RECORDS OF NORTH CAROLINA, Vol. 8, pp. 652-54. Ed. by William L. Saunders. Raleigh: P. M. Hall, Printer to the State, 1886-1890. Reprinted from John Haywood's Civil and Political History of Tennessee, 1823.

378. Weir, Robert M. "'The Violent Spirit,' the Reestablishment of Order, and the Continuity of Leadership in Post-Revolutionary South Carolina." In AN UNCIVIL WAR: THE SOUTHERN BACKCOUNTRY DURING THE AMERICAN REVOLUTION, pp. 70-98. Ed. by Ronald Hoffman, Thad W. Tate, and Peter J. Albert. Charlottesville: Univ. Press of Virginia,

1985. Includes vigilantism.

379. Whittenburg, James Penn.   "Backwoods Revolutionaries: Social Context and Constitutional Theories of the North Carolina Regulators, 1765-1771. Ph.D. diss., Univ. of Georgia, 1974.   See Diss. Ab. Intl., Vol. 35, No. 8 (Feb. 1975): 5327A-5328A.

380. Whittenburg, James Penn. "Planters, Merchants, and Lawyers: Social Change and the Origins of the North Carolina Regulation." WILLIAM AND MARY QUARTERLY, Third Series, Vol. 34, No. 2 (April 1977): 215-38.

381. Williams, Jack K. "Crime and Punishment in Alabama, 1819-1840." THE ALABAMA REVIEW, Vol. 6, No. 1 (Jan. 1953): 14-30.   See pp. 27-29 for vigilance committees.

382. Williams, Jack Kenny. VOGUES IN VILLAINY: CRIME AND RETRIBUTION IN ANTE-BELLUM SOUTH CAROLINA. Columbia: Univ. of South Carolina Press, 1959.   See "Lynch law" and "Vigilance societies" in index.

383. Wills, George S. "Lynch's Creek." THE NATION, Vol. 76, No. 1968 (March 19, 1903): 225-26.   Letter on the origin of term "lynch law."

384. Winters, Edwin.   THE TERRIBLE AND ALL ABSORBING NARRATIVE AND CONFESSION OF EDWIN WINTERS, WITH AN AUTHENTIC STATEMENT OF THE HORRIBLE ASSASSINATION OF MISS EUGENIE BLAKEMAN, ON BOARD A WESTERN STEAMER: WITH A CORRECT ACCOUNT OF THE UNFORTUNATE FATE OF MISS KATE BELMONT, TO WHICH IS ADDED A THRILL-ING ACCOUNT OF WINTERS' FEARFUL CONFLICT WITH AND ESCAPE FROM A BAND OF WESTERN DESPERADOES, WHO ATTEMPTED TO LYNCH HIM ON THE BANKS OF THE MISSIS-SIPPI RIVER, ALSO THE MOST STARTLING DEVELOPMENTS RELATIVE TO A CONSPIRACY TO REVOLUTIONIZE THE UNIT-ED STATES BY A WESTERN CONFEDERATION, WITH AN ACCOUNT OF THE CRUEL ASSASSINATION OF THEIR QUEEN IN AN UNDERGROUND PALACE IN ARKANSAS. New York: Barclay & Co., [1856?].   Attempted lynching is on pp. 16-17.

385. Wish, Harvey. "The Slave Insurrection Panic of 1856.   JOURNAL OF SOUTHERN HISTORY, Vol. 5, No. 2 (May 1939): 206-22.

386. Wright, Elizur, "Judge Lawless vs. Law." THE QUARTERLY ANTI-SLAVERY MAGAZINE, Vol. 1, No. 4 (July 1836): 400-09.   The part

about the lynching of McIntosh (St. Louis, 1836) is brief; article is mainly about words and actions of Judge Lawless (real name), who gave directions to grand jury.

387. Wright, John Livingston. "Elijah Parrish Lovejoy: The First Anti-slavery Martyr." THE COLORED AMERICAN MAGAZINE, Vol. 2, No. 3 (Jan. 1901): 163-68.   He was lynched at Alton, IL, 1837.

388. Wyatt-Brown, Bertram.   SOUTHERN HONOR: ETHICS AND BEHAVIOR IN THE OLD SOUTH. New York: Oxford Univ. Press, 1982. See Chapter 16, "Charivari and Lynch Law."

III

Civil War through 1881

389. Acheson, Sam, and O'Connell, Julie Ann Hudson, eds. GEORGE WASHINGTON DIAMOND'S ACCOUNT OF THE GREAT HANGING AT GAINESVILLE, 1862. Austin: Texas State Historical Association, 1963. Written in 1860s and '70s.

390. B., C. "Lynch Law in America." THE LEISURE HOUR [London], No. 903 (April 17, 1869 [sic; April 1, 1869; 1st p. of each issue gives a date later than the 1st of the month]): 245-47.

391. Baily, Joe. "The Magruder Murder." THE PACIFIC NORTHWEST-TERNER, Vol. 7, No. 2 (Spring 1963): 17-31. See p. 17 for earlier lynching of Nelson Scott, David English, and William Peoples (1863).

392. Barrett, Thomas. THE GREAT HANGING AT GAINESVILLE, COOKE COUNTY, TEXAS, OCTOBER, A.D. 1862. Gainesville, TX, 1885. Reprint ed.; Austin: Texas State Historical Assn., 1961.

393. Barrett, Thomas. "The Great Hanging at Gainesville, Texas, 1862." OLD WEST [Iola, WI], Vol. 17, No. 4, Whole No. 68 (Summer 1981): 49-66. Reprint of 1885 book with illustration added.

394. Betts, Vicki. "'Private and Amateur Hangings': The Lynching of W. W. Montgomery, March 15, 1863." SOUTHWESTERN HISTORICAL QUARTERLY, Vol. 88, No. 2 (Oct. 1984): 145-66. Confederates kidnapped him from Mexico.

395. Blackington, Alton H. YANKEE YARNS. New York: Dodd, Mead, 1954. See "Presque Isle Lynching," pp. 182-92. James Cullen was lynched in 1873 near Mapleton (then Ball's Mills), Aroostook County, Maine.

396. Bogue, Jesse Parker, Jr. "Violence and Oppression in North Carolina During Reconstruction 1865-1873." Ph.D. diss., Univ. of Maryland, 1973. See Diss. Ab. Intl., Vol. 34, No. 7 (Jan. 1974): 4139A.

397. Brasseaux, Carl A. "Ozeme Carriere and the St. Landry Jayhawkers, 1863-1865." ATTAKAPAS GAZETTE, Vol. 13, No. 4 (Winter 1978): 185-89. Mentions vigilantes.

398. Cantrell, Gregg. "Racial Violence and Reconstruction Policy in Texas, 1867-1868." SOUTHWESTERN HISTORICAL QUARTERLY, Vol. 93, No. 3 (Jan. 1990): 333-55. See pp. 350 and 351.

399. Carpenter, John A. "Atrocities in the Reconstruction Period." THE JOURNAL OF NEGRO HISTORY, Vol. 47, No. 4 (Oct. 1962): 234-47. Argues there was more violence against blacks in post-bellum South than many accounts would have one believe. Deals with few specific atrocities [but some would now be called lynchings].

400. Clark, James Lemuel. CIVIL WAR RECOLLECTIONS OF JAMES LEMUEL CLARK: INCLUDING PREVIOUSLY UNPUBLISHED MATERIAL ON THE GREAT HANGING AT GAINESVILLE, TEXAS IN OCTOBER, 1862. Edited and with an introduction by L. D. Clark. College Station: Texas A&M Univ. Press, 1984.

401. Cranfill, J. B. "The Story of a Mob." THE INDEPENDENT, Vol. 53, No. 2721 (Jan. 24, 1901): 213-14. Killing of a white man (Scoby) who taught at a school for blacks in Bastrop County, Texas, 1874.

402. Crouch, Barry A. "A Spirit of Lawlessness: White Violence; Texas Blacks, 1865-1868." JOURNAL OF SOCIAL HISTORY, Vol. 18, [No. 2] (Winter 1984): 217-32. Although the author does not refer to many of the acts of violence as lynchings, they could be so classified.

403. Davison, Charles Clement. "Race Friction in the South Since 1865." Ph.D. diss., Southern Baptist Theological Seminary, 1922.

404. Day, J. H. LYNCHED! A FIENDISH OUTRAGE--A TERRIBLE RETRIBUTION! COMPLETE HISTORY OF THE ARREST AND TRIAL OF ALEXANDER McLEOD, ABSALOM AND JACOB KIMMEL, FOR THE MURDER OF THE LITTLE GIRL, MARY ARABELLE SECAUR, IN MERCER COUNTY, OHIO; WITH AN ACCOUNT OF THE HANGING OF TWO OF THE MURDERERS BY AN ORGAN-IZED MOB, INCLUDING THE EVIDENCE TAKEN ON THE TRIAL, THE CONFESSION OF ABSALAM KIMMEL AND THE SPEECH OF McLEOD ON THE SCAFFOLD; ILLUSTRATED. Celina, OH: A. P. J.

Snyder, [1872?].   All involved were white. Lynching victims (July 1872) were A. Kimmel and A. McLeod.

405. Dorson, Richard M. "The Lynching of the McDonald Boys." THE AMERICAN MERCURY, Vol. 66, No. 294 (June 1948): 698-703. Two cousins. Menominee, Michigan, 1881.

406. Ellsworth, Lois Council. "San Antonio during the Civil War." M.A. thesis, Univ. of Texas, 1938.   Includes vigilantism.

407. Escott, Paul D. "White Republicanism and Ku Klux Klan Terror: The North Carolina Piedmont During Reconstruction." In RACE, CLASS, AND POLITICS IN SOUTHERN HISTORY: ESSAYS IN HONOR OF ROBERT F. DURDEN, pp. 3-34. Ed. by Jeffrey J. Crow, Paul D. Escott, and Charles L. Flynn, Jr. Baton Rouge: Louisiana State Univ. Press, 1989. Includes whippings.

408. Ezell, John Samuel.   THE SOUTH SINCE 1865.   New York: Macmillan, 1975.   See pp. 359-64, 401 for lynching. Page 401: governor of South Carolina pardoned three black lynchers of a white man [no date].

409. Gildrie, Richard P. "Lynch Law and the Great Clarksville Fire of 1878; Social Order in a New South Town." TENNESSEE HISTORICAL QUARTERLY, Vol. 42, No. 1 (Spring 1983): 58-75.

410. Graves, John William. TOWN AND COUNTRY: RACE RELA-TIONS IN AN URBAN-RURAL CONTEXT, ARKANSAS, 1865-1905. Fayetteville: Univ. of Arkansas Press, 1990.   See "Lynching" and "Violence" in index.

411. Hiatt, James M. MURDER AND MOB LAW IN INDIANA! THE SLAUGHTER OF THE PARK FAMILY!! AND THE LYNCHING OF THE NEGROES TAYLOR, DAVIS AND JOHNSON. A CHAPTER OF HORRORS UNEQUALLED IN THE HISTORY OF CRIME!! SHOW-ING THAT MOBS ARE MORE TO BE FEARED THAN CRIMINALS. Indianapolis: Indianapolis Printing and Publishing House, 1872.   Events in late 1871.

412. Hodes, Martha. "The Sexualization of Reconstruction Politics: White Women and Black Men in the South after the Civil War." JOURNAL OF THE HISTORY OF SEXUALITY, Vol. 3, No. 3 (Jan. 1993): 402-17. Includes lynching as a form of social control.

413. [Hopkins, Charles Ferren.] "Hell and the Survivor." AMERICAN HERITAGE, Vol. 33, No. 6 (Oct.-Nov. 1982): 78-93.   See pp. 83-85 for

gangs of robbers and murderers among prisoners at Andersonville, GA, and their punishment by other prisoners (called Regulators).

414. Horn, Stanley F., ed. "The Papers of Major Alonzo Wainwright." TENNESSEE HISTORICAL QUARTERLY, Vol. 12, No. 2 (June 1953): 182-84.   Report on a lynching in Knoxville, Feb. 13, 1866.   Victim: member of 16th U.S. Colored Infantry.

415. Howard, Gene L.   DEATH AT CROSS PLAINS: AN ALABAMA RECONSTRUCTION TRAGEDY.   University, AL: Univ. of Alabama Press, 1984.   The lynching of Canadian minister William Luke, a teacher of black railroad workers in Cross Plains.

416. Hughes, J. W. (Jack).   "Mob Action in '60s Took 40 Lives." FRONTIER TIMES [Bandera, TX], Vol. 11, No. 7 (April 1934): 321-23. Gainesville hangings.

417. Johnson, Nancy Rue.   "When Death Danced With Eleven."   THE JUNIOR HISTORIAN [Austin: Texas State Historical Assn.], Vol. 17, No. 6 (May 1957): 1-4, 22-23.   (Author was high school student.)   In 1872 Nance Hill, female, and five males were lynched because one of them had fatally wounded a man in Springtown, Parker County, Texas.   A few days later her mother and four adult sisters were also lynched.

418. Keener, Charles Virgil.   "Racial Turmoil in Texas, 1865-1874." M.A. thesis, North Texas State Univ., 1971.

419. Kharif, Wali Rashash.   "Establishing and Maintaining White Supremacy in Florida: 1876-1905." THE GRIOT, Vol. 12, No. 2 (Fall 1993): 21-34. Includes lynching.

420. Kiger, Joseph C.   "Social Thought as Voiced in Rural Middle Tennessee Newspapers, 1878-1898."   TENNESSEE HISTORICAL QUARTERLY, Vol. 9, No. 2 (June 1950): 131-54.   Has section on newspaper attitudes toward lynch law (pp. 145-46).

421. Kirwan, Albert D.   REVOLT OF THE REDNECKS: MISSISSIPPI POLITICS, 1876-1925. Lexington: Univ. of Kentucky Press, 1951.   See pp. 163-64 for lynching.

422. Klatt, Christine Granger. THEY DIED AT THEIR POSTS: A TRUE HISTORICAL ACCOUNT OF MURDER AND LYNCHING ON THE WISCONSIN FRONTIER 1881. Menomonie, WI: Dunn County Historical Society, 1976.   Ed Maxwell (aka Ed Williams) was hanged at Durand.

423. Kremm, Thomas Wesley. "Race Relations in Texas, 1865 to 1870." M.A. thesis, Univ. of Houston, 1970.

424. Logan, Rayford W. THE BETRAYAL OF THE NEGRO, FROM RUTHERFORD B. HAYES TO WOODROW WILSON. New ed.; New York: Collier Books, 1965.   Originally published as The Negro in American Life and Thought: The Nadir, 1877-1901 (New York: Dial Press, 1954). See "Lynching" in index.

425. [Madison, Henry.] THE MURDER OF THE GEOGLES AND LYNCHING OF THE FIEND SNYDER, BY THE OTHERWISE PEACEABLE AND LAW-ABIDING CITIZENS OF BETHLEHEM, PA., AND ITS VICINITY. A COLD-BLOODED MURDER, A SWIFT RETRIBUTION, A REMARKABLE CASE, AND THE FIRST RESORT TO LYNCH LAW IN PENNSYLVANIA. Philadelphia: Barclay & Co., [1881].

426. McCaslin, Richard B. TAINTED BREEZE: THE GREAT HANGING AT GAINESVILLE, TEXAS, 1862. Baton Rouge: Louisiana State Univ. Press, 1994.

427. McCornack, Elwin A. "When the Rebel Flag Flew on the Long Tom." LANE COUNTY HISTORIAN, Vol. 6, No. 1 (March 1961): 14-18.   Mob in Eugene, OR, (in 1862?) attacked jail holding Southerner from nearby community where Confederate flag was flying. Mob dispersed upon arrival of sheriff and posse. Mob's intent to lynch is only implied.

428. Miller, Jacqueline. "The Jayhawker Massacre: A Vermillion Parish Legend." ATTAKAPAS GAZETTE, Vol. 11, No. 1 (Spring 1976): 34-35. In April, 1863, vigilantes ambushed and killed 11 bandits called Jayhawkers.

429. Moffett, Cleveland. "The Destruction of the Reno Gang. Stories from the Archives of the Pinkerton Detective Agency." McCLURE'S MAGAZINE, Vol. 4, No. 6 (May 1895): 549-54.   Includes activities of Secret Vigilance Committee of Southern Indiana, 1868.

THE MURDER OF THE GEOGLES AND LYNCHING OF THE FIEND SNYDER . . . See [Madison, Henry.]

430. Noble, Madeleine M. "The White Caps of Harrison and Crawford County, Indiana: A Study in the Violent Enforcement of Morality." Ph.D. diss., Univ. of Michigan, 1973.   See Diss. Ab. Intl., Vol. 35, No. 1 (July 1974): 377A-378A.   Deals with southern IN, 1873-1893, where the term "white cap" originated as meaning "collective, violent, extra-legal actions, locally inspired."

431. Peek, Ralph L. "Aftermath of Military Reconstruction, 1868-1869." THE FLORIDA HISTORICAL QUARTERLY, Vol. 43, No. 2 (Oct. 1964): 123-41.   Page 125: Mob of Negroes gave Negro murderer of white woman 100 lashes, then hanged him.

432. Percy, Adrian. TWICE OUTLAWED: A PERSONAL HISTORY OF ED AND LON MAXWELL ALIAS THE WILLIAMS BROTHERS: A RECORD OF HIGHWAY ROBBERY, HORSE STEALING, ROMANCE, AND MURDER, TO WHICH IS ADDED A DETAILED AND GRAPHIC ACCOUNT OF THE ARREST AND LYNCHING OF EDWARD MAXWELL AT DURAND, WISCONSIN, NOVEMBER 19, 1881. Chicago: W. B. Conkey Co., [1882?].   Cover title: The Williams Brothers.

433. "'Regulators' Get 'A' in Deportment." MISSOURI HISTORICAL REVIEW, Vol. 44, No. 3 (April 1950): 335.   New group; about 200 came to Springfield, June 1866.   One paragraph.

434. Rice, Lawrence D. THE NEGRO IN TEXAS 1874-1900.   Baton Rouge: Louisiana State Univ. Press, 1971.   See "Lynching" and "Violence" in index.

435. Rice, Lawrence Delbert. "The Negro in Texas 1874-1900." Ph.D. diss., Texas Technological College, 1967.   See Diss. Ab., Vol. 28, No. 11 (May 1968): 4582A.

436. Rogers, William Warren. "The Boyd Incident: Black Belt Violence during Reconstruction." CIVIL WAR HISTORY, Vol. 21, No. 4 (Dec. 1975): 309-29.   Mob murder by Ku Klux Klan of A. Boyd at Eutaw, Alabama, 1870; and three lynchings (see pp. 325-26).

437. Rowell, George S. "A Maine Lynching: The Violent Death of James Cullen at Mapleton, 1873." MAINE HISTORICAL SOCIETY QUARTER-LY, Vol. 19, No. 4 (Spring 1980): 207-25.

438. Rutherford, Philip. "The Great Gainesville Hanging." CIVIL WAR TIMES ILLUSTRATED, Vol. 17, No. 1 (April 1978): 12-20. Forty-one pro-Union men were hanged in Texas, Oct. 1862.

439. Schrink, Jeffrey, and Schrink, Frances.   "Hangman's Crossing." INDIANA FOLKLORE, Vol. 11, No. 1 (1978): 87-97.   Vigilantes hanged three outlaws, 1868, near Seymour, Indiana.

440. Shapiro, Herbert.   "Afro-American Responses to Race Violence During Reconstruction." SCIENCE & SOCIETY, Vol. 36, No. 2 (Summer 1972): 158-70.   Hardly any reference to lynching (p. 167), but much

violence mentioned was tantamount to lynching.

441. "Sheriff Stubinger Murder." ATTAKAPAS GAZETTE [Louisiana], Vol. 14, No. 1 (Spring 1979): 43-44.   After black man named Christophe Robert killed the sheriff, he was lynched by hanging (Nov. 1869).

442. Simpson, Brooks D. "This Bloody and Monstrous Crime." CONSTI-TUTION, Vol. 4, No. 3 (Fall 1992): 38-47. Colfax, LA, massacre of over 100 blacks, 1873. Many deaths during Easter Sunday battle as whites attacked courthouse held by blacks. Arguable as to lynching, but 37 black prisoners were shot the evening after the battle.

443. Slabey, Vera, ed. DURAND 1881: MURDERS OF THE COLEMAN BROTHERS, SEARCH FOR THE WILLIAMS/MAXWELL BROTHERS, LAST LYNCHING IN WISCONSIN; VERBATIM EXCERPTS FROM THE PEPIN COUNTY COURIER [W. H. Huntington, ed.]. Durand, WI: Pepin County Historical Society, 1987.

444. Smallwood, James. "Disaffection in Confederate Texas: The Great Hanging at Gainesville." CIVIL WAR HISTORY, Vol. 22, No. 4 (Dec. 1976): 349-60.

445. Smith, Shirley M.   "The Negro 1877-1898, as Portrayed in the Cincinnati Enquirer." M.A. thesis, Howard Univ., 1948.   For this paper's treatment of lynching. See also Billingslea, Sebron, in Chapter IV in this bibliography.

446. Stearns, Charles. THE BLACK MAN OF THE SOUTH, AND THE REBELS; OR, THE CHARACTERISTICS OF THE FORMER, AND THE RECENT OUTRAGES OF THE LATTER. N.Y: American News Co.; Boston: N. E. News Co., 1872; reprint ed.: New York: Negro Universi-ties Press, 1969.   See Chapter XXXVII (pp. 398-411).

447. Swerkstrom, James R. "Double Vengeance." TRUE WEST [Iola, WI], Vol. 29, No. 5, Whole No. 176 (May 1982): 28-32.   Includes lynching of Ed Maxwell (alias Ed Williams) at Durand, Wisconsin, Nov. 1881.

448. Terrell, J. C. "Lynch Law in Texas in the Sixties." THE GREEN BAG, Vol. 14, No. 8 (Aug. 1902): 382-83.

449. Tindall, George Brown. SOUTH CAROLINA NEGROES: 1877-1900. Columbia, SC: Univ. of South Carolina Press, 1952.   See "Violence" in index. Chap. 12, "The Context of Violence" (pp. 233-59), is largely about lynching.

450. Trelease, Allen W. WHITE TERROR: THE KU KLUX KLAN CONSPIRACY AND SOUTHERN RECONSTRUCTION. New York: Harper & Row, 1971.   See "Lynchings and murders," "Mob violence," "Terrorism and violence," and states by name in index.

451. Trexler, H. A.   "Episode in Border History."   SOUTHWEST REVIEW, Vol. 16, No. 2 (Jan. 1931): 236-50.   Gainesville, Texas, hangings, Oct. 1862; also several hangings in Wise County. Less attention devoted to massacre of Unionists on Aug. 10, 1862, "on the Nueces about twenty miles from Fort Clark and forty from the Rio Grande" (p. 237).

452. U.S. Congress. Senate. LOUISIANA IN 1878. REPORT OF THE UNITED STATES SENATE COMMITTEE TO INQUIRE INTO ALLEGED FRAUDS AND VIOLENCE IN THE ELECTIONS OF 1878, WITH THE TESTIMONY AND DOCUMENTARY EVIDENCE. VOLUME I. LOUISIANA. Sen. Report No. 855, 45th Cong., 3d Sess. Washington, DC: Government Printing Office, 1879. Serial Set 1840.   Sen. Report 855, Part 2, pp. 761-78, contains supplementary evidence about Louisiana.

453. U.S. Congress. Senate. SOUTH CAROLINA IN 1878. REPORT OF THE UNITED STATES SENATE COMMITTEE TO INQUIRE INTO ALLEGED FRAUDS AND VIOLENCE IN THE ELECTIONS OF 1878, WITH THE TESTIMONY AND DOCUMENTARY EVIDENCE. VOL. II. SOUTH CAROLINA AND MISSISSIPPI. Sen. Report 855, Part 2, 45th Cong., 3d Sess. Washington, DC: Government Printing Office, 1879. Serial Set 1840.   The part about Mississippi is pp. 697-760.

454. Vandal, Gilles. "'Bloody Caddo': White Violence Against Blacks in a Louisiana Parish, 1865-1876." JOURNAL OF SOCIAL HISTORY, Vol. 25, No. 2 (Winter 1991): 373-88.

455. Vandal, Gilles. "The Policy of Violence in Caddo Parish, 1865-1884." LOUISIANA HISTORY, Vol. 32, No. 2 (Spring 1991): 159-82.   Many of the murders of blacks by whites in efforts at social and political control would now be classed as lynchings.

456. Volland, Robert F. "The Reno Gang of Seymour." M.A. thesis, Indiana Univ., 1948.

457. Walker, Wayne T. "When Vigilantes Turn Bad." GOLDEN WEST [Rockville Centre, NY], Vol. 8, No. 4 (March 1972): 6-9, 64-65.   Bald Knobbers of Missouri, 1880s.

458. Webb, Warren Franklin. "A History of Lynching in California Since

1875." M.A. thesis, Univ. of California, Berkeley, 1935.

459. Wells, James M. THE CHISOLM MASSACRE: A PICTURE OF "HOME RULE" IN MISSISSIPPI. 3d ed.; Chicago, 1877; reprint ed.: New York: Haskell House, 1969.   Five whites were murdered by Kemper County, Mississippi, mob, April, 1877.   See also James D. Lynch, <u>Kemper County Vindicated</u>.

460. Wharton, Vernon Lane. THE NEGRO IN MISSISSIPPI 1865-1890. Chapel Hill: Univ. of North Carolina Press, 1947; reprint: Westport, CT: Greenwood Press, 1984.   See the section "Interracial Violence" in Chapter XV (pp. 216-27) and especially pp. 224-27 on lynching.

461. White, Richard.   "Outlaw Gangs of the Middle Border: American Social Bandits." THE WESTERN HISTORICAL QUARTERLY, Vol. 12, No. 4 (Oct. 1981): 387-408.   Deals with Missouri, 1866-1882, and Oklahoma, 1890s. Includes gangs' relationship to vigilantism.

462. Williams, James C. "The Long Tom Rebellion." OREGON HISTOR-ICAL QUARTERLY,   Vol. 67, No. 1   (March 1966):   54-60. Attempted lynching of a Confederate sympathizer and later attempts to rescue him.

463. Windham, Allie Bayne.   "Methods and Mechanisms Used to Restore White Supremacy in Louisiana, 1872-1876." M.A. thesis, Louisiana State Univ., 1948.   Includes much violence which can be considered lynching.

464. Wingo, Horace Calvin. "Race Relations in Georgia, 1872-1908." Ph.D. diss., Univ. of Georgia, 1969.   See <u>Diss. Ab. Intl.</u>, Vol. 30, No. 12, Part 1 (June 1970): 5397A.   Mentions lynchings.

465. Wright, George C. RACIAL VIOLENCE IN KENTUCKY, 1865-1940: LYNCHINGS, MOB RULE, AND 'LEGAL LYNCHINGS.' Baton Rouge: Louisiana State Univ. Press, 1990.   Includes person-by-person list (pp. 307-23) of 353 "Victims of Lynchings," 1866-1934.

IV

1882 through 1916

466. "The Abbeville Lynching." THE CRISIS, Vol. 13, No. 3 (Jan. 1917): 120. Notes that the story appeared in The Independent for Dec. 11 [see Nash, Roy]; adds a bit to the account. Victim: Anthony Crawford; in South Carolina.

467. Abram, Morris B. "They Lynched an Innocent Man--as the Governor Tried to Save Him." TV GUIDE, Vol. 36, No. 4 (Jan. 23, 1988): 32-35. Leo Frank.

468. Adams, S. B. "Lynching and Its Remedy." In REPORT OF THE THIRTY-THIRD ANNUAL SESSION OF THE GEORGIA BAR ASSOCIATION, HELD AT TYBEE ISLAND, GEORGIA, JUNE 1-3, 1916, pp. 157-62. Ed. by Orville A. Park and Harry S. Strozier. Macon: J. W. Burke Co., 1916.

469. "Address of John Jay Chapman." HARPER'S WEEKLY, Vol. 56, No. 2909 (Sept. 21, 1912): 6. Speech at Coatesville, PA, Aug. 18, 1912, to commemorate lynching [of Zachariah Walker] in 1911. Title is first part of first sentence.

470. "An Address to the Public." THE COLORED AMERICAN MAGAZINE, Vol. 11, No. 5 (Nov. 1906): 332-34. Statement by Afro-American Council. Avers that "lynching is oftener the expression of race hatred than the punishment for any particular crime."

471. "Aftermaths." THE CRISIS, Vol. 6, No. 4 (Aug. 1913): 178-80. See p. 179 for two 1899 lynchings in Arkansas. One victim named Joe King.

472. Aked, Charles F. "Horrors of Lynching." CHRISTIAN LITERA-TURE AND THE REVIEW OF THE CHURCHES, Vol. 11, No. 4 [of

Christian Literature], Vol. 6, No. 4 [of Review of the Churches] (August 1894): 96-98.   Combined publication; the Christian Literature part has the letter "a" after each page number, while the other part does not.

473. Aked, Charles F.   "Lynch Law Rampant.   A Deep Disgrace to America. Miss Wells's Crusade." THE CHRISTIAN WORLD, Vol. 38, No. 1932 (April 12, 1894): 259.   Letter from Liverpool, England.

474. Aked, Charles F.   "The Race Problem in America." CONTEMPO-RARY REVIEW [London], Vol. 65, [No. 6] (June 1894): 818-27.   Pages 823-27 deal with lynching.

475. Alexander, Ann Field.   "'Like an Evil Wind': The Roanoke Riot of 1893 and the Lynching of Thomas Smith." THE VIRGINIA MAGAZINE OF HISTORY AND BIOGRAPHY, Vol. 100, No. 2 (April 1992): 173-206.

476. Alexander, Hooper.   "Race Riots and Lynch Law: The Cause and the Cure. I.--A Southern Lawyer's View." THE OUTLOOK, Vol. 85, No. 5 (Feb. 2, 1907): 259-63.   Continued by ". . . II. A Northern Professor's View," by J. E. Cutler (ibid., pp. 263-68).

477. Allison, Madeline G.   "A Lynching Map of the United States of America." THE CRISIS, Vol. 23, No. 4 (Feb. 1922): 168-69.   One dot on the map for each of 3,436 lynchings known to have taken place in the 32 years starting in 1889.

478. Alston, Robert C.   "Concerning Lynching." In REPORT OF THE THIRTY-THIRD ANNUAL SESSION OF THE GEORGIA BAR ASSOCIATION, HELD AT TYBEE ISLAND, GEORGIA, JUNE 1-3, 1916, pp. 141-56. Ed. by Orville A. Park and Harry S. Strozier. Macon: J. W. Burke Co., 1916.

479. "An American Atrocity." THE INDEPENDENT, Vol. 87, No. 3530 (July 31, 1916): 145-46.   Lynching of black teenager, Waco, Texas.

480. "The American Crime." THE CRISIS, Vol. 6, No. 2 (June 1913): 77. Comments on lynchings.

481. "Anarchy in Delaware." THE OUTLOOK, Vol. 74, No. 10 (July 4, 1903): 543-46.   Black man burned at stake in Wilmington, June, 1903, and subsequent violence between blacks and whites.

482. Anderson, Odin W.   "The Lynching of Hans Jakob Olson, 1889: the Story of a Norwegian-American Crime." NORWEGIAN-AMERICAN STUDIES, Vol. 29 (1983): 159-84.   Lynching near Blair, Wisconsin;

participants were tried and convicted.

483. "Another Victim at the Stake." THE VOICE OF THE NEGRO, Vol. 1, No. 4 (April 1904): 128.   Glenco Bays (black) burned at stake near Crossett, Arkansas.

484. "Anthony Crawford." THE CRISIS, Vol. 13, No. 2 (Dec. 1916): 67. Lynching of Crawford in Abbeville, South Carolina, Oct. 1916.

485. "Anti-American Riots in Mexico." THE INDEPENDENT, Vol. 69, No. 3233 (Nov. 17, 1910): 1061-62.   Mexican national burned at stake by Texas lynch mob.

486. "Anti-Semitism and the Frank Case." THE LITERARY DIGEST, Vol. 50, No. 3 (Jan. 16, 1915): 85-86.

487. Aptheker, Bettina. "The Suppression of the Free Speech: Ida B. Wells and the Memphis Lynching, 1892." SAN JOSE STUDIES, Vol. 3, No. 3 (Nov. 1977): 34-40.

488. Asbury, Herbert. THE FRENCH QUARTER: AN INFORMAL HISTORY OF THE NEW ORLEANS UNDERWORLD. New York: Knopf, 1936.   See pp. 403-16 passim, for mass lynching, 1891.

489. Asbury, Herbert. "Hearst Comes to Atlanta." THE AMERICAN MERCURY, Vol. 7, No. 25 (Jan. 1926): 87-95.   Has some material on the lynching of Leo Frank.

490. Ashbridge, George. "The Pennsylvania Lynching." THE NATION, Vol. 93, No. 2417 (Oct. 26, 1911): 392-93.   Letter. Coatesville.

491. THE ASHLAND TRAGEDY; THE CROW-BAR AND AX, THE SILENT WITNESSES. A HISTORY OF THE KILLING OF FANNY GIBBONS, EMMA CARICO, AND ROBBIE GIBBONS. Ashland, KY: J. M. Huff, [1883?]. Reprint ed.; Ashland, KY: Boyd County Historical Society, 1969. With "Note [by] W. J. Williamson, III" added. Facsimile of the 1883? edition. See also "Murder Will Out".

492. Aubrey, William. "Mob Law." In PROCEEDINGS OF THE SIX-TEENTH ANNUAL SESSION OF THE TEXAS BAR ASSOCIATION HELD IN THE CITY OF GALVESTON, JULY 28, 29 AND 30, 1897, pp 126-48. Austin: Texas Bar Assn., 1897.   Lynchings and the legal system. Same article: "Mob Law." The American Lawyer, Vol. V, No. 10 (Oct. 1897): 482-87.

493. "Auto-da-fe in Tyler, Texas." THE CRISIS, Vol. 4, No. 5 (Sept. 1912): 248.   Report from a St. Louis newspaper on the burning of a black man.

494. Babbitt, Dean Richmond.   "The Psychology of the Lynching Mob." THE ARENA, Vol. 32, No. 181 (Dec. 1904): 586-89.

495. Bacon, Leonard Woolsey.   LESSONS FROM THE RIOT IN CINCINNATI: A SERMON PREACHED TO THE WOODLAND CHURCH, WEST PHILADELPHIA, SUNDAY EVENING, APRIL 6TH 1884. Philadelphia: Siddall Brothers Printers, 1884.   Didactic; not very historical. [Riot flowed from attempt to lynch murderer who was only convicted of manslaughter.]

496. Bacote, Clarence A.   "Negro Proscriptions, Protests, and Proposed Solutions in Georgia, 1880-1908." THE JOURNAL OF SOUTHERN HISTORY, Vol. 25, No. 4 (Nov. 1959): 471-98.   Lynching: pp. 478-83.

497. "A Bad Week for Lynchers." THE INDEPENDENT, Vol. 46, No. 2389 (Sept. 13, 1894): 15 (1187).   Various recent lynchings, especially of two blacks in Alabama.

498. Bagozzi, Richard P. "Populism and Lynching in Louisiana (Comment on Inverarity, ASR April, 1976)."   AMERICAN SOCIOLOGICAL REVIEW, Vol. 42, No. 2 (April 1977): 355-58.   See Inverarity in this chapter.

499. Baiamonte, John V., Jr. SPIRIT OF VENGEANCE: NATIVISM AND LOUISIANA JUSTICE, 1921-1924. Baton Rouge, Louisiana State Univ. Press, 1986.   Includes Hennessey case, 1890-91, and lynching of 11 Italians. White caps in Tangipahoa Parish and other lynchings.

500. Baiamonte, John V., Jr.   "'Who Killa de Chief' Revisited: The Hennessey Assassination and Its Aftermath, 1890-1991 [sic]." LOUISIANA HISTORY, Vol. 33, No. 2 (Spring 1992): 117-46.

501. Bailey, J. W. "Some Thoughts on Lynching." THE SOUTH ATLAN-TIC QUARTERLY, Vol. 5, No. 4 (Oct. 1906): 353-54.   Part of sympo-sium; other parts by Charles B. Galloway and Robert Strange.

502. Baker, Ray Stannard. "The Thin Crust of Civilization; A Study of the Liquor Traffic in a Modern American City." THE AMERICAN MAGA-ZINE, Vol. 71, No. 6 (April 1911): 691-704.   July, 1910, lynching in Newark, Ohio, of a deputy participating in raids on illegal saloons.

503. Baker, Ray Stannard. "What Is a Lynching? A Study of Mob Justice,

South and North. I--Lynching in the South." McCLURE'S MAGAZINE, Vol. 24, No. 3 (Jan. 1905): 299-314.

504. Baker, Ray Stannard. "What Is a Lynching? A Study of Mob Justice, South and North. II. Lynching in the North." McCLURE'S MAGAZINE, Vol. 24, No. 4 (Feb. 1905): 422-30.

THE BALD KNOBBERS OR CITIZEN'S COMMITTEE OF TANEY AND CHRISTIAN COUNTIES, MISSOURI. See McConkey, F., and Groom, C. H.

505. Baldwin, D. P. "Lynch Law, Its Cause and Cure." THE INDIANA LAW JOURNAL, Vol. 1, No. 4 (April 1898): 143-48.

506. Ballard, Allen B. ONE MORE DAY'S JOURNEY: THE STORY OF A FAMILY AND A PEOPLE. New York: McGraw-Hill, 1984.   See chap. 9, 12, and 13 for violence, including lynching, in South Carolina in 50 years or so after Civil War.

507. ΒαρβαροϹ. "Lynch-Law in the United States." THE SPECTATOR [London], Vol. 73, No. 3454 (Sept. 8, 1894): 303.   Letter. Condemns lynching and vigilance committees.

Barnett, Ida B. See also Wells, Ida B., and Wells-Barnett, Ida B.

508. Barnett, Ida B. Wells.   "Lynching and the Excuse for It."   THE INDEPENDENT, Vol. 53, No. 2737 (May 16, 1901): 1133-36. See Addams, Jane, and Wells, Ida B.

509. Barrow, Elliott G. "On Lynching." THE NATION, Vol. 103, No. 2662 (July 6, 1916): 11.   Letter from man in Pensacola "not defending lynchings" but criticizing Northerners for not understanding that Southerners must defend their women from rape by "negro brutes."

510. Bauman, Mark K. "A Famous Atlanta Speaks Out Against Lynching: Bishop Warren Akin Candler and Social Justice."   THE ATLANTA HISTORICAL BULLETIN, Vol. 20, No. 1 (Spring 1976): 24-32. Occasioned by Andrew Sledd's article on lynching in 1902.

511. Baxter, Rex Mitchell. "A New Kind of Vigilance Committee." THE ARENA, Vol. 40, No. 228 (Dec. 1908): 572-76.   Citizens' committee, as in Lima, OH, working to get fair terms in granting of street railway franchises.

512. Beasley, Maurine. "The Muckrakers and Lynching: A Case Study in Racism." JOURNALISM HISTORY, Vol. 9, No. 3-4 (Autumn-Winter

1982-3): 86-91.   Some Progressive magazines were not aggressive in attacking lynching.

513. Beck, E. M.; Massey, James L.; and Tolnay, Stewart E. "The Gallows, The Mob, The Vote: Lethal Sanctioning of Blacks in North Carolina and Georgia, 1882-1930." LAW & SOCIETY REVIEW, Vol. 23, No. 2 (1989): 317-31.   Lynchings and executions relationship.

514. Beck, E. M., and Tolnay, Stewart E. "The Killing Fields of the Deep South: The Market for Cotton and the Lynching of Blacks, 1882-1930." AMERICAN SOCIOLOGICAL REVIEW, Vol. 55, No. 4 (Aug. 1990): 526-39.

515. Beck, E. M., and Tolnay, Stewart E. "A Season for Violence: The Lynching of Blacks and Labor Demand in the Agricultural Production Cycle in the American South." INTERNATIONAL REVIEW OF SOCIAL HISTORY, Vol. 37, Part 1 (1992): 1-24.   Title as given here on p. 1, but it's "A Season of . . ." on contents page. Deals with 1882-1930.

516. Beck, E. M., and Tolnay, Stewart E.   "Violence toward African Americans in the Era of the White Lynch Mob." In ETHNICITY, RACE, AND CRIME: PERSPECTIVES ACROSS TIME AND PLACE, pp. 121-44. Ed. by Darnell F. Hawkins. Albany: State University of New York Press, 1995.   Focuses on lynching, 1882-1930, and the extent to which interracial economic competition was a cause.

517. "'The Before Day Bogie.'" THE VOICE OF THE NEGRO, Vol. 1, No. 11 (Nov. 1904): 563-64.   Fantasy about Before Day Clubs has been used by whites to lynch, beat, and intimidate blacks.

518. Benjamin, R. C. O. SOUTHERN OUTRAGES; A STATISTICAL RECORD OF LAWLESS DOINGS. [Los Angeles?]: R. C. O. Benjamin, 1894.   Black author's 64-page book. Details of many lynchings, including Lee Walker (Memphis, 1892), multiple victims (Jefferson Parish, 1893), Henry Smith (Paris, TX, 1893), Ed Coy (Texarkana, 1892), John Peterson (taken from SC governor's mansion, 1893), and C. J. Miller (Bardsville, KY, 1893).

519. Berk, Richard A. "Proof? No. Evidence? No. A Skeptic's Comment on Inverarity's Use of Statistical Inference (Comment on Inverarity, ASR April 1976)." AMERICAN SOCIOLOGICAL REVIEW, Vol. 42, No. 4 (Aug. 1977): 652-56.   Concerned mainly with sampling, statistics, and inference. See Inverarity in this chapter.

520. Berry, Mary Frances. "Repression of Blacks in the South 1890-1945:

Enforcing the System of Segregation." In THE AGE OF SEGREGATION: RACE RELATIONS IN THE SOUTH, 1890-1945, pp. 29-43. Ed. by Robert Haws. Jackson: Univ. Press of Mississippi, 1978. See pp. 41-42 for lynching.

521. "The Best Defense." THE OUTLOOK, Vol. 74, No. 16 (Aug. 15, 1903): 927-29. Cause and cure of lynching and President Roosevelt's letter on the subject to Governor Durbin.

522. Billingslea, Sebron. "The Negro as Portrayed in the Cincinnati Enquirer, 1901-1920." M.A. thesis, Howard Univ., 1950. For this paper's treatment of lynching. See also Smith, Shirley M., in Chapter III in this bibliography.

523. Bischoff, Henry. "The Law's Delay No Excuse for Lynching." ALBANY LAW JOURNAL, Vol. 65, No. 11 (Nov. 1903): 337-41.

524. Bishop, Charles M. "The Causes, Consequences, and Cure of Mob Violence." In DEMOCRACY IN EARNEST: SOUTHERN SOCIOLOGI-CAL CONGRESS 1916-1918, pp. 191-200. Ed. by James E. McCulloch. Washington, DC: Southern Sociological Congress, 1918; reprint ed.; New York: Negro Universities Press, 1969.

525. Bishop, J. B. "An Instructive Parallel." THE NATION, Vol. 52, No. 1350 (May 14, 1891): 396. Three days of rioting in Cincinnati, March, 1884. Public perceived judicial system was incapable of condign punishment of criminals. Similar belief led to mass lynching in New Orleans, March, 1891; and other cities may be approaching same condition.

526. Bishop, Joseph B. "Lynching." THE INTERNATIONAL QUAR-TERLY, Vol. 8 (Sept.-Dec. 1903): 199-208.

527. Blair, Lewis H. "Lynching As A Fine Art." OUR DAY, Vol. 13, No. 76 (July-Aug. 1894): 307-14.

528. Bleckley, L. E. "Negro Outrage No Excuse for Lynching." THE FORUM, Vol. 16 (Nov. 1893): 300-02.

529. "A Blot on Civilization." THE OUTLOOK, Vol. 98, No. 17 (Aug. 26, 1911): 899. Coatesville, PA, lynching.

530. Bobbitt, L. B. "Lynching and Law." CHRISTIAN ADVOCATE [Nashville], Vol. 73, No. 27 (July 5, 1912): 12-13 (844-45). Anti-lynching article.

531. Boessenecker, John. "The Ruggles Boys' Death Treasure." WEST-ERNER [Encino, CA], Vol. 5, No. 3 (May-June 1973): 34-37.   Brothers John and Charlie were lynched at Redding, CA, 1892.

532. Bohrnstedt, George W.   "Use of the Multiple Indicators Multiple Causes (MIMIC) Model (Comment on Inverarity, ASR April 1976)." AMERICAN SOCIOLOGICAL REVIEW, Vol. 42, No. 4 (Aug. 1977): 656-63.   Says Inverarity's model "probably . . . should be rejected."   See Inverarity in this chapter.

533. Bonaparte, Charles J. "Lynch Law and Its Remedy." YALE LAW JOURNAL, Vol. 8, No. 8 (May 1899): 335-43.

534. Bonaparte, Chas. J. "Lynch law." LAW NOTES [Northport, N.Y.], Vol. 1, No. 12 (March 1898): 168-69.   Apologia for lynching.

535. Bontemps, Arna, and Conroy, Jack. ANYPLACE BUT HERE. New York: Hill & Wang, 1966.   [Earlier, shorter edition published as They Seek a City (Garden City, NY: Doubleday, Doran and Co., 1945).]   Black migration, especially from the South, and black life in new locales. See pp. 97-102 for Ida Wells and anti-lynching; pp. 147-50 for Springfield, IL, riot, 1908.

536. "Booker T. Washington on Lynching."   THE VOICE OF THE NEGRO, Vol. 1, No. 4 (April 1904): 166-67.

537. Botein, Barbara.   "The Hennessy Case: An Episode in American Nativism, 1890." Ph.D. diss., New York Univ., 1975.   See Diss. Ab. Intl., Vol. 36, No. 6 (Dec. 1975): 3918A.

538. Botein, Barbara. "The Hennessy Case: An Episode in Anti-Italian Nativism." LOUISIANA HISTORY, Vol., 20, No. 3 (Summer 1979): 261-79.   Italians were lynched in 1891.

539. "The Bottom Facts." THE INDEPENDENT, Vol. 46, No. 2357 (Feb. 1, 1894): 4 (132).   North Carolina resident asserts existence of large number of illicit sexual relations between blacks and whites; but discovery of such unions may result in lynching of black man (after white lover accuses him of rape).

540. "A Brave Sheriff." THE OUTLOOK, Vol. 94 (March 5, 1910): 511-12. Sheriff Nellis and a few deputies fought off a mob intent on lynching two blacks in Feb. 1910 in Cairo, IL; one of the mob leaders was killed.

541. Breckinridge, Clifton R.   "Is Lynching Advisable?"   In RACE

PROBLEMS OF THE SOUTH: REPORT OF THE PROCEEDINGS OF THE FIRST ANNUAL CONFERENCE HELD UNDER THE AUSPICES OF THE SOUTHERN SOCIETY FOR THE PROMOTION OF THE STUDY OF RACE CONDITIONS AND PROBLEMS IN THE SOUTH-- AT MONTGOMERY, ALABAMA, MAY 8, 9, 10, A. D. 1900, pp. 170-77 (in the section "Lynching as a Penalty"). Richmond, VA: B. F. Johnson Pub. Co. for The Southern Society, 1900.   Reprinted in John David Smith, ed., Racist Southern Paternalism, Vol. 2 of Anti-Black Thought 1863-1925: "The Negro Problem": An Eleven-Volume Anthology of Racist Writings (New York: Garland Publishing, 1993), pp. 286-93.

542. Breihan, Carl. "How They Hanged Jim Miller." REAL WEST [Derby, CT], Vol. 3, No. 10 (March 1960): 11, 47.   Some parts of this are identical to parts of the next item.

543. Breihan, Carl W. "Killing Jim Miller." REAL WEST [Derby, CT], Vol. 21, No. 158 (July 1978): 50-51.   Miller, a professional assassin and killer of Pat Garrett, was lynched with three other men in Ada, OK, 1909.

544. Bricker, L. O. "A Great American Tragedy." THE SHANE QUAR-TERLY, Vol. 4, No. 2 (April 1943): 89-95.   Leo Frank case. Letters by minister of church where Mary Phagan went to bible classes.

545. Brook, Kate Kinsey. "Side Lights on the Race Question." TO-MORROW, Vol. 3, No. 2 (Feb. 1907): 56-60.   George Young and sons were lynched for being "biggity" (p. 56). Analyzes rape as an alleged cause of lynching.

546. Brook, Kate Kinsey. "Side Lights on the Race Question." TO-MORROW, Vol. 3, No. 3 (March 1907): 33-38.   Some additional ideas on lynching and rape.

547. Brooks, R. P. "A Southern Professor on Lynching." THE NATION, Vol. 103, No. 2675 (Oct. 5, 1916): 321-22. Letter responding to Herbert L. Stewart's "The Casuistry of Lynch Law."

548. Brooks, Robert Preston.   GEORGIA STUDIES: SELECTED WRITINGS OF ROBERT PRESTON BROOKS. Ed. by Gregor Sebba. Athens: Univ. of Georgia Press, 1952.   See Chapter 8, "On Lynching" (pp. 216-22) for letter published in The Nation, Oct. 5, 1916, to which some comments by Brooks are here added.

549. Brophy, William Joseph. "The Black Texan, 1900-1950: A Quantitative History." Ph.D. diss., Vanderbilt Univ., 1974. See Diss. Ab. Intl., Vol. 35, No. 4 (Oct. 1974): 2165A. See pp. 253-62 for lynching.

550. Brown, Alexander. "Lynch Law." THE GREEN BAG, Vol. 5, No. 3 (March 1893): 116.   Corrections and additions to "The Lynch-Law Tree," in ibid., Vol. IV, No. 12 (Dec. 1892): 561-62.

551. Brown, L. J. "Philosophy of Lynching." THE VOICE OF THE NEGRO, Vol. 1, No. 11 (Nov. 1904): 554-59.   Popularly ascribed causes.

552. Brown, Tom Watson. "Review Essay: The Latest Works on the Leo Frank Case." ATLANTA HISTORY, Vol. 32, No. 1 (Spring 1988): 67-70. Reviews books by Mary Phagan, Robert Seitz Frey and Nancy Thompson-Frey, and Leonard Dinnerstein.

553. Bruce, John Edward. THE BLOOD RED RECORD. A REVIEW OF THE HORRIBLE LYNCHINGS AND BURNING OF NEGROES BY CIVILIZED WHITE MEN IN THE UNITED STATES, AS TAKEN FROM THE RECORDS. WITH COMMENTS BY JOHN EDWARD BRUCE. Albany: n.p., 1901.   Reprinted in The Selected Writings of John Edward Bruce: Militant Black Journalist, pp. 68-84. Ed. by Peter Gilbert. New York: Arno Press & The New York Times, 1971.

554. Bruce, W. Cabell. "Lynch Law in the South." THE NORTH AMERICAN REVIEW, Vol. 155, No. 430 (Sept. 1892): 379-81.   Though writing that lynching is wrong, author emphasizes his contention that the great amount of Southern lynching is an understandable effort by whites to protect their women from Negro ravishers.

555. Brundage, W. Fitzhugh. "The Darien 'Insurrection' of 1899: Black Protest During the Nadir of Race Relations." THE GEORGIA HISTORI-CAL QUARTERLY, Vol. 74, No. 2 (Summer 1990): 234-53.   Black responses to lynchings were varied--including violent prevention in McIntosh County, GA, 1899.   Page 248: criticizes Raper's account in Tragedy of Lynching of Darien 'Insurrection.' Page 251: map of lynchings, 1880-1930, of blacks in five different regions of Georgia.

556. Brundage, W. Fitzhugh. LYNCHING IN THE NEW SOUTH: GEORGIA AND VIRGINIA, 1880-1930. Urbana: Univ. of Illinois Press, 1993.

557. Brundage, W. Fitzhugh. "Mob Violence North and South, 1865-1940." THE GEORGIA HISTORICAL QUARTERLY, Vol. 75, No. 4 (Winter 1991): 748-70.   Review essay dealing with books by Downey and Hyser; Senechal; and Wright. Pages 759-60: criticism of Wright's explanation for decline of lynching.

558. Brundage, W. Fitzhugh. "The Varn Mill Riot of 1891: Lynchings,

Attempted Lynchings, and Justice in Ware County, Georgia." THE GEORGIA HISTORICAL QUARTERLY, Vol. 78, No. 2 (Summer 1994): 257-80.

559. Bruton, J. J., et al. BALD KNOB TRAGEDY OF TANEY AND CHRISTIAN COUNTIES, MISSOURI, IN EIGHT ACTS. Sparta, MO: J. J. Bruton, et al., 1887.   Creation and subsequent actions of Bald Knobbers. In National Union Catalog, Pre-1956, Vol. 31, p. 675, under Bald Knob.

560. Bryce, James. "Legal and Constitutional Aspects of the Lynching at New Orleans." THE NEW REVIEW [London], Vol. 4, No. 24 (May 1891): 835-97.   Victims: 11 Italians.

561. "The Burden."   THE CRISIS, Vol. 2, No. 3 (July 1911): 123-24. Lynchings, including six blacks at Lake City, Florida.

562. "The Burden." THE CRISIS, Vol. 2, No. 6 (Oct. 1911): 254-55. See last item on p. 255 for brief reference to lynching.

563. "The Burden." THE CRISIS, Vol. 3, No. 3 (Jan. 1912): 121.   Includes lynching comments.

564. "The Burden." THE CRISIS, Vol. 3, No. 5 (March 1912): 209.   Includes lynching statistics, comments, and a photograph.

565. "The Burden." THE CRISIS, Vol. 4, No. 1 (May 1912): 39.   Lynching statistics for 1885-1911.   Also in ibid., Vol. 4, No. 3 (July 1912): 147.

566. "The Burden." THE CRISIS, Vol. 7, No. 4 (Feb. 1914): 199-200. Lynchings in 1913. A list, by month and place. Includes many not reported in the listing compiled by the Chicago Tribune.

567. "The Burden." THE CRISIS, Vol. 7, No. 6 (April 1914): 302.   Two reports on lynching of two black men, Frank and Ernest Williams, in Louisiana.

568. "The Burden." THE CRISIS, Vol. 8, No. 4 (Aug. 1914): 197.   Lynching statistics, 1885-1913, and first half of 1914.

569. "The Burden." THE CRISIS, Vol. 9, No. 1 (Nov. 1914): 45.   Lynching statistics, 1885-1914.   Also in ibid., Vol. 9, No. 2 (Dec. 1914): 94; also in ibid., Vol. 9, No. 3 (Jan. 1915): 145.

570. "The Burden." THE CRISIS, Vol. 11, No. 3 (Jan. 1916): 144-45. Page 145: photos and text about burning of Will Stanley at Temple, Texas.

571. "The Burden.   Colored Men and Women Lynched Without Trial." THE CRISIS, Vol. 5, No. 6 (Feb. 1913): 194.   Statistics, 1885-1912.

572. "The Burden. Lynched a Woman." THE CRISIS, Vol. 4, No. 4 (Aug. 1912): 196-97.   Anne Bostwick, 60-year-old black woman, lynched at Pinehurst, GA. See also p. 227 in Sept. 1912 issue.

573. "The Burden. Lynchings, 1912." THE CRISIS, Vol. 5, No. 4 (Feb. 1913): 194-95.   A list, by date and place.

574. "Burning at the Stake." COLLIER'S WEEKLY, Vol. 31, No. 17 (July 25, 1903): 6.   Lynching barbarities in U.S. are worse than some cruelties in foreign lands. No specific case mentioned.

575. "A Burning Shame." THE INDEPENDENT, Vol. 77, No. 3400 (Feb. 2, 1914): 148.   Ex-President Taft urges federal law to protect aliens. Refers to New Orleans lynching of Italians and to cases of Chinese and Japanese victims of labor riots. See Taft in Chapter VII of this bibliography.

576. Burnside, Ronald D.   "Racism in the Administrations of Governor Cole Blease." THE PROCEEDINGS OF THE SOUTH CAROLINA HISTORICAL ASSOCIATION 1964, pp. 43-57.   See pp. 51-57 for lynching.

577. Busch, Francis X. GUILTY OR NOT GUILTY? AN ACCOUNT OF THE TRIALS OF THE LEO FRANK CASE, THE D. C. STEPHENSON CASE, THE SAMUEL INSULL CASE, THE ALGER HISS CASE. Indianapolis: Bobbs-Merrill, 1952.

578. Butler, Chas. C. "Lynching." THE AMERICAN LAW REVIEW, Vol. 44 (March-April 1910): 200-20.   Except for omission here of nine words at start of fifth paragraph, this is identical to pp. 48-69 of next item.

579. Butler, Chas. C.   "Lynching."   REPORT.   COLORADO BAR ASSOCIATION. TWELFTH ANNUAL MEETING, AT COLORADO SPRINGS, SEPTEMBER 3 AND 4, 1909. Vol. 12, pp. 48-69.

580. Butler, Chas. S.   "The Lynching of Negroes in America."   THE SPECTATOR [London], Vol. 73, No. 3452 (Aug. 25, 1894): 240. Letter. Anti-black. Asserts that cause of lynching for rape is "the law does not punish such offences [sic] by death."

581. Carroll, Richard L.   "The Impact of David C. Hennessey on New Orleans Society and the Consequences of the Assassination of Hennessey." M.A. thesis, Notre Dame Seminary [New Orleans], 1957.   See also Carroll,

Ralph Edward. "The Mafia in New Orleans, 1900-1907." M.A. thesis, Notre Dame Seminary [New Orleans], 1956.

582. Carter, David. "Outraged Justice: The Lynching of Postmaster Frazier Baker in Lake City, South Carolina, 1897-1899." Honors essay, Dept. of History, Univ. of North Carolina at Chapel Hill, 1992.

583. "The Case of Leo M. Frank." THE OUTLOOK, Vol. 110, No. 4 (May 26, 1915): 166-68.

584. Castleman, Harvey N. THE BALD KNOBBERS: THE STORY OF THE LAWLESS NIGHT-RIDERS WHO RULED SOUTHERN MISSOURI IN THE 80'S. Girard, KS: Haldeman-Julius Publications, 1944.

585. "Castration Instead of Lynching." ATLANTA JOURNAL-RECORD OF MEDICINE, Vol. 8, No. 7 (Oct. 1906): 456-58.

586. "The Cause of Lynching." THE CRISIS, Vol. 8, No. 3 (July 1914): 126-27.

587. "The Cause of Lynching." THE NATION, Vol. 61, No. 1591 (Dec. 26, 1895): 463.   A letter from Iowa (correspondent signed E.) saying lynching mostly flows from criminal tendencies of blacks and race prejudice among whites, both resulting largely from the institution of slavery.

588. "Causes of the Increase of Crimes and Lynchings in the Northern and Western States." THE CHRISTIAN ADVOCATE [New York], Vol. 69, No. 20 (May 17, 1894): 310-11.

589. Chafee, Zechariah, Jr. "Safeguarding Fundamental Human Rights: The Tasks of States and Nation." THE GEORGE WASHINGTON LAW REVIEW, Vol. 27, No. 4 (April 1959): 519-39.   Begins with New Orleans lynching of 11 men in 1891. Includes Sheriff Screws beating murder of Robert Hall, black man, in Georgia, 1943.

590. Cha-Jua, Sundiata Keita. "'Join hands and heart with law and order': The 1893 Lynching of Samuel J. Bush and the Response of Decatur's African American Community." ILLINOIS HISTORICAL JOURNAL, Vol. 83, No. 3 (Autumn 1990): 187-200.

591. Chaky, Doreen. "Hung and Shot Full of Holes." TRUE WEST [Stillwater, OK], Vol. 41, No. 7, Whole No. 315 (July 1994): 18-23.   C. M. Culbertson was lynched at Williston, North Dakota, Dec. 1913.

592. Chamberlayne, L. P. "Lynching." THE NATION, Vol. 103, No. 2663

(July 13, 1916): 34-35.   A letter from a South Carolina reader arguing against lynching and responding to a pro-lynching letter [see Winston, J. T., in this chapter].

593. Champion, Dale. "Lynching of the Ruggles Brothers." FRONTIER TIMES [Austin, TX], Vol. 35, No. 3, New Series No. 15 (Summer 1961): 14-15, 50.   Redding, California, July 1892.

594. Chandler, William E. "National Control of Elections." THE FORUM, Vol. 9 (Aug. 1890): 705-18.   See pp. 716-17 for about 40 blacks killed in Tallahatchie Co., Mississippi, 1889, in white suppression of Colored Farmers' Alliance. Killings seem to fit as lynchings.

595. Chapin, Earl V. "The Day They Hanged Ed Williams." REAL WEST [Derby, CT], Vol. 14, No. 98 (Nov. 1971): 33-34, 50-53.   Lynching of Ed Maxwell, Durand, Wisconsin, 1881.

596. Chapman, John Jay. "John Jay Chapman on Lynching." THE SOUTHERN WORKMAN, Vol. 42, No. 1 (Jan. 1913): 55-58.   Speech at Coatesville, Pennsylvania, Aug. 18, 1912.

597. Chapman, John Jay. "A Nation's Responsibility." EDUCATIONAL REVIEW, Vol. 44, [No. 5] (Dec. 1912): 460-65.   Editor's introduction and Chapman's speech in Coatesville, PA, one year after 1911 lynching.

598. "The Chautauqua Conference on the Mob Spirit." THE OUTLOOK, Vol. 74, No. 17 (Aug. 22, 1903): 960.   Lynching was conference topic.

599. "Chicago 'Indicts' the South." THE LITERARY DIGEST, Vol. 51, No. 14 (Oct. 2, 1915): 698-99.   In the wake of the Leo Frank lynching the Chicago Tribune described the South as "a region of illiteracy, blatant self-righteousness, cruelty, and violence." This elaborates on that and includes several Southern responses.

600. Chilton, William P. [No title, but sometimes listed as "Mobocracy," as in Index to Legal Periodicals to Dec. 1886, Vol. 1.] In PROCEEDINGS OF THE FOURTH ANNUAL MEETING OF THE ALABAMA STATE BAR ASSOCIATION HELD IN SUPREME COURT ROOM, MONTGOM-ERY, ALA., NOV. 20TH & 21ST, 1882, pp. 77-86. Montgomery: Barrett & Co., 1883.

601. "Christian Responsibility for Lynchings." CURRENT LITERATURE, Vol. 51, No. 4 (Oct. 1911): 404-05.   Includes quotations from article in The Continent by William T. Ellis on the Coatesville lynching.

602. "Christianity Versus Lynch Law." THE CONTINENT, Vol. 42, No. 36 (Sept. 7, 1911): 1269.   Editorial.

"City of New Orleans v Abbagnato." See ["Liability for Destruction . . ."]

603. "The Civilization of Mississippi." THE CRISIS, Vol. 7, No. 6 (April 1914): 285-86.   Lynching of Sam Petty, black man, in Mississippi, Feb. 1914.

604. Clark, Walter. "The True Remedy for Lynch Law." THE AMERI-CAN LAW REVIEW, Vol. 28 (Nov.-Dec., 1894): 801-07.

605. "Coatesville."   THE CRISIS, Vol. 5, No. 4 (Feb. 1913): 192-93. Pennsylvania.

606. "Coatesville Disgrace." THE CRISIS, Vol. 4, No. 2 (June 1912): 70-71.

607. "The Coatesville Fiasco." THE CRISIS, Vol. 3, No. 1 (Nov. 1911): 13.

608. "Coatesville Lynchers Free." THE LITERARY DIGEST, Vol. 44, No. 20 (May 18, 1912): 1023-24.

609. "The Coatesville Lynching." AMERICA, Vol. 5, No. 20 (Aug. 26, 1911): 470-71.

610. "The Coatesville Lynching." THE CRISIS, Vol. 2, No. 5 (Sept. 1911): 188.

611. "A Collegiate Move on Lynching." THE LITERARY DIGEST, Vol. 52, No. 4 (Jan. 22, 1916): 178.

612. "Colored Men Lynched Without Trial." THE CRISIS, Vol. 1, No. 2 (Dec. 1910): 26.

613. "Colored Men Lynched Without Trial." THE CRISIS, Vol. 1, No. 6 (April 1911): 28.   A list of yearly numbers from 1885 thru 1910. Also in ibid., Vol. 2, No. 2 (June 1911): 76; Vol. 2, No. 3 (July 1911): 123; Vol. 2, No. 6 (Oct. 1911): 254; Vol. 3, No. 1 (Nov. 1911): 34; Vol. 3, No. 2 (Dec. 1911): 76.

614. "Colored Men Lynched Without Trial." THE CRISIS, Vol. 3, No. 5 (March 1912): 209.   Gives statistics, 1885-1911, but says The Crisis believes many more were lynched in 1911 than the figures provided by the Chicago Tribune indicate. Accompanied by photo of lynching victim.

615. "Colored Men and Women Lynched Without Trial." THE CRISIS, Vol. 7, No. 4 (Feb. 1914): 199-200.

616. [Colored National League.]   OPEN LETTER TO PRESIDENT McKINLEY BY COLORED PEOPLE OF MASSACHUSETTS . . . [Boston, 1899.]   Complaints that McKinley was not acting to protect blacks from mob violence in the South. Reprinted as "Open Letter to President McKinley from Massachusetts Negroes" in A TASTE OF FREEDOM 1854-1927, pp. 93-101, ed. by Mortimer J. Adler and Charles Van Doren, Vol. II of The Negro in American History (3 vols.; [Chicago]: Encyclopaedia Britannica Educational Corp., 1969).

617. "Comments on the President's Letter." THE OUTLOOK, Vol. 74, No. 17 (Aug. 22, 1903): 959-60.   T. Roosevelt's lynching letter to Governor Durbin of Indiana.

618. Connolly, C. P. "The Frank Case." COLLIER'S, Vol. 54, No. 14 (Dec. 19, 1914): 6-7, 22-24.

619. Connolly, C. P. "The Frank Case." COLLIER'S, Vol. 54, No. 15 (Dec. 26, 1914): 18-20, 23-25.

620. Connolly, Christopher Powell. THE TRUTH ABOUT THE FRANK CASE. New York: Vail-Ballou Co., 1915.   Partly from Collier's.

621. "Contagion of Mob Violence; Vengeance of the Mob as a Check upon Crime; Blaming the Courts for Lynching; The Cure for Mobs." CASE AND COMMENT, Vol. 10, No. 2 (July 1903): 13-15.   Special reference to recent lynching at Wilmington, [Delaware].

622. "A Contagious Social Disease." THE INDEPENDENT, Vol. 85, No. 3505 (Feb. 7, 1916): 178.

623. Cook, Waldo L.   "Wars and Labor Wars." INTERNATIONAL JOURNAL OF ETHICS, Vol. 18, No. 3 (April 1908): 323-42.   Includes comments on lynching (pp. 332-33).

624. "The Cossack Regime in San Diego." MOTHER EARTH, Vol. 7, No. 4 (June 1912): 97-107.   Action against free-speech effort. One section is "Vigilante Committee."

625. "A Courageous Governor." THE OUTLOOK, Vol. 110, No. 9 (June 30, 1915): 492-93.   Governor Slaton's commutation of Leo Frank's death sentence; also on nature of mobs.

626. "Courts and Crime." THE CRISIS, Vol. 9, No. 6 (April 1915): 272. Several lynchings.

627. "Cowardice." THE CRISIS, Vol. 12, No. 6 (Oct. 1916): 270-71. Recent lynching in Gainesville, Florida.

628. Coxe, John E. "The New Orleans Mafia Incident." THE LOUISIANA HISTORICAL QUARTERLY, Vol. 20, No. 4 (Oct. 1937): 1067-1110. Lynching of 11 Italians, 1891. Originally a Master's thesis, Louisiana State Univ., 1928.

629. "Crime." THE CRISIS, Vol. 2, No. 1 (May 1911): 7. Includes: "The cases [sic] against the members of the mob who murdered twenty Negroes in Palestine, Tex., last July has [sic] not yet come to trial."

630-75. "Crime." THE CRISIS, Vol. 2, No. 2 (June 1911): 53. Many subsequent issues of this periodical have a section titled "Crime" which often has items dealing with lynching and mob violence. Those which need no special annotation are as follows: Vol. 2, No. 3 (July 1911): 99-100; Vol. 2, No. 4 (Aug. 1911): 142-44; Vol. 3, No. 1 (Nov. 1911): 11-12; Vol. 3, No. 2 (Dec. 1911): 56-57; Vol. 3, No. 5 (March 1912): 189; Vol. 3, No. 6 (April 1912): 233; Vol. 4, No. 1 (May 1912): 11-12; Vol. 4, No. 2 (June 1912): 65-66; Vol. 4, No. 3 (July 1912): 137; Vol. 4, No. 4 (Aug. 1912): 167-68; Vol. 4, No. 5 (Sept. 1912): 221; Vol. 5, No. 1 (Nov. 1912): 13-14; Vol. 5, No. 2 (Dec. 1912): 65; Vol. 5, No. 3 (Jan. 1913): 118; Vol. 5, No. 5 (March 1913): 222; Vol. 5, No. 6 (April 1913): 273; Vol. 6, No. 1 (May 1913): 15; Vol. 6, No. 2 (June 1913): 68; Vol. 6, No. 4 (Aug. 1913): 169-71; Vol. 6, No. 5 (Sept. 1913): 221; Vol. 6, No. 6 (Oct. 1913): 27; Vol. 6, No. 7 [sic; should be Vol. 7, No. 1] (Nov. 1913): 324; Vol. 7, No. 2 (Dec. 1913): 64; Vol. 7, No. 3 (Jan. 1913): 118; Vol. 7, No. 4 (Feb. 1913): 170; Vol. 7, No. 5 (March 1914): 222; Vol. 7, No. 6 (April 1914): 271; Vol. 8, No. 1 (May 1914): 12; Vol. 8, No. 3 (July 1914): 116; Vol. 8, No. 4 (Aug. 1914): 168; Vol. 8, No. 5 (Sept. 1914): 220; Vol. 8, No. 3 (Oct. 1914): 273; Vol. 9, No. 1 (Nov. 1914): 11; Vol. 9, No. 2 (Dec. 1914): 64; Vol. 9, No. 3 (Jan. 1915): 115; Vol. 9, No. 5 (March 1915): 220; Vol. 10, No. 1 (May 1915): 12; Vol. 10, No. 2 (June 1915): 64; Vol. 10, No. 3 (July 1915): 117; Vol. 10, No. 4 (Aug. 1915): 168; Vol. 10, No. 5 (Sept. 1915): 220; Vol. 10, No. 6 (Oct. 1915): 273; Vol. 11, No. 1 (Nov. 1915): 12; Vol. 11, No. 2 (Dec. 1915): 66; Vol. 11, No. 3 (Jan. 1916): 117.

676. "Crime." THE CRISIS, Vol. 2, No. 5 (Sept. 1911): 185-86. Coatesville. See also p. 194 for NAACP telegram to Pennsylvania governor.

677. "Crime." THE CRISIS, Vol. 3, No. 4 (Feb. 1912): 143-44. Several items on lynching and mob violence. See first item in "Courts" on p. 145.

678. "Crime." THE CRISIS, Vol. 6, No. 3 (July 1913): 121.   Several lynching items. Also item on 1900 riot in Akron, Ohio, in which "the city hall was burned and two persons killed" after black man was falsely accused of "assault upon a white child."

679. "Crime." THE CRISIS, Vol. 8, No. 2 (June 1914): 64.   Three lynching items and one item on James Conley and the Frank case.

680. "Crime." THE CRISIS, Vol. 9, No. 4 (Feb. 1915): 168.   Lynching in 1914 and two black men lynched in Jan. 1915.

681. "Crime." THE CRISIS, Vol. 11, No. 4 (Feb. 1916): 168.   Recent lynchings and race conflicts. Includes "Armed Negroes helped to stop the lynching of two of their race at Muskogee, Okla. . . ."

682. "Crime and Lynching." THE CRISIS, Vol. 3, No. 3 (Jan. 1912): 113-14.   Governor Gilchrist on lynching of six blacks at Lake City, FL, and editorial comment.

683. "Crimes and Lynchings." THE CHRISTIAN ADVOCATE [New York], Vol. 69, No. 18 (May 3, 1894): 277-78.   Continued by "Causes of the Increase . . ."

684. "Criminal Procedure: Necessity of Pleading to the Indictment--Technicality versus Common Sense." THE AMERICAN LAW REVIEW, Vol. 30 (Nov.-Dec. 1896): 939-40. Overturning convictions because of minor technicalities "provokes, and in some measure justifies, what is called 'Lynch Law.'"

685. Crowe, Charles. "Tom Watson, Populists, and Blacks Reconsidered." THE JOURNAL OF NEGRO HISTORY, Vol. 55, No. 2 (April 1970): 99-116.   See brief references to lynching on pp. 99-100 (Leo Frank case), 101, 102, 105, 107, and 110.

686. Crudele, Juanita W. "A Lynching Bee: Butler County Style." THE ALABAMA HISTORICAL QUARTERLY, Vol. 42, No. 1-2 (Spring and Summer 1980): 59-71.   Late 1800s. Black victim.

687. Cumberland, Charles C. "Border Raids on the Lower Rio Grande Valley, 1915." SOUTHWESTERN HISTORICAL QUARTERLY, Vol. 57, No. 3 (Jan. 1954): 285-311.   Raids from Mexico into U.S. led to violent American retaliation, including "lynchings."

688. Cunningham, Robert E. TRIAL BY MOB. Stillwater, OK: Redland Press, 1957.   Pamphlet; 24 pages. Second section, "The White Caps of

Oklahoma," includes corporal and lethal lynching. Third section, "Indian Scare," includes lynch burning of two Seminole Indians in Oklahoma, 1898.

689. "The Cure for Lynching." THE COLORED AMERICAN MAGA-ZINE, Vol. 3, No. 6 (Oct 1901): 455-56, 458-59.

690. Curran, John W. "The Leo Frank Case Again." JOURNAL OF CRIMINAL LAW AND CRIMINOLOGY, Vol. 34, No. 6 (March-April 1944): 363-64.   Judge Arthur G. Powell, in a volume of reminiscences [I Can Go Home Again (Chapel Hill: Univ. of North Carolina Press, 1943)] claims to know who really killed Mary Phagan but says he cannot reveal the information.

691. Curtis, George Ticknor. "The Law and the Lynchers." NORTH AMERICAN REVIEW, Vol. 152, No. 415 (June 1891): 691-95.   Mass lynching of Italians in New Orleans, 1891.

692. Cutler, J[ames] E[lbert]. "Race Riots and Lynch Law: The Cause and Cure. II.--A Northern Professor's View." THE OUTLOOK, Vol. 85, No. 5 (Feb. 2, 1907): 263-268.   See also Alexander, Hooper, ibid., pp. 259-63. See also "The Medicine for the Mob," ibid., pp. 249-50; a commentary on the articles by Alexander and Cutler.

693. Daniel, Pete. STANDING AT THE CROSSROADS: SOUTHERN LIFE SINCE 1900. New York: Hill and Wang, 1986.   See "lynching" and "whitecapping" in index.

694. Darling, William E. THE MURDER OF SALLIE E. DEAN. Denton, MD: Baker Printing Co., 1971.   Marshall Price, white, was lynched in 1895 for this murder in Maryland.

695. Dawson, Marion L. "The South and the Negro." THE NORTH AMERICAN REVIEW, Vol. 172, No. 531 (Feb. 1901): 279-84.   Lynching is mainly caused by black rape of whites.   Lesser cause is delay and uncertainty in convictions of criminals.

696. "Deception." THE CRISIS, Vol. 12, No. 2 (June 1916): 81-82. Mentions lynching.

697. "The 'Decline' of Lynching." THE CRISIS, Vol. 8, No. 1 (May 1914): 19-21.   Includes description of lynching in Leland, Mississippi. Victims not named.

698. "The Decrease in Lynchings." THE VOICE OF THE NEGRO, Vol. 3, No. 2 (Feb. 1906): 89-90.

699. Deems, Charles F. "Lynching." THE CENTURY MAGAZINE, Vol. 13 (New Series), Vol. 34 (Old Series), No. 1 (Nov. 1887): 166.   Letter saying since so many murderers are not punished by law, better law enforcement would reduce the number of lynchings.

700. "The Delaware Firebrand." THE VOICE OF THE NEGRO, Vol. 1, No. 3 (March 1904): 82.   Reverend Elwood encouraged lynching.

701. "The Delaware Lynching." LAW NOTES [Northport, N.Y.], Vol. 7, No. 5 (Aug. 1903): 81.   Followed by "A Brave Sheriff" (p. 81), "Administration of Criminal Law" (pp. 81-82), "Speedy Justice" (p. 82), "The Crime that Leads to Lynching" (p. 82), and "Lynching and the Race Question" (p. 82).

702. "The Delaware Lynching." THE LITERARY DIGEST, Vol. 27, No. 1 (July 4, 1903): 4-5.   George F. White, black, was taken from prison in Wilmington and burned at the stake.

703. "Demoralizations of the Lynching Habit." THE CONTINENT, Vol. 42, No. 42 (Oct. 19, 1911): 1478.

704. Dennis, Alfred Pearce.   "The Political and Ethical Aspects of Lynching." INTERNATIONAL JOURNAL OF ETHICS, Vol. 15, No. 2 (Jan. 1905): 149-61.

705. "The Devil's Country." THE SPECTATOR [London], Vol. 110, No. 4,418 (March 1, 1913): 348-49.   Anti-lynching editorial occasioned by news of two lynchings at Houston, Mississippi.

706. "Did you send my letter open?" THE CRISIS, Vol. 4, No. 6 (Oct. 1912): 302.   Details of lynching at Andalusia, Alabama. For photo of it see "Holmes on Lynching," ibid., Vol. 3, No. 3 (Jan. 1912): 110.

707. Diggs, James R. L.   "Is It Ignorance or Slander: The Answer to Thomas Nelson Page." THE VOICE OF THE NEGRO, Vol. 1, No. 6 (June 1904): 228-33.   Criticism of Page's "The Lynching of Negroes--Its Cause and Its Prevention."

708. Diner, Hasia R. IN THE ALMOST PROMISED LAND: AMERICAN JEWS AND BLACKS, 1915-1935. Westport, CT: Greenwood Press, 1977.   See "Frank, Leo," and "Lynching" in index.

709. Dinnerstein, Leonard. "A Dreyfus Affair in Georgia." In ANTISEMITISM IN THE UNITED STATES, pp. 87-101. Ed. by Leonard Dinnerstein. American Problem Studies. New York: Holt, Rinehart and Winston, 1971. Leo Frank case. Originally published as "Atlanta in the Progressive Era:

A Dreyfus Affair in Georgia," in The Age of Industrialism in America: Essays in Social Structure and Cultural Values, pp. 127-57. Edited by Frederick Cople Jaher (New York: Free Press, 1968).

710. Dinnerstein, Leonard. THE LEO FRANK CASE. New York: Columbia Univ. Press, 1968. This was a Ph.D. diss., Columbia Univ., 1966 (title: "The Leo Frank Case"). See Diss. Ab., Vol. 27, No 8 (Feb. 1967), pp. 2474A-2475A.

711. Dinnerstein, Leonard. "Leo M. Frank and the American Jewish Community." IN CRITICAL STUDIES IN AMERICAN JEWISH HISTORY: SELECTED ARTICLES FROM AMERICAN JEWISH ARCHIVES, Vol. 3, pp. 34-51. Publications of the American Jewish Archives No. 4. 3 vols.; Cincinnati: American Jewish Archives; New York: KTAV Publishing House, 1971. From American Jewish Archives, Vol. 20, No. 2 (Nov. 1968): 107-26.

712. "The Disgrace of Georgia and Alabama." CURRENT LITERATURE, Vol. 37, No. 4 (Oct. 1904): 294-96. Recent lynchings.

713. Dittmer, John. BLACK GEORGIA IN THE PROGRESSIVE ERA, 1900-1920. Urbana: Univ. of Illinois Press, 1977. See "Lynching" in index.

714. Dixon, Thomas. "Lynching." THE INTERCOLLEGIATE LAW JOURNAL, Vol. 2, No. 5 (April 1893): 163-64.

715. "The Docket." THE AMERICAN LAW REVIEW, Vol. 49 (Sept.-Oct. 1915): 776-80. Lynch law; the Frank case.

716. "The Doddsville Savagery." THE VOICE OF THE NEGRO, Vol. 1, No. 3 (March 1904): 81-82. Lynching of Luther Holbert and wife in Mississippi.

717. "A Double Lynching in Virginia." THE INDEPENDENT, Vol. 52, No. 2678 (March 29, 1900): 783-84.

718. Douglass, Frederick. "Introduction to the Reason Why the Colored American is Not in the World's Columbian Exposition." In THE LIFE AND WRITINGS OF FREDERICK DOUGLASS, Vol. IV, pp. 469-77. Ed. by Philip S. Foner. 4 vols.; New York: International Publishers, 1950-1955. Includes references to rape and lynch law. See The Reason Why the Colored American is not in the World's Columbian Exposition.

719. Douglass, Frederick. "Lynch Law in the South." NORTH AMERICAN REVIEW, Vol. 155, No. 428 (July 1892): 17-24. Explanations about

Southern lynching; suggestions for its reduction.

720. Douglass, Frederick. "Lynching Black People Because They are Black."
OUR DAY, Vol. 13, No. 76 (July-Aug. 1894): 298-306. Title is listed in
contents as "Lynching Black Men Because They are Black."

721. Douglass, Frederick. WHY IS THE NEGRO LYNCHED? ("The
Lesson of the Hour.") Bridgewater, Eng.: J. Whitby & Sons, 1895.
Reprinted from The A.M.E. Church Review, with headings and divisions
added. Reprinted in The Life and Writings of Frederick Douglass, Vol. 4,
Reconstruction and After, pp. 491-523, edited by Philip S. Foner (4 vols.;
New York: International Publishers, 1950-1955 [see Foner's text, pp. 140-43].
Slightly different version as Chapter 11, "The Lessons of the Hour (1894)"
in William L. Andrews, editor, The Oxford Frederick Douglass Reader (New
York: Oxford Univ. Press, 1996), pp. 339-66; reprinted from the pamphlet
Address by Hon. Frederick Douglass, Delivered in the Metropolitan A.M.E.
Church, Washington, D.C., Tuesday, January 9th, 1894 on The Lessons of
Hour (Baltimore: Thomas & Evans, 1894).

722. Downey, Dennis B., and Hyser, Raymond M. "'A Crooked Death':
Coatesville, Pennsylvania and the Lynching of Zachariah Walker." PENN-
SYLVANIA HISTORY, Vol. 54, No. 2 (April 1987): 85-102.

723. Downey, Dennis B., and Hyser, Raymond M. NO CROOKED
DEATH: COATESVILLE, PENNSYLVANIA, AND THE LYNCHING OF
ZACHARIAH WALKER. Urbana and Chicago: Univ. of Illinois Press,
1991.

724. DuBois, W. E. Burghardt. "The Over-Look: Editorial Opinion." THE
HORIZON, Vol. 5, No. 4 (Feb. 1910): 1-4.   Item on pp. 2-3 titled "1909"
includes Governor Deneen's refusal to reinstate sheriff who did not prevent
lynching of William James and Henry Salzner at Cairo, Illinois. Committee
of Chicago blacks encouraged Deneen's action.

725. DuBois, W. E. Burghardt. "Violations of Property Rights." THE
CRISIS, Vol. 2, No. 1 (May 1911): 28-32. See pp. 31-32 on how mob
violence in the South discourages Negroes from saving and investing--and
encourages them to move to cities.

726. "Due Process of Law in the Frank Case." HARVARD LAW
REVIEW, Vol. 28, No. 8 (June 1915): 793-95.

727. Durbin, Winfield T. "The Mob and the Law." THE INDEPENDENT,
Vol. 55, No. 2852 (July 30, 1903): 1790-93.

728. "Durbin of Indiana." HARPER'S WEEKLY, Vol. 47, No. 2436 (Aug. 29, 1903): 1396-97.   Praise for his action to suppress mob violence.

729. Earl, Phillip I. "The Lynching of Adam Uber." NEVADA HISTORI- CAL SOCIETY QUARTERLY, Vol. 16, No. 1 (Spring 1973): 2-19. Occurred in 1897 in Nevada.

730. Early, J[unius] M. "AN EYE FOR AN EYE;" OR, THE FIEND AND THE FAGOT.   AN UNVARNISHED ACCOUNT OF THE BURNING OF HENRY SMITH AT PARIS, TEXAS, FEBRUARY 1, 1893, AND THE REASON HE WAS TORTURED. Paris, TX: Marshall's Print. House, 1893.

731. "Echo of a Questionable Sermon." THE CHRISTIAN ADVOCATE [New York], Vol. 78, No. 48 (Nov. 26, 1903): 1903.   Baltimore Synod directs reconsideration of case of Reverend Ellwood of Wilmington, Delaware (regarding lynching of George White). Ellwood says he did not mean to incite the crowd.

732. "Editorial." THE CHRISTIAN ADVOCATE [New York], Vol. 62, No. 18 (May 5, 1887), p. 285.   Manifesto from a lyncher.

733. "Editorial." THE CHRISTIAN ADVOCATE [New York], Vol. 69, No. 12 (March 22, 1894): 177.   Black man lynched in Strousburg [no state listed]. He "was captured by a Negro, who cut up the rope with which he was hanged and sold it on the street for 25 cents a piece." [See #1155 in this bibliography for black man lynched in Stroudsburg, Pennsylvania.]

734. "Editorial." THE CRISIS, Vol. 11, No. 6 (April 1916): 302-06. Includes a photo on p. 303 of the lynching of five blacks in Lee County, Georgia, Jan. 20, 1916, and text (pp. 301, 304-05) about the lynching.

735. [Editorial Comment.] THE NATION, Vol. 103, No. 2675 (Oct. 5, 1916): 322.   Deplores lack of criticism in Waco, Texas, about recent lynching there.

736. [Editorial Comment.] THE NATION, Vol. 103, No. 2687 (Dec. 28, 1916): 609.   Three lines accepting correction for previous editorial comment, Oct. 5, 1916.

737. "Editorial. Two Letters. The One Which Was Not Written to Georgia." THE CRISIS, Vol. 12, No. 4 (Aug. 1916): 163-64. Supposedly from President Wilson on lynching.

738. "Education." THE CRISIS, Vol. 7, No. 5 (March 1914): 231. Includes

a paragraph on lynching in 1913.

739. "Education the Chief Remedy." THE AMERICAN MONTHLY REVIEW OF REVIEWS, Vol. 28, No. 2 (Aug. 1903): 136.

740. Elliott, Jeffrey M.   "A Legacy of Violence: The Opera House Lynching." NEGRO HISTORY BULLETIN, Vol. 37, No. 6 (Oct./Nov. 1974): 303.   Livermore, Kentucky, 1911. Victim: M. Potter, black.

741. Ellis, Mary Louise. "A Lynching Averted: The Ordeal of John Miller." THE GEORGIA HISTORICAL QUARTERLY, Vol. 70, No. 2 (Summer 1986): 306-16.   Events in 1899.

742. Ellis, Mary Louise. "'Rain Down Fire': The Lynching of Sam Hose." Ph.D. diss., Florida State Univ., 1992.   See Diss. Ab. Intl., Vol. 53, No. 10 (April 1993): 3650A.   Georgia, 1899.

743. Ellis, William T.   "Civilization's Failure at Coatesville."   THE CONTINENT, Vol. 42, No. 34 (Aug. 24, 1911): 1211-12.   Pennsylvania.

744. "The End of the Frank Case." THE OUTLOOK, Vol. 111, No. 3 (Sept. 15, 1915): 114-15.   Georgia.

745. "English Feeling Upon America's Lynchings." THE LITERARY DIGEST, Vol. 9, No. 11 (July 14, 1894): 8 (308).   Feelings stirred up by Ida B. Wells' activities in England. Press comments.

746. "An Englishman's View of the New Orleans Affair." THE REVIEW OF REVIEWS [American Edition], Vol. 5, No. 26 (March 1892): 196. Reports on N. J. D. Kennedy's second of two articles on lynch law in the January Juridical Review.

747. "The Epidemic of Savagery." THE OUTLOOK, Vol. 69, No. 1 (Sept. 7, 1901): 9-11.   Bad effects of lynching.

748. "Every Man's Right to Justice." THE CONTINENT, Vol. 42, No. 34 (Aug. 24, 1911): 1208-09.   Coatesville, Pennsylvania.

749. Ewing, Quincy. "How Can Lynching be Checked in the South?" THE OUTLOOK, Vol. 69, No. 6 (Oct. 12, 1901): 359-61.

750. Ex parte Wall, 107 U.S. 265 (1882). This case relates to the disbarment of a prominent Florida attorney who was a passive participant in the lynching of a black man outside the courthouse in Tampa on March 6, 1882. See also In re Wall, 13 F. 814 (Cir. S.D. 1882).

751. "Ex-Communication for Christian (?) Murderers and Lynchers." THE VOICE OF THE NEGRO, Vol. 1, No. 10 (Oct. 1904): 490-91.   Georgia minister tried to prevent lynching of Cato and Reed and asked mob members in congregation to repent or withdraw. Reference to Before Day clubs.

752. "The Exodus from Mississippi." THE VOICE OF THE NEGRO, Vol. 1, No. 6 (June 1904): 258-59.   Blacks leaving because of bad conditions such as lynching.

753. "Exterminating the Mafia." ILLUSTRATED AMERICAN, Vol. 6 (Supplement to March 28, 1891): 1-15.   Mass lynching in New Orleans.

754. An Ex-Vigilante. "An Apology for the Short Shrift." THE SATUR-DAY REVIEW [London], Vol. 85, No. 2222 (May 28, 1898): 717-18. Extremely reactionary, anti-black letter with some pro-lynching views.

755. "Facts About the Atlanta Murders." THE WORLD'S WORK, Vol. 13, No. 1 (Nov. 1906): 8147-48.   Lynching and the race riot in Atlanta.

756. THE FACTS IN THE CASE OF THE HORRIBLE MURDER OF LITTLE MYRTLE VANCE AND ITS FEARFUL EXPIATION AT PARIS, TEXAS, FEBRUARY 1ST, 1893. Paris, TX: P. L. James, 1893.

757. Feldman, Glenn. "Lynching in Alabama, 1889-1921." THE ALA-BAMA REVIEW, Vol. 48, No. 2 (April 1995): 114-41.

758. "Fewer Lynchings in 1904." THE AMERICAN LAW REVIEW, Vol. 39, [No. 1] (Jan.-Feb. 1905): 104.

759. "A Fifty Year Record of Lynchings." INTERRACIAL REVIEW, Vol. 13, No. 1 (Jan. 1940): 10.   A graph, from The New York Times.

760. "The Finale of the Statesboro Disgrace." THE VOICE OF THE NEGRO, Vol. 1, No. 12 (Dec. 1904): 588-89.   Georgia.

761. Finnegan, Terence Robert. "'At the hands of parties unknown': Lynching in Mississippi and South Carolina, 1881-1940." Ph.D. diss., Univ. of Illinois at Urbana-Champaign, 1993.   See Diss. Ab. Intl., Vol. 54, No. 5 (Nov. 1993): 1923A.

762. Fletcher, Marvin. "The Black Volunteers In The Spanish-American War." MILITARY AFFAIRS, Vol. 38, No. 2 (April 1974): 48-53.   Includes black soldiers invading Jim Crow park in Macon, Georgia, and destroying tree used for lynching. Others rescue buddies from jail because of fear of

white justice.

763. Flower, B. O. "The Burning of Negroes in the South: A Protest and a Warning." THE ARENA, Vol. 7, No. 41 (April 1893): 630-40. Especially on Paris, Texas, lynching of Henry Smith, 1893.

764. Flower, B. O. "The Rise of Anarchy in the United States." THE ARENA, Vol. 30, No. 3 (Sept. 1903): 305-11.   Deplores lawlessness of lynch mobs.

765. Floyd, Josephine Bone.   "Rebecca Latimer Felton, Champion of Women's Rights." THE GEORGIA HISTORICAL QUARTERLY, Vol. 30, No. 2 (June 1946): 81-104.   In an 1897 speech, she said, "If it needs lynching to protect woman's dearest possession from the raving human beasts--then I say lynch; a thousand times a week if necessary" (pp. 83-84).

766. "For Civilization at Evansville." THE INDEPENDENT, Vol. 55, No. 2850 (July 16, 1903): 1694-95. Attempted lynching in Indiana.

767. Ford, E. C. "A Horrible Blot on the Fair Name of Kansas." THE NEGRO HISTORY BULLETIN, Vol. 19, No. 2 (Nov. 1955): 42.   Eye-witness account of burning of innocent black man in unnamed city. Undated. [Could this be Leavenworth lynching of Fred Alexander in 1901?]

768. "Frank." THE CRISIS, Vol. 10, No. 4 (Aug. 1915): 177.   Leo Frank case, but not his lynching.

769. "Frank." THE CRISIS, Vol. 10, No. 6 (Oct. 1915): 276-78.   Leo Frank's lynching.   Includes (pp. 277-78) recent burning of black man in public square in Temple, Texas, in front of crowd of 10,000.

770. "The Frank Case." THE OUTLOOK, Vol. 108, No. 16 (Dec. 16, 1914): 859-60.

771. "The Frank Case." THE OHIO LAW BULLETIN, Vol. 60, No. 38 (Sept. 20, 1915): 395-96.   Deplores the lynching.

772. "Frank's Prophesy of Vindication Comes True 10 Years After Georgia Mob Hangs Him as Slayer." THE JEWISH ADVOCATE [Boston], Vol. 42, No. 8 (Oct. 18, 1923): 20.   Reprinted from The Boston Traveler, Oct. 6.

773. Freshman, Clark Jack. "Beyond Pontius Pilate and Judge Lynch: The Pardoning Power in Theory and Practice As Illustrated in the Leo Frank Case." Thesis (A.B., Honors), Harvard Univ., 1986.

774. Frey, Robert Seitz, and Thompson-Frey, Nancy. THE SILENT AND THE DAMNED: THE MURDER OF MARY PHAGAN AND THE LYNCHING OF LEO FRANK. Lanham, MD; New York; and London: Madison Books, 1988.

775. "A Friend of the Mob." THE NATION, Vol. 77, No. 1990 (Aug. 20, 1903): 146-47.   Comment on an apologia for lynching in speech by a Mr. Graves of Georgia.

776. "Friendly Interference into the Domestic Affairs of Other Countries." THE AMERICAN LAW REVIEW, Vol. 28 (Nov.-Dec. 1894): 904-06. Negative response to news that a committee from England will come to U.S. investigate lynching.

777. "From Atlanta, Ga." THE CRISIS, Vol. 12, No. 2 (June 1916): 82. Mentions lynching.

778. G., R. H. [Gault, Robert H.] Lynchings in 1912." JOURNAL OF THE AMERICAN INSTITUTE OF CRIMINAL LAW AND CRIMINOL- OGY, Vol. 4, No. 1 (May 1913): 130.   Statistics.

779. G., R. H. [Gault, Robert H.] "Vindicating the law." JOURNAL OF THE AMERICAN INSTITUTE OF CRIMINAL LAW AND CRIMINOL- OGY, Vol. 4, No. 4 (Nov. 1913): 610-12.   Lynching statistics.

780. Gabrilowitsch, Ossip.   "A Georgian Investigation."   HARPER'S WEEKLY, Vol. 61, No. 3067 (Oct. 2, 1915): 335. Coroner's jury investigat- ing Leo Frank's lynching elicited almost no information despite existence of detailed press reports.

781. Galloway, Charles B. "Some Thoughts on Lynching." THE SOUTH ATLANTIC QUARTERLY, Vol. 5, No. 4 (Oct. 1906): 351-53.   Part of symposium; other parts by J. W. Bailey and Robert Strange.

782. Galloway, Chas. B. "The South and the Negro." THE METHODIST QUARTERLY REVIEW, Vol. 53, No. 3 (July 1904): 501-12. Incudes lynching.

783. Galloway, J. C. "Lynching in the South." THE INDEPENDENT, Vol. 46, No. 2357 (Feb. 1, 1894): 2-3 (130-31).   Relates lynching to "atrocities on females" and claims "a large majority of those lynched are for the last- named crime."

784. Galvin, Kathleen Ann. "The Springfield Riots of 1904 and 1906." M.A. thesis, Ohio State Univ., 1971.   Ohio.   Lynching of black man in 1904

preceded burning part of black section. Lynchings were prevented in 1906, but again part of black section was burned.

785. Gambino, Richard.   VENDETTA: A TRUE STORY OF THE WORST LYNCHING IN AMERICA, THE MASS MURDER OF ITALIAN-AMERICANS IN NEW ORLEANS IN 1891, THE VICIOUS MOTIVATIONS BEHIND IT, AND THE TRAGIC REPERCUSSIONS THAT LINGER TO THIS DAY. Garden City, NY: Doubleday, 1977.

786. Garner, James Wilford.   "Lynching and the Criminal Law."   THE SOUTH ATLANTIC QUARTERLY, Vol. 5, No. 4 (Oct. 1906): 333-41.

787. "Georgia: A Political Suicide." TIME, Vol. 65, No. 4 (Jan. 24, 1955): 19.   Governor John Slaton and the Leo Frank lynching.

788. "Georgia and the Nation." THE NEW REPUBLIC, Vol. 4, No. 42 (Aug. 21, 1915): 56.   Leo Frank lynching.

789. "Georgia at Statesboro and Manassas."   THE VOICE OF THE NEGRO, Vol. 1, No. 12 (Dec. 1904): 589-90.   "Georgia troops, fresh from the saturnalia at Statesboro, on the way to the summer maneuvers at Manassas" robbed, beat, and terrorized blacks.

790. Georgia. Governor, 1913-1915 (Slaton). SUPPLEMENT TO MES-SAGE OF THE GOVERNOR TO THE GENERAL ASSEMBLY OF GEORGIA, JUNE 23, 1915. OPINION IN THE CASE OF THE STATE VS. LEO FRANK. Atlanta: C. P. Byrd, State Printer, 1915.

791. "Georgia's 'Right to Lynch.'" THE LITERARY DIGEST, Vol. 53, No. 11 (Sept. 9, 1916): 593.

792. "Georgia's Shame." THE INDEPENDENT, Vol. 83, No. 3482 (Aug. 30, 1915): 280-81.   Lynching of Leo Frank.

793. Gerard, C. E., and Griffey, M. G., eds. LYNCHED! THE STORY OF AMER GREEN. Delphi, IN: Indiana Graphic Arts Co., 1974.   Lynching of alleged murderer in Indiana, 1887. This is a compilation of contemporary articles from local newspapers.

794. "Ghetto." THE CRISIS, Vol. 11, No. 5 (March 1916): 223.   Includes recent lynchings.

795. "Ghetto." THE CRISIS, Vol. 11, No. 6 (April 1916): 289.   Includes recent lynchings.

796. Gibbons, J. Cardinal. "Lynch Law: Its Causes and Remedy." NORTH AMERICAN REVIEW, Vol. 181, No. 587 (Oct. 1905): 502-09.

797. Gilbert, John Wesley. "A Voice from the Negro Race." THE METHODIST REVIEW QUARTERLY, Vol. 60, No. 4 (Oct. 1911): 717-30. See pp. 726-27 for rape and lynching.

798. Ginn, Duane E. "Racial Violence in Texas, 1884-1900." M.A. thesis, Univ. of Houston, 1974.

799. Giordano, Paolo. "Italian Immigration in the State of Louisiana: Its Causes, Effects, and Results." ITALIAN AMERICANA, Vol. 5, No. 2 (Spring/Summer 1979): 160-77.   Includes Italian lynchings in 1896 and 1899.

800. Gipson, Henry E. "Delay of the Law as an Excuse for Lynching." THE AMERICAN LAWYER, Vol. 12, No. 12 (Dec. 1904): 531-32.

801. Glasrud, Bruce A. "Child or Beast?: White Texas' View of Blacks, 1900-1910." EAST TEXAS HISTORICAL JOURNAL, Vol. 15, No. 2 (1977): 38-44.

802. Glasrud, Bruce A. "Enforcing White Supremacy in Texas, 1900-1910." RED RIVER VALLEY HISTORICAL REVIEW, Vol. 4, No. 4 (Fall 1979): 65-74.

803. Glasrud, Bruce Allen. "Black Texans, 1900-1930: A History." Ph.D. diss., Texas Technological College, 1969.   See Diss. Ab. Intl., Vol. 30, No. 8 (Feb. 1970): 3398A.   See Chapter V for lynching, and pp. 150-51, 160, for whitecapping.

804. Glass, Mary Ellen. "A Curse Upon Lynchers." WESTERN FOLK-LORE, Vol. 28, No. 3 (July 1969): 207-10.   Alleged curse laid by Adam Uber on his killers in Nevada (1897).

805. Glasson, William H. "The Statistics of Lynching." THE SOUTH ATLANTIC QUARTERLY, Vol. 5, No. 4 (Oct. 1906): 342-48.

806. Golden, Harry. A LITTLE GIRL IS DEAD. Cleveland: World Pub. Co., 1965.   Leo Frank case.

807. Goldenweiser, A. A. "Atlanta Riots and the Origin of Magic." THE NEW REPUBLIC, Vol. 3, No. 35 (July 3, 1915): 225.   Rioters were against Governor Slaton because he commuted Leo Frank's death sentence.

808. Goldin, Gullie B. "The United States Supreme Court and the Frank Case." THE CENTRAL LAW JOURNAL, Vol. 80, No. 2 (Jan. 8, 1915): 29-32.

809. Goldman, Eric. "Summer Sunday." AMERICAN HERITAGE, Vol. 15, No. 4 (June 1964): 50-53, 83-89.   Coatesville, PA, lynching, 1911.

810. Gordon, Edward C. "Mob Violence: 'The National Crime.'" THE INDEPENDENT, Vol. 46, No. 2396 (Nov. 1, 1894): 4-5 (1400-01).

811. "Government By Murderous Vigilantes." MOTHER EARTH, Vol. 11, No. 10 (Dec. 1916): 694-97.   Recent activity: Everett massacre in Washington state.

812. "Governor Atkinson's Message on Lynch Law." THE AMERICAN LAWYER, Vol. 4, No. 12 (Dec. 1896): 531-32.   Georgia's governor.

813. Graham, Stephen.   CHILDREN OF THE SLAVES.   London: Macmillan, 1920.   See numerous entries under "Lynching" in index.   Also: "Atrocities," "Burning them to death," "Governors and lynching," "Jew lynched at Milledgeville" [sic; Leo Frank], "Macon," "Make 'em die slow," "Mayor," "Newspaper accounts," "Pensacola," and "Photographs."   Published in United States as The Soul of John Brown (New York: Macmillan, 1920).

814. "Grand Jurors Condemn Coatesville." THE CONTINENT, Vol. 42, No. 39 (Sept. 28, 1911): 1370.   Pennsylvania.

815. Grant, John H. "Some of the Evils which are Producing Desperadoes and Murderers Among the Negroes, and the Remedies." THE VOICE OF THE NEGRO, Vol. 2, No. 8 (Aug. 1905): 544-47.   Page 546: for blacks who hurt whites in fights, lynching "has become such a law in the South that Negroes accept death in defying the officers of the law rather than fall in the hands of the law to be turned over to a murderous mob."

816. Grimke, Francis James. THE LYNCHING OF NEGROES IN THE SOUTH. ITS CAUSES AND REMEDY.   Washington, DC: 1899.   Also in The Works of Francis J. Grimke, Vol. I, pp. 291-333, as "Lynching: Its Causes--A Low State of Civilization and Race Hatred." Edited by Carter G. Woodson.   4 vols.; Washington, DC: Associated Publishers, 1942.

817. Groves, Billy. "Lookout Lynching." TRUE WEST [Austin, TX], Vol. 12, No. 4, Whole No. 68 (March-April 1965): 34-35, 62-63.   Father and four sons hung, Modoc County, California, 1906.   Conflicts and killings during effort to hold trial of alleged lynchers.

818. "A Growing Social Effort in the South." THE SURVEY, Vol. 36, No. 8 (May 20, 1916): 196.   Protests against lynching.

819. H., M. A. "Another Lynching." THE CRISIS, Vol. 12, No. 6 (Oct. 1916): 275-76.   Lynching of five blacks (including two women) near Gainesville, Florida, Aug. 1916.

820. Haas, Edward F. "Guns, Goats, and Italians: The Tallulah Lynching of 1899." NORTH LOUISIANA HISTORICAL ASSOCIATION JOUR-NAL, Vol. 13, No. 2 and 3 (Spring and Summer 1982): 45-58 (illustration on p. v).   Five Sicilians were lynched in July; two together, another group of two, and one by himself (Joseph and Charles Defatta, Frank Defatta and Rosario Fiducia, and John Cerano).

821. Hale, Richard W. "Lynching Unnecessary. A Report on Common-wealth v. Christian." THE AMERICAN LAW REVIEW, Vol. 45 (Nov.-Dec. 1911): 875-83.   The capture, trial, and electrocution of a murderer in Virginia in 1909.

822. Harris, Mark. "The Great Springfield Race War." NEGRO DIGEST, Vol. 8, No. 1 (Nov. 1949): 52-57.   Illinois riot (1908) began after mob was frustrated in desire to lynch black man accused of rape.   Accuser later admitted charge was false.

823. Harrison, Russell Sage. "The Attitude of the Methodist Episcopal Church, South Toward the Lynching of Negroes Since 1885." B.D. thesis, Duke Univ., 1934.

824. Hart, Albert Bushnell. "The Outcome of the Southern Race Ques-tion." THE NORTH AMERICAN REVIEW, Vol. 188, No. 632 (July 1908): 50-61.   Includes a section on "Remedy of Violence" in the South, which is largely about lynching.

825. Hartman, Mary, and Ingenthron, Elmo.   BALD KNOBBERS; VIGILANTES ON THE OZARKS FRONTIER. Gretna, LA: Pelican Pub. Co., 1988.

826. Hartman, Viola R. "Terror In the Night: The Bald Knobbers." OLD WEST [Iola, WI], Vol. 20, No. 1, Whole No. 77 (Fall 1983): 48-51, 63. Missouri, 1880s.

827. Haswell, A. M. "The Story of the Bald Knobbers.: THE MISSOURI HISTORICAL REVIEW, Vol. 18, No. 1 (Oct. 1923): 27-35.   Missouri, 1880s.

828. Haygood, Atticus G.   "The Black Shadow in the South."   THE FORUM, Vol. 16, [No. 2] (Oct. 1893): 167-75.

829. Haygood, Atticus G.   "Lynching by Wholesale."   THE INDEPEN-DENT, Vol. 46, No. 2378 (June 28, 1894): 1 (817).   Labor riots; see [no author; no title], ibid., p. 12 (828).

830. Haynesworth, H. J.   "The Spirit of Lynch Law and Its Control."   In TRANSACTIONS OF THE TWELFTH ANNUAL MEETING OF THE SOUTH CAROLINA BAR ASSOCIATION, JANUARY 19-20, 1905, pp. 67-78. Columbia: R. L. Bryan Co., 1905.

831. Hays, Arthur Garfield. TRIAL BY PREJUDICE. New York: Covici, Friede, 1933.   Includes Leo Frank case.

832. "Healthy Southern Sentiment." THE VOICE OF THE NEGRO, Vol. 1, No. 11 (Nov. 1904): 513.   Increasing opposition to lynching.

833. Henri, Florette.   BLACK MIGRATION: MOVEMENT NORTH, 1900-1920. Garden City, NY: Anchor, 1975.   See "Lynching" in index.

834. Hertzberg, Steven. STRANGERS WITHIN THE GATE CITY: THE JEWS OF ATLANTA, 1845-1915. Philadelphia: Jewish Publications Society of America, 1978.   See "Frank, Leo M.," in index. See Chapter 9, "The Leo Frank Case," pp. 202-15.

835. Higgins, Ray E., Jr. "Strange Fruit: Lynching in South Carolina, 1900-1914." M.A. thesis, Univ. of South Carolina, 1961. This is listed in Hall, Revolt Against Chivalry, p. 399, but an interlibrary loan request elicited information that the closest item to this is the thesis by Jack Simpson Mullins, which see.

836. Hillyer, George. "Criminal law administration." JOURNAL OF THE AMERICAN INSTITUTE OF CRIMINAL LAW AND CRIMINOLOGY, Vol. 7, No. 1 (May 1916): 114-17.   A plea for better methods; relates to lynchings. Letter from Atlanta Constitution, Feb. 18, 1916.

837. Hines, Mary Elizabeth. "Death at the Hands of Persons Unknown: The Geography of Lynching in the Deep South, 1882 to 1910." Ph.D. diss., Louisiana State University and Agricultural and Mechanical College, 1992. See Diss. Ab. Intl., Vol. 53, No. 9 (March 1993): 3327A.

838. Hobson, Will. ABOUT THE HANGING OF ROBERT HARPER, BY A MOB, WEDNESDAY, DECEMBER 28, 1892, AT BOWLING GREEN, KY. N.p., n.d.

839. Holmes, John Haynes. "The Contagion of the South." THE CRISIS, Vol. 2, No. 6 (Oct. 1911): 251-52.   Letter regarding Coatesville, Pennsylvania.

840. "Holmes on Lynching." THE CRISIS, Vol. 3, No. 3 (Jan. 1912): 109, 111.   Speech by John Haynes Holmes, a Unitarian minister in New York City.   Page 110 consists of reproductions of front and back of a postcard from Alabama with a pro-lynching message to Holmes and a photo of a lynching at Andalusia, Alabama. [See "Did you send my letter open?" The Crisis, Vol. 4, No. 6 (Oct. 1912), p. 302, for details of that lynching.]

841. Holmes, William F.   "The Leflore County Massacre and the Demise of the Colored Farmers' Alliance." PHYLON, Vol. 34, No. 3 (Sep 1973): 267-74.   The murders of perhaps 25 blacks by whites in Mississippi, 1889. Some of the deaths may have been lynchings under some definitions.

842. Holmes, William F.   "Moonshiners and Whitecaps in Alabama, 1893." THE ALABAMA REVIEW, Vol. 34, No. 1 (Jan. 1981): 31-49.

843. Holmes, William F.   "Whitecapping: Agrarian Violence in Mississippi, 1902-1906." THE JOURNAL OF SOUTHERN HISTORY, Vol. 35, No. 2 (May 1969): 165-85.   Violence against blacks.

844. Holmes, William F.   "Whitecapping: Anti-Semitism in the Populist Era." AMERICAN JEWISH HISTORICAL QUARTERLY, Vol. 63, No. 3 (March 1974): 244-61.

845. Holmes, William F.   "Whitecapping in Georgia: Carroll and Houston Counties, 1893." THE GEORGIA HISTORICAL QUARTERLY, Vol. 64, No. 4 (Winter 1980): 388-404.

846. Holmes, William F.   "Whitecapping in Late Nineteenth-Century Georgia." In FROM THE OLD SOUTH TO THE NEW: ESSAYS ON THE TRANSITIONAL SOUTH, pp. 121-32. Ed. by Walter J. Fraser, Jr., and Winfred B. Moore, Jr. Contributions in American History, Number 93. Westport, CT: Greenwood Press, 1981.

847. Holmes, William F.   "Whitecapping in Mississippi: Agrarian Violence in the Populist Era." MID-AMERICA, Vol. 55, No. 2 (April 1973): 134-48.

848. Holt, George C.   "Lynching and Mobs." JOURNAL OF SOCIAL SCIENCE, No. 32 (Nov. 1894): 67-81.   Includes details of several cases; in one, blacks and whites cooperated in lynching a white man, and there were prosecutions but no convictions.

849. HON. BENJAMIN FRANKLIN LONG, JUDGE OF THE SUPE-
RIOR COURTS OF NORTH CAROLINA. PUBLISHED OPINIONS ON
TWO IMPORTANT CASES: STATE VS. SOUTHERN RAILWAY CO.,
ET AL[.], [AND] STATE VS. GEORGE HALL; TOGETHER WITH AN
INTRODUCTORY LETTER TO HIS SON BY HENRY JEROME
STOCKARD. N.p.: n.p., n.d. [Raleigh, 1912?]   See pp. 13-16, "The
Lynching Case, 1906," for newspaper opinions of Judge Long's action in
sentencing George Hall to 15 years in prison for leading a mob in lynching
blacks near Charlotte in Aug., 1906.

850. Hope, Welborn. FOUR MEN HANGING: THE END OF THE OLD
WEST. Oklahoma City: Century Press, 1974.   Masons lynched four men
in Ada, Oklahoma, April 19, 1909.

851. "Hopeful Signs in Mississippi." THE VOICE OF THE NEGRO, Vol.
1, No. 5 (May 1904): 173.   A sheriff saved a black man from lynching, and
a meeting of Confederate veterans condemned lynching.

852. "The Horizon." THE CRISIS, Vol. 13, No. 1 (Nov. 1916): 28-36. See
p. 36 for several recent lynchings.

853. "The Horizon. Crime." THE CRISIS, Vol. 12, No. 6 (Oct. 1916): 300.
Includes lynching.

854. "The Horizon. Ghetto." THE CRISIS, Vol. 13, No. 1 (Nov. 1916): 35-
36.   Includes recent lynchings.

855. "The Horizon. Ghetto." THE CRISIS, Vol. 13, No. 2 (Dec. 1916): 94.
Includes lynching and Anti-Lynching Fund.

856. Hoss, E. E. "Lynching. Its Cause and Cure. The Great National
Disgrace. Apology and Denunciation. Why It Is Not Suppressed. Lynch
Law and the Southern Press." THE INDEPENDENT, Vol. 46, No. 2357
(Feb. 1, 1894): 1-2 (129-30). Extensive quotations from his writings against
lynching by editor of Nashville Christian Advocate.

857. "How Can Lynching Be Stopped?" THE LITERARY DIGEST, Vol.
27, No. 6 (Aug. 8, 1903): 156-57.   Includes William James's article
reprinted from Springfield Daily Republican, July 23, 1903. Also includes
some of Indiana Governor Durbin's views from The Independent, July 30,
1903.

858. "How to Prevent Lynching." THE CHRISTIAN ADVOCATE [New
York], Vol. 78, No. 34 (Aug. 20, 1903): 1335.   Views of judges Brewer,
Lore, and Woodward.

859. "How to Put Down Lynching." THE NATION, Vol. 77, No. 1987 (July 30, 1903): 86.

860. "How to Stop Lynching." THE WOMEN'S ERA, Vol. 1, No. 2 (1894): 8-9. In Black Women in White America: A Documentary History, pp. 194-95. Ed. by Gerda Lerner. New York: Pantheon Books, 1972. Editorial. Lynching county would pay pension to family of lynching victim.

861. "The Howard Association on Lynchings." THE VOICE OF THE NEGRO, Vol. 1, No. 5 (May 1904): 207. The Humanitarian Association of England is investigating lynching and peonage in the U.S.

862. Hoyt, James A. THE PHOENIX RIOT: NOVEMBER 8, 1898. [Greenwood, SC?: Greenwood Index-Journal?, 1938?] Election-day violence in South Carolina led to lynchings of several blacks in succeeding days.

863. Hubbard, George U. "The Lynching of 'Killer' Miller." TRUE FRONTIER, SPECIAL ISSUE NO. 1: THE BAD MEN [New York] (1971): 46-47, 54, 56-57. Jim Miller and three other men were lynched at Ada, Oklahoma, April 1909.

864. Hunt, Robert V., Jr. "'Reddy' Wilson's Fatal Encounter." OLD WEST [Stillwater, OK], Vol. 32, No. 2, Whole No. 126 (Winter 1995): 40-45. He was lynched in Iowa, 1894.

865. Hunt, Robert V., Jr. "Wyoming Sheriff Killer's Final Days." TRUE WEST [Stillwater, OK], Vol. 41, No. 4, Whole No. 312 (April 1994): 30-36. Charles Woodward was lynched on the scaffold built for his legal hanging, Casper, Wyoming, 1902.

866. "The Huntsville Lynchers." THE VOICE OF THE NEGRO, Vol. 1, No. 11 (Nov. 1904): 513-14. Alabama. Victim: Horace Maples. Grand jury indicted 26, and three were actually tried; no result mentioned. Soldiers were dismissed in disgrace after failure to protect jail from burning.

867. Ianniello, Lynne. "'Trial by Prejudice.'" THE ADL BULLETIN, Vol. 20, No. 3 (March 1963): 6-7. Leo Frank case.

868. "If Lincoln Could Return." THE CENTURY MAGAZINE, Vol. 85, No. 1 (Nov. 1912): 153-54. Briefly mentions lynching.

869. "Inability of the Governor of Kentucky to Bring Lynchers to Justice." AMERICAN LAW REVIEW, Vol. 34, [No. 2] (March-April 1900): 238-39.

870. "Increase of Lynching During the Year 1914." THE SURVEY, Vol. 33, No. 26 (March 27, 1915): 685.

871. "An Indiana Instance." THE AMERICAN MONTHLY REVIEW OF REVIEWS, Vol. 28, No. 2 (Aug. 1903): 134-35.   Frustration of Evansville mob's desire to lynch black man led to rioting and killing of several rioters by soldiers.

872. "The Indiana Lynching." PUBLIC OPINION, Vol. 23, No. 13 (Sept. 23, 1897): 389.   Five thieves were hanged at Versailles, Ripley County, Sept. 15, 1897. Followed by "Press Comment," pp. 389-90.

873. Ingalls, Robert P. "General Joseph B. Wall and Lynch Law in Tampa." THE FLORIDA HISTORICAL QUARTERLY, Vol. 63, No. 1 (July 1984): 51-70.   Lynching of a white man named Charles Owens in 1882 and its aftermath.

874. Ingalls, Robert P. "Lynching and Establishment Violence in Tampa, 1858-1935." JOURNAL OF SOUTHERN HISTORY, Vol. 53, No. 4 (Nov. 1987): 613-44.

875. Ingalls, Robert P. URBAN VIGILANTES IN THE NEW SOUTH: TAMPA, 1882-1936. Knoxville: Univ. of Tennessee Press, 1988.   Violence against blacks, immigrants, labor organizers, and radicals.

876. Ingenthron, Elmo, and Hartman, Mary. "Death of the Bald Knobbers." OLD WEST [Stillwater, OK], Vol. 25, No. 1, Whole No. 97 (Fall 1988): 44-49.   An excerpt from Bald Knobbers: Vigilantes on the Ozarks Frontier by Hartman and Ingenthron.

877. "An Insult to the Nation." THE OUTLOOK, Vol. 82, No. 13 (March 31, 1906): 721.   Black man lynched in Tennessee after his case was appealed to the U.S. Supreme Court.

878. Inverarity, James M. "Populism and Lynching in Louisiana, 1889-1896: A Test of Erickson's Theory of the Relationship Between Boundary Crises and Repressive Justice." AMERICAN SOCIOLOGICAL REVIEW, Vol. 41, No. 2 (April 1976): 262-80. See critiques in ibid., pp. 359-69 [numbers 498, 519, 532, 1231, and 1447 in this bibliography].

879. Inverarity, James M. "Reply to Bagozzi, Berk, Bohrnstedt, Pope and Ragin, and Wasserman." AMERICAN SOCIOLOGICAL REVIEW, Vol. 42, No. 4 (Aug. 1977): 663-67. Corrections to original article leave percent black as "the only significant causal variable" and "one could dispense with mechanical solidarity as a cause of lynchings."

880. Inverarity, James Michael. "The Relationship of Social Solidarity to the Incidence and Form of Adjudication: A Sociological Investigation of Lynching in the American South, 1890-1920." Ph.D. diss., Stanford Univ., 1976. See Diss. Ab. Intl., Vol. 36, No. 12 (June 1976): 8311A-8312A. Uses Southern lynching, the Solid South, and the disruption of solidarity by the Populist movement to examine Emile Durkheim's thesis "that repressive justice serves as a ritual to reinforce social solidarity." Finds the thesis valuable in this context.

881. "Is Burning at the Stake to Continue?" THE OUTLOOK, Vol. 99, No. 10 (Nov. 4, 1911): 551-52.   Coatesville, Pennsylvania, lynching.

882. "The Italian Lynchings." THE OUTLOOK, Vol. 62, No. 14 (Aug. 5, 1899): 735.   Five Italians lynched recently at Tallulah, Louisiana.

883. Jackson, Harvey H. "The Middle-Class Democracy Victorious: The Mitcham War of Clarke County, Alabama, 1893." JOURNAL OF SOUTHERN HISTORY, Vol. 57, No. 3 (Aug. 1991): 453-78.   Lynching and vigilantism, 1892-1893.

884. Jackson, Joy. "Crime and the Conscience of a City." LOUISIANA HISTORY, Vol. 9, No. 3 (Summer 1968): 229-44.   See pp. 234-35 for vigilante groups in New Orleans. See pp. 235-44 for Hennessy murder and lynching of Italians.

885. Jewett, Charles L. "Is Our Criminal Code Partly Responsible?" THE INDIANA LAW JOURNAL, Vol. 1, No. 5 (May 1898): 177-82.   Relates in part to lynching of five people in Ripley County [Sept. 1897].

886. Jones, Calico. "Wyoming's Mob Murder." REAL WEST [Derby, CT], Vol. XI, No. 62 (Aug. 1968): 10-11, 47-48, 60-61, 66.   William Clifton was lynched at Newcastle, 1902 [sic; should be 1903].

887. Jordan, D. E. "Mob Law." THE PRESBYTERIAN QUARTERLY, Vol. 4 (Oct. 1890): 590-613.   Deals with lynch mobs and mobs of striking workers.

888. "Judge Lynch and the Race Wars." COLLIER'S WEEKLY, Vol. 31, No. 15 (July 11, 1903): 6.   George White, black man, lynched at Wilmington, Delaware, June 22.   On June 24 "armed negroes [sic] ran amuck through the city."

889. "Judge Lynch as an Educator." THE NATION, Vol. 57, No. 1474 (Sept. 28, 1893): 222-23.   Argues that community sentiment which makes lynching possible makes certain the conviction of blacks in courts, and

lynching teaches blacks and whites disrespect for law and thereby weakens society.

890. "Judge Lynch's Reports, Annotated." THE NATIONAL CORPORA-TION REPORTER, Vol. 37, No. 1 (Aug. 20, 1908): 9.

891. "'Judicial Lynching at Brownsville': November 9, 1906." THE CRISIS, Vol. 80, No. 1 (Jan. 1973): 15-17. Discharge of black soldiers, only some of whom may have been guilty of rioting.

892. "The Jury to the Rescue." THE NATION, Vol. 77, No. 1988 (Aug. 6, 1903): 106-07.   Juries should convict lynchers.

893. "Justice Brewer on Cures for Lynching." THE OUTLOOK, Vol. 74, No. 17 (Aug. 22, 1903): 960-61.

894. Kaltenbach, Peter J. "The Man Who Was Hanged Twice." REAL WEST [Derby, CT], Vol. 17, No. 128 (July 1974): 46-49.   Joe (Hootch) Simpson was lynched in Skidoo, California, 1908. After burial he was dug up and hanged again so press could take photos.

895. "Kansas versus New Jersey." THE COLORED AMERICAN MAGAZINE, Vol. 2, No. 4 (Feb. 1901): 314-15. Includes item about a black man named Fred Alexander who was burned at the stake in Leaven-worth.

896. Karlin, J. Alexander. "The Italo-American Incident of 1891 and the Road to Reunion." JOURNAL OF SOUTHERN HISTORY, Vol. 8, No. 2 (May 1942): 242-46.   The "war scare" resulting from the lynching of Italians in New Orleans led to increased national unity.

897. Karlin, J. Alexander.   "New Orleans Lynching of 1891 and the American Press." THE LOUISIANA HISTORICAL QUARTERLY, Vol. 24, No. 1 (Jan. 1941): 187-204.

898. Karlin, J. Alexander. "Some Repercussions of the New Orleans Mafia Incident of 1891." RESEARCH STUDIES OF THE STATE COLLEGE OF WASHINGTON, Vol. 11, No. 4 (Dec. 1943): 267-82.

899. Karlin, Jules Alexander. "The Indemnification of Aliens Injured by Mob Violence." THE SOUTHWESTERN SOCIAL SCIENCE QUAR-TERLY, Vol. 25, No. 4 (March 1945): 235-46.

900. Katz, Allan. "The Hennessy Affair: A Centennial." NEW ORLEANS MAGAZINE, Vol. 25, No. 2 (Oct. 1990): 58-61, 81.   Includes "Who Really

Killed The Chief?" (pp. 61-62), by A.K.

901. Kendall, John S. "Who Killa de Chief?" THE LOUISIANA HISTORICAL QUARTERLY, Vol. 22, No. 2 (April 1939): 492-530. Anti-Italian riot and lynchings in New Orleans, 1891.

902. Kennedy, N. J. D. "Lynch." THE JURIDICAL REVIEW [London], Vol. 3, No. 3 (1891): 213-22.

903. Kennedy, N. J. D. "Lynch." "Lynch. II.--Its International Aspect." THE JURIDICAL REVIEW [London], Vol. 4, No. 1 (1892): 44-57. On protection of foreigners and a government's responsibility for violence done to them. See especially for the lynching of Italians in New Orleans.

904. Kernan, Thomas J. "The Jurisprudence of Lawlessness." REPORTS OF AMERICAN BAR ASSOCIATION, Vol. 29, Part 1 (1906): 450-67. Situations in which Americans believe it proper to take the law into their own hands, as in lynching.

905. Kernan, Thomas J. "The Jurisprudence of Lawlessness." THE GREEN BAG, Vol. 18, No. 11 (Nov. 1906): 588-97. Includes lynching.

906. Kesler, J. L. "In Justice to Waco." THE NATION, Vol. 103, No. 2687 (Dec. 28, 1916): 609. Letter about Waco response to May 15 lynching.

907. Kilgo, John Carlisle. "An Inquiry Concerning Lynchings." THE SOUTH ATLANTIC QUARTERLY, Vol. 1, No. 1 (Jan. 1902): 4-13.

908. "Killing and Lying." THE CRISIS, Vol. 12, No. 2 (June 1916): 72-74. Several lynching items.

909. King, Alex. C. "The Punishment of Crimes Against Women, Existing Legal Remedies and Their Sufficiency." In RACE PROBLEMS OF THE SOUTH: REPORT OF THE PROCEEDINGS OF THE FIRST ANNUAL CONFERENCE HELD UNDER THE AUSPICES OF THE SOUTHERN SOCIETY FOR THE PROMOTION OF THE STUDY OF RACE CONDITIONS AND PROBLEMS IN THE SOUTH--AT MONTGOM-ERY, ALABAMA, MAY 8, 9, 10, A. D. 1900, pp. 160-70 (in section "Lynching as a Penalty"). Richmond, VA: B. F. Johnson Pub. Co. for The Southern Society, 1900. Reprinted in John David Smith, ed., Racist Southern Paternalism, Vol. 2 of Anti-Black Thought 1863-1925: "The Negro Problem": An Eleven-Volume Anthology of Racist Writings (New York: Garland Publishing, 1993): 276-86.

910. Kleine, W. Laird. "Anatomy of a Riot." Historical and Philosophical

Society of Ohio BULLETIN,   Vol. 20, No. 4 (Oct. 1962):   234-44.
Cincinnati, 1884; attempt to lynch murderer who was only convicted of
manslaughter led to more general riot and destruction of courthouse.

911. Kleinschmidt, Bruce Lee.   "The Phoenix Riot."   THE FURMAN
REVIEW, Vol. 5, No. 1 (Spring Term 1974): 27-31. Election-day violence
in South Carolina led to lynchings of several blacks in succeeding days, Nov.
1898.

912. Kouris, Diana Allen.   "The Lynching: Calamity in Brown's Park."
TRUE WEST [Stillwater, OK], Vol. 42, No. 9, Whole No. 329 (Sept. 1995):
20-25. Victim: John Bennett; in northwestern Colorado, March 2, 1898.

913. Kwasny, Mark V.   "A Test for the Ohio National Guard: The
Cincinnati Riot of 1884." OHIO HISTORY, Vol. 98 (Winter-Spring 1989):
23-51.   Riot began as effort to lynch killer convicted only of manslaughter.

914. LaGumina, Salvatore, J., ed. WOP: A DOCUMENTARY HISTORY
OF ANTI-ITALIAN DISCRIMINATION IN THE UNITED STATES. San
Francisco: Straight Arrow Books; dist. by Quick Fox Inc., New York, 1973.
See pp. 73-89 for Hennessy's murder and resultant lynching of 11 Italians.

915. Lamon, Lester C. BLACK TENNESSEANS 1900-1930.   Knoxville:
Univ. of Tennessee Press, 1977.   See "Lynching" and "Racial violence" in
index.

916. Lamon, Lester Crawford. "Negroes in Tennessee, 1900-1930." Ph.D.
diss., Univ. of North Carolina at Chapel Hill, 1971.   See Diss. Ab. Intl.,
Vol. 32, No. 5 (Nov. 1971): 2608A-2609A.

917. Lane, Mills, ed. STANDING UPON THE MOUTH OF A VOL-
CANO: NEW SOUTH GEORGIA, A DOCUMENTARY HISTORY.
Savannah, GA: Beehive Press, 1993.   See "lynching" in index. Includes "A
Lynching in Statesboro, 1904," pp. 198-203, from Ray Stannard Baker,
Following the Color Line (New York, 1908), which deals with Paul Reed
and Will Cato.

918. Langston, Whitley. "The Statesboro Tragedies." THE CHRISTIAN
ADVOCATE [New York], Vol. 79, No. 35 (Sept. 1, 1904): 1425-26. Lynching of Cato and Reid [sic] in GA.

919. [Lansing, Robert.]   "Address of Mr. Robert Lansing of Watertown,
N. Y."   In PROCEEDINGS OF THE AMERICAN SOCIETY OF
INTERNATIONAL LAW . . . 1908, pp. 44-60.   New York: American
Society of International Law, 1908.   On protection of civil rights of aliens,

as from mob violence. Discussion on pp. 60-67.

920. "The Last Legal Stage of the Frank Case." THE OUTLOOK, Vol. 109, No. 17 (April 28, 1915): 958-59.

921. "The Latest Lynching Case." THE LITERARY DIGEST, Vol. 9, No. 20 (Sept. 15, 1894): 7 (577).   Recent lynching of six black prisoners near Memphis. [See also No author; no title; The Independent (Sept. 20, 1894)].

922. "Law and Lynching in Georgia." THE OUTLOOK, Vol. 112, No. 9 (March 1, 1916): 484.   Little about lynching per se; mostly deals with removal of Atlanta police chief for enforcing law relating to clubs called "blind tigers."

923. "Law Instead of Lynching." THE OUTLOOK, Vol. 76, No. 9 (Feb. 27, 1904): 487-88.   Governor Montague, Virginia, ensured trial of black man accused of rape.

924. "Law or Lynching." THE CENTURY MAGAZINE, Vol. 20 (New Series), Vol. XLII (Old Series), No. 2 (June 1891): 313-14.   Lynching of 11 men in New Orleans in 1891.

925. Law, R. A. "Stirring Up Race Hatred." THE NATION, Vol. 99, No. 2561 (July 30, 1914): 132-33.   Letter mentioning attempted lynching of an innocent black person in South Carolina.

926. Law, Robert Adger. "Punishment for Lynching." THE NATION, Vol. 100, No. 2595 (March 25, 1915): 330-31.   Letter telling of white members of a mob which attempted to lynch a black in South Carolina being convicted of riot, assault and battery, and being sentenced to prison in 1914.

927. "Leaders of the Murderous Vigilantes Pilloried." MOTHER EARTH, Vol. 7, No. 4 (June 1912): 108.   San Diego free speech conflict.

928. Leake, Graydon Boyd, III. "The Case of Mary Phagan and Leo Frank, 1913-1986: Seventy-Three Years of Fact, Fiction, and Opinion." M.A. thesis, Georgia State Univ., 1990.

929. "The Leavenworth Lynching." THE AMERICAN REVIEW OF REVIEWS, Vol. 23, No. 3 (March 1901): 262-63.

930. Lee, Thomas Zanslaur. "Lynching in 1916." AMERICA, Vol. 16, No. 21 (March 3, 1917): 495.   Letter.

931. "Legal Impotency and Lynching." OHIO LAW BULLETIN, Vol. 61,

No. 51 (Dec. 18, 1916): 407-09.   Reprint from New York Law Journal, Vol. LVI, No. 59 (Dec. 12, 1916): 932.

932. "Leo Frank." THE NEW REPUBLIC, Vol. 3, No. 38 (July 24, 1915): 300.

933. "Leo Frank and the Liberty of the Press." AMERICA, Vol. 13, No. 20 (Aug. 28, 1915): 494.

934. "Less Work for Judge Lynch." THE LITERARY DIGEST, Vol. 46, No. 17 (April 26, 1913): 936.   Fewer lynchings in 1912.

935. "Lessons of Coatesville." THE NATION, Vol. 93, No. 2409 (Aug. 31, 1911): 183-84.   Describes the Coatesville, PA, lynching from the study by William T. Ellis in The Continent.

936. "Letter Box." THE CRISIS, Vol. 6, No. 7 [sic; should be Vol. 7, No. 1] (Nov. 1913): 348.   Includes a letter advising The Crisis to stop dealing so much with lynching.

937. Level [sic], William Hayne. "Lynching--From a Southern Standpoint." THE BAR [West Virginia], Vol. 9, No. 1 (Jan. 1902): 27-31.

938. Levell, William Hayne. "On Lynching in the South." THE OUT-LOOK, Vol. 69, No. 11 (Nov. 16, 1901): 731-33.   Gives reasons for lynching, especially for rape.

939. Levi, Steven C. "San Francisco's Law and Order Committee, 1916." JOURNAL OF THE WEST, Vol. 12, No. 1 (Jan. 1973): 53-70.   Committee was established to promote open shop.

940. Levy, Eugene. "'Is the Jew a White Man?': Press Reaction to the Leo Frank Case, 1913-15." PHYLON, Vol. 35, No. 2 (June 1974): 212-22.

941. Lewis, H. T. "Is Lynch Law Due to Defects in the Criminal Law, or Its Administration?" In REPORT OF THE FOURTEENTH ANNUAL SESSION OF THE GEORGIA BAR ASSOCIATION, HELD AT WARM SPRINGS, GA., ON THURSDAY, JULY 1, AND FRIDAY, JULY 2, 1897, pp. 164-68 (Appendix 7). Atlanta: Franklin Printing and Publishing Co., 1897.   See also: Thomas, Lewis W.; [same title]; ibid., pp. 169-78 (Appendix 8). McDonald, John C.; [same title]; ibid., pp. 179-80 (Appendix 9). Munro, G. P.; [same title]; ibid., pp. 181-84 (Appendix 10). Smith, Burton; [same title]; ibid., pp. 196-97 (Appendix 12). Glenn, W. C.; "The Reform of Criminal Procedure," ibid., pp. 185-95 (Appendix 11); technical errors by which a defendant escapes conviction in a trial "contribute sensibly to the

spirit of the lynch law idea" (p. 190).

942. ["Liability for Destruction of Life or Property by Mob. Annotated Case."] In AMERICAN RAILROAD AND CORPORATION REPORTS, Vol. 10, pp. 721-37, as "City of New Orleans v. Abbagnato" (U. S. Circuit Court of Appeals, Fifth Circuit, May 29, 1894). Ed. by John Lewis. Chicago: E. B. Myers and Co., 1895.   Case involving lynching of 11 Italians in New Orleans, March 1891, after murder of Police Chief Hennessy in 1890. Title given here in brackets is in Index to Legal Periodicals, Vol. 2 (1887-1899): 342.

943. "The Life of Saver Vardaman." THE VOICE OF THE NEGRO, Vol. 1, No. 4 (April 1904): 127-28.   Governor Vardaman, Mississippi, prevented a lynching.

944. Lindemann, Albert S.   THE JEW ACCUSED: THREE ANTI-SEMITIC AFFAIRS (DREYFUS, BEILIS, FRANK) 1894-1915. New York: Cambridge Univ. Press, 1991.

945. Lineberger, Lois. "The Death of Sam Hose: A Study in the Ritual of Lynching." Honors thesis, Univ. of North Carolina at Chapel Hill, 1984. He was lynched in Georgia, 1899.

946. Livingston, David W. "The Lynching of Negroes in Texas, 1900-1925." M.A. thesis, East Texas State Univ., 1972.

947. "Local Mistakes About Sovereignty--Lynching." THE AMERICAN LAW REVIEW, Vol. 51 (Jan.-Feb. 1907): 112-13. Report on speech by Robert W. Shand, president of South Carolina Bar Association, with quotations. People may think themselves sovereign over their law officers.

948. Lockhart, Walter Samuel, III. "Lynching in North Carolina, 1888-1906." M.A. thesis, Univ. of North Carolina, Chapel Hill, 1972.

949. Lodge, Henry Cabot. "Lynch Law and Unrestricted Immigration." NORTH AMERICAN REVIEW, Vol. 152, No. 414 (May 1891): 602-12. In response to the mass lynching of Italians in New Orleans, 1891, advocates immigration restriction to keep out ignorant and criminal people and to prevent race and nationality antagonisms.

950. "The Looking Glass. The Burning Question." THE CRISIS, Vol. 12, No. 5 (Sept. 1916): 233-34.   Lynching.

951. "The Looking Glass. Lynching." THE CRISIS, Vol. 12, No. 4 (Aug. 1916): 188-89.   Waco, Texas, lynching.

952. "The Looking Glass. Mob Murder." THE CRISIS, Vol. 13, No. 1 (Nov. 1916): 24-25.

953. "The Looking Glass. Our Lynching Culture." THE CRISIS, Vol. 12, No. 6 (Oct. 1916): 283-84, 289.

954. Lopez, Claira S. "James K. Vardaman and the Negro: The Foundation of Mississippi's Racial Policy." THE SOUTHERN QUARTERLY, Vol. 3, No. 2 (Jan. 1965): 155-80.   Though Vardaman said he would lead a lynch mob as a private citizen, as governor he acted to enforce laws and prevent lynching (pp. 174-76).

955. Lore, Charles B. "The Relation of Law to the Manifestation of the Mob Spirit." THE CHRISTIAN ADVOCATE [New York], Vol. 78, No. 35 (Aug. 27, 1903): 1388-89.   Speech on Aug. 14 at Chautauqua conference on mobs, lynching, and feuds.

956. "Lynch Law." THE NATION, Vol. 65, No. 1670 (July 1, 1897): 6-7. Editorial. Not about a specific case.

957. "Lynch Law." POLITICAL SCIENCE QUARTERLY, Vol. 18, No. 4 (Dec. 1903): 733-34.   Recent lynchings.

958. "Lynch Law." THE SATURDAY REVIEW [London], Vol. 71, No. 1857 (May 30, 1891): 643.   Refers to various lynchings. Americans prefer anarchy to reform of courts, whose delays are often excuse for lynching.

959. "Lynch Law Again." LAW NOTES [Northport, NY], Vol. 1, No. 12 (March 1898): 161.

960. "Lynch Law and Riot in Ohio." THE INDEPENDENT, Vol. 56, No. 2885 (March 17, 1904): 580.   Lynching of Richard Dixon, black man, in Springfield, 1904, and subsequent riot.

961. "Lynch Law in America." CHRISTIAN WORLD, Vol. 38 (April 19, 1894): 287.   Two paragraphs; three quotations.

962. "Lynch Law in America." THE SOLICITORS' JOURNAL AND WEEKLY REPORTER, Vol. 59, (Aug. 28, 1915): 713.

963. "Lynch-Law in America." THE SPECTATOR [London], Vol. 72, No. 3440 (June 2, 1894): 743-44.   Editorial occasioned by Mr. Aked's article in Contemporary Review.

964. "Lynch Law in America and the Efforts Made to Stamp It Out."

CENTRAL LAW JOURNAL, Vol. 57, No. 1 (July 3, 1903): 1-4.

965. "Lynch Law in Iowa." THE INDEPENDENT, Vol. 62, No. 3033 (Jan. 17, 1907): 117.   Recent lynching at Waterloo of James Cullen. Also, references to Virginia and Mississippi.

966. "Lynch Law in New Orleans." THE REVIEW OF REVIEWS [London], Vol. 5, No. 26 (Feb. 1892): 153.   Quotes from N. J. D. Kennedy, "Lynch Law," Juridical Review, (Jan. 1892).

967. "Lynch Law in Pennsylvania." THE LITERARY DIGEST, Vol. 43, No. 9 (Aug. 26, 1911): 301-02.   Coatesville lynching.

968. "Lynch Law in the South." THE INDEPENDENT, Vol. 61, No. 3019 (Oct. 11, 1906): 842-43.

969. "Lynched a Woman." THE CRISIS, Vol. 4, No. 4 (Aug. 1912): 196-97. The lynching of a black woman about 60 years old in Pinehurst, Georgia, June 24, 1912.

970. "Lynchers Triumphant." THE CRISIS, Vol. 3, No. 2 (Dec. 1911): 60-61.   Various lynchings.

971. "Lynchers Triumphant." THE NATION, Vol. 93, No. 2417 (Oct. 26, 1911): 386.   Deals with Coatesville, Pennsylvania; a lynching in Durant, Oklahoma; a lynching near Charleston, South Carolina; and with anti-black violence (some by police) in New York City.

972. "Lynching." THE CRISIS, Vol. 2, No. 4 (Aug. 1911): 158.   No specific case.

973. "Lynching." THE CRISIS, Vol. 2, No. 6 (Oct. 1911): 232-33. Reports on several incidents on lynching and mob violence, including Coatesville, Pennsylvania.

974. "Lynching." THE CRISIS, Vol. 3, No. 4 (Feb. 1912): 149.   Press comments on the lynchings of 1911.

975. "Lynching." THE CRISIS, Vol. 3, No. 6 (April 1912): 238.   Reprint from a Sacramento newspaper.

976. "Lynching." THE CRISIS, Vol. 4, No. 1 (May 1912): 19-20.   Reprint from a New York newspaper.

977. "Lynching." THE CRISIS, Vol. 6, No. 6 (Oct. 1913): 283.   Two cases.

978. "Lynching." THE CRISIS, Vol. 7, No. 3 (Jan. 1914): 125.   Several items.

979. "Lynching." THE CRISIS, Vol. 7, No. 5 (March 1914): 239.   More lynchings occurred in 1912 and 1913 than were reported.

980. "Lynching." THE CRISIS, Vol. 8, No. 6 (Oct. 1914): 279-81.   Several items including 17-year-old white male "killed by a mob of Negroes" in Clarksville, Tennessee.

981. "Lynching." THE CRISIS, Vol. 9, No. 4 (Feb. 1915): 178-79.   Several items.

982. "Lynching." THE CRISIS, Vol. 9, No. 5 (March 1915): 225-29.

983. "Lynching." THE CRISIS, Vol. 10, No. 2 (June 1915): 71-72.   Lynching of man named Brooks in Tennessee.   Lynching of black man in a southwest Georgia county.

984. "Lynching." THE CRISIS, Vol. 10, No. 5 (Sept. 1915): 226-28.   Statistics and several cases.

985. "Lynching." THE CRISIS, Vol. 11, No. 6 (April 1916): 293-95.   Lynching in Georgia. See ibid., p. 303, for photo of "The Lynching in Lee County, Ga., Jan. 20, 1916."

986. "Lynching." THE CRISIS, Vol. 12, No. 3 (July 1916): 135.

987. "Lynching." THE NATION, Vol. 69, No. 1798 (Dec. 14, 1899): 440. Seeks to correct the misimpression that lynching occurs only as punishment for rape. Deplores the barbarism of lynching, as in recent case in Maysville, KY, where the victim's eyes were burned out with acid. Points out the hypocrisy of purporting to civilize the Philippines while practicing or condoning lynching at home. Mentions a boy who told his mother "that he had seen a man hanged, and he did so want to see one burned."

988. "Lynching." THE OUTLOOK, Vol. 93, No. 13 (Nov. 27, 1909): 637*-38* [sic].   Black man and white man lynched in Cairo, IL, Nov., 1909.

989. "Lynching a Family." THE LITERARY DIGEST, Vol. 50, No. 5 (Jan. 30, 1915): 178-79.   Four blacks lynched in Monticello, Georgia.

990. "The Lynching Affair at New Orleans." THE SPECTATOR [London], Vol. 66, No. 3273 (March 21, 1891): 400-02.   Murder of Hennessy [sic] and resultant lynching of Italians. Related untitled story on p. 398.

991. "The Lynching Affair at Tallulah." THE CHRISTIAN ADVOCATE [New York], Vol. 74, No. 33 (Aug. 17, 1899): 1294.

992. "Lynching Again." THE CRISIS, Vol. 4, No. 1 (May 1912): 27. Reaction to Justice Department stance.

993. "Lynching and Criminal Law." THE AMERICAN MONTHLY REVIEW OF REVIEWS, Vol. 34, No. 6 (Dec. 1906): 751-52.

994. "Lynching and Criminal Procedure." THE OUTLOOK, Vol. 83, No. 6 (June 9, 1906): 301.

995. "Lynching and Federal Law." THE CHAUTAUQUAN, Vol. 40, No. 5 (Jan. 1905): 408-09.

996. "Lynching and Its Cause." THE NATIONAL CORPORATION REPORTER, Vol. 40, No. 22 (July 14, 1910): 757.

997. "Lynching and Illiteracy." THE WORLD'S WORK, Vol. 30, No. 6 (Oct. 1915): 637-38.

998. "Lynching and Public Sentiment." THE OUTLOOK, Vol. 98, No. 6 (June 10, 1911): 289-91.   Contrasts recent lynching of six blacks in Lake City, Florida, and lack of outrage in the newspapers with the published protest against a Georgia newspaper reference to lynchers as a "mob."

999. "Lynching and Southern Opinion." THE OUTLOOK, Vol. 62, No. 5 (June 3, 1899): 242-43.

1000. "Lynching and Southern Sentiment." THE OUTLOOK, Vol. 62, No. 4 (May 27, 1899): 200-01.   Selections from Southern press show opposition to lynching.

1001. "Lynching and the Franchise Rights of the Negro." ANNALS OF THE AMERICAN ACADEMY OF POLITICAL AND SOCIAL SCIENCE, Vol. 15, No. 3 (May 1900): 181-85 (493-97).   Most of this is a quotation from a recent speech and pamphlet by the Reverend Edgar G. Murphy, saying lynch mobs are now dominated by a lower class of person; lynching encourages crime through power of suggestion. The topic seemingly in the title is not in the text.

1002. "Lynching and the New Negro Crime." HARPER'S WEEKLY, Vol. 47, No. 2436 (Aug. 29, 1903): 1395-96. The 'new Negro crime' was assault on a white woman by a black.

1003. THE LYNCHING AT CORUNNA. Mount Pleasant, MI: Private Press of John Cumming, 1980.   Victim: William Sullivan. Michigan, 1893.

1004. "The Lynching at Wewoka." THE CRISIS, Vol. 7, No. 3 (Jan. 1914): 146.   The victim was John Cudjo. [This occurred in Seminole County, OK, in November, 1913.]

1005. "The Lynching at Wilmington, Del." THE CHRISTIAN ADVO-CATE [New York], Vol. 78, No. 28 (July 9, 1903): 1093-94. Black man was victim.   He apparently murdered a Miss Bishop.   See also "A Noble Utterance . . ."

1006. "Lynching by Wholesale." THE AMERICAN MONTHLY REVIEW OF REVIEWS, Vol. 16, No. 4 (Oct. 1897): 390-91.   Five men (alleged to have committed a small burglary) were lynched at Versailles, IN, Sept. 14, 1897.   Further comments on lynching under headings "Growth of Rural Disorder" (p. 391) and "Some Faults in Our National Character" (p. 392).

1007. "The Lynching 'Championship.'" THE LITERARY DIGEST, Vol. 52, No. 6 (Feb. 5, 1916): 274-75.

1008. "The Lynching Habit." THE INDEPENDENT, Vol. 53, No. 2727 (March 7, 1901): 575.

1009. "The Lynching Horror." THE NATION, Vol. 73, No. 1887 (Aug. 29, 1901): 162.   Three blacks lynched, homes of some blacks burned, other blacks driven from their homes, Pierce City, MO, August, 1901. Black man burned alive in Grayson County, TX, and another in Winchester, TN.

1010. "Lynching: How Far the Courts are Responsible for its Prevalence." THE AMERICAN LAW REVIEW, Vol. 33 (July-Aug. 1899): 596-98.

1011. "Lynching--Immunity for Witnesses--Pardoning Power."   THE AMERICAN LAW REVIEW, Vol. 42 (Jan.-Feb. 1908): 130.   North Carolina law was upheld in court case.

1012. "Lynching in America." CHAMBER'S JOURNAL OF POPULAR LITERATURE, SCIENCE, AND ART [Edinburgh], Fifth Series, Vol. 7, No. 333 (May 17, 1890): 317-19.   Includes account of lynching at Fort Collins, Colorado, of John Howe in late 1880s.

1013. "Lynching in America and English Interference." THE SPECTATOR [London], Vol. 73, No. 3450 (Aug. 11, 1894): 169-70.   Argues against such interference--despite the pleas of Miss Ida Wells.

1014. "A Lynching in Arkansas." THE COLORED AMERICAN MAGA-ZINE, Vol. 9, No. 2 (Aug. 1905): 409.   Black man named Jos. Woodman was lynched for running away with a white girl.

"A Lynching in Statesboro, 1904." See Lane, Mills.

1015. A LYNCHING IN VIRGINIA.   CHARLOTTESVILLE, OCTO-BER 1. JIM RHODES THE MURDERER OF THE MASSIE FAMILY WAS TAKEN OUT OF JAIL . . . AND HUNG TO A TREE.   Poster, 1882. In University of Virginia library.

1016. "The Lynching Industry." THE CRISIS, Vol. 9, No. 4 (Feb. 1915): 196, 198.   Black men lynched in 1914, by month and state.

1017. "The Lynching Industry." THE CRISIS, Vol. 11, No. 4 (Feb. 1916): 198-99.   Gives details of blacks lynched in 1915, by name, state, and date.

1018. "Lynching. Its Causes and Cure. The Great National Disgrace. . . ." THE INDEPENDENT, Vol. 46, No. 2357 (Feb. 1, 1894): 1-4 (129-32). A symposium. See E. E. Hoss, Fanny M. Preston, Geo. C. Rowe, and A Resident in North Carolina.

1019. "The Lynching Madness." THE NATION, Vol. 77, No. 1983 (July 2, 1903): 4.   Mania for lynching spreads from place to place. Not about any particular lynching.

1020. "The Lynching Mania at Large." THE AMERICAN MONTHLY REVIEW OF REVIEWS, Vol. 23, No. 3 (March 1901): 263.

1021. "The Lynching Problem." THE AMERICAN LAW REVIEW, Vol. 39 (Jan.-Feb. 1905): 98-101.

1022. "The Lynching Problem in America." THE OUTLOOK [London], Vol. 14, No. 355 (Nov. 19, 1904): 473-74.

1023. "The Lynching Record." CHRISTIAN ADVOCATE [Nashville], Vol. 78, No. 2 (Jan. 12, 1917): (2) 26.   Brief paragraph about 1916.

1024. "The Lynching Record." THE OUTLOOK, Vol. 106, No 9 (Feb. 28, 1914): 434.   Notes decline in lynchings per year but a vastly greater decline in number of whites lynched per year. Lists trivial "offenses" for which blacks were lynched.

1025. "The Lynching Record of 1903." PUBLIC OPINION, Vol. 36, No. 2 (Jan. 14, 1904): 40.   Subtitle: "Number, Geographical Distribution, and

Cause of the Mob Executions of Last Year."

1026. "Lynching--Removal of Derelict Sheriff." THE AMERICAN LAW REVIEW, Vol. 44 (Jan.-Feb. 1910): 115.   Alabama case.

1027. "The Lynching Spirit Again." THE VOICE OF THE NEGRO, Vol. 2, No. 11 (Nov. 1905): 750.   Includes reports that a lynch mob composed of blacks lynched a black on Oct. 7 at Bainbridge, South Carolina.

1028. "A Lynching 'Talk-Fest.'" THE CRISIS, Vol. 11, No. 5, (March 1916): 232-33.   Comments on lynching.

1029. "Lynching--The Great American Pastime." THE SURVEY, Vol. 35, No. 16 (Jan. 15, 1916): 453.

1030. "Lynchings." THE CRISIS, Vol. 4, No. 6 (Oct. 1912): 275.   Several items.

1031. "Lynchings and the Federal Power." THE CHAUTAUQUAN, Vol. 35, No. 6 (Sept. 1902): 539-40.

1032. "Lynchings by States and Counties in the United States 1900 to 1931." In I TOO AM AMERICA: DOCUMENTS FROM 1619 TO THE PRESENT, p. 202.   Ed. by Patricia W. Romero.   Vol. 3 of INTERNATION-AL LIBRARY OF NEGRO LIFE AND HISTORY.   10 vols.; New York: Publishers Co., under the auspices of The Association for the Study of Negro Life and History, 1968.   A map.

1033. "Lynchings During 1913." JOURNAL OF CRIMINAL LAW AND CRIMINOLOGY, Vol. 4, No. 6 (March 1914): 927-30.

1034. "Lynchings in the South." THE OUTLOOK, Vol. 69, No. 11 (Nov. 16, 1901): 678-79.

1035. LYNCHINGS IN THE UNITED STATES A NATIONAL DIS-GRACE AND A MENACE TO HIGHER CIVILIZATION; OR, A CONSENSUS OF OPINION FOR AND AGAINST LYNCHINGS WITH COMMENTS. Washington, DC: Age Print. Co., 1898.

1036. "Lynchings North and South." GUNTON'S MAGAZINE, Vol. 25 (Aug. 1903): 179-81.

1037. "Lynchings of 1906." THE COLORED AMERICAN MAGAZINE, Vol. 12, No. 3 (March 1907): 225.

1038. "Lynchings South and North." CURRENT LITERATURE, Vol. 36, No. 4 (April 1904): 376-77.   Lynchings prevented by Governor Vardaman, Mississippi, and Governor Montague, Virginia, but lynching and riot occurred in Springfield, Ohio.

1039. MacLean, Nancy. "The Leo Frank Case Reconsidered: Gender and Sexual Politics in the Making of Reactionary Populism." THE JOURNAL OF AMERICAN HISTORY, Vol. 78, No. 3 (Dec. 1991): 917-48.

1040. Macrae, David.   "The Lynching of Negroes in America."   THE SPEAKER [London], Vol. 14 (Aug. 4, 1906): 408-09.   Letter.

1041. "The Mafia and What Led to the Lynching." HARPER'S WEEKLY, Vol. 35, No. 1788 (March 28, 1891): 226.   New Orleans. Followed by "The Massacre at the Parish Prison," pp. 226-27. Cover (p. 217) has illustration, "The Killing of Six of the Italians in the Yard of the Parish Prison."

1042. "'The Mafia' in New Orleans." HARPER'S WEEKLY, Vol. 34, No. 1768 (Nov. 8, 1890): 874.   Assassination of Hennessy. See illustration on p. 872.

1043. Malone, James H. "Judge Lynch and the Jury Laws." In PROCEED-INGS OF THE THIRTEENTH ANNUAL MEETING OF THE BAR ASSOCIATION OF TENNESSEE HELD AT LOOKOUT INN, LOOK-OUT, TENN., AUGUST 7, 8, 9, 1894, pp. 108-13. Nashville: Marshall & Bruce Co., 1894.

1044. Malone, James H. "Judge Lynch and the Jury Laws." THE AMERI-CAN LAWYER, Vol. 3, No. 2 (Feb. 1895): 57-58.

1045. Marr, Robt. H., Jr. "The New Orleans Mafia Case." THE AMERI-CAN LAW REVIEW, Vol. 25 (May-June 1891): 414-31.   Assassination of police chief Hennessy, trial of the accused, and lynching of 11 Italians.

1046. Martin, E. S. "This Busy World." HARPER'S WEEKLY, Vol. 43, No. 2212 (May 13, 1899): 469.   Includes lynchings of Sam Hose in Georgia and a black prisoner named Strickland. Brief.

1047. "Massachusetts as an Example." THE AMERICAN MONTHLY REVIEW OF REVIEWS, Vol. 23, No. 3 (March 1901): 263-64.   Massa-chusetts does not engage in lynching, as Kansas did in the recent burning at Leavenworth.

"The Massacre at the Parish Prison." See "The Mafia and What Led to the Lynching."

1048. Massey, James. L., and Myers, Martha A. "Patterns of Repressive Social Control in Post-Reconstruction Georgia, 1882-1935." SOCIAL FORCES, Vol. 68, No. 2 (Dec. 1989): 458-88. Finds "little evidence of relationship among trends in the lynching, execution, and incarceration of black males during this period."

1049. Matthews, Janet Snyder. "'He Has Carried His Life in His Hands': The 'Sarasota Assassination Society' of 1884." THE FLORIDA HISTORI-CAL QUARTERLY, Vol. 58, No. 1 (July 1979): 1-21. Murders by vigilantes whose leaders were motivated by personal gain.

1050. Matthews, John Michael. "Studies in Race Relations in Georgia, 1890-1930." Ph.D. diss., Duke Univ., 1970. See pp. 154-77 for lynching. See Diss. Ab. Intl., Vol. 31, No. 10 (April 1971): 5327A.

1051. Maxey, Edwin. "The Court v. the Mob." THE AMERICAN LAW REVIEW, Vol. 40 (Nov.-Dec. 1906): 864-68. An argument against lynching.

1052. Maxey, Edwin. "Mob Rule." THE ARENA, Vol. 30, No. 4 (Oct. 1903): 377-81. Deals with strike-riots and lynchings.

1053. [McAllister, Henry.] ["What Can Be Done to Stop Lynching?"] THE AMERICAN LAW REVIEW, Vol. 39 (Jan.-Feb. 1905): 101-03. Report of a speech given to the Colorado Bar Association, 1904.

1054. McAllister, Henry, Jr. "What Can Be Done to Stop Lynching?" In REPORT OF THE SEVENTH ANNUAL MEETING OF THE COLO-RADO BAR ASSOCIATION, pp. 123-36. N.p.: n.p., n.d. See entry in this chapter under "What Can Be Done to Stop Lynching . . ."

1055. McConkey, F., and Groom, C. H. THE BALD KNOBBERS; OR, CITIZENS COMMITTEE OF TANEY AND CHRISTIAN COUNTIES, MISSOURI; A HISTORY OF SOUTHWEST MISSOURI'S FAMOUS ORGANIZATION. Forsyth, MO: Groom & McConkey, 1887.

1056. McGuire, Hunter, and Lydston, G. Frank. "Sexual Crimes Among the Southern Negroes--Scientifically Considered--An Open Correspondence between Hunter McGuire . . . and G. Frank Lydston . . ." VIRGINIA MEDICAL MONTHLY, Vol. 20, No. 2 (May 1893): 105-25. Includes lynching (pp. 105-06, 121-22). Lydston favors castration or emasculation.

1057. McIver, H. M. "'Water Bound in Arkansas.'" Part II. THE ARKANSAS HISTORICAL QUARTERLY, Vol. 14, No. 3 (Autumn 1955): 225-51. See p. 232 for 1899 incident in which blacks asked to hang and burn black accused of murder--but whites performed the lynching.

1058. McKay, W. "Lynching in Georgia: A Correction." THE SPECTA-
TOR [London], Vol. 73, No. 3448 (July 28, 1894): 111.   Letter from
Macon, GA. Some lynching stories, such as the skinning of a black man and
"the woman rolled in a barrel stuck full of nails," are untrue.

1059. McKemy, Al, submitter. "Negro Murderer Lynched." MISSOURI
STATE GENEALOGICAL ASSOCIATION JOURNAL, Vol. 13, No. 3
(Summer 1993): 168-70.   Lynchee: Arthur McNeal; at Richmond, MO,
March, 1901. Reprint of newspaper article.

1060. McKinney, Gordon B. "Industrialization and Violence in Appalachia
in the 1890's." In AN APPALACHIAN SYMPOSIUM: ESSAYS WRIT-
TEN IN HONOR OF CRATIS D. WILLIAMS, pp. 131-44. Ed. by J. W.
Williamson. Boone, NC: Appalachian State Univ. Press, 1977. Includes
lynching, especially lynching and riot in Roanoke, VA, 1893.

1061. McLagan, Elizabeth. A PECULIAR PARADISE: A HISTORY OF
BLACKS IN OREGON, 1788-1940.   Oregon Black History Project.
Portland: Georgian Press, 1980.   See pp. 135-39 for lynchings and near-
lynchings. Victims: Alonzo Tucker, 1902; Timothy Pettis, 1924. Both at
Marshfield, now Coos Bay.

1062. McMillen, Neil R. DARK JOURNEY: BLACK MISSISSIPPIANS
IN THE AGE OF JIM CROW. Urbana: Univ. of Illinois, 1989.   See
"lynching," "violence," and "Whitecapping" in index, and especially Chap. 7,
"Judge Lynch's Court" (pp. 224-53).

1063. McQuiston, J. A. C.   "Lynching." THE HOMILETIC REVIEW,
Vol. 28, No. 3 (Sept. 1894): 219-24.   Argues against it.

1064. McSwain, J. J. "What Shall Be Done With the Mob." CENTRAL
LAW JOURNAL, Vol. 67, No. 20 (Nov. 13, 1908): 375-76.

1065. McTeer, Will A.   "The Mountaineers of East Tennessee and
Kentucky." THE AMERICAN LAW REVIEW, Vol. 26 (May-June 1892):
469-70.   Letter; author objects to lynchings and says eastern Tennessee has
had few.   Editorial comment follows: in 1891 some mountaineers [in
Tennessee and Kentucky] tied a naked, 16-year-old girl to a tree and
"whipped her to death for the crime of marrying an old widower."

1066. "The Medicine for the Mob." THE OUTLOOK, Vol. 85, No. 5 (Feb.
2, 1907): 249-50.   Reviews the arguments advanced by Hooper Alexander
and J. E. Cutler on the causes of race riots and lynching in two articles in
this issue of The Outlook.

1067. Meier, Gary. "Where is the Ruggles' Gold?" OLD WEST [Stillwater, OK], Vol. 28, No. 1, Whole No. 109 (Fall 1991): 54-58.   The two brothers were lynched at Redding, California, 1892.

1068. Melzer, John T. "The Danville Riot, November 3, 1883." M.A. thesis, Univ. of Virginia, 1963.

1069. "Messrs. Blease and Johnson." THE CRISIS, Vol. 5, No. 3 (Jan. 1913): 123-24.   Newspaper comments on Governor Cole Blease's defense of lynching.

1070. "A Mexican Boycott." THE INDEPENDENT, Vol. 69, No. 3233 (Nov. 17, 1910): 1111-12.   Mexican national burned at the stake by Texas lynch mob. Victim name and location not given. Also: general comments.

1071. Miller, Kelly. "The Attitude of the Intelligent Negro Toward Lynching." THE VOICE OF THE NEGRO, Vol. 2, No. 5 (May 1905): 307-12.

1072. Miller, Kelly. "Possible Remedies for Lynching." THE SOUTHERN WORKMAN AND HAMPTON SCHOOL RECORD, Vol. 28, No. 11 (Nov. 1899): 418-23.

1073. Miller, Kelly.   RADICALISM AND CONSERVATIVES AND OTHER ESSAYS ON THE NEGRO IN AMERICA. New York: Schocken Books, 1968.   Includes "An Appeal to Reason on the Race Problem: An Open Letter to John Temple Graves Suggested by the Atlanta Riot" (pp. 71-101), which includes lynching.

1074. Miller, William D. "Myth and New South City Murder Rates." THE MISSISSIPPI QUARTERLY, Vol. 26, No. 2 (Spring 1973): 143-53.   See pp. 152-53 for lynching.

1075. "A Minimum of Race Friction." THE AMERICAN MONTHLY REVIEW OF REVIEWS, Vol. 28, No. 2 (Aug. 1903): 139.   Brief mention of lynchings says they "are neither sectional nor racial."

1076. THE MINNEAPOLIS TRAGEDY: FULL ACCOUNT OF THE CRIME OF THE FIEND FRANK McMANUS, AND THE SWIFT RETRIBUTION OF AN OUTRAGED COMMUNITY. Minneapolis: Haywood & Kruckeberg, 1882.   A lynching in 1882.

1077. "Miscellaneous." THE CRISIS, Vol. 10, No. 5 (Sept. 1915): 228-29. Reprint from Afro-American Ledger on proposal for vigilance committees in Washington, DC, and state capitals and ability of NAACP branches to perform function of watchdogs on legislative matters of interest to blacks.

1078. "Miscellaneous Editorial Paragraphs." THE CHRISTIAN ADVO-
CATE [New York], Vol. 76, No. 4 (Jan. 24, 1901): 143.   Recalls predic-
tions of increase in lynching. New York Tribune editorial "Judge Lynch at
His Worst" notes lynching is unknown in Europe.

1079. "Mississippi Whitecappers Convicted." THE VOICE OF THE
NEGRO, Vol. 2, No. 2 (Feb. 1905): 87.   "Reign of terror" against blacks
caused labor scarcity and made white farmers organize "to root up the evil."

1080. Mitchell, John, Jr. "Shall the Wheels of Race Agitation Be Stopped?"
THE COLORED AMERICAN MAGAZINE, Vol. 5, No. 5 (Sept. 1902):
386-91.   Several references to lynching.

1081. "The Mob at Springfield, Ohio." THE INDEPENDENT, Vol. 60, No.
2988 (March 8, 1906): 582-84.   Frustrated in their effort to lynch two
blacks, rioters attacked and burned part of black section of town.

1082. "The Mob Ceremonial." THE INDEPENDENT, Vol. 64, No. 3108
(June 25, 1908): 1459-60.   Former mob fury, as in lynchings, is being
replaced by form and ceremony, as in political conventions and football
crowds.

1083. "The Mob is Not Yet Dead." THE COLORED AMERICAN
MAGAZINE, Vol. 9, No. 2 (Aug. 1905): 404-05.

1084. "Mob Law." THE CRISIS, Vol. 7, No. 2 (Dec. 1913): 71-72.
Lynching; includes comments from magazines in Japan and London.

1085. "Mob Law." TOLEDO LEGAL NEWS, Vol. 1 [of OHIO LEGAL
NEWS] (May 19, 1894): 98.   Judge's charge to Logan County Grand Jury
regarding April, 1893, lynching at Rushsylvania of Seymour Newlin.

1086. "Mob-Law and Prosperity." THE NATION, Vol. 92, No. 2385
(March 16, 1911): 259-60.   Southern lynchings and race riots hurt the
section's economy.

1087. "Mob Law in Georgia." THE LITERARY DIGEST, Vol. 51, No. 9
(Aug. 28, 1915): 392.   Lynching of Leo Frank.

1088. "'Mob Law' is Anarchy." THE AMERICAN LAW REVIEW, Vol.
38 (Jan.-Feb. 1904): 97-98.   Examples of lynching of innocent men.

1089. Mob-Murder." THE CRISIS, Vol. 12, No. 1 (May 1916): 22-24.

Several lynching items.

1090. "Mob or Court?" THE OUTLOOK, Vol. 88, No. 14 (April 4, 1908): 768-69.   U.S. is moving toward greater racial justice despite some riots and lynchings.

1091. "Mob Rule." PUBLIC OPINION, Vol. 14, No. 19 (Feb. 11, 1893): 447-48.   Two newspaper stories on lynching.

1092. "The Mob Spirit." THE CHAUTAUQUAN, Vol. 38, No. 1 (Sept. 1903): 11-13.   Reports of speeches on mountain feuds, lynching, and strike violence at 1903 conference.

1093. "The Mob Spirit,--A Delaware Instance."   THE AMERICAN MONTHLY REVIEW OF REVIEWS, Vol. 28, No. 2 (Aug. 1903): 134. Black man burned at the stake near Wilmington.

1094. THE MOB SPIRIT IN AMERICA. Springfield, OH: Chautauqua Press, 1903.   Reprint of speeches from 1903 conference; see "The Mob Spirit."

1095. "'The Mob Spirit, Lynchings, and Feuds.'"   THE CHRISTIAN ADVOCATE [New York], Vol. 78, No. 36 (Sept. 3, 1903): 1414-17. Reports of Chautauqua conference speeches by William G. Frost ("The Mountain Feud"), Henry M. Brock, John Temple Graves ("The Mob Spirit in the South," especially on lynching), and James M. Buckley.

1096. "'The Mob Spirit, Lynchings, and Feuds.'"   THE CHRISTIAN ADVOCATE [New York], Vol. 78, No. 37 (Sept. 10, 1903): 1455-57. More on Chautauqua conference.

1097. "'The Mob Spirit, Lynchings, and Feuds.'" THE CHRISTIAN ADVOCATE [New York], Vol. 78, No. 38 (Sept. 17, 1903): 1495-97. Concluding article on Chautauqua conference. This part includes labor violence and part of speech "The Law and the Mob Spirit" by John Woodward (which includes material on lynching).

1098. "Mob Violence, North and South." THE INDEPENDENT, Vol. 55, No. 2852 (July 30, 1903): 1769-70.   Various lynchings and attempted lynchings.

1099. "Monticello." THE CRISIS, Vol. 9, No. 5 (March 1915): 237.   Recent lynching in Monticello, Georgia.

1100. Mooney, C. W.   "Burned Alive At The Stake."   WILD WEST

[Sepulveda, CA], Vol. 2, No. 1 (March 1970): 50-56. Two Seminole Indians were lynched in Oklahoma, Jan. 1898.

1101. "More Lynch Law." THE AMERICAN LAW REVIEW, Vol. 26 (March-April 1892): 248-49. Mob took three black men from Memphis jail and shot them.

1102. Morris, Lucile. BALD KNOBBERS. Caldwell, ID: Caxton Printers, 1939. Ozark night riders.

1103. Moseley, Charlton, and Brogdon, Frederick. "A Lynching at Statesboro: The Story of Paul Reed and Will Cato." THE GEORGIA HISTORICAL QUARTERLY, Vol. 65, No. 2 (Summer 1981): 104-18. Two black men were burned alive in 1904.

1104. Moseley, Charlton. "Latent Klanism in Georgia, 1890-1915." THE GEORGIA HISTORICAL QUARTERLY, Vol. 56, No. 3 (Fall 1972): 365-86. Pages 377-78 examine causes of violence against Leo Frank.

1105. Moseley, Clement Charlton. "The Case of Leo M. Frank, 1913-1915." THE GEORGIA HISTORICAL QUARTERLY, Vol. 51, No. 1 (March 1967): 42-62. Middle name is Charlton on p. 42 but Carlton on contents page.

1106. Moses, Adolph. "Growth of Mob Spirit." THE NATIONAL CORPORATION REPORTER, Vol. 27, No. 3 (Sept. 10, 1903): 70. Argument against lynching occasioned by two recent lynchings in Illinois.

1107. "Moving Against Lynching." THE NATION, Vol. 103, No. 2666 (Aug. 3, 1916): 101-02.

1108. Mowry, Duane. "Lynch-Law and Lynching." THE GREEN BAG, Vol. 17, No. 11 (Nov. 1905): 638-43.

1109. Mowry, Duane. "Mob Law in America." THE GREEN BAG, Vol. 16, No. 8 (Aug. 1904): 524-27.

1110. Mowry, Duane. "What Shall Be Done With the Mobs?" CENTRAL LAW JOURNAL, Vol. 67, No. 17 (Oct. 23, 1908): 315-16.

1111. Mullins, Jack Simpson. "Lynching in South Carolina, 1900-1914." M.A. thesis, Univ. of South Carolina, 1961.

1112. "Municipal Liability Under Statutes for Injuries by Mobs." LAW NOTES [Northport, NY], Vol. 3 (June 1899): 43-46. The last part of this article deals with lynching.

1113. "Murder." THE CRISIS, Vol. 5, No. 5 (March 1913): 232-33. See p. 233 for comments on lynching.

1114. "Murder." THE CRISIS, Vol. 5, No. 6 (April 1913): 277-78. Some references to lynching.

1115. "Murder." THE CRISIS, Vol. 11, No. 4 (Feb. 1916): 172-73. Includes comments on lynching of blacks.

1116. "Murder." THE OUTLOOK, Vol. 74, No. 15 (Aug. 8, 1903): 877-80. Lynching is part of a general disregard for life and the law in the U.S. The remedies are: (1) swifter and more certain justice against rapists, (2) greater stigmatization of and action against lynchers as murderers, (3) greater respect for law and a redefinition of liberty away from the idea that "liberty is the right of every man to do what he will, and that majorities can do no wrong."

1117. "Murder and the Law." THE NATION, Vol. 96, No. 2492 (April 3, 1913): 326-27. Growing sentiment in the South against lynching. Lynching and individual homicide show disrespect for law.

1118. "The Murder of Frank Carmichael." THE VOICE OF THE NEGRO, Vol. 3, No. 9 (Sept. 1906): 625-26. Black victim of mob near Lakewood, Georgia, because of alleged rape.

1119. "MURDER WILL OUT"; THE ASHLAND TRAGEDY; THE CROW-BAR AND AX, THE SILENT WITNESSES. A HISTORY OF THE KILLING OF FANNY GIBBONS, EMMA CARICO AND ROBBIE GIBBONS. Ashland, KY: J. M. Huff, [1883?]. Reprint ed.; Lexington, KY: Gallows Press, 1985. Triple murder in Kentucky, 1881, resulted in 1882 lynching of one perpetrator. During attempted lynching later that year of the other two, state militia soldiers on boat going down Ohio River fired at innocent bystanders on shore, killing and wounding several.

1120. Murphy, Edgar Gardner. "The Georgia Atrocity and Southern Opinion." THE OUTLOOK, Vol. 62, No. 3 (May 20, 1899): 179-80. Lynching letter.

1121. Murphy, Edgar Gardner. THE WHITE MAN AND THE NEGRO IN THE SOUTH. AN ADDRESS DELIVERED UNDER INVITATION OF THE AMERICAN ACADEMY OF POLITICAL AND SOCIAL SCIENCE... IN THE CHURCH OF THE HOLY TRINITY, PHILADEL-PHIA, ON THE EVENING OF MARCH 8TH, A.D. 1900. [Montgomery?

AL, 1900]   See "Lynching and the Franchise Rights of the Negro."

1122. [NAACP]. [Ad for contributions to NAACP Anti-Lynching Fund.] THE CRISIS, Vol. 12, No. 4 (Aug. 1916): 202.

1123. "The N. A. A. C. P." THE CRISIS, Vol. 2, No. 2 (June 1911): 60-61. On p. 61 there is a letter from the governor of Kentucky giving facts about a lynching in a theater in Livermore.

1124. "The N. A. A. C. P." THE CRISIS, Vol. 2, No. 3 (July 1911): 107-09. See pages 108-09 for lynching of six blacks at Lake City, Florida.

1125. "The N. A. A. C. P." THE CRISIS, Vol. 3, No. 2 (Dec. 1911): 64. See last item for New York City meeting to protest lynching.

1126. Nance, Lee. A REPUBLIC OR DESPOTISM, WHICH? Chicago: Louis Nash and Co., 1894.   Black author. Includes numerous instances of lynching.

1127. Nash, Roy. THE LYNCHING OF ANTHONY CRAWFORD. New York: NAACP, 1916.   South Carolina, 1916.

1128. Nash, Roy. "The Lynching of Anthony Crawford." THE INDEPEN-DENT, Vol. 88, No. 3549 (Dec. 11, 1916): 456, 458, 460-62.   South Carolina, 1916.

1129. Nash, Royal Freeman. "The Cherokee Fires. An N. A. A. C. P. Investigation." THE CRISIS, Vol. 11, No. 5 (March 1916): 265-68, 270. Relates several fires in Dec., 1915, in Cherokee County, Georgia, to an anti-Negro "pogrom" in Forsyth and Dawson counties in Georgia in 1912. Also describes a lynching in Forsyth County in 1912.

1130. National Association for the Advancement of Colored People. NOTES ON LYNCHING IN THE UNITED STATES: COMPILED FROM THE CRISIS . . . New York: NAACP, 1912.

1131. National Association for the Advancement of Colored People. THIRTY YEARS OF LYNCHING IN THE UNITED STATES, 1889-1918. New York: NAACP, 1919; reprint: New York: Arno Press and the New York Times, 1969.   Includes "The Story of One Hundred Lynchings" (pp. 11-28) and "Chronological List of Persons Lynched in United States, 1889 to 1918, inclusive, arranged by States" (pp. 43-103), and "List of Persons Lynched in 1918, by States" (pp. 104-05).

1132. "The National Crime." THE INDEPENDENT, Vol. 46, No. 2357

(Feb. 1, 1894): 10 (138).   Editorial on lynching.

1133. [National Governors' Conference, 1912.] PROCEEDINGS OF THE FIFTH MEETING OF THE GOVERNORS OF THE STATES OF THE UNION HELD AT RICHMOND, VIRGINIA, DECEMBER 3-7, 1912. See pp. 246-59 for remarks and resolutions on remarks of the Governor of South Carolina [Blease] concerning lynch law [made at this conference on the preceding Thursday].

1134. "A Nation's Responsibility." EDUCATIONAL REVIEW, Vol. 44, No. 5 (Dec. 1912): 460-65.   Editor's introduction, and text of a speech by John Jay Chapman about Coatesville, PA, lynching, Aug. 1911.

1135. Neal, Diane. "Ben Tillman--No Apologies for Lynching." THE PROCEEDINGS OF THE SOUTH CAROLINA HISTORICAL ASSOCI-ATION 1971, pp. 5-15.   Perspicacious examination of lynching and Tillman's sometimes inconsistent attitudes toward it.

1136. "The Negro National Council." THE CHRISTIAN ADVOCATE [New York], Vol. 68, No. 50 (Dec. 14, 1893): 801.   Includes statistics on murder, executions, lynching, and rape.

1137. "The Negroes in the United States: Reassuring Statement by Dr. Albert Shaw." THE REVIEW OF REVIEWS [London], Vol. 28, No. 164 (Aug. 1903): 166.   In American Review of Reviews for August, Shaw says yearly number of lynchings is declining.

1138. "Negroes Lynched in Missouri." THE INDEPENDENT, Vol. 60, No. 2994 (April 19, 1906): 892.   Horace Duncan, James Copeland, and William Allen; Springfield, 1906. Fourteen other jail inmates escaped during mob activity.

1139. "The New Abolition." THE CRISIS, Vol. 9, No. 6 (April 1915): 280-82.   Includes a paragraph on lynching (pp. 280-81).

1140. "New Orleans' War on the Mafia." ILLUSTRATED AMERICAN, Vol. 6 (April 4, 1891): 319-23.   Mass lynching in New Orleans.

1141. "A New Way to Prevent Lynching." THE INDEPENDENT, Vol. 57, No. 2913 (Sept. 29, 1904): 747-48.   The 'new way' is "punishing in a mild way, and disgracing in a severe way, the officers . . . who have not protected prisoners under their charge" (p. 747).

1142. Newby, I. A. JIM CROW'S DEFENSE: ANTI-NEGRO THOUGHT IN AMERICA, 1900-30. Baton Rouge: Louisiana State Univ. Press, 1965.

See "Lynching" in index. See pp. 137-39 for justification of lynching by racists.

1143. Newby, Idus A. "The Negro and American Racism, 1900-1930." Ph.D. diss., Univ. of California, Los Angeles, 1962.

1144. Newman, Ewell L. "'Death in the Heart of This People.'" THE CRISIS, Vol. 80, No. 2 (Feb. 1973): 51-53, 56-57.   Coatesville, Pennsylvania, lynching 1911.

1145. Newman, Harvey K. "Piety and Segregation--White Protestant Attitudes Toward Blacks in Atlanta, 1865-1905."   THE GEORGIA HISTORICAL QUARTERLY, Vol. 63, No. 2 (Summer 1979): 238-51. A lynching in August, 1906, preceded the September riot (p. 247). Quotations (pp. 248-49) from minister who would not oppose lynching as long as raping continued.

1146. [No author. No title.] THE AMERICAN LAW REVIEW, Vol. 17 (Sept.-Oct. 1883): 775-77.   Lynchings in Iowa and Missouri.

1147. [No author.   No title; in section "News of the Week."]   THE SPECTATOR [London], Vol. 64, No. 3211 (Jan. 11, 1890): 39.   Eight black prisoners lynched in Barnwell County, South Carolina.

1148. [No author.   No title; in section "News of the Week."]   THE SPECTATOR [London], Vol. 64, No. 3220 (March 15, 1890): 359.   Statistics on murders, legal executions, and lynchings in U.S.

1149. [No author.   No title; in section "News of the Week."] THE SPECTATOR [London], Vol. 66, No. 3273 (March 21, 1891): 398.   Lynching of Italians at New Orleans.

1150. [No author.   No title; in section "News of the Week."]   THE SPECTATOR [London], Vol. 66, No. 3275 (April 4, 1891): 461.   U.S. problems with Italy because of lynchings in New Orleans.

1151. [No author.   No title; in section "News of the Week."]   THE SPECTATOR [London], Vol. 66, No. 3276 (April 11, 1891): 499.   U.S. problems with Italy regarding lynchings in New Orleans.

1152. [No author.   No title; in section "News of the Week."]   THE SPECTATOR [London], Vol. 66, No. 3277 (April 18, 1891): 531.   U.S. problems with Italy regarding lynchings in New Orleans.

1153. [No author.   No title; in section "News of the Week."]   THE

SPECTATOR [London], Vol. 66, No. 3278 (April 25, 1891): 578. U.S. problems with Italy regarding lynchings in New Orleans.

1154. [No author. No title; in section "News of the Week."] THE SPECTATOR [London], Vol. 66, No. 3280 (May 9, 1891): 646-47. No indictments in New Orleans lynchings. Brief.

1155. [No author. No title; in section "Editorial Notes."] THE INDEPEN-DENT, Vol. 46, No. 2364 (March 22, 1894): 14 (366). Black man recently lynched in Stroudsburg, Pennsylvania.

1156. [No author. No title; in section "Editorial Notes."] THE INDEPEN-DENT, Vol. 46, No. 2370 (May 3, 1894): 12 (560).

1157. [No author. No title; in section "News of the Week."] THE SPECTATOR [London], Vol. 72, No. 3442 (June 16, 1894): 810. Report of a black man skinned alive by a lynch mob in Georgia. (See McKay, W., for assertion this was untrue.)

1158. [No author. No title; in section "Editorial Notes."] THE INDEPEN-DENT, Vol. 46, No. 2378 (June 28, 1894): 12 (828). On Bishop Haygood referring to labor riots as "lynching by wholesale." [See Haygood.]

1159. [No author. No title; in section "Editorial Notes."] THE INDEPEN-DENT, Vol. 46, No. 2384 (Aug. 9, 1894): 12 (1024).   Mob of blacks lynched a white man in Elkhorn, West Virginia.

1160. [No author. No title; in section "Editorial Notes."] THE INDEPEN-DENT, Vol. 46, No. 2390 (Sept. 20, 1894): 12 (1216).   Recent lynching of six blacks near Memphis. [See also "The Latest Lynching Case."]

1161. [No author. No title.] THE OUTLOOK, Vol. 56, No. 7 (June 12, 1897): 386.   Lynching of black man in Urbana, Ohio, after militia killed at least two members of attacking mob.

1162. [No author. No title.] THE OUTLOOK, Vol. 56, No. 10 (July 3, 1897): 524-25.   Governor Johnston of Alabama prevented lynching of two blacks.

1163. [No author. No title.] THE OUTLOOK, Vol. 57, No. 4 (Sept. 25, 1897): 205-06. Five men were lynched at Versailles, IN. Black postmaster was murdered at Hogansville, GA--might fit definition of lynching.

1164. [No author. No title.] THE NATION, Vol. 65, No. 1683 (Sept. 30, 1897): 253.   Editorial. Attempted lynching at Jonesboro, GA, has produced indictments against eight men for "conspiracy to lynch."

1165. [No author. No title.] THE NATION, Vol. 69, No. 1798 (Dec. 14, 1899): 438.   Links injustice of recent lynching of black man in Maysville, KY, to injustice of House of Representatives' refusal to seat Mr. Roberts of Utah.

1166. [No author. No title.] THE INDEPENDENT, Vol. 52, No. 2667 (Jan. 11, 1900): 140.   Lynching statistics for 1899.

1167. [No author.   No title; in section "News of the Week."]   THE SPECTATOR [London], Vol. 88, No. 3858 (June 7, 1902): 867. President Roosevelt said "the men who condemned these crimes [of cruelty by U.S. soldiers in the Philippines], . . . condoned the much more cruel lynching of negroes [sic] in their own communities. Was all America responsible for those crimes, or only the actual lynchers?"

1168. [No author.   No title; in section "News of the Week."]   THE SPECTATOR [London], Vol. 91, No. 3916 (July 18, 1903): 78. Racial bitterness and lynching are increasing in the South. A remedy might be to try "prisoners accused of certain crimes by Court-Martial or Special Commission."

1169. [No author.   No title; in section "News of the Week."]   THE SPECTATOR [London],   Vol. 91, No. 3920 (Aug. 15, 1903):   225-26. Report on Roosevelt's letter on lynching to Governor Durbin of Indiana.

1170. [No author.   No title; in section "News of the Week."]   THE SPECTATOR [London], Vol. 92, No. 3950 (March 12, 1904): 398. There was no need to lynch black murderer in Springfield, Ohio, on March 7 (which led to widespread riot and killing).

1171. [No author.   No title; in section "News of the Week."]   THE SPECTATOR [London], Vol. 93, No. 3983 (Oct. 29, 1904): 623.   Black man named Blount was recently lynched at Norfolk, Virginia.

1172. [No author.   No title; in section "News of the Week."]   THE SPECTATOR [London],   Vol. 97,   No. 4083 (Sept. 29, 1906):   422. Massacre of blacks at Atlanta. Cause: "newspaper campaign advocating lynching, and even, it is alleged, offering rewards for killing negroes accused of assaults on white women."

1173. [No author. No title.] THE CRISIS, Vol. 1, No. 1 (Nov. 1910): 11. Two Italian Americans were lynched in Florida.

1174. [No author. No title.] THE NATION, Vol. 100, No. 2589 (Feb. 11, 1915): 158.   Reaction to quadruple lynching at Monticello, Georgia.

1175. [No author. No title.] THE NATION, Vol. 102, No. 2655 (May 18, 1916): 530-31.   Burning of a black man at Waco, Texas.

1176. [No author. No title.] AMERICA, Vol. 15, No. 17 (Aug. 5, 1916): 412.   In contents as "Our Lynching Record." Brief; largely a quote from Richmond Times Dispatch.

1177. "No Safety but in the Law."   THE AMERICAN MONTHLY REVIEW OF REVIEWS, Vol. 23, No. 3 (March 1901): 263.

1178. [No title.] SEEN AND HEARD [by Megargee], Vol. 3, No. 130 (July 1, 1903): 2497-2510.   Includes lynching.

1179. Noa, F. M. "Southern Lynchings." THE NATION, Vol. 61, No. 1588 (Dec. 5, 1895): 407-08.   Letter advocating harsh penalties for lynching.

1180. "A Noble Utterance in the Face of an Atrocious and Deplorable Crime." THE CHRISTIAN ADVOCATE [New York], Vol. 78, No. 27 (July 2, 1903): 1051-52.   Relates to "The Lynching at Wilmington, Del."

1181. Nock, Albert Jay. "What We All Stand For."   THE AMERICAN MAGAZINE, Vol. 75, No. 4 (Feb. 1913): 53-57. Coatesville, PA, lynching.

1182. "A North Carolina Uprising." THE NATION, Vol. 83, No. 2147 (Aug. 23, 1906): 158-59.   Applauds criticism in North Carolina of recent multiple lynching of blacks in Salisbury.

1183. "A Northern Lynching." THE OUTLOOK, Vol. 95, (July 23, 1910): 597-98.   Newark, Ohio, mob hanging of a white man who was a detective for the Anti-Saloon League and had killed a saloon keeper.

1184. "Not a Sectional Problem Any Longer." THE CONTINENT, Vol. 42, No. 36 (Sept. 7, 1911): 1273.

1185. "Not by Violence." THE INDEPENDENT, Vol. 53, No. 2731 (April 4, 1901): 796-97.   Southern lynching and general climate of violence in the South.

1186. O'Brien, John M., Jr. "The Story of Old Ruby." THE PACIFIC NORTHWESTERN, Vol. 4, No. 2 (Spring 1960): 27-32.   See pp. 28-29 for 1891 lynching in Washington state of an Indian named Steven.

1187. "Observations and Comments." MOTHER EARTH, Vol. 5, No. 11 (Jan. 1911): 338-39.   Second item: Fresno, CA, papers wanted "Vigilance Committee" to deal with free-speech radicals; mob attacked Wobblies and threatened to lynch 50 or so I.W.W. men in jail. Third item: two union men were lynched in Tampa, Florida.

1188. Oehler, Herbert E.   "Murder Avenged By Burning At the Stake." REAL WEST [Derby, CT], Vol. 20, No. 149 (Jan. 1977): 46-47, 56-58. Lynchee: Antonio Rodriques (also Rodriquez); Texas, Nov. 1910.

1189. "Oh Lord! How Long?" THE VOICE OF THE NEGRO, Vol. 1, No. 9 (Sept. 1904): 411-13.   Lynching of Cato and Reed in Georgia.

1190. "The Ohio Lynching." THE LITERARY DIGEST, Vol. 28, No. 12 (March 19, 1904): 394-96.   And subsequent riot, Springfield, Ohio.

1191. "The Ohio Lynching." THE LITERARY DIGEST, Vol. 41, No. 4 (July 23, 1910): 119-21.   Victim: private detective who killed local man while raiding illegal saloons in Newark.

1192. "Ohio's Diabolism." THE VOICE OF THE NEGRO, Vol. 1, No. 4 (April 1904): 126-27.   Lynching of Richard Dixon, black. Next night a white mob burned part of black section of Springfield.

1193. "The Oklahoma Lynching." THE CRISIS, Vol. 2, No. 4 (Aug. 1911): 153-54.   Letter from the governor about the lynching at Okemah of a black woman and her child.

1194. Olzak, Susan. "Impact of Economic and Political Competition on Lynching and Urban Racial Violence, 1882-1915." Ithaca, NY: Cornell Univ., Dept. of Sociology, 1988. Technical Report 88-4.   Economic competition increased both kinds of anti-black violence, and political competition increased the lynching of blacks.

1195. Olzak, Susan. "The Political Context of Competition: Lynching and Urban Racial Violence, 1882-1914." SOCIAL FORCES, Vol. 69, No. 2 (Dec. 1990): 395-421.

1196. O'Malley, Stephen. "The Salisbury Lynching, 1906." M.A. thesis, Univ. of North Carolina, 1977.   This is listed in Hall, Revolt Against Chivalry, p. 340, but in 1994 UNC-Chapel Hill said it could not locate it.

1197. "The One Remedy for Mobs." THE WORLD'S WORK, Vol. 6, No. 5 (Sept. 1903): 3829-30.

1198. Oney, Steve. "The Lynching of Leo Frank." ESQUIRE, Vol. 104, No. 3 (Sept. 1985): 90-94, 96, 100-01, 104.

1199. Oppenheim, James. "The Lynching of Robert Johnson." THE INDEPENDENT, Vol. 73, No. 3332 (Oct. 10, 1912): 823-27. Lynching in Princeton, West Virginia, Sept. 1912. Comment on origin of this article is on p. 864.

1200. Oppenheimer, Moses. "The Black Franks." THE CRISIS, Vol. 10, No. 6 (Oct. 1915): 291-92. Contrasts excitement over the lynching of Leo Frank (white) with apathy regarding so many lynched blacks.

1201. Oswald, F. L. "Lynch Epidemics." NORTH AMERICAN REVIEW, Vol. 165, No. 488 (July 1897): 119-21. Makes excuses for lynching (too many pardons and incompetent jurors) but condemns whitecapping.

"Our Lynching Record." See [No author. No title.], Aug. 5, 1916.

1202. "An Outlaw State." THE OUTLOOK, Vol. 110, No. 17 (Aug. 25, 1915): 945-47. Lynching of Leo Frank.

1203. Page, Thomas Nelson. "The Great American Question: The Special Plea of a Southerner." McCLURE'S MAGAZINE, Vol. 28, No. 5 (March 1907): 565-72. White supremacist argument. Lynching references on pp. 565n. and 570.

1204. Page, Thomas Nelson. "The Lynching of Negroes--Its Cause and Its Prevention." NORTH AMERICAN REVIEW, Vol. 178, No. 566 (Jan. 1904): 33-48.

1205. Page, Walter H. "The Last Hold of the Southern Bully." THE FORUM, Vol. 16 (Nov. 1893): 303-14. Lynching.

1206. Parden, N. W. "The Case of Ed Johnson." THE VOICE OF THE NEGRO, Vol. 3, No. 5 (May 1906): 361-63. Black man lynched in Chattanooga. Same case as on pp. 323-24; see "The Supremacy of the Mob."

1207. Parker, D. M. "A Georgian on Justice." THE NEW REPUBLIC, Vol. 4, No. 1 [sic; should be No. 40.] (Aug. 7, 1915): 23. Leo Frank case; letter to editor.

1208. Paterson, A. H. "Lynch Law." MACMILLAN'S MAGAZINE [London], Vol. 55, No. 329 (March 1887): 342-50. A participant's account of a lynching in New Mexico; name of town and other participants are fictionalized.

1209. Peckham, Charles A. "The Ohio National Guard and Its Police Duties, 1894." OHIO HISTORY, Vol. 83, No. 1 (Winter 1974): 51-67. Guard was involved in various violent events--attempted lynching and labor disputes.

1210. Pederson, Jane M. "Gender, Justice, and a Wisconsin Lynching, 1889-1890." AGRICULTURAL HISTORY, Vol. 67, No. 2 (Spring 1993): 65-82. Hans Jacob Olson was lynched in 1889 for being wife abuser and local troublemaker. Four people were convicted and sentenced to life in prison, including widow of victim.

1211. Pell, Edward Leigh. "The Prevention of Lynch-Law Epidemics." THE AMERICAN MONTHLY REVIEW OF REVIEWS, Vol. 17, No. 3 (March 1898): 321-25.

1212. Pemberton, Caroline H. "The Barbarism of Civilization." THE ARENA, Vol. 23, No. 1 (Jan. 1900): 5-15. Includes Southern lynching.

1213. Pendleton, Leila Amos. "An Apostrophe to the Lynched." THE CRISIS, Vol. 12, No. 2 (June 1916): 86. Four paragraphs calling for lynching victims to hang in view until vengeance strikes the nation and it realizes more about liberty, justice, and Christianity.

1214. "A Penitent at Coatesville." THE LITERARY DIGEST, Vol. 45, No. 14 (Oct. 5, 1912): 566-67. A report, taken largely from Harper's Weekly, Vol. 56, No. 2909 (Sept. 21, 1912): 6, about John Jay Chapman's effort at penance for the Coatesville, Pennsylvania, lynching a year earlier--though he was not a participant.

1215. People ex rel. Davis v. Nellis 94 N.E. 165 (Ill., 1911). Gives the facts of an Illinois case upholding the removal of the sheriff of Alexander County after two prisoners were taken from his custody and lynched.

1216. Perkins, Randy. "The Lynching of Danny Arata." TRUE WEST [Stillwater, OK], Vol. 35, No. 7 (July 1988): 37-39. Denver; July 1893.

1217. Persico, Joseph E. "Vendetta in New Orleans." AMERICAN HERITAGE, Vol. 24, No. 4 (June 1973): 65-72. Murder of police chief Hennessey, 1890, and lynching of alleged perpetrators, 1891.

1218. Pfeifer, Michael J. "The Ritual of Lynching: Extralegal Justice in Missouri, 1890-1942." GATEWAY HERITAGE, Vol. 13, No. 3 (Winter 1993): 22-33.

1219. Pfeifer, Michael James. "Iowa's Last Lynching: The Charles City Mob of 1907 and Iowa Progressivism." THE ANNALS OF IOWA, Third Series, Vol. 53, No. 4 (Fall 1994): 305-28.   Victim: 62-year-old white man, James Cullen.

1220. Phagan, Mary. THE MURDER OF LITTLE MARY PHAGAN. Far Hills: NJ: New Horizon Press, 1987.   By the great niece of the murdered girl. Leo Frank case.

1221. Phillips, Charles David. "Exploring Relations Among Forms of Social Control: The Lynching and Execution of Blacks in North Carolina, 1889-1918." LAW & SOCIETY REVIEW, Vol. 21, No. 3 (1987): 361-74. Relationship was more social conflict than social control of individual deviance.

1222. Pickens, William. THE NEW NEGRO: HIS POLITICAL, CIVIL AND MENTAL STATUS AND RELATED ESSAYS.   Reprint; New York: Negro Universities Press, 1969; originally published in 1916. See "Lynching" chapter (pp. 190-205)

1223. Pickens, Wm. "The Story of a 'Desperado.'" THE CRISIS, Vol. 3, No. 2 (Dec. 1911): 74-75.   Newspaper misrepresentation could lead to lynching.

1224. Pickett, William P.   THE NEGRO PROBLEM: ABRAHAM LINCOLN'S SOLUTION. New York: G. P. Putnam's Sons, 1909.   See Book II, Chapter II, "Lynching as an Element of the Problem" (pp. 178-203).

1225. Pierantoni, Augusto. "Italian Feeling on American Lynching." THE INDEPENDENT, Vol. 55, No. 2856 (Aug. 27, 1903): 2040-42.   Refers to several lynchings of Italians.

1226. Pincus, Samuel N. THE VIRGINIA SUPREME COURT, BLACKS AND THE LAW, 1870-1902. Distinguished Studies in American Legal and Constitutional History, No. 20. New York and London: Garland Publishing, 1990. See Chapter 11, "The Official Response to Lynching and the Case of the Lunenburg Prisoners" (pp. 209-45). See p. 215 for black mob lynching white man in 1900.

1227. Pittman, Walter E., Jr.   "The Mel Cheatham Affair: Interracial Murder in Mississippi in 1889." THE JOURNAL OF MISSISSIPPI HISTORY, Vol. 43, No. 2 (May 1981): 127-33.   Page 133: "Many, if not most, lynchings [at that time and place?] had no racial basis but were based on criminal acts, although most of the victims were blacks."

1228. Plattner, Steven W. "Days of Dread." QUEEN CITY HERITAGE,

Vol. 42, No. 1 (Spring 1984): 13-38.   Riot in Cincinnati, 1884, over attempted lynching after lenient sentence for a murderer.

1229. Poe, Clarence H. "Lynching: A Southern View." THE ATLANTIC MONTHLY, Vol. 93, No. 556, (Feb. 1904): 155-65.

1230. "A Political Suicide." TIME, Vol. 65, No. 4 (Jan. 24, 1955): 19. Death of ex-governor Slaton is reminder of Leo Frank case.

1231. Pope, Whitney, and Ragin, Charles.   "Mechanical Solidarity, Repressive Justice, and Lynchings in Louisiana (Comment on Inverarity, ASR April, 1976)." AMERICAN SOCIOLOGICAL REVIEW, Vol. 42, No. 2 (April 1977): 363-69.   Part of "Comments on Inverarity." See Inverarity in this chapter.

1232. "Posthumous Pardon." THE CHRISTIAN CENTURY, Vol. 103, No. 11 (April 2, 1986): 321.   Leo Frank pardon was granted.

1233. Powell, E. P. "Mobs and Torture." THE ALBANY LAW JOUR-NAL, Vol. 48, No. 14 (Sept. 30, 1893): 273-75.

1234. "Preparedness." THE CRISIS, Vol. 11, No. 5 (March 1916): 242-43. Anti-lynching letter signed by "white college professors in eleven Southern states."

1235. "The President on Lynching." THE NATION, Vol. 77, No. 1989 (Aug. 13, 1903): 126.   A report on T. Roosevelt's condemnation of lynching.

1236. "The President on Negro Lynching." THE AMERICAN MONTHLY REVIEW OF REVIEWS, Vol. 28, No. 3 (Sept. 1903): 265-66.

1237. "President Roosevelt on Lynching." THE NATIONAL CORPORA-TION REPORTER, Vol. 27, No. 2 (Sept. 3, 1903): 36.   Letter to Governor Durbin of Indiana.

1238. "President Roosevelt on Lynching." THE SPECTATOR [London], Vol. 91, No. 3920 (Aug. 15, 1903): 231.

1239. "The President's Words Fulfilled." THE CHRISTIAN ADVOCATE [New York], Vol. 78, No. 34 (Aug. 20, 1903), p. 1332.   Mob runs to a lynching "as jackals and hyenas to carrion" (quote from California, not President). Praises T. Roosevelt letter to Governor Durbin regarding anti-lynching.

1240. Presley, Samuel C. NEGRO LYNCHING IN THE SOUTH. TREATING OF THE NEGRO. HIS PAST AND PRESENT CONDI- TION; OF THE CAUSE OF LYNCHING, AND OF THE MEANS TO REMEDY THE EVIL. PRESENTING THE NORTHERN AND THE SOUTHERN VIEW. ACCURATE ACCOUNTS OF MANY NOTABLE CRIMES AND LYNCHINGS, INCLUDING THAT OF THE MAFIA IN NEW ORLEANS. Washington, DC: Thos. W. Cadick, 1899.   Includes several good full-page illustrations.

1241. Preston, Fanny M. "The South Yet in the Saddle." THE INDEPEN- DENT, Vol. 46, No. 2357 (Feb. 1, 1894): 2 (130).   Floridian defends lynching. Better lynch an innocent man "than for all women and children to be in constant danger."

1242. "The Prevailing 'Epidemic of Lawlessness.'" THE LITERARY DIGEST, Vol. 27, No. 3 (July 18, 1903): 67-68.   Especially about recent lynching and riot in Evansville, Indiana.

1243. "The Prevalence of Lynching." THE AMERICAN MONTHLY REVIEW OF REVIEWS, Vol. 28, No. 2 (Aug. 1903): 135.

1244. Proctor, Henry Hugh. "The Atlanta Race Riot: Fundamental Causes and Reactionary Results." THE SOUTHERN WORKMAN, Vol. 36, No. 8 (Aug. 1907): 425-26.   Lynching threat was part of the background.

1245. Proffit, Joseph Edwin. "Lynching: Its Cause and Cure." YALE LAW JOURNAL, Vol. 7, No. 6 (March 1898): 264-67.

1246. "Proposed Remedies for Lynching." THE LITERARY DIGEST, Vol. 27, No. 4 (July 25, 1903): 94-95.   Remarks of Justice Brewer, U.S. Supreme Court, and responses thereto.

1247. "Protests Against Mob Savagery." THE OUTLOOK, Vol. 76, No. 11 (March 12, 1904): 620.   References to Booker T. Washington's anti- lynching appeal in the Age Herald and to Governor Vardaman, Mississippi, saving a black man from mob burning.

1248. A Public Man of Georgia. "Why Was Frank Lynched: Was It Race Hatred, Dirty Politics, Yellow Journalism?" THE FORUM, Vol. 56, [No. 6] (Dec. 1916): 677-92.   Title is "Why Frank Was Lynched" on contents and at top of every page of the article except the title page.

1249. "Public Responsibility for Mob Violence." THE OUTLOOK, Vol. 82 (April 28, 1906): 920-22.   Controversy about prevention and punishment of mob actions against blacks in Springfield, Ohio, and Springfield, Missouri.

1250. "Punishment for Lynchers." THE INDEPENDENT, Vol. 60, No. 2998 (May 17, 1906): 1177.   Lynchers in Springfield, Ohio, [March 1904] were not punished, but several of subsequent rioters were.

1251. "Questions to Specialists." OUR DAY, Vol. 13, No. 75 (May-June 1894): 272-75.   Includes statements of Prince Momolu Massaquoi and General Morgan on lynchings in Southern states.

1252. Quillin, Frank U. THE COLOR LINE IN OHIO: A HISTORY OF RACE PREJUDICE IN A TYPICAL NORTHERN STATE.   Univ. of Michigan Historical Studies, III. Ann Arbor: George Wahr, 1913.   See lynchings, pp. 114-16; Springfield race riots of 1904 and 1906, pp. 141-43.

1253. "Race Conflict in Louisiana." THE INDEPENDENT, Vol. 53, No. 2762 (Nov. 7, 1901): 2615-16.   Battle after a recent lynching; three whites and 11 blacks were killed.

1254. "Race Riots and Murders in Atlanta." THE INDEPENDENT, Vol. 61, No. 3017 (Sept. 27, 1906): 713-14.   Includes brief mention that an Atlanta newspaper suggested lynching as way to deal with recent alleged assaults by black men on white women, which helped cause the riots.

1255. "Race Riots in Ohio." THE OUTLOOK, Vol. 82 (March 10, 1906): 536.   Springfield, 1906.

1256. Ramage, B. J. "Homicide in the Southern States." THE SEWANEE REVIEW, Vol. 4, No. 2 (Feb. 1896): 212-32.   Advances reasons for the low regard for human life in the South (e.g., the influence of slavery) and suggests remedies. Mentions lynchings (pp. 218-19, 230).

1257. Raun, Gerald G. "Seventeen Days in November: The Lynching of Antonio Rodriguez and American-Mexican Relations, November 3-19, 1910." THE JOURNAL OF BIG BEND STUDIES, Vol. 7 (Jan. 1995): 157-79. Rock Springs [Rocksprings], Texas.

1258. Ready, Milton L. "Georgia's Entry Into World War I.   THE GEORGIA HISTORICAL QUARTERLY, Vol. 52, No. 3 (Sept. 1968): 256-64. Shame of most Georgians because of national criticism of Leo Frank lynching helped cause them "to embrace the most nationalistic cause of all, preparedness" (pp. 260-61).

1259. "Real Reasons." THE CRISIS, Vol. 10, No. 6 (Oct. 1915): 278-80. "Lynchings and lawlessness rest on theft."

1260. "Reaping the Whirlwind." THE AMERICAN LAW REVIEW, Vol.

39 (Jan.-Feb. 1905): 104-05.   Report of investigation of lynching of John T. Morrison at Kershaw, South Carolina.

1261. "Reaping the Whirlwind." THE NATION, Vol. 87, No. 2262 (Nov. 5, 1908): 428-29.   Lynching harms victims, perpetrators and the community at large.   Mentions that the sheriff in Wetumpka, AL, arrested those engaged in "nigger-killing," and some were sent to a chain gang.

1262. THE REASON WHY THE COLORED AMERICAN IS NOT IN THE WORLD'S COLUMBIAN EXPOSITION. Chicago: [Ida B. Wells], 1893.   Reprinted in Trudier Harris, ed., Selected Works of Ida B. Wells-Barnett, The Schomburg Library of Nineteenth-Century Black Women Writers, ed. by Henry Louis Gates, Jr. New York: Oxford Univ. Press, 1991. Lynching is included in Chapter I, "Introduction," by Frederick Douglass (pp. 2-12), and Chapter IV, "Lynch Law," by Ida B. Wells (pp. 25-39).

1263. "Recent Comments on Lynching and the New Negro Crime." HARPER'S WEEKLY, Vol. 47, No. 2436 (Aug. 29, 1903): 1395-96.

1264. "Recent Lynchings in the South." PUBLIC OPINION, Vol. 15, No. 26 (Sept. 30, 1893): 618-19.   Items from several newspapers.

1265. Reedy, William Marion.   "Reflections: Justice for Leo Frank." REEDY'S MIRROR, Vol. 24, No. 18 (June 25, 1915): 3.   Comment.

1266. Reedy, William Marion. "Reflections: The Frank Case." REEDY'S MIRROR, Vol. 24, No. 9 (April 23, 1915): 1.   Brief comment.

1267. "The Reign of Terror." THE CRISIS, Vol. 2, No. 6 (Oct. 1911): 237-39.   Press comments on recent lynchings.

1268. Reitman, Ben L. "The Respectable Mob." MOTHER EARTH, Vol. 7, No. 4 (June 1912): 109-14.   Author tells of beating and torture he suffered in San Diego, May 1912, by men he termed vigilantes--[during IWW free speech effort].

1269. "Remedy for Lynch Law." AMERICA, Vol. 8, No. 25 (March 29, 1913): 591.   Editorial. London Spectator suggests depriving citizens in lynching districts of the franchise.

1270. "A Reply to Mr. Holmes from Alabama." THE CRISIS, Vol. 3, No. 3 (Jan. 1912): 110.   Illustration of both sides of postcard; on one side is a photo of "A Lynching at Andalusia, Ala."

1271. "The Reputation of Georgia at Stake." THE VOICE OF THE

NEGRO, Vol. 2, No. 8 (Aug. 1905): 529-30.   Watkinsville lynchings.

1272. Rescorla, Richard.   "'Killing Jim' Miller."   GOLDEN WEST [Freeport, NY], Vol. 6, No. 1 (Nov. 1969): 16-17, 49-50.   He and three others were lynched in Ada, Oklahoma, 1909.

1273. A Resident in North Carolina. "The Bottom Facts." THE INDE-PENDENT, Vol. 46, No. 2357 (Feb. 1, 1894): 4 (132). Interracial sex and lynching.

1274. "The Rev. Quincy Ewing on Lynching." THE INDEPENDENT, Vol. 53, No. 2752 (Aug. 29, 1901): 2059-61.

1275. "A Reversion to Savagery." THE OUTLOOK, Vol. 110, No. 15 (Aug. 11, 1915): 835-36.   Deplores the burning alive of Will Stanley, black, in Temple, Texas, on July 3, 1915.

1276. Reynolds, Wm.   "The Remedy for Lynch Law." YALE LAW JOURNAL, Vol. 7, No. 1 (Oct. 1897): 20-25.

1277. Rice, Harvey F. "The Lynching of Antonio Rodriguez." M.A. thesis, Univ. of Texas at Austin, 1990.   Rock Springs [Rocksprings], TX, 1910.

1278. Richmond, Robert W.   "Gallows on the Treeless Plains."   TRUE WEST [Austin, TX], Vol. 20, No. 2, Whole No. 114 (Nov.-Dec. 1972): 25, 46-47.   Lynching of J. G. Burton, William Gay, and John Gay, Russell, Kansas, 1894. Includes 2 photos of lynching victims.

1279. Rimanelli, Marco, and Postman, Sheryl L., eds. THE 1891 NEW ORLEANS LYNCHING AND U.S.-ITALIAN RELATIONS: A LOOK BACK. Studies in Southern Italian and Italian-American Culture, Vol. 2. New York: Peter Lang, 1992.   Contains Marco Rimanelli and Sheryl L. Postman, "Introduction: A Centennial Retrospective on the 1891 New Orleans Lynchings"; Giose Rimanelli, "An Introspective Preface: New Orleans and 'Nonno Slim' Dominick"; Sheryl L. Postman, "Parallels of Life Style: Southern Italians in the United States South -- New Orleans, 1891"; Giose Rimanelli, "The 1891 New Orleans Lynching: Southern Politics, Mafia, Immigration and the American Press"; Marco Rimanelli, "The New Orleans Lynching and U.S.-Italian Relations from Harmony to War-Scare: Immigration, Mafia, Diplomacy"; Marco Rimanelli, "The 1891-92 U.S.-Italian Diplomatic Crisis and War-Scare: Foreign and Domestic Policies of the Harrison and Di Rudini Governments": Carol J. Bradley, "The 1891-92 New Orleans Negotiations through the Italian Documents"; Liborio Casilli, "The Impact of the 1891 New Orleans Incident on the Italian Press"; Francis X. Femminella, "A Socio-Literary Analysis of Police Captain J. Howard's Novel:

'The New Orleans Mafia, or Police Chief Hennessy Avenged!'"; Sheryl L. Postman, "An Hypnogogic Journey Through Time in Giose Rimanelli's Novel: 'Una Posizione Sociale'"; Marco Rimanelli and Sheryl L. Postman, "Conclusion: The 1891-92 New Orleans Crisis and U.S.-Italian Relations in Retrospect."

1280. "The Riot at Springfield." THE OUTLOOK, Vol. 89, No. 17 (Aug. 22, 1908): 869-70.   Illinois.

1281. Riss, Jean F. "The Lynching of Francisco Torres." THE JOURNAL OF MEXICAN AMERICAN HISTORY, Vol. 2, No. 2 (Spring 1972): 90-121.   Hanged in Orange County, California, 21 Aug. 1892.

1282. Robertson, Dorothy. "Frontier Justice at Lookout." REAL WEST [Derby, CT], Vol. 21, No. 157 (May 1978): 54-59.   Lynching of the "Hall gang" (five men) in California, 1901.

1283. Roche, John P. "The Curbing of the Militant Majority: A dissent from the classic liberal interpretation of civil liberties in America." THE REPORTER, Vol. 29, No. 2 (July 18, 1963): 34-38.   See pp. 37-38 for Leo Frank case.

1284. Rodabaugh, James H. "The Cincinnati Riot of 1884." MUSEUM ECHOES, Vol. 32, No. 12 (Dec. 1959): 91-94.   Effort to lynch man found guilty of manslaughter instead of murder led to major riot.

1285. Rogers, William Curran. "A Comparison of the Coverage of the Leo Frank Case by the Hearst-Controlled Atlanta Georgian and the Home-Owned Atlanta Journal, April 28, 1913-August 30, 1913." Master's thesis, Univ. of Georgia, 1950.

1286. Rogers, William Warren, and Ward, Robert David.   AUGUST RECKONING: JACK TURNER AND RACISM IN POST-CIVIL WAR ALABAMA. Baton Rouge: Louisiana State Univ. Press, 1973.   Turner was a black leader who was lynched in 1882 for allegedly planning a massacre of local whites.

1287. Roosevelt, Theodore. "The Enforcement of Law." THE FORUM, Vol. 20 (Sept. 1895): 1-10.   One paragraph (p. 8) on disrespect for law causing lynchings and Whitecap outrages.

1288. Roosevelt, Theodore. "The Foreign Policy of President Harrison." THE INDEPENDENT, Vol. 44, No. 2280 (Aug. 11, 1892): 1-3 (1113-1115). Includes praise of Harrison's handling of relations with Italy after New Orleans mob lynched some Italian immigrants (p. 2).

1289. Roosevelt, Theodore. "Lynching and the Miscarriage of Justice." THE OUTLOOK, Vol. 99, No. 13 (Nov. 25, 1911): 706-07.   Society must share the blame for mob violence when it does not enact laws to ensure quick and appropriate punishment of rapists.

1290. Rosenbaum, Stanley N. "'Our Willie' and the Leo Frank Case." THE CHRISTIAN CENTURY, Vol. 102, No. 30 (Oct. 9, 1985): 887-88.

1291. Ross, Mary. "Where Lynching Is a Habit." THE SURVEY, Vol. 49, No. 10 (Feb. 15, 1923): 626-27.   Counties with most lynchings in five Southern states, 1889-1922.

1292. Rowe, Geo. C. "How to Prevent Lynching." THE INDEPENDENT, Vol. 46, No. 2357 (Feb. 1, 1894): 3-4 (131-32).   1: enforce and respect law; 2: create proper public sentiment. Also, white preachers must teach white men "to respect the chastity of black women; which will offer a worthy example for the black man to follow." Not rape but race prejudice is at the heart of lynching.

1293. "A Rude Awakening." THE VOICE OF THE NEGRO, Vol. 1, No. 10 (Oct. 1904): 442-43.   Lynching of Cato and Reed in Georgia.

1294. S., H. E. "Lynch-Law In America." THE SPECTATOR [London], Vol. 73, No. 3445 (July 7, 1894): 16.   Letter. Anti-black. Says lynching in Tennessee is mainly for rape and incendiarism and does not involve torture.

1295. S., J. M. "Lynching." THE NATION, Vol. 103, No. 2663 (July 13, 1916): 35.   Letter. Negro is not punished for crime against Negroes; that leads to rape (against whites) and lynching.

1296. Saban, Vera. "20th Century Vigilante Justice." OLD WEST [Austin, TX], Vol. 14, No. 2, Whole No. 54 (Winter 1977): 12-13, 40-43.   Lynchers killed two murderers and a deputy at Basin City, Wyoming, 1903.

1297. "Sackcloth and Ashes." THE CRISIS, Vol. 5, No. 2 (Dec. 1912): 87-88.   John Jay Chapman's atonement at Coatesville, Pennsylvania, and quotations from Harper's Weekly of what he said.

1298. Saunders, Robert. "Southern Populists and the Negro 1893-1895." THE JOURNAL OF NEGRO HISTORY, Vol. 54, No. 3 (July 1969): 240-61.   See pp. 248-49 and 259 n.37.

1299. "Savagery as a Civilizer." THE NATION, Vol. 68, No. 1767 (May 11, 1899): 847.   Refers to recent paper by Reverend Robert Campbell about lynching--occasioned by recent lynching in Georgia.

1300. "The Scapegoat." THE CRISIS, Vol. 4, No. 5 (Sept. 1912): 248. Apparent lynching.

1301. "The Scarcity of Farm Labor." THE VOICE OF THE NEGRO, Vol. 3, No. 9 (Sept. 1906): 620-21.   Blacks are leaving Southern rural areas because of "murders, lynchings, peonage, white-caps, chaingangs [sic], forced ignorance--a veritable reign of terror and tyranny."

1302. Schmier, Louis E. "'No Jew Can Murder': Memories of Tom Watson and the Lichtenstein Murder Case of 1901." THE GEORGIA HISTORI-CAL QUARTERLY, Vol. 70, No. 3 (Fall 1986): 433-55.   Watson's campaign against Leo Frank was balanced by his successful defense of Lichtenstein.

1303. Schofield, Henry. "Federal Courts and Mob Domination of State Courts: Leo Frank's Case." ILLINOIS LAW REVIEW, Vol. 10, No. 7 (Feb. 1916): 479-506.

1304. "A Scotch View of Lynch Law in Louisiana." THE AMERICAN LAW REVIEW, Vol. 25, No. 3 (May-June 1891): 461-62.   Lynching of 11 Italians in New Orleans.   From Journal of Jurisprudence (Edinborough [sic]).

1305. Scroggs, William O. MOB VIOLENCE: AN ENEMY OF BOTH RACES. N.p.: n.p, 1916. "An address before the Southern Sociological Congress at New Orleans, La., April 19, 1916." Also in James E. Mc-Culloch, ed., Democracy in Earnest (New York: Negro Universities Press, 1969), pp. 185-90.

1306. Secrest, William B. "The Last Ride." TRUE WEST [Austin, TX], Vol. 14, No. 3, Whole No. 79 (Jan.-Feb. 1967): 6-9, 46, 48, 50-52.   Includes lynching of James Miller and three others at Ada, Oklahoma, 1909.

1307. "Secretary Dickinson on Lynch Law." THE CRISIS, Vol. 1, No. 6 (April 1911): 13.   Speech by U.S. Secretary of War.

1308. Sedgwick, Bob [pseud. of Robert L. Harper]. AMONG THE BALD KNOBBERS. A HISTORY OF DESPERADOES OF THE OZARK MOUNTAINS--THEIR ATROCIOUS DEEDS--RENDEZVOUS--HOMES AND HABITS. THE ARREST AND CONVICTION. Clinton [?], MO, 1880.

1309. Sena, Mitchell C. "Third Rate Henchman of a First Rate Terror." TRUE WEST [Austin, TX], Vol. 17, No. 3, Whole No. 97 (Jan.-Feb. 1970): 28-29, 40-44.   Cecilio Lucero was lynched in Las Vegas, NM, 1893.

1310. Senechal, Roberta. THE SOCIOGENESIS OF A RACE RIOT: SPRINGFIELD, ILLINOIS, IN 1908. Urbana: Univ. of Illinois Press, 1990. Riot began as lynching attempt.

1311. "The Shame of Pennsylvania." THE INDEPENDENT, Vol. 71, No. 3273 (Aug. 24, 1911): 437-39.   Critical of recent burning at stake of a wounded black murderer who was seized by a mob from a hospital; lack of specific detail. [Coatesville.]

1312. Shaw, Barton C. THE WOOL-HAT BOYS: GEORGIA'S POPU-LIST PARTY. Baton Rouge: Louisiana State Univ. Press, 1984.   See "Lynching" in index.

1313. SHELBY COUNTY'S SHAME.   STORY OF BIG CREEK LYNCHING AND TRIAL. N.p., 1895.   Mob took Tom Moss, Calvin McDowell, and Will Stewart, blacks, from jail at Memphis and lynched them, March 1892; mob took Lee Walker, black, from Memphis jail and lynched him, July 1893; in Big Creek bottom mob lynched six manacled blacks on their way to Memphis, Aug. 1894.   Pamphlet gives details of all three lynchings but devotes majority of its pages to the third.

1314. Sheldon, Winthrop D.   "Shall Lynching Be Suppressed?"   THE OUTLOOK, Vol. 111, No. 3 (Sept. 15, 1915): 152.   Letter.

1315. Sheldon, Winthrop D.   "Shall Lynching Be Suppressed, and How?" THE ARENA, Vol. 36, No. 202 (Sept. 1906): 225-33.

1316. Shofner, Jerrell H.   "Florida and the Black Migration."   THE FLORIDA HISTORICAL QUARTERLY, Vol. 57, No. 3 (Jan. 1979): 267-88.   See lynchings on pp. 280-81, 284-86.

1317. Shufeldt, R[obert]. W. AMERICA'S GREATEST PROBLEM: THE NEGRO.   Philadelphia: F. A. Davis Co., 1915.   See Chapter VIII, "Criminality of the Negro: Lynch Law" (pp. 145-62); this chapter is almost word-for-word from selected paragraphs in Chapter VIII, The Negro: A Menace to American Civilization.

1318. Shufeldt, R[obert]. W. THE NEGRO: A MENACE TO AMERI-CAN CIVILIZATION. Boston: Richard G. Badger, 1907. See Chapter VII, "Passion and Criminality in the Negro: Lynch Law and Other Questions" (pp. 124-51), and pp. 167-68, 176-77, 206-25, 232-46. Includes five full-page photos regarding Henry Smith's lynching, Paris, Texas, 1893. Includes lynching of George White at Wilmington, Delaware (1903): pp. 210-20, 224-25.

1319. Simkins, Francis B. PITCHFORK BEN TILLMAN. Baton Rouge: Louisiana State Univ. Press, 1944.   See pp. 396-98, 405, for Tillman's pro-lynching views and the connection to black rape of white women. He was governor of South Carolina in 1890s and later a U.S. Senator.

1320. Sims, L. Moody. "A Voice of Dissent: John Jay Chapman and the 'Great Wickedness.'"   NEGRO HISTORY BULLETIN, Vol. 32, No. 3 (March 1969): 12-13.   Coatesville, Pennsylvania, lynching.

1321. "Six Women."   THE CRISIS, Vol. 8, No. 1 (May 1914): 21-22. Includes black woman lynched at Wagoner, Oklahoma.

1322. Sledd, Andrew.   "The Negro: Another View."   THE ATLANTIC MONTHLY, Vol. 90, No. 537 (July 1902): 65-73. Includes lynchings in the South; argues that Negroes, though inferior, should be accorded fairness and certain rights.

1323. Smith, Chas. H. "Have American Negroes Too Much Liberty?" THE FORUM, Vol. 16 (Oct. 1893): 176-83.   Burning black rapists is too mild (p. 182).

1324. Smith, John Douglas. "Statesboro Blues." M.A. thesis, Univ. of Virginia, 1993.   Lynching of Paul Reed and Will Cato, blacks, in Georgia, Aug. 1904.

1325. Smith, Rembert G. "Some Lurid Lessons from the Frank Case." THE PUBLIC, Vol. 18, No. 913 (Oct. 1, 1915): 952-53.

1326. Smith, Robert Barr.   "Killer In Deacon's Clothing."   WILD WEST [Leesburg, VA], Vol. 5, No. 2 (Aug. 1992): 34-40.   James P. Miller. Lynched at Ada, Oklahoma, along with three others, 1909.

1327. Smith, Robert Benjamin.   "Cornered Killer."   WILD WEST [Leesburg, VA], Vol. 5, No. 4 (Dec. 1992): 34-40.   Effort to kill Rafael Lopez by smoke and starvation in Utah mine tunnels, 1913.

1328. Smith, Rogers Melton. "The Waco Lynching of 1916: Perspective and Analysis." M.A. thesis, Baylor Univ., 1971.

1329. Smith, T. Lynn. "The Redistribution of the Negro Population of the United States, 1910-1960." THE JOURNAL OF NEGRO HISTORY, Vol. 51, No. 3 (July 1966): 155-73.

1330. Snyder, Henry N. "Lawlessness in the South: An Analysis of Conditions." THE METHODIST QUARTERLY REVIEW, Vol. 53, No. 1 (Jan.

1904): 81-96.   Anti-black. See pp. 91-92 for rape and lynching. Says rape is a big problem.

1331. "The So-Called Race Riot at Springfield, Illinois." CHARITIES AND THE COMMONS, Vol. 20 (Sept. 19, 1908): 709-11.   The riot began as a lynching attempt.

1332. "Some Southern Logic." THE CRISIS, Vol. 6, No. 7 [sic; should be Vol. 7, No. 1] (Nov. 1913): 328-31.   Three items which include comments on lynching.

1333. Somerville, Henderson M.   "Some Co-operating Causes of Negro Lynching." THE NORTH AMERICAN REVIEW, Vol. 177, No. 563 (Oct. 1903): 506-12.

1334. SoRelle, James M.   "The 'Waco Horror': The Lynching of Jesse Washington." SOUTHWESTERN HISTORICAL QUARTERLY, Vol. 86, No. 4 (April 1983): 517-36.   Occurred in 1916.

1335. Soule, Sarah. "Populism and Black Lynching in Georgia, 1890-1900." SOCIAL FORCES, Vol. 71, No. 2 (Dec. 1992): 431-49.   Increased black/white economic competition led to more lynchings of blacks.

1336. Soule, Sarah Anne. "Populism and Lynching in Georgia: 1890-1900." M.A. thesis, Cornell Univ., 1991.

1337. "South Carolina's Protest." THE CRISIS, Vol. 3, No. 2 (Dec. 1911): 61-62.   Lynching at Honeapath.

1338. Souther, James Otto. LEGEND INTO HISTORY: FACT AND FICTION OF THE LOOKOUT LYNCHING. New York: Vantage Press, 1968. Lynching of five men, Modoc County, CA, May 31, 1901.

1339. "The Southern Campaign Against Lynching." THE VOICE OF THE NEGRO, Vol. 1, No. 11 (Nov. 1904): 564-65.

1340. "Southern Defenses of Lynching." THE LITERARY DIGEST, Vol. 32, No. 14 (April 7, 1906): 508-09.   Reactions to lynching of Edward Johnson, black man, at Chattanooga, Tennessee.

1341. "Southern Governors on English Critics."   THE LITERARY DIGEST, Vol. 9, No. 21 (Sept. 22, 1894): 1-2 (601-02).   Most condemn the British efforts initiated by Ida B. Wells.

1342. A Southern Lawyer. "Remedies for Lynch Law." THE SEWANEE

REVIEW, Vol. 8, No. 1 (Jan. 1900): 1-11.

1343. "Southern Lynching." THE NATION, Vol. 57, No. 1479 (Nov. 2, 1893): 322-23.   Argues that rapes, a common excuse for lynching, occur less than rumored, and Southern supersensitivity about women helps cause lynching and should be reduced to a more civilized level.

1344. "Southern Press on the Georgia Lynching." THE LITERARY DIGEST, Vol. 31, No. 3 (July 15, 1905): 71-72.   Victims: one white man and six or seven black men taken from Watkinsville, GA, jail.

1345. "A Southern Protest Against Lynching." THE OUTLOOK, Vol. 112, No. 3 (Jan. 19, 1916): 124-25.

1346. "A Southern Reform League." THE VOICE OF THE NEGRO, Vol. 3, No. 2 (Feb. 1906): 90-92.   "It is nothing out of the way these days to hear Negroes say that certain men ought to be lynched. They have been taught to so believe by white people" (pp. 91-92).

1347. Southern Society for the Promotion of the Study of Race Conditions and Problems in the South.   RACE PROBLEMS OF THE SOUTH: REPORT OF THE PROCEEDINGS OF THE FIRST ANNUAL CON-FERENCE HELD UNDER THE AUSPICES OF THE SOUTHERN SOCIETY FOR THE PROMOTION OF THE STUDY OF RACE CONDITIONS AND PROBLEMS IN THE SOUTH, AT MONTGOM-ERY, ALABAMA, MAY 8, 9, 10, A.D. 1900.   Richmond, VA: B. F. Johnson Pub. Co., 1900.   Reprint; New York: Negro Universities Press, 1969.   See section on "Lynching as a Penalty," with speeches by Alex C. King (pp. 160-70) and Clifton R. Breckinridge (pp. 170-77). See also pp. 29-30, 36, 37, 202-04.

1348. "A Southerner's Protest." THE CRISIS, Vol. 3, No. 4 (Feb. 1912): 148-49.   Anti-lynching editorial from a North Carolina newspaper.

1349. "Speech of Charles E. Hughes Delivered at Bethel A.M.E. Church, New York City, November 6, 1906." THE CRISIS, Vol. 13, No. 1 (Nov. 1916): 7-8.   An appeal for blacks to vote for Hughes and "the Entire Republican Ticket" because Hughes spoke against lynching in 1906.

1350. "The Springfield Mob." THE VOICE OF THE NEGRO, Vol. 3, No. 4 (April 1906): 245-46.   Anti-black riot in Ohio after black killed a white and was hurried out of town to prevent lynching.

1351. "The Statesboro Savagery." THE VOICE OF THE NEGRO, Vol. 1, No. 9 (Sept. 1904): 375-76.   Lynching of Cato and Reed in Georgia.

1352. Steinthal, S. Alfred. "Lynching in America." THE SPECTATOR [London], Vol. 73, No. 3449 (Aug. 4, 1894): 142. Letter responding to that of W. McKay. Hostile to lynching.

1353. "Stern Force as a Remedy." THE AMERICAN MONTHLY REVIEW OF REVIEWS, Vol. 28, No. 2 (Aug. 1903): 135-36. Best way to prevent mob violence.

1354. Stern, Joseph S., Jr. "It Was the Best of Times: It Was the Worst of Times." QUEEN CITY HERITAGE, Vol. 42, No. 1 (Spring 1984): 3-12. Riot in 1884 in Cincinnati over attempted lynching.

1355. Stevens, Lois. "Five Lynchings in Lookout." TRUE WEST [Iola, WI], Vol. 29, No. 1, Whole No. 172 (Jan. 1982): 38-40. Frank Hall, James Hall, Calvin Hall, Dan Yantis, and Martin Wilson were lynched near Lookout, California, May 1901.

1356. Stevens, W. LeConte. "Lynching and the Law's Delay." THE NATION, Vol. 61, No. 1589 (Dec. 12, 1895): 426. Advocates curtailing the right of appeal as a way to swifter justice and few lynchings.

1357. Stewart, Herbert L. "The Casuistry of Lynch Law." THE NATION, Vol. 103, No. 2669 (Aug. 24, 1916): 173-74. An attack on pro-lynching arguments.

1358. Stone, J. M. "The Suppression of Lawlessness in the South." NORTH AMERICAN REVIEW, Vol. 158, No. 449 (April 1894): 500-06. Apologia by Mississippi governor. Deals briefly with "White-capism" and lynching. Says, "Conflicts between the races have happily ceased to occur" (p. 503).

1359. Storey, Moorfield. ADDRESS ON LAWLESSNESS. N.p.: n.p., 1904. Lynching: pp. 2-3, 4, 12.

1360. Stovall, Mary E. "The Chicago Defender in the Progressive Era." ILLINOIS HISTORICAL JOURNAL, Vol. 83, No. 3 (Autumn 1990): 159-72.

1361. Strange, Robert. "Some Thoughts on Lynching." THE SOUTH ATLANTIC QUARTERLY, Vol. 5, No. 4 (Oct. 1906): 349-51. Part of symposium; other parts by J. W. Bailey and Charles B. Galloway.

1362. Strickland, John J. "Are the Courts Responsible for Lynchings, and If So, Why?" In REPORT OF THE SIXTEENTH ANNUAL SESSION OF THE GEORGIA BAR ASSOCIATION HELD AT WARM SPRINGS,

GA., THURSDAY, JULY 6TH, AND FRIDAY, JULY 7TH, 1899, pp. 184-90. Ed. by Orville A. Park. Atlanta: Franklin Printing and Pub. Co., 1899.

1363. Stuckert, Robert P. "Racial Violence in Southern Appalachia, 1880-1940." APPALACHIAN HERITAGE, Vol. 20 (Spring 1992): 35-41.

1364. "Suffering Natural Consequences of Its Action." THE CHRISTIAN ADVOCATE [New York], Vol. 75, No. 22 (May 31, 1900):   868-69. Colorado abolished capital punishment and lynching of an escaped murderer named Reynolds resulted.   Also, Calvin Kunblern, black, was lynched at Pueblo, May 22.

1365. Sullivan, Joseph Matthew.   "The Lynching Record for 1916." JOURNAL OF THE AMERICAN INSTITUTE OF CRIMINAL LAW AND CRIMINOLOGY, Vol. 8, No. 2 (July 1917): 302-03.

1366. Sullivan, Kathleen Alicia.   "Judge Lynch in South Carolina: the Frazier B. Baker Case." M.A. thesis, Univ. of Georgia, 1970.   Events in 1898.

1367. "The Sunny South." THE CRISIS, Vol. 11, No. 2 (Dec. 1915): 73-75. Includes comment on Leo Frank's lynching.

1368. "A Supine State." THE AMERICAN MONTHLY REVIEW OF REVIEWS, Vol. 28, No. 2 (Aug. 1903): 134.   Black man burned at stake in Delaware; continuation of "The Mob Spirit,--A Delaware Instance."

1369. "The Supremacy of the Mob." THE VOICE OF THE NEGRO, Vol. 3, No. 5 (May 1906): 323-24.   Black man named Johnson was lynched in Tennessee on March 19. Three blacks were lynched at Springfield, Missouri. See also Parden, N. W., in this chapter.

1370. Swain, John D. "A Warning To the South." THE VOICE OF THE NEGRO, Vol. 3, No. 6 (June 1906): 426-30. Recent lynching of three black men at Springfield, Missouri.

1371. Sweetman, Alice M.   "Mondak: Planned City of Hope Astride Montana-Dakota Border." MONTANA, THE MAGAZINE OF WESTERN HISTORY, Vol. 15, No. 4 (Oct. 1965): 12-27. Includes lynching of black man J. C. Collins, 1913.

1372. Taber, S. R. "A Remedy for Lynching." THE NATION, Vol. 75, No. 1955 (Dec. 18, 1902): 478-79.   Letter to the editor. Remedy: teach children kindness to animals.

1373. Taylor, Graham. "The Race Riot in Lincoln's City." CHARITIES AND THE COMMONS, Vol. 20 (Aug. 29, 1908): 627-28. Problems in Springfield, Illinois; little detail.

1374. Taylor, Hannis. "The True Remedy for Lynch Law." THE AMERICAN LAW REVIEW, Vol. 41 (March-April 1907): 255-66. Remedy: limit unsubstantial appeals of convictions.

1375. Taylor, Jonathan, Jr. "Riot Law." THE GREEN BAG, Vol. 13, No. 8 (Aug. 1901): 279-84. Deals especially with Ohio and an attempted-lynching riot at Akron (no date given) [probably 1899-1901].

1376. Terrell, Mary Church. "Lynching from a Negro's Point of View." THE NORTH AMERICAN REVIEW, Vol. 178, No. 571 (June 1904): 853-68.

1377. Terrell, Mary Church. "A Plea for the White South by a Coloured Woman." THE NINETEENTH CENTURY AND AFTER [London], Vol. 60, No. 353 (July 1906): 70-84. Brief references to lynching: pp. 70, 76, 76-77, 77, 80.

1378. "The Terrorists." THE CRISIS, Vol. 3, No. 5 (March 1912): 192-94. Various comments on lynching.

1379. Texas. Governor. MESSAGE OF GOVERNOR J. S. HOGG, OF TEXAS, TO THE TWENTY-THIRD LEGISLATURE, ON THE SUBJECT OF LYNCH LAW. Austin, 1893.

1380. "The Texas Horror." PUBLIC OPINION, Vol. 14, No. 19 (Feb. 11, 1893): 448. Three newspaper stories on lynching of Henry Smith in Texas.

1381. "That Iowa Lynching." THE INDEPENDENT, Vol. 62, No. 3035 (Jan. 31, 1907): 278-79. Man named Cullen was lynched at Charles City.

1382. "Thirteen Lynched in Arkansas." THE VOICE OF THE NEGRO, Vol. 1, No. 5 (May 1904): 173. Blacks were shot and killed "last month."

1383. Thomas, Larry Coyle. THE DOUBLE AX MURDER OF THE GUNTER'S [sic] AND FINCH'S [sic] FAMILY OF CHATHAM COUNTY, N.C. Sanford, NC: Larry Coyle Thomas, [1990?]. Poor quality book of 109 pages. Double murder, Dec. 1883, and triple murder, July 1885, led to lynching of four blacks, 9-28-1885.

1384. Thompson, Maurice. "The Court of Judge Lynch." LIPPINCOTT'S MONTHLY MAGAZINE, Vol. 64, No. 380 (Aug. 1899): 254-62.

Accounts of various lynchings and attitudes, mostly Southern. Author tried to prevent one. Includes one black victim of a black mob.

1385. Thornbrough, Emma Lou. THE NEGRO IN INDIANA BEFORE 1900: A STUDY OF A MINORITY. 2d ed.; Bloomington: Indiana Univ. Press, 1993.   See "Lynchings of Negroes" and "Racial violence" in index.

1386. "Those Before-Day Clubs." THE VOICE OF THE NEGRO, Vol. 1, No. 10 (Oct. 1904): 445-46.   No such organization of Negro criminals despite press report of one at Statesboro.

1387. "Three Significant Lynchings." THE VOICE OF THE NEGRO, Vol. 3, No. 7 (July 1906): 468.   White man Robert T. Rogers was lynched on May 29 at Tallaulah [sic], Louisiana. White man J. V. Johnson was lynched on May 28 at Wadesboro, North Carolina. White child (male) was burned at stake by playmates on May 31 at Cedar Grove, West Virginia.

1388. Tobias, D. E. "A Negro on the Position of the Negro in America." THE NINETEENTH CENTURY [New York and London], Vol. 46, No. 274 (Dec. 1899): 957-73.   See "A Few Remarks on the Lynching Problem in the South," pp. 966-68.

1389. Togo, Hashimura (Per Wallace Irwin). "Letters of a Japanese School-boy. Atrocities." LIFE, Vol. 65, No. 1689 (March 11, 1915): 411-12.   When Germans murder a Belgian family isn't it called an atrocity? But when Georgians lynch a black family, what is it called? Social unrest.

1390. Tolbert, R. R. "The Election Tragedy at Phoenix." THE INDEPEN-DENT, Vol. 50, No. 2608 (Nov. 24, 1898): 1492-96.   South Carolina Democrats attacked Republicans and blacks, killing many of the latter, 1898.

1391. Tolnay, Stewart E., and Beck, E. M. "Black Flight: Lethal Violence and the Great Migration, 1900-1930." SOCIAL SCIENCE HISTORY, Vol. 14, No. 3 (Fall 1990): 347-70.   Seeks to correct previous neglect of racial violence, such as lynching as a cause of black migration. Also argues that black exodus caused southern whites to reduce anti-black violence.

1392. Tolnay, Stewart E., and Beck, E. M. A FESTIVAL OF VIOLENCE: AN ANALYSIS OF SOUTHERN LYNCHINGS, 1882-1930. Urbana: Univ. of Illinois Press, 1995.

1393. Tolnay, Stewart E., and Beck, E. M. "Lethal Social Control in the South: Lynchings and Executions Between 1880 and 1930." In INEQUAL-ITY, CRIME AND SOCIAL CONTROL, pp. 176-94. Ed. by George S. Bridges and Martha A. Myers. Boulder: Westview, 1994.

1394. Tolnay, Stewart E., and Beck, E. M.   "Racial Violence and Black Migration in the American South, 1910 to 1930." AMERICAN SOCIO-LOGICAL REVIEW, Vol. 57, No. 1 (Feb. 1992): 103-16. Odd-numbered pages 105-15 have heading "Black Migration and Lynching in the South."

1395. Tolnay, Stewart E., and Beck, E. M. "Rethinking the Role of Racial Violence in the Great Migration." In BLACK EXODUS: THE GREAT MIGRATION FROM THE AMERICAN SOUTH, pp. 20-35. Ed. by Alferdteen Harrison. Jackson: University Press of Mississippi, 1992.

1396. Tolnay, Stewart E.; Beck, E. M.; and Massey, James L.   "Black Competition and White Vengeance: Legal Execution of Blacks as Social Control in the Cotton South, 1890 to 1929." SOCIAL SCIENCE QUAR-TERLY, Vol. 73, No. 3 (Sept. 1992): 627-44.   Includes some consideration of lynchings.

1397. "Torture and Lynching." THE OUTLOOK, Vol. 71, No. 9 (June 28, 1902): 533-34.   Burning of a black man at Lansing, Texas, May, 1902.

1398. Train, Arthur.   "Did Leo Frank get Justice?"   EVERYBODY'S MAGAZINE, Vol. 32, No. 3 (March 1915): 314-17.   Written before the lynching.

1399. "The Trial of Leo M. Frank for the Murder of Mary Phagan, Atlanta, Georgia, 1913." In AMERICAN STATE TRIALS, Vol. 10, pp. 182-414. Ed. by John D. Lawson. 17 vols.; St. Louis: F. H. Thomas Law Book Co., 1914-1936 [this vol.: 1918].

1400. "Trials: Right to a Fair Trial--Threatening Demonstrations on the Part of the Audience Influencing the Jury Against the Prisoner--'Indirect Lynching.'" THE AMERICAN LAW REVIEW, Vol. 36 (Nov.-Dec. 1902): 934-35.   Courtroom spectators threatened a lynching.

1401. Tucker, David M.   "Miss Ida B. Wells and Memphis Lynching." PHYLON, Vol. 32, No. 2 (Summer 1971): 112-22.   Lynchings in 1892, 1893, and 1894.

1402. Tunison, J[oseph] S[alathiel]. THE CINCINNATI RIOT: ITS CAUSES AND RESULTS. Cincinnati: Keating & Co., 1886.   Riot in 1884 when crowds protested light sentence given murderer; in three days at least 50 people were killed.

1403. [Turner, George.]   "Address of Mr. George Turner of Spokane, Washington."   In PROCEEDINGS OF AMERICAN SOCIETY OF INTERNATIONAL LAW . . . 1908, pp. 21-34. New York: American

Society of International Law, 1908.   Protection of civil rights of aliens, as from mob violence. Discussion on pp. 34-44.

1404. Twain, Mark. "The United States of Lyncherdom." In EUROPE AND ELSEWHERE, pp. 239-49. By Mark Twain. Ed. by Albert Bigelow Paine. New York: Harper & Brothers, 1923.   Twain was moved to write this in 1901 by the lynching of three blacks in Missouri [see Philip S. Foner, Mark Twain: Social Critic (New York: International Publishers, 1958), pp. 219-20].

1405. "Two Lynchings." THE INDEPENDENT, Vol. 52, No. 2687 (May 31, 1900): 1332-33.   One black was lynched in Colorado, and another in Georgia.

1406. Ulmer, Christina. "Southern Lynching: The Prototypical Lynching County, 1882-1911." Honors thesis, College of William and Mary, 1972.

1407. "The Unwritten Law and Lynching." THE COLORED AMERICAN MAGAZINE, Vol. 11, No. 3 (Sept. 1906): 144-45. White man in South Carolina was recently sentenced to prison for participation in a lynching.

1408. Upton, George P. "The Facts About Lynching." THE INDEPEN-DENT, Vol. 57, No. 2913 (Sept. 29, 1904): 719-21.

1409. "The Urbana Lynching." PUBLIC OPINION, Vol. 22, No. 24 (June 17, 1897): 741-42.   Press comments on lynching of black man in Ohio. Militia killed and wounded several mob members.

1410. U.S. Congress. Senate. Committee on Foreign Relations. LYNCH-ING OF FLORENTINO SUASTE. . . . REPORT. Senate Report No. 1832, 56th Cong., 2d Sess. [Jan. 9, 1901]. Serial Set 4064 (SENATE REPORTS. Vol. 2).   Occurred in Texas; see #1421 below.

1411. U.S. Department of Justice. BURNING OF TWO INDIANS IN OKLAHOMA. . . . COMMUNICATION FROM THE UNITED STATES ATTORNEY OF OKLAHOMA TERRITORY IN REFERENCE TO THE BURNING OF THE TWO INDIANS IN OKLAHOMA TERRITORY. Senate Doc. No. 99, Pt. 3, 55th Cong., 2d Sess. [Feb. 7, 1898]. Serial Set 3593 (SENATE DOCUMENTS. Vol. 4).

1412. U.S. Department of Justice. BURNING OF TWO SEMINOLE INDIANS.   . . . LETTER FROM THE UNITED STATES ATTORNEY RELATIVE TO THE BURNING OF TWO SEMINOLE INDIANS IN OKLAHOMA TERRITORY. Senate Doc. No. 99, Pt. 2, 55th Cong., 2d Sess. [Feb. 2, 1898]. Serial Set 3593 (SENATE DOCUMENTS. Vol. 4).

1413. U.S. Department of Justice. KILLING OF MRS. LAIRD BY SEMINOLE INDIANS. . . . PAPERS AND CORRESPONDENCE . . . RELATING TO THE KILLING OF MRS. LAIRD IN THE SEMINOLE NATION, AND THE SUBSEQUENT BURNING TO DEATH OF M'GEISY AND SAMPSON BY A MOB. Senate Doc. No. 99 [Pt. 1], 55th Cong., 2d Sess. [Jan. 28, 1898]. Serial Set 3593 (SENATE DOCUMENTS. Vol. 4).

1414. U.S. Department of State. "Correspondence in Relation to the Killing of Prisoners in New Orleans, March 14, 1891." In PAPERS RELATING TO THE FOREIGN RELATIONS OF THE UNITED STATES, TRANSMITTED TO CONGRESS, WITH THE ANNUAL MESSAGE OF THE PRESIDENT, DECEMBER 9, 1891, . . ., pp. 658-728. Washington, DC: GPO, 1891. Supt. of Doc. #: S1.1:891

1415. U.S. Department of State. CORRESPONDENCE REGARDING THE LYNCHING OF CERTAIN ITALIAN SUBJECTS. . . . Senate Doc. No. 104, 55th Cong., 1st Sess. [May 25, 1897]. Serial Set 3562 (SENATE DOCUMENTS. Vol. 5). Lynching of Arena, Venturella, and Salardino at Hahnville, Louisiana, on Aug. 8, 1896.

1416. U.S. Department of State. GIUSEPPE DEFINA, ETC. . . . REPORT . . . RELATING TO THE CLAIM OF GIUSEPPE DEFINA, AND RELATING TO THE LYNCHING OF CERTAIN ITALIAN SUBJECTS AT TALLULAH, LA. [July 20, 1899]. Senate Doc. No. 95, 57th Cong., 1st Sess. [Jan. 8, 1902]. Serial Set 4226 (SENATE DOCU-MENTS. Vol. 8).   Defina had to abandon his home and business in Millikins Bend, Louisiana, to avoid being lynched.

1417. U.S. Department of State. HEIRS OF CERTAIN CITIZENS OF ITALY. . . . COMMUNICATION . . . RELATING TO THE OUTRAGES . . . UPON CITIZENS OF ITALY, AND RECOMMENDING AN APPROPRIATION . . . FOR THE RELIEF OF THE HEIRS OF THE SUFFERERS. House Doc. No. 37, 55th Cong., 1st Sess. [May 3, 1897]. Serial Set 3571 (HOUSE DOCUMENTS. Vol. 1).   Lynching at Hahnville, Louisiana, on Aug. 8, 1896, of three Italians named Salvatore Arena, Giuseppe Venturella, and Lorenzo Salardino.

1418. U.S. Department of State. INDEMNITY TO RELATIVES OF LUIS MORENO. . . . REPORT . . . TOUCHING THE LYNCHING IN 1895 AT YREKA, CAL., OF LUIS MORENO, A MEXICAN CITIZEN, AND THE DEMAND OF MEXICAN GOVERNMENT FOR INDEM-NITY. House Doc. No. 237, 55th Cong., 2d Sess. [Jan. 18, 1898]. Serial Set 3679 (HOUSE DOCUMENTS. Vol. 51).

1419. U.S. Department of State. KILLING OF ITALIAN SUBJECTS AT ERWIN, MISS. . . . REPORT . . . IN REGARD TO THE KILLING OF JULY 11, 1901, BY A MOB AT ERWIN, MISS., OF GIOVANNI AND VINCENZO SERIO, AND THE WOUNDING OF SALVATORI [Salvatore] LIBERTO . . . Senate Doc. No. 40, 57th Cong., 2d Sess. [Dec. 15, 1902]. Serial Set 4420 (SENATE DOCUMENTS. Vol. 5).

1420. U.S. Department of State. LYNCHING OF CERTAIN ITALIAN SUBJECTS AT TALLULAH, LA. . . . REPORT . . . TOUCHING A CLAIM FOR FIVE THOUSAND DOLLARS PRESENTED BY THE ITALIAN AMBASSADOR ON BEHALF OF GUISEPPE [Giuseppe] DEFINA. 1901. Senate Doc. No. 194, 56th Cong., 2d Sess. [Feb. 26, 1901]. Serial Set 4042 (SENATE DOCUMENTS. Vol. 14).

1421. U.S. Department of State. LYNCHING OF FLORENTINO SUASTE. . . . REPORT . . . IN RELATION TO THE LYNCHING, IN LASALLE COUNTY, TEX., ON OCTOBER 5, 1895, OF FLORENTINO SUASTE, A MEXICAN CITIZEN. House Doc. No. 142, 56th Cong., 2d Sess. Serial Set 4138 (HOUSE DOCUMENTS. Vol. 64).

1422. U.S. Department of State. LYNCHING OF ITALIAN SUBJECTS AT TALLULAH, LA. . . . REPORT . . . RELATING TO THE LYNCH-ING OF TWO ITALIAN SUBJECTS AT TALLULAH, LA., JULY 20, 1899. Senate Doc. No. 125, 56th Cong., 2d Sess. [Jan. 29, 1901]. Serial Set 4039 (SENATE DOCUMENTS. Vol. 11).

1423. U.S. Department of the Interior. KILLING OF A WOMAN IN OKLAHOMA BY SEMINOLE INDIANS, ETC. . . . CORRESPOND-ENCE RELATIVE TO THE KILLING OF A WOMAN IN OKLAHOMA TERRITORY BY SEMINOLE INDIANS AND THE BURNING TO DEATH OF TWO SEMINOLE INDIANS BY A MOB . . . Senate Doc. No. 98, 55th Cong., 2d Sess. [Jan. 27, 1898]. Serial Set 3593 (SENATE DOCUMENTS. Vol. 4).

1424. U.S. President. INDEMNITIES PAID BY THE UNITED STATES TO ALIENS. MESSAGE FROM THE PRESIDENT OF THE UNITED STATES . . . Senate Doc. No. 17, 55th Cong., 1st Sess. [March 31, 1897]. Serial Set 3559 (SENATE DOCUMENTS, Vol. 2). Three pages. Includes massacre of Italian prisoners in New Orleans, March 14, 1891.

1425. Verax. "The Springfield Riot." THE NATION, Vol. 87, No. 2256 (Sept. 24, 1908): 284-85.   Illinois. Letter.

Vermont lynching. See THE NEW YORK TIMES INDEX, May 21, 1911.

1426. Vernier, C. G. "Local Sentiment and Lynching in Pennsylvania." JOURNAL OF THE AMERICAN INSTITUTE OF CRIMINAL LAW AND CRIMINOLOGY, Vol. 3, No. 2 (July 1912): 171-73.

1427. "The Vigilance Committee." AMERICA, Vol. 8, No. 16 (Jan. 25, 1913): 374-75.   Massachusetts effort to protect boys and girls from moral dangers. Editorial.

1428. "The Vigilance Committee: A Call to Arms." THE CRISIS, Vol. 6, No. 1 (May 1913): 26-29.   Local organization of blacks to protect their communities from aggression. Objectives of NAACP.

1429. "'Vilifying' a State." THE NATION, Vol. 101, No. 2617 (Aug. 26, 1915): 251-52.   Leo Frank case in Georgia.

1430. Vyzralek, Frank E. "Murder in Masquerade: A Commentary on Lynching and Mob Violence in North Dakota's Past, 1882-1931." NORTH DAKOTA HISTORY, Vol. 57, No. 1 (Winter 1990): 20-29.

1431. "The Waco Horror." THE CRISIS, Vol. 12, No. 3 (July 1916): supplement of eight pages numbered 1-8, following p. 154. Includes eight photos. Burning of Jesse Washington, May, 1916.

1432. Waits, John Anderson. "Roanoke's Tragedy: The Lynch Riot of 1893." M.A. thesis, Univ. of Virginia, 1972. After battle between mob and militia left 17 dead and 25 wounded, mob lynched Thomas Smith, black man. Several mob members later received light sentences or were acquitted.

1433. Waldrep, Christopher. "Augustus E. Willson and the Night Riders." THE FILSON CLUB HISTORY QUARTERLY, Vol. 58, No. 2 (April 1984): 237-52.   Economic violence, early 1900s.

1434. Waldrep, Christopher. "'Human Wolves': The Night Riders and the Killing of Axiom Cooper." REGISTER OF THE KENTUCKY HISTORI-CAL SOCIETY, Vol. 81, No. 4 (1983): 407-24.   Early 1900s night riders began as vigilantes among farmers resisting tobacco trust.

1435. Waldrep, Christopher. "The Law, the Night Riders, and Community Consensus: The Prosecution of Dr. David Amos." REGISTER OF THE KENTUCKY HISTORICAL SOCIETY, Vol. 82, No. 3 (1984): 235-56. Economic violence, early 1900s.

1436. Walker, Dale L. "Brann, the Iconoclast." REAL WEST [Derby, CT], Vol. 22, No. 162 (March 1979): 14-17, 64.   W. C. Brann was almost lynched in Waco, Texas, 1897.

1437. Walker, Dale L. "Fire Brann of Six-Shooter Depot." THE WEST [Freeport, NY], Vol. 13, No. 1 (June 1970): 10-11, 68-70.   Life of W. C. Brann. Lynching threatened, 1897.

1438. Walker, Norman. "Tallulah's Shame." HARPER'S WEEKLY, Vol. 43, No. 2224 (Aug. 5, 1899): 779.   Lynching of five Sicilians in Louisiana, July 20, 1899.

1439. Wall, James M. "Anti-Semitism and the Sinai Withdrawal." THE CHRISTIAN CENTURY, Vol. 99, No. 17 (May 12, 1982): 555-56. Includes Leo Frank case.

1440. Walling, William English. "The Race War in the North." THE INDEPENDENT, Vol. 65, No. 3118 (Sept. 3, 1908): 529-34.   Riot in Springfield, IL, Aug. 1908. Refers to blacks lynched during riot (p. 531).

1441. Warnock, Henry Y. "Andrew Sledd, Southern Methodists, and the Negro: A Case History." THE JOURNAL OF SOUTHERN HISTORY, Vol. 31, No. 3 (Aug. 1965): 251-71.   Professor Sledd lost his job at Emory College because of his 1902 article which included criticism of lynching.

1442. Washington, Booker T. "The Case of the Negro." THE ATLANTIC MONTHLY, Vol. 84, No. 505 (Nov. 1899): 577-87.   See pp. 578, 586 (quoting Reverend Vance) for lynching.

1443. Washington, Booker T. "Is the Negro Having a Fair Chance?" THE CENTURY MAGAZINE, Vol. 85 (New Series, Vol. LXIII), No. 1 (Nov. 1912): 46-55.   See section "The Crime of Lynching" (p. 55).

1444. Washington, Booker T. "Lynching in the South." THE SOUTHERN WORKMAN AND HAMPTON SCHOOL RECORD, Vol. 28, No. 10 (Oct. 1899): 373-76.   Text of a letter by B. T. W. to a New Orleans newspaper.

1445. Washington, Booker T. "Lynchings and International Peace." THE OUTLOOK, Vol. 100, No. 10 (March 9, 1912): 554-55.   Mainly on recent lynching record of U.S. and how to stop lynchings.

1446. Washington, Booker T. "Lynchings During 1913." JOURNAL OF THE AMERICAN INSTITUTE OF CRIMINAL LAW AND CRIMINOL-OGY, Vol. 4, No. 6 (March 1914): 927-30.   Reprinted from Chicago Record-Herald, Dec. 31, 1913. Case-by-case listing.

1447. Wasserman, Ira M. "Southern Violence and the Political Process. (Comment on Inverarity, ASR April 1976)." AMERICAN SOCIOLOGI-CAL REVIEW, Vol. 42, No. 2 (April 1977): 359-62.   See the Inverarity entry in this chapter.

1448. "The Watkinsville Lynching." THE VOICE OF THE NEGRO, Vol. 2, No. 8 (Aug. 1905): 529.   Eight men (one white, seven black) were lynched in Georgia.

1449. Weatherford, W. D. LYNCHING, REMOVING ITS CAUSES: ADDRESS DELIVERED BEFORE THE SOUTHERN SOCIOLOGICAL CONGRESS, NEW ORLEANS, LA., APRIL 14, 1916. Nashville: Southern Sociological Congress, 1916.   Very small pamphlet of 12 pages.

1450. Webb, Harry. "'Hangin' him just wasn't enough!'" WESTERNER [Encino, CA], Vol. 4, No. 6 (Nov.-Dec. 1972): 10-11, 29, 34. Lynching of Slim Clifton (aka Bill Clinton) decapitated him, Newcastle, WY, 1901 [sic; should be 1903].

1451. "The Week" [1st item]. THE NATION, Vol. 68, No. 1765 (April 27, 1899): 303.   Comments on burning humans alive in U.S.

1452. "The Week" [10th item]. THE NATION, Vol. 68, No. 1766 (May 4, 1899): 323-24.   Black preacher Lige Strickland was hung in aftermath of Sam Hose lynching, and mob would have lynched another black preacher by mistake but for correction of misidentification. Georgia.

1453. "A Week's Mob Violence." THE OUTLOOK, Vol. 74, No. 15 (Aug. 8, 1903): 867.   Includes hanging and burning of a black man in Danville, Illinois, followed by the arrests of nearly twenty mob members; and includes lynching of an innocent black man in Georgia. See editorial comment under heading "Murder" on pp. 877-80.

1454. Wells, F. Lyman. "Lynching." THE NATION, Vol. 103, No. 2663 (July 13, 1916): 35.   Letter.

1455. Wells, Ida B. "Lynch Law in all its Phases." OUR DAY, Vol. 11, No. 65 (May 1893): 333-47.

1456. Wells, Ida B. A RED RECORD: TABULATED STATISTICS AND ALLEGED CAUSES OF LYNCHINGS IN THE UNITED STATES, 1892-1893-1894. Chicago: Donohue & Henneberry, 1895.   Reprinted in Ida B. Wells-Barnett, On Lynchings (1969); see below, #1464.

1457. Wells, Ida B. UNITED STATES ATROCITIES. LYNCH LAW. London: "Lux" Newspaper and Publishing Co., 1892.   See National Union Catalog, Pre-1956, Vol. 655, p.391.

1458. Wells, Tom Henderson. "The Phoenix Election Riot." PHYLON, Vol. 31, No. 1 (Spring [March] 1970): 58-69.   Anti-black riot in South Carolina, 1898.

1459. Wells-Barnett, Ida B. "Lynch Law in America." THE ARENA, Vol. 23, No. 1 (Jan. 1900): 15-24.   Part III of the "White Man's Problem."

1460. Wells-Barnett, Ida B. LYNCH LAW IN GEORGIA. A SIX-WEEKS' RECORD IN THE CENTER OF SOUTHERN CIVILIZATION, AS FAITHFULLY CHRONICLED BY THE "ATLANTA JOURNAL" AND THE "ATLANTA CONSTITUTION." ALSO THE FULL REPORT OF LOUIS P. LE VIN, THE CHICAGO DETECTIVE SENT TO INVESTIGATE THE BURNING OF SAMUEL HOSE, THE TORTURE AND HANGING OF ELIJAH STICKLAND, THE COLORED PREACHER, AND THE LYNCHING OF NINE MEN FOR ALLEGED ARSON. Chicago, 1899?   See National Union Catalog, Pre-1956, Vol. 655, p. 467. Hose: Georgia. Strickland: Georgia.

1461. Wells Barnett, Ida B. "Lynching and the Excuse for It." THE INDEPENDENT, Vol. 53, No. 2737 (May 16, 1901): 1133-36.

1462. Wells-Barnett, Ida. "Lynching[:] Our National Crime." In PROCEEDINGS OF THE NATIONAL NEGRO CONFERENCE 1909. Reprint; New York: Arno Press and The New York Times, 1969.

1463. Wells Barnett, Ida B. "The Negro's Case in Equity." THE INDEPENDENT, Vol. 52, No. 2682 (April 26, 1900): 1010-11.

1464. Wells-Barnett, Ida B. ON LYNCHINGS: SOUTHERN HORRORS; A RED RECORD; MOB RULE IN NEW ORLEANS. New York: Arno Press and The New York Times, 1969.

1465. Wells-Barnett, Ida B. "Our Country's Lynching Record." THE SURVEY, Vol. 29, No. 18 (Feb. 1, 1913): 573-74.

1466. Wells-Barnett, Ida B. SELECTED WORKS OF IDA B. WELLS-BARNETT. Ed. by Trudier Harris. New York: Oxford Univ. Press, 1991. Includes Mob Rule in New Orleans: Robert Charles and His Fight to the Death, in which see "Burning Human Beings Alive" (pp. 314-20) and "Lynching Record" (pp. 320-22).

1467. Weston County Heritage Group. WESTON COUNTY WYOMING [title on spine: HISTORY OF WESTON COUNTY WYOMING]. Dallas: Curtis Media Corp., 1988.   See p. 14 for lynching of Tom Waggoner near Newcastle, June 1891.   See pp. 101-02 for "The Demise of 'Diamond L

Slim'" by Alex Mitich, about the Newcastle lynching of W. C. Clifton, 1903.

1468. "What Can be Done to Stop Lynching . . ." THE AMERICAN LAW REVIEW, Vol. 39 (Jan.-Feb. 1905): 101-03.   Report of speech by Henry McAllister at Colorado Bar Association meeting, Sept. 1904.

1469. "When Men Become Beasts." FRONTIER TIMES [Bandera, TX], Vol. 11, No. 7 (April 1934): 319-20.   Burning of Henry Smith, black man, Paris, Texas, 1893.

1470. "When Lynch Law Becomes a Necessity." CANADA LAW JOUR-NAL, Vol. 50, No. 11 and 12 (June 1914): 370-71.   Advocates lynching of suffragettes in England. Does not deal with U.S.A.

1471. THE WHITE CAPS: A HISTORY OF THE ORGANIZATION IN SEVIER COUNTY. E. W. Crozier, publisher. Knoxville: Bean, Warters & Gaut, printers and binders, 1899.   Activities in Tennessee, 1890s. The publisher seems to have functioned as the editor.

1472. White, Frank. "Municipal Liability for Damages by Mobs." NORTH-WESTERN LAW REVIEW, Vol. 4, No. 1 (Oct. 1895): 1-23.   Brief mention of lynching on p. 9.

1473. "Who are White Cappers and Lynchers?" THE VOICE OF THE NEGRO, Vol. 2, No. 6 (June 1905): 423-24.   They are not entirely low-lifes but are also Southern leaders.

1474. "Why Crimes and Lynchings?" THE CHRISTIAN ADVOCATE [New York], Vol. 80, No. 30 (July 27, 1905): 1164.   Recent address of Secretary Taft.

"Why Frank Was Lynched" and "Why Was Frank Lynched." See A Public Man of Georgia.

1475. Wiggins, Gene. "The Socio-Political Works of Fiddlin' John and Moonshine Kate." SOUTHERN FOLKLORE QUARTERLY, Vol. 41 (1977): 97-118.   On p. 97 vol. number is incorrectly listed as 40. Includes material and song lyrics about Mary Phagan and Leo Frank (see pp. 100-04).

1476. Wilkinson, J. L. THE TRANS-CEDAR LYNCHING AND THE TEXAS PENITENTIARY. Ed. by Bertha E. Drager. New York: Carlton Press, 1974.   Lynching of Jim Humphreys and his two sons, May, 1893. Author served 12 years in prison for the crime.

1477. Willcox, Walter F. "Negro Criminality." In STUDIES IN THE

AMERICAN RACE PROBLEM, pp. 443-75. Alfred Holt Stone. New York: Doubleday, Page & Co., 1908. For lynching see pp. 460-75. Deals especially with Sam Hose case in Georgia.

1478. Williams, Charleea H. "Recent Developments in 'the Land of the Free.'" THE COLORED AMERICAN MAGAZINE, Vol. 5, No. 4 (Aug. 1902): 284-93.   Lynching and massacre at Ball Town, Louisiana; lynching of Louis F. Wright at New Madrid, Missouri; a lynching in western Kentucky; race war at Madrid Bend, Kentucky; lynching of James Walker at Washington, North Carolina; lynching of Wm. H. Wallace at La Junta, Colorado; etc.

1479. Williams, Chas. H. THE NEGRO PROBLEM: WHEN, IN THE COURSE OF HUMAN EVENTS . . . Baraboo, WI, 1900.   Four-page pamphlet 56-266 in library of State Historical Society of Wisconsin. Includes lynching--and desire of blacks in Marshalltown, Iowa, to lynch two white tramps who had murdered an elderly black man.

1480. Williams, Chas. H.   THE RACE PROBLEM: INHERITANCE FROM PLANTATION TYRANNY, AGAIN ILLUSTRATED BY THE BARBAROUS LYNCHING OF TWO COLORED BOYS AND OTHER BARBARIAN ACTS IN THE SOUTHERN STATES. Baraboo. WI, 1902. Two-page pamphlet 56-275 in library of State Historical Society of Wisconsin.

1481. Williams, Chas. H. THE RACE PROBLEM: WHY MEN OF THE "SUPERIOR RACE" ARE LYNCHED IN THE SOUTH. Baraboo, WI, 1899.   Two-page pamphlet.   White men are lynched "because of their outspoken sympathy for colored people." See National Union Catalog, Pre-1956, Vol. 664, p. 580 for this and other short pamphlets by this author.

1482. Williamson, Edward C. "Black Belt Political Crisis: The Savage-James Lynching, 1882." THE FLORIDA HISTORICAL QUARTERLY, Vol. 45, No. 4 (April 1967): 402-09.   Victims were two black men who were Republicans in Madison County, Florida.

1483. Williamson, Joel. "How Black Was Rhett Butler?"   In THE EVOLUTION OF SOUTHERN CULTURE, pp. 87-107. Ed. by Numan V. Bartley. Athens: Univ. of Georgia Press, 1988.   Includes influences on Margaret Mitchell, such as the South of alleged black rapists, lynchings (details on Sam Hose lynching near Newnan, Georgia, 1899), and race riots (especially Atlanta, 1906).

1484. Williamson, Joel. WILLIAM FAULKNER AND SOUTHERN HISTORY. New York: Oxford Univ. Press, 1993.   See pp. 157-61 for former U.S. Senator William Sullivan leading mob which lynched Nelse Patton, black man, at Oxford, Mississippi, 1908.

1485. "The Will-to-Lynch." THE NEW REPUBLIC, Vol. 8, No. 102 (Oct. 14, 1916): 261-62.   Argues that the lynching spirit, "this volcano of communal savagery," rested by 1916 not on concern for justice, revenge, or an alleged crime, but on "an impersonal hunger for blood" in which "certain classes in the community express their hatred of an 'inferior race,' their contempt for law, their sense of the predominance of the Anglo-Saxon, [and] the gallantry of the predatory male."

1486. Wilson, Edward E. "The Negro in the President's Message." THE VOICE, Vol. 3, No. 12 (Dec. 1906): 575-80.   Sees positives and negatives in Roosevelt's remarks about lynching.   See also editorial comment, "The Negro in the Message," pp. 536-37.

1487. Wilson, Gary C. "When the Devil Went Down to Waco." TRUE WEST, Vol. 32, No. 7 (Dec. 1985): 12-18.   W. C. Brann, his conflicts with Baylor Univ., his near lynching [1897], his murder, etc.

1488. Wilson, Jon L. "Days of Fear: A Lynching in St. Petersburg." TAMPA BAY HISTORY, Vol. 5, No. 2 (Fall/Winter 1983): 4-26.   Hanging of John Evans, black suspect in murder and possible rape cases, 1914.

1489. Wimpy, W. E. "Lynching, an Evil of County Government." MANU-FACTURERS RECORD, Vol. 70 (Aug. 24, 1916): 49-50.   Includes extensive quotations from "Concerning Lynching," a 21-page speech by Robert C. Alston to the Georgia Bar Association in 1916.

1490. Winn, Bill. "Lynching on Wynn's Hill." SOUTHERN EXPOSURE, Vol. 15, No. 3-4 (Fall-Winter 1987): 17-24.   Georgia lynching of black youth named T. Z. McElhaney, 1912.

1491. Winston, J. T. "Lynching Defended." THE NATION, Vol. 102, No. 2660 (June 22, 1916): 671.   Letter from a transplanted Northerner in Bryan, Texas, advocating lynching for rapists whether black or white--but the emphasis is on blacks.

1492. Winter, Rogers. "A Man Is Hanged." In STAR REPORTERS AND 34 OF THEIR STORIES, pp. 131-42. Ed. by Ward Greene. New York: Random House, 1948.   Leo Frank was lynched in Georgia.

1493. "Wiping Off a Smirch." THE OUTLOOK, Vol. 100, No. 1 (Jan. 6, 1912): 7-8.   Efforts for justice (including indictments and convictions) in Newark, Ohio, after a lynching in 1903.

1494. Wolf, Charlotte. "Constructions of a Lynching." SOCIOLOGICAL INQUIRY, Vol. 62, No. 1 (Winter 1992): 83-97. Two black brothers were lynched in Tennessee in Jan. 1900; related lynching of a black man a week later. Identities of town and victims concealed by fictitious names. [In Jan. 1900 brothers Henry and George Giveney were lynched in Ripley, TN; see NAACP, Thirty Years of Lynching in the United States, 1889-1918, p. 93.]

1495. Wolfe, George D. "Utah's Greatest Manhunt." FRONTIER TIMES [Austin, TX], Vol. 36, No. 4, New Series No. 20 (Fall 1962): 32-33, 61-62. A posse tried to kill Rafael Lopez by building fires at entrance to sealed mine, 1913. But Lopez's body was never found.

1496. "Women Lynched." THE CRISIS, Vol. 42, No. 1 (Jan. 1935): 22. Brief review of the number of cases by state since 1889, making a total of 83 (65 black women and 18 whites).

1497. Woodbridge, W. A. "Why the Difference?" THE INDEPENDENT, Vol. 65, No. 3119 (Sept. 10, 1908): 605-06. Lynching of black man was averted in Portsmouth, VA; anti-black rioting occurred in Springfield, IL.

1498. Woods, Henry. "The Crime at Marietta." AMERICA, Vol. 13, No. 22 (Sept. 11, 1915): 535-37. Leo Frank was lynched in Georgia.

1499. Woodward, C. Vann. TOM WATSON: AGRARIAN REBEL. 2d ed.; Savannah: Beehive Press, 1973. Leo Frank case: pp. 376-89.

1500. Work, M. N. "Negro Criminality in the South." THE ANNALS OF THE AMERICAN ACADEMY OF POLITICAL AND SOCIAL SCIENCE, Vol. 49 (Sept. 1913): 74-80. Lynchings mentioned on pp. 75-76; positive correlation between years of most lynchings and years of highest amount of Negro crime. Otherwise not about collective violence.

1501. "The World War." THE CRISIS, Vol. 9, No. 1 (Nov. 1914): 15-17. Lynchings in U.S. as barbaric as European atrocities.

1502. "Worries and Concerns." COLORADO HERITAGE, [no vol. # or issue #] (Winter 1991): 26-27. Includes lynching (burning alive) of black youth named Preston Porter in Colorado, Nov. 1900 (with full-page illustration from contemporary newspaper).

1503. Wreszin, Michael. "Albert Jay Nock and the Anarchist Elitist Tradition in America." AMERICAN QUARTERLY, Vol. 21, No. 2, Pt. 1 (Summer 1969): 165-89. See p. 170 for the lynching in Coatesville, Pennsylvania, in 1911 and Nock's interest in it. [See also Nock in this bibliography.]

1504. "The Writhing South." THE CRISIS, Vol. 10, No. 3 (July 1915): 126-28.   Includes lynching.

1505. Wyllie, Irvin G.   "Race and Class Conflict on Missouri's Cotton Frontier." THE JOURNAL OF SOUTHERN HISTORY, Vol. 20, No. 2 (May 1954): 183-96.   Anti-black violence culminating in lynching of A. B. Richardson, black, in Oct. 1911, in Pemiscot County.

1506. X. "Lynch Law and the Governor." THE INDIANA LAW JOURNAL, Vol. 1, No. 4 (April 1898): 135-43.   Partly on a governor's legal relation to the suppression of lynching.

1507. Zanjani, Sally Springmeyer.   "The Curse of the Uber Lynching." AMERICAN WEST, Vol. 19, No. 5 (Sept./Oct. 1982): 59-61, 67-69. Victim Adam Uber placed a curse on the lynchers, Genoa, Nevada, 1897.

1508. Ziglar, William. "'Community on Trial': The Coatesville Lynching of 1911." THE PENNSYLVANIA MAGAZINE OF HISTORY AND BIOGRAPHY, Vol. 106, No. 2 (April 1982): 245-70.

1509. Ziglar, William L. "The Decline of Lynching in America." INTERNATIONAL SOCIAL SCIENCE REVIEW, Vol. 63, No. 1 (Winter 1988): 14-25.   Misleading title; this is largely about T. Roosevelt's ideas and actions. Limited insight into causes of lynching's decline.

V

1917 through 1996

1510. Abernathy, Mollie C. (Davis). "Southern Women, Social Reconstruction, and the Church in the 1920s." LOUISIANA STUDIES, Vol. 13, No. 4 (Winter 1974): 289-312.   See lynching on pp. 294, 295, 296, 304-06.

1511. "Acquittals in Tampa Murder Case." INTERNATIONAL JURIDICAL ASSOCIATION MONTHLY BULLETIN, Vol. 6, No. 5 (Nov. 1937): 58-59.   Shoemaker, et al.   Florida.

1512. "Action of Vigilantes." INTERNATIONAL JURIDICAL ASSOCIATION MONTHLY BULLETIN, Vol. 5, No. 5 (Nov. 1936): 51. Mobs interfering with Communist Party speakers.

1513. "Again the Till Case." LOOK, Vol. 20, No. 6 (March 20, 1956): 164-71.   Two letters. Mississippi murder, 1955.

1514. "After All the Sacrifice--This!" THE CRUSADER, Vol. 1, No. 11 (July 1919): 4.   Lynching headlines.

1515. "Aftermath: Rolph's Lynching Stand Causes National Storm." NEWSWEEK [sic], Vol. 2, No. 20 (Dec. 16, 1933): 8-10.   California governor criticized for praising San Jose lynchers; mention of several other actual or threatened lynchings. Photo of San Jose lynching tree being cut down.

1516. Age, Arthur V. "The Omaha Riot of 1919." M.A. thesis, Creighton Univ., 1964.   Successful effort to lynch a black rapist. Courthouse destroyed. Mayor almost lynched.

1517. "Aiken." THE CRISIS, Vol. 33, No. 3 (Jan. 1927): 141-42.   Public furor stirred up by the stories in New York World about lynching of three blacks in Aiken, South Carolina, Oct. 1926.

1518. "Aiken." THE CRISIS, Vol. 34, No. 1 (March 1927): 34.   Nothing being done against recent lynchers.

1519. "Ala. Klansman Gets Life Term For Lynching Black." JET, Vol. 68, No. 8 (May 6, 1985): 28.   Michael Donald killing, 1981.

1520. "Ala. Klansman Indicted In 1981 Slaying Of Black Man." JET, Vol. 67, No. 10 (Nov. 12, 1984): 44.   Michael Donald killing.

1521. "Alabama Policemen Mete Out Death."   THE SOUTHERN FRONTIER, Vol. 2, No. 5 (May 1941): [p. 3].

1522. Allen, James S. SMASH THE SCOTTSBORO LYNCH VERDICT. New York: Workers Library Publishers, 1933.

1523. Allison, M. G. "The Lynching Industry, 1920." THE CRISIS, Vol. 21, No. 4 (Feb. 1921): 160-62.   Gives names of victims, dates of lynchings, and alleged causes.   Includes a map of Georgia showing locations of lynchings, 1885-1920. Includes a photo of three white men lynched in Santa Rosa, California.

1524. "The American Lynching Record."   THE SOCIAL SERVICE REVIEW, Vol. 24, No. 3 (Sept. 1950): 399-400. Lynchings in 1949. Mainly quotations from New York Times editorial.

1525. "Americanism in Action." THE WORLD TOMORROW, Vol. 16, No. 25 (Oct. 26, 1933): 581-82.   George Armwood lynching in Maryland.

1526. "America's Burning Shame." THE CRISIS, Vol. 42, No. 1 (Jan. 1935): 26.   State-by-state figures on the 45 people burned alive by lynch mobs in the United States, 1919-1934.

1527. "America's Citizen Crime Fighters." READER'S DIGEST, Vol. 96, No. 575 (June 1970): 225-26, 228-30.   Organizations have been formed in various localities. Condensed from "Citizens' War on Crime," U.S. News & World Report (March 23, 1970).

1528. "America's Supreme National Shame." THE CHRISTIAN CENTURY, Vol. 53, No. 31 (July 29, 1936): 1029-30.   Lynching.

1529. Ames, Jessie Daniel. "Can Newspapers Harmonize Their Editorial Policy on Lynching and Their News Stories on Lynching?" In THE CHANGING CHARACTER OF LYNCHING, pp. 55-58.   A 1936 speech.

1530. Ames, Jessie Daniel.   THE CHANGING CHARACTER OF

LYNCHING: REVIEW OF LYNCHING, 1931-1941, WITH A DISCUS-SION OF RECENT DEVELOPMENTS IN THIS FIELD. Atlanta: Commission on Interracial Cooperation, 1942; New York: AMS Press, 1973. Includes Jessie Daniel Ames, "Editorial Treatment of Lynchings," pp. 51-54; "Can Newspapers Harmonize Their Editorial Policy on Lynching and Their News Stories on Lynching?" pp. 55-58; "Toward Lynchless America," pp. 59-62; Lewis T. Nordyke, "Ladies and Lynchings," pp. 63-68.

1531. Ames, Jessie Daniel. "Editorial Treatment of Lynchings." THE PUBLIC OPINION QUARTERLY, Vol. 2., No. 1 (Jan. 1938): 77-84. Also in Ames, The Changing Character of Lynching.

1532. Ames, Jessie Daniel. "Men Who Came Back." NEGRO DIGEST, Vol. 1, No. 5 (March 1943): 12. Two prevented lynchings and one case of mob returning black man to jail. Condensed from Changing Character of Lynching.

1533. Ames, Jessie Daniel. "The Shame of a Christian People." THE WORLD OUTLOOK, Vol. 24 (Feb. 1934): 21, 32.

1534. Ames, Jessie Daniel. TOWARD LYNCHLESS AMERICA. Washington, DC: American Council on Public Affairs, [1940?] Also in Ames, The Changing Character of Lynching.

1535. Ames, Jessie Daniels [sic]. "Whither Leads the Mob?" THE MISSIONARY VOICE, Vol. 22, No. 1 (Jan. 1932): 20, 46. Especially on lynchings and attempted lynchings in 1931 and on legal lynching.

1536. Amis, B. D. LYNCH JUSTICE AT WORK. [New York: Workers Library Publishers], [1930?].

1537. "Anarchy at Maryville." AMERICA, Vol. 44, No. 20 (Feb. 21, 1931): 469-70. Editorial on Missouri lynching.

1538. "Announced Lynching Takes Place." INTERNATIONAL JURIDI-CAL ASSOCIATION MONTHLY BULLETIN, Vol. 3, No. 5 (Oct. 1934): 4-5. Claude Neal, in Florida.

1539. "Another Cause of Lynchings." THE CRISIS, Vol. 41, No. 10 (Oct. 1934): 301. "The desire to look after matters personally rather than take their chances in organized society."

1540. "Another Lynching." THE COMMONWEAL, Vol. 21, No. 2 (Nov. 9, 1934): 49. [Claude Neal] taken from Alabama to Florida.

1541. "Another Lynching." INTERNATIONAL JURIDICAL ASSOCIATION MONTHLY BULLETIN, Vol. 7, No. 6 (Dec. 1938): 63.   Wilder McGowan, black man; Wiggins, Mississippi.

1542. "Another Lynching in Florida." INTERNATIONAL JURIDICAL ASSOCIATION MONTHLY BULLETIN, Vol. 7, No. 12 (June 1939): 138. Lee Snell, black, killed by two men. Deals also with several other lynchings.

1543. "Another Lynching in Georgia." INTERNATIONAL JURIDICAL ASSOCIATION MONTHLY BULLETIN, Vol. 4, No. 12 (June 1936): 2-3. John Rushin [sic], black man.

1544. "Another Lynching Whitewashed." INTERNATIONAL JURIDICAL ASSOCIATION MONTHLY BULLETIN, Vol. 7, No. 6 (Dec. 1938): 63-64. Case of W. C. Williams, reported last month.

1545. "Another Newspaper Takes a Stand." THE SOUTHERN WORKMAN, Vol. 46, No. 7 (July 1937): 214-16.

1546. "Anti-Lynching Remedies." THE PUBLIC [New York], Vol. 22, No. 1102 (May 17, 1919): 511.

1547. "'Any Negro Will Do.'" THE CRISIS, Vol. 44, No. 7 (July 1937): 209. Editorial with details of the lynching at Abbeville, Alabama, Feb. 1937.

1548. "Applied Violence." THE NEW REPUBLIC, Vol. 28, No. 352 (Aug. 31, 1921): 5-6.   Deplores recent increase of various types of violence in U.S. Includes beatings and tarring and feathering but not lethal lynching.

1549. "At Princess Anne." TIME, Vol. 22, No. 18 (Oct. 30, 1933): 12. Lengthy story on lynching of George Armwood in Maryland.

1550. "At the Store." TIME, Vol. 35, No. 4 (Jan. 22, 1940): 18-19.   Lynching tensions in Mississippi, and Gavagan anti-lynching bill passed House.

1551. "The Attempted Lynching of Lube Martin." THE CRISIS, Vol. 13, No. 5 (March 1917): 226-27.   Governor Stanley went to Murray, Calloway County, Kentucky, Jan. 1917, to prevent the lynching.

1552. "Attorney General Gregory on Lynching." THE NATIONAL CORPORATION REPORTER, Vol. 56, No. 26 (Aug. 1, 1918): 981.

1553. "Authors and Artists as 'Vigilantes.'" THE LITERARY DIGEST, Vol. 54, No. 15 (April 14, 1917): 1061-62.   Effort to promote patriotism and support war effort.

1554. "Back to Lynching." THE NEW REPUBLIC, Vol. 107, No. 18 (Nov. 2, 1942): 560-61. Three lynchings in one week in Mississippi. Continued on p. 561 by one paragraph entitled "Call in the FBI."

1555. "Bad Men Hang." THE COMMONWEAL, Vol. 18, No. 4 (May 26, 1933): 89-90. Lynching article occasioned by Arthur Raper's The Tragedy of Lynching.

1556. Bagnall, Robert. "An Oklahoma Lynching." THE CRISIS, Vol. 37, No. 8 (Aug. 1930): 274, 284-85. Chickasha, Oklahoma, mob attacked jail and killed black teenager named Henry Argo in May, 1930.

1557. Barnard, Harry. "Emmett Lewis [sic] Till." THE NATION, Vol. 181, No. 12 [sic; should be No. 13] (Sept. 24, 1955): inside front cover [p. 252]. Letter. Mississippi murder, 1955.

1558. Barton, Belle. "Things Happen in Alabama." LABOR DEFENDER, Vol. 10, No. 11 (Dec. 1936): 10. Beating of Joseph Gelders.

1559. "The Beast is Loose." THE SURVEY, Vol. 69, No. 12 (Dec. 1933): 413. Refers to recent lynchings in California, Maryland, and Missouri.

1560. Beatty-Brown, Florence Rebekah. "The Negro as Portrayed by the St. Louis Post-Dispatch from 1920-1950." Ph.D. diss., U. of Illinois, 1951. See Diss. Ab., Vol. 12, No. 1 (1952): 109-10.

1561. Beck, Earl R. "German Views of Negro Life in the United States, 1919-1933." THE JOURNAL OF NEGRO HISTORY, Vol. 48, No. 1 (Jan. 1963): 22-32. Includes criticism of lynching.

1562. Beers, Paul G. "The Wythe County Lynching of Raymond Bird: Progressivism vs. Mob Violence in the '20s." APPALACHIAN JOURNAL, Vol. 22 (Fall 1994): 34-59. Virginia.

1563. "Behind the Lynchers." NEW SOUTH, Vol. 2, No. 7 (July 1947): 7.

1564. "Behind the Terror in Racine, Wisconsin." INTERNATIONAL JURIDICAL ASSOCIATION MONTHLY BULLETIN, Vol. 3, No. 8 (Jan. 1935): 6-7. "Vigilantes" attacking workers.

1565. Belknap, Michal R. FEDERAL LAW AND SOUTHERN ORDER: RACIAL VIOLENCE AND CONSTITUTIONAL CONFLICT IN THE POST-BROWN SOUTH. Athens: Univ. of Georgia Press, 1987. See Chapter 1, "Law and Violence in the Lynching Era." In index see "Chaney," "Goodman," "Schwerner," and "Till" [Mississippi victims].

1566. Berkman, Alexander. "The Lynching." THE BLAST, Vol. 2, No. 3 (March 15, 1917): 3.   Conviction of Tom Mooney in California. Other than title, this has nothing to do with lynching, unless one considers it was a legal lynching.

1567. Besig, Ernest. "Vigilantes Use Guns and Fire at Salinas." THE OPEN FORUM, Vol. 11, No. 40 (Oct. 6, 1934): [first page].   Violence against striking Filipino lettuce workers in California.

1568. Bims, Hamilton. "Deacons For Defense.: EBONY, Vol. 20, No. 11 (Sept. 1965): 25-28, 30.   Black protective organization in South, especially in Bogalusa, Louisiana.

1569. "Black Legion." TIME, Vol. 27, No. 22 (June 1, 1936): 12-13.   Mob murder of Charles Poole near Dearborn, Michigan, and arrest of 16 Black Legionnaires.

1570. "The Black Legion." LABOR DEFENDER, Vol. 10, No. 7 (July 1936): 4.   Claims this Michigan (and elsewhere) organization has been involved in 43-48 murders and several floggings.

1571. "Black Shirts and Lynching." THE WORLD TOMORROW, Vol. 13, No. 11 (Nov. 1930): 437-38.   Includes men's idleness as one cause of lynching.

1572. BLACK SPOTS ON THE MAP. A CHALLENGE TO EVERY AMERICAN CITIZEN. Atlanta: Commission on Interracial Cooperation, 1924.

1573. Blagden, Willie Sue. "Arkansas Flogging." THE NEW REPUBLIC, Vol. 87, No. 1126 (July 1, 1936): 236-37.   White men whipped a Southern white woman who was trying to find out if a black man had been lynched.

1574. Blagden, Willie Sue. "Is it TRUE what they SAY about DIXIE?" LABOR DEFENDER, Vol. 10, No. 8 (Aug. 1936): 7, 19.   Floggings, head shavings, beatings of supporters of Southern Tenant Farmers' Union.

1575. Blake, Morgan. "And So They Got Away With It." NEGRO DIGEST, Vol. 5, No. 5 (March 1947): 62-63.   Lynchers of four blacks in Walton County, Georgia.

1576. Blakely, Paul L. "Lynching." AMERICA, Vol. 50, No. 11 (Dec 16, 1933): 253-54.   Statistics; lynchers are low-lifes; state laws; get rid of complaisant officials like California governor Rolph.

1577. Blakely, Paul L. "The Right not to Be Lynched." AMERICA, Vol. 52, No. 6 (Nov. 17, 1934): 134-35.   Reprinted in Interracial Review, Vol. 7 (Dec. 1934), pp. 142-43.

1578. "The Bloody Blot." THE CRISIS, Vol. 33, No. 4 (Feb. 1927): 212-13. Lynching of a black man at LaBelle, Florida.

1579. "The Blot Darkens." INTERRACIAL REVIEW, Vol. 8, No. 11 (Nov. 1935): 165.   Lynching increase.   Reprint from The Southwest Courier (Oklahoma City).

1580. "The Blot on the Flag." THE INDEPENDENT, Vol. 105, No. 3754 (Jan. 15, 1921): 65.   Lynching statistics for 1920, with comments.

1581. Boardman, Helen. "Grand Jury Adjourns: Laurens County Fails to Indict Dendy Lynchers." THE CRISIS, Vol. 41, No. 5 (May 1934): 140. Norris Dendy was lynched in South Carolina on July 4, 1933.

1582. Boffey, Philip M. "Dissent and Reaction: Vigilante Activity at NBS Labs in Boulder." SCIENCE, Vol. 169, No. 3941 (July 10, 1970): 163-64. Alleged harassment of one worker by others.

1583. Bond, Horace M. "What Lies Behind Lynching." THE NATION, Vol. 128, No. 3325 (March 27, 1929): 370-71.

1584. Bongartz, Roy. "Superjew." ESQUIRE, Vol. 74, No. 2A (Aug. 1970): 110-11, 126-28.   Meir Kahane and the Jewish Defense League.

1585. Booker, Simeon. "30 Years Ago: How Emmett Till's Lynching Launched Civil Rights Drive." JET, Vol. 68, No. 14 (June 17, 1985): 12-15, 18.   He was murdered in Mississippi, 1955.

1586. "Books.--Children of the Slaves." THE SPECTATOR [London], Vol. 125, No. 4822 (Nov. 27, 1920): 703-05.   Information and comments on lynching in the U.S. occasioned by Stephen Graham's book The Children of the Slaves (1920).

1587. "A Boy Goes Home." NEWSWEEK, Vol. 46, No. 11 (Sept. 12, 1955): 32.   Funeral of Emmett Till, Mississippi murder victim.

1588. Boyd, Thomas. "Defying the Klan." THE FORUM, Vol. 76, No. 1 (July 1926): 48-56.   Includes criticism by Julian Harris (son of Joel Chandler Harris), editor and publisher of Columbus, GA, newspaper named Enquirer-Sun, of Georgia's lynching of Negro lunatic Willie Dixon.

1589. Bradley, Rose. "Back of the Maryland Lynching." THE NATION, Vol. 137, No. 3571 (Dec. 13, 1933): 672-73.   Lynching of black man named George Armwood--and its causes.

1590. Braffet, Mark P. POLITICS HERE IN CARBON COUNTY. Price, UT: Printed by the Sun, [192-?].   One folded sheet (4 pp.).   Comments on performance of incumbent sheriff on lynching. Yale Library Catalog.

1591. Brearley, H. C.   "Ba-ad Nigger."   THE SOUTH ATLANTIC QUARTERLY, Vol. 38, No. 1 (Jan. 1939): 75-81.   Says some blacks engage in reckless bravado, such as rowdy horseplay or insults to white civilians or policemen; to do so with impunity is admired, and thus "bad" is "good." Such activity sometimes causes interracial homicides and lynchings.

1592. Breed, Warren. "Comparative Newspaper Handling Of the Emmett Till Case." JOURNALISM QUARTERLY, Vol. 35, No. 3 (Summer 1958): 291-98.   Till was murdered in Mississippi, 1955.

1593. Breskin, David. "Leave it to Beaver." ROLLING STONE, Issue 457, (Sept. 26, 1985): 66-68, 70, 105, 109-10.   Legion of Doom at Paschal High School in Ft. Worth, Texas.

1594. Briggs, Cyril V. "The American Race Problem. No. 2. The White Man's Solution." THE CRUSADER, Vol. 1, No. 2 (Oct. 1918): 12, 31-32. Includes quotations from Walter White in September issue of The Crisis on lynching of Mary Turner in Georgia.

1595. Brill, A. A. "Psychologists Analyze Neal Lynching." THE CRISIS, Vol. 42, No. 1 (Jan. 1935): 18.   Florida.

1596. "Brisk Start of the 1923 Lynchings." THE LITERARY DIGEST, Vol. 76, No. 3 (Jan 20, 1923): 11-12.   Includes race riot at Rosewood, Florida, and two Rosewood photos.

1597. "Brotherhood Week Lynching." EVENTS AND TRENDS IN RACE RELATIONS: A MONTHLY SUMMARY, Vol. 4, No. 8 (March 1947): 247.   Willie Earle; South Carolina, 1947.

1598. "Brothers, Come North." THE CRISIS, Vol. 19, No. 3 (Jan. 1920): 105-06.   Mentions lynching as a reason the South is "a Hell."

1599. Brown, Richard Maxwell. "An Escape from Paranoia." THE AMER-ICAN WEST, Vol. 7, No. 1 (Jan. 1970): 48.   Contemporary urban vigilantism; advances five proposals for "law and order with justice in the 1970s."

1600. Brown, Richard Maxwell. "Southern Violence vs. the Civil Rights Movement, 1954-1968." In PERSPECTIVES ON THE AMERICAN SOUTH, Vol. 1, pp. 49-69. Ed. by Merle Black and John Shelton Reed. New York: Gordon and Breach Scientific Publishers, 1981. Distinguishes Southern traditionalist opponents of civil rights for blacks from violent, right-wing, extremist ideologues. Shows the latter did not have the community support of the KKK of Reconstruction or turn-of-the-century lynch mobs.

1601. Browne, Porter Emerson. "The Vigilantes: Who and Why and What They Are." THE OUTLOOK, Vol. 119 (May 8, 1918): 67-69. Writers and artists promoting patriotism and preparedness.

1602. Buckmiller, Helen. [Letter against lynching.] THE CRISIS, Vol. 21, No. 3 (Jan. 1921): 126.

1603. "The Bullock Case." THE CRISIS, Vol. 23, No. 6 (April 1922): 263-64. On the lynching of two blacks in Norlina, North Carolina, in January 1921, and the subsequent unsuccessful effort to extradite from Canada the brother of one of the victims.

1604. Bunker, Edward. "Imprisoned Black Rage: The Lynching of Vinson Harris." THE NATION, Vol. 242, No. 19 (May 17, 1986): 681, 697-99. Some people might not count this as a lynching; black prisoner killed by white guards on prison bus in North Carolina, 1986.

1605. Burnham, Louis. BEHIND THE LYNCHING OF EMMET LOUIS TILL. New York: Freedom Associates, 1955. He was murdered in Mississippi in 1955. This book spells "Emmet" as given here.

1606. "The Burning at Dyersburg. An N. A. A. C. P. Investigation." THE CRISIS, Vol. 15, No. 4 (Feb. 1918): 178-83. The torture and burning at the stake of a black man named Lation Scott in Dyersburg, TN, Dec. 1917.

1607. "Bury Miss. Lynch Victim As His Threatened Mother Flees State." JET, Vol. 16, No. 4 (May 21, 1959): 8-9. Includes photo of Mack Parker's body.

1608. "The Business of Us All." COMMONWEAL, Vol. 116, No. 16 (Sept. 22, 1989): 484-85. Racial murders of Emmett Till (1955) and Yusuf Hawkins (1989 in Brooklyn).

1609. Butler, Hilton. "Lynch Law in Action." THE NEW REPUBLIC, Vol. 67, No. 868 (July 22, 1931): 256-58. Descriptions of several lynchings and ideas about general causes (such as lack of amusements and existence of types of jobs that permit temporary absence of workers).

1610. Butler, Hilton. "Murder for the Job." THE NATION, Vol. 137, No. 3549 (July 12, 1933): 44.   Black workers were killed and wounded in Mississippi so whites could get their jobs.   No lethal lynchings but one flogging.

1611. "The Butte Lynching." THE OUTLOOK, Vol. 116, No. 16 (Aug. 15, 1917): 572.   Victim: Frank Little.   Montana.

1612. Cabaniss, Allen.   "Governor White Deplores Duck Hill Lynching." THE CHRISTIAN CENTURY, Vol. 54, No. 20 (May 19, 1937): 654.   Mississippi.

1613. Cabaniss, Allen. "State Congratulated on No-Lynching Record." THE CHRISTIAN CENTURY, Vol. 54, No. 13 (March 31, 1937): 432.   Mississippi, during 1936.   Tuskegee report says Mississippi had one lynching in 1936.   One brief paragraph.

1614. Cagin, Seth, and Dray, Philip.   WE ARE NOT AFRAID: THE STORY OF GOODMAN, SCHWERNER, AND CHANEY AND THE CIVIL RIGHTS CAMPAIGN IN MISSISSIPPI. New York: Macmillan, 1988.   They were lynched in 1964.

1615. Caldwell, Erskine.   "'Parties Unknown' in Georgia."   In NEW MASSES: AN ANTHOLOGY OF THE REBEL THIRTIES, pp. 137-41. Ed. by Joseph North.   New York: International Publishers, 1969.   Known and suspected lynchings, Bartow, Georgia.   From New Masses, Vol. 10, No. 4 (Jan. 23, 1934), pp. 16, 18.

1616. Caldwell, Erskine, and Bourke-White, Margaret. YOU HAVE SEEN THEIR FACES. New York: Viking Press, 1937; reprint: New York: Arno Press, 1975.   See lynching on pp. 51, 75-76, 112, 139.

1617. "The California Lynching of 3 White Men, December 10, 1920." THE CRISIS, Vol. 21, No. 4 (Feb. 1921): 162.   A photo.   Accompanying text indicates it happened in Santa Rosa.

1618. "California Vigilantes Attack 'Reds.'" INTERNATIONAL JURIDICAL ASSOCIATION MONTHLY BULLETIN, Vol. 4, No. 3 (Aug. 1935): 1.   Tarring and feathering.

1619. "California Vigilantes Run the Government." INTERNATIONAL JURIDICAL ASSOCIATION MONTHLY BULLETIN, Vol. 5, No. 5 (Nov. 1936): 54.   Salinas, California.   See "Attacks on Steel Organizers" on same page. "Call in the FBI." See "Back to Lynching."

1620. Calvin, Floyd J. "The Present South." THE MESSENGER, Vol. 5, No. 1 (Jan. 1923): 576-77. Conclusion of series "Eight Weeks in Dixie." A black worker from Kansas was taken off train and shot by mob near Texarkana, AR. Just days later many blacks emigrated to the North.

1621. Cameron, James. LYNCHINGS AND THE IDEA OF THE KU KLUX KLAN IN AMERICA; A FEW OF THE SORDID FACTS. Milwaukee: James Cameron, 1983. Pamphlet; 21 pages.

1622. Cameron, James. A TIME OF TERROR. Milwaukee: TD Publications, 1982. Reprint ed.; Baltimore: Black Classic Press, 1994. Marion, IN, lynchings, 1930. [Cameron is founder and director of America's Black Holocaust Museum, 2233 N. 4th St. Milwaukee, WI 53212, which is devoted primarily to lynching.]

1623. "Can the South Stop Lynch Gangs?" NEGRO DIGEST, Vol. 5, No. 11 (Sept. 1947): 83-86.

1624. "Can the States Stop Lynching?" THE CRISIS, Vol. 43, No. 1 (Jan. 1936): 6-7, 18. A review of the lynchings in 1935. See related editorials, p. 17.

1625. "Can the States Stop Lynching?" THE CRISIS, Vol. 45, No. 1 (Jan. 1938): 12-13. A review of the lynching record of 1937 and the progress of the anti-lynching bill.

1626. "Can the States Stop Lynching?" THE CRISIS, Vol. 46, No. 1 (Jan. 1939): 9. A review of the seven lynchings of 1938.

1627. "The Cancer of Lynching." THE SOUTHERN WORKMAN, Vol. 63, No. 2 (Feb. 1934): 40-44.

1628. Cannon, James P. "Frank Little, the Rebel--On the Ninth Anniversary of His Death." LABOR DEFENDER, Vol. 1, No. 8 (Aug. 1926): 132-33. He was lynched in Butte, MT.

1629. Cansler, Fritz. "Lynching Statistics." THE CHRISTIAN CENTURY, Vol. 55, No. 34 (Aug. 24, 1938): 1016. Tuskegee Institute statistics on numbers of lynchings are probably too low.

1630. Cantwell, Robert. "Lynchers in Maryland." THE NEW REPUBLIC, Vol. 77, No. 995 (Dec. 27, 1933): 199. Letter responding to Gerald W. Johnson's Dec. 20 article. Armwood case.

1631. Capeci, Dominic J., Jr. "The Lynching of Cleo Wright: Federal Protection of Constitutional Rights during World War II." THE JOURNAL OF AMERICAN HISTORY, Vol. 72, No. 4 (March 1986): 859-87. Missouri.

1632. Carroll, Ginny. "An Ugly Silence in a Prison Death." NEWSWEEK, Vol. 108, No. 5 (Aug. 4, 1986): 19. Death by asphyxiation of black federal prisoner Vinson Harris in North Carolina.

1633. Carter, Charles Frederick. "The Lynching Infamy." CURRENT HISTORY, Vol. 15, No. 6 (March 1922): 897-902.

1634. Carter, Proctor Neal. "Lynch-Law and the Press of Missouri." M.A. thesis, Univ. of Missouri, 1933. Begins with 1900.

1635. Cartwright, Marguerite. "The Mob Still Rides." THE NEGRO HISTORY BULLETIN, Vol. 19, No. 5 (Feb. 1956): 105-06. Reprinted from The Crisis, Vol. 60, No. 4 (April 1953): 222-23. Followed here by two letters to Dr. Cartwright in response to her article in The Crisis.

1636. Cartwright, Marguerite. "The Mob Still Rides--Tuskegee Notwithstanding." THE CRISIS, Vol. 60, No. 4 (April 1953): 222-23. The first "lynch-less year" was recently achieved only because Tuskegee Institute's definition of lynching is too "technical and doctrinaire."

1637. Cason, Clarence. 90° IN THE SHADE. Chapel Hill: Univ. of North Carolina Press, 1935. See pp. 111-20 for lynchings, especially those in Tuscaloosa, Alabama, in 1933 (Pippen and Harden).

1638. "Catholic Magazine Asks Coughlin to Hit Lynching." INTERRACIAL REVIEW, Vol. 8, No. 4 (April 1935): 65. Brief.

1639. "The Cause and Cure of Mob Violence." CENTRAL LAW JOURNAL, Vol. 89, No. 15 (Oct. 10, 1919): 257-58.

1640. "The Cause Of and Remedy For Race Riots." THE MESSENGER, Vol. 2, No. 9 (Sept. 1919): 14-21. Brief references to lynching.

1641. Chadbourn, James H. "Plan for Survey of Lynching and the Judicial Process." NORTH CAROLINA LAW REVIEW, Vol. 9, No. 3 (April 1931): 330-36.

1642. Chadwick, John S. "Jury Refuses to Indict Lynchers." THE CHRISTIAN CENTURY, Vol. 54, No. 25 (June 23, 1937): 816. Alabama. One paragraph.

1643. "The Challenge which Lynching Brings to the Churches." FEDERAL COUNCIL BULLETIN, Vol. 6, No. 2 (Feb.-March 1923): 14-15.

1644. Chamberlain, Bernard Peyton. THE NEGRO AND CRIME IN VIRGINIA. [Charlottesville]: Univ. of Virginia, 1936. (Publications of the University of Virginia Phelps-Stokes Fellowship Papers no. 15.) Lynching: pp. 61-74.

1645. Chamblee, George W. "I.--The Motives of Judge Lynch." THE FORUM, Vol. 76, No. 6 (Dec. 1926): 811-17. Part of "Is Lynching Ever Defensible?" Second part (pp. 818-22) is by John P. Fort.

1646. Chang, David. "Lynching and Terrorism, Speech, and R.A.V.: The Constitutionality of Wisconsin's Hate Crimes Statute." NEW YORK LAW SCHOOL JOURNAL OF HUMAN RIGHTS, Vol. 10, Part 2 (Spring 1993): 455-512. Includes argument that lynching is any assault committed with the intent to send a message and does not have to be committed by a mob, and that it is therefore unprotected speech under the First Amendment.

1647. "Change of Name to Avoid Vigilantes Lawful." INTERNATIONAL JURIDICAL ASSOCIATION MONTHLY BULLETIN, Vol. 4, No. 6 (Nov. 1935): 10.

1648. Chaplin, Ralph. "Frank Little and the War." LABOR DEFENDER, Vol. 1, No. 8 (Aug. 1926): 135-36.

1649. Chase, Daniel W. "To Stop Lynching." THE NATION, Vol. 108, No. 2815 (June 14, 1919): 946. Letter.

1650. Cheers, D. Michael. "Time Heals Few Wounds For Emmett Till's Mother." JET, Vol. 66, No. 5 (April 9, 1984): 54-56. He was murdered in Mississippi in 1955.

1651. "Chicago Boy." THE NATION, Vol. 181, No. 12 (Sept. 17, 1955): 234-35. Editorial about Emmett Till, Mississippi murder victim, 1955.

1652. "Chicago's Black Vigilantes." NEWSWEEK, Vol. 78, No. 13 (Sept. 27, 1971): 75, 77. Afro-American Group Attack Team working to drive drug pushers and junkies out of ghetto.

1653. "Chicago's 71st Street is Renamed For Emmett Till." JET, Vol. 80, No. 17 (Aug. 12, 1991): 4-5. Mississippi murder victim, 1955.

1654. "The Churches and Lynchings." THE CHRISTIAN CENTURY, Vol.

47 [sic; should be 48], No. 13 (April 1, 1931): 429.

1655. "Churches Stop a Lynching." THE CHRISTIAN CENTURY, Vol. 54, No. 3 (Jan. 20, 1937): 69.   Dalton, Georgia; January 1937.

1656. "Citizens' War on Crime: Spreading Across U.S." U.S. NEWS & WORLD REPORT, Vol. 68, No. 12 (March 23, 1970): 55-58.   Various groups which "are not vigilantes" (p. 55).

1657. "Civil Liberty Passing." THE MESSENGER, Vol. 5, No. 1 (Jan. 1923): 563.   Annual report of American Civil Liberties Union on mob violence; includes lynching.

1658. Civil Rights Congress.   "'We Charge Genocide.'" MASSES & MAINSTREAM, Vol. 4, No. 5 (May 1951): 22-29.   Introduction to petition about mass murder of blacks in the U.S. (includes lynching).

1659. "Civil Rights in 1960." THE COMMONWEAL, Vol. 71, No. 16 (Jan. 15, 1960): 434.   Mack Charles Parker lynching; Mississippi, 1959.

1660. "Civil Rights Chairman Demands Federal Probe of Miss. Jail Hangings." JET, Vol. 83, No. 23 (April 5, 1993): 28.

1661. "Civil Rights: The Deacons." NEWSWEEK, Vol. 66, No. 5 (Aug. 2, 1965): 28-29.   Black defensive and counter-intimidation organization, here referred to as vigilantes, in the South, especially Bogalusa, Louisiana.

1662. "Civilization in the South." THE CRISIS, Vol. 13, No. 5 (March 1917): 215-16.   Includes lynching.

1663. "Civilization in the United States, 1930." THE CRISIS, Vol. 37, No. 10 (Oct. 1930): 348.   Photo of "lynching of Tom Shipp and Abe Smith at Marion, Indiana, August 7, 'by party or parties unknown.'"

1664. Claiborne, William L. "New Yorkers Fight Back: The Tilt Toward Vigilantism." NEW YORK, Vol. 6, No. 42 (Oct. 15, 1973): 49-53.

1665. Clarke, Edwin L. WHITE WOMEN IN A BIRACIAL SOCIETY. Atlanta: Association of Southern Women for the Prevention of Lynching, 1942.   Only two brief references to lynching in this five-page pamphlet.

1666. Clawar, Stanley S. "Neo-Vigilantism in America: An Analysis of the Jewish Defense League." Ph.D. diss., Bryn Mawr College, 1976.   See Diss. Ab. Intl., Vol. 37, No. 9 (March 1977): 6069A.

1667. "Climate of Fear." THE COMMONWEAL, Vol. 63, No. 2 (Oct. 14, 1955): 28-29.   Till case, Mississippi, 1955.

1668. Cline, Leonard Lanson. "In Darkest Louisiana." THE NATION, Vol. 116, No. 3010 (March 14, 1923): 292-93.   KKK violence as part of rivalry between towns of Bastrop and Mer Rouge. Torture murders of Daniel and Richards.

1669. Cohen, Julius.   "The Screws Case: Federal Protection of Negro Rights." COLUMBIA LAW REVIEW, Vol. 46, No. 1 (Jan. 1946): 94-106. Sheriff Screws and two other officers arrested Robert Hall, black, and beat him to death [Baker County, Georgia].

1670. Cohen, William.   "Riots, Racism, and Hysteria: The Response of Federal Investigative Officials to the Race Riots of 1919." THE MASSA-CHUSETTS REVIEW, Vol. 13, No. 3 (Summer 1972): 373-400.   See page 399 for James E. Cutler and lynching.

1671. Cohn, David L.   WHERE I WAS BORN AND RAISED.   Boston: Houghton Mifflin, 1948.   Part I was published in 1935 as God Shakes Creation. Page 66: white woman gave birth to Negro child; her brother tried to kill her, and the Negro was lynched.

1672. "Col. Lawton on Mob Action."   THE JOURNAL OF SOCIAL FORCES, Vol. 1, No. 5 (Sept. 1923): 589-90.

1673. Coleman, Frank. "Freedom from Fear on the Home Front: Federal Prosecution of 'Village Tyrants' and Lynch-Mobs." IOWA LAW REVIEW, Vol. 29, No. 3 (March 1944): 415-29.   Briefly describes some instances of violence. Deals especially with Sikeston, Missouri, lynching of Cleo Wright (and use made of it by Japanese propagandists).

1674. Coleman, J. Winston, Jr.   DEATH AT THE COURT-HOUSE: AN ACCOUNT OF THE MOB ACTION IN LEXINGTON, KENTUCKY, ON FEBRUARY 9TH, 1920, AND THE EVENTS LEADING UP TO IT. Lexington: Winburn Press, 1952.   Mob stormed court-house to lynch black killer but was repulsed by soldiers, who killed six mob members and wounded many more.

1675. Collins, Winfield H.   THE TRUTH ABOUT LYNCHING AND THE NEGRO IN THE SOUTH IN WHICH THE AUTHOR PLEADS THAT THE SOUTH BE MADE SAFE FOR THE WHITE RACE.   New York: Neale Pub. Co., 1918.

1676. Colman, Louis.   "Protest 3rd Lynch Verdict Against Heywood

Patterson in Shops, Streets, Schools, Churches--Demand Unconditional Safe Release of the Scottsboro Boys--The Lynchers Shall Not Succeed!" LABOR DEFENDER, Vol. 9, No. 11 (Dec. 1933): 79.   Refers to the judge as a lyncher. Claims "46 lynchings already reported this year."

1677. Commission on Interracial Cooperation. BURNT CORK AND CRIME: STORIES SUMMARIZED FROM PRESS REPORTS. Atlanta: Commission on Interracial Cooperation, 193-? Brief pamphlet. Whites sometimes blackened their faces when committing crimes so blacks would be blamed. Or whites would falsely accuse blacks, as in the case of the lynching in 1930 of an innocent black.

1678. Commission on Interracial Cooperation. THE CRIME OF MOB MURDER: A CHALLENGE TO EVERY AMERICAN CITIZEN. Atlanta: Commission on Interracial Cooperation, [1935?].   Brief.

1679. Commission on Interracial Cooperation. THE MOB STILL RIDES: A REVIEW OF THE LYNCHING RECORD, 1931-1935. 2nd ed.; Atlanta: Commission on Interracial Cooperation, 1936.   Page 3: "This little volume, in which Dr. [Arthur F.] Raper summarizes the results of careful studies, made by himself and Prof. Walter Chivers, of the eighty-four lynchings of the past five years."

Committee for the Defense of Civil Rights in Tampa.   See National Committee for the Defense of Civil Rights in Tampa.

1680. "Communal Liability for Mob Violence."   HARVARD LAW REVIEW, Vol. 49, No. 8 (June 1936): 1362-1369.   Includes lynching.

1681. Communist Party of the United States of America (Va.) PUNISH LYNCHERS OF EMMETT TILL: AN OPEN LETTER TO THE PEOPLE OF VIRGINIA.   Broadside.   Univ. of Virginia Library.   He was murdered in Mississippi, 1955.

1682. "'The Compleat Lyncher.'" THE CRISIS, Vol. 13, No. 6 (April 1917): 288-89.

1683. "Concerning Mob Violence." THE CRISIS, Vol. 23, No. 1 (Nov. 1921): 30-32.

1684. "Congress Committee Urged To Include Lynchings In 'Un-American' Probe." INTERRACIAL REVIEW, Vol. 11, No. 7 (July 1938): 112.

1685. Conklin, John E. THE IMPACT OF CRIME. New York: Macmillan, 1975.   See Chap. 8: "Collective Response to Crime: Vigilante

Movements and Civilian Patrol Groups."

1686. "Continue Probe Of Suspected Lynching in Ga." JET, Vol. 11, No. 23 (April 11, 1957): 5.   Victim: Willie Jo Sanford.

1687. "Conviction of Lynchers."   INTERNATIONAL JURIDICAL ASSOCIATION MONTHLY BULLETIN, Vol. 3, No. 8 (Jan. 1935): 2. White killers of Dick Wilkerson, black man, in Tennessee were convicted of manslaughter.

1688. Copeland, Tom. "Wesley Everest, IWW Martyr." PACIFIC NORTH-WEST QUARTERLY, Vol. 77, No. 4 (Oct. 1986): 122-29.   Page 127: Everest was probably not castrated when lynched; John Dos Passos in his novel 1919 first gave the story wide circulation (1932).

1689. Cothran, Ben.   "South of Scottsboro."   THE FORUM AND CENTURY, Vol. 93, No. 6 (June 1935): 323-29. Causes and cures, if any, of white and black maladjustment in the South. Ends with illustration of whites chasing one black man.

1690. "Council Investigates Maryville Lynching." FEDERAL COUNCIL BULLETIN, Vol. 14, No. 3 (March 1931): 10.   Victim: Raymond Gunn, in Missouri.

1691. "County Made to Pay Damages to Widow of Negro Lynched." In NEGRO YEAR BOOK . . . 1921-1922, p. 70.   Ed. by Monroe N. Work. Tuskegee Institute, AL: Negro Year Book Pub. Co., 1922.

1692. Cousins, Norman. "Bystanders Become Active." THE SATURDAY REVIEW OF LITERATURE, Vol. 30, No. 35 (Aug. 30, 1947): 20, 26. Only two sentences on lynching.

1693. Cox, Oliver C. "Lynching and the Status Quo." THE JOURNAL OF NEGRO EDUCATION, Vol. 14, No. 4 (Fall 1945): 576-88.

1694. Crabb, Beth. "May 1930: White Man's Justice for a Black Man's Crime." THE JOURNAL OF NEGRO HISTORY, Vol. 75, No. 1-2 (Winter, Spring 1990): 29-40.   Lynchings of George Hughes in Sherman, Texas; Sam Johnson, at Honey Grove, Texas; and Henry Argo, at Chickasha, Oklahoma.

1695. Crabb, Myra Elizabeth. "The Killing of a Black Man: The Case of George Hughes." M.A. thesis, East Texas State Univ., 1987.   He was lynched at Sherman, Texas, in 1930.

1696. "Crackdown on the Klan." TIME, Vol. 59, No. 8 (Feb. 25, 1952): 28. KKK floggings of blacks and whites in North Carolina.

1697. Crawford, Bruce. "The South versus the C.I.O." NEW MASSES, Vol. 24, No. 11 (Sept. 7, 1937): 6-7.   Subtitle: "The bourbon agents of Wall Street are resorting to every weapon, including 'Divine Providence,' lynch law and even anti-lynch law."

1698. "Crime: Lynch Week." TIME, Vol. 40, No. 17 (Oct. 26, 1942): 23-24. Three lynchings in Mississippi. Victims: two 14-year-old boys (not named) and Howard Wash.

1699. "Crime: Lynchers Due." NEWSWEEK, Vol. 29, No. 9 (March 3, 1947): 26.   Willie Earle case, South Carolina.

1700. "Crime: Rope Over a Limb Takes Care of a Louisiana Negro." NEWS-WEEK [sic], Vol. 4, No. 3 (July 21, 1934): 8.   Victim: Andrew McLeod.

1701. "The Crime of Lynching." In TO SECURE THESE RIGHTS, THE REPORT OF THE PRESIDENT'S COMMITTEE ON CIVIL RIGHTS, pp. 20-25.   U.S. President's Committee on Civil Rights.   Washington, DC: USGPO, 1947; New York: Simon and Schuster, 1947.   Deals largely with lynchings in 1946 and 1947 and with attempted lynchings during 1937-1946.

1702. ["Critic."] "A London Diary."   THE NEW STATESMAN AND NATION [London], Vol. 33, No. 847 (May 31, 1947): 388-89.   Commentary about lynching (slow burning). Also: the acquittal of 28 self-confessed lynchers in the South [Willie Earle case in South Carolina].

1703. Crosswaith, Frank R., and Lewis, Alfred Baker.   "Discrimination, Incorporated." SOCIAL ACTION, Vol. 8, No. 1 (Jan. 15, 1942): 4-37. Includes lynching (pp. 4-6, 8-9).

Cumming, Jos. B.   See Davison, J. H., in this chapter.

1704. Cunard, Nancy, ed. NEGRO ANTHOLOGY MADE BY NANCY CUNARD 1931-1933. Reprint; New York: Negro Universities Press, 1969; originally published in 1934.   Includes: "The American Congo--Burning of Henry Lowry," by William Pickens, pp. 29-31; "A Roman Holiday," by William Pickens, pp. 32-35 (burning of Charley Sheppard); photograph of a different lynching victim, p. 33; "Aftermath of a Lynching," by William Pickens, pp. 35-38 (Marion, Indiana) [photo of 2 lynched blacks at Marion, p. 38]; "Lynching, Terrorisation [sic], Injustice. Cases contributed by the Rev. Clarence Wimley," pp. 176-78; "Furies of Florida," by William Pickens, pp.

178-79 (killing which might be considered a lynching); "Lynching and Murder," pp. 182-84; "Terrorisation [sic] and Violence," pp. 185-88; "Say Preacher Led Mississippi Mob of Lynchers," pp. 193-94; "Scottsboro--and other Scottsboros," by Nancy Cunard, pp. 245-69 (see pp. 248-49 for list of 47 whites and blacks lynched or otherwise murdered, Jan.-June 1933, compiled by International Labor Defense; "Lynching in the Quiet Manner," by Josephine Herbst, pp. 269-71.

1705. Curriden, Mark. "Suicide or Lynching? Human rights commission holds hearings on jail hangings." ABA JOURNAL, Vol. 79 (June 1993): 14. Says "47 people, a majority of them black, . . . have died by hanging in local jails in Mississippi since 1987."

1706. "Curse of Lynching Agitates the Nation." THE LITERARY DIGEST, Vol. 116, No. 24 (Dec. 9, 1933): 5, 34. Governors' responses to lynchings, as in the San Jose, California, case.

1707. "Damages Awarded for Lynching." INTERNATIONAL JURIDICAL ASSOCIATION MONTHLY BULLETIN, Vol. 5, No. 1 (July 1936): 4. Federal court action in case of Freddie Moore, black, Napoleonville, Louisiana.

1708. Damon, Anna. "We Accuse." LABOR DEFENDER, Vol. 10, No. 8 (Aug. 1936): 14-15. Black Legion [Michigan and elsewhere]. With reply from United States Assistant Attorney General.

1709. Daniels, Jonathan. "A Native at Large." THE NATION, Vol. 151, No. 11 (Sept. 14, 1940): 219. Reported decrease in number of lynchings conceals fact that blacks are killed in the South by other methods.

1710. Daniels, Jonathan. "A Native at Large: Lynching without Bloodshed." THE NATION, Vol. 152, No. 6 (Feb. 8, 1941): 158. The "skilled Negro worker has been lynched" by discrimination which has largely eliminated him.

1711. "Darkest Mississippi. An N. A. A. C. P. Investigation." THE CRISIS, Vol. 18, No. 3 (July 1919): 142. About the Delta and nearby regions being a frontier (i.e., "a region not yet fully civilized") where mobs engage in murder, blacks are denied their humanity, and black resentment may cause a catastrophe. Mentions women.

1712. Dashiell, Alfred. "Moscow Comes to Maryland." THE NEW REPUBLIC, Vol. 70, No. 898 (Feb. 17, 1932): 20-21. Letter. Response to lynching of Matthew Williams.

1713. Davis, Horace B. "A Substitute for Lynching." THE NATION, Vol. 130, No. 3365 (Jan. 1, 1930): 12-14.   Reported decrease in number of lynchings conceals fact that blacks in the South are increasingly killed by other means.

1714. Davis, Jack E. "Shades of Justice: The Lynching of Jesse James Payne and Its Aftermath." M.A. thesis, University of South Florida, 1989.   He was lynched in Florida in 1945.

1715. Davis, Jack E. "'Whitewash' in Florida: The Lynching of Jesse James Payne and its Aftermath." THE FLORIDA HISTORICAL QUARTERLY, Vol. 68, No. 3 (Jan. 1990): 277-98.   Lynching of a black man in Oct., 1945, and successful libel trials of Collier's magazine (Governor Caldwell, plaintiff).

1716. Davis, Mike. "Behind the Orange Curtain: Legal Lynching in San Clemente." THE NATION, Vol. 259, No. 14 (Oct. 31, 1994): 485-86, 488, 490.   Murder indictments of six Latino youths in California.

1717. Davison, J. H. "Lynching in the Southern States." THE SPECTA-TOR [London], Vol. 126, No. 4832 (Feb. 5, 1921): 166-67.   Letter from Georgia and an extract from a pamphlet on lynching by Major Jos. B. Cumming.

1718. "Dawn." THE CRISIS, Vol. 13, No. 6 (April 1917): 267-68.   Includes lynching.

1719. "The Deacons Go North." NEWSWEEK, Vol. 67, No. 18 (May 2, 1966): 20-21.   Effort to expand a 'guns-for-Negroes' vigilante organization from the South to Chicago.

1720. "Death Flag." THE CRISIS, Vol. 43, No. 10 (Oct. 1936): cover. Photo showing flag saying, "A Man Was Lynched Yesterday" hanging from a window of NAACP office in New York to mark lynching of A. L. McCamy on Sept. 6, 1936, in Dalton, Georgia.

1721. "Death in Mississippi." THE COMMONWEAL, Vol. 62, No. 25 (Sept. 23, 1955): 603-04.   Emmett Till.

1722. "Death of Picky Pie." TIME, Vol. 53, No. 24 (June 13, 1949): 23. Lists this as "1949's first lynching" but advances no information for more than two killers. He was lynched at Irwinton, Georgia.

1723. "A Decrease in Lynching." THE OUTLOOK, Vol. 134, No. 10 (July 25, 1923): 449.   Includes "The Lynching of Samuel Petty." [It took place at

Leland, Mississippi, in 1914].

1724. "Decrease in Lynchings." AMERICA, Vol. 29, No. 13 (July 14, 1923): 311.   Editorial.   Brief.

1725. "Deep Down Under Lynching." THE WORLD TOMORROW, Vol. 16, No. 29 (Dec. 21, 1933): 678.   Lawlessness and crime are encouraged by the American political, economic, and social system.

1726. "A Defeat for Judge Lynch." THE LITERARY DIGEST, Vol. 105, No. 2 (April 12, 1930): 24.   Black man acquitted of rape in Alabama, and governor stationed solders in and out of courtroom in Montgomery to prevent lynching.

1727. "Defeat Scottsboro Lynchers." LABOR DEFENDER, Vol. 10, No. 1 (Jan. 1934): 2.   Alabama.

1728. "Democracy Versus Demo-n-cracy." THE SURVEY, Vol. 40, No. 18 (Aug. 3, 1918): 511-12.   Several blacks were lynched in May, 1918, in Brooks and Lowndes counties in Georgia.

1729. "Dendy Lynching Unpunished." INTERNATIONAL JURIDICAL ASSOCIATION MONTHLY BULLETIN, Vol. 2, No. 10 (March 1934): 3. South Carolina, 1933.

1730. De Santis, John. FOR THE COLOR OF HIS SKIN: THE MUR- DER OF YUSUF HAWKINS AND THE TRIAL OF BENSONHURST. New York: Pharos Books, 1991.   Hawkins was killed in Brooklyn, New York, in 1989.

1731. "Developments in the Gelders Case." INTERNATIONAL JURIDI- CAL ASSOCIATION MONTHLY BULLETIN, Vol. 5, No. 8 (Feb. 1937): 84.   Alabama.

1732. Devine, Edward T. "Lawlessness." THE CHRISTIAN ADVOCATE [New York], Vol. 106, No. 45 (Nov. 5, 1931): 1347-48.   Includes brief references to lynch law and vigilance committees.

1733. Dew, Lee A. "The Lynching of 'Boll Weevil.'" THE MIDWEST QUARTERLY, Vol. 12, No. 2 (Jan. 1971): 145-53.   Jonesboro, Arkansas, Dec. 1920. "Boll Weevil" was a black man named Wade Thomas.

1734. Dewey, Edward R. "An 8-Year Cycle in Violence--Lynchings in the United States." CYCLES, Vol. 20, No. 1 (Jan. 1969): 15-17.

1735. Dileva, Frank D. "Attempt to Hang Iowa Judge." ANNALS OF IOWA, Third Series, Vol. 32, No. 5 (July 1954): 337-64. Depression violence because of mortgage foreclosures and sales of farms.

1736. "Dishonoring America." AMERICA, Vol. 19, No. 18 (Aug. 10, 1918): 432-33. Editorial. President Wilson on lynch law.

1737. "Dixie Debunks Lynching." THE LITERARY DIGEST, Vol. 111, No. 8 (Nov. 21, 1931): 10. Report of Southern Commission on Lynching [sic].

1738. "Dixie Justice." NEGRO DIGEST, Vol. 2, No. 2 (Dec. 1943): 6. Includes two lynching jokes.

1739. "Do Lynching Pictures Create Race Hatred?" THE CRISIS, Vol. 44, No. 2 (Feb. 1937): 61.

1740. "Do Lynching Pictures Create Race Hatred?" THE CRISIS, Vol. 44, No. 3 (March 1937): 93. Letters from readers.

1741. "A Document the Nation Should Read." THE CHRISTIAN CENTURY, Vol. 51, No. 1 (Jan 3, 1934): 10. Document: "The Plight of Tuscaloosa," [Alabama] about lynchings there. Issued by Southern Commission on the Study of Lynchings.

1742. Doran, J. T. "Murder in Centralia." THE LIBERATOR [New York], Vol. 3, No. 2 (Feb. 1920): 16-18. Wesley Everest was lynched in Washington state.

1743. Dos Passos, John. "Scottsboro's Testimony." LABOR DEFENDER, Vol. 6, No. 7 (July 1931): 131. Some references to lynching.

1744. "Double Murder in Mississippi." THE CHRISTIAN CENTURY, Vol. 72, No. 40 (Oct. 5, 1955): 1132. Victims: Emmett Till and "Mississippi justice in the ensuing trial."

1745. Dowd, Wilbur J. "Vigilance Committees." THE FORUM, Vol. 85, No. 5 (May 1931): xxviii-xxix. Letter advocating vigilance committees for combating organized crime.

1746. Dreiser, Theodore. "Lynching Negro Children in Southern Courts." LABOR DEFENDER, Vol. 6, No. 6 (June 1931): 108-09. Scottsboro case in Alabama. See ad on back page of this issue: "Stop the Scottsboro Legal Lynching of 9 Negro Boys."

1747. DuBois, W. E. B. "Aiken." THE CRISIS, Vol. 34, No. 1 (March 1927): 34.   Outrage that South Carolina lynchers in Aiken will not be punished.

1748. DuBois, W. E. B. "The Governors." THE CRISIS, Vol. 19, No. 1 (Nov. 1919): 336.   "The most prevalent crime in the United States that provokes mob violence is the crime of being black."

1749. DuBois, W. E. B. "The Migration of Negroes." THE CRISIS, Vol. 14, No. 2 (June 1917): 63-66.   Cites mob violence in the South as one reason blacks moved to the North.

1750. DuBois, W. E. B. "Postscript." THE CRISIS, Vol. 34, No. 6 (Aug. 1927): 203-04.   Page 203 includes a section entitled "Lynchings," saying the U.S. government seems uninterested in the recent burning alive of black people in Louisville, MS, who aroused white wrath by driving too slowly. Includes a section entitled "Mob Tactics," about how blacks are unfairly victimized; urges blacks to use firearms to defend themselves.

1751. DuBois, W. E. B. "Postscript." THE CRISIS, Vol. 39 [sic; should be 38], No. 4 (April 1931): 138.   Hope that Southern Commission on the study of lynching will examine causes honestly.

1752. DuBois, W. E. B. "Postscript: The Athens of Texas." THE CRISIS, Vol. 37, No. 7 (July 1930): 245-46.   Quotes Heywood Broun's column on lynching in Sherman, Texas; inspired by Atlanta Constitution defense of a mob.

1753. DuBois, W. E. B. "Postscript: Coffeeville, Kansas." THE CRISIS, Vol. 34, No. 5 (July 1927): 167.   Riot because of attempted lynching of a black man.

1754. DuBois, W. E. B. "Postscript: Lynch Laws." THE CRISIS, Vol. 41 [sic; should be 39], No. 5 (May 1932): 158.   Letter from Tom Mooney requesting copy of lynching article from The Crisis, 1918.   Mooney's California conviction had nothing to do with lynching, unless one calls it a legal lynching.

1755. DuBois, W. E. B. "Postscript: Lynching." THE CRISIS, Vol. 35, No. 9 (Sept. 1928): 312.   Presents photo of nameless black man lynched in Florida.

1756. DuBois, W. E. B. "Postscript: Lynchings." THE CRISIS, Vol. 41 [sic; should be 39], No. 2 (Feb. 1932): 58.   Report of Southern Commission on the Study of Lynching.

1757. DuBois, W. E. B. "Postscript: Marion." THE CRISIS, Vol. 37, No. 10 (Oct. 1930): 353.   Two black men lynched in Marion, Indiana.

1758. DuBois, W. E. B. "Postscript: Misrepresentation." THE CRISIS, Vol. 40 [sic; should be 38], No. 5 (May 1931): 171.   Includes statistics on lynchings in Georgia, 1930.

1759. DuBois, W. E. B. "Postscript: Mob Tactics." THE CRISIS, Vol. 34, No. 6 (Aug. 1927): 204.   References to lynching and rioting.

1760. DuBois, W. E. B. "Postscript: Violence." THE CRISIS, Vol. 41, No. 5 (May 1934): 147-48.   Opposes use of violence by blacks to gain rights.

1761. "DuBois, W. E. B. "Rape." THE CRISIS, Vol. 18, No. 1 (May 1919): 12-13.   "The charge of rape against colored Americans was invented by the white South after Reconstruction to excuse mob violence." Rape is alleged in less than one-fourth of cases of lynched blacks.

1762. DuBois, W. E. B.; Garfield, John; Hammerstein, Oscar, II, et. al. AMERICAN CRUSADE TO END LYNCHING.   Throw-away pamphlet, 1946. In "Lynching" folder, Schomburg Collection, New York City Public Library.

1763. "Duck Hill Lynchings." INTERNATIONAL JURIDICAL ASSOCIA-TION MONTHLY BULLETIN, Vol. 5, No. 11 (May 1937): 127.   Missis-sippi.

1764. Dudley, J. Wayne. "'Hate' Organizations of the 1940s: The Colum-bians, Inc." PHYLON, Vol. 42, No. 3 (Sept. 1981): 262-74.   Increased racial tensions after World War II, exemplified by lynchings and riots, led to emergence of racist groups.

1765. Duffus, Robert L. "How the Ku Klux Klan Sells Hate." THE WORLD'S WORK, Vol. 46, No. 2 (June 1923): 174-83.   See pp. 174-76 for Aug. 24, 1922, Mer Rouge, Louisiana, mob murders of white men Watt Daniel and Tom Richards.

1766. "Duluth." THE CRISIS, Vol. 20, No. 4 (Aug. 1920): 179.   Activities of St. Paul and Minneapolis branches of NAACP in investigating lynching of three blacks recently at Duluth.

1767. "Duluth." THE CRISIS, Vol. 20, No. 5 (Sept. 1920): 231.   Three blacks were lynched there on June 15.

1768. "The Duluth Cases," THE CRISIS, Vol. 21, No. 4 (Feb. 1921): 165-66.

1769. Dunne, William F. "August, 1917, in Butte: The Murder of Frank Little." LABOR DEFENDER, Vol. 1, No. 8 (Aug. 1926): 123-24, 142-43.

1770. Ebony, The Editors of. THE NEGRO HANDBOOK. Chicago: Johnson Pub. Co., 1966. See pp. 75-82, "Civil Rights Murders: 1964-1965."

1771. "Editorial." THE CHRISTIAN ADVOCATE, Vol. 107, No. 34 (Aug. 25, 1932): 883.   Criticism of conditions in foreign countries is nullified by U.S. lynching record.

1772. "Editorial." THE LAWYER AND BANKER AND SOUTHERN BENCH AND BAR REVIEW, Vol. 19, No. 2 (March-April 1926): 66-69. Lynch law.

1773. "Editorial Comment." THE CATHOLIC WORLD, Vol. 138 (Feb. 1934): 521-23.   Governor Ritchie and the recent lynching in Maryland.

1774. "Editorial Comment: Mobs Governors Citizens." THE CATHOLIC WORLD, Vol. 138 (Jan. 1934): 385-90.   San Jose, CA, lynchings.

1775. "Editorial of the Month." THE CRISIS, Vol. 42, No. 1 (Jan. 1935): 19.   St. Augustine, Florida, Record supports Wagner-Costigan bill.

1776. "Editorial of the Month: Lynching." INTERRACIAL REVIEW, Vol. 10, No. 9 (Sept. 1937): 130.   Four lynchings in first six months of 1937. From The Observer, Pittsburgh.

1777. "Editorial of the Week." INTERRACIAL REVIEW, Vol. 8, No. 11 (Nov. 1935): 175.   From Washington Daily News. Brief.

1778. "Editorial of the Week." INTERRACIAL REVIEW, Vol. 10, No. 5 (May 1937): 79.   Danville, Virginia, Register reverses itself and favors federal anti-lynching law because of blow-torch lynchings at Duck Hill, Mississippi.

1779. "Editorials." THE CRISIS, Vol. 43, No. 1 (Jan. 1936): 17.   Several items on lynching.

1780. Edmonds, Henry M. "THE COST OF THE MOB." Atlanta: Commission on Interracial Cooperation, [1933?].   Pamphlet; 7 pages. Reprinted from Birmingham Age-Herald, Oct. 8, 1933. Title page also includes heading "LET 'ER BURN DOWN; THE TAXPAYERS WILL PUT 'ER BACK!" Sermon on "The Cost of Lynching," with extensive quotations from Raper, The Tragedy of Lynching.

1781. Edwards, John Carver. "America's Vigilantes and the Great War, 1916-1918." ARMY QUARTERLY AND DEFENCE JOURNAL [Great Britain], Vol. 106, No. 3 (July 1976): 277-86.

1782. Egerton, John. "A case of prejudice: Maurice Mays and the Knoxville Race Riot of 1919." SOUTHERN EXPOSURE, Vol. 11, No. 4 (July/Aug. 1983): 56-65.   Arrest of innocent black man for murder of white woman caused riot by white lynch mob.

1783. "Eighty Per Cent of Lynchings For Crimes Other Than Rape." In NEGRO YEAR BOOK . . . 1921-1922, p. 72. Ed. by Monroe N. Work. Tuskegee Institute, AL: Negro Year Book Pub. Co., 1922.

1784. Eleazer, R. B. "Judge Lynch and His Court." THE SOUTHERN WORKMAN, Vol. 61, No. 2 (Feb. 1932): 60-64.   Summary of Commission on Interracial Cooperation's report "Lynchings and What They Mean."

1785. Elliff, John T. "Aspects of Federal Civil Rights Enforcement: The Justice Department and the FBI, 1939-1964." In PERSPECTIVES IN AMERICAN HISTORY, Vol. 5, pp. 603-73. Ed. by Donald Fleming and Bernard Bailyn. Cambridge: Charles Warren Center for Studies in American History, Harvard Univ., 1971.

1786. Elliott, Lawrence. "Day Judge Lynch Cried Hang!" CORONET, Vol. 40, No. 2 (June 1956): 113-17.   San Jose, California, lynchings.

1787. Ellison, Ralph. "Judge Lynch in New York." NEW MASSES, Vol. 32, No. 8 (Aug. 15, 1939): 15-16.   Various beatings of blacks in Washington Heights section for purpose of confining them to Harlem.

1788. Emmart, A. D. "Lynching and Mob Rule." THE SPECTATOR [London], Vol. 151, No. 5502 (Dec. 8, 1933): 841-42.   Deals with the U.S.

1789. "The Emmett Till Case." LOOK, Vol. 20, No. 5 (March 6, 1956): 12. Letters to the editor.   Till was murdered in Mississippi, 1955.

1790. "Emmett Till's Day in Court." LIFE, Vol. 39, No. 14 (Oct. 3, 1955): 36-38.   Acquittal of his alleged killers, Bryant and Milam.

1791. "Emmett Till's Mother Remembers Her Son On His 50th Birthday." JET, Vol. 80, No. 17 (Aug. 12, 1991): 6, 10.   Till was murdered in Mississippi, 1955.

1792. "Employer-Vigilante-Police Conspiracy Held Outside Scope of Federal Constitutional Protection."   INTERNATIONAL JURIDICAL

ASSOCIATION MONTHLY BULLETIN, Vol. 7, No. 1 (July 1938): 161.

1793. Engdahl, J. Louis. "On Bread and Water." LABOR DEFENDER, Vol. 5, No. 9 (Sept. 1930): 175-76.   Includes lynching as an example of "capitalist class justice."

1794. "Estill Springs Burning." THE CRISIS, Vol. 15, No. 6 (April 1918): 281-82.   Telegram from NAACP to President Wilson about the burning at the stake of Jim M'IlKeron [sic] in Tennessee on Lincoln's birthday, 1918.

1795. Evanier, David.   "Invisible Man: The Lynching of Yankel Rosenbaum." THE NEW REPUBLIC, Vol. 205, No. 16 (Oct. 14, 1991): 21-26. He was murdered by blacks in Crown Heights, Brooklyn, New York.

1796. "Extracts from Letters." THE NEW REPUBLIC, Vol. 77, No. 995 (Dec. 27, 1933): 199.   Two statements on San Jose, CA, lynchings.

1797. "Extradition Cases." THE CRISIS, Vol. 20, No. 1 (May 1920): 5. Black man extradited from Michigan arrived back in Kentucky on Monday and was lynched on Tuesday.

1798. "Extra-Legal Violence Against Minorities." EQUAL JUSTICE, Vol. 15, No. 3 (Winter 1941): 50-52.   Includes details of lynchings in 1939, 1940, 1941, and a map.

1799. "The Facts about Lynching." FEDERAL COUNCIL BULLETIN, Vol. 7, No. 2 (Mar.-Apr. 1924): 8.

1800. Fairclough, Adam. "Racial Repression in World War Two: The New Iberia Incident." LOUISIANA HISTORY, Vol. 32, No. 2 (Spring 1991): 183-207.   A dozen blacks were run out of this Louisiana town in May, 1944. Second sentence says one was beaten so much that he soon died--but this is never referred to in the rest of the article. See pp. 205-06 for causes of decline of lynching.

1801. Faris, Robert E. L. SOCIAL DISORGANIZATION. New York: Ronald Press Co., 1948.   See "Lynchings" (pp. 386-88) and "The Leeville Affair: an Account of a Lynching" (pp. 388-93), which is drawn from Pruden, "A Texas Lynching." See Pruden in this chapter.

1802. "Farm Riots: Martial Law in Turbulent Iowa Counties After Mobbing of Judge and Deputies." NEWS-WEEK [sic], Vol. 1, No. 12 (May 6, 1933): 9.   See Dileva, Frank D., in this chapter.

1803. Farrell, Harry. SWIFT JUSTICE: MURDER AND VENGEANCE

IN A CALIFORNIA TOWN. New York: St. Martin's Press, 1992.   San Jose lynching of Holmes and Thurmond, Nov. 1933.

1804. "Federal Action Coming Against Lynching." THE CHRISTIAN CENTURY, Vol. 51, No. 46 (Nov. 14, 1934): 1444-45.   Recent lynching at Greenwood, Florida, with advance publicity, no official effort to prevent it, picnic and political-campaign atmosphere. [See "Lynching in the Raw," ibid., Vol. LII, No. 1 (Jan. 2, 1935): 10-11, to see the Claude Neal lynching stated as having occurred "in Greenwood, Florida."]

1805. "A Federal Campaign Against Mob Violence." THE SURVEY, Vol. 40, No. 8 (May 25, 1918): 225-26.   Lynching of Prager at Collinsville, IL.

1806. "Federal Council Denounces Florida Lynching." THE CHRISTIAN CENTURY, Vol. 51, No. 46 (Nov. 14, 1934): 1461.   Dr. Cavert, General Secretary of Federal Council of Churches, protested Marianna, Florida, lynching to Governor David Sholtz.   One paragraph.

1807. Federal Council of the Churches of Christ in America.   MOB MURDER IN AMERICA: THE CHALLENGE WHICH LYNCHING BRINGS TO THE CHURCHES.   New York: Federal Council of the Churches of Christ in America, 1923.

1808. Federal Council of the Churches of Christ in America, Department of Research and Education; National Catholic Welfare Conference, Social Action Department; Central Conference of American Rabbis, Social Justice Commission.   THE CENTRALIA CASE: A JOINT REPORT ON THE ARMISTICE DAY TRAGEDY AT CENTRALIA, WASHINGTON, NOVEMBER 11, 1919. [New York: Brooklyn Eagle Press], 1930.

1809. "Federal Court Gives Award To Lynch Victims." THE CATHOLIC WORKER, Vol. 7, No. 9 (June 1940): 3.   Blacks who were beaten in Cranbury, New Jersey, Aug. 1939.

1810. "The Federal Government Tackles The Custom of Lynching--1943." THE SOUTHERN FRONTIER, Vol. 4, No. 7 (July 1943): [1-2].

1811. "Federal Grand Jury Indicts Mississippi Lynchers." THE SOUTH-ERN FRONTIER, Vol. 4, No. 1 (Jan. 1943): [p. 1].

1812. Fedo, Michael W. "THEY WAS JUST NIGGERS." Ontario, CA: Brasch and Brasch, 1979.   Three blacks were lynched in Duluth, MN, 1920.

1813. "Fewer Lynchings." THE LITERARY DIGEST, Vol. 68, No. 4 (Jan. 22, 1921): 15-16.   Commentary on 61 lynchings in 1920 compared to 83 in

1919.   Extensive quotation from editorial in San Antonio <u>Express</u>.

1814.   "The Fight in Texas Against Lynching."   THE WORLD'S WORK, Vol. 37, No. 6 (April 1919): 615-16.

1815.   "Fight Lynch Law."   LABOR DEFENDER, Vol. 9, No. 11 (Dec. 1933): 74, 93.   "The appeal of Governor Rolph [California] to lynch violence places the open sanction of high authority upon this fascist weapon of the ruling class."

1816.   "First Lynching in 1935."   INTERNATIONAL JURIDICAL ASSOCIATION MONTHLY BULLETIN, Vol. 3, No. 9 (Feb. 1935): 2. Brief paragraph.   Jerome Wilson at Franklinton, Louisiana.   Citation to Louisiana Supreme Court decision.

1817.   "First Lynching of the Year."   INTERNATIONAL JURIDICAL ASSOCIATION MONTHLY BULLETIN, Vol. 5, No. 9 (March 1937): 99. Wes Johnson, black, near Abbeyville [sic], Alabama.

1818.   "The First 1934 Lynching."   THE LITERARY DIGEST, Vol. 117, No. 6 (Feb. 10, 1934): 16.   Black man named Rex Scott, in Kentucky.

1819.   "The First War-Lynching."   THE LITERARY DIGEST, Vol. 57, No. 3 (April 20, 1918): 16-17.   Lynching on April 4, 1918, in Collinsville, IL, of Robert Prager for allegedly seditious remarks.

1820.   Fitelson, H. William.   "The Murders at Monroe."   THE NEW REPUBLIC, Vol. 115, No. 9 (Sept. 2, 1946): 258-60.   Recent lynching of Roger Malcolm and three other blacks in Georgia.

1821.   "Florida."   THE CRISIS, Vol. 32, No. 5 (Sept. 1926): 246-47.   Includes one lynching item.

1822.   "Florida ILD Fights Lynch Whitewash."   EQUAL JUSTICE, Vol. 13, No. 4 (June 1939): 5.   Two brothers shot Lee Snell, black, who was in police custody.

1823.   "Florida Lynching."   INTERNATIONAL JURIDICAL ASSOCIATION MONTHLY BULLETIN, Vol. 4, No. 2 (July 1935): 2.   Rubin Stacey, black.

1824.   "Florida Lynching."   INTERNATIONAL JURIDICAL ASSOCIATION MONTHLY BULLETIN, Vol. 9, No. 12 (June 1941): 135.   Two separate efforts on separate days to kill A. C. Williams, black.

1825. "Florida's Third Lynching." INTERNATIONAL JURIDICAL ASSOCIATION MONTHLY BULLETIN, Vol. 6, No. 5 (Nov. 1937): 57. J. C. Evans, black.

1826. "Flouting the Law." THE PUBLIC, Vol. 22, No. 1113 (Aug. 2, 1919): 816.   Argument against lynching.

1827. "Foiled Lynchers Burn A Courthouse." THE CHRISTIAN CENTURY, Vol. 52, No. 1 (Jan. 2, 1935): 4.   Shelbyville, Tennessee.

1828. Foner, Philip S., and Lewis, Ronald L., eds.   THE BLACK WORKER FROM THE FOUNDING OF THE CIO TO THE AFL-CIO MERGER, 1936-1955. Vol. VII of THE BLACK WORKER: A DOCUMENTARY HISTORY FROM COLONIAL TIMES TO THE PRESENT. 8 Vols.; Philadelphia: Temple U.P., 1978-1984.   See Part I, #76: "Brophy Raps Lynching at Negro Parley."

1829. "For Everything Except Lynching." THE CRISIS, Vol. 41, No. 9 (Sept. 1934): 268.   Federal government acts in all ways to make U.S. better except regarding lynching.

1830. "For Hanging Judge Lynch." THE LITERARY DIGEST, Vol. 105, No. 7 (May 17, 1930): 26.   Lynchings in the South.

1831. Forster, Henry A. "Do Our Laws Protect Criminals? Why the United States Leads the World in the Relative Proportion of Murders, Lynchings and Other Felonies, and Why the Anglo-Saxon Countries Not Under the American Flag Have the Least Proportion of Murders and Felonies and Know No Lynchings." THE AMERICAN LAW REVIEW, Vol. 51, [No. 2] (March-April 1917): 239-48.

1832. Forster, Henry A. "Our Criminals: Why the United States Leads the World in the Relative Proportion of Murders, Lynchings and Other Felonies, and Why the Anglo-Saxon Countries Not Under the American Flag Have the Least Proportion of Murders and Felonies and Know No Lynchings." DOCKET, Vol. 2, No. 341 (Nov. 1917): 1875-78, 1880.   This article is virtually identical to that in the immediately preceding entry.

1833. Forster, Henry A. "Why the United States Leads the World in the Relative Proportion of Murders, Lynchings and Other Felonies, and Why the Anglo-Saxon Countries Not Under the American Flag Have the Least Proportion of Murders and Felonies and Know No Lynchings." CENTRAL LAW JOURNAL, Vol. 85, No. 17 (Oct. 26, 1917): 299-304.   This article is basically the same as those listed in the two immediately preceding entries.

1834. [Forster] Foster, Henry A. "Our Criminals. Why the United States Leads the World." CHICAGO LEGAL NEWS, Vol. 51, No. 36 (April 3, 1919): 283-84, 286.

1835. Fort, John P. "II.--The Mind of the Lynching Mob." THE FORUM, Vol. 76, No. 6 (Dec. 1926): 818-22.   Part of "Is Lynching Ever Defensible?" The other part (pp. 811-17) is by George W. Chamblee.

1836. "Forty-Four Lynched Upholding Tradition."   THE SOUTHERN FRONTIER, Vol. 2, No. 1 (Jan. 1941): [3].

1837. "4 Lynchings, or Only 2?" THE SOUTHERN FRONTIER, Vol. 3, No. 1 (Jan. 1942): [2].

1838. "Four Months Without Lynchings." THE LITERARY DIGEST, Vol. 97, No. 9 (June 2, 1928): 9.

1839. "468th & 469th; 248th." TIME, Vol. 27, No. 19 (May 11, 1936): 19. Lynchings in Georgia and Arkansas. Black victims: Lint Shaw, John Ruskin [sic], Willie Kees.

1840. "A Fourteen Point Indictment of Lynching."   INTERRACIAL REVIEW, Vol. 10, No. 4 (April 1937): 51-52.

1841. "Fourteenth Annual Convention." THE CRISIS, Vol. 26, No. 6 (Oct. 1923): 259-62.   Pages 259-61 include lynching remarks by Representative Dyer and some details about lynchings during the first six months of 1923.

1842. Francis, John L. "Again the Till Case." LOOK, Vol. 20, No. 6 (March 20, 1956): 25.   Letter. He was murdered in Mississippi, 1955.

1843. Franklin, John Hope.   RACE AND HISTORY: SELECTED ESSAYS, 1938-1988.   Baton Rouge: Louisiana State Univ. Press, 1989. See p. 281 for three sentences about lynching of Cordie Cheek, black student at Fisk University, Nashville, 1933, because he slightly injured a white child while riding his bicycle.

1844. "Frightfulness at Home." THE BELLMAN, Vol. 24, No. 614 (April 20, 1918): 425-26.   "Patriotic" violence in support of war effort, including tarring and feathering.

1845. Fuller, Tony. "Marshals of Southie." NEWSWEEK, Vol. 87, No. 21 (May 24, 1976): 30.   Citizen patrols in racial violence area of South Boston, Massachusetts. Referred to as vigilantes.

1846. Fulton, Vera. "Aristocracy on the Eastern Shore." THE NEW REPUBLIC, Vol. 78, No. 1007 (March 21, 1934): 162.   Letter regarding Gerald W. Johnson's Dec. 20 article.

1847. "Further Lynchings in Mississippi." INTERNATIONAL JURIDICAL ASSOCIATION MONTHLY BULLETIN, Vol. 4, No. 2 (July 1935): 2. Bert Moore and Morton Dooley, blacks, in Columbus.

1848. Gardner, Virginia. "Slow Lynching in Baltimore." NEW MASSES, Vol. 61, No. 6 (Nov. 5, 1946): 9-12.   Some bad things about life in areas where blacks are segregated; also, some paragraphs on actual lynchings and "legal lynchings."

1849. Garris, Susan P. "The Decline of Lynching in South Carolina, 1915-1947." M.A. thesis, Univ. of South Carolina, 1973.

1850. "Gelders Flogged." INTERNATIONAL JURIDICAL ASSOCIA-TION MONTHLY BULLETIN, Vol. 5, No. 5 (Nov. 1936): 53. Birming-ham, Alabama.

1851. Gellhorn, Martha. "Justice at Night." THE SPECTATOR [London], Vol. 157, No. 5,643 (Aug. 21, 1936): 304-05.   Eyewitness account of Hyacinth's lynching in Mississippi, Sept. [19??]. Condensed, with same title, in Reader's Digest, Vol. 30, No. 179 (March 1937): 43-46.

1852. "General Race News." THE HALF-CENTURY MAGAZINE, Vol. 2, No. 6 (June 1917): 9. Bishop Gailor (Episcopal) of Memphis told white congregation "so long as they made no effort to stop the lynching and mobbing that they were guilty of murder."

1853. "General Race News." THE HALF-CENTURY MAGAZINE, Vol. 6, No. 3 (March 1919): 10.   Representative Saunders of North Carolina introduced bill to abolish capital punishment and argued that lynchings are encouraged by capital punishment.

1854. "General Race News." THE HALF-CENTURY MAGAZINE, Vol. 7, No. 1 (July 1919): 15.   First four paragraphs are about lynching.

1855. "General Race News." THE HALF-CENTURY MAGAZINE, Vol. 7, No. 5 (Nov. 1919): 8. Federal Council of Churches of Christ in America has announced program against mob violence.

1856. "General Race News." THE HALF-CENTURY MAGAZINE, Vol. 7, No. 6 (Dec. 1919): 8. White preacher in Pine Bluff, AR, who endorsed lynching in his sermon was interrupted by congregation and told to leave.

1857. "General Race News." THE HALF-CENTURY MAGAZINE, Vol. 8, No. 2 (Feb. 1920): 8. Lynching is the 7th agenda item for a Lincoln League of America convention in Chicago, Feb. 11-12, 1920.

1858. "General Race News." THE HALF-CENTURY MAGAZINE, Vol. 9, No. 2 (Aug.-Sept. 1920): 8. Harding's and Coolidge's acceptance speeches oppose lynching.

1859. "General Race News." THE HALF-CENTURY MAGAZINE, Vol. 14, No. 3 (May-June 1923): 9. Blacks in Mississippi recently held mass meeting to explain exodus to whites. Reasons: poor schools, low wages, lynching, no service, disfranchisement.

1860. "General Race News." THE HALF-CENTURY MAGAZINE, Vol. 16, No. 2 (March-April 1924): 8. Decline in lynching due to migration, Dyer bill, and publicity.

1861. George, Paul S. "Colored Town: Miami's Black Community, 1896-1930." THE FLORIDA HISTORICAL QUARTERLY, Vol. 56, No. 4 (April 1978): 432-47. Includes 1923 lynching of two blacks near Homestead, Florida.

1862. Georgia. Governor, 1917-1921 (Hugh M. Dorsey). A STATEMENT FROM GOVERNOR HUGH M. DORSEY AS TO THE NEGRO IN GEORGIA. [Atlanta?: Committee on Race Relations for Georgia?, 1921.] Has 135 cases of lynching and other outrages against blacks in Georgia.

1863. "Georgia: 'Just Another Killing.'" TIME, Vol. 52, No. 23 (Dec. 6, 1948): 23. Robert Mallard, black, was shot by "white-robed men."

1864. "Georgia Lynching." INTERNATIONAL JURIDICAL ASSOCIATION MONTHLY BULLETIN, Vol. 4, No. 11 (April 1936): 3. Philip Baker, black, near Cusseta.

1865. "Georgia Needs the Marines, Too." NEW MASSES, Vol. 4, No. 1 (June 1928): 13. Photo of black lynching victim.

1866. "Georgia: The Best People Won't Talk." TIME, Vol. 48, No. 6 (Aug. 5, 1946): 25. One black man lynched for voting; two black couples lynched.

1867. "Georgia: Trial by Jury." NEWSWEEK, Vol. 33, No. 4 (Jan. 24, 1949): 20, 23. White man was acquitted for lynching black man named Robert Mallard. Two jurors testified for defense.

1868. "Georgia's Body-Blow at Mob Murder." THE LITERARY DIGEST,

Vol. 91, No. 10 (Dec. 4, 1926): 10.   Life sentence for the white leader of a mob that lynched a white man.

1869. "Georgia's Indictment." THE SURVEY, Vol. 46, No. 6 (May 7, 1921): 183, 190-91.   Governor's concern about various racist actions against blacks, including mob violence.

1870. "Georgians Convict Lynchers." THE CRISIS, Vol. 50, No. 11 (Nov. 1943): 327.

1871. Gillard, John T. "Can Law Stop Lynching?" THE COMMON-WEAL, Vol. 19, No. 9 (Dec. 29, 1933): 235-37.

1872. Gillard, John T. "Lynching and Lunching." THE COMMONWEAL, Vol. 20, No. 4 (May 25, 1934): 95-97.

1873. Gillard, John T. "Lynching and the Law." THE COMMONWEAL, Vol. 19, No. 7 (Dec. 15, 1933): 175-77.

1874. Gillis, James M.   "Participants in Lynching Are Murderers." INTERRACIAL REVIEW, Vol. 9, No. 1 (Jan. 1936): 16.

1875. Gilmore, Eddie. "The Reporter and the Mob." In NEWS STORIES OF 1933: A COLLECTION OF SOME OF THE BEST NEWS AND FEATURE STORIES OF VARIOUS TYPES WHICH APPEARED AMERICAN NEWSPAPERS IN 1933, pp. 127-30. Ed. by Frank Luther Mott. Iowa City: Clio Press, 1934.   Mob in Salisbury [Maryland] stormed hotel in effort to attack seven newsmen and photographers. Mob had forced soldiers to leave Salisbury.

1876. Gilmour, Austin. "Lynching in America." VANITY FAIR, Vol. 44, No. 4 (June 1935): 17, 62.   Condensed as "Mob Murder" in Reader's Digest, Vol. 28, No. 167 (March 1936): 83-85. Includes 1931 lynching of Raymond Gunn in Maryville, Missouri.

1877. "Going After the Klan." NEWSWEEK, Vol. 109, No. 8 (Feb. 23, 1987): 29.   Verdict in case of Michael Donald, lynched in Alabama, 1981.

1878. Gold, Michael. "Lynchers in Frockcoats." NEW MASSES, Vol. 3, No. 5 (Sept. 1927): 6.   Sacco and Vanzetti case in Massachusetts.

1879. "A Good Negro." THE CRISIS, Vol. 25, No. 4 (Feb. 1923): 183-84. A black man in North Carolina was whipped by a white mob which seems to have thought he supported Dyer Anti-Lynching Bill and was organizing blacks.

1880. "Good News on Lynching." COLLIER'S, Vol. 121, No. 7 (Feb. 14, 1948): 82.

1881. Goolrick, William K. "Dixie Town's Feud with the FBI." LIFE, Vol. 46, No. 22 (June 1, 1959): 24-25.   See also "The Feds vs. Gangland Lynchland," ibid., p. 19. Poplarville, Mississippi, and Mack Parker case, 1959.

1882. Gould, Benjamin. "San Jose Ministers on Lynching." THE CHRISTIAN CENTURY, Vol. 50, No. 52 (Dec. 20, 1933): 1611-12.   Letter, with enclosure. California.

1883. "Governor Lynch and His Mob." THE NATION, Vol. 137, No. 3571 (Dec. 13, 1933): 666 (with cartoon on p. 667).   California governor's approval of San Jose double lynching and expected results.

1884. "The Governor of Kentucky." AMERICA, Vol. 16, No. 16 (Jan. 27, 1917): 377-78.   He went to Murray to prevent a lynching. Editorial.

1885. Gray, Frank H. "'Just Another Negro Dead.'" THE SOUTHERN FRONTIER, Vol. 2, No. 7 (July 1941): [pp. 3-4].   Includes: "For every one Negro lynched during the past several years, more than a thousand Negroes have been killed by other Negroes."

1886. Gray, R. L. "Winning the War on Lynching." THE WORLD'S WORK, Vol. 50, No. 5 (Sept. 1925): 507-11.

1887. "The Great American Specialty." THE CRISIS, Vol. 27, No. 4 (Feb. 1924): 168.   The record of lynchings in 1923, with a map.

1888. "The Great American Specialty: Lynchings of 1923." THE CRISIS, Vol. 27, No. 4 (Feb. 1924): 168.

1889. "The Great American Sport." THE CRISIS, Vol. 20, No. 1 (May 1920): 45.   Refers to Beulah Amidon Ratliff's article in April Atlantic Monthly of a "nigger chase" in Mississippi which resulted in lynching of a black man.

1890. "Greenville After the Willie Earle Lynching: A Community Struggles to Change." CAROLOGUE: A PUBLICATION OF THE SOUTH CAROLINA HISTORICAL SOCIETY, Vol. 8, No. 4 (Winter 1992): 6. Introduction to papers from a symposium held at Furman University, Nov. 1990. Earle was lynched in South Carolina in 1947.

1891. Gregg, James E. "Lynching: A National Menace." THE SOUTH-

ERN WORKMAN, Vol. 48, No. 7 (July 1919): 329-30. Separate reprint which includes several additional sentences: Lynching: A National Menace--The White South's Protest Against Lynching (Hampton, VA: Press of Hampton Normal and Agricultural Institute, [1919]).

1892. Gregg, Richard B. "Following a Lynching." THE CHRISTIAN CENTURY, Vol. 51, No. 45 (Nov. 7, 1934): 1426. Letter. After every lynching whites should contribute money or service to help blacks.

1893. Griffin, Larry J. "Narrative, Event-Structure Analysis, and Causal Interpretation in Historical Sociology." AMERICAN JOURNAL OF SOCIOLOGY, Vol. 98, No. 5 (March 1993): 1094-1133. Abstract: "Through . . . [the lynching of David Harris, black] in Mississippi in 1930, this article shows how event-structure analysis can be used to build replicable and generalizable causal interpretations of events."

1894. Grill, Johnpeter Horst, and Jenkins, Robert L. "The Nazis and the American South in the 1930s: A Mirror Image?" THE JOURNAL OF SOUTHERN HISTORY, Vol. 58, No. 4 (Nov. 1992): 667-94. Includes responses in Germany to lynchings (pp. 671, 674, 676) and Southern newspaper responses to relation of lynchings to Germany (p. 686).

1895. "The Grim Facts." EQUAL JUSTICE, Vol. 16, No. 3 (Summer 1942): 2-10. Survey of recent violence against blacks, including lynching.

1896. "Growing Sentiment Against Mob Action." THE JOURNAL OF SOCIAL FORCES, Vol. 1, No. 5 (Sept. 1923): 389.

1897. Gruening, Martha. "The Lynching of Norris Dendy." THE NEW REPUBLIC, Vol. 79, No. 1018 (June 6, 1934): 96-98. At Clinton, South Carolina, July 4, 1933.

1898. Gruening, Martha. "Reflections on the South." THE NATION, Vol. 140, No. 2644 (May 8, 1935): 539-40. South Carolina lynching of black man Norris Dendy shows need for passage of Costigan-Wagner anti-lynching bill.

1899. Gunther, John. INSIDE U. S. A. Rev. ed.; New York: Harper & Brothers, 1951. See "Lynching" in index.

1900. Gutfeld, Arnon. "The Murder of Frank Little: Radical Labor Agitation in Butte, Montana, 1917." LABOR HISTORY, Vol. 10, No. 2 (Spring 1969): 177-92.

1901. Guzman, Jessie P., and Hughes, W. Hardin. "Lynching--Crime." In NEGRO YEAR BOOK: A REVIEW OF EVENTS AFFECTING NEGRO

LIFE 1941-46, pp. 302-19. Ed. by Jessie Parkhurst Guzman. Tuskegee, AL: Tuskegee Institute, 1947.

1902. Guzman, Jessie Parkhurst, ed.   "Lynching."   In 1952 NEGRO YEARBOOK: A REVIEW OF EVENTS AFFECTING NEGRO LIFE, pp. 277-79. New York: William H. Wise, 1952.

1903. Hackett, Chauncey. "Lynching in America." THE SPECTATOR [London], Vol. 126, No. 4828 (Jan. 8, 1921): 46.   Letter.

1904. Hagedorn, H. "What Is the Vigilantes. What Is It Doing for this Country?" THE TOUCHSTONE, Vol. 2, No. 1 (Oct. 1917): 91-93, 112. No "?" after "Vigilantes" on contents page and on p. 91, but is included at top of pp. 92-93 and on p. 112. Page 91: "The avowed purpose of The Vigilantes, a non-partisan organization of authors, artists and others is to arouse the country to a realization of the importance of the war problems confronting the American people; . . ."

1905. Hairston, Julie B. "Killing Kittens, Bombing Clinics." SOUTHERN EXPOSURE, Vol. 18, No. 2 (Summer 1990): 14-16, 18.   Anti-abortion vigilantes.

1906. Haldeman-Julius, Marcet. THE STORY OF A LYNCHING: AN EXPLORATION OF SOUTHERN PSYCHOLOGY. Little Blue Book No. 1260. Girard, KS: Haldeman-Julius Publications, 1927.   Includes (1) 1927 rape and murder of 11-year-old girl and desire of mob in Little Rock to lynch her alleged black attacker, Lonnie Dixon, and (2) 1927 lynching of John Carter, black, near Little Rock, Arkansas.

1907. Hallanan, Walter S. "West Virginia and the Negro." THE CRISIS, Vol. 38, No. 1 (Jan. 1931): 10-11, 34.   See section on "Lynching" on p. 11.

1908. Hare, Nathan. "The Passing of the Jim Crow Vigilantes." NEGRO HISTORY BULLETIN, Vol. 24, No. 8 (May 1961): 181-82, 184.   Key to lynching decline was 1920 use of militia by governor of Kentucky; six mob members were killed and 50 wounded.

1909. Harman, Everett Radcliff. "What is Law." THE COMMONWEAL, Vol. 19, No. 16 (Feb. 16, 1934): 438-39. Letter. Favors people "taking the law into their own hands" (as in lynching) under certain conditions.

1910. Harrington, Oliver W. TERROR IN TENNESSEE: THE TRUTH ABOUT THE COLUMBIA OUTRAGES. [Columbia]: National Committee for Justice in Columbia, Tenn., 1946.

1911. Harris, J. William. "Etiquette, Lynching, and Racial Boundaries in Southern History: A Mississippi Example." THE AMERICAN HISTORICAL REVIEW, Vol. 100, No. 2 (April 1995): 387-410.   Tarring and feathering, July, 1918, by "whitecappers." Hanging and burning of Lloyd Clay, black, May, 1919, Vicksburg.

1912. Hartt, Rollin Lynde. "The New Negro." THE INDEPENDENT, Vol. 105, No. 3754 (Jan. 15, 1921): 59-60, 76.   Blacks will fight to defend lives, property, and rights against white lynchers, etc.

1913. Haskell, H. J. "Martial Law in Oklahoma." THE OUTLOOK, Vol. 135, No. 4 (Sept. 26, 1923): 133.   Response to whippings by mobs (perhaps KKK involvement).

1914. [Haskin, Sara Estelle.] H., S. E. "Southern Women and Mob Violence." THE MISSIONARY VOICE, Vol. 22, No. 2 (Feb. 1932): 34.

1915. Haslam, Gerald. "Posse Comitatus: Every Man a Sheriff." THE NATION, Vol. 221, No. 21 (Dec. 20, 1975): 659-60.   Penultimate sentence refers to "vigilante activities."

1916. Hawkins, W. E. "When Negroes Shot a Lynching Bee Into Perdition." THE MESSENGER, Vol. 2, No. 9 (Sept. 1919): 28-29.   Recent Washington, DC, riot.

1917. Haywood, H[arry]., and Howard, M[ilton]. LYNCHING. International Pamphlets, No. 25. New York: International Publishers, 1932.

1918. "He Should Have been Impeached." THE CHRISTIAN CENTURY, Vol. 53, No. 37 (Sept. 9, 1936): 1182.   Pennsylvania judge who spoke in favor of lynching when sentencing a black man.

1919. Hendricks, John. ONCE UPON A LYNCHING: THE JEROME BOYETT STORY. Second printing; [Huntsville?], TN: Scott County Historical Society, 1985.   June, 1933, lynching of alleged murderers Jerome Boyett and Harry (Harvey) Winchester in Tennessee. A deputy who died about same time may have been shot during participation in the lynching.

1920. Herbst, Josephine. "Lynching in the Quiet Manner." In NEGRO: AN ANTHOLOGY, pp. 174-76. Ed. by Nancy Cunard and Hugh Ford. New York: Frederick Ungar Pub. Co., 1970.   Deals with the Scottsboro case in Alabama and legal methods of keeping blacks downtrodden; not about lynching per se. Originally published in New Masses, July 1931. See Cunard, Nancy, in this bibliography for another copy of this.

1921. "Hernando Hanging (Concl.)." TIME, Vol. 23, No. 13 (March 26, 1934): 10.   Legal execution of 3 Mississippi blacks after their lynching was prevented and after failure of bill to permit offended father of white girl from hanging them personally.

1922. "Hernando Hangman." TIME, Vol. 23, No. 12 (March 19, 1934): 14. Lynching of 3 black rapists was avoided, but bill in legislature would let rape victim's father act as hangman.

1923. Hickey, Donald R.   "The Prager Affair: A Study In Wartime Hysteria."   JOURNAL OF THE ILLINOIS STATE HISTORICAL SOCIETY, Vol. 62, No. 2 (Summer 1969): 117-34.   Lynching of Robert Paul Prager in Illinois, 1918.

1924. Higgins, Chester. "Meredith March Shows Brutal Side of Mississippi: Bury Victim of Mississippi Klansmen's Senseless Shot-Gun Slaying." JET, Vol. 30, No. 13 (July 7, 1966): 14-20.

1925. Higgins, Renelda.   "A Nation's Shame: Brutal Lynch/Murder in Alabama." THE CRISIS, Vol. 88, No. 5 (June 1981): 226-28, 230-31, 257-58. Victim: Michael Lee Donald.

1926. Hixson, Richard.   "Special Master's Final Report."   Tallahassee: Florida House of Representatives, March 21, 1994.   Fifteen-page report on the incident at Rosewood, FL, Jan. 1923. For further documentation by the state of Florida see Jones, Maxine D., et al., in this bibliography.

1927. Hoffman, Edwin D.   "The Genesis of the Modern Movement for Equal Rights in South Carolina, 1930-1939." THE JOURNAL OF NEGRO HISTORY, Vol. 44, No. 4 (Oct. 1959): 346-69.   For anti-lynching sentiments and efforts see pp. 350-51, 356, 363.   For KKK and police violence see pp. 359-60.

1928. Holland, Endesha Ida Mae.   "Memories of the Mississippi Delta." MICHIGAN QUARTERLY REVIEW, Vol. 26, No. 1 (Winter 1987): 246-58.   Introductory paragraph has several factual errors about Emmett Till murder in Mississippi, 1955.

1929. Holt, Len. THE SUMMER THAT DIDN'T END. NY.: Morrow, 1965.   Includes lynching of Chaney, Goodman, and Schwerner in Mississippi in 1964.

1930. "Honor Roll of States Free from Lynching." FEDERAL COUNCIL BULLETIN, Vol. 15, No. 3 (March 1932): 23.   Deals especially with 1931.

1931. "Honor Roll Shows Forty-three States Free of the Lynching Evil." FEDERAL COUNCIL BULLETIN, Vol. 13, No. 5 (May 1930): 23.

1932. Hope, Cecil S.   "The Flames of Lynch-Law Spread." LABOR DEFENDER, Vol. 7, No. 12 (Dec. 1931): 237.   Frightened bosses are increasingly getting rid of undesirables by lynching and "a new method of lynching--through due process of law."

1933. Hope, Cecil S. "Halt Lynch Terror!" LABOR DEFENDER, Vol. 8, No. 2 (Feb. 1932): 26, 38.   Deplores various forms of oppression of Negroes and support of it by "a host of Negro sycophants."

1934-1976. "The Horizon. Crime." THE CRISIS, Vol. 14, No. 4 (Aug. 1917): 197.   Includes lynching. Many subsequent issues of this periodical have a section with this title with items dealing with recent lynchings. Those which need no special annotation are as follows: Vol. 14, No. 5 (Sept. 1917): 264; Vol. 15, No. 1 (Nov. 1917): 41; Vol. 15, No. 2 (Dec. 1917): 91; Vol. 15, No. 3 (Jan. 1918): 145; Vol. 15, No. 5 (March 1918): 249; Vol. 16, No. 1 (May 1918): 36; Vol. 16, No. 2 (June 1918): 88; Vol. 16, No. 3 (July 1918): 141; Vol. 16, No. 4 (Aug. 1918): 192; Vol. 16, No. 5 (Sept. 1918): 242; Vol. 16, No. 6 (Oct. 1918): 297; Vol. 17, No. 1 (Nov. 1918): 37; Vol. 17, No. 2 (Dec. 1918): 90; Vol. 17, No. 3 (Jan. 1919): 144; Vol. 17, No. 5 (March 1919): 247; Vol. 18, No. 1 (May 1919): 36; Vol. 18, No. 3 (July 1919): 155;   Vol. 18, No. 4 (Aug. 1919): 207; Vol. 18, No. 5 (Sept. 1919): 257; Vol. 18, No. 6 (Oct. 1919): 309;   Vol. 19, No. 1 (Nov. 1919): 349; Vol. 19, No. 2 (Dec. 1919): 82; Vol. 19, No. 3 (Jan. 1920): 147; Vol. 19, No. 5 (March 1920): 277; Vol. 20, No. 1 (May 1920): 50; Vol. 20, No. 2 (June 1920): 102; Vol. 20, No. 3 (July 1920): 148; Vol. 20, No. 4 (Aug. 1920): 195; Vol. 20, No. 5 (Sept. 1920): 242; Vol. 20, No. 6 (Oct. 1920): 291; Vol. 21, No. 1 (Nov. 1920): 36; Vol. 21, No. 2 (Dec. 1920): 80; Vol. 21, No. 3 (Jan. 1921): 130; Vol. 21, No. 5 (March 1921): 225; Vol. 21, No. 6 (April 1921): 274; Vol. 22, No. 1 (May 1921): 31; Vol. 22, No. 3 (July 1921): 131-32; Vol. 22, No. 5 (Sept. 1921): 228; Vol. 22, No. 6 (Oct. 1921): 276; Vol. 23, No. 1 (Nov. 1921): 36; Vol. 23, No. 2 (Dec. 1921): 83.

1977. "The Horizon. Ghetto." THE CRISIS, Vol. 13, No. 3 (Jan. 1917): 146-47.   Includes $1,000 compensation for Arkansas black man beaten by a mob; also Anthony Crawford, lynched in South Carolina.

1978. "The Horizon. Ghetto." THE CRISIS, Vol. 13, No. 6 (April 1917): 301, 303.   Includes lynching. One item reports $50,000 lawsuit by George Fryar, husband of woman killed by Waco, Texas, lynching victim, against Paul Quinn College (black) because student newspaper said he was suspected of the murder.

1979-1986. "The Horizon. Ghetto." THE CRISIS, Vol. 14, No. 1 (May 1917): 44.   Includes lynching.   Some subsequent issues of this periodical have a section with this title with items on recent lynchings.   Those which need no special annotation are as follows: Vol. 14, No. 3 (July 1917): 145; Vol. 14, No. 5 (Sept. 1917): 264; Vol. 14, No. 6 (Oct. 1917): 316; Vol. 15, No. 5 (March 1918): 249; Vol. 16, No. 2 (June 1918): 88; Vol. 17, No. 1 (Nov. 1918): 37; Vol. 22, No. 2 (June 1921): 81.

1987. "The Horror at Sacramento." AMERICA, Vol. 50, No. 10 (Dec. 9, 1933): 219.   Governor Rolph's approval of San Jose, CA, lynchings.

1988. "The Horror at Sherman." AMERICA, Vol. 43, No. 7 (May 24, 1930): 149-50.   Editorial.   Events in Texas.

1989. "The Horror of Lynching." AMERICA, Vol. 52, No. 11 (Dec. 22, 1934): 243-44.   Claude Neal's lynching in Florida.

1990. "Horrors." THE CRUSADER, Vol. 2, No. 7 (March 1920): 8. Hearst's The New York American, Feb. 8, 1920, argues for annexation of Mexico with photo of 13-year-old Mexican boy who was lynched.   Contrasted with lynchings in U.S.

"How a Town Was Lynched." See Taylor, John.

1991. "How Just is Our Justice?" NEW SOUTH, Vol. 22, No. 1 (Winter 1967): 44-45.   Reprint of Montgomery newspaper editorial.   Includes comparative comment on lynching.

1992. "How Lynchings Happen." THE CRISIS, Vol. 23, No. 4 (Feb. 1922): 167.   An innocent black man accused of assaulting a white woman near Knoxville was saved from being lynched, but more than 20 of the attacking mob were wounded by the sheriff and his deputies.

1993. "How Shall the Black Man's Burden Be Lifted?" CURRENT OPINION, Vol. 67, No. 2 (Aug. 1919): 111-12.

1994. "How Tampa Treats Lynchers." THE LITERARY DIGEST, Vol. 93, No. 12 (June 18, 1927): 12-13.   Five killed and 32 injured when troops fired on mob to prevent lynching of a white man.   Florida.

1995. "How To Stop Lynching." THE MESSENGER, Vol. 2, No. 8 (Aug. 1919): 8-10.   Blacks should organize armed volunteers to oppose lynching.

1996. Howard, George Elliott.   "The Social Cost of Southern Race Prejudice." THE AMERICAN JOURNAL OF SOCIOLOGY, Vol. 22, No.

5 (March 1917): 577-93.   Lynching: pp. 588-89, 593.

1997. Howard, Walter. "'A Blot on Tampa's History': The 1934 Lynching of Robert Johnson." TAMPA BAY HISTORY, Vol. 6, No. 2 (Fall/Winter 1984): 5-18.   Florida.

1998. Howard, Walter T. "Beaches and Hanging Trees: Lynch Law in Florida, 1930-1940." CARVER, Vol. 10 (Spring 1992): 7-20.

1999. Howard, Walter T. "A Hillsborough County Tragedy: The 1930 Lynching of John Hodaz." TAMPA BAY HISTORY, Vol. 11, No. 2 (Fall/Winter 1989): 34-51.   Florida. Hodaz was only white person lynched in 1930 (p. 50, n. 52).

2000. Howard, Walter T. "In the Shadow of Scottsboro: The 1937 Robert Hinds Case." GULF COAST HISTORICAL REVIEW, Vol. 4 (Fall 1988): 64-81.   In a legal lynching, Florida officials tried and executed this black teenager, partly to avert an actual lynching.

2001. Howard, Walter T. LYNCHINGS: EXTRALEGAL VIOLENCE IN FLORIDA DURING THE 1930S. Selinsgrove: Susquehanna Univ. Press [Cranbury, NJ: Associated University Press], 1995.

2002. Howard, Walter T. "Vigilante Justice and National Reaction: The 1937 Tallahassee Double Lynching." FLORIDA HISTORICAL QUAR-TERLY, Vol. 66, No. 1 (July 1988): 41-69.   Florida.

2003. Howard, Walter Thomas. "Vigilante Justice: Extra-Legal Executions in Florida, 1930-1940." Ph.D. diss., Florida State Univ., 1987.   See Diss. Ab. Intl., Vol. 48, No. 2 (Aug. 1987): 467A. Detailed accounts of Florida's 15 lynchings in 1930s.

2004. Howe, Frederic C. "Lynch Law and the Immigrant Alien." THE NATION, Vol. 110, No. 2850 (Feb. 14, 1920): 194-95.   Not about lynching; deals with deportation of aliens.

2005. Huber, Patrick J. "The Lynching of James T. Scott: The Underside of a College Town." GATEWAY HERITAGE, Vol. 12, No. 1 (Summer 1991): 18-37.   Missouri, 1923.

2006. Huberman, Leo. "Lynching in America." SCHOLASTIC, Vol. 25, No. 9 (Nov. 17, 1934): 21.

2007. Hudson, Clenora Frances (Hudson-Weems, Clenora). "Emmett Till: The Impetus for the Modern Civil Rights Movement." Ph.D. diss., Univ. of

Iowa, 1988.   See <u>Diss. Ab. Intl.</u>, Vol. 49, No. 8 (Feb. 1989): 2281A.   Till was murdered in Mississippi, 1955.

2008. Huie, William Bradford.   "The Shocking Story of Approved Killing in Mississippi." LOOK, Vol. 20, No. 2 (Jan. 24, 1956): 46-48, 50.   Two white men murdered Emmett Till in Mississippi, 1955.

2009. Huie, William Bradford. THREE LIVES FOR MISSISSIPPI. New York: WCC Books, 1965.   Chaney, Goodman, and Schwerner; murdered in 1964.

2010. Huie, William Bradford. "The True Story Behind . . . The Rape-Lynch That Rocked America." CAVALIER, Vol. 10, No. 83 (May 1960): 10-15, 61-67.   Mack Parker case in Mississippi, 1959.

2011. Huie, William Bradford.   "What's Happened to the Emmett Till Killers?" LOOK, Vol. 21, No. 2 (Jan. 22, 1957): 63-66, 68.   Legally exonerated but largely ostracized. Mississippi.

2012. Hull, Robert R. "Lynch Law in Indiana." AMERICA, Vol. 43, No. 23 (Sept. 13, 1930): 543-44.   Marion lynching of Thomas Shipp and Abram Smith, 1930.

2013. "Hun News." THE INDEPENDENT, Vol. 93, No. 3608 (Jan. 26, 1918): 133.   Tuskegee Institute lynching statistics for 1917.

2014. "The Huns." THE INDEPENDENT, Vol. 90, No. 3574 (June 2, 1917): 398.   "Last week a large and enthusiastic throng of the 'best citizens' of Memphis, Tennessee, burned a negro [sic] at the stake after soaking him in oil and cutting off his ears."

2015. "The Huns of America." THE CRUSADER, Vol. 2, No. 4 (Dec. 1919): 29.   Lynchers and race rioters provoke derision in Europe and Mexico.

2016. Hux, Roger K. "The Ku Klux Klan in Macon, 1919-1925." THE GEORGIA HISTORICAL QUARTERLY, Vol. 62, No. 2 (Summer 1978): 155-68.   Floggings of "moral offenders" in Georgia.

2017. Hyman, Alvin D. "The San Jose Lynchings." In NEWS STORIES OF 1933: A COLLECTION OF SOME OF THE BEST NEWS AND FEATURE STORIES OF VARIOUS TYPES WHICH APPEARED IN AMERICAN NEWSPAPERS IN 1933, pp. 118-26. Ed. by Frank Luther Mott. Iowa City, IA: Clio Press, 1934.   California.

2018. Hynes, Charles J, and Drury, Bob. INCIDENT AT HOWARD BEACH: THE CASE FOR MURDER. New York: G. P. Putnam's Sons, 1990. Michael Griffith's beating and subsequent traffic death in New York City, 1986.

2019. "ILD Calls for Texas Investigation." EQUAL JUSTICE, Vol. 13, No. 3 (May 1939): 6. Whipping of a black teenager.

2020. "I.L.D. Exposes 'Lynchless Year.'" EQUAL JUSTICE, Vol. 14, No. 2 (May 1940): 5. Details of five lynchings in 1940 during time (May 8, 1939-May 8, 1940) when there were no lynchings according to Jessie Daniel Ames.

2021. "'Ill-Chosen Symbol.'" TIME, Vol. 66, No. 21 (Nov. 21, 1955): 21. Byrant and Milam indicted for Till kidnaping [sic] in Mississippi.

2022. "'I'm trying to forgive them,' Says Mack Parker's Mother." JET, Vol. 16, No. 5 (May 28, 1959): 14-15. Interview in California about Mississippi lynching.

2023. "Immunity for Lynchers." AMERICA, Vol. 50, No. 20 (Feb. 17, 1934): 465. Failure to convict Missouri lynchers of Lloyd Warner.

2024. "Important Statistical Study Of Lynchings." INTERRACIAL REVIEW, Vol. 8, No. 3 (March 1935): 48. Statistics from NAACP.

2025. "In Georgia." THE CRISIS, Vol. 20, No. 4 (Aug. 1920): 167. Beatings of blacks, some by mobs, in Spalding County.

2026. "In Kentucky and Mississippi." THE CRISIS, Vol. 31, No. 6 (April 1926): 300-01. Several lynching items.

2027. "In Memorium, Emmett Till." LIFE, Vol. 39, No. 15 (Oct. 10, 1955): 48. Emmett was murdered in Mississippi, 1955. Says Till's father was "killed in France fighting for the American proposition that all men are equal." [According to William M. Simpson, "it was later revealed that Private Louis Till had been executed in Italy by the U.S. Army in the summer of 1945 for a series of rape-murder convictions"; see Simpson item, p. 190n.]

2028. "In Spite of Evidence To The Contrary It Is Still Maintained That Lynchings Are For The One Cause." In NEGRO YEAR BOOK . . . 1921-1922, pp. 71-72. Ed. by Monroe N. Work. Tuskegee Institute, AL: Negro Year Book Pub. Co., 1922.

2029. "In the Land of the Free." THE CRISIS, Vol. 23, No. 4 (Feb. 1922): 181.   Quote from <u>Vardaman's Weekly</u> about black man who was "thrashed" by whites in Mississippi.

2030. "Incident at Pikeville." NEWSWEEK, Vol. 24, No. 23 (Dec. 4, 1944): 48-49.   Lynching of James Scales in Tennessee.

2031. Ingalls, Robert. "The Murder of Joseph Shoemaker." SOUTHERN EXPOSURE, Vol. 8, No. 2 (Summer 1980): 64-68.   Flogging by a mob near Tampa, 1935.

2032. Ingalls, Robert P. "Anti-labor Vigilantes in the South During the 1930s." SOUTHERN EXPOSURE, Vol. 12, No. 6 (Nov./Dec. 1984): 72-78.

2033. Ingalls, Robert P. "Antiradical Violence in Birmingham During the 1930s." THE JOURNAL OF SOUTHERN HISTORY, Vol. 47, No. 4 (Nov. 1981): 521-44.   Includes actions of vigilantes in Alabama. Deals especially with Florida flogging of Joseph Gelders.

2034. Ingalls, Robert P. "The Flogging of Joseph Gelders: A Policeman's View." LABOR HISTORY, Vol. 20, No. 4 (Fall 1979): 576-78.   Beating in 1936 of a radical who was supporting imprisoned communist in Alabama.

2035. Ingalls, Robert P. "Radicals and Vigilantes: The 1931 Strike of Tampa Cigar Workers." In SOUTHERN WORKERS AND THEIR UNIONS, 1880-1975: SELECTED PAPERS, THE SECOND SOUTHERN LABOR HISTORY CONFERENCE, 1978, pp. 44-53. Ed. by Merle E. Reed, Leslie S. Hough, and Gary M. Fink. Westport, CT: Greenwood Press, 1981.

2036. Ingalls, Robert P. "Strikes and Vigilante Violence in Tampa's Cigar Industry." TAMPA BAY HISTORY, Vol. 7, No. 2 (Fall/Winter 1985): 117-34.

2037. Ingalls, Robert P. "The Tampa Flogging Case, Urban Vigilantism." THE FLORIDA HISTORICAL QUARTERLY, Vol. 56, No. 1 (July 1977): 13-27.   Murder of Joseph Shoemaker. Floggings and murder in 1935 to prevent political reform.

2038. Ingalls, Robert P. "Vanquished But Not Convinced: Worker Militancy and Vigilante Violence in Tampa." SOUTHERN EXPOSURE, Vol. 14, No. 1 (Jan./Feb. 1986): 51-58.

2039. Innerst, J. Stuart. "Capital Punishment and Lynching." THE CHRISTIAN CENTURY, Vol. 47 [sic; should be 48], No. 11 (March 18,

1931): 381.   Letter.

2040. "Insane Negro Lynched in North Carolina."   INTERNATIONAL JURIDICAL ASSOCIATION MONTHLY BULLETIN, Vol. 4, No. 2 (July 1935): 2.   Sweat Ward, 10 miles from Louisburg.

2041. "Investigating Lynching." AMERICA, Vol. 44, No. 2 (Oct. 18, 1930): 30.   Editorial.

2042. "Investigation of 1935 Lynchings Is Approved." THE CATHOLIC WORKER, Vol. 3, No. 9 (Feb. 1936): 1.   Action by Senate Judiciary Committee.

2043. "The Invincible Power of Public Opinion." EQUAL JUSTICE, Vol. 13, No. 3 (May 1939): 5.   Excerpts from speech by Attorney General Frank Murphy. Refers to lynching. Includes cartoon with caption "The victim, lynched and lying dead, has no appeal."

2044. "Invisible Injustice." THE OUTLOOK, Vol. 133, No. 1 (Jan. 3, 1923): 7.   Secret bands of "regulators" often commit injustice. One paragraph on Mer Rouge, Louisiana, murders and two on recent burnings of Catholic churches in Canada.

2045. "The Irwinton Story." In CHANGING PATTERNS IN THE NEW SOUTH, pp. 18-19 (Vol. 10, No. 1 (Jan. 1955) of NEW SOUTH.   Lynching of Caleb Hill in Georgia. From New South, Vol. 4, No. 7 (July 1949): 1, 8.

2046. "Is a Lynchless Year Coming?" THE LITERARY DIGEST, Vol. 89, No. 4 (April 24, 1926): 14.

2047. "Is Lynching Crime?" THE CRISIS, Vol. 41, No. 11 (Nov. 1934): 341. Lynching seems not to be on agenda of National Conference on crime which will meet in December.

2048. "Is Lynching Ever Defensible?" THE FORUM, Vol. 76, No. 6 (Dec. 1926): 811-22.   Includes: "I.--The Motives of Judge Lynch," by George W. Chamblee (pp. 811-17); "II.--The Mind of the Lynching Mob," by John P. Fort.

2049. "Is Lynching Justified?" NEGRO DIGEST, Vol. 1, No. 2 (Dec. 1942): 60-61.   Condensed from PM. Consists of "No . . .," by Albert Deutsch, pp. 60-61, and "Yes . . .," by J. L. Rushing, p. 61.

2050. "Is Mississippi Hushing Up a Lynching? Mississippi Gunmen Take

Life Of Militant Negro Minister." JET, Vol. 8, No. 3 (May 26, 1955): 8-11. George Lee was shot in Belzoni, Mississippi.

2051. "Is the Mob to Rule?" THE CHRISTIAN CENTURY, Vol. 50, No. 51 (Dec. 13, 1933): 1568-70.   Recent lynchings in San Jose, Maryland, and Missouri. Also, Lincoln's anti-lynching advice in 1837 on the topic "The Perpetuation of Our Political Institutions." Page 1570: "Lynching in the United States is generally accounted to date from the burning of a Negro in St. Louis in 1836."

2052. "It would have been futile to call out the militia." NEW MASSES, Vol. 13, No. 6 (Nov. 6, 1934): 3.   Illustration of lynching of Claude Neal in Florida. See also untitled text on page 6.

2053. "It's Not the Law." THE NEW REPUBLIC, Vol. 140, No. 24 (June 15, 1959): 2.   Mack Parker case in Mississippi emphasizes that lynching does not violate federal law.

2054. Ivins, Molly. "Beulah Mae Donald." MS., Vol. 16, No. 7 (Jan. 1988): 52-54, 56, 88.   Woman who successfully sued KKK after her son was lynched in Mobile.

2055. Jackson, Juanita E. "Youth and the Lynching Evil." INTERRACIAL REVIEW, Vol. 10, No. 2 (Feb. 1937): 26-27.

2056. Jacobs, Sally. "The Death of Vinson P. Harris." SOUTHERN EXPOSURE, Vol. 15, No. 3-4 (Fall-Winter 1987): 45-49.   North Carolina death of federal prisoner.

2057. Jakira, A. "As if to slaughter." LABOR DEFENDER, Vol. 5, No. 6 (June 1930): 126.   Especially about lynching of George Hughes at Sherman, Texas. Includes photos of Hughes before and after. Includes cartoon.

2058. "Japan on American Lynching." THE MESSENGER, Vol. 3, No. 3 (Aug. 1921): 225.   Quotation from Asian Review on burning of Henry Lowery [sic]. Includes editorial comment by The Messenger. Turkish ambassador was forced to be recalled for comparing Armenian massacre to U.S. lynchings.

2059. "Jet Reconstructs Lynching Of Mack Charles Parker." JET, Vol. 16, No. 7 (June 11, 1959): 6-8.   Mississippi.

2060. "Jewish Vigilantes." TIME, Vol. 94, No. 1 (July 4, 1969): 22.   Meir Kahane's Jewish Defense League.

2061. "The Jewish Vigilantes." NEWSWEEK, Vol. 75, No. 2 (Jan. 12, 1970): 35-36.   Meir Kahane's Jewish Defense League.

2062. Jiggetts, Louis M.   "Without Benefit of Law."   BLACKWOOD'S MAGAZINE, Vol. 220, No. 1330 (Aug. 1926): 204-09.   Lynching in the U.S., with some details of 1925 cases.

2063. Johnson, Ben.   "Christopher Wilson: Lynching by Burning." THE CRISIS, Vol. 100, No. 2 (Feb. 1993): 21, 27.   Wilson, a black man, was set on fire in Florida in 1993.

2064. Johnson, Charles S.   "How Much is the Migration a Flight From Persecution?" OPPORTUNITY, Vol. 1, No. 9 (Sept. 1923): 272-74.   Lynchings did not seem to cause reductions of black population in Southern counties with high numbers of lynchings.

2065. Johnson, Gerald W. "Lynchers in Maryland." THE NEW REPUB-LIC, Vol. 77, No. 995 (Dec. 27, 1933): 199.   Letter about Armwood case, responding to Robert Cantwell's letter in same issue.

2066. Johnson, Gerald W.   "Maryland: Storm Warning."   THE NEW REPUBLIC, Vol. 77, No. 994 (Dec. 20, 1933): 159-61.   Armwood lynching and mob battle with soldiers when some of alleged lynchers were arrested.

2067. Johnson, Gerald W.   "The Superficial Aspect.   The Flight from Liberty." THE NEW REPUBLIC, Vol. 140, No. 24 (June 15, 1959): 14. Mack Parker's lynching in Mississippi is not the only "relic of barbarism in the country."

2068. Johnson, Guy B.   "What Happened at Columbia." NEW SOUTH, Vol. 1, No. 5 (May 1946): 1-8.   Tennessee.

2069. Johnson, James Weldon.   "Lynching." THE FORUM, Vol. 77, No. 2 (Feb. 1927): 308-09.   Letter.

2070. Johnson, James Weldon.   "Lynching--America's National Disgrace." CURRENT HISTORY, Vol. 19, No. 4 (Jan. 1924): 596-601.

2071. Johnson, James Weldon.   "The Practice of Lynching."   THE CENTURY MAGAZINE, Vol. 115 (New Series, Vol. XCIII), No. 1 (Nov. 1927): 65-70.

2072. Johnson, Joseph. [No title.] THE NEGRO HISTORY BULLETIN, Vol. 19, No. 5 (Feb. 1956): 106.   A letter to Dr. Marguerite Cartwright in response to her April, 1953, article about lynching in The Crisis.   Refers to his 1939 manuscript "The Social Basis of Lynching" not being published.

2073. Jones, Edwin. "Again the Till Case." LOOK, Vol. 20, No. 6 (March 20, 1956): 25.   Letter. Till was murdered in Mississippi, 1955.

2074. Jones, Ellis O. "Was An Innocent Man Lynched at San Jose?" THE NEW REPUBLIC, Vol. 77, No. 1001 (Feb. 7, 1934): 365-66.   Letter about Jack Holmes. California.

2075. Jones, Maxine D., et. al. A DOCUMENTED HISTORY OF THE INCIDENT WHICH OCCURRED AT ROSEWOOD, FLORIDA IN JANUARY 1923.   SUBMITTED TO THE FLORIDA BOARD OF REGENTS 22 DECEMBER 1993. Tallahassee: Florida House of Representatives, 1993.   Bound document of 93 pages; numerous references to lynching. Unbound "Appendices" of 461 pages can be obtained separately; has sections titled "Lynching Statistics," covering 1906-1934 (pp. 82-108); "Victims of Lynchings in Florida, 1882-1930" (pp. 109-18); "Unconfirmed and Problem Lynchings: Florida" (pp. 119-20). See also "Brisk Start of the 1923 Lynchings"; Hixson, Richard; Taylor, John.

2076. Jordan, Joe.   "Lynchers Don't Like Lead."   THE ATLANTIC MONTHLY, Vol. 177, No. 2 (Feb. 1946): 103-08.   In February, 1920, in Lexington, Kentucky, a white mob bent on lynching a black man being tried in the courthouse was fired on by state soldiers. Six civilians were killed and many more wounded. Author feels this action caused a decline in lynching. Condensed in Negro Digest, Vol. IV, No. 6 (April 1946): 67-78.

2077. "A Journalistic Blunder." THE NATION, Vol. 137, No. 3573 (Dec. 27, 1933): 723.   Comment on Westbrook Pegler's defense of lynching. Reference to Writers' League Against Lynching.

2078. Judge, Frank. "Slaying the Dragon." THE AMERICAN LAWYER, Vol. 9, No. 7 (Sept. 1987): 83-89.   Michael Donald lynching in Alabama, 1981, and legal case against KKK.

2079. "Judge Lynch." CURRENT HISTORY, Vol. 51, No. 6 (Feb. 1940): 6.

2080. "Judge Lynch and John Law." THE NEW REPUBLIC, Vol. 77, No. 996 (Jan. 3, 1934): 213.   Response to James Chadbourn's recent book.

2081. "Judge Lynch and the Pole Cat." NEWSWEEK, Vol. 19, No. 6 (Feb. 9, 1942): 59.   Lynching at Sikeston, Missouri, was filmed.

2082. "'Judge Lynch' Becoming Unpopular." THE LITERARY DIGEST,

Vol. 80, No. 5 (Feb. 2, 1924): 31-32.

2083. "Judge Lynch in Decline." THE LITERARY DIGEST, Vol. 86, No. 1840 (July 25, 1925): 32.

2084. "Judge Lynch in New York." NEW MASSES, Vol. 32, No. 8 (Aug. 15, 1939): 15-16.   Blacks were beaten in New York City, 1939.

2085. "Judicial Advocacy of Lynching." INTERNATIONAL JURIDICAL ASSOCIATION MONTHLY BULLETIN, Vol. 5, No. 3 (Sept. 1936): 26. Several cases, two of which seem questionable regarding "advocacy."

2086. "A Jury Betrays Southern Justice." NEW SOUTH, Vol. 2, No. 7 (July 1947): 4-5.   Acquittals in Willie Earle case in South Carolina.

2087. "Justice Department Urges FBI To Investigate Miss. Lynching." JET, Vol. 8, No. 4 (June 2, 1955): 4-5.   Shooting of Reverend George Lee.

2088. "Justice Dept. Explores Black Prisoner's Death." JET, Vol. 70, No. 23 (Aug. 25, 1986): 33.   Case of V. Harris in North Carolina.

2089. "'Justice': Floridians Stage 'A Lynching Up to Cannidy's.'" NEWS-WEEK [sic], Vol. 4, No. 18 (Nov. 3, 1934): 38.   Victim: Claude Neal.

2090. Kahn, Albert E. HIGH TREASON: THE PLOT AGAINST THE PEOPLE. 2d ed.; New York: Hour Publishers, 1950.   Covers 1919-1950. Includes, inter alia, activities of the Black Legion [Michigan and elsewhere]; anti-black riot in Columbia, Tennessee, in 1946; miscellaneous lynchings and murders of blacks in 1947.

2091. Kantor, MacKinlay. MISSOURI BITTERSWEET. Garden City, NY: Doubleday, 1969.   See Chap. 12, "Maryville," pp. 140-69, for Missouri lynching of Raymond Gunn, Jan. 1931.

2092. Kendrick, Alexander. "Spotlight on Vigilanteism." NEW MASSES, Vol. 25, No. 2 (Oct. 5, 1937): 13-15.   Subtitle: "The N.L.R.B. hearings on Bethlehem Steel's anti-union activities show how employers cultivate native fascism."

2093. Kendrick, Schaefer B. "What kind of place was Greenville in 1947?" CAROLOGUE: A PUBLICATION OF THE SOUTH CAROLINA HISTORICAL SOCIETY, Vol. 8, No. 4 (Winter 1992): 7, 14.   Willie Earle lynching in South Carolina.

2094. Kennedy, David M. OVER HERE: THE FIRST WORLD WAR

AND AMERICAN SOCIETY. New York: Oxford Univ. Press, 1980.   See "Lynching" and "Vigilantism" in index.

2095. "The Kentucky Cure for Lynching." THE LITERARY DIGEST, Vol. 64, No. 9 (Feb. 28, 1920): 20-21.   Mob attack at Lexington failed to obtain black man for lynching, but six died and many were wounded. See Jordan, Joe.

2096. Kerby, Elizabeth.   "Violence in Silver City: Who Caused the Trouble?" FRONTIER, Vol. 4, No. 7 (May 1953): 5-10.   Vigilantism while the movie "Salt of the Earth" was being filmed.

2097. Kerlin, Robert T., ed. THE VOICE OF THE NEGRO. New York: Dutton, 1920. Reprint ed.; New York: Arno Press & New York Times, 1968.   Compilation from the black press in 1919; see Chapter VI, "Lynchings" (pp. 100-25).

2098. Kessler, Sidney H. "The Negro in Labor Strikes." THE MIDWEST JOURNAL, Vol. 6, No. 2 (Summer 1954): 16-35.   Includes violence; see p. 31 for lynching.

2099. [Kester, Howard.] THE LYNCHING OF CLAUDE NEAL. New York: NAACP, 1934; [Montgomery, AL: Reprint by the Southern Rural Welfare Assn., Inc., 1971].   Florida, 1934. Reprint of a 1934 report issued by the National Association for the Advancement of Colored People. See Robert F. Martin, Howard Kester and the Struggle for Social Justice in the South, 1904-77 (Charlottesville: Univ. Press of Virginia, 1991): 76-77; 175, n. 29; 176, n. 32; and compare cited sections of National Association for the Advancement of Colored People, The Lynching of Claude Neal, to see that Kester was its anonymous author.

2100. "The Keystone Vigilantes." THE CHRISTIAN CENTURY, Vol. 35, No. 10 (March 6, 1968): 283-84.   Proposal of Cook County, Illinois, sheriff to deputize a 1,000-man posse of blacks and whites for riot duty. Refers to this encouragement of "vigilante action."

2101. "Killed by Kluxers." NEWSWEEK, Vol. 35, No. 11 (March 13, 1950): 22-23.   Five KKK members murdered a [white?] man in Alabama because he "didn't work" and "argued with his neighbors."

2102. "King Mob Runs Amuck in Texas." THE LITERARY DIGEST, Vol. 105, No. 8 (May 24, 1930): 11.   George Hughes was burned alive in destruction of courthouse at Sherman, Texas.

2103. Kornbluth, J. "The woman who beat the Klan." THE NEW YORK

TIMES MAGAZINE, Vol. 137, No. 47,310 (Nov. 1, 1987): 26-32, 34, 36, 38-39.   Michael Donald lynching in Mobile, Alabama, 1981.

2104. Kotecha, Kanti C., and Walker, James L.   "Police Vigilantes." SOCIETY, Vol. 13, No. 3 (March/April 1976): 48-52.   Deals with 1970s.

2105. Kumler, Donna J.   "'They have gone from Sherman': The Courthouse Riot of 1930 and Its Impact on the Black Professional Class." Ph.D. diss., Univ. of North Texas, 1995. See Diss. Ab. Intl., Vol. 56, No. 12 (June 1996): 4901A.

2106. Kunen, James S. "Seeking Justice for Her Lynched Son, an Alabama Mother Ruins the Klan That Killed Him." PEOPLE WEEKLY, Vol. 27, No. 23 (June 8, 1987): 55-56, 61.   M. Donald case.

2107. Lacy, Steve. THE LYNCHING OF ROBERT MARSHALL. Prince, UT: Castle Press, 1978.   Black victim, June 1925, near Price, Utah.

2108. "L'affaire Till in the French Press." THE CRISIS, Vol. 62 (Dec. 1955): 596-602.   Till was murdered in Mississippi in 1955.

2109. Lamon, Lester C. "Document: Charles W. Cansler to the Honorable Tom C. Rye, Governor of Tennessee, February 1918." THE JOURNAL OF NEGRO HISTORY, Vol. 57, No. 4 (Oct. 1972): 407-14.   Letter about lynchings in Tennessee, 1917-18.

2110. Lane, Emerson. "A Lynching Incident." THE CRISIS, Vol. 42, No. 11 (Nov. 1935): 332, 340.

2111. Larsen, Laurence H., and Cottrell, Barbara J. THE GATE CITY: A HISTORY OF OMAHA. N.p.: Pruett Pub. Co., 1982.   Courthouse riot and lynching, 1919: pp. 168-75.

2112. Larsson, Clotye Murdock. "Land of the Till Murder Revisited." EBONY, Vol. 41, No. 5 (March 1986): 53-54, 56-58.   Mississippi.

2113. "Last Year's Lynchings." THE LITERARY DIGEST, Vol. 54, No. 4 (Jan. 27, 1917): 178.

2114. "Last Year's Lynching Record." THE OUTLOOK, Vol. 115, No. 3 (Jan. 17, 1917): 97.

2115. "Law-and-Order Anarchy." THE NATION, Vol. 113, No. 2926 (Aug. 3, 1921): 113.   Tarring-feathering and lynching.

2116. Law and Order Conference (1917: Blue Ridge, NC). LAWLESS-NESS OR CIVILIZATION--WHICH? REPORT OF ADDRESSES AND DISCUSSION IN THE LAW AND ORDER CONFERENCE, HELD AT BLUE RIDGE, N.C., AUGUST 4TH, 5TH AND 6TH, NINETEEN HUNDRED AND SEVENTEEN. Ed. by W. D. Weatherford. Nashville: Williams Print. Co., [1917].

2117. "Law and Order for the Negro." THE SURVEY, Vol. 38, No. 20 (Aug. 18, 1917): 443-44. Report on Conference on Mob Violence, Blue Ridge, North Carolina. Photo of conference members on p. 445.

2118. "The Law and the Mob." INTERNATIONAL JURIDICAL ASSOCIATION MONTHLY BULLETIN, Vol. 2, No. 5 (Oct. 1933): 4-5. Four cases in four states in "Lynchings" section.

2119. "The Law Gaining on Lynching." THE LITERARY DIGEST, Vol. 76, No. 2 (Jan. 13, 1923): 13-14. Includes two cartoons.

2120. "The Law Gains Ground." In CHANGING PATTERNS IN THE NEW SOUTH, pp. 20-22 [Vol. 10, No. 1 (Jan. 1955) of NEW SOUTH]. The two lynchings of 1950 and definitions of lynching. From New South, Vol. 6, No. 1 (Jan. 1951).

2121. "The Law Punishes Lynchers." In NEGRO YEAR BOOK . . . 1921-1922, p. 70. Ed. by Monroe N. Work. Tuskegee Institute, AL: Negro Year Book Pub. Co., 1922.   Instances of indictments and, in some cases, punishment "during the year."

2122. "The Law Takes Its Course." INTERNATIONAL JURIDICAL ASSOCIATION MONTHLY BULLETIN, Vol. 2, No. 10 (March 1934): 6. Lynching as issue and mob as threat during trial of three blacks at Hernando, Mississippi.

2123. Lawson, Michael. "Omaha, a City in Ferment: Summer of 1919." NEBRASKA HISTORY, Vol. 58, No. 3 (Fall 1977): 395-417.   Provides background for September race riot and some description of riot.

2124. Lay, Shawn. WAR, REVOLUTION, AND THE KU KLUX KLAN: A STUDY OF INTOLERANCE IN A BORDER CITY. El Paso: Texas Western Press, Univ. of Texas at El Paso, 1985.   See Chap. 3, "The Heyday of the Vigilante: El Paso During the Great War."

2125. "Legal Lynching Again Disapproved." INTERNATIONAL JURIDICAL ASSOCIATION MONTHLY BULLETIN, Vol. 1, No. 9 (Jan. 1933): [3-4].

2126. "Legal Lynching Disapproved." INTERNATIONAL JURIDICAL ASSOCIATION MONTHLY BULLETIN, Vol. 1, No. 6 (Oct. 1932): [7]. Convictions of blacks in Missouri and Oklahoma were reversed.

2127. "Legion of Doom: Young Vigilantes?" NEWSWEEK, Vol. 105, No. 14 (April 8, 1985): 27.　Ft. Worth, Texas, high school students may have used violence against thieves, drug users, and minorities.

2128. Leonard, George B., Jr. "Memo from Mississippi." LOOK, Vol. 24, No. 2 (Jan. 19, 1960): 82-83.　Mack Parker case, 1959.

2129. Lesesne, Henry. "Lynching By Law." NEGRO DIGEST, Vol. 9, No. 11 (Sept. 1951): 94-96.　Fewer lynchings in South but more police and mob violence.

2130. "Less Inclined to Lynch." THE OUTLOOK, Vol. 142, No. 13 (March 31, 1926): 481-82.

2131. "Lesson Learned." TIME, Vol. 22, No. 24 (Dec. 11, 1933): 14-15. Lynching of Lloyd Warner, black, in St. Joseph, Missouri, and influence on it of Governor Rolph of California.　Also Maryland governor's action in Armwood lynching.

2132. Lester, V. L.　THE MOB VIOLENCE AND THE AMERICAN NEGRO: "MY EXPERIENCE IN THE SUNNY SOUTH." [Memphis: Dobbin Print. Co., 1919.]　Pages 40-48: Lester persuaded mob not to lynch him.　Pages 71, 73, 74-75: lynching references.

2133. "Letters." TIME, Vol. 47, No. 5 (Feb. 4, 1946): 4, 6.　Three-item apology by editor for statements in story about Governor Caldwell (Florida) in Jan. 7 issue (see "The South: Two Governors") about shooting death of black man named Jesse James Payne.

2134. Levenson, Lew. "California Casualty List." THE NATION, Vol. 139, No. 3608 (Aug. 29, 1934): 243-45.　Record for July, 1934, of workers, radicals, etc., suffering violence at hands of police, vigilantes, etc.

2135. Levi, Steven C.　COMMITTEE OF VIGILANCE: THE SAN FRANCISCO CHAMBER OF COMMERCE LAW AND ORDER COMMITTEE, 1916-1919: A CASE STUDY IN OFFICIAL HYSTERIA. Jefferson, NC: McFarland, 1983.

2136. "Levon Carlock, Lynched by Memphis Police." LABOR DEFENDER, Vol. 9, No. 3 (March 1933): 31.　Tennessee.

2137. Lewis, Todd E. "Mob Justice in the 'American Congo': 'Judge Lynch' in Arkansas During the Decade After World War I." THE ARKANSAS HISTORICAL QUARTERLY, Vol. LII, No. 2 (Summer 1993): 156-84.

2138. "Life and Liberty." THE COMMONWEAL, Vol. 46, No. 8 (June 6, 1947): 180. Willie Earle case in South Carolina and two nonlynching incidents.

2139. Lomax, Louis E.; Griffin, John Howard; and Gregory, Dick. MISSISSIPPI EYEWITNESS: THREE CIVIL RIGHTS WORKERS-- HOW THEY WERE MURDERED. A special issue of RAMPARTS MAGAZINE (1964). Chaney, Goodman, and Schwerner were lynched in 1964.

2140. "A London Diary." THE NEW STATESMAN AND NATION [London], Vol. 33, No. 847 (May 31, 1947): 388-89. First two sections deal with U.S. lynching.

2141. "Look Before You Lynch." THE OUTLOOK, Vol. 133, No. 6 (Feb. 7, 1923): 253. Attempted lynching in Mississippi. From Piney Woods and Its Story by Laurence C. Jones, pp. 111-14. New York: Fleming H. Revell Co., 1922.

2142. "The Looking Glass." THE CRISIS, Vol. 19, No. 5 (March 1920): 267-71. Includes comment on newspaper headlines which falsely identify blacks as perpetrators of crime; sentencing of white-cappers in Mississippi; and the first lynching of a black veteran of the fighting in France (in Georgia).

2143. "The Looking Glass. America's Blot." THE CRISIS, Vol. 19, No. 6 (April 1920): 330.

2144. "The Looking Glass. As To Lynching In Texas." THE CRISIS, Vol. 16, No. 6 (Oct. 1918): 279.

2145. "The Looking Glass. Contrasts." THE CRISIS, Vol. 20, No. 2 (June 1920): 95-96. One item is about a black man named Price in St. Augustine, Texas, who was captured at 4:30 P.M. one day, legally tried, and executed at 11:00 the next day.

2146. "The Looking Glass. Impossible Atrocities." THE CRISIS, Vol. 16, No. 1 (May 1918): 24-25. Especially about Estill Springs, Tennessee, lynching. [Jim McIlherron]

2147. "The Looking Glass. Lynch Law." THE CRISIS, Vol. 16, No. 2

(June 1918): 71-72.   Attorney General Gregory on lynching.

2148. "The Looking Glass. Lynching and Southern Women." THE CRISIS, Vol. 18, No. 4 (Aug. 1919): 197-98.

2149. "The Looking Glass. Mob Action." THE CRISIS, Vol. 16, No. 5 (Sept. 1918): 227-28.   President Wilson's letter of July 26 on lynching.

2150. "The Looking Glass. The Present South." THE CRISIS, Vol. 15, No. 6 (April 1918): 288-90.   Includes item, p. 289, from Little Rock, Arkansas, Daily News which can be read as favoring lynching.

2151. "The Looking Glass. The Protest of a Nation." THE CRISIS, Vol. 16, No. 4 (Aug. 1918): 180-82.   Lynchings.

2152. "The Looking Glass. Sheriff Eley." THE CRISIS, Vol. 13, No. 4 (Feb. 1917): 184.   Ohio sheriff prevented lynching of a black prisoner.

2153. "Looking Toward a Lynchless Year."   FEDERAL COUNCIL BULLETIN, Vol. 11, No. 4 (April 1928): 2.

2154. "Louder Than Words." NEW REPUBLIC, Vol. 116, No. 12 (March 24, 1947): 8.   Willie Earle lynching in South Carolina.

2155. "Louisiana Lynchings." THE CRISIS, Vol. 15, No. 6 (April 1918): 282.   Inquiries about the recent lynchings of four black men.

2156. "Louisiana: Quiet Week." TIME, Vol. 48, No. 9 (Aug. 26, 1946): 21. John Johnson was whipped to death.

2157. Loveless, Dawn. "Lynch Law in Oregon." LABOR DEFENDER, Vol. 10, No. 4 (April 1934): 15.   Black worker sentenced to hang, but Oregon Supreme Court has granted petition for a rehearing.

2158. Lovin, Hugh T. "World War Vigilantes in Idaho, 1917-1918." IDAHO YESTERDAYS, Vol. 18, No. 3 (Fall 1974): 2-11.   Only minor violence.

2159. Lowell, Esther. "A Steel-Trust Lynching." LABOR DEFENDER, Vol. 4, No. 12 (Dec. 1929): 260.   Victim: Matt Lucas, black, at Birmingham, Alabama.

2160. Lurie, David.   "Vigilante Headquarters, Johnston, Pa." LABOR DEFENDER, Vol. 11, No. 8 (Sept. 1937): 11, 16.   The Johnstown Plan for crushing unionism.

2161. "Lynch & Anti-Lynch." TIME, Vol. 29, No. 17 (April 26, 1937): 16-17.   Report on Duck Hill, Mississippi, lynching of McDaniels and Townes while House of Representatives debated Gavagan bill.

2162. "Lynch-Free Year." NEWSWEEK, Vol. 41, No. 2 (Jan. 12, 1953): 25.

2163. "A Lynch Jury in San Francisco Convicts Thomas Mooney." MOTHER EARTH, Vol. 12, No. 1 (March 1917): 11-14.

2164. "Lynch Law." AMERICA, Vol. 57, No. 22 (Sept. 4, 1937): 518. Lynching will continue as long as communities have superstition, vice, illiteracy, and general ignorance.

2165. "Lynch Law." THE ECONOMIST [London], Vol. 194, No. 6074 (Jan. 23, 1960): 310, 313.   No charges against the lynchers in 1959 at Poplarville, Mississippi, of Charles Mack Parker, black, despite a 378-page report on it by the FBI. [The report is unpublished.]

2166. "Lynch Law and the President." CHRISTIAN ADVOCATE [Nashville], Vol. 79, No. 33 (Aug. 16, 1918): (5) 965.   Brief editorial.

2167. "Lynch-Law and Treason." THE LITERARY DIGEST, Vol. 55, No. 7 (Aug. 18, 1917): 12-13.   Lynching of Frank Little in Montana.

2168. "Lynch-Law as Treason." THE LITERARY DIGEST, Vol. 58, No. 6 (Aug. 10, 1918): 13.   President Wilson's open letter against lynching.

2169. "Lynch Law in 1930." THE SURVEY, Vol. 65, No. 2 (Oct. 15, 1930): 69.   Includes membership of new commission which will examine lynchings.

2170. "Lynch Law Speeds On." LABOR DEFENDER, Vol. 8, No. 9 (Sept. 1932): 165.   Virtually nothing on conventional lynching.

"The Lynch Mob and the Preacher." See Robertson, Minns S.

2171. "Lynch Mob Discharges Jury." INTERNATIONAL JURIDICAL ASSOCIATION MONTHLY BULLETIN, Vol. 4, No. 4 (Sept. 1935): 2. Ellwood Higginbotham, black, was lynched at Oxford, Mississippi.

2172. "Lynch Rumors Surround Torn Body Of Miss. Negro Trucker." JET, Vol. 17, No. 3 (Nov. 12, 1959): 12-13.   Victim: Booker T. Mixon.

2173. "Lynch Stuff." NEW MASSES, Vol. 33, No. 5 (Oct. 24, 1939): 19. Potpourri of quotations.

2174. "Lynch Terror Fails To Stop Share Croppers' Union Growth." THE CATHOLIC WORKER, Vol. 3, No. 6 (Nov. 1935): 1.

2175. "Lynch the Legislators' Prize Department." STATE GOVERN-MENT, Vol. 4, No. 11 (Nov. 1931): 16.   Announcement of money which will be paid by this journal to readers who submit abusive or appreciative quotations and cartoons about state legislators or legislatures. See Vol. 4, No. 12 (Dec. 1931): 14; Vol. 5, No. 1 (Jan. 1932): 14; Vol. 5, No. 2 (Feb. 1932): 22.

2176. "Lynch Trial Makes Southern History." LIFE, Vol. 22, No. 22 (June 2, 1947): 27-31.   Willie Earle case in South Carolina.

2177. "Lynched." THE CRISIS, Vol. 41 [sic; should be 39], No. 6 (June 1932): 192.   Brief report of 60-year-old Davis Tillus being lynched because he frightened a white woman near Crockett, Texas.

2178. "Lynched." EQUAL JUSTICE, Vol. 13, No. 11 (Feb. 1940): 3.   List of authenticated 1939 lynchings, but at least 20 more blacks in Mississippi were victims of "quiet lynchings" that were unreported.

2179. "Lynched" and "Averted Lynchings." EQUAL JUSTICE, Vol. 16, No. 1 (Winter 1942): 2.   Many details. See also "Murder, Shooting, Beating" on pp. 2-3 for wanton killings of blacks.

2180. "Lynched." LABOR DEFENDER, Vol. 10, No. 2 (Feb. 1934): 5. List of 47 victims in 1933. This page also has note on recent anti-lynching conference in Birmingham with attendant publicity.

2181. "'Lynched' Georgia Man Says He 'Knows It Ain't So.'" THE SOUTHERN FRONTIER, Vol. 1, No. 1 (Jan. 1940): [1].   Charlie E. Williams is alive.

2182. "Lynched in the U.S.A. During the Year 1937." EQUAL JUSTICE, Vol. 12, No. 1 (Jan. 1938): 1.

2183. "Lynchers and Vigilantes." AMERICA, Vol. 21, No. 6 (May 17, 1919): 153.   Editorial. Lynching murders and anti-labor beatings.

2184. "Lynchers Identified But Not Indicted." THE CHRISTIAN CEN-TURY, Vol. 76, No. 23 (June 10, 1959): 691.   Mack Charles Parker lynching in Mississippi, 1959.

2185. "Lynchers Prepare Blood-Bath in Alabama." LABOR DEFENDER, Vol. 9, No. 3 (March 1933): 35.   There will be a legal or an "extra-legal" lynching for the Scottsboro boys.

2186-90. "Lynching." AMERICA, Vol. 45, No. 17 (Aug. 1, 1931): 389. Editorial. More editorials with same title in same journal: Vol. 46, No. 7 (Nov. 21, 1931): 150; Vol. 46, No. 16 (Jan. 23, 1932): 373-74; Vol. 50, No. 5 (Nov. 4, 1933): 99; Vol. 50, No. 13 (Dec. 30, 1933): 291-92.

2191. "Lynching." AMERICA, Vol. 54, No. 15 (Jan. 18, 1936): 343-44. Tuskegee statistics for 1935.

2192. "Lynching." CHRISTIAN ADVOCATE [Nashville], Vol. 86, No. 27 (July 3, 1925): (4) 932.   Editorial.

2193. "Lynching." THE CRISIS, Vol. 13, No. 3 (Jan. 1917): 112-13.   Two recent lynchings.

2194. "Lynching." THE CRISIS, Vol. 13, No. 3 (Jan. 1917): 135-37.   Several items--including the argument that lynchings hurt the economy of the South.

2195. "Lynching." THE CRISIS, Vol. 33, No. 3 (Jan. 1927): 131. Increased number of lynchings during 1926.

2196. "Lynching." THE CRISIS, Vol. 33, No. 4 (Feb. 1927): 180-81. Upsurge in 1926.

2197. "Lynching." INTERNATIONAL JURIDICAL ASSOCIATION MONTHLY BULLETIN, Vol. 6, No. 4 (Oct. 1937): 43.   Will Kirby, black, Mount Vernon, Georgia.

2198. "Lynching." JOURNAL OF CRIMINAL LAW AND CRIMINOLOGY, Vol. 22, No. 1 (May 1931): 151.   Tuskegee statistics for 1931.

2199. ["Lynching."] THE LAWYER AND BANKER AND SOUTHERN BENCH AND BAR REVIEW, Vol. 19, No. 2 (March-April 1926): 66-69. Editorial.

2200. "Lynching." A MONTHLY SUMMARY OF EVENTS AND TRENDS IN RACE RELATIONS, Vol. 2, No. 4 (Nov. 1944): 100.   Victim: James T. Scales, at Pikeville, Tennessee.

2201. "Lynching." A MONTHLY SUMMARY OF EVENTS AND TRENDS IN RACE RELATIONS, Vol. 4, No. 4 (Nov. 1946): 104-05.

2202. "Lynching." A MONTHLY SUMMARY OF EVENTS AND

TRENDS IN RACE RELATIONS, Vol. 4, No. 5 (Dec. 1946): 138.

2203. "The Lynching." THE NATION, Vol. 188, No. 19 (May 9, 1959): 418. Poplarville, Mississippi, lynching.

2204. "Lynching." THE NEW REPUBLIC, Vol. 116, No. 9 (March 3, 1947): 9-10.   Willie Earle lynching in South Carolina. Includes illustration.

2205. "Lynching." NEWSWEEK, Vol. 19, No. 5 (Feb. 2, 1942): 28.   Cleo Wright was dragged to death behind a car at Sikeston, Missouri.

2206. "Lynching a Domestic Question." THE MESSENGER, Vol. 2, No. 7 (July 1919): 7.   Lynching is not a domestic question.

2207. "Lynching a National Evil." THE OUTLOOK, Vol. 132, No. 14 (Dec. 6, 1922): 596-97.

2208. "Lynching, a National Evil: What Are the Facts?"   INTERNA-TIONAL JOURNAL OF RELIGIOUS EDUCATION, Vol. 13, No. 10 (June 1937): 18, 40.   Includes suggestions for eradicating lynching, in addition to passage of federal law.

2209. "Lynching--A Service To Tradition." THE SOUTHERN FRONTIER, Vol. 2, No. 1 (Jan. 1941): [2].   One paragraph.

2210. "Lynching Again on the Increase." THE CHRISTIAN CENTURY, Vol. 48, No. 1 (Jan. 7, 1931): 5.

2211. "Lynching: An American Kulture?" THE NEW REPUBLIC, Vol. 14, No. 180 (April 13, 1918): 311-12.   Lynching of Robert Prager at Collins-ville, Illinois, as part of American culture.

2212. "Lynching and Communism." INTERRACIAL REVIEW, Vol. 9, No. 10 (Oct. 1936): 147-48.   Lynching outrages help communism. Editorial.

2213. "Lynching and Other Mob Outrages." INTERRACIAL REVIEW, Vol. 9, No. 8 (Aug. 1936): 115-16.   Black Legion members in Detroit, Michigan, killed "an available Negro 'just to see how it would feel.'"

2214. "Lynching and Riots." THE CRISIS, Vol. 19, No. 5 (March 1919): 243.

2215. "Lynching and the Axis." THE COMMONWEAL, Vol. 37, No. 2 (Oct. 30, 1942): 27-28.   Lynching of 3 blacks in Mississippi is a boon to Axis propaganda.

2216. "Lynching and the Law's 'Leniency.'" THE CRISIS, Vol. 42, No. 1 (Jan. 1935): 18.   Disputes the idea "that there has been any great leniency or delay in the punishment of Negroes accused of crime."

2217. "Lynching and the Physician." AMERICA, Vol. 54, No. 9 (Dec. 7, 1935): 194.   Lynching or killing of patient by doctor are murder--whether community approves or patient requests it.

2218. "Lynching and Treason." INTERRACIAL REVIEW, Vol. 14, No. 5 (May 1941): 80.

2219. "Lynching at All-Time Low." THE CHRISTIAN CENTURY, Vol. 63, No. 3 (Jan. 16, 1946): 67.

2220. "The Lynching at Houston." LABOR DEFENDER, Vol. 3, No. 8 (Aug. 1928): 173.   Victim: Robert Powell, black. Includes photo of four lynched blacks. Texas.

2221. "The Lynching at Memphis." THE CRISIS, Vol. 14, No. 4 (Aug. 1917): 185-88.   The burning of a black man named Ell Person near Memphis in May 1917.

2222. "Lynching County Seeks Fresh Prey." THE CRISIS, Vol. 41, No. 10 (Oct. 1934): 302.   Maury County, Tennessee, where Cordie Cheek was lynched in Dec., 1933, is seeking extradition of a black man from Illinois.

2223. "Lynching Decreasing." THE LITERARY DIGEST, Vol. 90, No. 4 (July 24, 1926): 30.

2224. "Lynching: Dixie Blowtorch Sets Yankee Congressmen Afire." NEWS-WEEK [sic], Vol. 9, No. 17 (April 24, 1937): 12.   Duck Hill, Mississippi. Says Roosevelt Townes was burned to death and that shots killed Bootjack McDaniels [sic].

2225. "Lynching Ebbs and Flows." AMERICA, Vol. 43, No. 24 (Sept. 20, 1930): 560.   Editorial.

2226. "Lynching et Al."[sic] THE COMMONWEAL, Vol. 18, No. 18 (Sept. 1, 1933): 417-18.   In section titled "Week by Week." Double lynching in Alabama with third victim escaping.

2227. "The Lynching Evil." THE NEW REPUBLIC, Vol. 19, No. 235 (May 3, 1919): 7-8.   Says lynching has disgraced the nation; it is not done primarily against accused rapists; hopes for remedies, perhaps from the National Conference on Lynching.

2228. "The Lynching Evil from a Southern Standpoint." THE AMERICAN REVIEW OF REVIEWS, Vol. 60, No. 5 (Nov. 1919): 531-32.   Report on Robert R. Moton's ideas in South Atlantic Quarterly on how to end lynching.

2229. "The Lynching Evil--Readers' Replies." THE LITERARY DIGEST, Vol. 117, No. 5 (Feb. 3, 1934): 47.   Responses to article by A. R. W. Mackreth.

2230. "Lynching: Excitement Over Picky Pie." NEWSWEEK, Vol. 33, No. 24 (June 13, 1949): 19-20.   Death of Caleb "Picky Pie" Hill, Jr., in Georgia.

2231. "Lynching for Drunkenness." INTERNATIONAL JURIDICAL ASSOCIATION MONTHLY BULLETIN, Vol. 4, No. 5 (Oct. 1935): 3. Lewis Harris, black, near Vienna, Georgia.

2232. LYNCHING GOES UNDERGROUND: A REPORT ON A NEW TECHNIQUE. Sponsored by Senators Robert Wagner and Arthur Capper, and Representatives Joseph A. Cavagan [sic; should be Gavagan] and Hamilton Fish. N.p.: n.p., Jan. 1940.   Eight page pamphlet. Page 1: ". . . countless Negroes are lynched yearly, but their disappearance is shrouded in mystery, for they are dispatched quietly and without general knowledge. In some lonely swamp a small body of men do the job formerly done by a vast, howling blood-thirsty mob . . ." Page 2: "The author of this report, who must remain anonymous, is a white native southerner who has . . . made a number of investigations of lynchings." [Possibly Howard Kester.]

2233. "Lynching in America: Today's Facts." THE CHRISTIAN CENTURY, Vol. 53, No. 15 (April 8, 1936): 526.

2234. "Lynching in Covington, Tennessee." INTERNATIONAL JURIDICAL ASSOCIATION MONTHLY BULLETIN, Vol. 6, No. 3 (Sept. 1937): 32.   Albert Gooden, black.

2235. "Lynching in Mississippi." INTERNATIONAL JURIDICAL ASSOCIATION MONTHLY BULLETIN, Vol. 4, No. 1 (June 1935): 3. R. D. McGee, black, at Wiggins.

2236. "Lynching in Montana. THE INDEPENDENT, Vol. 91, No. 3584 (Aug. 11, 1917): 216.   Frank Little.

2237. "Lynching in 1940." INTERRACIAL REVIEW, Vol. 13, No. 1 (Jan. 1940): 4-5.   Editorial.

2238. "Lynching in Omaha." In RACIAL VIOLENCE IN THE UNITED

STATES, pp. 92-94. Ed. by Allen D. Grimshaw. Chicago: Aldine, 1969. Originally published in The New York Times, September 30, 1919, under the headline "700 Federal Troops Quiet Omaha; Mayor Recovering; Omaha Mob Rule Defended by Most of the Population."

2239. "A Lynching in the Making." INDEPENDENT WOMAN, Vol. 14 (Jan. 1935): 6-7, 33. Names of people and town involved are not given. Includes arguments for and against lynching.

2240. "Lynching in the Raw." THE CHRISTIAN CENTURY, Vol. 52, No. 1 (Jan. 2, 1935): 10-11. Personal letter about lynching of Claude Neal in Florida, "By Eye Witness."

2241. "The Lynching Industry." THE CRISIS, Vol. 13, No. 4 (Feb. 1917): 178-79.

2242. "The Lynching Industry." THE CRISIS, Vol. 13, No. 5 (March 1917): 226-27.

2243. "The Lynching Industry, 1919." THE CRISIS, Vol. 19, No. 4 (Feb. 1920): 183-86. Gives names of victims, dates of lynchings, and alleged causes. Includes a map (p. 184) of where lynchings and race riots occurred in the U.S. in 1919.

2244. "Lynching Is No Crime." THE CRISIS, Vol. 43, No. 6 (June 1936): 179. Editorial from Philadelphia Tribune. Congress and the Franklin Roosevelt administration do nothing against lynching.

2245. "Lynching: Jury Makes Sheriff Pay for Negro's Lawless Death." NEWS-WEEK [sic], Vol. 7, No. 22 (May 30, 1936): 36. White jury in Louisiana awarded damages to parents of black lynching victim Freddy Moore. Precedent in Indiana 36 years ago.

2246. "Lynching Map of the United States for Past Decade." THE SOUTHERN FRONTIER, Vol. 2, No. 1 (Jan. 1941): [3].

"A Lynching Map of the United States of America." See Allison, Madeline G., in Chapter IV of this bibliography.

2247. "Lynching Maps of the United States for Two Decades." THE SOUTHERN FRONTIER, Vol. 3, No. 1 (Jan. 1942): [4]. Five maps.

2248. "Lynching: Maryland Judge Is Censured for Tragedy." NEWS-WEEK [sic], Vol. 2, No. 13 (Oct. 28, 1933): 8. Armwood lynching.

2249. "Lynching Must Be Stopped." THE CHRISTIAN CENTURY, Vol. 54, No. 17 (April 28, 1937): 544-46.

2250. "Lynching Must Go!" INTERRACIAL REVIEW, Vol. 9, No. 12 (Dec. 1936): 179.   Editorial.

2251. "Lynching Must Stop." CHRISTIAN ADVOCATE [Nashville], Vol. 90, No. 6 (Feb. 8, 1929): (3-4) 163-64.   Editorial.

2252. "Lynching, 1950: The Law Gains Ground." NEW SOUTH, Vol. 5, No. 12, Vol. 6, No. 1 (Dec.-Jan. 1950-51): 4-5, 8.

2253. "Lynching: 1936 Score Jumps to Six, Catching Up With 1935." NEWS-WEEK [sic], Vol. 7, No. 19 (May 9, 1936): 11-12.

2254. LYNCHING NORTHERN STYLE. New York: Committee to Free the Trenton Six, Civil Rights Congress, [1948?].

2255. "Lynching Number One, 1942; Women Protest--Editor Gloats." THE SOUTHERN FRONTIER, Vol. 3, No. 2 (Feb. 1942): [4].

2256. "The Lynching of Justice." THE COMMONWEAL, Vol. 19, No. 6 (Dec. 8, 1933): 141-42.   Double lynching in San Jose, California.

2257. "Lynching on the Decrease." THE OUTLOOK, Vol. 136, No. 2 (Jan. 9, 1924): 49.

2258. "Lynching on the Wane." AMERICA, Vol. 38, No. 14 (Jan. 14, 1928): 335.

2259. "Lynching on the Wane." THE LITERARY DIGEST, Vol. 82, No. 8 (Aug. 23, 1924): 31.

2260. "Lynching Rate Cut In Half." THE CHRISTIAN CENTURY, Vol. 57, No. 1 (Jan. 3, 1940): 5.

2261. "Lynching Record." JOURNAL OF CRIMINAL LAW AND CRIMINOLOGY, Vol. 22, No. 3 (Sept. 1931): 448.   Statistics for first half of 1931.

2262. "Lynching Record." THE JOURNAL OF CRIMINAL LAW AND CRIMINOLOGY, Vol. 23, No. 3 (Sept.-Oct. 1932): 498.   Tuskegee statistics for first half of 1932.

2263. "The Lynching Record for 1921." CHRISTIAN ADVOCATE

[Nashville], Vol. 83, No. 1 (Jan. 6, 1922): 22-23.

2264. "Lynching Record for 1927." CHRISTIAN ADVOCATE [Nashville], Vol. 88, No. 31 (Aug. 5, 1927): (21) 981. R. R. Moton's statistics 'for first half of 1927.

2265. "Lynching Record for the Year 1918." THE CRISIS, Vol. 17, No. 4 (Feb. 1919): 180-81.   A history.

2266. "Lynching Record, 1938." THE JOURNAL OF CRIMINAL LAW AND CRIMINOLOGY, Vol. 29, No. 5 (Jan.-Feb. 1939): 755-56.

2267. "Lynching Record For 1921." In NEGRO YEAR BOOK . . . 1921-1922, p. 72. Ed. by Monroe N. Work. Tuskegee Institute, AL: Negro Year Book Pub. Co., 1922.

2268. "Lynching Record for the Year 1918." THE CRISIS, Vol. 17, No. 4 (Feb. 1919): 180-81.   Gives names of victims, dates of lynchings, and alleged causes of the lynchings.

2269. "Lynching Record Shows Continued Gains." THE CHRISTIAN CENTURY, Vol. 57, No. 22 (May 29, 1940): 692.   First 12 months with dates, names of victims, and alleged reasons for lynchings since record keeping started in 1882.

2270. "Lynching Remains." INTERRACIAL REVIEW, Vol. 11, No. 8 (Aug. 1938): 116.   Editorial.

2271. "Lynching Report." THE CRISIS, Vol. 60, No. 2 (Feb. 1953): 103. Tuskegee reports there was no lynching in U.S. in 1952, first such year since record keeping began.   But other forms of anti-Negro violence have not declined.

2272. "The Lynching Roll of Honor." THE LITERARY DIGEST, Vol. 81, No. 1 (April 5, 1924): 32-33.

2273. "The Lynching Spirit Finds a New Technique." INTERRACIAL REVIEW, Vol. 12, No. 3 (March 1939): 37-38.   Flogging instead of lethal lynching.

2274. "Lynching the Innocent." THE NATION, Vol. 133, No. 3464 (Nov. 25, 1931): 561.   Report of Southern Commission on the Study of Lynching and lynchings in 1930.

2275. "Lynching Toll for 1938." EQUAL JUSTICE, Vol. 12, No. 12 (Jan.

1939): 7.   Dates, places, names of victims, and attendant circumstances.

2276. "Lynching: Troops Called Out in Shelbyville; Four Die; Court House in Ruins; Negro Spirited Away." NEWS-WEEK [sic], Vol. 4, No. 26 (Dec. 29, 1934): 5.   Mob members slain by National Guard in Tennessee. Two photos.

2277. A LYNCHING UNCOVERED BY THE NATIONAL ASSOCIA-TION FOR THE ADVANCEMENT OF COLORED PEOPLE. THE RESULTS: INVESTIGATION AND CONFIRMATION BY THE "ATLANTA CONSTITUTION." $1,500 REWARD OFFERED BY GOVERNOR DORSEY OF GEORGIA. [New York?: NAACP?, 1919?] Victim: Berry Washington, 72, black, at Milan, Georgia, May 1919.

2278. "A Lynching? We're Too Busy." NEW MASSES, Vol. 10, No. 8 (Feb. 20, 1934): 19.   Former governor Ferguson's reaction to lynching of David Gregory, black man, at Kountze, Texas.

2279. "Lynchings." COMMON SENSE, Vol. 5, No. 1 (Jan. 1936): 5.   Pro-tests by radicals have so far saved the Scottsboro boys [Alabama] and Angelo Herndon [Georgia] from "Legal lynching."

2280. "Lynchings." THE CRISIS, Vol. 33, No. 1 (Nov. 1926): 42.   Four recent victims.

2281. "Lynchings."   INTERNATIONAL JURIDICAL ASSOCIATION MONTHLY BULLETIN, Vol. 3, No. 10 (March 1935): 2.   Brief item.

2282. "Lynchings." OUTLOOK AND INDEPENDENT, Vol. 156, No. 13 (Nov. 26, 1930): 489-90.

2283. "Lynchings--A Further Note." INTERNATIONAL JURIDICAL ASSOCIATION MONTHLY BULLETIN, Vol. 2, No. 7 (Dec. 1933): [9-10].

2284. "Lynchings and Mob Murders, 1917." THE CRISIS, Vol. 15, No. 4 (Feb. 1918): 183-84.   Gives dates, names of victims, and alleged reasons for lynchings.

2285. "Lynchings and Mobs." THE CRISIS, Vol. 22, No. 4 (Aug. 1921): 149.

2286. "Lynchings Decline to Three in 1939." INTERRACIAL REVIEW, Vol. 13, No. 1 (Jan. 1940): 16.

2287. "Lynchings During 1935."   INTERNATIONAL JURIDICAL

ASSOCIATION MONTHLY BULLETIN, Vol. 4, No. 8 (Jan. 1936): 2. Difference in numbers between figures of NAACP and International Labor Defense.

2288. "Lynchings During 1934." INTERNATIONAL JURIDICAL ASSOCIATION MONTHLY BULLETIN, Vol. 3, No. 9 (Feb. 1935): 2. Brief paragraph. The NAACP set the number at 16; the International Labor Defense set it at 25.

2289. "Lynchings During 1934." SIGN, Vol. 14, No. 8 (March 1935): 477. Letter from R. R. Moton.

2290. "Lynchings during 1926." JOURNAL OF THE AMERICAN INSTITUTE OF CRIMINAL LAW AND CRIMINOLOGY, Vol. 18, No. 2 (Aug. 1927): 272.   Tuskegee statistics.

2291. "Lynchings for 1919." CHRISTIAN ADVOCATE [Nashville], Vol. 81, No. 2 (Jan. 9, 1920): (3) 35.   Statistics from Dr. Moton.

2292. "Lynchings for 1922." CHRISTIAN ADVOCATE [Nashville], Vol. 83, No. 52 (Dec. 29, 1922): (19) 1651.   Tuskegee statistics.

2293. "The Lynchings in Indiana." THE CHRISTIAN CENTURY, Vol. 47, No. 33 (Aug. 20, 1930): 1003.   Marion.

2294. "Lynchings in 1919." THE LITERARY DIGEST, Vol. 64, No. 3 (Jan. 17, 1920): 20.

2295. "Lynchings in 1931." JOURNAL OF CRIMINAL LAW AND CRIMINOLOGY, Vol. 22, No. 6 (March 1932): 922.   Tuskegee statistics for 1931.

2296. "Lynchings in 1928." CHRISTIAN ADVOCATE [Nashville], Vol. 90, No. 2 (Jan. 11, 1929): (23) 55.   R. R. Moton's Tuskegee statistics for 1928.

2297. "Lynchings in the United States." AMERICA, Vol. 28, No. 25 (April 7, 1923): 599.   Editorial. Brief.

2298. "Lynchings in the United States." THE CRISIS, Vol. 23, No. 4 (Feb. 1922): 165-66.

2299. "Lynchings Increase in 1940." THE CHRISTIAN CENTURY, Vol. 58, No. 3 (Jan. 15, 1941): 76.

2300. "Lynchings--More or Less--1941." THE SOUTHERN FRONTIER,

Vol. 3, No. 1 (Jan. 1942): [2].

2301. "The Lynchings of 1934." THE LITERARY DIGEST, Vol. 119, No. 2 (Jan. 12, 1935): 18.

2302. "The Lynchings of Two Days." THE CHRISTIAN CENTURY, Vol. 52, No. 48 (Nov. 27, 1935): 1509.

2303. "Lynching's Ominous Growth." THE LITERARY DIGEST, Vol. 117, No. 2 (Jan. 13, 1934): 7.

2304. "Lynchings Protested." THE CHRISTIAN ADVOCATE [New York], Vol. 107, No. 6 (Feb. 11, 1932): 160.   Methodist Episcopal Church condemnation of recent lynchings in Lewisburg, West Virginia, and Salisbury, Maryland.

2305. "Lynchings Stir Southern Debate." THE LITERARY DIGEST, Vol. 120, No. 21 (Nov. 23, 1935): 6.

2306. "Lynchings: Texas v. The Supreme Court."   INTERNATIONAL JURIDICAL ASSOCIATION MONTHLY BULLETIN, Vol. 9, No. 12 (June 1941): 134.   Doesn't seem to qualify as a lynching.

2307. "Lynchings: The First Lynching, 1942." THE SOUTHERN FRONTIER, Vol. 3, No. 7 (July 1942): [3].

2308. "A Lynchless South in 1933." THE COMMONWEAL, Vol. 17, No. 5 (Nov. 30, 1932): 116.   Hope of the Association of Southern Women for the Prevention of Lynching.

2309. Mack, Mary. "This Year's Crop in Georgia." LABOR DEFENDER, Vol. 10, No. 6 (June 1936): 15, 17.   Recent lynchings of Lint Shaw in Cordele, GA, and John Rushin [sic] in Pavo, Georgia, have spurred renewed anti-lynching activity.

2310. Mackreth, A. R. W. "The Lynching Evil and Church Responsibility." THE LITERARY DIGEST, Vol. 116, No. 26 (Dec. 23, 1933): 19-20.

2311. MacLean, Harry N. IN BROAD DAYLIGHT: A MURDER IN SKIDMORE, MISSOURI. New York: Dell, 1990.   Sometimes considered a lynching. July, 1981.

2312. MacLean, Nancy. BEHIND THE MASK OF CHIVALRY: THE MAKING OF THE SECOND KU KLUX KLAN. New York: Oxford Univ. Press, 1994.   See "Lynching" and "Vigilantism" in index. Based on author's

Ph.D. diss., Univ. of Wisconsin, Madison, 1989; see <u>Diss. Ab. Intl.</u>, Vol. 50, No. 11 (May 1990): 3718A; abstract says, "Chapter 8 explores the local Klan's vigilantism . . ."

2313. Madison, Mary Jo. "Shots in the Dark: Lynching in Tuscaloosa, Alabama, 1933." M.A. thesis, Auburn Univ., 1991. Victims: Dan Pippen, Jr., A. T. Harden, and (later) Dennis Cross, blacks.

2314. Magil, A. B. "Gastonia Prepares a Lynching." LABOR DEFENDER, Vol. 4, No. 7 (July 1929): 136-37. Anti-labor activity; not actual lynching. North Carolina.

2315. "Making Lynching Less Attractive." OPPORTUNITY, A JOURNAL OF NEGRO LIFE, Vol. 6, No. 3 (March 1928): 68.

2316. "Man Who Was Almost Lynched." EBONY, Vol. 35, No. 6 (April 1980): 148-50, 152, 154. James Cameron and lynchings at Marion, Indiana, Aug. 1930.

2317. Marcantonio, Vito. "Lynching Must Go!" EQUAL JUSTICE, Vol. 16, No. 2 (Spring 1942): 2. Letter to President Roosevelt.

2318. Marcantonio, Vito. "The Menace of Vigilantism." LABOR DEFENDER, Vol. 11, No. 7 (Aug. 1937): 7, 15. Anti-labor activities.

2319. "Marianna Lynching Report." THE CRISIS, Vol. 42, No. 1 (Jan. 1935): 27. Report on Claude Neal lynching in Florida is for sale.

2320. "Marion." THE CRISIS, Vol. 37, No. 10 (Oct. 1930): 353. Indiana lynching of Tom Shipp and Abe Smith. For photo see "Civilization in the United States," p. 348.

2321. Mars, Florence, with Eden, Lynn. WITNESS IN PHILADELPHIA. Baton Rouge: Louisiana State Univ. Press, 1977. Chaney, Goodman, and Schwerner in Mississippi, 1964.

2322. Marshall, Marilyn. "Beulah Mae Donald: The Black Woman Who Beat The Ku Klux Klan." EBONY, Vol. 43, No. 5 (March 1988): 148-49, 152-53. Michael Donald was lynched in Mobile, Alabama, 1981.

2323. "Martyrs For Black Freedom." EBONY, Vol. 30, No. 10 (Aug. 1975): 138-40. Review of lynching, 1890s-1940s, but emphasis on post-1954 civil rights movement.

2324. Marx, Gary T., and Archer, Dane. "Community Self-Defense."

SOCIETY, Vol. 13, No. 3 (March-April 1976): 38-43.   Part of symposium on American vigilantes.

2325. "Maryland Has a Lynching." OUTLOOK AND INDEPENDENT, Vol. 159, No. 17 (Dec. 23, 1931): 521.   Victim: Matthews Williams. Location: Salisbury. See cartoon on p. 520.

2326. "The Masked Floggers of Tulsa." THE LITERARY DIGEST, Vol. 78, No. 12 (Sept. 22, 1923): 17.   Oklahoma governor proclaimed martial law.

2327. "Mass Murder in America." THE NEW REPUBLIC, Vol. 77, No. 993 (Dec. 13, 1933): 116-17.   Lynchings in Maryland, Missouri, and San Jose, California.

2328. "Mass Murders or Civilized Society?" THE SIGN, Vol. 13, No. 6 (Jan. 1934): 324.   Recent lynchings in Maryland, Missouri, and California.

2329. Matelis, Valentine. "Merrily Lynching Along!" THE COMMON-WEAL, Vol. 16, No. 19 (Sept. 7, 1932): 443-45.   Lynching of Matthew Williams in Maryland and efforts against lynchers in various states, including prison sentences for seven Alabama lynchers in 1926.

2330. "A Matter of Manners." THE CRISIS, Vol. 19, No. 4 (Feb. 1920): 170.   Includes information that a black youth was lynched in Roanoke, Virginia, for offering a helping hand to a white girl who had fallen down.

2331. Matthews, Donald R., and Prothro, James W. "Political Factors and Negro Voter Registration in the South." THE AMERICAN POLITICAL SCIENCE REVIEW, Vol. 57, No. 2 (June 1963): 355-67.   See pp. 364-66 for lynching.

2332. Maurer, George. "It Takes a Mass Fight to Defeat Deportation, Lynching and Boss Terror!" LABOR DEFENDER, Vol. 6, No. 4 (April 1931): 76.

2333. Maxwell, Joe. "Racial Healing in the Land of Lynching: How 24,000 Mississippi Christians are beating racism one friendship at a time." CHRISTIANITY TODAY, Vol. 38, No. 1 (Jan. 10, 1994): 24-26.

2334. McClelland, John M., Jr. "Terror on Tower Avenue." PACIFIC NORTHWEST QUARTERLY, Vol. 57, No. 2 (April 1966): 65-72.   Centralia, Washington, 1919.

2335. McGinty, Brian. "Shadows in St. James Park." CALIFORNIA

HISTORY, Vol. 57, No. 4 (Winter 1978-79): 290-307.   A 1933 double-lynching in California known as "San Jose's shame."

2336. McGovern, James R.   ANATOMY OF A LYNCHING: THE KILLING OF CLAUDE NEAL. Baton Rouge: Louisiana State Univ. Press, 1982.   Florida, 1934.

2337. McGovern, James R., and Howard, Walter T. "Private Justice and National Concern: The Lynching of Claude Neal." THE HISTORIAN, Vol. 43, No. 4 (Aug. 1981): 546-59.   Florida, 1934.

2338. McLellan, Howard. "Corn Belt Vigilantes.: THE WORLD'S WORK, Vol. 56, No. 6 (Oct. 1928): 639-47.   In 1920 bankers in Iowa organized citizens as deputies to combat robberies. Followed by other states.

2339. McRea, John. "Wesley Everest's Soliloquy." LABOR DEFENDER, Vol. 2, No. 5 (May 1927): 72.   He was lynched at Centralia, Washington, 1919.

2340. Mecklin, John M. "Confessio Nominis Non Examinatio Criminis." THE NATION, Vol. 104, No. 2694 (Feb. 15, 1917): 186-87.   Problems with stopping lynching in the South.

2341. "Meditations on Poplarville." THE NATION, Vol. 188, No. 23 (June 6, 1959): 505-06.   Mack Charles Parker lynching in Mississippi, 1959.

2342. "Members of Lynch Mob Slain." INTERNATIONAL JURIDICAL ASSOCIATION MONTHLY BULLETIN, Vol. 3, No. 7 (Dec. 1934): 3. Shelbyville, TN. "This is the first known case in which the authorities protected a Negro from a lynch mob at the cost of white lives."

2343. "Memento of a Lynching Mob." LIFE, Vol. 46, No. 18 (May 4, 1959): 44.   Mack Charles Parker lynching, Mississippi, 1959.

2344. "Memo from Mississippi." LOOK, Vol. 24, No. 2 (Jan. 19, 1960): 82-83.   Poplarville and Mack Parker, 1959.

2345. "Memphis." THE CRISIS, Vol. 14, No. 3 (July 1917): 133-35.   Ell Person lynching in Tennessee. Includes photo. Quotes from Harvard Crimson, S.F. Bulletin, The New Republic, and The Independent. Part of "The Looking Glass."

2346. "Memphis. May 22, A.D., 1917." THE CRISIS, Vol. 14, No. 3 (July 1917) [or No. 6 (Oct. 1917)], Supplement, pp. 1-4.   Listed at top of page 1 as "Supplement to The Crisis, July, 1917, Vol. 14, No. 3" but in microfilm copy of The Crisis is at end of Oct. issue. In hard-copy reprint edition of The Crisis (New York: Negro Universities Press, 1969) is at end of July issue. Ell Persons [sic] case in Memphis white newspapers.

2347. "The Memphis Supplement." THE CRISIS, Vol. 15, No. 3 (Jan. 1918): 127.   Anonymous letter from Memphis on Ell Person lynching.

2348. Mendelsohn, Jack.   THE MARTYRS: SIXTEEN WHO GAVE THEIR LIVES FOR RACIAL JUSTICE. New York: Harper & Row, 1966. See pp. 1-20 for Rev. George Lee, shot while driving his car, Belzoni, Mississippi, May, 1955 (not a "traditional" lynching). See pp. 109-32 for Chaney, Goodman, and Schwerner, lynched in Mississippi, 1964.

2349. "Mer Rouge Murders Unpunished." THE LITERARY DIGEST, Vol. 76, No. 13 (March 31, 1923): 10-11.   Two men killed in Louisiana, possibly by KKK.

2350. "Michael Donald Buried: Police Still Unsure Of Motive in Ala. Lynching." JET, Vol. 60, No. 5 (April 16, 1981): 6-8.

2351. "Migration Will Stop Lynching in the South." THE MESSENGER, Vol. 5, No. 8 (Aug. 1923): 784.

2352. Miller, Gene. INVITATION TO A LYNCHING. Garden City, NY: Doubleday, 1975.   No actual lynching as term is commonly understood. Two black men were convicted for 1963 murders.

2353. Miller, Kelly. "The Disgrace of Democracy." THE CRISIS, Vol. 15, No. 3 (Jan. 1918): 149.   Ad for open letter on lynching and race riots by a Howard University professor.

2354. Miller, Kelly.   THE DISGRACE OF DEMOCRACY--OPEN LETTER TO PRESIDENT WOODROW WILSON. [Washington, DC]: n.p., [1917].

2355. Miller, Kelly. THE EVERLASTING STAIN. Washington, DC: Associated Publishers, 1924.   Reprinted in Race Adjustment and The Everlasting Stain (New York: Arno Press & The New York Times, 1968). Pages 5-43 of The Everlasting Stain are "Radicalism and the Negro" (Chap. II); pp. 57-87 are "An Appeal to Reason on the Race Problem: An Open Letter to John Temple Graves Suggested by the Atlanta Riot"; pp. 136-60 are "Disgrace of Democracy (Open Letter to President Wilson)" (dated Aug. 4, 1917) (Chapter VI); pp. 314-32 are "The Sport of the Ghouls" (Chapter XXII). See pp. 66-84 of Race Adjustment for lynching.

2356. Miller, Kelly. "Radicalism and the Negro." THE COMPETITOR, Vol. 1, No. 3 (March 1920): 33-37. Includes this paraphrase of a statement of Frederick Douglass: "The people who are lynched the easiest
Will be lynched oftenest" (p. 36).

2357. Miller, Malcolm F. "Lynching as a Substitute for Capital Punishment." THE CHRISTIAN CENTURY, Vol. 48, No. 8 (Feb. 25, 1931): 275-76. Letter commenting on "North Dakota's Lynching" in Feb. 11, 1931, issue. The lynching "would probably not have occurred" if North Dakota had legal capital punishment.

2358. Miller, Robert Moats. AMERICAN PROTESTANTISM AND SOCIAL ISSUES, 1919-1939. Chapel Hill: Univ. of North Carolina Press, 1958. See Chapter IX, "The Churches and Lynching" (pp. 131-36). "Substantial portions" were originally in The Journal of Negro History, Vol. XLII (April 1957).

2359. Miller, Robert Moats. "The Protestant Churches and Lynching, 1919-1939." THE JOURNAL OF NEGRO HISTORY, Vol. 42, No. 2 (April 1957): 118-31. Argues that Protestant churches, even in the South, were more outspoken against lynching than was commonly thought.

2360. Miller, William D. MEMPHIS DURING THE PROGRESSIVE ERA, 1900-1917. Memphis: Memphis State Univ. Press, 1957. See pp. 191-95 for Eli [sic] Persons lynching in Tennessee.

2361. Mills, Nicolaus. LIKE A HOLY CRUSADE: MISSISSIPPI 1964--THE TURNING OF THE CIVIL RIGHTS MOVEMENT IN AMERICA. Chicago: Ivan R. Dee, 1992. See Chaney, Goodman, and Schwerner in index.

2362. Milton, George Fort. "The Impeachment of Judge Lynch." THE VIRGINIA QUARTERLY REVIEW, Vol. 8, No. 2 (April 1932): 247-56. The chairman of the Southern Commission on the Study of Lynching reports the background and conclusions of its study, which dealt especially with the year 1930.

2363. "Milwaukee Is Talking . . ." NEWSWEEK, Vol. 123, No. 12 (March 21, 1994): 14. James Cameron and his new book A Time of Terror about 1930 Marion, Indiana, lynching. One paragraph.

2364. Minor, Robert. LYNCHING AND FRAME-UP IN TENNESSEE. New York: New Century Publishers, 1946. Confrontation between a mob of whites and blacks trying to prevent lynching at Columbia, Tennessee, Feb. 1946. Eventually 30 blacks were indicted; most were acquitted, but some got long prison sentences.

2365. "Minority Groups and Mob Violence." INTERRACIAL REVIEW, Vol. 9, No. 7 (July 1936): 99-100.   Editorial. Catholics, Jews, blacks should work together against lynching.

2366. Minton, Bruce. "The Klan Turns to Murder." NEW MASSES, Vol. 17, No. 11 (Dec. 10, 1935): 13-16. Murder of Florida labor organizer Frank Norman. Lured from his home on pretext of identifying a black who had been lynched. [See also Bruce Minton, "Fred Bass and the Norman Case," ibid., Vol. 17, No. 12 (Dec. 17, 1935): 12-14.]

2367. "Miss West at Greenville." NEWSWEEK, Vol. 29, No. 25 (June 23, 1947): 63.   Rebecca West's New Yorker article about the trial of Willie Earle's alleged lynchers in South Carolina.

2368. MISSISSIPPI AND THE MOB. STATE OFFICIALS, OFFICERS AND OUTSTANDING MEMBERS OF STATE BAR ASSOCIATION, AND OTHER PROMINENT MISSISSIPPIANS CONDEMN MOB VIOLENCE AND CALL ON OFFICERS TO DO THEIR SWORN DUTY. Jackson, MS: Jackson Printing Co., [1925?].

2369. "Mississippi: Back to the Courts." NEWSWEEK, Vol. 55, No. 3 (Jan. 18, 1960): 23-24.   Mack Parker case presented to federal grand jury.

2370. "Mississippi Barbarism." THE CRISIS, Vol. 62 (Oct. 1955): 480. Emmett Till. Editorial.

2371. "Mississippi: Case Closed." TIME, Vol. 73, No. 23 (June 8, 1959): 20. Mack Charles Parker.

2372. "Mississippi Murder." THE SOUTHERN FRONTIER, Vol. 5, No. 10 (Oct. 1944): [1].

2373. "Mississippi: 'Nothing Can Save Us.'" TIME, Vol. 73, No. 22 (June 1, 1959): 18-19.   Mack Charles Parker.

2374. "Mississippi: Officials Express Concern At Poplarville Incident." SOUTHERN SCHOOL NEWS, Vol. 5, No. 11 (May 1959): 8.   Mack Charles Parker.

2375. "Mississippi: On Behalf of Lynch Law." TIME, Vol. 74, No. 20 (Nov. 16, 1959): 33.   Mack Charles Parker.

2376. "Mississippi Tense After Lynching of Natchez Negro." JET, Vol. 30,

No. 12 (June 30, 1966): 4-5.   Victim: Ben (Chester) White, 67 years old.

2377. "Mississippi's Seventh Lynching." INTERNATIONAL JURIDICAL ASSOCIATION MONTHLY BULLETIN, Vol. 4, No. 3 (Aug. 1935): 1-2. Bodie Bates, black, in Calhoun County. One victim in other lynching was a black, H. T. Tyrone, who "was apparently just too prosperous to suit his white neighbors."

2378. "Missouri Heads 1931 Lynching Parade." THE LITERARY DIGEST, Vol. 108, No. 5 (Jan. 31, 1931): 17-18.   Includes photo.

2379. "Missouri Lynching." INTERNATIONAL JURIDICAL ASSOCIATION MONTHLY BULLETIN, Vol. 10, No. 9 (March 1942): 94.   Cleo Wright, black, at Sikeston.

2380. "Missouri Mob Murder." OUTLOOK AND INDEPENDENT, Vol. 157, No. 4 (Jan. 28, 1931): 123-24.   Black man was lynched at Maryville.

2381. "The Mob." THE INDEPENDENT, Vol. 92, No. 3597 (Nov. 10, 1917): 275.   "Patriot" mob took Cincinnati, Ohio, minister to Kentucky and whipped him.   Action of Memphis, Tennessee, mob in burning and beheading a black man was widely publicized in Germany.

2382. "Mob Law." THE CRISIS, Vol. 31, No. 1 (Nov. 1925): 40-42.   Several lynching items and two photos. Especially about the burning of Jim Ivy in Mississippi.

2383. "Mob Law and the Negro." THE PUBLIC, Vol. 20, No. 1012 (Aug. 24, 1917): 810-11.

2384. "Mob Law: Substitution of 'Judge Lynch' for More Leisurely Justice Inflames National Controversy." NEWS-WEEK [sic], Vol. 2, No. 19 (Dec. 9, 1933): 6-8.   Lynchings in general and recent ones in San Jose, CA, Princess Anne, Maryland, and St. Joseph, Missouri.

2385. "Mob Lynches Prisoner, Takes Negro From Ambulance." THE SOUTHERN FRONTIER, Vol. 2, No. 5 (May 1941): [3].   Florida.

2386. "Mob Members Who Pleaded Guilty to Assaulting Negro, Paroled." INTERNATIONAL JURIDICAL ASSOCIATION MONTHLY BULLETIN, Vol. 8, No. 5 (Nov. 1939): 44.   Refers to mob members as vigilantes.

2387. "Mob Murder." OUTLOOK AND INDEPENDENT, Vol. 155, No. 3 (May 21, 1930): 96.   Victim: George Hughes; Sherman, Texas, 1930.

2388. "Mob-Rule As a National Menace." THE LITERARY DIGEST, Vol. 63, No. 3 (Oct. 18, 1919): 9-11.   Lynchings and race riots, with comments from newspapers.

2389. MOB VIOLENCE, A PHOTOGRAPHIC REVIEW AND DESCRIPTIVE ACCOUNT OF THE APPALLING LYNCHING OF THREE NEGROES BY A REVENGEFUL MOB AFTER ALLEGED ASSAULT ON A YOUNG WHITE GIRL, AT DULUTH, MINNESOTA, JUNE 15, 1920. Duluth: Duluth Pub. Co., 1920.

2390. "Mob Violence and War Psychology." THE NEW REPUBLIC, Vol. 16, No. 196 (Aug. 3, 1918): 5-7.   Increase in violence, including lynching, because of U.S. participation in World War I.

2391. "Mob Violence in the United States." THE SURVEY, Vol. 40, No. 4 (April 27, 1918): 101-02.   Deals with several cases, especially violence against some IWW men (and others) at Tulsa, Oklahoma, Nov. 1917.

2392. "The Mobilization of Black Strength." LIFE, Vol. 65, No. 23 (Dec. 6, 1968): 93-106.   See p. 94 for lynching, and photo with cutline on p. 95, of black man named Rubin Stacy who was lynched at Fort Lauderdale, Florida, in 1935.

2393. "Mobs Act, While -- U.S. Senators Talk." THE CRISIS, Vol. 43, No. 6 (June 1936): 172-73.   A photo of the lynching of Lint Shaw near Royston, Georgia, in April, 1936, and an extract from the Congressional Record, May 22, 1936.

2394. "Mobs Are Tougher Than Women." THE CRISIS, Vol. 42, No. 1 (Jan. 1935): 16.   Attorney General Cummings is silent on "clear-cut interstate kidnap-lynching of Claude Neal." Abducted in Alabama; lynched in Florida.

2395. "Mobs, Governors, Citizens." THE CATHOLIC WORLD, Vol. 138, No. 826 (Jan. 1934): 385-90.   Editorial. San Jose, California, lynching.

2396. "Mobs, No Lynchings, But the Year Is Young." THE SOUTHERN FRONTIER, Vol. 1, No. 2 (Feb. 1940): [4].

2397. Moncrief, Adiel J., Jr.   "Stanley Jones Leads in Condemning Lynching." THE CHRISTIAN CENTURY, Vol. 51, No. 7 (Feb. 14, 1934): 235-36.   Speech at Tampa Protestant conference regarding recent lynching at Tampa.

2398. "The Monroe, Georgia Lynching Case. A MONTHLY SUMMARY

OF EVENTS AND TRENDS IN RACE RELATIONS, Vol. 4, No. 3 (Oct. 1946): 77-78.

2399. Moore, A. M. "Brotherly Love Must Abide Throughout the Land." THE COMPETITOR, Vol. 3, No. 2 (April 1921): 9-11.   Lynching and rape; four paragraphs.

2400. Moore, Richard B. "We must Counter-attack." LABOR DEFEND-ER, Vol. 6, No. 4 (April 1931): 70-71.   Includes claim that white workers are joining Negro workers in fight against lynching. Page 71: misidentifica-tion of photo; is actually that of black man lynched at Marion, Indiana, in 1930.

2401. Moore, Trudy S. "Black Lawyer Forces KKK to Pay $7 Million For Lynching Black, 19." JET, Vol. 71, No. 24 (March 9, 1987): 6-8.   Michael Donald was lynched in Alabama, 1981.

2402. "Moral Lashes for Alabama Floggers." THE LITERARY DIGEST, Vol. 95, No. 12 (Dec. 17, 1927): 32.

2403. "A Moral Void." THE CRISIS, Vol. 14, No. 1 (May 1917): 9. Includes lynching.

2404. "More and Faster Lynchings." AMERICA, Vol. 43, No. 15 (July 19, 1930): 343.   Editorial.

2405. "More Nonsense. THE CRUSADER, Vol. 2, No. 1 (Sept. 1919): 9. Disputes claim that "no Negro with a high school or college education has ever been lynched or accused of the heinous crimes which are cited as excuse for lynchings."

2406. Morgan, Charles T. "Lynched Death." THE CHRISTIAN CEN-TURY, Vol. 56, No. 6 (Feb. 8, 1939): 182-84.   Victim: Rex Manning, Jr. No location given.

2407. Moseley, Bill. "Terror's General Headquarters." LABOR DEFEND-ER, Vol. 11, No. 10 (Oct. 1935): 10, 22.   Violence against workers and radicals. Some cases might be considered lynchings (corporal and lethal).

2408. Moses, Kingsley. "The Negro Comes North." THE FORUM, Vol. 58, No. 2 (Aug. 1917): 181-90.   Section on "Lynching and Terrorism" (pp. 187-88) minimizes lynching as migration motivation.

2409. "Mother of Slain Black Son Takes Possession of KKK Building Won in Lawsuit." JET, Vol. 72, No. 11 (June 8, 1987): 8.   Mother of Michael

Donald, who was lynched in Mobile, Alabama, 1981.

2410. Moton, R. R. "The Lynching Record." CHRISTIAN ADVOCATE [Nashville], Vol. 87, No. 28 (July 9, 1926): (31) 873.   Statistics for first half of 1926.

2411. Moton, R. R.   "Lynching Record for First Six Months of 1924." CHRISTIAN ADVOCATE [Nashville], Vol. 85, No. 29 (July 18, 1924): (22) 918.

2412. Moton, R. R. "The Lynching Record for 1920." THE CRUSADER, Vol. 3, No. 6 (Feb. 1921): 27.

2413. Moton, R. R. "The Lynching Record for the First Six Months of 1923." CHRISTIAN ADVOCATE [Nashville], Vol. 84, No. 28 (July 13, 1923): (22) 886.

2414. Moton, R. R. "The Lynching Record for the First Six Months of 1922." CHRISTIAN ADVOCATE [Nashville], Vol. 83, No. 29 (July 21, 1922): (29) 925.

2415. Moton, Robert R. "The Lynching Record for 1918." THE OUT-LOOK, Vol. 121, No. 4 (Jan. 22, 1919): 159.   Letter from principal of Tuskegee Institute.

2416. Moton, Robert R. "Lynchings Last Year." THE FORUM, Vol. 79, No. 3 (March 1928): 475-76.   Letter from principal of Tuskegee Institute.

2417. Moton, Robert R.   "The South and the Lynching Evil."   THE SOUTH ATLANTIC QUARTERLY, Vol. 18, No. 3 (July 1919): 191-96.

2418. "Moton Again Squirms Into the Limelight." THE CRUSADER, Vol. 2, No. 8 (April 1920): 9.   Ridicules Robert Moton's optimism that lynching of blacks in the South will end "in a few years."

2419. "A Movement to Watch." THE NATION, Vol. 218, No. 18 (May 4, 1974): 550.   Posse comitatus movement in Eugene, Oregon, and other parts of the Northwest should make people uneasy who know "history of vigilante action in the Northwest," as when "armed deputies and Chamber of Commerce vigilantes" battled mostly-unarmed Wobblies at Everett, Washington.

2420. "The Murders of Mer Rouge." THE LITERARY DIGEST, Vol. 76, No. 2 (Jan. 13, 1923): 10-12.   KKK murder of two white men (Daniels and Richards) in Louisiana.

2421. Murphy, Edward F. "The Blood of Able." THE CATHOLIC MIND, Vol. 42, No. 981 (Sept. 1944): 554-56. Three lynchings of blacks in one recent week in Mississippi occasion this plea against lynching and for Christian treatment of blacks. Reprinted from Our Colored Missions (New York).

2422. Murray, Florence. "The Negro and Civil Liberties During World War II." SOCIAL FORCES, Vol. 24, No. 2 (Dec. 1945): 211-16. See pp. 212-13 for lynchings.

2423. Murray, Florence, ed. THE NEGRO HANDBOOK. New York: Wendell Malliet and Co., 1942. See lynchings, pp. 51-53.

2424. Murray, Florence, ed. THE NEGRO HANDBOOK 1944. New York: Current Reference Publications, 1944. See "Lynchings" and "Riot" in index. See same in later editions.

2425. Murray, Florence, ed. THE NEGRO HANDBOOK 1949. New York: Macmillan, 1949. See lynchings, pp. 91-100.

2426. "My Country 'Tis of Thee. Sweet Land of Liberty --." THE CRISIS, Vol. 41, No. 11 (Nov. 1934): 342. Lynching photo and statistics (as of Oct. 15). Repeated on p. 370 of December issue, with figures as of Nov. 15.

2427. "N. A. A. C. P. Annual Meeting." THE CRISIS, Vol. 23, No. 4 (Feb. 1922): 166-67.

2428. "The N.A.A.C.P. Overlooks 26 Lynchings! A Joint Statement by the I.L.D. and L.S.N.R." LABOR DEFENDER, Vol. 9, No. 2 (Feb. 1933): 5, 18. International Labor Defense and League of Struggle for Negro Rights have broader definition of lynching.

2429. "N.A.A.C.P. Urges Coughlin to Score Lynching." INTERRACIAL REVIEW, Vol. 8, No. 4 (April 1935): 65. Brief.

2430. "Nashville Pastors Condemn Lynching." THE CHRISTIAN CENTURY, Vol. 51, No. 1 (Jan. 1934): 38. Nashville, Tennessee, grand jury did not indict black youth who was then lynched.

2431. "Nation Cheers as Tennessee Prevents Lynching." THE LITERARY DIGEST, Vol. 118, No. 26 (Dec. 29, 1934): 6. Shelbyville courthouse burned. Four mob members killed by National Guard.

2432. "Nation Horrified by Murder Of Kidnaped [sic] Chicago Youth." JET, Vol. 80, No. 17 (Aug. 12, 1991): 8-9. Emmett Till was murdered in

Mississippi in 1955.

2433. "The National American Sport Lynching." THE CRUSADER, Vol. 1, No. 6 (Feb. 1919): 16-17. Moorfield Storey's description of Dyersburg, TN, lynching [1917], in The Negro Question.

2434. National Association for the Advancement of Colored People. AN AMERICAN LYNCHING. BEING THE BURNING AT THE STAKE OF HENRY LOWRY AT NODENA, ARKANSAS, JANUARY 26, 1921, AS TOLD IN AMERICAN NEWSPAPERS. New York: NAACP, [1921].

2435. National Association for the Advancement of Colored People. AN APPEAL TO THE CONSCIENCE OF THE CIVILIZED WORLD. New York: NAACP, 1920. Photos and text on lynching.

2436. National Association for the Advancement of Colored People. AN APPEAL TO THE WORLD! A STATEMENT ON THE DENIAL OF HUMAN RIGHTS TO MINORITIES IN THE CASE OF CITIZENS OF NEGRO DESCENT IN THE UNITED STATES OF AMERICA AND AN APPEAL TO THE UNITED NATIONS FOR REDRESS. Ed. by W. E. Burghardt Du Bois. New York: NAACP, 1947. Material on lynching is brief (pp. 16-17, 40-41, 49-50, 60).

2437. National Association for the Advancement of Colored People. BURNING AT STAKE IN THE UNITED STATES. A RECORD OF THE PUBLIC BURNING BY MOBS OF FIVE MEN, DURING THE FIRST FIVE MONTHS OF 1919, IN THE STATES OF ARKANSAS, FLORIDA, GEORGIA, MISSISSIPPI, AND TEXAS. New York: NAACP, 1919. Reprint with new afterword by Kinya Kiongozi; Baltimore: Black Classic Press, 1986.

2438. National Association for the Advancement of Colored People. CAN THE STATES STOP LYNCHING? New York: NAACP, [1937].

National Association for the Advancement of Colored People. THE LYNCHING OF CLAUDE NEAL. See [Kester, Howard].

2439. National Association for the Advancement of Colored People. THE LYNCHINGS OF MAY, 1918 IN BROOKS AND LOWNDES COUN-TIES, GEORGIA. New York: NAACP, 1918. See also "The Work of a Mob."

2440. National Association for the Advancement of Colored People. M IS FOR MISSISSIPPI AND MURDER. New York: NAACP, 1955. Eight-page pamphlet; mainly on murders of Rev. George W. Lee, Lamar Smith, and Emmett Till.

2441. National Association for the Advancement of Colored People. A RECORD OF MOB VIOLENCE AND RACE CLASHES IN THE UNITED STATES, 1947. N.p., 1948.

2442. National Association for the Advancement of Colored People. A STATEMENT ON THE DENIAL OF HUMAN RIGHTS TO MINORI- TIES IN THE CASE OF CITIZENS OF NEGRO DESCENT IN THE UNITED STATES OF AMERICA AND AN APPEAL TO THE UNITED NATIONS FOR REDRESS. Ed. by W. E. B. DuBois. New York: NAACP, [1942?].

2443. National Association for the Advancement of Colored People. THE SHAME OF AMERICA. New York: NAACP, [1922].   A broadside. Available at Rare Books, Houghton Library, Harvard University.

2444. National Committee for the Defense of Civil Rights in Tampa. TAMPA -- TAR AND TERROR. New York: National Committee for the Defense of Civil Rights in Tampa, [1935].   Murder of Joseph Shoemaker, 1935; also other violence.

2445. NATIONAL CONFERENCE ON LYNCHING TO BE HELD IN NEW YORK CITY MAY FIFTH AND SIXTH NINETEEN HUNDRED AND NINETEEN. New York: n.p., [1919?].   Pamphlet: program and objectives.

2446. Navarre, Carl. "High Noon in Skidmore." PLAYBOY, Vol. 29, No. 7 (July 1982): 111, 144, 154, 156, 194-209.   Lynching of a bully in Missouri.

2447. "A Near Outrage and Its Moral." THE SOUTHERN WORKMAN, Vol. 60, No. 10 (Oct. 1931): 443.   White girl in North Carolina falsely said she had been criminally assaulted. Almost resulted in a lynching.

2448. "The Negro and Lynching." In NEGRO YEAR BOOK . . . 1937- 1938, pp. 153-59. Ed. by Monroe N. Work. Tuskegee Institute, AL: Negro Year Book Pub. Co., 1937.

2449. "The Negro at Bay." THE NATION, Vol. 108, No. 2815 (June 14, 1919): 931.   Lynching is one of several injustices toward blacks which need correcting.

2450. "Negro Is Lynched by Missouri Crowd." INTERRACIAL REVIEW, Vol. 15, No. 2 (Feb. 1942): 32.

2451. "The Negro Lives in a World of Fear." THE CHRISTIAN CEN-
TURY, Vol. 72, No. 42 (Oct. 19, 1955): 1197.   Two witnesses at trial of
men accused in Emmett Till case in Mississippi.

2452. "Negro Lynched With Sheriff's Gun." INTERNATIONAL JURIDI-
CAL ASSOCIATION MONTHLY BULLETIN, Vol. 4, No. 6 (Nov. 1935):
2.   Baxter Bell, at White Bluff, Tennessee.

2453. "Negro Preacher Flogged to Death." THE MESSENGER, Vol. 5,
No. 6 (June 1923): 737.   Elder Burton was beaten because he bought his
wife nice home and car.

2454. "The Negro Silent Parade." THE CRISIS, Vol. 14, No. 5 (Sept.
1917): 241-44.   Protest against recent race riots and outrages.

2455. "Negro Sues Mob for Assault." INTERNATIONAL JURIDICAL
ASSOCIATION MONTHLY BULLETIN, Vol. 4, No. 2 (July 1935): 2.
Adam Avie in Louisiana.

2456. "Neither Censorship nor Puritanism Involved." THE CHRISTIAN
CENTURY, Vol. 47, No. 12 (March 19, 1930): 357-58.   Illinois vigilance
association and indecent literature.

2457. "Neither Do We." THE CRUSADER, Vol. 4, No. 3 (May 1921): 27.
Letter saying lynching is 100% American and there would be more lynchings
in the North if it were as free of "foreigners" as the South.

2458. "A New Attack on Lynching." THE SOCIAL SERVICE REVIEW,
Vol. 17, No. 1 (March 1943): 93.   Federal government is acting, without an
anti-lynching law, by federal indictment of "five alleged leaders of the mob
in Mississippi who took a Negro out of jail and lynched him last fall."

2459. "A New Record for the Country." THE SOUTHERN FRONTIER,
Vol. 1, No. 7 (July 1940): [2].   Few lynchings.

2460. Newberry, Mike. "Lynch Ropes on Birch Boughs." MAINSTREAM,
Vol. 15 (Feb. 1962): 33-39.   Men such as Kent Courtney, John Birch
Society "Coordinator" for Louisiana, are replacing mob action with more
sophisticated racist activities.

2461. "News Item." INTERRACIAL REVIEW, Vol. 9, No. 9 (Sept. 1936):
136.   Black Legion members in Detroit killed Silas Coleman, black man,
May 25, 1935, because one wanted "to see how it felt to shoot a Negro."
Accompanied by illustration "What you have done to the least of these you
have done to me."

2462. "The News of One Day." THE CRUSADER, Vol. 2, No. 3 (Nov. 1919): 32.   Lynchings and a Brooklyn judge who seemed to approve of lynching.

2463. "Newspaper Thoughts on Lynching." NEW SOUTH, Vol. 2, No. 2 (Feb. 1947): 7.

2464. Newton, Herbert. "Georgia Tops the List in Lynchings." LABOR DEFENDER, Vol. 5, No. 12 (Dec. 1930): 257.   Includes St. Louis meeting of American Negro Labor Congress opposition to lynching.

2465. "1940 Lynchings." INTERNATIONAL JURIDICAL ASSOCIATION MONTHLY BULLETIN, Vol. 9, No. 3 (Sept. 1940): 22.   Includes Sarah Rawls, Benton Ford, and Isaac Gaston, whites, in Georgia.; "Texas Red," black, at Port Gideon, Mississippi; Elbert Williams, black, at Brownsville, Tennessee.

2466. "1935 Lynching Record Aids Anti-Lynching Bill." THE CATHOLIC WORKER, Vol. 3, No. 6 (Nov. 1935): 2.

2467. "1935 Lynchings Show Increase." INTERRACIAL REVIEW, Vol. 9, No. 1 (Jan. 1936): 16.

2468. "1933 Lynching Record." THE WORLD TOMORROW, Vol. 17, No. 2 (Jan. 18, 1934): 39.

2469. [No author. No title.] THE NEW REPUBLIC, Vol. 11, No. 135 (June 2, 1917): 120.   Comment on the lynching of Ell Person in Tennessee.

2470. [No author. No title.] THE NATION, Vol. 112, No. 2916 (May 25, 1921): 727.   Governor Dorsey, Georgia, faces impeachment effort because his pamphlet The Negro in Georgia deals with peonage, lynching, etc.

2471. [No author. No title. Section does not have a title.] THE NATION, Vol. 131, No. 3404 (Oct. 1, 1930): 337.   Appointment and membership of commission to investigate recent lynchings.

2472. [No author. No title.] THE CHRISTIAN ADVOCATE [New York], Vol. 107, No. 3 (Jan. 21, 1932): 55.   Editorial against lynching.

2473. [No author. No title; in section titled "The Week."] THE NEW REPUBLIC, Vol. 73, No. 945 (Jan. 11, 1933): 226.   Fewer lynchings in 1932, but definition of lynching minimizes true number.

2474. [No author. No title; in section titled "The Week."] THE NEW

REPUBLIC, Vol. 76, No. 978 (Aug. 30, 1933): 58.   Grand jury is considering lynching of three blacks (two died, one survived) in Tuscaloosa, Alabama. Mob earlier tried to lynch three lawyers.

2475. [No author. No title; in section titled "The Week."] THE NEW REPUBLIC, Vol. 76, No. 983 (Oct. 4, 1933): 197.   Dallas, Texas, police prevented double lynching, but "organized killings" continue elsewhere, as in whipping death of black named Joe Soles in Benton, Alabama.

2476. [No author. No title.] THE NATION, Vol. 137, No. 3565 (Nov. 1, 1933): 497.   Armwood lynching in Maryland.

2477. [No author. No title; in section titled "The Week."] THE NEW REPUBLIC, Vol. 76, No. 988 (Nov. 8, 1933): 348.   Armwood lynching in Maryland.

2478. [No author. No title.] THE NATION, Vol. 137, No. 3570 (Dec. 6, 1933): 635-36.   Aftermath of a lynching in Princess Anne, Maryland, on Oct. 18.

2479. [No author. No title; in section titled "The Week."] THE NEW REPUBLIC, Vol. 77, No. 995 (Dec. 27, 1933): 181.   Lynching of black man Cord Cheek at Columbia, Tennessee.

2480. [No author. No title.] NEW MASSES, Vol. 10, No. 2 (Jan. 9, 1934): 6.   Lynchings in 1933.

2481. [No author. No title; in section titled "The Week."] THE NEW REPUBLIC, Vol. 80, No. 1040 (Nov. 7, 1934): 350.   Claude Neal lynching in Florida.

2482. [No author. No title.] SOCIAL PROCESS, Vol. 13, No. 3 (March 1935): 399.   Lynchings for 1934.

2483. [No author. No title.] AMERICA, Vol. 59, No. 17 (July 30, 1938): 388.   No lynchings for six months while Wagner-Van Nuys bill was pending in Congress, but lynchings resumed after Congress adjourned.

2484. [No author. No title.] NEW SOUTH, Vol. 1, No. 7 (July 1946): 2. Rewards for arrest of lynchers of four blacks near Monroe, Georgia.

2485. [No author. No title; 2d item in section titled "The Shape of Things."] THE NATION, Vol. 163, No. 5 (Aug. 3, 1946): 113.   Two black couples shot to death by whites in Georgia.

2486. [No author. No title; in section titled "The Shape of Things."] THE NATION, Vol. 163, No. 9 (Aug. 31, 1946): 225-26.   "Nine Negroes have been lynched in the last two months," and power of Southerners, such as Senator Bilbo, in Congress prevents remedial legislation.

2487. [No author. No title; in section titled "The Shape of Things."] THE NATION, Vol. 164, No. 21 (May 24, 1947): 615.   Trial in South Carolina of 31 whites for lynching Willie Earle.

2488. [No author.   No title; in section "The Shape of Things."]   THE NATION, Vol. 164, No. 22 (May 31, 1947): 643-44.   Editorial. Acquittal of 28 self-confessed lynchers in Greenville, South Carolina.

2489. [No author. No title.] NEW SOUTH, Vol. 2, No. 7 (July 1947): 5-6. Press comments on lynching.

2490. [No author. No title.] THE CRISIS, Vol. 55, No. 3 (March 1948): 70-71.   Lynching statistics for 1947.

2491. "No Christian Condonation of Lynching."   THE LITERARY DIGEST, Vol. 74, No. 11 (Sept. 9, 1922): 35.   Not about any specific case.

2492. "No-Lynching Honor Roll Published."   FEDERAL COUNCIL BULLETIN, Vol. 17, No. 3 (March 1934): 8.   States without lynchings.

2493. "No Lynching in Forty States During 1932." FEDERAL COUNCIL BULLETIN, Vol. 16, No. 3 (March 1933): 11.

2494. "No Lynching in Texas, State Uses New Method." THE SOUTHERN FRONTIER, Vol. 3, No. 1 (Jan. 1942): [2].   Individuals kill blacks or mob mutilates but does not kill.

2495. "No Remedy in Law." THE NEW REPUBLIC, Vol. 133, No. 21 (Nov. 21, 1955): 5.   Emmet [sic] Till case in Mississippi; calls it a lynching.

2496. "No Rights for Lynchers." NEW MASSES, Vol. 10, No. 1 (Jan. 2, 1934): 6.   Westbrook Pegler's recent newspaper column defending lynching occasioned this editorial saying democratic rights should be denied to lynchers and Fascists.

2497. "No U. S. Lynching In 3 Years, Says FBI." JET, Vol. 7, No. 11 (Jan. 20, 1955): 6.   Brief.

2498. Nordyke, Lewis T. "Ladies and Lynchings." SURVEY GRAPHIC, Vol. 28, No. 11 (Nov. 1939): 683-86.

2499. Nordyke, Lewis T. "The Ladies and the Lynchers." READER'S DIGEST, Vol. 35, No. 211 (Nov. 1939): 110-13.   Condensed from Nov. 1939 issue of Survey Graphic.

2500. "Norman Thibodaux's Story." LABOR DEFENDER, Vol. 10, No. 2 (Feb. 1934): 21-22.   Lynchers in Louisiana killed Moore and almost killed Thibodaux (hanged but survived when cut down, 1933).

2501. "Norris Dendy's Children." THE CRISIS, Vol. 41, No. 10 (Oct. 1934): 300.   Dendy was lynched in South Carolina on July 4, 1933. Message from his children.

2502. "North Carolina Courts Act Against Lynchers." THE SOUTHERN FRONTIER, Vol. 2, No. 7 (July 1941): [2].

2503. "North Carolina Slips." OUTLOOK AND INDEPENDENT, Vol. 156, No. 1 (Sept. 3, 1930): 14.   Victim: Oliver Moore (black man).

2504. "North Carolina: The Klan Is Guilty." NEWSWEEK, Vol. 39, No. 21 (May 26, 1952): 31.   Convictions and sentencing of KKK members who flogged a white couple for alleged immorality.

2505. "North Dakota's Lynching." THE CHRISTIAN CENTURY, Vol. 48, No. 6 (Feb. 11, 1931): 195.   A man was lynched at Schafer on Jan. 29.

2506. North, Joseph. LYNCHING NEGRO CHILDREN IN SOUTHERN COURTS. New York: International Labor Defense, [1931?].   Scottsboro case in Alabama.

2507. "The North Mississippi Conference Condemns Lynching." CHRISTIAN ADVOCATE [Nashville], Vol. 86, No. 51 (Dec. 18, 1925): (30) 1726.

2508. Nossiter, Adam.   "Legal Lynching in Louisiana: The Case That Refuses to Die." THE NATION, Vol. 250, No. 10 (March 12, 1990): 337-41. Gary Tyler, black, was convicted of killing Timothy Weber, white, in 1974.

2509. "'Not Interested.'" THE CRISIS, Vol. 41, No. 12 (Dec. 1934): 365. Attorney General Homer S. Cummings is not interested in lynching.

2510. "A Note on Lynchings." SCRIBNER'S COMMENTATOR, Vol. 9, No. 6 (April 1941): 68.   Lynchings in 1940.

2511. "Notes on Lynching." THE CRISIS, Vol. 24, No. 2 (June 1922): 80-81.

2512. Oak, Liston M. "The Industrialization of the South and the Negroes." LABOR DEFENDER, Vol. 4, No. 2 (Feb. 1929): 30-31.   Includes lynching.

2513. O'Donnell, T. C. "Our Own Pogroms." CARTOONS MAGAZINE, Vol. 16, No. 4 (Oct. 1919): 586-91.   Lynchings and race riots in earlier years did not produce positive change; result: a holocaust of race riots in 1919. Includes mob law cartoon by Rehse.

2514. Odum, Howard W.   "Lynchings, Fears, and Folkways."   THE NATION, Vol. 133, No. 3469 (Dec. 30, 1931): 719-20.   Thoughts from reading recent lynching report. Lynching widespread in South and not elsewhere because of fears, folkways which defeat stateways, and high homicide rate in South (which "reflects a lack of respect for human life").

2515. "The Old Story." INTERRACIAL REVIEW, Vol. 10, No. 11 (Nov. 1937): 164-65.   Pattern of lynchings in which prisoners are taken from lawmen.

2516. "Omaha." THE NATION, Vol. 109, No. 2832 (Oct. 11, 1919): 491. Rape issue and lynching, with suggested remedies. Nebraska.

2517. "Omaha." THE LITERARY DIGEST, Vol. 63, No. 2 (Oct. 11, 1919): 16.   Lynching riot in Nebraska.

2518. OMAHA'S RIOT IN STORY AND PICTURE. Omaha: Educational Publishing Co., n.d. [1919 or 192?].   Successful Nebraska attempt to lynch a black rapist, September 1919.

2519. "An Ominous Growl." THE CHRISTIAN ADVOCATE [New York], Vol. 107, No. 4 (Jan. 28, 1932): 86.   Murder of a native Hawaiian by whites [Thalia Massey case] elicited editorials in some U.S. newspapers favoring such protection of white women; relates this to lynching.

2520. "Once More--The Annual Lynching Record." THE CHRISTIAN CENTURY, Vol. 47, No. 2 (Jan. 8, 1930): 37.

2521. "One of the Advocates of 'The League of Nations.'" THE CRU-SADER, Vol. 2, No. 3 (Nov. 1919): 29-30.   Senator Williams of Mississippi spoke in approval of Omaha, Nebraska, lynching.

2522. "One Woman and a Mob." THE EPWORTH HIGHROAD, Vol. 1, No. 7 (July 1932): 21, 54.   Sheriff's wife in Huntingdon, Tennessee, prevented a lynching in 1931.

2523. "Only One-Sixth of Lynchings for Rape." THE CRISIS, Vol. 42, No. 1 (Jan. 1935): 14.

2524. "Other Lynching Mobs." THE CRISIS, Vol. 15, No. 6 (April 1918): 283.

2525. "Our National Disgrace." AMERICA, Vol. 26, No. 17 (Feb. 11, 1922): 407-08.   Editorial. Tuskegee statistics for 1921. Brief.

2526. Ovington, Mary White. "Is Mob Violence the Texas Solution of the Race Problem?" THE INDEPENDENT, Vol. 99, No. 3691 (Sept. 6, 1919): 320.   Several men in Austin beat up John R. Shillady, secretary of the NAACP, and said he should be lynched.

2527. Ovington, Mary White. "Revisiting the South." THE CRISIS, Vol. 34, No. 2 (April 1927): 42-43, 60-61. Brief references to lynching on pages 60 and 61.

2528. Owen, Chandler. "Peonage, Riots & Lynching." THE MESSEN-GER, Vol. 3, No. 3 (Aug. 1921): 232-34.

2529. Owen, Chandler. THE REMEDY. New York: Cosmo-Advocate Pub. Co., [1917].   Pages 9-16 (as "The Remedy for Lynching") in pamphlet with Asa Philip Randolph, The Truth About Lynching.

2530. Page, Myra. "Lynching and Pay Checks." LABOR DEFENDER, Vol. 5, No. 10 (Oct. 1930): 196-97.   Lynching as a weapon of capitalist oppression.

2531. Page, Thomas Walker. "Lynching and Race Relations in the South." NORTH AMERICAN REVIEW, Vol. 206, No. 741 (Aug. 1917): 241-50.

2532. Painter, Nell Irvin. "Who Was Lynched?" THE NATION, Vol. 253, No. 16 (Nov. 11, 1991): 577.   Lynching history as context for Judge Clarence Thomas casting himself as lynching victim during his confirmation hearings.

2533. Parker, George Wells. "The Omaha Mob." THE CRUSADER, Vol. 2, No. 3 (Nov. 1919): 11-12.   Will Brown, black man accused of rape, was lynched in Nebraska after mob tried to lynch the mayor during attack on courthouse jail.

2534. Parrott, Lisbeth. "Making History of Lynching." THE SURVEY, Vol. 67, No. 10 (Feb. 15, 1932): 532-33.

2535. Parsons, Malcolm B. "Violence and Caste in Southern Justice." THE SOUTH ATLANTIC QUARTERLY, Vol. 60, No. 4 (Fall 1961): 455-68. Includes lynching and reasons for its decline.

2536. "The Passing of Judge Lynch." THE LITERARY DIGEST, Vol. 84, No. 5 (Jan. 31, 1925): 30-31.   Reduced number of lynchings, 1924.

2537. "Pattern of Violence." NEW SOUTH, Vol. 4, No. 3 (March 1949): 3-5.   Chronological listing for 1948-1949; includes lynchings.

2538. "Pattern of Violence." In CHANGING PATTERNS IN THE NEW SOUTH, pp. 16-17 [Vol. 10, No. 1 (Jan. 1955) of NEW SOUTH].   Editorial against KKK and mob violence. From New South (March 1949).

2539. Patterson, F. D. "The Lynching Record For The First Six Months, 1941." THE SOUTHERN FRONTIER, Vol. 2, No. 7 (July 1941): [2]. Letter.

2540. Patterson, F. D. "Lynchings in 1939." THE SPECTATOR [London], Vol. 164, No. 5821 (Jan. 19, 1940): 81.   Letter from Tuskegee Institute's president.

2541. Patterson, F. D.   "Tuskegee Reports on Victims of Lynching." INTERRACIAL REVIEW, Vol. 12, No. 7 (July 1939): 112.   Letter.

2542. Patterson, W. L. "Judge Lynch Goes to Court." LABOR DEFEND-ER, Vol. 6, No. 5 (May 1931): 84, 99.   Scottsboro case in Alabama.

2543. Patterson, William L. SIKESTON: HITLERITE CRIME AGAINST AMERICA. St. Louis: Communist Party of Missouri, 1942.   Cover lists author's initial as H.; but later pages have it as L.   Booklet of 23 pages. Lynching of Cleo Wright in Missouri.

2544. Patterson, William L., ed.   WE CHARGE GENOCIDE; THE HISTORIC PETITION TO THE UNITED NATIONS FOR RELIEF FROM A CRIME OF THE UNITED STATES GOVERNMENT AGAINST THE NEGRO PEOPLE. Originally published in 1951. New ed.; New York: International Publishers, 1970.   See especially "Part III, The Evidence," which includes lynchings during 1945-1951.

2545. Patterson, William L. "We Indict the Alabama Lynchers." LABOR DEFENDER, Vol. 9, No. 3 (March 1933): 28, 37.   Legal lynching (Scottsboro) and other forms of oppression.

2546. Pearce, J. E. "The Mob Spirit in the United States." THE TEXAS

REVIEW, Vol. 4, No. 3 (April 1919): 205-28.

2547. Peet, Hubert W. "Why More Lynchings?" THE SPECTATOR [London], Vol. 146, No. 5352 (Jan. 24, 1931): 104-05.

2548. "The People's Forum." THE HALF-CENTURY MAGAZINE, Vol. 8, No. 4 (April 1920): 17.   Letter signed JMG, saying author came from Georgia recently and is never returning because of so many lynchings there.

2549. "Perhaps a Lex Talionis Is Better Than No Lex." THE CHRISTIAN CENTURY, Vol. 51, No. 12 (March 21, 1934): 381.   Lynching of three blacks may have been prevented by agreement that father of girl they attacked could spring the trap for their Mississippi execution.

2550. "Persons Have Been Lynched For These 'Crimes.'" THE CRISIS, Vol. 42, No. 1 (Jan. 1935): 12.   A list.

2551. Petrie, John Clarence. "Citizens Protest Killing by Police: Claim Made That 'Justifiable Homicides' Are Disguised Lynchings." THE CHRISTIAN CENTURY, Vol. 55, No. 8 (Feb. 23, 1938): 248.   Memphis, Tennessee.

2552. Petrie, John Clarence. "Flogging Arouses Varied Opinions." THE CHRISTIAN CENTURY, Vol. 53, No. 30 (July 22, 1936): 1021.   Earle, Arkansas, beatings of Reverend Claude Williams and Miss Willie Sue Blagden.

2553. Petrie, John Clarence. "Lynching Shows Need for Federal Law." THE CHRISTIAN CENTURY, Vol. 51, No. 4 (Jan. 24, 1934): 133.   Victim: Cordie Cheek, black, at Columbia, Tennessee.

2554. Phillips, Charles David.   "Social Structure and Social Control: Modeling the Discriminatory Execution of Blacks in Georgia and North Carolina, 1925-35." SOCIAL FORCES, Vol. 65, No. 2 (Dec. 1986): 458-75. Several references to lynching, especially as unofficial executions.

2555. Pickens, William. "Aftermath of a Lynching." THE NATION, Vol. 132, No. 3432 (April 15, 1931): 406-07.   Lynching of two black men in Marion, Indiana, Aug. 7, 1930.

2556. Pickens, William. "The American Congo--Burning of Henry Lowry." THE NATION, Vol. 112, No. 2907 (March 23, 1921): 426-28.   Arkansas.

2557. Pickens, William. "Behind the Evil of the Lynching of Negroes." LABOR DEFENDER, Vol. 3, No. 4 (April 1928): 82-83.

2558. Pickens, William. LYNCHING AND DEBT SLAVERY. New York: American Civil Liberties Union, 1921.

2559. Pickens, William. "A Roman Holiday." THE CRISIS, Vol. 36, No. 3 (March 1929): 79-80, 96.   Charley Sheppard, black, was burned alive near Rome, Mississippi, on New Year's Eve, 1928, in front of enormous mob.

2560. Pirie, Madsen. "Taking it to the Streets." THE SPECTATOR [London], Vol. 271, No. 8631 (Dec. 11, 1993): 24-26.   "Predicts rising vigilantism in response to the collapse of law and order" in England and United States.

2561. "The Pity Of It." THE CRISIS, Vol. 17, No. 6 (April 1919): 291-92. Comments about lynching from other periodicals and newspapers.

2562. "The Place, the Acquittal." NEWSWEEK, Vol. 46, No. 14 (Oct 3, 1955): 24, 29-30.   Bryant and Milam (Till case in Mississippi).

2563. "Pogram in Tennessee--And the Part Politics Plays." THE NEW REPUBLIC, Vol. 114, No. 13 (April 1, 1946): 429.   Blacks indicted after conflict between white lawmen and blacks in Columbia.

2564. "The Political Power of the South." THE CRISIS, Vol. 29, No. 1 (Nov. 1924): 27-28.   Includes map showing South has had 73 percent of lynchings.

2565. Pooley, Eric. "Frontier Justice." NEW YORK, Vol. 23, No. 28 (July 23, 1990): 32-39.   Mainly about individuals in New York City taking the law into their own hands.

2566. "Postulates." INTERRACIAL REVIEW, Vol. 9, No. 10 (Oct. 1936): contents page.   Anti-lynching statement which appears in longer list of "Postulates" in this and many other issues of this journal.

2567. "Poverty in South Leads to Negro Lynching Orgy." THE CATHOLIC WORKER, Vol. 2, No. 7 (Dec. 1934): 1, 8.   Claude Neal was lynched in Florida.

2568. Pozzetta, George E. "Lynching in the South: Some Observations and Suggestions." INTERNATIONAL BEHAVIOURAL SCIENTIST, Vol. 7, No. 2 (June 1975): 37-45.   Considers white rationales for lynching of blacks; suggests areas for further study.

2569. "A Practical Way to Cut Down Lynchings." THE SURVEY, Vol. 37, No. 16 (Jan. 20, 1917): 461.   Governor Stanley went to Murray, Kentucky, and spoke to the mob, 1917.

2570. Preece, Harold. "Texas Holiday." THE CRISIS, Vol. 43, No. 1 (Jan. 1936): 20-21.   Lynching of two black teenagers in Columbus, Texas, 1935.

2571. "Prejudice Moves Northward." THE SOUTHERN WORKMAN, Vol. 60, No. 4 (April 1931): 148-49.   Survey done by Federal Council of Churches in Maryville, MO, showed little negative reaction to recent lynching there.

2572. "The President and the Mob Spirit." THE NATION, Vol. 107, No. 2770 (Aug. 3, 1918): 114.   Commends Wilson's exhortation against mob violence; lists several incidents of such activity.

2573. "President Roosevelt Deplores Lynching." THE SIGN, Vol. 14, No. 6 (Jan. 1935): 325.

2574. "President Wilson on Mob Violence." THE SURVEY, Vol. 40, No. 18 (Aug. 3, 1918): 512.   Text of statement.

2575. "The President's Address on Lynching." THE CRUSADER, Vol. 1, No. 1 (Sept. 1918): 15-16.

2576. "The Press and Emmett Till." NEW SOUTH, Vol. 10, No. 10 (Oct. 1955): 10-11.   He was murdered in Mississippi in 1955.

2577. "Press Opinion: From Editorials and Columns." EVENTS AND TRENDS IN RACE RELATIONS: A MONTHLY SUMMARY, Vol. IV, No. 12 (July 1947): 378-82.   Leads with lynching.

2578. Preston, C. Thomas, Jr. "Characterizing the Issue: Metaphor and Contemporary Impromptu Discussions of Gender." ARGUMENTATION AND ADVOCACY: THE JOURNAL OF THE AMERICAN FORENSIC ASSOCIATION, Vol. 28, No. 4 (Spring 1992): 185-91.   Includes use of lynching metaphor in Clarence Thomas hearings, 1991, to transform "the issue from one of gender to one of race" (p. 187).

2579. "Prevented Lynchings in February." THE SOUTHERN FRONTIER, Vol. 1, No. 3 (March 1940): [3].

2580. "Preventing Lynchings." FEDERAL COUNCIL BULLETIN, Vol. 9, No. 3 (May-June 1926): 14.

2581. "The Prevention of Lynching." THE OUTLOOK, Vol. 140, No. 9 (July 1, 1925): 318, 320.   Refers to report by Commission on Race

Relations of the Federal Council of Churches.

2582. "Programs of Action: Action on Columbia Riot." A MONTHLY SUMMARY OF EVENTS AND TRENDS IN RACE RELATIONS, Vol. 3, No. 9 (April 1946): 273.

2583. "Programs of Action: Action Taken on Monroe, Georgia Lynching." A MONTHLY SUMMARY OF EVENTS AND TRENDS IN RACE RELATIONS, Vol. 4, Nos. 1 and 2 (Aug.-Sept. 1946): 29-30.

2584. "Protests From Georgia and Arkansas." THE CRISIS, Vol. 19, No. 3 (Jan. 1920): 141-42.   Lynching.

2585. Pruden, Durward. "A Sociological Study of a Texas Lynching." M.A. thesis, Southern Methodist Univ., 1935.   May, 1930, lynching of George Hughes in Sherman; but this study uses fictitious names.

2586. Pruden, Durward. "A Texas Lynching." THE CRISIS, Vol. 44, No. 1 (Jan. 1937): 6-7, 18, 20. Reprinted from Southern Methodist University, Studies in Sociology, Vol. I, No. 1 (Summer 1936): 3-9, with title "A Sociological Study of a Texas Lynching."   May, 1930, lynching of George Hughes in Sherman; but this article uses fictitious names.

2587. "'Public Confession of the Sin of Lynching.'" FEDERAL COUNCIL BULLETIN, Vol. 16, No. 9 and 10 (Nov.-Dec. 1933): 12-13.   Dr. Cavert says churches should do this because of October lynching in Princess Anne, Maryland.

2588. "Public Enemy Number One!" THE CRISIS, Vol. 42, No. 1 (Jan. 1935): 6-7, 22-23.   A symposium on lynching. Contributions by Oswald Garrison Villard, DuBose Heyward, W. E. Woodward, James Weldon Johnson, Fannie Hurst, Edward P. Costigan, Robert F. Wagner, William Pickens, Gertrude Atherton, Sherwood Anderson, George Fort Milton, and Pearl S. Buck.

2589. "Race War." THE CRISIS, Vol. 18, No. 5 (Sept. 1919): 247-49. Includes comments on lynching.

2590. "Races: A Flogging for the Klan." TIME, Vol. 60, No. 6 (Aug. 11, 1952): 21.   Convictions of KKK members for flogging blacks in North Carolina in 1951.

2591. "Races: Judge Lynch Overruled." TIME, Vol. 38, No. 1 (July 7, 1941): 13-14.   Mob in Georgia decided not to lynch a black man and returned him to jail.

2592. "Races: Lynch and Anti-Lynch." TIME, Vol. 29, No. 17 (April 26, 1937): 16-17.   Double lynching at Duck Hill, Mississippi; anti-lynching bill in House of Representatives.

2593. "Races: Mink Slide: The Aftermath." TIME, Vol. 48, No. 16 (Oct. 14, 1946): 29.   Trial of 25 blacks for riot at Columbia, Tennessee; 23 were acquitted.

2594. "Races: 'Unusual & Different Punishment.'" TIME, Vol. 41, No. 4 (Jan. 25, 1943): 24.   Several indictments by federal grand jury in the Mississippi lynching of Howard Wash.

2595. "Racial: Lynch-Free Year." NEWSWEEK, Vol. 41, No. 2 (Jan. 12, 1953): 25.   No lynchings in 1952. First lynchless year in decades, but other forms of similar violence still exist, especially against blacks.

2596. "Racial: Men With Guns." NEWSWEEK, 28, No. 6 (Aug. 5, 1946): 24.   Lynching of Roger Malcolm and three other blacks in Georgia.

2597. "Racial: Story of a Lynching." NEWSWEEK, Vol. 29, No. 21 (May 26, 1947): 29-30.   Willie Earle case, South Carolina.

2598. "Racial: Trial and Terror." NEWSWEEK, Vol. 28, No. 19 (Nov. 4, 1946): 33.   Lynching in Mississippi of black man named Leon McAtee and acquittal of accused whites.

2599. "Racialism and Violence." RACE RELATIONS: A MONTHLY SUMMARY OF EVENTS AND TRENDS, Vol. 5, Nos. 1 and 2 (Oct.-Nov. 1947): 28.   Violence against prisoners; lynching; and reprint of Georgia editorial promoting mob violence in cases of blacks raping white women.

2600. "Racialism and Violence." RACE RELATIONS: A MONTHLY SUMMARY OF EVENTS AND TRENDS, Vol. 5, Nos. 3 and 4 (Dec. 1947-Jan. 1948): 85-87.   Includes averted lynchings.

2601. "Racialism and Violence." RACE RELATIONS: A MONTHLY SUMMARY OF EVENTS AND TRENDS, Vol. 5, No. 5 (Feb. 1948): 116-18.   Includes lynching.

2602. "Racialism and Violence." RACE RELATIONS: A MONTHLY SUMMARY OF EVENTS AND TRENDS, Vol. 5, No. 6 (March 1948): 137, 143.   Includes lynching.

2603. "A Racist Editorial." INTERRACIAL REVIEW, Vol. 16, No. 7 (July 1943): 101.   Long Island, New York, weekly supports lynching "to curb crimes committed by Negroes."

2604. Ragan, Sandra L.; Bystrom, Dianne G.; Kaid, Lynda Lee; and Beck, Christina S., eds.   THE LYNCHING OF LANGUAGE: GENDER, POLITICS, AND POWER IN THE HILL-THOMAS HEARINGS. Urbana: Univ. of Illinois Press, 1996.

2605. Raines, Howell. MY SOUL IS RESTED: MOVEMENT DAYS IN THE DEEP SOUTH REMEMBERED. New York: G. P. Putnam's Sons, 1977. See pp. 131-33 for lynching (George W. Lee, Lamar Smith, Emmett Till in Mississippi); pp. 275-78, 389-93 for Chaney, Goodman, and Schwerner in Mississippi; pp. 389, 392-93 for Till; pp. 416-23 for Bogalusa, Louisiana, and Deacons for Defense and Justice.

2606. Randolph, A. Philip. "How To Stop Lynching." THE MESSEN-GER, Vol. 2 (March 1919): 9-12.

2607. Randolph, A. Philip. "Lynching: Capitalism Its Cause; Socialism Its Cure." THE MESSENGER, [Vol. 2] (March 1919): 9-12. Listed on cover as "The Truth About Lynching."

2608. Randolph, Asa Philip. THE TRUTH ABOUT LYNCHING. New York: Cosmo-Advocate Pub. Co., [1917].   Pages 2-8 (as "Causes and Effects of Lynching") in pamphlet with Chandler Owen, The Remedy.

2609. Randolph, Thomas [pseud.]. "The Governor and the Mob." THE INDEPENDENT, Vol. 89, No. 3560 (Feb. 26, 1917): 347-48.   Governor A. O. Stanley faced down a lynch mob in Murray, Kentucky, in Jan. 1917.

2610. Ransom, Leon A. "Lynching. . . . In All Its Forms." LABOR DEFENDER, Vol. 11, No. 6 (July 1937): 8.

2611. Raper, Arthur F. THE TRAGEDY OF LYNCHING. Chapel Hill: Univ. of North Carolina Press, 1933; New York: Arno Press, 1969.   Important book on 1930 lynchings.

2612. Ratliff, Beulah Amidon. "In the Delta: The Story of a Man-Hunt." THE ATLANTIC MONTHLY, Vol. 125, No. 4 (April 1920): 456-61. Search for black man named Will Lane, an alleged murderer, and his capture near Itta Bena, Mississippi, April 1919. Sheriff will cooperate so mob can "overpower" him and lynch the prisoner. Includes story of earlier chase which resulted in escape of black murderer named Filly and lynching of black man named Martin suspected of helping him.

2613. "The Real Causes of Two Race Riots." THE CRISIS, Vol. 19, No.

2 (Dec. 1919): 56-62.   Phillips County, Arkansas, and Omaha, Nebraska. The latter includes lynching of a man named Brown.

2614. "The Real Story Behind Lynching of Miss. Negro." JET, Vol. 16, No. 3 (May 14, 1959): 12-15.   Mack Parker.

2615. Reddick, L. D. "The Lynching of Pickie Pie." THE CRISIS, Vol. 57, No. 3 (March 1950): 141-43, 198-99.   Caleb Hill; Irwinton, Georgia; May 1949.

2616. Reed, Roy. "The Deacons, Too, Ride by Night." THE NEW YORK TIMES MAGAZINE, Vol. 114, No. 39,285 (Aug. 15, 1965): 10-11, 20, 22, 24.   Black protective organization called Deacons for Defense and Justice. Chartered by state of Louisiana.

2617. Reedy, William Marion. "The Black Man's Burden." REEDY'S MIRROR, Vol. 28, No. 24 (June 19, 1919): 402-03.   Response to articles by Herbert Seligman, Edward Raymond Turner, and W. E. B. Du Bois. Includes lynching.

2618. "The Reign of the Tar-bucket." THE LITERARY DIGEST, Vol. 70, No. 9 (Aug. 27, 1921): 12-13.   Violence by the new KKK.

2619. Reilly, Louis W. "Lynching: A National Crime." THE CATHOLIC WORLD, Vol. 127, No. 760 (July 1928): 396-403.

2620. "Repair Court House, But Destroy State." THE COMPETITOR, Vol. 3, No. 2 (April 1921): 4-5.   White man was convicted in Georgia "of leading a mob against a courthouse in an effort to lynch a colored man charged with murder."

2621. "Report on Claude Neal Case." INTERNATIONAL JURIDICAL ASSOCIATION MONTHLY BULLETIN, Vol. 3, No. 6 (Nov. 1934): 2. Florida lynching.   Brief.

2622. "The Report That Didn't Come." THE CHRISTIAN CENTURY, Vol. 72, No. 2 (Jan. 12, 1955): 35.   Tuskegee Institute recently issued no annual report on lynching because there hadn't been one since 1951.

2623. "Report Three Lynchings in First Half of Year." INTERRACIAL REVIEW, Vol. 14, No. 7 (July 1941): 112.

2624. "Reported Lynchings--Not Confirmed." THE SOUTHERN FRON-TIER, Vol. 3, No. 7 (July 1942): [3].

2625. "Reprints Showing Preparations for the Lynching of John Hartfield." THE CRISIS, Vol. 18, No. 4 (Aug. 1919): 208.   Advance newspaper publicity about a lynching in June, 1919.

2626. "A Resolution To Investigate Lynchings." INTERRACIAL REVIEW, Vol. 9, No. 2 (Feb. 1936): 20-21. Senator Van Nuys introduced resolution in the Senate.

2627. "Respect for Law." THE CRISIS, Vol. 42, No. 1 (Jan. 1935): 16. "Tolerance of lynching" has helped crime and disrespect for law to flourish.

2628. "Revival of Mass Lynchings in the South: An Analysis of Editorial Opinion on the Lynching of Four Negroes in Georgia, July 25th." A MONTHLY SUMMARY OF EVENTS AND TRENDS IN RACE RELATIONS, Vol. 4, Nos. 1 and 2 (Aug.-Sept. 1946): 59-61.

2629. "Rewards to Catch Lynchers." THE NATION, Vol. 107, No. 2774 (Aug. 31, 1918): 218-19.

2630. Richardson, William H. "No More Lynchings! How North Carolina Has Solved the Problem." THE AMERICAN REVIEW OF REVIEWS, Vol. 69, No. 4 (April 1924): 401-04.

2631. "The Right to Murder Labor." THE LITERARY DIGEST, Vol. 76, No. 5 (Feb. 3, 1923): 13.   Railroad striker E. C. Gregor was lynched at Harrison, Arkansas.   Includes other violence against strikers and their supporters.

2632. "The Riots at Charleston, Longview, Omaha And Knoxville." In NEGRO YEAR BOOK . . . 1921-1922, pp. 74-75. Ed. by Monroe N. Work. Tuskegee Institute, AL: Negro Year Book Pub. Co., 1922.

2633. "The Riots at Duluth, Ocoee, Independence And Springfield." In NEGRO YEAR BOOK . . . 1921-1922, p. 74. Ed. by Monroe N. Work. Tuskegee Institute, AL: Negro Year Book Pub. Co., 1922.   Includes lynchings. This was the Springfield in Ohio.

2634. "Rising Above the Mob Spirit." THE HALF-CENTURY MAGA-ZINE, Vol. 16, No. 3 (May-June 1924): 6.   Lynching declining because (1) campaigns of NAACP, etc., (2) threat of Dyer bill, (3) state anti-lynching legislation, (4) migration of blacks out of lynching states, (5) education that "violence breeds mutual loss." Widow of South Carolina black lynch victim recently obtained verdict for $2,000.

2635. Robb, Arthur. "Shop Talk at Thirty." EDITOR & PUBLISHER,

Vol. 73, No. 1 (Jan. 6, 1940): 48.   See section "Mob Lynchings Now Rare, But Always News."

2636. Robertson, Minns S. "They Meant to Lynch Him." NEW REPUB-LIC, Vol. 119, No. 16 (Oct. 18, 1948): 16-17.   Preacher in Winnsboro, Louisiana, protected black soldier from mob. On cover as "The Lynch Mob and the Preacher."

2637. Rogers, J. A. "Critical Excursions and Reflections." THE MESSEN-GER, Vol. 6, No. 10 (Oct. 1924): 329-30.   Includes section titled "What Is the Real Cause for the Decline in Lynching?"

2638. Rogers, John. THE MURDERS OF MER ROUGE. St. Louis: Security Pub. Co., 1923.   Louisiana.

2639. Romero, Patricia W., ed.   INTERNATIONAL LIBRARY OF NEGRO LIFE AND HISTORY.   Vol. 3: I TOO AM AMERICA: DOCUMENTS FROM 1619 TO THE PRESENT.   10 vols.; New York: Publishers Company & Association for the Study of Negro Life and History, 1967-1969.   See pp. ii, 201-12, 219, 221, 229 for lynching.   Includes "Herbert J. Seligmann on Lynching" (from NAACP Papers), description of lynching of Eugene Green at Belzoni, Mississippi, March 1919; map of "Lynchings By States and Counties In the United States 1900 to 1931"; and two cartoons.

2640. Rubin, Anne Sarah. "Reflections on the Death of Emmett Till." SOUTHERN CULTURES, Vol. 2, No. 1 (Fall 1995): 45-66.

2641. "Rustlers Ride: Stream-lined Trucks in Cattle-Stealing Replace Old West's Cow-Ponies." THE LITERARY DIGEST, Vol. 123, No. 23 (June 5, 1937): 6-7.   Mentions vigilantes.

2642. "S. Carolina Residents Say Youth Lynched, Castrated, For Dating White Girl." JET, Vol. 56, No. 20 (Aug. 2, 1979): 5.   Police say Mickey M. Poag died from hit-and-run accident.

2643. S., R. A.   "The Halter Around the Negro's Neck." LABOR DEFENDER, Vol. 3, No. 3 (March 1928): 58.   Lynching.

2644. "Safe for Democracy." THE CRISIS, Vol. 15, No. 6 (April 1918): 270.   A comparison of violence in Russia and the U.S. (the burning of a black man named Jim McIlherron [sic] at Estill Springs).

2645. Sancton, Thomas. "The Greenville Acquittals." SURVEY GRAPH-IC, Vol. 36, No. 6 (June 1947): 349, 362.   Willie Earle. South Carolina.

2646. "Savagery--Borneo vs. America." INTERRACIAL REVIEW, Vol. 10, No. 6 (June 1937): 94.

2647. "Savagery Unchained." AMERICA, Vol. 44, No. 16 (Jan. 24, 1931): 375.   Missouri lynching of man chained to ridgepole of schoolhouse.

2648. "Savages Are Ever Cowards." THE CATHOLIC WORLD, Vol. 138, No. 825 (Dec. 1933): 261-62.   George Armwood lynching. Continuation of "Shame Upon Maryland."

2649. "Says Miss. Lynch Victim Had No GI Criminal Record." JET, Vol. 16, No. 5 (May 28, 1959): 5.   Mack Parker.

2650. Scanlan, Patrick F. "Mob Violence." INTERRACIAL REVIEW, Vol. 9, No. 10 (Oct. 1936): 157.   Reprint of anti-lynching editorial from The Brooklyn Tablet.

2651. "The Scape Goat." THE CRISIS, Vol. 20, No. 6 (Oct. 1920): 283-84. Includes lynching of Red Roach in North Carolina.

2652. Schneier, Edward V. "White-Collar Violence and Anticommunism." SOCIETY, Vol. 13, No. 3 (March/April 1976): 33-37.   McCarthyism, HUAC activities, and blacklisting as vigilantism.

2653. Schwantes, Carlos A. "Making the World Unsafe for Democracy: Vigilantes, Grangers and the Walla Walla 'Outrage' of June 1918." MONTANA, THE MAGAZINE OF WESTERN HISTORY, Vol. 31, No. 1 (Jan. 1981): 18-29.   Actions by locals against state convention of the Grange because of alleged Grange sympathies for the Nonpartisan League and the I.W.W.

2654. Scott, Emmett J. NEGRO MIGRATION DURING THE WAR. New York: Oxford Univ. Press, 1920.   See "Lynchings" in index.

2655. "Scottsboro Boys Face Lynching!" LABOR DEFENDER, Vol. 9, No. 4 (April 1933): 1-2.   Alabama.

2656. Scroggs, Wm. O. "Interstate Migration of Negro Population." THE JOURNAL OF POLITICAL ECONOMY, Vol. 25, No. 10 (Dec. 1917): 1034-43.   See p. 1041: Lynching and other adverse conditions in the South were not main cause of black emigration because they were worse in 1880s and 1890s; so main cause was better opportunities, such as jobs in the North, to escape those adverse conditions by 1917.

2657. "The Second Battle of Lexington." THE CRISIS, Vol. 19, No. 6

(April 1920): 298.   Five men killed in Kentucky. Reference to lynch law. See also "The Horizon. Crime," ibid., Vol. 20, No. 1 (May 1920), p. 50.

2658. Seligmann, Herbert J. "Lynching and Its Prevention." AMERICA, Vol. 44, No. 1 (Oct. 11, 1930): 24.   Letter followed by editorial comment opposing anti-lynching law.

2659. Seligmann, Herbert J. "The Press Abets the Mob." THE NATION, Vol. 109, No. 2831 (Oct. 4, 1919): 460-61.   Mob beating of John R. Shillady in Austin, Texas.

2660. Seligmann, Herbert J. "Protecting Southern Womanhood." THE NATION, Vol. 108, No. 2815 (June 14, 1919): 938-39.   Lynching of blacks. Especially about cases of George Bolden (Louisiana) and Lloyd Clay (Mississippi). Next to last paragraph deals with some causes of lynching.

2661. Sellers, Cleveland, with Terrell, Robert.   THE RIVER OF NO RETURN: THE AUTOBIOGRAPHY OF A BLACK MILITANT AND THE LIFE AND DEATH OF SNCC. New York: William Morrow, 1973. See Chaney, Goodman, and Schwerner in index. Lynched in Mississippi, 1964.

2662. "Senate Resolution Calls For Lynching Inquiry." INTERRACIAL REVIEW, Vol. 9, No. 2 (Feb. 1936): 32.

2663. "The Sequel to Scottsboro." THE NEW REPUBLIC, Vol. 76, No. 977 (Aug. 23, 1933): 34-35.   Alabama lynching of Pippen and Harden.

2664. "Seven Miss. Negro Leaders Marked For Death By Whites." JET, Vol. 8, No. 5 (June 9, 1955): 4-5.   Aftermath of George Lee murder.

2665. "Seven Were Lynched With Impunity." INTERRACIAL REVIEW, Vol. 12, No. 2 (Feb. 1939): 20.   Editorial on 1939 lynchings.

2666. "Seventy-two Lynchings." AMERICA, Vol. 55, No. 6 (May 16, 1936): 124.   Roy Wilkins sent telegram to Franklin Roosevelt on lynchings since he became President.

2667. "Shame to Mississippi." THE NATION, Vol. 128, No. 3315 (Jan. 16, 1929): 62.   Five lynchings in 1928 including that of Charley Shepherd at Parchman on Dec. 31.

2668. "Shame Upon Maryland" THE CATHOLIC WORLD, Vol. 138, No. 825 (Dec. 1933): 261-62.   George Armwood lynching. Continued by "Savages Are Ever Cowards."

2669. "The Shape of Things." THE NATION, Vol. 163, No. 5 (Aug. 3, 1946): 113.   Second item in this section. Comment on recent quadruple lynching in Georgia.

2670. "The Shape of Things." THE NATION, Vol. 163, No. 9 (Aug. 31, 1946): 225-26.   Third item in this section.   Comments occasioned by lynching of nine blacks in last two months.

2671. "The Shape of Things." THE NATION, Vol. 164, No. 21 (May 24, 1947): 615.   First item in this section. Greenville, South Carolina, trial of 31 whites for lynching Willie Earle in 1947.

2672. Sheean, Vincent. "Lawrenceburg Verdict." THE NEW REPUBLIC, Vol. 115, No. 15 (Oct. 14, 1946): 472-73.   Acquittal of 23 of 25 black men for shooting Will Willsford during disorders at Columbia, Tennessee.

2673. Sheean, Vincent. "The Tragedy of Mink Slide." In A TREASURY OF GREAT REPORTING: "LITERATURE UNDER PRESSURE" FROM THE SIXTEENTH CENTURY TO OUR OWN TIME, pp. 758-61. Ed. Louis L. Snyder and Richard B. Morris. New York: Simon & Schuster, 1949.   Columbia, Tennessee.

2674. "The Shelbyville Affair." THE COMMONWEAL, Vol. 21, No. 10 (Jan. 4, 1935): 273.   Battle between National Guard and would-be lynchers in Tennessee followed by destruction of courthouse.

2675. "The Shelbyville Mob." CRIME SURVEY, Vol. 1, No. 1 (April 1935): 9.   Would-be lynchers burned Tennessee courthouse. From Toledo Blade.

2676. Shepherd, William G. "The Whip Hand." COLLIER'S, Vol. 81, No. 1 (Jan. 7, 1928): 8-9, 44-45.   Modern KKK and floggings in Alabama.

2677. Shepherd, William G. "The Whip Wins." COLLIER'S, Vol. 81, No. 2 (Jan. 14, 1928): 10-11, 30, 32.   Modern KKK and floggings in Alabama.

2678. "Sheriff or Coroner?." THE LAWYER AND BANKER AND SOUTHERN BENCH AND BAR REVIEW, Vol. 19, No. 1 (Jan.-Feb. 1926): 1-3.   Editorial favoring lynching. [By Charles E. George; see contents page listing him as editor of this journal.]   Reprinted in Virginia Law Register, Vol. XI (New Series), No. 10 (Feb. 1926): 629-30.

2679. "Sheriffs Protect Property Not Life In United States: Mob in Florida Mutilates, Shoots and Hangs Negro." THE CATHOLIC WORKER, Vol. 2, No. 6 (Nov. 1934): 1.   Claude Neal.

2680. Sherman, Scott. "Preserving Black History." THE PROGRESSIVE, Vol. 55, No. 12 (Dec. 1991): 15.   Black Holocaust Museum, Milwaukee. Created by James Cameron, who was almost lynched with two victims who died, at Marion, Indiana, 1930.

2681. Shofner, Jerrell H.   "Judge Herbert Rider and the Lynching at Labelle." THE FLORIDA HISTORICAL QUARTERLY, Vol. 59, No. 3 (Jan. 1981): 292-306.   Florida torture and lynching of a black man named Henry Patterson, who accidentally frightened a white woman (1926).

2682. "Shooting Straight." AMERICA, Vol. 23, No. 15 (July 31, 1920): 353. Editorial against lynching.

2683. Shostak, David A. "Crosby Smith: Forgotten Witness to a Mississippi Nightmare." NEGRO HISTORY BULLETIN, Vol. 38, No. 1 (Dec. 1974-Jan. 1975): 320-25.   Emmett Till case, 1955.

2684. Shotland, R. Lance. "Spontaneous Vigilantes." SOCIETY, Vol. 13, No. 3 (March/April 1976): 30-32.   Bystander intervention, especially in New York City in 1970s. Brief comparison to lynchings in 1930 (p. 31).

2685. Shotland, R. Lance.   "Spontaneous Vigilantism: A Bystander Response to Criminal Behavior." In VIGILANTE POLITICS, pp. 30-44. Ed. by H. Jon Rosenbaum and Peter C. Sederberg.   Philadelphia: Univ. of Pennsylvania Press, 1976.

2686. "The Shubata Lynchings." THE CRISIS, Vol. 18, No. 1 (May 1919): 24-25.   Four black victims in Mississippi.

2687. Shull, Carol Edwards. "Lynching and the American Negro's Progress During the 1920's." M.A. thesis, Univ. of Texas at Austin, 1969.

2688. "Sikeston Lynching--Continued and Closed." THE SOUTHERN FRONTIER, Vol. 3, No. 8 (Aug. 1942): [2].   Missouri.

2689. "Silent Sentinel." NEW REPUBLIC, Vol. 116, No. 21 (May 26, 1947): 8-10.   Trial of 31 white men for lynching Willie Earle in South Carolina in 1947.

2690. Simpson, William M. "Reflections on a Murder: The Emmett Till Case."   In SOUTHERN MISCELLANY: ESSAYS IN HONOR OF GLOVER MOORE, pp. 177-200.   Ed. by Frank Allen Dennis.   Jackson: Univ. Press of Mississippi, 1981.   He was murdered in Mississippi in 1955.

2691. Sitkoff, Harvard.   A NEW DEAL FOR BLACKS: THE EMER-

GENCE OF CIVIL RIGHTS AS A NATIONAL ISSUE. VOL. I: THE DEPRESSION DECADE. New York: Oxford Univ. Press, 1978.   See "Anti-lynching" and "Lynching" in index.

2692. Sitkoff, Harvard. "Racial Militancy and Interracial Violence in the Second World War." THE JOURNAL OF AMERICAN HISTORY, Vol. 58, No. 3 (Dec. 1971): 661-81.

2693. "Six Months Sans Lynching." THE SOUTHERN FRONTIER, Vol. 1, No. 7 (July 1940): [2].

2694. "Sixth Lynching of Year 1938 Is Whitewashed." EQUAL JUSTICE, Vol. 12, No. 10 (Nov. 1938): 1.

2695. "A 'Sleeping Giant' Stirs." NEWSWEEK, Vol. 75, No. 11 (March 16, 1970): 76.   Violence in Berkeley, California, prompts mayor's plan for patrols by block wardens, which critics say would be "an ill-disguised troop of vigilantes."

2696. "Smallest Lynching Record in 1924." FEDERAL COUNCIL BULLETIN, Vol. 8, No. 1 (Jan.-Feb. 1925): 7.

2697. Smead, Edwin Howard. "The Lynching of Mack Charles Parker in Poplarville, Mississippi, April 25, 1959." Ph.D. diss., Univ. of Maryland, 1979.   See Diss. Ab. Intl., Vol. 41, No. 2 (Aug. 1980): 775A.

2698. Smead, Howard. BLOOD JUSTICE: THE LYNCHING OF MACK CHARLES PARKER. New York: Oxford Univ. Press, 1986.   One of the last Southern lynchings (Mississippi, 1959).

2699. Smith, Alfred E. [editor of this journal]   "Two Governors." NEW OUTLOOK, Vol. 163, No. 1 (Jan. 1934): 11-12.   Lynchings in California and Maryland.

2700. Smith, Bolton. "The Memphis Lynching." THE NEW REPUBLIC, Vol. 12, No. 145 (Aug. 11, 1917): 51.   Letter claiming Tennessee lynching victim Ell Person was guilty.

2701. Smith, J. Clay, Jr. "The 'Lynching' at Howard Beach: An Annotated Bibliographic Index." NATIONAL BLACK LAW JOURNAL, Vol. 12, No. 1 (Spring 1990): 29-60.   Beating and traffic death of black man Michael Griffith in New York City, 1986.

2702. Smith, Walker C. WAS IT MURDER? AUTHENTIC RECORD OF THE CAUSES LEADING TO, THE ACTUAL EVENTS OF, AND

THE TRIAL THAT FOLLOWED THE ARMISTICE DAY TRAGEDY AT CENTRALIA, WASH., NOV. 11, '19 . . . Seattle: Northwest District Defense Committee, 1922.   Title given here is the one on the cover; title given on page 1 is WAS IT MURDER? THE TRUTH ABOUT CENTRALIA. There was a revised ed.; Seattle, 1927.

2703. Snell, William R. "Fiery Crosses in the Roaring Twenties: Activities of the Revised Klan in Alabama, 1915-1930." THE ALABAMA REVIEW, Vol. 23, No. 4 (Oct. 1970): 256-76.   See pp. 273-75 for floggings.

2704. Snell, William R. "Masked Men in the Magic City: Activities of the Revised Klan in Birmingham, 1916-1940." ALABAMA HISTORICAL QUARTERLY, Vol. 34, No. 3-4 (Fall and Winter 1972): 206-27.   Some violence, such as flogging non-Klansmen.

2705. Snowden, Frank M. "The Italian Press Views America's Attitude Toward Civil Rights and the Negro." THE JOURNAL OF NEGRO EDUCATION, Vol. 21, No. 1 (Winter 1952): 20-26.   See p. 23 for mention of article in Il Momento (June 1950) on lynching.

2706. Snyder, Howard. "Negro Migration and the Cotton Crop." THE NORTH AMERICAN REVIEW, Vol. 219, No. 818 (Jan. 1924): 21-29. Lynching helps cause migration [one paragraph on p. 26].

2707. "The Social Front." A MONTHLY SUMMARY OF EVENTS AND TRENDS IN RACE RELATIONS, Vol. 1, No. 1 (Aug. 1943): 6-11.   Includes "Race Riots," "Minor Outbreaks," "Rumors of Riots That Did Not Happen," "Soldier Violence," and "Lynching."

2708. "The Social Front: Lynching." EVENTS AND TRENDS IN RACE RELATIONS: A MONTHLY SUMMARY, Vol. 4, No. 8 (March 1947): 233-34.

2709. "The Social Front: Violence." A MONTHLY SUMMARY OF EVENTS AND TRENDS IN RACE RELATIONS, Vol. 3, No. 8 (March 1946): 233-36.   Mainly about Columbia, Tennessee.   On Columbia see also Vol. 3, No. 9 (April 1946): 266-67; Vol. 3, No. 11 (June 1946): 33; Vol. 4, Nos. 1 and 2 (Aug-Sept. 1946): 8-9; Vol. 4, No. 3 (Oct. 1946): 68-69, 93-94; Vol. 4, No. 4 (Nov. 1946): 105.

2710. "The Social Front: Violence." EVENTS AND TRENDS IN RACE RELATIONS: A MONTHLY SUMMARY, Vol. 4, No. 12 (July 1947): 365-68.   Willie Earle (South Carolina), etc.

2711. "The Social Front: Violence: Lynchings." A MONTHLY SUM-

MARY OF EVENTS AND TRENDS IN RACE RELATIONS, Vol. 4, Nos. 1 and 2 (Aug.-Sept. 1946): 3-5.

2712. "Some Un-American Activities Congressman Dies Didn't Investigate: Vigilante Attacks On Labor In 1938." EQUAL JUSTICE, Vol. 12, No. 12 (Jan. 1939): 3.

2713. "Somewhere in America, 1942." COLLIER'S Vol. 109, No. 13 (March 28, 1942): 70.   Lynching in Sikeston, Missouri.

2714. SoRelle, James M. "Race Relations in 'Heavenly Houston,' 1919-45." In BLACK DIXIE: AFRO-TEXAN HISTORY AND CULTURE IN HOUSTON, pp. 175-91. Ed. by Howard Beeth and Cary D. Wintz. College Station: Texas A&M [sic] Univ. Press, 1992.   See pp. 178-80 for 1928 lynching of Robert Powell, black man.

2715. Sosna, Morton. IN SEARCH OF THE SILENT SOUTH: SOUTH-ERN LIBERALS AND THE RACE ISSUE. New York: Columbia Univ. Press, 1977.   See "Lynching" in index.

2716. Sosna, Morton Philip.   "In Search of the Silent South: White Southern Racial Liberalism, 1920-1950." Ph.D. diss., Univ. of Wisconsin, 1972.   See Diss. Ab. Intl., Vol. 33, No. 12, Part I (June 1973): 6853A-6854A.

2717. "The Soul of a Lyncher." THE COMPETITOR, Vol. 2, No. 3 (Oct.-Nov. 1920): 192.   Comment on reprint of anti-Negro letter by P. N. Pittenger to editor of Atlanta Journal.

2718. Soule, Isobel Walker. THE VIGILANTES HIDE BEHIND THE FLAG. [New York]: International Labor Defense, 1937.   Anti-labor organizations.

2719. "South Approves Conditions Which Cause Lynching."   THE SOUTHERN FRONTIER, Vol. 2, No. 1 (Jan. 1941): [2].

2720. "South Carolina: By the Clock." TIME, Vol. 49, No. 8 (Feb. 24, 1947): 29.   Lynching of a black man named Willie Earle.

2721. "South Carolina: New Twist." TIME, Vol. 49, No. 9 (March 3, 1947): 25.   Arrests of Willie Earle's alleged lynchers.

2722. "South Carolina: Trial by Jury." TIME, Vol. 49, No. 21 (May 26, 1947): 27.   Willie Earle case.

2723. "South Carolina's Shame." THE NATION, Vol. 123, No. 3203 (Nov. 17, 1926): 497.   Walter White's investigation of the lynching of blacks named Lowman.

2724. "The South Lifts Its Head." In CHANGING PATTERNS IN THE NEW SOUTH, p. 24 [Vol. 10, No. 1 (Jan. 1955) of NEW SOUTH]. Response to Tuskegee report of no lynchings in 1952. From New South (Jan. 1953).

2725. "The South: Two Governors." TIME, Vol. 47, No. 1 (Jan. 7, 1946): 16.   Governors of North Carolina and Florida.   The latter allegedly claimed Jesse James Payne was not lynched and condoned his death at the hands of a mob. [See "Letters," ibid. Vol. XLVII, No. 5 (Feb. 4, 1946): 4, 60, for editor's apology.]

2726. "Southern Church Speaks Out Against Lynching." THE CHRISTIAN CENTURY, Vol. 47, No. 43 (Oct. 22, 1930): 1268.   Methodist Episcopal Church, South.

2727. Southern Commission on the Study of Lynching. LYNCHINGS AND WHAT THEY MEAN: GENERAL FINDINGS OF THE SOUTH-ERN COMMISSION ON THE STUDY OF LYNCHING.   Atlanta: Southern Commission on the Study of Lynching, 1931.

2728. Southern Commission on the Study of Lynching.   THE MOB MURDER OF S. S. MINCEY, WITH THE ADDED STORY OF A THREATENED LYNCHING FOILED. Atlanta: Southern Commission on the Study of Lynching, 1932.

2729. Southern Commission on the Study of Lynching. THE PLIGHT OF TUSCALOOSA: A CASE STUDY OF CONDITIONS IN TUSCALOOSA COUNTY, ALABAMA, 1933. Atlanta: Southern Commission on the Study of Lynching, 1933. Cover title: THE PLIGHT OF TUSCALOOSA: MOB MURDERS, COMMUNITY HYSTERIA, OFFICIAL INCOMPETENCE. Lynching of Pippen, Harden, and (later) Cross; all were blacks.

2730. Southern Commission on the Study of Lynching.   SOUTHERN LEADERS IMPEACH JUDGE LYNCH: HIGHLIGHTS FROM RE-PORT OF COMMISSION ON THE STUDY OF LYNCHING. Atlanta: Commission on Interracial Cooperation, 1931.

2731. "Southern Commission Reports on Lynching." THE CHRISTIAN CENTURY, Vol. 48, No. 47 (Nov. 25, 1931): 1477.   Date Nov. 26, 1931, is listed on p. 1475, but on cover and on pp. 1474, 1476, etc., it is Nov. 25. Preceding issue was Nov. 18.

2732. Southern Conference for Human Welfare. THE TRUTH ABOUT COLUMBIA TENNESSEE CASES. Nashville: Southern Conference for Human Welfare, [1946?].   Failed attempt to lynch blacks led to white attack on black section of town and arrests of many blacks, some of whom were killed in jail.

2733. "Southern Conscience Speaks." NEW SOUTH, Vol. 2, No. 7 (July 1947): 2-3.   Acquittals in Willie Earle case in South Carolina.

2734. "Southern Leaders Out to Track Down Judge Lynch."   THE LITERARY DIGEST, Vol. 107, No. 3 (Oct. 18, 1930): 24-25.

2735. "The Southern Mob." THE CRISIS, Vol. 35, No. 4 (April 1928): 132. Example of would-be lynchers seeking innocent black male.

2736. "Southern Protests Against Lynching." THE OUTLOOK, Vol. 122, No. 13 (July 30, 1919): 493.

2737. "Southern Women and Lynching." THE SOUTHERN FRONTIER, Vol. 1, No. 7 (July 1940): [2].

2738. "Southern Women Speak Out." THE WORLD TOMORROW, Vol. 13 (Dec. 1930): 487.

2739. "The South's Fight Against Mob Murders."   THE LITERARY DIGEST, Vol. 84, No. 3 (Jan. 17, 1925): 30-31.

2740. Spain, David M. "Mississippi Autopsy." RAMPARTS special edition, 1964.   Chaney, Goodman, and Schwerner, 1964.

2741. Spearman, Walter, and Meyer, Sylvan. RACIAL CRISIS AND THE PRESS. Atlanta: Southern Regional Council, 1960.   Contains "Racial Stories in the News," by Walter Spearman, and "The Press and the Schools," by Sylvan Meyer.   See pp. 20-21 in the former for "The Poplarville Lynching--April 1959" (lynching of Mack C. Parker in Mississippi).

2742. Spence, Alex W. "Lynching and the Nation." THE COMMON-WEAL, Vol. 15, No. 24 (April 13, 1932): 658-59.   Report of the Southern Commission on the Study of Lynching,

2743. Spivak, John L. "Who Backs the Black Legion?" NEW MASSES, Vol. 19, No. 11 (June 9, 1936): 9-10; Vol. 19, No. 12 (June 16, 1936): 9-10; Vol. 19, No. 13 (June 23, 1936): 13-14; Vol. 20, No. 1 (June 30, 1936): 6. Michigan and elsewhere.

2744. "SRC Investigates Columbia Incident, Consults With Justice Department." NEW SOUTH, 1, No. 4 (April 1946): 3-4.   Tennessee.

2745. "SRC Investigates Lynchings." NEW SOUTH, Vol. 1, No. 8 (Aug. 1946): 5-6.

2746. Stanton, Bill. KLANWATCH: BRINGING THE KU KLUX KLAN TO JUSTICE. New York: Grove Weidenfeld, 1991.   See "lynchings" and "Donald, Michael, murder case" [Alabama] in index.

2747. "State Police: A Cure for Lynchings." THE WORLD'S WORK, Vol. 35, No. 6 (April 1918): 585-86.

2748. Stephens, Harold W.   "Mask and Lash in Crenshaw."   NORTH AMERICAN REVIEW, Vol. 225, No. 842 (April 1928): 435-42.   KKK violence in Alabama.

2749. Stewart, Herbert L.   "The Southern View of Lynching."   THE NATION, Vol. 104, No. 2691 (Jan. 25, 1917): 102-03.

2750. "Still With Us." THE COMMONWEAL, Vol. 79, No. 18 (Jan. 31, 1964): 495-96.   Vigilantism as blacklisting and an Indiana law against peaceful assembly to advocate government overthrow "by force, violence, or any unlawful means."

2751. Stolberg, Benjamin. "Vigilantism, 1937." THE NATION, Vol. 145, No. 7 (Aug. 14, 1937): 166-68.   Sees vigilantism as a mechanism of class exploitation.

2752. Stolberg, Benjamin. "Vigilantism, 1937--II." THE NATION, Vol. 145, No. 8 (Aug. 21, 1937): 191-93.   Continuation of idea in preceding issue.

2753. Storey, Moorfield.   THE NEGRO QUESTION: AN ADDRESS DELIVERED BEFORE THE WISCONSIN BAR ASSOCIATION BY MOORFIELD STOREY, JUNE 27, 1918. N.p.: n.p., [1918].   Lynching: pp. 7-14, 25-27.   Details on Dyersburg, Tennessee, and Estill Springs, Tennessee.

2754. Storey, Moorfield. OBEDIENCE TO THE LAW. AN ADDRESS AT THE OPENING OF PETIGRU COLLEGE IN COLUMBIA, SOUTH CAROLINA. Boston: Press of Geo. H. Ellis Co., 1919.   Lynching: pp. 13-19.

2755. "The Strange Trial Of The Till Kidnaping." [sic] JET, Vol. 80, No.

17 (Aug. 12, 1991): 12-15.   Mississippi, 1955.

2756. Street, James Howell. LOOK AWAY! A DIXIE NOTEBOOK. New York: Viking Press, 1936; Westport, CT: Greenwood Press, 1977, ©1936. Newspaperman's reminiscences, especially about lynching and racial violence.

2757. "Streicher Reminds America Of Lynching Disgrace." THE CHRISTIAN CENTURY, Vol. 52, No. 35 (Aug. 28, 1935): 1077.   Report of speech by a leading Nazi.

2758. Strong, Edward E.   "The Till Case and the Negro Liberation Movement." POLITICAL AFFAIRS, Vol. 34, No. 12 (Dec. 1955): 35-51. Till was murdered in Mississippi in 1955.

2759. "The Struggle Against Lynching Goes On."   THE CHRISTIAN CENTURY, Vol. 64, No. 34 (Aug. 20, 1947): 988.   Action by North Carolina governor against attempted lynchers.

2760. "Suit Filed Against KKK In Death of Black Youth." JET, Vol. 66, No. 18 (July 9, 1984): 39.   Michael Donald. Mobile, Alabama, 1981.

2761. Sullivan, Edward S.   "The Brooke Hart Kidnap-Murder And The California Lynch Mob." MASTER DETECTIVE, Vol. 64, No. 2 (May 1962): 58-65, 87-91.

2762. Sullivan, Joseph Matthew. "Lynching Statistics." JOURNAL OF THE AMERICAN INSTITUTE OF CRIMINAL LAW AND CRIMINOLOGY, Vol. 9, No. 1 (May 1918): 144-46.   Page 145: "In the southern states ignorant, vicious, and illiterate white officers take an intense delight in bragging about the number of 'niggers' they kill in the course of their careers."

2763. "Summer Lynching Rate Is One Every 6 Days." INTERRACIAL REVIEW, Vol. 8, No. 9 (Sept. 1935): 145. Brief.

2764. Summerbell, Carlyle.   "Following a Lynching Further."   THE CHRISTIAN CENTURY, Vol. 51, No. 47 (Nov. 21, 1934): 1491.   Letter. Not about any one lynching. Suggestions for preventing lynchings.

2765. "A Summons Against Mob Violence." THE LITERARY DIGEST, Vol. 96, No. 5 (Feb. 4, 1928): 31-32.

2766. Sydnor, Charles S. "The Southerner and the Laws." THE JOURNAL OF SOUTHERN HISTORY, Vol. 6, No. 1 (Feb. 1940): 3-23.

2767. Sykes, Leonard, Jr. "Jim Crow, Lynchings and a Return to Business As Usual." BLACK BOOKS BULLETIN, Vol. 7, No. 3 (1981): 18-20. Includes Michael Donald lynching [Alabama, 1981] and mock lynching in 1976.

2768. Sykes, Leonard, Jr. "Black Youth, 19, Lynched In Ala., Motive Probed." JET, Vol. 60, No. 4 (April 9, 1981): 6-8, 55.   Victim: Michael Donald.

2769. "Talking Points." THE CRUSADER, Vol. 4, No. 5 (July 1921): 30. Includes this: "Negroes from Croweburg, Kan., a mining camp, made an attack upon the whites of Mulberry, Kan., where a Negro was lynched, following an alleged attack upon a white girl."

2770. "Tallahassee Double Lynching." INTERNATIONAL JURIDICAL ASSOCIATION MONTHLY BULLETIN, Vol. 6, No. 2 (Aug. 1937): 20. Richard Hawkins and Ernest Ponder, blacks.

2771. "The Tampa Floggings." INTERNATIONAL JURIDICAL ASSOCIATION MONTHLY BULLETIN, Vol. 5, No. 1 (July 1936): 10-13. Shoemaker, et al.

2772. "Tampa Kidnapping Conviction Reversed." INTERNATIONAL JURIDICAL ASSOCIATION MONTHLY BULLETIN, Vol. 6, No. 2 (Aug. 1937): 20-21.

2773. "Tampa's Fatal Flogging." THE LITERARY DIGEST, Vol. 120, No. 26 (Dec. 28, 1935): 7.   Death of Joseph Shoemaker.

2774. "Tampa's Murders." NEW MASSES, Vol. 18, No. 10 [sic; should be 11] (March 10, 1936): 4.   Two deaths in aftermath of Shoemaker murder.

2775. "Tampa's Political Murder." NEW MASSES, Vol. 19, No. 3 (April 14, 1936): 6, 8.   Shoemaker case.

2776. Tannebaum, Frank. DARKER PHASES OF THE SOUTH. New York: G.P. Putnam's Sons, 1924.   Pages 20-30: dullness of small-town and rural life (worse in the South than elsewhere because of single-crop economy, idleness of some whites who depend on black laborers, poorer means of communication, and greater illiteracy) has helped promote KKK and lynchings.

2777. "Tarred and Feathered: The Facts: Told by Archdeacon Irwin Himself and Bishop Mann." THE INDEPENDENT, Vol. 106, No. 3783 (Sept. 17, 1921): 115-16.   Violence by whites in Miami, Florida, against an Episcopal

minister because of his alleged aid to blacks, 1921. Followed by "Bishop
Mann Sums Up the Case," ibid., pp. 116, 130-31.

2778. Taub, Allan. "Prelude to a Lynching." NEW MASSES, Vol. 8, No.
12 (Aug. 1933): 6-7.   Some events prior to lynching of Dan Pippen and A.
T. Harden in Alabama. See also illustration by Hugo Gellert on p. 7.

2779. Taylor, Alva W.   "Law Officers Show More Resolution."   THE
CHRISTIAN CENTURY, Vol. 54, No. 51 (Dec. 22, 1937): 1603.

2780. Taylor, Alva W. "Lynchers Still Go Unpunished." THE CHRISTIAN
CENTURY, Vol. 51, No. 6 (Feb. 7, 1934): 200. Unnamed black victim was
lynched in Maury County, Tennessee, in Dec. 1933.

2781. Taylor, Alva W.   "Lynchings on Decrease."   THE CHRISTIAN
CENTURY, Vol. 54, No. 51 (Dec. 22, 1937): 1602-03.

2782. Taylor, Alva W. "Racial Tensions Rock the South." THE CHRIS-
TIAN CENTURY, Vol. 63, No. 38 (Sept. 18, 1946): 1124, 1126. Floggings,
murders, and lynchings.

2783. Taylor, Alva W. "Report on Responsibility for Lynchings." THE
CHRISTIAN CENTURY, Vol. 50, No. 48 (Nov. 29, 1933): 1509.   Recent
report (written by Arthur Raper) by interracial commission.

2784. Taylor, John. "The Rosewood Massacre." ESQUIRE, Vol. 122, No.
1 (July 1994): 46-54.   Includes lynching, Florida, 1923. Listed on cover as
"How a Town Was Lynched."

2785. "$10,000 Reward Offered In Donald Lynching Case." JET, Vol. 60,
No. 17 (July 9, 1981): 24.   Mobile, Alabama, 1981.

2786. "Tennessee: Morning in Bledsoe County." TIME, Vol. 44, No. 23
(Dec. 4, 1944): 22.   Lynching of James Scales, black teenager.

2787. "Tennessee to the Fore." AMERICA, Vol. 52, No. 13 (Jan. 5, 1935):
291.   Governor sent troops to prevent lynching and four would-be lynchers
were killed.

2788. "Terror Against the Negro People." EQUAL JUSTICE, Vol. 15, No.
3 (Winter 1941): 52-54.   Wanton killings not listed as lynchings are
increasing in number.

2789. "Terror in Alabama." NEW MASSES, Vol. 15, No. 10 (June 4, 1935):
5.   Anti-black violence; beatings.

2790. "Terror in Mink Slide." NEWSWEEK, Vol. 27, No. 10 (March 11, 1946): 28-29.   Columbia, Tennessee, racial violence.

2791. "Terror Stalks the Negro People." EQUAL JUSTICE, Vol. 15, No. 5 (Autumn 1941): 5-6.   Facts from I.L.D. Civil Right [sic] Survey.   Includes lynchings.

2792. Terry, John. "The Terror in San Jose." THE NATION, Vol. 139, No. 3605 (Aug. 8, 1934): 161-62.   Anti-red "vigilantes" in California rounded up 13 alleged radicals, beat them, and drove them out of Santa Clara County.

2793. "A Texas Horror." THE CRISIS, Vol. 24, No. 3 (July 1922): 121-22. Lynchings of several blacks (three by burning alive) after a white girl was murdered in Kirwin, Texas.

2794. "Texas Officials Approve Lynching of Negroes Too Young for Capital Punishment." INTERNATIONAL JURIDICAL ASSOCIATION MONTH-LY BULLETIN, Vol. 4, No. 6 (Nov. 1935): 2.   Victims: Bennie Mitchell and Ernest Collins.

2795. "Texas Stages First Lynching in Six Years." THE SOUTHERN FRONTIER, Vol. 3, No. 7 (July 1942): [3].

2796. "They Are Still Lynching." INTERRACIAL REVIEW, Vol. 14, No. 1 (Jan. 1941): 5.

2797. "Thirteen Lynchings." OUTLOOK AND INDEPENDENT, Vol. 160, No. 1 (Jan. 6, 1932): 7.   Number of lynchings in 1931 compared to other years.

2798. "Thirteen Lynchings In 1936 According to the N. A. A. C. P." [sic] INTERRACIAL REVIEW, Vol. 10, No. 2 (Feb. 1936): 32.   Brief note.

2799. "A Thirty Years' Record in Lynching." THE WORLD'S WORK, Vol. 39, No. 5 (March 1920): 433-34.

2800. "This Lawless Nation." THE NATION, Vol. 129, No. 3344 (Aug. 7, 1929): 134.   Briefly includes lynching.

2801. Thomas, Norman. "Socialism's Appeal to Negroes." THE CRISIS, Vol. 43, No. 10 (Oct. 1936): 294-95, 315.   See section subtitled "About Lynching."

2802. Thornton, William. "A Southern Comment on Lynching." THE

NATION, Vol. 131, No. 3407 (Oct. 22, 1930): 444. Letter.

2803. "Three Important Cases." THE CRISIS, Vol. 30, No. 1 (May 1925): 35-36. One is a court case in Arkansas to collect damages from the 1922 lynchers of John Harrison, a black man.

2804. "Three Lynch Affidavits. By Alabama Sharecroppers." NEW MASSES, Vol. 17, No. 4 (Oct. 22, 1935): 16-18. Lynching and other violence by white mobs against blacks in Lowndes County who joined Sharecroppers' Union.

2805. "3,000 Will Burn Negro." THE CRISIS, Vol. 18, No. 4 (Aug. 1919): 209. Reprints from two Southern newspapers. Expected lynching of John Hartfield at Ellisville, Mississippi, June, 1919

2806. "Throwback to Lynch Law." THE ECONOMIST [London], Vol. 191, No. 6037 (May 9, 1959): 529. Comment about lynching in Poplarville, Mississippi, in April, 1959, of a black man accused of rape.

2807. "The Till Case." NEW SOUTH, Vol. 10, No. 9 (Sept. 1955): 1-2. He was murdered in Mississippi, 1955.

2808. Tippett, Tom. "Short Cut to Lynching." THE CRISIS, Vol. 43, No. 1 (Jan. 1936): 8-10, 26. Deaths of two blacks (Henry Freeman and Dave Hart) in Gretna, Louisiana.

2809. "To De-bunk Lynching." INTERRACIAL REVIEW, Vol. 10, No. 4 (April 1937): 64. Editorial from Cleveland Plain Dealer. J. D. Ames says, "Economic greed is the cause of many more lynchings than the protection of white women's honor." Brief.

2810. "'To Hell With Law' Mob Tells Sheriff." INTERRACIAL REVIEW, Vol. 10, No. 9 (Sept. 1937): 143. Lynching victim: Albert Gooden, black. Near Covington, Tennessee.

2811. "To Lynch or Not to Lynch?" THE OUTLOOK, Vol. 115, No. 4 (Jan. 24, 1917): 137-38. Governor Stanley, Kentucky, faced down lynch mob at Murray. Governor Manning, South Carolina, and his courage to prosecute lynchers. The "Waco Horror" [Texas].

2812. "'Too Rich To Be a Niggar [sic].'" THE CRISIS, Vol. 40, No. 12 (Dec. 1933): 282-83. Background of lynching of Norris Dendy; South Carolina, 1933.

2813. Toppin, Edgar A. "A Half-century of Struggle for Equal Rights,

1916-1965." NEGRO HISTORY BULLETIN, Vol. 28, No. 8 (Special Summer Issue, 1965): 176-77, 188-89.   See p. 177 for lynching. It ended because of publicity from NAACP and "organized protest of Southern ladies."

2814. "The Tragedy of Afro-America."   THE NATION AND THE ATHENAEUM [London], Vol. 27 (April 24, 1920): 106-07.   Mainly on lynching, but also on Sandburg's The Chicago Race Riots.

2815. Trapp, Charles N. "Mob Victim: The Story of a Man Who Barely Missed Being One." THE NEW REPUBLIC, Vol. 56, No. 758 (Nov. 14, 1928): 345-46.   Mob could not work up enough courage to hang the author. No place or date given.

2816. "Trial by Jury." TIME, Vol. 66, No. 14 (Oct. 3, 1955): 18-19. Bryant and Milam (Till case in Mississippi).

2817. Tribble, Edwin. "Impeaching Judge Lynch." THE NEW REPUBLIC, Vol. 67, No. 867 (July 15, 1931): 226-27. Battle between National Guard and mob trying to lynch John Downer at Elberton, Georgia. Downer was later tried and convicted.

2818. Trimmer, J. Maurice. "Strikers Tried As Lynchers." THE CHRIS-TIAN CENTURY, Vol. 54, No. 35 (Sept. 1, 1937): 1082.   Result of economic violence in Virginia.

"The Truth About Lynching." See Randolph, A. Philip.

2819. "Trying To Stamp Out Peonage in Georgia." CURRENT OPINION, Vol. 71, No. 1 (July 1921): 76-77. Some references to lynching on p. 77.

2820. Tucker, William.   VIGILANTE: THE BACKLASH AGAINST CRIME IN AMERICA. New York: Stein & Day, 1985.   Mainly about U.S. in second half of 20th century.

2821. Turner, Edward Raymond. "The Habit of Torture." THE NATION, Vol. 108, No. 2809 (May 3, 1919): 686-89.   Accounts of torture in various times and places. Includes lynching in U.S. (pp. 688-89).

2822. Turner, William Douglas, Jr. "The Dallas Express as a Forum on Lynching, 1919-1921." M.A. thesis, Southern Methodist Univ., 1974.

2823. "Tuskegee Institute No Longer Issues Report Of Lynchings." JET, Vol. 60, No. 4 (April 9, 1981): 55. Total number of blacks lynched, 1882-1961, plus Michael Donald [Alabama, 1981].

2824. "Tuskegee Lists Five Lynchings." INTERRACIAL REVIEW, Vol. 15, No. 2 (Feb. 1943): 33.

2825. "Tuskegee Lists One Lynching in 1945, Florida Governor and SRC Disagree." NEW SOUTH, Vol. 1, No. 1 (Jan. 1946): 9.

2826. Tuttle, Elbert P. "Reflections on the Law of Habeas Corpus." JOURNAL OF PUBLIC LAW, Vol. 22, No. 2 (Fall 1973): 325-34. Includes how Tuttle helped save two black prisoners from lynching in Georgia in 1931.

2827. "Twelve Good Men and True." NEW REPUBLIC, Vol. 116, No. 22 (June 2, 1947): 9. Acquittals of white men accused of lynching Willie Earle in South Carolina, 1947.

2828. "28 Lynchings in 1933." THE SURVEY, Vol. 70, No. 2 (Feb. 1934): 49.

2829. "Two Governors on Race Problems." COLLIER'S, Vol. 117, No. 8 (Feb. 23, 1946): 94. Editorial about Florida lynching (of Jesse James Payne) which led to successful libel suit by Governor Millard Caldwell.

2830. "Two Juries Make History In the South." THE CHRISTIAN CENTURY, Vol. 53, No. 23 (June 3, 1936): 789. One made an award of damages to parents of black lynching victim Fred Moore. He was lynched in Assumption Parish, Louisiana, in 1933.

2831. "Two Lynchings in April." INTERNATIONAL JURIDICAL ASSO-CIATION MONTHLY BULLETIN, Vol. 4, No. 11a (May 1936): 3. Lint Shaw, black, near Royston, Georgia; and Willie Kees, black, at Lepanto, Arkansas.

2832. "Two Lynchings Last Year." THE CHRISTIAN CENTURY, Vol. 66, No. 3 (Jan. 19, 1949): 67.

2833. "Two Methods." THE CRISIS, Vol. 20, No. 3 (July 1920): 118. A Des Moines, Iowa, vigilance committee has a program for the betterment of black children in mixed schools.

2834. "Two More Lynchings." INTERNATIONAL JURIDICAL ASSOCI-ATION MONTHLY BULLETIN, Vol. 3, No. 4 (Sept. 1934): 3.

2835. "Two More Lynchings." INTERNATIONAL JURIDICAL ASSOCI-ATION MONTHLY BULLETIN, Vol. 7, No. 5 (Nov. 1938): 51. One victim was Otis Price, black man, Perry, Florida; the other was R. C.

Williams, black man, Ruston, Louisiana.

2836. "Two More Lynchings." THE SOUTHERN FRONTIER, Vol. 5, No. 11 (Nov. 1944): [3].

2837. Tyler, Robert L. "Violence at Centralia, 1919." PACIFIC NORTH-WEST QUARTERLY, Vol. 45, No. 4 (Oct. 1954): 116-24.   Washington state.

2838. Tyre, Nedra. "You All Are a Bunch of Nigger Lovers." In RED WINE FIRST, pp. 112-23. New York: Simon and Schuster, 1947. Account told to a Southern case worker, 1940-1945. Anonymous narrator describes lynching of black man in which he participated.

2839. "The Undermining of Civilization." THE CHRISTIAN CENTURY, Vol. 50, No. 50 (Dec. 6, 1933): 1525-26.   San Jose, CA, lynching.

2840. "Unfortunate Mistake." THE SOUTHERN FRONTIER, Vol. 1, No. 1 (Jan. 1940): [4].   KKK flogged Lamar Pruitt in South Carolina.

2841. "A University Course in Lynching." THE CRISIS, Vol. 26, No. 2 (June 1923): 55.   Lynching of James T. Scott, a janitor at the University of Missouri.

2842. "The Unsolved Race Problem: A Review of Events in 1920." THE WORLD TOMORROW, Vol. 4, No. 2 (Feb. 1921): 51-53.   Begins with 1920 lynchings. Tuskegee and NAACP statistics don't agree.

2843. U.S. Commission on Civil Rights. JUSTICE: 1961 COMMISSION ON CIVIL RIGHTS REPORT. Washington, DC: USGPO, [1961?]. Supt. of Doc. #: CR1.1:961/bk.5 Includes some references to lynching, especially that of Mack Parker in Mississippi in 1959.

2844. U.S. Congress. House. THE KU-KLUX KLAN. HEARINGS BEFORE THE COMMITTEE ON RULES, HOUSE OF REPRESENTA-TIVES, SIXTY-SEVENTH CONGRESS, FIRST SESSION. Washington, DC: Government Printing Office, 1921.   Supt. of Doc. #: Y4.R86/1:K95 See pp. 63-66 for violence on Nov. 2, 1920, at Ocoee, Florida; several blacks and whites were killed.

2845. U.S. Congress. Senate. Committee on the Judiciary. INVESTIGA-TION OF LYNCHINGS, REPORT TO ACCOMPANY S. RES. 211. Senate Report No. 1561, 74th Cong., 2d Sess. Serial Set 9990.

2846. U.S. President. [Circular letter, July 26, 1918, concerning mob spirit in United States.] Supt. of Doc. #: PR28.2:M71

2847. U.S. President. MOB VIOLENCE. STATEMENT OF THE PRESIDENT OF THE UNITED STATES DENOUNCING MOB VIOLENCE . . . Senate Document No. 272, 65th Cong., 2d Sess. [Aug. 22, 1918]. Serial Set 7330 (SENATE DOCUMENTS. Vol. 20).

2848. U.S. President's Committee on Civil Rights. TO SECURE THESE RIGHTS, THE REPORT OF THE PRESIDENT'S COMMITTEE ON CIVIL RIGHTS. Washington, DC: USGPO, 1947. Supt. of Doc. #: Pr33.2:R449. New York: Simon & Schuster, 1947.   See subsection of chapter II entitled "The Crime of Lynching," pp. 20-25. It deals largely with lynching in 1946 and 1947 and with attempted lynchings during 1937-1946.

2849. Usher, Roland G. "Primitive Law and the Negro." THE JOURNAL OF NEGRO HISTORY, Vol. 4, No. 1 (Jan. 1919): 1-6.   Lynching is a form of self-help by aggrieved persons (pp. 4-5).

2850. Valentine, C. "Hand Grenades." THE CRUSADER, Vol. 6, No. 1 (Jan.-Feb. [1922]): 6.   If Negro lynch victims fought lynchers, lynching would end. When mob gets a Negro, he's going to die anyway, so he might as well die fighting.

2851. Valentine, C. "The Man Whom They Lynched." THE CRUSADER, Vol. 2, No. 3 (Nov. 1919): 14-15.   Will Brown at Omaha, Nebraska.

2852. Valentine, C. "Why Lynching Persists." THE CRUSADER, Vol. 2, No. 1 (Sept. 1919): 6-7.   Some Negro publications say Negroes are satisfied.

2853. Van Slingerland, Peter. SOMETHING TERRIBLE HAS HAP-PENED. New York: Harper & Row, 1966.   Thalia Massie case in Hawaii. See pp. 144-49 for kidnapping and murder of Joseph Kahahawai.

2854. Vernimont, Raymond. "'The Horror at Sherman.'" AMERICA, Vol. 43, No. 9 (June 7, 1930): 216.   Letter regarding May 24 editorial. Texas.

2855. "A Victory and Defeat." THE CRISIS, Vol. 21, No. 6 (April 1921): 253-54.   Lynching as an issue in extradition cases.

2856. "Victory Over Lynchers In Minneapolis." LABOR DEFENDER, Vol. 10, No. 1 (Jan. 1934): 4.   Charges of murder and assault dropped against two blacks who defended themselves against a lynch mob.

2857. "Vigilance Against Mobs." CHRISTIAN ADVOCATE [Nashville],

Vol. 86, No. 1 (Jan. 2, 1925): 3.   Recent Nashville, Tennessee, lynching of Negro taken from hospital shows need to be on guard.

2858. "Vigilante Brutality." COMMON SENSE, Vol. 5, No. 1 (Jan. 1936): 5.   Beating death of Joseph Shoemaker, Tampa, 1935.   Brief.

2859. "Vigilante Held Not Deportable." INTERNATIONAL JURIDICAL ASSOCIATION MONTHLY BULLETIN, Vol. 8, No. 3 (Sept. 1939): 21.

2860. "Vigilante Organizations." EQUAL JUSTICE, Vol. 15, No. 3 (Winter 1941): 55-56.   List of some of them.

2861. "Vigilante Organizations--Vintage of 1939." EQUAL JUSTICE, Vol. 13, No. 12 (March 1940): 5-6.   Anti-union, anti-radical, anti-black.

2862. "Vigilante Terror 'Exiles' Gold Miners on Coast." EQUAL JUS-TICE, Vol. 12, No. 5 (May 1938): 3.   Anti-labor activities in Nevada County, California.

2863. "Vigilante Terror Spreading." EQUAL JUSTICE, Vol. 12, No. 6 (June 1938): 2, 4.   Anti-labor, anti-progressive.

2864. "The Vigilantes." THE BOOKMAN, Vol. 45, No. 4 (June 1917): 420. Society of authors and illustrators whose slogan is "For Patriotic Purposes."

2865. "The Vigilantes." THE OUTLOOK, Vol. 116, No. 8 (June 20, 1917): 286-87.   An "American organization of writers and artists who are engaged in putting the best thoughts on the war into the hands of the greatest possible number of Americans" (pp. 286-87).

2866. "Vigilantes and Cops: The Cops Were Not There." NEW MASSES, Vol. 16, No. 12 (Sept. 17, 1935): 16-17.   Anti-communist violence in Santa Rosa, California.

2867. "Vigilantes in Tampa." INTERNATIONAL JURIDICAL ASSOCIA-TION MONTHLY BULLETIN, Vol. 4, No. 7 (Dec. 1935): 3.   Joseph Shoemaker case in Florida.

2868. "Vigilantes: Women in Phoenix, Arizona, Organize to Fight Vice and Graft." THE LITERARY DIGEST, Vol. 122, No. 25 (Dec. 19, 1936): 13.

2869. "Vigilantism and Official Lawlessness." INTERNATIONAL JURIDICAL ASSOCIATION MONTHLY BULLETIN, Vol. 6, No. 2 (Aug. 1937): 17-19.   Various items, including recent labor troubles; not traditional vigilantism.

2870. "Vigilantism and Official Lawlessness." INTERNATIONAL JURIDICAL ASSOCIATION MONTHLY BULLETIN, Vol. 6, No. 3 (Sept. 1937): 30-31.

2871. "Vigilantism in Vermont." INTERNATIONAL JURIDICAL ASSOCIATION MONTHLY BULLETIN, Vol. 9, No. 4 (Oct. 1940): 35. Anti-conscription "communists" were attacked in Bristol.

2872. Wakefield, Dan. "Justice in Sumner: Land of the Free." THE NATION, Vol. 181, No. 14 (Oct. 1, 1955): 284-85. Emmett Till case in Mississippi; trial of Bryant and Milam.

2873. Wallace, Henry. "Violence and Hope in the South." NEW REPUBLIC, Vol. 117, No. 23 (Dec. 8, 1947): 14-16. One paragraph on lynching still existing in the South, but "the technique now is quietly to murder a Negro, one man doing the killing instead of a mob." Jim Crow is more against underprivileged than for race hatred.

2874. "The Wane of Lynching." THE OUTLOOK, Vol. 137, No. 12 (July 23, 1924): 459.

2875. Warren, N. J. "Inside Facts from Shelbyville." THE CHRISTIAN CENTURY, Vol. 52, No. 5 (Jan. 30, 1935): 146-47. Tennessee mob tried to lynch black man; mob burned courthouse. Some mob members killed by soldiers. December, 1934.

2876. "Was Melker Lynched? North Carolinians Say 'No!'" THE SOUTHERN FRONTIER, Vol. 2, No. 10 (Oct. 1941): [3]. Case in 1941 of four white men who killed a black man and were convicted of second degree murder.

2877. "We Need Grand Jury Evidence." THE SOUTHERN FRONTIER, Vol. 1, No. 7 (July 1940): [2]. Federal government should investigate reported lynchings.

2878. "'We Refuse to Accept Your Lynch Verdicts!'" LABOR DEFENDER, Vol. 10, No. 9 (Oct. 1934): 11. "Legal lynchings" of Scottsboro boys [Alabama] and Angelo Herndon [Georgia].

2879. West, Rebecca. "Lynching Trials in America." THE MEDICO-LEGAL JOURNAL, Vol. 17, Part 3 (1949): 90-99. Only one trial: Willie Earle case in South Carolina, 1947.

2880. West, Rebecca. "Opera in Greenville." THE NEW YORKER, Vol. 23, No. 17 (June 14, 1947): 31-36, 39-42, 44-46, 48-50, 52-56, 58-62, 65.

Willie Earle case, South Carolina, 1947.

2881. "What a White Paper and a Negro Paper of Mississippi Say About Verdict." THE SOUTHERN FRONTIER, Vol. 4, No. 5 (May 1943): [3]. Lynching at Laurel, Mississippi.

2882. "What Alabama Thinks of Her Lynching." THE LITERARY DIGEST, Vol. 116, No. 10 (Sept. 2, 1933): 8.   Three blacks were seized and shot by lynchers; one survived.

"What Is the Real Cause for the Decline in Lynching?" See Rogers, J. A.

2883. "'What You Have Done To the Least Of These You Have Done To Me.'" INTERRACIAL REVIEW, Vol. 9, No. 9 (Sept. 1936): 136.   Black Legion members in Michigan killed Silas Coleman "to see how it felt to shoot a Negro." See "'The Thrill Murder'" in Chapter VIII.

2884. "When a State Means to Stop Lynching." THE CHRISTIAN CENTURY, Vol. 48, No. 21 (May 27, 1931): 701.   Lynching prevented at Elberton, Georgia.

2885. "When Is a Lynching?" THE CHRISTIAN CENTURY, Vol. 55, No. 32 (Aug. 10, 1938): 957.   Decline in number of lynchings may be because some are being listed under another name, such as "Justifiable homicide."

2886. Whitaker, Hugh Stephen. "A Case Study in Southern Justice: The Emmett Till Case." M.A. thesis, Florida State Univ., 1963.   He was murdered in Mississippi in 1955.

2887. White, Daniel. R. "America's Most Wanted." ABA JOURNAL, Vol. 75, No. 10 (Oct. 1989): 92-94, 96.   Contents (p. 4): "Catching crooks by television: Is it public service or electronic vigilantism?"

2888. White, John T. "As to Mobs." MISSOURI BAR JOURNAL, Vol. 5, No. 1 (Jan. 1934): 10.   Mobs only lynch poor people.

2889. "White Lynching in California." INTERNATIONAL JURIDICAL ASSOCIATION MONTHLY BULLETIN, Vol. 4, No. 3 (Aug. 1935): 1. Clyde L. Johnson, at Dunsmuir or Yreka.

2890. "The White South's Protest Against Lynching: A Press Symposium." THE SOUTHERN WORKMAN, Vol. 48, No. 7 (July 1919): 350-61.

2891. White, Walter. "I Investigate Lynchings." THE AMERICAN MERCURY, Vol. 16, No. 61 (Jan. 1929): 77-84.

2892. White, Walter. "The Shambles of South Carolina." THE CRISIS, Vol. 33, No. 2 (Dec. 1926): 72-75.   Oct. 8 lynching of three blacks, including one woman, in Aiken.

2893. White, Walter F. "The Burning of Jim McIlherron. An N. A. A. C. P. Investigation." THE CRISIS, Vol. 16, No. 1 (May 1918): 16-20.   The torture and burning of a black man in Estill Springs, Tennessee, in February, 1918. Photo on p. 16 has no cutline. Photo on p. 20 is of lynching of George McNeal in Monroe, LA, March 16, 1918.

2894. White, Walter F.   "U.S. Department of (White) Justice."   THE CRISIS, Vol. 42, No. 10 (Oct. 1935): 309-10.   Refusal of the Department of Justice to act against lynching, especially in several recent cases which are detailed here.

2895. White, Walter F. "The Work of a Mob." THE CRISIS, Vol. 16, No. 5 (Sept. 1918): 221-23.   A report on 11 lynchings of blacks in May, 1918, near Valdosta, Georgia, in the wake of the murder of one white man by a black. Description of especially barbaric lynching of a black woman who was eight months pregnant.

2896. Whitfield, Stephen J. A DEATH IN THE DELTA: THE STORY OF EMMETT TILL. New York: Free Press, 1988.   He was murdered in Mississippi in 1955.

2897. "Who Is to Blame for Mob Murders?" THE LITERARY DIGEST, Vol. 106, No. 3 (July 19, 1930): 22.

2898. "Why Lynching Has Slumped." THE LITERARY DIGEST, Vol. 78, No. 4 (July 28, 1923): 16.   Includes good cartoon "The Exodus from Dixie" from The Liberator.

2899. "Why Not Intervention?" THE CRUSADER, Vol. 4, No. 2 (April 1921): 9-10.   Because lynchings occur in the U.S., perhaps Mexico and Haiti should intervene in the U.S. to establish law and order.

2900. Wilkins, Roy. "Two Against 5,000." THE CRISIS, Vol. 43, No. 6 (June 1936): 169-70.   Mob murder of elderly, black brother and sister (William and Cora Wales) in Gordonsville, Virginia, May, 1936.

2901. Williams, Juan. EYES ON THE PRIZE: AMERICA'S CIVIL RIGHTS YEARS, 1954-1965. New York: Viking, 1987.   See Chapter 2, "Standing For Justice: Mississippi and the Till Case."   Till was murdered in Mississippi, 1955.

2902. "Willie Earle is on the Conscience of the Nation." THE SOUTH-ERN PATRIOT, Vol. 5, No. 3 (April 1947): 5.   He was lynched in South Carolina in 1947.

2903. Wilson, Sharon. "The Sheriff Who Outsmarted the Mob." FRON-TIER TIMES [Austin, TX], Vol. 40, No. 1, New Series No. 39 (Dec.-Jan. 1966): 28-29, 53-54.   Jesse Phillips prevented a lynching in Atoka, Oklahoma, 1922.

2904. Wimpy, W. E. "Lynching, an Evil of County Government." JOUR-NAL OF THE AMERICAN INSTITUTE OF CRIMINAL LAW AND CRIMINOLOGY, Vol. 11, No. 1 (May 1920): 127-31.   From Manufactur-ers' Record, Aug. 24, 1916.

2905. Wimpy, W. E. "Mob Lynching Lynches the Law." MANUFACTUR-ERS RECORD, Vol. 76 (Dec. 25, 1919): 113-14.

2906. Winter, Ella. "California's Little Hitlers." THE NEW REPUBLIC, Vol. 77, No. 995 (Dec. 27, 1933): 188-90.   Mob spirit at work in San Jose double lynching and in actions against agricultural strikers, 1933.

2907. Wise, James Waterman. "Vigilantism--Streamline Model." LABOR DEFENDER, Vol. 11, No. 9 (Oct. 1937): 4-5.   Definition used here: "Lawlessness and violence employed against workers in the name of law and order."

2908. "'With My Own Body!'" THE INDEPENDENT, Vol. 89, No. 3555 (Jan. 22, 1917): 135.   Governor Stanley prevented a lynching at Murray, Kentucky.

2909. Wolf, Herman. "And Southern Death." COMMON SENSE, Vol. 5, No. 2 (Feb. 1936): 12-14.   Joseph Shoemaker's kidnapping and death in Florida; other beatings.

2910. Wolfe, Alan. "Extralegality and American Power." SOCIETY, Vol. 13, No. 3 (March/April 1976): 44-47.   Part of symposium on American vigilantes.

2911. "Woman Awarded $7 million Against KKK Dies Without Will; Daughters Administer." JET, Vol. 76, No. 3 (April 24, 1989): 12.   Michael Donald killing in Alabama, 1981.

2912. Woodley, Richard. "A Recollection of Michael Schwerner." THE REPORTER, Vol. 31, No. 2 (July 16, 1964): 23-24.   He was lynched in Mississippi, 1964.

2913. "Wool Hat Temper." NEWSWEEK, Vol. 32, No. 26 (Dec. 20, 1948): 22.   Lynching of Robert Mallard in Georgia.

2914. "Word Protests." THE CRUSADER, Vol. 1, No. 9 (May 1919): 4. Lynching protests by the Advancement Association [NAACP], as in the lynching of Eugene Green in Mississippi, are ineffective, especially as so much of it is composed of whites.

2915. "The Work of a Mob." THE CRISIS, Vol. 16, No. 5 (Sept. 1918): 221-23.   Walter White's investigation of recent lynchings in Brooks and Lowndes counties in Georgia. Reprinted by NAACP as The Lynchings of May, 1918 in Brooks and Lowndes Counties, Georgia.

2916. Work, Monroe N., ed. THE LAW VERSUS THE MOB. New York: Federal Council of the Churches of Christ in America, Commission on the Church and Race Relations, 1925.

2917. Work, Monroe N. "Lynchings in the United States Since 1885." THE MISSIONARY REVIEW OF THE WORLD [New York], Vol. 54, No. 8 (Aug. 1931): 620.   Statistics compiled by Work for 1931 World Almanac.

2918. "Working for a Lynchless Year." THE LITERARY DIGEST, Vol. 115, No. 1 (Jan. 7, 1933): 19.

2919. Wren, William C.; Hyman, Alvin D.; and Eppinger, Josua. "Judge Lynch in California." In STAR REPORTERS AND 34 OF THEIR STORIES, pp. 382-91. Ed. by Ward Greene. New York: Random House, 1948.   Thomas Thurmond and Jack Holmes in San Jose, 1933.

2920. Wright, Eva.   "Our Women Take Part in Suffrage Memorial Ceremonies." THE COMPETITOR, Vol. 3, No. 2 (April 1921): 30-31. Hallie Q. Brown spoke against lynching.

2921. Wright, John D., Jr. "Lexington's Suppression of the 1920 Will Lockett Lynch Mob." THE REGISTER OF THE KENTUCKY HISTORI-CAL SOCIETY, Vol. 84, No. 3 (Summer 1986): 263-79.

2922. "The Wrong Way." AMERICA, Vol. 17, No. 18 (Aug. 11, 1917): 451. Lynching of Frank Little in Montana. Editorial.

2923. "The Year's Lynchings." THE CRISIS, Vol. 13, No. 4 (Feb. 1917): 195-96.   A list, by date, place, and name.

2924. "Year's Record of Lynchings, Attempted Lynchings." THE SOUTH-ERN FRONTIER, Vol. 5, No. 1 (Jan. 1944): [1-2].

2925. Young, Marguerite. "Steel's G.O.P. Vigilantes." NEW MASSES, Vol. 20, No. 6 (Aug. 4, 1936): 9-12.   Anti-labor activities in Aliquippa, Pennsylvania.

2926. Young, N. Clifford. "A Case Study of the Tarboro Lynching." M.A. thesis, Univ. of North Carolina, 1931.   Oliver Moore, black man, lynched in North Carolina, Aug. 1930.

2927. Ziegenhagen, Eduard A., and Brosnan, Dolores. "Citizen Orientations Toward State and Non-State Policing." LAW & POLICY, Vol. 13, No. 3 (July 1991): 245-57.   Survey of New York City subway riders showed support for Guardian Angels.

VI

Frontier West, through 1890

2928. Adams, Ramon F., ed. WESTERN WORDS, A DICTIONARY OF THE AMERICAN WEST. Rev. ed.; Norman: Univ. of Oklahoma Press, 1968. See "Hanging."

2929. Aikman, Duncan. CALAMITY JANE AND THE LADY WILD-CATS. New York: H. Holt and Co., 1927. Biographical sketches of some notorious women in the West. See pp. 128-57 for Ella Watson (Cattle Kate) and her lynching in Wyoming, 1889.

2930. Alfrey, Genie, and Alfrey, Gaylord. "The Innocent Be Damned!" FRONTIER TIMES [Austin, TX], Vol. 41, No. 2, New Series No. 46 (Feb.-March 1967): 16-17, 47-49. Lynching of five Indians at Helltown, California, 1863, and violent aftermath.

2931. Anderson, Pete. "The Hanging of Cattle Kate." TRUE WESTERN ADVENTURES [Greenwich, CT], Vol. 3, No. 17 (Dec. 1960): 28-29. Wyoming, 1889.

2932. Ayres, W. O. "Personal Recollections of the Vigilance Committee." THE OVERLAND MONTHLY, Vol. 8, Second Series, No. 44 (Aug. 1886): 160-76. San Francisco, 1856.

2933. Bair, Bruce. "They Hanged Joe North." TRUE WEST [Austin, TX], Vol. 25, No. 3, Whole No. 145 (Jan.-Feb. 1978): 18-19, 48-50. He was lynched in Wallace, Kansas, 1874.

2934. Baker, Jack, as told to S. H. Logan. "They Hanged Me--Twice." TRUE WESTERN ADVENTURES [Greenwich, CT], No. 3 (Summer 1958): 15. Man survived lynching; Deadwood, South Dakota, 1890.

2935. Ballenger, Dean.   "The Hooray Hanging of Jeff Glover."   WEST-ERNER [Encino, CA], Vol. 5, No. 2 (March-April 1973): 8-11, 31-32, 54. Colorado land hog lynched several people, such as Rolly Yates in 1868, as part of a criminal scheme before his own legal hanging.

2936. Bancroft, Hubert Howe.   POPULAR TRIBUNALS.   2 vols.; San Francisco: History Company, Publishers, 1887.   Standard work on Western vigilantes.

2937. Bancroft, Hubert Howe.   RETROSPECTION: POLITICAL AND PERSONAL.   New York: The Bancroft Co., 1912.   Chapter X, "The Mills of the Gods" (pp. 172-93) deals with vigilantism in California.

2938. THE BANDITTI OF THE ROCKY MOUNTAINS AND VIGI-LANCE COMMITTEE IN IDAHO.   AN AUTHENTIC RECORD OF STARTLING ADVENTURES IN THE GOLD MINES OF IDAHO. 20TH THOUSAND. New York: Wilson and Co., 1865.   Henry Plummer and his gang.   See the edition with preface, notes, and bibliography by Jerome Peltier (Minneapolis: Ross & Haines, 1964)--especially valuable for preface information on meaning of "20th thousand," date of publication (prior to Dimsdale, Vigilantes of Montana), and authorship [not Olga Bandel; but possibly J. L. Campbell, whose book Idaho and Montana Gold Regions (Chicago: J. L. Campbell, 1865), p. 46, contains an ad for "just published" book Banditti of Idaho with illustration similar to those in Banditti of the Rocky Mountains].

2939. Banks, Leo W.   "The Bisbee Massacre."   ARIZONA HIGHWAYS, Vol. 69, No. 1 (Jan. 1993): 18-21.   John Heith was lynched in Tombstone, Arizona, on Feb. 22, 1884, as an accessory to the Dec. 8, 1883, robbery which resulted in five people killed by the robbers.

2940. Barbour, C.   "Two Vigilance Committees."   THE OVERLAND MONTHLY, Vol. 10, Second Series, No. 57 (Sept. 1887): 285-91.   Montana, 1863-1864, with some comparison to San Francisco committee of 1856.

2941. Barrows, William. THE UNITED STATES OF YESTERDAY AND OF TO-MORROW.   Boston: Roberts Brothers, 1888.   See Chapter X, "Lynch Law" (pp. 221-62); first half deals with Montana, 1862-65, and Vigilantes in Bannack and Nevada City area; then San Francisco Vigilance Committees of 1851 and 1856; finally, popular justice in other American frontier areas.

2942. Beachy, E. B. Dykes.   "The Saga of Cattle Kate."   FRONTIER TIMES [Austin, TX], Vol. 38, No. 2, New Series No. 28 (Feb.-March 1964): 22-23, 54.   Lynched in Wyoming.

2943. Beal, Merrill D.   "Rustlers and Robbers: Idaho Cattle Thieves in Territorial Days." IDAHO YESTERDAYS, Vol. 7, No. 1 (Spring 1963): 24-28.

2944. Benson, V. G. "Black Monday." OLD WEST [Austin, TX], Vol. 8, No. 1, Whole No. 29 (Fall 1971): 19, 68-69.   Mob entered jail intent on hanging but shot two Hawks brothers to death, Flagstaff, Arizona, 1887.

2945. Bergenroth, Gustav Adolf.   "The First Vigilance Committees." HOUSEHOLD WORDS, Vol. 14, No. 347 (Nov. 15, 1856): 409-16.   California committees.

2946. Bernson, Sara L., and Eggers, Robert J.   "Black People in South Dakota History." SOUTH DAKOTA HISTORY, Vol. 7, No. 3 (Summer 1977): 241-70.   See pp. 247-49 for a lynching and other violence in 1885.

2947. Bird, Roy. "They Lynched Nat Oliphant." REAL WEST [Derby, CT], Vol. 24, No. 180 (Oct. 1981): 40-42, 49, 54.   Topeka, Kansas, June, 1889.

2948. Birney, Hoffman. "Vigilante." SATURDAY EVENING POST, Vol. 201, No. 34 (Feb. 23, 1929): 3-5, 86, 88-89, 92.   The first in a series of articles. Montana, 1860s. See also Vol. 201, No. 35 (March 2, 1929): 33-35, 107-08, 111; Vol. 201, No. 36 (March 9, 1929): 24-25, 149-50, 152, 154; Vol. 201, No. 37 (March 16, 1929): 20-21, 65-66, 69; Vol. 201, No. 38 (March 23, 1929): 37, 40, 110, 114, 119 (last article).

2949. Birney, Hoffman. VIGILANTES: A CHRONICLE OF THE RISE AND FALL OF THE PLUMMER GANG OF OUTLAWS IN AND ABOUT VIRGINIA CITY MONTANA IN THE EARLY '60'S. Philadelphia: Penn Publishing, 1929.

2950. Bishop, Luckett P., Sr. "Shoot-Out on Christmas Day." FRONTIER TIMES [Austin, TX], Vol. 39, No. 4, New Series No. 36 (June-July 1965): 6-11, 59-62, 64.   Includes vigilantes and lynchings, central Texas, 1870s-1880s.

2951. Black, Paul Walton. "Attempted Lynchings in Iowa." ANNALS OF IOWA, Third Series, Vol. 11, No. 4 (Jan. 1914): 260-85.

2952. Black, Paul Walton. "Lynchings in Iowa." THE IOWA JOURNAL OF HISTORY AND POLITICS, Vol. 10, No. 2 (April 1912): 151-254.

2953. Blew, Robert W. "Vigilantism in Los Angeles, 1835-1874." SOUTHERN CALIFORNIA QUARTERLY, Vol. 54, No. 1 (Spring 1972): 11-30.

2954. Bloom, Lansing, B., ed. "A Lynching at Tucson in 1873; As written up by John G. Bourke." NEW MEXICO HISTORICAL REVIEW, Vol. 19, No. 3 (July 1944): 233-42.

2955. Bloom, Lansing, B., ed. "A Tucson Tragedy: A True Tale of Terror: The Court of Judge Lynch: The Execution. II, Identifying the Murderers." NEW MEXICO HISTORICAL REVIEW, Vol. 19, No. 4 (Oct. 1944): 312-18.   Conclusion of "A Lynching at Tucson in 1873."

2956. Boren, Kerry Ross. "Jack Slade's Grave Located." FRONTIER TIMES [Austin, TX], Vol. 50, No. 3, New Series No. 101 (April-May 1976): 24-25, 56-57.   Though lynched in Montana [sic], he was buried in Salt Lake City.

2957. Botkin, J. T. "Justice Was Swift and Sure in Early Kansas." KANSAS HISTORICAL COLLECTIONS [COLLECTIONS OF THE KANSAS STATE HISTORICAL SOCIETY 1923-1925], Vol. 16 (1923-1925): 488-93. Two legal hangings and one lynching. [Contents page gives title as "Justice Was Swift and Sure in Early Days," and that is at top of pages of article in briefer form except for title page.]

2958. Boynton, S. S.   "The Miners' Vengeance."   THE OVERLAND MONTHLY, Vol. 22, Second Series, No. 129 (Sept. 1893): 303-07.   John Ross and Robert Williams were lynched in California, July, 18--.

2959. Bradley, Betty J. "Tale of the Bloody Cottonwood." FRONTIER TIMES [Austin, TX], Vol. 49, No. 3, New Series No. 95 (April-May 1975): 20-21, 46-48.   Robert Wilson was lynched at Columbus, Nebraska, 1867.

2960. Bradley, Ralph. "Carnival of Crime." OLD WEST [Stillwater, OK], Vol. 30, No. 2, Whole No. 118 (Winter 1993): 28-31.   Double lynching, Phoenix, Arizona Territory, 1879.

2961. Breihan, Carl. "Joe Slade--Gunfighter." WESTERNER [Encino, CA], Vol. 4, No. 2 (March-April 1972): 38-40, 59-60, 62-63.   He was lynched by vigilantes in Montana [Idaho Territory], 1864.

2962. Breihan, Carl. "The Outlaw Who Became A Pair of Shoes." TRUE WEST [Iola, WI], Vol. 30, No. 1, Whole No. 184 (Jan. 1983): 44-46.   This article is nearly identical to Breihan's "Big Nose George Parrott" and tells of his career and lynching in Rawlins, Wyoming, March 22, 1881.

2963. Breihan, Carl. "The Vigilante Sheriff." WESTERNER [Encino, CA], Vol. 3, No. 7 (Oct. 1971): 48-51.   Henry Plummer.

2964. Breihan, Carl W. "Big Nose George Parrott." REAL WEST [Derby, CT], Vol. 11, No. 63 (Sept. 1968): 26-28.   Reprinted in REAL WEST, Vol. 17, No. 133 (Dec. 1974): 46-48, 55.   Lynched at Rawlins, Wyoming, 1881. Includes "The Lynching of Big Nose George," a ballad [by Jean Osborne?].

2965. Breihan, Carl W. "Captain Joe Slade, the Big Wolf." REAL WEST [Derby, CT], Vol. 11, No. 60 (June 1968): 46-49, 76-77.   Includes Slade's lynching at Virginia City, Montana [sic], 1864.

2966. Breihan, Carl W.   "Henry Plummer's Horrendous Masquerade." GOLDEN WEST [Freeport, NY], Vol. 4, No. 3 (March 1968): 22-25, 56-60. Includes Montana [sic], 1863-1864.

2967. Briggs, John E. "Pioneer Gangsters." THE PALIMPSEST, Vol. 21, No. 3 (March 1940): 73-90.   Crime in Iowa, 1840s, led to vigilante activity.

2968. Brooks, Noah.   "The San Francisco Vigilantes."   HARPER'S WEEKLY, Vol. 37, No. 1928 (Dec. 2, 1893): 1147.   William T. Coleman and the committees of 1851, 1856, and 1877.

2969. Brown, Lee. "The Lackey Tragedy in Blanco County." FRONTIER TIMES [Bandera, TX], Vol. 13, No. 6 (April 1936): 348-49.   Al Lackey was lynched for murder near Blanco, Texas, Aug. 1885.

2970. Brown, Richard Maxwell. "Pivot of American Vigilantism: The San Francisco Vigilance Committee of 1856." In REFLECTIONS OF WEST-ERN HISTORIANS, pp. 105-19. Ed. by John Alexander Carroll. Tucson: Univ. of Arizona Press, 1969.

2971. Brown, Richard Maxwell.   "Western Violence: Structure, Values, Myth." THE WESTERN HISTORICAL QUARTERLY, Vol. 24, No. 1 (Feb. 1993): 5-20.   References to vigilantes, vigilantism, etc.

2972. Buecker, Thomas R. "Confrontation at Sturgis: An Episode in Civil-Military Race Relations, 1885." SOUTH DAKOTA HISTORY, Vol. 14, No. 3 (Fall 1984): 238-61.   See pp. 250-51 for the lynch hanging of a black soldier at Sturgis, South Dakota, August 25, 1885.

2973. Burg, Richard. "Vigilantes in Lawless Denver: The City of the Plains." GREAT PLAINS JOURNAL, Vol. 6, No. 2 (Spring 1967): 68-84.

2974. Burlingame, Merrill G.   "Montana's Righteous Hangmen: A Reconsideration." MONTANA, THE MAGAZINE OF WESTERN HIS-TORY, Vol. 28, No. 4 (Oct. 1978): 36-49.   Vigilante executions.

2975. Burt, Olive W. "Last Words From The Scaffold." REAL WEST [Derby, CT], Vol. 18, No. 140 (July 1975): 36-39, 52, 60, 62.   Includes words of some Western lynching victims.

2976. Callaway, Lew [Llewellyn Link].   MONTANA'S RIGHTEOUS HANGMEN: THE VIGILANTES IN ACTION.   Norman: Univ. of Oklahoma Press, 1982.   On spine: VIGILANTES: TWO TRUE TALES OF THE WILD WEST. Originally published in 1973 as Two True Tales of the Wild West (Oakland, CA: Maud Gonne Press, 1973).   Lives and deaths of Captain James Williams and Joseph Alfred Slade.

2977. Callaway, Lew L. "Joseph Alfred Slade: Killer or Victim?" THE MONTANA MAGAZINE OF HISTORY, Vol. 3, No. 1 (Jan. 1953): 4-34. Vigilantes lynched him at Virginia City, Montana Territory [sic], 1864.

2978. Carey, Elton.   "Reign of the Vigilantes."   FRONTIER TIMES [Austin, TX], Vol. 44, No. 1, New Series No. 63 (Dec.-Jan. 1970): 34-35, 48-50.   Crook County Vigilante Committee in Oregon killed several people in and near Prineville, 1882-1883. A counter-organization was formed to stop the excessive violence.

2979. Carothers, June E. "Ouray's Ghastly Corpse: The first woman lynched in Colorado." THE DENVER WESTERNERS MONTHLY ROUNDUP, Vol. 11, No. 1 (Jan. 1955): 12-15.   Husband and wife were lynched, 1884.

2980. Carroll, Jane Lamm. "Criminal Justice on the Minnesota Frontier, 1820-1857." Ph.D. diss., U of Minnesota, 1991.   See Diss. Ab. Intl., Vol. 52, No. 5 (Nov. 1991): 1868A-1869A.

2981. Carroll, Murray L. "A Fatal Necktie Party: The Lynching of Si Partridge." OLD WEST, Vol. 23, No. 1, Whole No. 89 (Fall 1986): 22-27. Near Laramie, Wyoming, 1885.

2982. Carroll, Murray L. "Judge Lynch Rides the Rails." TRUE WEST [Stillwater, OK], Vol. 42, No. 10, Whole No. 330 (Oct. 1995): 12-19.   Vigilantes and lynchings, Laramie, Wyoming, 1868-1869.

2983. Carson, Xanthus. "The Bisbee Massacre." WESTERNER [Encino, CA], Vol. 2, No. 7 (Nov. 1970): 48-49, 65-66.   Includes text and photo of lynching of John Heith [sic] at Tombstone, Arizona, 1884.

2984. Carter, James L. "Who Killed Print Olive?" REAL WEST [Derby, CT], Vol. 3, No. 10 (March 1960): 22-23, 66-69.   Includes lynching of Luther Mitchell and Ami Ketchum in Nebraska, 1878.

2985. Cary, Thomas G. "The First San Francisco Vigilance Committee." THE INTERNATIONAL REVIEW, Vol. 11, [No. 1] (July 1881): 78-88.

2986. Cary, Thomas G. "The San Francisco Vigilance Committee." THE ATLANTIC MONTHLY, Vol. 40, No. 242 (Dec. 1877): 702-09.   Committee of 1856.

2987. Cary, Thomas G.   THE VIGILANCE COMMITTEE OF SAN FRANCISCO, 1856. N.p.: n.p., 1884.

2988. Castel, Albert.   "The Day the Marshal Tried to Rob the Bank." AMERICAN HISTORY ILLUSTRATED, Vol. 15, No. 5 (Aug. 1980): 14-22.   Henry Brown, marshal of Caldwell, Kansas, tried to rob bank in Medicine Lodge in 1884; he and his three accomplices were lynched.

2989. [Cazneau, Mrs. William Leslie]. EAGLE PASS; OR, LIFE ON THE BORDER. By Cora Montgomery (pseud.). New York: George P. Putnam & Co., 1852.   Consult "Lynch Law" section (pp. 153-54) and p. 167.

2990. Chamberlain, C. W. "Last of the Badmen." NEGRO DIGEST, Vol. 5, No. 1 (Nov. 1946): 26-28.   Dodge City, Kansas, vigilantes hanged seven men at one time, but heel tendons of black man named Ben Hodges were severed in lieu of hanging.

2991. Champney, Freeman. "The Justice of the People." THE ANTIOCH REVIEW, Vol. 7, No. 2 (Summer 1947): 231-42. San Francisco committees of 1851, 1856, and 1877; anti-Chinese violence in 1877, and the perversion of vigilantism in more recent times.

2992. Cheney, Louise. "James King of William." REAL WEST [Derby, CT], Vol. 18, No. 138 (May 1975): 30-34. Includes vigilante lynching of Cora and Casey. San Francisco, 1850s.

2993. "The Child Killer of Julesburg Junction." WESTERNER [Encino, CA], Vol. 5, No. 1 (Jan.-Feb. 1973): 28-31, 57-58.   Immigrants lynched Holon Godfrey in Colorado Territory [near present town of Merino], 1865, because his greed caused people to drown in a marsh. Page 28 says some photos are from author's collection, but author is not named.

2994. Chrisman, Harry E. "When 'Slow Elk' Came High." TRUE WEST [Austin, TX] , Vol. 1, No. 3 (Winter 1953): 26-27, 53-54.   Lynching of Luther Mitchell and Ami Ketchum in Nebraska, 1878. Reprinted in Old West [Austin, TX], Vol. 1, No. 4 (Summer 1965): 46-48.

2995. Clampitt, John W. "The Vigilantes of California, Idaho, and Montana." HARPER'S NEW MONTHLY MAGAZINE, Vol. 83, No. 495 (Aug. 1891): 442-51.

2996. Cline, Donald. "Socorro Killer." FRONTIER TIMES [Austin, TX], Vol. 48, No. 2, New Series No. 88 (Feb.-March 1974): 26-28, 45.   Joel Fowler, convicted murderer, was lynched at Socorro, New Mexico, 1883.

2997. Cobb, Ronald Lee. "Guthrie Mound and the Hanging of John Guthrie." KANSAS HISTORY, Vol. 5, No. 3 (Autumn 1982): 177-83. Lynching of an anti-slavery sympathizer by pro-slavery men in 1860.

2998. Coblentz, Stanton A.   VILLAINS AND VIGILANTES: THE STORY OF JAMES KING OF WILLIAM AND PIONEER JUSTICE IN CALIFORNIA. New York: Wilson-Erickson, 1936.

2999. Coleman, William T. "San Francisco Vigilance Committees. By the Chairman of the Committees of 1851, 1856, and 1877." THE CENTURY MAGAZINE, Vol. 43 (New Series, Vol. 21), No. 1 (Nov. 1891): 133-50. Reprinted as "San Francisco Vigilance Committees" in GOLDEN WEST [Freeport, NY], Vol. 1, No. 3 (March 1965): 43-45, 65-69.

3000. Committee of Vigilance. San Francisco. ALTA CALIFORNIA SUPPLEMENT. SAN FRANCISCO, SEPT. 5, 1856. THE ADDRESS OF THE EXECUTIVE . . . THE EXECUTIVE COMMITTEE TO THE GENERAL COMMITTEE OF VIGILANCE . . . [San Francisco, 1856.]

3001. Committee of Vigilance. San Francisco. [Certificate of membership.] [San Francisco: Excelsior print., 1856.]

3002. Committee of Vigilance. San Francisco. CONSTITUTION AND ADDRESS OF THE COMMITTEE OF VIGILANCE OF SAN FRAN-CISCO. San Francisco: Morning Globe print, 1856.

3003. Committee of Vigilance. San Francisco. EXCITING EVENTS OF SATURDAY, JUNE 21ST, 1856. San Francisco: Daily Town Talk Office, 1856.

3004. Committee of Vigilance. San Francisco. [Form of Application for enrollment.] [San Francisco, 1856?]

3005. Committee of Vigilance. San Francisco. PAPERS OF THE SAN FRANCISCO COMMITTEE OF VIGILANCE OF 1851.   See Garnett, Porter, and Williams, Mary Floyd.

3006. Committee of Vigilance. San Francisco. PROCLAMATION OF

THE VIGILANCE COMMITTEE OF SAN FRANCISCO, JUNE 9TH, 1856. San Francisco: Hutchings & Co., 1856.

3007. Considine, John L. "The Bandit Who Became Sheriff." SUNSET, Vol. 49, No. 2 (Aug. 1922): 33. 54. 56.   Henry Plummer.

3008. Considine, John L. "How the Law Came to Lewiston." SUNSET, Vol. 49, No. 1 (July 1922): 41-42. Lynching of three men. Also, information on Henry Plummer.

3009. Considine, John L. "Primitive Tribunals of Early Nevada." SUNSET, Vol. 49, No. 4 (Oct. 1922): 19-20.   Includes cutting off ears as punishment.

3010. Considine, John L. "The Vigilantes of the Comstock." SUNSET, Vol. 48, No. 6 (June 1922): 16.

3011. Considine, John L. "When Downieville Hanged a Woman." SUNSET, Vol. 50, No. 1 (Jan. 1923): 20, 56, 58. Victim named Juanita was lynched in July [1851] in California. Includes also the lynching of John Barclay at Columbia, California, Oct. 10, 1855.

3012. Cook, D. J., as told to Zoltan Malocsay.   "'Hang Musgrove!'" WESTERNER [Encino, CA], Vol. 6, No. 2 (March-April 1974): 34-35. Lynching; Denver, Colorado, 1868.

3013. Cook, D. J., as told to Zoltan Malocsay. "The Noose Didn't Fit." WESTERNER [Encino, CA], Vol. 6, No. 2 (March-April 1974): 36-37. Lynching of Duggan, Denver, Colorado [1868?]. See Hart, George, "The Lynching of Sanford Dougan," in this bibliography.

3014. Cook, D[avid] J.   HANDS UP; OR, TWENTY YEARS OF DETECTIVE LIFE IN THE MOUNTAINS AND ON THE PLAINS. REMINISCENCES OF GENERAL D. J. COOK, CHIEF OF THE ROCKY MOUNTAIN DETECTIVE ASSOCIATION. Denver: Republican Pub. Co., 1882.   Includes various lynchings in Colorado and Wyoming.

3015. Cook, John W., ed. HANDS UP; OR, THIRTY-FIVE YEARS OF DETECTIVE LIFE IN THE MOUNTAINS AND ON THE PLAINS. REMINISCENCES OF GENERAL D. J. COOK, CHIEF OF THE ROCKY MOUNTAIN DETECTIVE ASSOCIATION. Denver: The W. F. Robinson Printing Co., 1897.   A later edition with added years.

3016. Dahl, Victor C. "Granville Stuart: Author and Subject of Western History." PACIFIC HISTORICAL REVIEW, Vol. 39, No. 4 (Nov. 1970): 493-511.

3017. Dakis, Ruth, and Dakis, Mike N. "Guilty or Not Guilty? Vigilantes on Trial." IDAHO YESTERDAYS, Vol. 12, No. 4 (Winter 1968): 2-5. Controversy in Idaho, 1860s. Title here is what is on page 2; on contents page it is merely "Vigilantes on Trial."

3018. Darwin, Wayne. "Who Really Condemned Slade to Hang?" GOLD-EN WEST [Freeport, NY], Vol. 5, No. 5 (July 1969): 10-13, 42-44. Vigilantes lynched him at Virginia City, Montana [sic], 1864.

3019. Decker, Peter R. FORTUNES AND FAILURES: WHITE-COLLAR MOBILITY IN NINETEENTH CENTURY SAN FRANCISCO. Cambridge: Harvard Univ. Press, 1978.   Includes material on Vigilance Committee, 1856. Based on "Social Mobility on the Urban Frontier: the San Francisco Merchants, 1850-1880," Ph.D. diss., Columbia Univ., 1974; see Diss. Ab. Intl., Vol. 35, No. 11 (May 1975), p. 7221A.

3020. Demarest, Dave. "Mother Lode Massacre." FRONTIER TIMES [Austin, TX], Vol. 49, No. 2, New Series No. 94 (Feb.-March 1975): 12-13, 35-36.   After Mexicans attacked town of Rancheria, California, Anglos retaliated with lynchings and destruction, 1855.

3021. DeMattos, Jack. "Gunfighters Of The Real West: Henry Plummer." REAL WEST [Derby, CT], Vol. 28, No. 204 (Aug. 1985): 42-44, 46, 48, 50.

3022. DeNevi, Don. "Two Lynchings Closer to Law and Order." REAL WEST [Derby, CT], Vol. 24, No. 177 (June 1981): 26-28, 54.   Juanita, at Downieville, CA [1851]. John Barclay, at Columbia, CA, 1855. The photos of these two people (and of Jack Cannon, the man Juanita killed) are from "Author's collection," and one might question their authenticity.

3023. Dewald, Margaret. "Oscar Samson: Northeast Nebraska Vigilante of 1868." NEBRASKA HISTORY MAGAZINE, Vol. 15 (1934): 96-100.

3024. Dick, Nevada. "Horse Thief." TRUE WEST [Austin, TX], Vol. 3, No. 6, Whole No. 16 (July-Aug. 1956): 17, 36-37.   Includes text and illustration on Horse Thief Canyon, west of Dodge City, as place where 3 men were lynched. Includes claim that vigilantes lynched 10 horse thieves near Cimarron, Kansas, about 18 miles west of Dodge City, [1870s or 1880s].

3025. Dimsdale, Thomas J. "The Arrest and Execution of Captain J. A. Slade, With a Short Account of His Previous Career." From THE VIGILANTES OF MONTANA, OR POPULAR JUSTICE IN THE ROCKY MOUNTAINS, pp. 194-205. Norman: Univ. of Oklahoma Press, 1953.

3026. Dimsdale, Thomas J. THE VIGILANTES OF MONTANA, OR POPULAR JUSTICE IN THE ROCKY MOUNTAINS. Norman: Univ. of Oklahoma Press, 1953; originally published in 1866.

3027. Dodge, Matt. "The Lynchers." REAL WEST [Derby, CT], Vol. 26, No. 192 (Aug. 1983): 22-27.   Concentrates on lynchings along emigrant trails to the West, Denver in 1860, Wyoming in 1868, Arizona from 1873 to 1917, and a few other locales.

3028. Dodge, Matt. "The Vigilantes: Nebraska's Public Defenders." REAL WEST [Derby, CT], Vol. 27, No. 199 (Oct. 1984): 10-15.   Deals mainly with 1850s and 1870s-1880s.

3029. Donohue, Charlie. "Swift Justice." FRONTIER TIMES [Austin, TX], Vol. 35, No. 4, New Series No. 16 (Fall 1961): 41, 51-52.   Jud Palmer killed Mary Woods in Iowa, 1870, and was lynched next morning.

3030. Dosch, Henry Ernst. VIGILANTE DAYS AT VIRGINIA CITY: PERSONAL NARRATIVE OF COL. HENRY DOSCH . . . By Fred Lockley. Portland, OR: F. Lockley, 1924.

3031. Dozier, Jack. "Hanging of the Highbinders." FRONTIER TIMES [Austin, TX], Vol. 38, No. 5, New Series No. 31 (Aug.-Sept. 1964): 26-27, 67.   Five Chinese were lynched for murder near Pierce City, Idaho, 1885.

3032. Drago, Harry Sinclair. NOTORIOUS LADIES OF THE FRON-TIER. New York: Dodd, Mead and Co., 1969.   Chapter XVI (pp. 156-70) deals with several lynchings, including that of Elizabeth Taylor in Nebraska, 1885.   Chapter XXI (pp. 223-35): lynching of Jim Averell [sic] and Ella Watson in Wyoming, 1889.

3033. Drannan, William F. THIRTY-ONE YEARS ON THE PLAINS AND IN THE MOUNTAINS; OR, THE LAST VOICE FROM THE PLAINS. AN AUTHENTIC RECORD OF A LIFE TIME OF HUNTING, TRAPPING, SCOUTING AND INDIAN FIGHTING IN THE FAR WEST. Chicago: Thos. W. Jackson Pub. Co., 1900.   See pp. 448-52 in Chapter XXVII for Virginia City [Montana] vigilantes and lynchings of Jack Gallagher, Boone, Helm, Hank Parrish, Clubfoot George, and [Jack] Slade.

3034. Drees, James D. "The Hays City Vigilante Period, 1868-1869." Masters thesis, Fort Hays State Univ., 1983.

3035. Ducomb, Dean. "A Silent Drum Beside the Okaw: The Story of Jack Slade, Outlaw." THE WESTERNERS NEW YORK POSSE BRAND BOOK, Vol. 4, No. 1 (1957): 1, 3-4, 6-8.   Hanged in Montana [sic], 1864.

3036. Dunklee, Edward V. "Justice Comes to Denver." In DENVER POSSE THE WESTERNERS BRAND BOOK, Vol. 3, pp. 195-204. Ed. by Herbert O. Brayer. Denver: The Westerners, 1949. Citizen courts hanged criminals.

3037. Edgerton, Ralph P. "Montana Vigilantism." THE PACIFIC NORTHWESTERNER, Vol. 8, No. 4 (Fall 1964): 49-57.

3038. Edwards, Harold L. "Trouble in Socorro." OLD WEST [Stillwater, OK], Vol. 27, No. 2, Whole No. 106 (Winter 1990): 42-47.   Includes lynching of Enofre Baca, New Mexico Territory, 1881.

3039. Edwards, John Carver. "Daniel-Potter Feud." OLD WEST [Iola, WI], Vol. 17, No. 1, Whole No. 65 (Fall 1980): 8-15.   Includes 1883 Danville, Arkansas, lynching of John Coker and John Flood.

3040. Ege, Robert J. "Montana's Mob Hanging." REAL WEST [Derby, CT], Vol. 14, No. 96 (Sept. 1971): 19-22. Lynching near Choteau, 1881. Title is listed on contents page as "Montana's Hanging Mob."

3041. Eherts, Walter. "Vigilantes of the Far West." TRUE WEST [Iola, WI], Vol. 30, No. 1, Whole No. 184 (Jan. 1983): 34-37.   Mainly about San Francisco, 1850s.

3042. Elliott, Lee. "Sheriff Burns' Battle with Los Angeles Vigilantes." OLD WEST [Stillwater, OK], Vol. 30, No. 4, Whole No. 120 (Summer 1994): 30-34.   A lynching in 1870 and mob murders of Chinese in 1871.

3043. Emenhiser, JeDon Allen.   "Armed Politics: An Analysis and Comparison of Six Cases in the United States."   Ph.D. diss., Univ. of Minnesota, 1962. See Diss. Ab., Vol. 23, No. 11 (May 1963): 4407.   One of the six is San Francisco Vigilance Committee (1856).

3044. Emery, Wesley P. "The Execution of 'Bill' Hunter." In CONTRIBU-TIONS TO THE HISTORICAL SOCIETY OF MONTANA, Vol. 7 (1910), pp. 165-74. Helena: Montana Historical and Miscellaneous Library, 1910. Lynching by Montana [sic] vigilantes, 1864.

3045. Everett, George. "Gunfighters & Lawmen: Whether called Big Nose George or some other name, this Wyoming-born outlaw had a nose for trouble." WILD WEST [Leesburg, VA], [Vol. 6, No. 3] (Oct. 1993): 10, 14, 16. He was lynched in Wyoming in 1881.

3046. Farley, Wayne. "The Montana Stranglers." TRUE WESTERN ADVENTURES [Greenwich, CT], No. 9 (Aug. 1959): 31.   Vigilantes lynched numerous cattle rustlers in 1884.

3047. Faulk, Odie B.   "Law & the Land: The Legal Heritage of the American Southwest." THE AMERICAN WEST, Vol. 7, No. 1 (Jan. 1970): 14-16, 57.   Has some material on vigilantism and a lynching (see illustration).

3048. Fergusson, Erna B. MURDER & MYSTERY IN NEW MEXICO. Albuquerque: Merle Armitage, 1948.   Includes "The Vigilantes of Socorro" (1880-1883).

3049. Fieldsome, George. "The Hangings That Named Two Towns." THE WEST [Freeport, NY], Vol. 2, No. 1 (Dec. 1964): 44, 64.   Two Old West mining camps [in California?] were named First Garrote and Second Garrote after murderers were lynched in them. Exactly the same author, title, and article appeared in The West [Rockville Centre, NY], Vol. 15, No. 8 (Jan. 1972): 13, 50.

3050. Fink, Clarence M. "Saved From Hanging." REAL WEST [Derby, CT], Vol. 17, No. 127 (May 1974): 56-57.   Mob was talked out of a lynching. California, 1850s.

3051. "The First Vigilance Committees." HOUSEHOLD WORDS, Vol. 14, No. 347 (Nov. 15, 1856): 409-16.   Various locations in northern California, 1850-1851.

3052. Fisher, Robert B.   "Ad Hoc Justice Documented: The 'Paper Daguerreotypes' of George Robinson Fardon." JOURNAL OF THE WEST, Vol. 33, No. 2 (April 1994): 6-12.   Text about San Francisco Vigilance Committees of 1851 and 1856. Fardon's photos of 1856 activities.

3053. "Five Men Hanged at Tombstone." FRONTIER TIMES [Bandera, TX], Vol. 5, No. 10 (July 1928): 412-14.   Includes lynching of John Heath, 1884.

3054. Flint, Edward P. "My Recollections of Vigilante Days." SUNSET, Vol. 32, No. 6 (June 1914): 1219-27.   San Francisco, 1850s.

3055. Florcken, Herbert G., ed.   "The Law and Order View of the San Francisco Vigilance Committee of 1856. Taken from the Correspondence of Governor J. Neely Johnson." CALIFORNIA HISTORICAL SOCIETY QUARTERLY, Vol. 14, No. 4 (Dec. 1935): 350-74; Vol. XV, No. 1 (March 1936): 70-87; Vol. XV, No. 2 (June 1936): 143-62; Vol. XV, No. 3 (Sept. 1936): 247-75.

3056. Forrest, Earle R. ARIZONA'S DARK AND BLOODY GROUND. Rev. ed.; Caldwell, ID: Caxton Printers, 1950. Includes Chapter XV, "Lynching of Stott, Scott, and Wilson" (1888).

3057. "Fort Gunnybags. The Old Stronghold of the Vigilante Committee." OVERLAND MONTHLY, Vol. 72, No. 6 (Dec. 1918): 574-81. Committee of 1856. Includes parts of Theodore H. Hittell's History of California.

3058. "Fort 'Gunnybags, the Old Stronghold of the Vigilance Committee. Shall It Be Marked?" OVERLAND MONTHLY, Vol. 31 (Second Series), No. 181 (Jan. 1898): 73-77. Site of headquarters of San Francisco 1856 committee.

3059. Frederick, J. V. "The Vigilantes in Early Beaver." CHRONICLES OF OKLAHOMA, Vol. 16, No. 2 (June 1938): 190-96.

3060. Freeman, G. D. MIDNIGHT AND NOONDAY, OR THE INCIDENTAL HISTORY OF SOUTHERN KANSAS AND THE INDIAN TERRITORY . . . AND INCIDENTS HAPPENING IN AND AROUND CALDWELL, KANSAS, FROM 1871 UNTIL 1890. Caldwell: G. D. Freeman, 1890 (reprint 1892). See pp. 97, 99, 107-08, 111, 132, 178-81, 253-59, 260-64, 320-24, 355-60, 381-85, for lynchings, attempted lynchings, and vigilantes.

3061. Gannett, Henry. "The Vigilantes of Montana." THE CALIFOR-NIAN, AND OVERLAND MONTHLY, Vol. 6, No. 34 (Oct. 1882): 363-67.

3062. Gard, Wayne. FRONTIER JUSTICE. Norman: Univ. of Oklahoma Press, 1949. See "Vigilantes" in index.

3063. Garnett, Porter, ed. PAPERS OF THE SAN FRANCISCO COMMITTEE OF VIGILANCE OF 1851 I. Publications of the Academy of Pacific Coast History, Vol. 1, No. 7. Berkeley: Univ. of California, 1910.

3064. Garnett, Porter, ed. PAPERS OF THE SAN FRANCISCO COMMITTEE OF VIGILANCE OF 1851: LIST OF NAMES APPROVED BY THE COMMITTEE ON QUALIFICATIONS. Publications of the Academy of Pacific Coast History, Vol. 2, No. 2. Berkeley: Univ. of California, 1911.

3065. Gass, Olive. "The Vigilantes, Nebraska's First Defenders." NEBRAS-KA HISTORY MAGAZINE, Vol. 14, No. 1 (Jan.-March 1933): 3-18. Contents page lists title as "Vigilantes of Eastern Nebraska."

3066. Gerlach, Larry R. "Ogden's 'Horrible Tragedy': The Lynching of

George Segal." UTAH HISTORICAL QUARTERLY, Vol. 49, No. 2 (Spring 1981): 157-72.   Utah lynching in 1884. Segal was Japanese.

3067. Gilfert, Shirley. "Nebraska City Mobocracy." OLD WEST [Stillwater, OK], Vol. 26, No. 4, Whole No. 104 (Summer 1990): 44-48.   Casper Diercks was lynched, 1866. Henry Jackson and Henry Martin, blacks, were lynched, 1878. Lee Shellenberger was lynched, 1887.

3068. Gill, Larry. "Montana Stranglers: Vigilante Activity of the Montana Cattlemen in 1884." THE PACIFIC NORTHWESTERNER, Vol. 11, No. 3 (Summer 1967): 39-43.

3069. Gipson, Fred. "The Hanging of Bob Augustine." TRUE WESTERN ADVENTURES [Greenwich, CT], No. 2 (Spring 1958): 21-22, 55.   This lynching in 1864 was first of 20 hangings by vigilantes in less than two weeks in San Antonio, Texas.

3070. Givens, Hank. "Fair Play Meant a Hanging." FRONTIER TIMES [Austin, TX], Vol. 46, No. 6, New Series No. 80 (Oct.-Nov. 1972): 20-21, 62. John Hoover was lynched in Fairplay, Colorado, 1880.

3071. Goar, J. C. "Bloody Times in Blanco County." FRONTIER TIMES [Bandera, TX], Vol. 6, No. 11 (Aug. 1929), 446-47.   Texas mob shot Tom Blasingame and his father to death. [Compare article by Kemp, L. W.]

3072. Gordan, John D., III. AUTHORIZED BY NO LAW: THE SAN FRANCISCO COMMITTEE OF VIGILANCE OR 1856 AND THE UNITED STATES CIRCUIT COURT FOR THE DISTRICTS OF CALIFORNIA. Pasadena: Ninth Judicial Circuit Historical Society; San Francisco: United States District Court for the Northern District of California Historical Society, 1987.

3073. Goss, Helen Rocca. THE CALIFORNIA WHITE CAP MURDERS: AN EPISODE IN VIGILANTISM. Santa Barbara: Helen Rocca Goss, 1969.   In Oct., 1890, a group (not White Caps, but inspired by them) raided saloon in Lake County to whip, tar, and feather bartender, but killed owner's wife (and one of their own leaders). Book is by daughter of man involved in prosecution and pardons/commutations controversy.

3074. Gould, Lewis L. "A. S. Mercer and the Johnson County War.: A Reappraisal." ARIZONA AND THE WEST, [Vol. 7, No. 1 (Spring 1965)]: 5-20.

3075. Gower, Calvin W. "Vigilantes." THE COLORADO MAGAZINE, Vol. 41, No. 2 (Spring 1964): 93-104.   In 1860 James Gordon murdered a

man in Denver, Kansas Territory. A mob tried to lynch him in Leavenworth. Back in Denver, he was subjected to a "vigilante" trial, was found
guilty, and was hanged.

3076. Graham, C. M. "Have You Ever Heard of the White Caps?" NEW
MEXICO GENEALOGIST, Vol. 6 , No. 4 (Dec. 1967): 3-8.   Gorras
Blancas of New Mexico, 1888-1890.

3077. Grahame, Orville F. "The Vigilance Committees." THE PAL-
IMPSEST, Vol. 6, No. 10 (Oct. 1925): 359-70.   Iowa committees.

3078. Grant, Ben O. "Citizen Law Enforcement Bodies: A Little More
About The Vigilantes." WEST TEXAS HISTORICAL ASSOCIATION
YEAR BOOK, Vol. 39 (Oct. 1963): 155-61.   Vigilantism and lynching in
several West Texas counties, 1870s.

3079. Greenfield, Charles D. "Clean-up of Laramie in '68." TRUE WEST
[Austin, TX], Vol. 18, No. 3, Whole No. 103 (Jan.-Feb. 1971): 26-27, 70, 72.
Vigilantes and lynching in Wyoming.

3080. Gregg, Andrew. "How They Hung Indestructible Gus." REAL
WEST [Derby, CT], Vol. 5, No. 23 (May 1962): 8-11, 53-54.   Gus Mentzer
was lynched at Raton, New Mexico, 1882.

3081. Gustafson, Carl Stanley. "History of Vigilante and Mob Activity in
Wyoming." M.A. thesis, Univ. of Wyoming, 1961.

3082. Gustafson, Stan. VIGILANTES OF WYOMING: LYNCHINGS
AND OTHER MOB ACTIVITY, 1867-1910. New York: Carlton Press,
1971.   Based on author's thesis.

3083. Haefele, Walter R. "Vigilante Justice Dispensed." WILD WEST
[Leesburg, VA], Vol. 2, No. 2 (Aug. 1989): 26-33.   San Francisco
Committees of Vigilance.

3084. Haines, Francis D., Jr. "An Inquest on David Updike." IDAHO
YESTERDAYS, Vol. 15, No. 3 (Fall 1971): 28-32.   Vigilante hanging,
1866.

3085. Hamilton, Wade. "They Hanged Him Too Soon." TRUE WEST
[Austin, TX], Vol. 11, No. 4, Whole No. 62 (March-April 1964): 49, 67.
Victor Monego was lynched in Columbus (California or Nevada), Jan. 1,
1874.

3086. Hansen, Baird. "The Vigilantes." REAL WEST [Derby, CT], Vol. 4,

No. 18 (July 1961): 14-16, 44-45. Arkansas River valley, Colorado, 1874.

3087. Hanson, James E. "The Killer Who Called Himself The Law." TRUE WESTERN ADVENTURES [Greenwich, CT], No. 7 (April 1959): 34-36, 59-61.   Jack Slade; he was lynched in Montana [Idaho Territory], 1864.

3088. Harper, C. W. "Committees of Vigilance and Vigilante Justice." JOURNAL OF THE WEST, Vol. 17, No. 1 (Jan. 1978): 3-7.   Action in mining areas of West, 1849-1880s.

3089. Harrison, Fred.   "Innocent and Hanged."   GOLDEN WEST [Freeport, NY], Vol. 1, No. 6 (Sept. 1965): 8, 65-66.   Lynching of John Callaham [sic] (and a guilty man) near Dodge City, Kansas, April 1876. Same author, title, and article in The West [Rockville Centre, NY], Vol. 15, No. 10 (March 1972): 46-47.

3090. Harrison, John. "Montana's Horse Thief War." GREAT WEST [New York], Vol. 7, No. 2 (Oct. 1973): 16-19, 43-44.   Vigilantes, 1884.

3091. Harrison, John H. "The Vigilantes." TRUE FRONTIER [New York], No. 56 (April 1978): 30-33, 44-46.   San Francisco, 1851, 1856; Montana (Idaho Territory), 1862-1865.

3092. Hart, George. "The Hanging of Big Ned Wilson." REAL WEST [Derby, CT], Vol. 13, No. 81 (April 1970): 12-13, 78.   Four men were hanged at Laramie, Wyoming, 1868.

3093. Hart, George. "The Lynching of Sanford Dougan." REAL WEST [Derby, CT], Vol. 12, No. 74 (Sept. 1969): 50-51.   Denver, 1868. See Cook, D. J., as told to Zoltan Malocsay, in this bibliography.

3094. Hartley, William B. "The Men Who Wouldn't Be Lynched." TRUE WESTERN ADVENTURES [Greenwich, CT], No. 9 (Aug. 1959): 8-9, 57-60.   Marlow brothers; Texas, late 1880s.

3095. Hartley, William B. "Outlaw Sheriff." TRUE WESTERN ADVEN-TURES [Greenwich, CT], No. 8 (June [1959]): 38-52.   Henry Plummer.

3096. Harvey, Mark. "Legacy of a Range War." WYOMING ANNALS, Vol. 65, No. 4 (Winter 1993): 4-5, 74-75.   Johnson County War. Includes remarks on vigilantism.

3097. Haugen, T. Josephine. "The Lynching of Kid Wade." NEBRASKA HISTORY MAGAZINE, Vol. 14, No. 1 (January-March 1933): 18-34. Vigilante action, 1884; lynching near Bassett, Rock County, Nebraska.

3098. Haumont, Jules. "Pioneer Years in Custer County." NEBRASKA HISTORY MAGAZINE, Vol. 13, No. 4 (Oct.-Dec. 1932): 223-37.   See "Vigilantes and Horse Thieves," pp. 232-33.

3099. Hawthorne, Roger. "Conflict and Conspiracy. Events Leading to the Johnson County War of 1892: The Lynching of Tom Waggoner." TRUE WEST [Iola, WI], Vol. 31, No. 6, Whole No. 201 (June 1984): 12-17. Examines issues related to this 1891 event--about 20 miles west of Newcastle, Wyoming, in Weston County.

3100. Henn, Roger E. "Equality for Women in the West: Lynching." THE WESTERNERS BRAND BOOK [Chicago Corral], Vol. 36, No. 4 (Sept.-Oct. 1979): 25-27.   Vigilante hangings of Mike and Margaret Cuddigan, Ouray, Colorado, 1884.

3101. Henry, Edwin C. "More Than Mighty!" FRONTIER TIMES [Austin, TX], Vol. 33, No. 1, New Series No. 5 (Winter 1958-59): 18-19, 28.   Jack Slade, lynched by Montana [sic] vigilantes.

3102. Herff, Charles A. "San Antonio Vigilantes Hanged Ten In One Day." FRONTIER TIMES [Bandera, TX], Vol. 6, No. 5 (Feb. 1929): 197-99.   In about 1864. Reprinted in ibid., Vol. 29, No. 6 (March 1952): 162-66. See also Gipson, Fred, in this bibliography.

3103. Hewitt, James W. "The Fatal Fall of Barrett Scott: Vigilantes on the Niobrara." GREAT PLAINS QUARTERLY, Vol. 12, No. 2 (Spring 1992): 107-20.   Vigilantism in Nebraska, 1880s.

3104. Hilger, David. "Vigilante Trial and Execution." ROCKY MOUNTAIN MAGAZINE, Vol. 2, No. 2 (April 1901): 632-36.   Helena, Montana, hanging of Joseph Wilson and Arthur L. Compton, April 30, 1870.

3105. Hogan, Richard Lawrence. "'Law and Order' in Colorado: 1858-1888." Ph.D. diss., Univ. of Michigan, 1982.   See Diss. Ab. Intl., Vol. 43, No. 6 (Dec. 1982): 2126A.   Conflict between local governing authority (Carnival), often controlled by producers, and private, unofficial governance (Caucus), often controlled by nonproducers.

3106. Holben, Dick. "Biography of a Lynching." THE WEST [Rockville Centre, NY], Vol. 16, No. 12 (July 1973): 34-37, 42-43.   Three victims at Las Vegas, New Mexico, 1880.

3107. Holben, Dick. "The Day They Hanged Gus Mentzer." REAL WEST [Derby, CT], Vol. 16, No. 118 (Aug. 1973): 26-28, 61.   Lynching at Raton, New Mexico, 1882.

3108. Hornung, Chuck. "The Lynching Of Gus Mentzer." REAL WEST [Derby, CT], Vol. 28, No. 202 (April 1985): 10-16.   Raton, New Mexico, 1882.

3109. Hough, Emerson. THE STORY OF THE OUTLAW: A STUDY OF THE WESTERN DESPERADO WITH HISTORICAL NARRATIVES OF FAMOUS OUTLAWS; THE STORIES OF NOTED BORDER WARS; VIGILANTE MOVEMENTS AND ARMED CONFLICTS ON THE FRONTIER. New York: Outing Pub. Co., 1907.

3110. Housman, R. L. "The Vigilante Movement and Its Press in Montana." AMERICANA, Vol. 35, No. 1 (Jan. 1941): 34-50.

3111. Hufsmith, George W. THE WYOMING LYNCHING OF CATTLE KATE, 1889. Glendo, WY: High Plains Press, 1993.

3112. Hufsmith, George W., and Hufsmith, Eleanor. "The Sweetwater Lynching." Libretto for an opera about Cattle Kate and Jim Averill which was performed in various Wyoming towns in 1976. Copy at American Heritage Center, University of Wyoming.

3113. Hunt, Robert V., Jr. "Cicero C. Simms: Villain or Victim?" OLD WEST [Stillwater, OK], Vol. 31, No. 1, Whole No. 121 (Fall 1994): 40-45. Lynching of John Hoover at Fairplay, Colorado, 1880, may have intimidated jury that convicted Simms.

3114. Hunt, Rockwell D. "The Committees of Vigilance of California." OVERLAND MONTHLY, Vol. 49, New Series, No. 1 (Jan. 1907): 31-39.

3115. Hunt, T. Dwight. SERMON SUGGESTED BY THE EXECUTION OF JENKINS ON THE PLAZA, BY THE PEOPLE OF SAN FRANCISCO DURING THE NIGHT OF THE 10TH OF JUNE, 1851. San Francisco: Marvin & Hitchcock, 1851.

3116. Hunter, George. "The Vigilante Years." TRUE WEST [Iola, WI], Vol. 27, No. 3, Whole No. 157 (Jan.-Feb. 1980): 12-13, 42-44, 46-48. Montana, Idaho, Oregon, and Washington, 1860s. Very little on vigilantes. From Reminiscences of an Old Timer (San Francisco: H. S. Crocker & Co., 1887.

3117. Hunter, J. Marvin. "The Hoo-Doo War in Mason County." FRONTIER TIMES [Bandera, TX], Vol. 14 [sic; should be Vol. 15], No. 4 (Jan. 1938): 171-75. Texas, 1870s. Mob shot Tim Williamson to death. Mob also hanged three men and shot another; one of hanged men survived.

3118. Huston, Fred. "They Hung Him as a Drunk." PIONEER WEST [Sepulveda, CA], Vol. 3, No. 2 (May 1969): 22-25. Joseph A. "Jack" Slade was lynched at Virginia City, Montana [Idaho Territory].

3119. Hutton, Harold. VIGILANTE DAYS: FRONTIER JUSTICE ALONG THE NIOBRARA. Chicago: Swallow Press, 1978. Nebraska.

3120. Johnson, David A. "Vigilance and the Law: The Moral Authority of Popular Justice in the Far West." AMERICAN QUARTERLY, Vol. 33, No. 5 (Winter 1981): 558-86.

3121. Johnson, Dorothy M. THE BLOODY BOZEMAN: THE PERIL-OUS TRAIL TO MONTANA'S GOLD. New York: McGraw-Hill, 1971. Includes vigilantes.

3122. Johnson, Edward W. "Deputy Marshal Johnson Breaks a Long Silence." TRUE WEST [Iola, WI], Vol. 27, No. 3, Whole No. 157 (Jan.-Feb. 1980): 6-11, 48-49, 52-54. Includes mob actions against the Marlow Brothers in Texas, 1889.

3123. Johnson, Howard A. "Pioneer Law and Justice in Montana." THE WESTERNERS BRAND BOOK (Chicago Corral of Westerners), Vol. 5, No. 2 (April 1948): 5-7, 9-12; Vol. V, No. 3 (May 1948): 18-20. Includes vigilantes, 1863-1864.

3124. Jones, Calico. "They Hanged Them High." PIONEER WEST [Van Nuys, CA], Vol. 2, No. 3 (May 1968): 42-45, 47-49. Includes lynching of two men in Globe, Arizona, 1882.

3125. Jones, Charles A. "The Lynching of Bert Wilkinson." Ed. by Clifford B. Jones. In PIONEERS OF THE SAN JUAN COUNTRY, Vol. 3, by Sarah Platt Decker Chapter N.S.D.A.R., Durango, Colorado, pp. 68-76. Durango, CO: Durango Printing Co., 1952. In Sept. 1881 the marshal of Silverton, Colorado, was killed. A man named Brown was immediately lynched for it; Wilkinson was captured through treachery a few days later and lynched at Silverton.

3126. Jordan, Phil. "Mysterious Juanita." WESTERNER [Encino, CA], Vol. 6, No. 5 (Sept.-Oct. 1974): 18-20, 57. Lynched at Downieville, California, 1851. Photo of Jack Cannon, man Juanita killed, and portrait of her were provided by author; are they authentic?

3127. Jordan, Philip D. "Frontier Law and Order." NORTH DAKOTA HISTORY, Vol. 39, No. 1 (Winter 1972): 6-12. Little on lynching.

3128. Jordan, Philip D. FRONTIER LAW & ORDER: TEN ESSAYS. Lincoln: Univ. of Nebraska Press, 1970.   See "Lynching," "Mobs," and "Riots" in index.

3129. JUDGES AND CRIMINALS: SHADOWS OF THE PAST. HISTORY OF THE VIGILANCE COMMITTEE OF SAN FRANCISCO, CAL., WITH THE NAMES OF ITS OFFICERS. San Francisco: Printed for the author, 1858.   In National Union Catalog, Pre-1956, Vol. 211, p. 266, under Gray, Henry Martin, supposed author.

3130. Jury, John G. "Lynch Law in California." THE GREEN BAG, Vol. 14, No. 6 (June 1902): 291-94.   From an article in History of the Bench and Bar of California . . ., ed. by Oscar T. Shuck (Los Angeles: The Commercial Printing House, 1901).

3131. Kelly, Joseph M.   "Shifting Interpretations of the San Francisco Vigilantes." JOURNAL OF THE WEST, Vol. 24, No. 1 (Jan. 1985): 39-46.

3132. Kelly, William R.   "Homesteading . . . Ella Watson's (Cattle Kate) Capital Crime." THE DENVER WESTERNERS MONTHLY ROUNDUP, Vol. 19, No. 5 (May 1963): 10, 15-21.   She was lynched in Wyoming, 1889.

3133. Kemp, L. W. "A Blanco County Tragedy." FRONTIER TIMES [Bandera, TX], Vol. 11, No. 8 [sic; should be No. 9] (June 1934): 412-16. Texas mob shot to death Woodson Blassingame and son Calvin, 1856. [Compare article by Goar, J. C., in this chapter.]

3134. Kendall, Jan. "Nine Lives of Captain Wakeman." THE WEST [Freeport, NY], Vol. 2, No. 1 (Dec. 1964): 22-24, 68-71.   Only a cutline on p. 24 and one paragraph on p. 69 relate to Wakeman's role as head of the Water Police for the San Francisco Vigilance Committee, 1851.

3135. Kennelley, Joseph.   "Vengeance Riders of The Monte." TRUE WEST [Austin, TX], Vol. 13, No. 3, Whole No. 73 (Jan.-Feb. 1966): 32-33, 53-54.   Vigilantism and lynching in southern California, 1850s-1860s.

3136. Kerby, Phil. "Los Angeles: Western Justice." THE NATION, Vol. 205, No. 4 (Aug. 14, 1967): 104-05; in a section on "The Violence."   Violence was incited and condoned by public officials in California from an 1854 lynching to the June 23, 1967, peace march.

3137. Kildare, Maurice. "The Bisbee Massacre Hangings." REAL WEST [Derby, CT], Vol. 14, No. 95 (Aug. 1971): 16-19, 54-56.   Five men committed robbery in Bisbee, Arizona Territory, Dec. 1883, and murdered four people.   Five innocent men were convicted and legally hanged at

Tombstone, March 1884. One innocent man, John Heith, was lynched in Tombstone, Feb. 1884, as an accessory to the robbery and murders.

3138. Kildare, Maurice. "Hanging At Grizzly Flats." WILD WEST [Sepulveda, CA], Vol. 2, No. 3 (Sept. 1970): 13-16, 66. Sam Pritcher was lynched in California, 1851.

3139. Kildare, Maurice. "Hell Gate Hanging Bee." REAL WEST [Derby, CT], Vol. 10, No. 52 (March 1967): 27-31, 68-69, 80. Jan. 1864. Virginia City vigilantes led by James Williams and John X. Beidler went to area of present Missoula, Montana, and lynched six men during two-day period.

3140. Kildare, Maurice. "Henry Plummer's Golden Loot." FRONTIER TIMES [Austin, TX], Vol. 39, No. 3, New Series No. 35 (April-May 1965): 6-8, 55-58. Includes vigilantes and lynching, 1863-1864. Montana [Idaho Territory].

3141. Kildare, Maurice. "Sun River Vigilantes." THE WEST [Freeport, NY], Vol. 4, No. 3 (Feb. 1966): 16-19, 65-68. Montana, 1870s-1880s.

3142. Kildare, Maurice. "Vigilante's Doublecross." WESTERNER [Encino, CA], Vol. 1, No. 1 (March-April 1969): 44-48, 72-73. Was Henry Plummer a victim of justice or "a greedy pack of killers"? Montana [Idaho Territory].

3143. King, Joseph L. "The Vigilance Committee of '56." OVERLAND MONTHLY, Vol. 68, No. 6 (Dec. 1916): 509-20. By the son of murdered James King of William. California.

3144. Knight, Maria. "Early Days in San Francisco: A Near View of Vigilante Times." OVERLAND MONTHLY, Vol. 30 (Second Series), No. 177 (Sept. 1897): 252-59.

3145. Knight, Maria. "Early Days in San Francisco: A Near View of Vigilante Times." OVERLAND MONTHLY, Vol. 30 (Second Series), No. 178 (Oct. 1897): 313-22.

3146. Koop, W. E. "A Rope for One-Armed Charlie." TRUE WEST [Austin, TX], Vol. 14, No. 3, Whole No. 79 (Jan.-Feb. 1967): 22-24, 56-57, 62-65. Includes lynchings of Tom Smith (Tom Ford) in Kansas, 1872, and Charlie Smith (Charles Ford), L. B. Hasbrouck, and Billy Brooks at Wellington, Kansas, 1874.

3147. Kubista, Bob. "Aftermath of the Bisbee Hanging." REAL WEST [Derby, CT], Vol. 8, No. 44 (Nov. 1965): 22-23. Largely about the lynching of John Heath at Tombstone, Arizona, 1884.

3148. Kubista, Bob. "The Hanging of George Johnson." GOLDEN WEST [Rockville Centre, NY], Vol. 9, No. 11 (Oct. 1973): 11, 50.   He was lynched at Tombstone, Arizona, 1882.

3149. Kutz, Jack. "Las Gorras Blancas: Vigilantes Storm Into the Night." NEW MEXICO MAGAZINE, Vol. 70, No. 3 (March 1992): 58-62.   Fence cutting and conflict over land grants.

3150. Ladd, Robert E. EIGHT ROPES TO ETERNITY. Tombstone, AZ: Tombstone Epitaph, 1965.   Deals seven legal hangings and one lynching (John Heith, 1884) in Tombstone.

3151. Lalire, Gregory.   "Gunfighters & Lawmen: Despite their secret nickname, Henry Plummer and his road agents were no 'Innocents.'" WILD WEST [Leesburg, VA], Vol. 5, No. 1 (June 1992): 8, 56, 58-60.   Montana [sic; Idaho Territory] .

3152. Landes, Cheryl. "Blood on the Junipers." TRUE WEST [Stillwater, OK], Vol. 37, No. 3 (March 1990): 44-47.   Vigilantism in Central Oregon, 1882-1884.

3153. Langford, Nathaniel P. VIGILANTE DAYS AND WAYS; THE PIONEERS OF THE ROCKIES, THE MAKERS AND MAKING OF MONTANA, IDAHO, OREGON, WASHINGTON, AND WYOMING. Introduction by Dorothy M. Johnson. Missoula: Montana State Univ. Press, 1957.   Originally published in 1890.

3154. Larson, Robert W. "The White Caps of New Mexico: A Study of Ethnic Militancy in the Southwest." PACIFIC HISTORICAL REVIEW, Vol. 44, No. 2 (May 1975): 171-85. Mexican-American vigilantes protected "native" rights to land.

3155. "The Last of 'Plummer's Gang.'" THE LITERARY DIGEST, Vol. 44, No. 11 (March 16, 1912): 558-61.   Excerpts from Nathaniel P. Langford's book Vigilante Days and Ways [see above].

3156. Layne, J. Gregg. "Gun Fights and Lynchings in Early Los Angeles." THE WESTERNERS BRAND BOOK [Los Angeles Corral], [Vol. 1] (1947): 19-25.   Includes sections on California's first and last vigilance committees.

3157. Leary, Hal. "A Rope for Mary Rose." FRONTIER TIMES [Austin, TX], Vol. 48, No. 1, New Series No. 87 (Dec.-Jan. 1974): 32-33, 53-54. Michael Cuddigan and his pregnant wife Margaret were lynched near Ouray, Colorado, for murdering an 11-year-old girl, 1884.

3158. Leavitt, Harry. "Vigilante 601." TRUE WEST [Austin, TX], Vol. 9, No. 5, Whole No. 51 (May-June 1962): 34-35.   Deals with vigilantes in Bodie, California, 1880, and lynching of man named De Roche.

3159. LeBaron, A. D. "Bisbee's Five Black Ghosts." TRUE WEST [Austin, TX], Vol. 7, No. 6, Whole No. 40 (July-Aug. 1960): 12-14, 56-57.   Includes lynching (with photo) of John Heath at Tombstone, Arizona, 1884.

3160. Lee, Wayne C. "The Badman of Kearney." TRUE WEST, Vol. 37, No. 2 (Feb. 1990): 28-32.   Attempted lynching in Nebraska, 1878.

3161. Leeson, Michael A., ed. HISTORY OF MONTANA, 1739-1885. A HISTORY OF ITS . . . INDIANS AND INDIAN WARS, VIGILANTES . . . Chicago: Warner, Beers and Co., 1885.

3162. Leigh, Sharon. "Ella Watson: Rustler or Homesteader?" WYO-MING ANNALS, Vol. 64, Nos. 3/4 (Summer/Fall 1992): 49-56.   Lynched in Wyoming, 1889.

3163. Lewis, Steve. "Hang 'Em!" GREAT WEST [New York], Vol. 4, No. 3 (Aug. 1970): 14-15, 42-44.   Sept. 1860: three horse thieves were lynched in or near Denver, two by hanging and one by shooting.

3164. Lindsey, David. "The Reign of the Vigilantes." AMERICAN HISTORY ILLUSTRATED, Vol. 8, No. 3 (June 1973): 22-32.   San Francisco, 1856.

3165. Lockley, Fred. VIGILANTE DAYS AT VIRGINIA CITY: PERSONAL NARRATIVE OF COL. HENRY E. DOSCH, MEMBER OF FREMONT'S BODY GUARD AND ONE-TIME PONY EXPRESS RIDER. Portland, OR: Fred Lockley, n.d.

3166. Long, J. A. "How Red Jack Almer Died." THE WEST [New York], Vol. 1, No. 5 (Oct. 1964): 46-47, 54-56.   Includes lynching of two bandits in Arizona Territory, 1883.

3167. Long, James A. "Strange Truth About Jack Slade." THE WEST [Freeport, NY], Vol. 4, No. 3 (Feb. 1966): 26-28, 54-55.   He was lynched in Montana [Idaho Territory], 1864.

3168. Long, Phil S. "Last Victim of the Vigilantes." TRUE WEST [Austin, TX], Vol. 15, No. 6, Whole No. 88 (July-Aug. 1968): 24-25, 48-50.   Near East Helena, Montana Territory, Jan. 1885.

3169. Los Angeles Star. EXPEDITION TO SANTA BARBARA--

EXECUTION OF TWO MEN. [Los Angeles, 1857].

3170. "Lynch Law in California." THE GREEN BAG, Vol. 14, No. 6 (June 1902): 291-94. Lynchings in 1849, 1851 (a woman victim), 1855, and 1856 (by San Francisco Vigilance Committee).

3171. Malin, George. "Trial By Fury." THE WEST [Freeport, NY], Vol. 4, No. 3 (Feb. 1966): 38-40, 69-70. Various lynchings in frontier CA, CO, NV, and WY. Reprinted in The West [Rockville Centre, NY], Vol. 15, No. 9 (Feb. 1972): 38-41 [bottom of p. 40 incorrectly says article continues on p. 67; article continues and concludes on p. 41].

3172. Malsbory, George. "Old San Francisco's Summer of Death." WESTERNER [Encino, CA], Vol. 2, No. 8 (Dec. 1970): 39-41, 58-59. Sam Brannan and 1851 Committee of Vigilance.

3173. Marshall, Paul D. "The Bonsall Tragedy." FRONTIER TIMES [Austin, TX], Vol. 49, No. 6, New Series No. 98 (Oct.-Nov. 1975): 16-19, 50. Two or three Indians were lynched for murder in Porterville, California, 1870.

3174. Martin, Cy. "Playing Fair In Fairplay." REAL WEST [Derby, CT], Vol. 17, No. 124 (Feb. 1974): 18-23, 75. Includes Colorado lynchings of John J. Hooper, 1888, and Sam Porter, approximately 1888.

3175. Martin, Cy. WHISKEY AND WILD WOMEN: AN AMUSING ACCOUNT OF THE SALOONS AND BAWDS OF THE OLD WEST. New York: Hart Pub. Co., 1974. See pp. 75-77 for Juanita, lynched in California, 1851. See pp. 119-24 for Ella Watson, lynched in Wyoming, 1889. See pp. 124-28 for Elizabeth Taylor, lynched in Nebraska, 1885.

3176. Martin, G. K. "Land of the Noose: Yegua Knobbs." OLD WEST [Austin, TX], Vol. 5, No. 3, Whole No. 19 (Spring 1969): 2-9, 36, 38, 40, 42-45. See pp. 5-9 for vigilantes and lynchings in central Texas, 1870s-1880s.

3177. Mason, Frank. "Hanging Bill Coons Was Such Fun!" FRONTIER TIMES [Austin, TX], Vol. 34, No. 2, New Series No. 10 (Spring 1960): 24-25, 54. Reprinted in Old West [Austin, TX], Vol. 15, No. 4, Whole No. 60 (Summer 1979): 14-15, 38. Lynched in New Mexico for murder, 1881.

3178. Mather, R. E. "Cyrus and Nellie and the Vigilantes." TRUE WEST, Vol. 34, No. 5 (May 1987): 20-26. Montana, 1864.

3179. Mather, R. E. "Gunfighters & Lawmen: Was Henry Plummer a lawman-gone-bad or the innocent victim of ruthless vigilantes?" WILD

WEST [Leesburg, VA], [Vol. 6, No. 2] (Aug. 1993): 14, 16, 20, 22, 24. Montana [sic; Idaho Territory].

3180. Mather, R. E. "Last Lynching at Bannack, Montana." TRUE WEST, Vol. 38, No. 4 (April 1991): 14-19.   Title given as on p. 14; on contents page title is "Last Lynching in Bannack." D. C. Rawleigh was lynched Oct., 1864, for criticizing the vigilantes.

3181. Mather, R. E., and Boswell, F. E. HANGING THE SHERIFF: A BIOGRAPHY OF HENRY PLUMMER. Salt Lake City: Univ. of Utah Press, 1987.   Revisionist work which sees Plummer more favorably.

3182. Mather, R. E., and Boswell, F. E.   VIGILANTE VICTIMS: MONTANA'S 1864 HANGING SPREE. San Jose: History West Pub. Co., 1991.

3183. Mazzulla, Fred M. "Undue Process of Law--Here and There." THE DENVER WESTERNERS MONTHLY ROUNDUP, Vol. 20, No. 10 (Oct. 1964): 3-17. Also published as "Undue Process of Law, Here and There," in Volume XX of the Brand Book of the Denver Westerners, pp. 255-79. Ed. by Francis B. Rizzari. Denver: The Westerners, 1965.   Includes lynching of George Witherill in Colorado, 1888; Dutch Charley in Wyoming, 1878; and "Big Nose" George Parrotti in Wyoming, 1881.

3184. McConnell, William J., with Driggs, Howard R. FRONTIER LAW: A STORY OF VIGILANTE DAYS. Yonkers-on-Hudson, NY: World Book Co., 1924.   Idaho.   Rather autobiographical.

3185. McCray, E. Ward.   "Stuart's Stranglers."   TRUE WESTERN ADVENTURES [Greenwich, CT], Vol. 4, No. 18 (Feb. 1961): 10-12, 43-45. Montana Territory, 1884. America's deadliest vigilante movement.

3186. McGinty, Brian. "Hung be the Heavens with Black." AMERICAN HISTORY ILLUSTRATED, Vol. 17, No. 10 (Feb. 1983): 31-39.   San Francisco vigilantes, 1850s.

3187. McGowan, Edward. NARRATIVE OF EDWARD McGOWAN, INCLUDING A FULL ACCOUNT OF THE AUTHOR'S ADVENTURES AND PERILS WHILE PERSECUTED BY THE SAN FRANCISCO VIGILANCE COMMITTEE OF 1856. . . . San Francisco: The Author, 1857.   McGowan vs. California Vigilantes is a reprint.

3188. McGrath, Roger D. "Frontier Violence in the Trans-Sierra West." Ph.D. diss., Univ. of California, Los Angeles, 1978.   See Diss. Ab. Intl., Vol. 39, No. 7 (Jan. 1979): 4449A.

3189. McGrath, Roger D.   GUNFIGHTERS, HIGHWAYMEN, & VIGILANTES: VIOLENCE ON THE FRONTIER. Berkeley: Univ. of California Press, 1984.   Focus is on two California towns.

3190. McGuckin, Andrew J. "San Francisco's Vigilantes Versus the U.S. Navy." THE WEST [Rockville Centre, NY], Vol. 18, No. 3 (Oct. 1974): 28-31, 42-43.

3191. McKanna, Bud. "Gallows and Gunfights in Old San Diego." TRUE WEST, Vol. 33, No. 6, Whole No. 218 (June 1986): 26-30.   Includes vigilantism and lynching.

3192. McKelvey, Nat. "Riddle of the Redfield Robbers." TRUE WEST [Austin, TX], Vol. 5, No. 3, Whole No. 25 (Jan.-Feb. 1958): 24-25, 30-32. Includes lynching of Joe Tuttle and Lem Redfield, Florence, Arizona Territory, Sept. 1883.

3193. McKinnon, L. C. "The Devil's Sanctuary." REAL WEST [Derby, CT], Vol. 26, No. 192 (Aug. 1983): 36-39.   Plummer's gang, Montana [Idaho Territory], and lynchings of some of them.

3194. McMillan, Mark. "Lucky Bill gets the Noose." TRUE WEST [Austin, TX], Vol. 1, No. 4 (Spring 1954): 22-23, 33-34. Reprinted in Old West [Austin, TX], Vol. 2, No. 1 (Fall 1965): 24-25, 32. Also reprinted in Badman [Austin, TX], Vol. 1, No. 1 (1971): 22-23, 46.   Vigilantes lynched Bill Thorrington in Nevada, 1858.

3195. Meketa, Jacqueline D. "The Socorro Stranglers." TRUE WEST, Vol. 34, No. 9 (Sept. 1987): 22-25.   Vigilantes in New Mexico.

3196. Meldrum, John W. "The Taming of 'Big Nosed George'--and Others." THE UNION PACIFIC MAGAZINE, Vol. 5, No. 11 (Nov. 1926): 8-9.   Includes lynchings of Dutch Charley and Parrott in Wyoming; by court official who interviewed Parrott.

3197. "Members of the V.C." ALL THE YEAR ROUND [London], Vol. 6, No. 146 (Feb. 8, 1862): 477-80.   Removal of prisoners from San Francisco Vigilance Committee only temporarily saved them from hanging.

3198. "Mercy of Judge Lynch." ALL THE YEAR ROUND [London], Vol. 6, No. 140 (Dec. 28, 1861): 321-23.   An acquittal by a jury of miners, Gila City, New Mexico Territory (later [1863] Arizona Territory), 1858.

3199. Michelson, Charles. "The Vigilantes of the West." MUNSEY'S MAGAZINE, Vol. 25, No. 2 (May 1901): 200-12.   Mainly about San

Francisco, 1851, but also 1856, and other places in California, Nevada, and the Northwest.

3200. Miller, Henry M. THE MOB'S VERDICT: SILENCE AT THE END OF THE ROPE. Chatsworth, CA: Barclay House, 1974.   Chapter 1: lynching of Juanita at Downieville; Chapter 2: Vigilantes, Bannack and Virginia City, 1863-1864; Chapter 3: lynchings and vigilantes in the West more generally; Chapter 6: Leo Frank; Chapters 8 and 9: various lynchings of Southern blacks; Chapter 10: Thalia Massie case in Hawaii; Chapter 11: lynching of Holmes and Thurmond in San Jose.

3201. Miller, Michael. "Las Gorras Blancas: Night Riders of Las Vegas." EL PALACIO, Vol. 91, No. 3 (Winter/Spring 1986): 16-21.   Vigilantism by Hispanics in New Mexico because of land disputes, late 1800s.

3202. Miller, Nyle H., and Snell, Joseph W.   WHY THE WEST WAS WILD: A CONTEMPORARY LOOK AT THE ANTICS OF SOME HIGHLY PUBLICIZED KANSAS COWTOWN PERSONALITIES. Topeka: Kansas State Historical Society, 1963.

3203. Miranda, Ben. "The Cherry Creek Vigilantes." REAL WEST [Derby, CT], Vol. 16, No. 122 (Dec. 1973): 38-41.   Area that later became Denver, 1859-[1860?].   On p. 39 author is given as Ben Miranda--but listed in contents as Ernest H. Hart.

3204. "A Mob Scene at Rough and Ready." In THE MINING FRONTIER: CONTEMPORARY ACCOUNTS FROM THE AMERICAN WEST IN THE NINETEENTH CENTURY, pp. 21-28.   Ed. by Marvin Lewis. Norman: Univ. of Oklahoma Press, 1967.   A store owner was whipped to death in Nevada County, California, 1850. Taken from T. H. Hittell, History of California, which deals further with vigilante activity.

3205. Montana Territory Vigilance Committee. NOTICE! Helena, MT: Sept. 19, 1865.   A broadside.

3206. "Monthly Record of Current Events." HARPER'S NEW MONTHLY MAGAZINE, Vol. 3, No. 16 (Sept. 1851): 557-67.   See p. 559 for San Francisco Committee of Vigilance and its first two executions.

3207. Morando, B. "Montana's Stranglers." REAL WEST [Derby, CT], Vol. 17, No. 128 (July 1974): 36-39.   Horse thieves were hanged by Granville Stuart's vigilantes, 1880s. [See Miranda, Ben.]

3208. Moyer, Paul. "'Lynch Justice': No Man Should Die the Way They Killed Rollie Judkins." FRONTIER WEST [New York], Vol. 1, No. 4 (Oct.

1971): 40-43, 67-68.   Lynching at Bogart, Nevada, 1866.

3209. Mueller, Oscar O. "The Central Montana Vigilante Raids of 1884."
THE MONTANA MAGAZINE OF HISTORY, Vol. 1, No. 1 (Jan. 1951):
23-35.

3210. Mueller, Richard K. "Granville Stuart and the Montana Vigilantes
of 1884." M.A. thesis, Univ. of Oregon, 1980.   See Masters Abstracts, Vol.
19, No. 1 (March 1981): 66.

3211. Mullen, Kevin J.   LET JUSTICE BE DONE: CRIME AND
POLITICS IN EARLY SAN FRANCISCO. Reno: Univ. of Nevada Press,
1989.   See "Vigilance" in index.

3212. Mumey, Nolie. "Behind a Woman's Skirt: The Saga of 'Cattle Kate.'"
1950 BRAND BOOK [The Westerners, Denver, CO], Vol. 6 (Dec. 1950):
77-89.   She was lynched in Wyoming, 1889.

3213. Muyskens, Joan. "Iowa Desperadoes Captured and Lynched in 1883."
ANNALS OF IOWA, Third Series, Vol. 39, No. 2 (Fall 1967): 149-57.

3214. Myers, John Myers. SAN FRANCISCO'S REIGN OF TERROR.
Garden City, NY: Doubleday, 1966.   Though dealing with vigilantism, this
is more a biography of Ned McGowan, one of the main operators of David
C. Broderick's political machine in the early 1850s.

3215. Myers, Rex C. "Vigilante Numbers: A Re-examination." MON-
TANA, THE MAGAZINE OF WESTERN HISTORY, Vol. 24, No. 4 (Oct.
1974): 67-70.   Title here is from contents, but title on p. 67 is "the fateful
numbers 3-7-77 a re-examination."

3216. "New Look at San Francisco's Vigilantes." USA TODAY [magazine],
Vol. 115, No. 2499 (Dec. 1986): 10-12. Ideas of Robert M. Senkewicz in his
book Vigilantes in Gold Rush San Francisco.

3217. Newton, Allen.   "Explosion on Powder River."   WESTERNER
[Encino, CA], Vol. 1, No. 3 (July-Aug. 1969): 16-19, 59-61.   Subtitle:
"When the Wyoming Cattle Barons Turned To Lynching to Save Their
Empires." Starts with 1889 lynching of Jim Averill and Cattle Kate and then
deals with Johnson County War.

3218. [No author.] "They Hung Henry Plummer." GREAT WEST [St.
Louis], Vol. 2, No. 6 (Dec. 1968): 14-19, 56, 58, 60.   Montana vigilantes.

3219. "No. '3, 7, 77.'"   CHAMBERS'S JOURNAL OF POPULAR

LITERATURE, SCIENCE, AND ART [Edinburgh], Fifth Series, Vol. 11, No. 544 (June 2, 1894): 351-52.   These numbers are "the warning notice and the signature of the Vigilantes of the Far West." No indication of numbers' origin. Title in volume's index is "Vigilantes--No. '3, 7, 77.'"

3220. Nolan, Patrick B. VIGILANTES ON THE MIDDLE BORDER: A STUDY OF SELF-APPOINTED LAW ENFORCEMENT IN THE STATES OF THE UPPER MISSISSIPPI FROM 1840 TO 1880. New York: Garland, 1987.   Originally a Ph.D. diss., Univ. of Minnesota, 1971; same title; see Diss. Ab. Intl., Vol. 32, No. 11 (May 1972): 6318A-6319A. States of Wisconsin, Illinois, Minnesota, and Missouri. Finds evidence for legalized or sanctioned vigilantism.

3221. Noll, Lowell H. "Southern Idaho Vigilantism." THE PACIFIC NORTHWESTERNER, Vol. 2, No. 2 (Spring 1958): 25-32.

Numbers 3, 7, 77. See "No. '3, 7, 77.'"

3222. Nunis, Doyce B., ed.   THE SAN FRANCISCO VIGILANCE COMMITTEE OF 1856: THREE VIEWS [by] WILLIAM T. COLEMAN, WILLIAM T. SHERMAN [and] JAMES O'MEARA. Los Angeles: Los Angeles Westerners, 1971.   Contains William T. Coleman, "San Francisco Vigilance Committees," facsimile from Century Magazine, Nov. 1891; William T. Sherman, "Sherman and the San Francisco Vigilantes," facsimile from Century Magazine, Dec. 1891; A Pioneer Journalist, "The Vigilance Committee of 1856," facsimile account by James O'Meara; "Portfolio of Pictorial Letter Sheets On the Vigilance Committee of 1856"; "Appendix I: 'The Vigilantes of 1856,' William T. Coleman's Record of Early Days," facsimile from the San Francisco Call, April 20, 1884; "Appendix II: Corrections to 'Sherman and the San Francisco Vigilantes"; "Appendix III: 'The Vigilance Committee of 1856,'" by William T. Sherman, facsimile from Overland Monthly, Feb. 1874.

3223. O'Dell, Roy. "Gold Camp Ruffian." OLD WEST [Stillwater, OK], Vol. 29, No. 3, Whole No. 115 (Spring 1993): 46-51. See p. 49 for lynching of Tom Bell in California, 1856.

3224. O'Donnell, Jeff. "The Committee of 33." OLD WEST [Stillwater, OK], Vol. 24, No. 2, Whole No. 94 (Winter 1987): 26-29. Two men were lynched at Hastings, Nebraska, 1883.

3225. O'Donnell, Jeff. "Lynching at Spring Ranch." OLD WEST [Stillwater, OK], Vol. 28, No. 4, Whole No. 112 (Summer 1992): 22-24, 26-27. Victims: Elizabeth Taylor and her brother Thomas Jones. Nebraska, 1885.

3226. Offen, C. N. [sic] "Vigilante Justice on the Prairies." THE WEST [Freeport, NY], Vol. 2, No. 5 (April 1965): 22-24, 55-56.   Vigilantes lynched eight men near Douglass, Kansas, Nov.-Dec. 1870.

3227. Offen, Charlotte M. "Kansas Avengers Mete Out Unjustified Justice." TRUE WEST, Vol. 35, No. 4 (April 1988): 44-49.   Three brothers were lynched in Anthony, Kansas, 1886.

3228. Offen, Charlotte M. "Penalty for a Midnight Robbery." OLD WEST [Austin, TX], Vol. 11, No. 2, Whole No. 42 (Winter 1974): 20-21, 54-56. Nat Oliphant was lynched in Topeka, Kansas, June 1889.

3229. Olmsted, Roger. "San Francisco and the Vigilante Style: I. Let Each Man Be His Own Executioner." THE AMERICAN WEST, Vol. 7, No. 1 (Jan. 1970): 6-11, 63-64.   Mainly on 1851 vigilance committee.

3230. Olmsted, Roger. "San Francisco and the Vigilante Style: II. 'Absolute Obedience, Absolute Secrecy.'" THE AMERICAN WEST, Vol. 7, No. 2 (March 1970): 20-27, 60-62.   Mainly on 1856 Committee.

3231. Olsen, Barton Clark. "Lawlessness and Vigilantes in America, An Historical Analysis Emphasizing California and Montana." Ph.D. diss., Univ. of Utah, 1968.   See Diss. Ab., Vol. 29, No. 8 (Feb. 1969): 2645A. Vigilantism arose because too many people were uninterested in civic affairs, thus creating imbalance between individual freedom and responsibility.

3232. Olsen, Barton Clark. "The Vigilantes of Montana: A Second Look." M.A. thesis, Univ. of Utah, 1966.

3233. [O'Meara, James.] THE VIGILANCE COMMITTEE OF 1856. San Francisco: James H. Barry, 1887 (cover dated 1890).

3234. O'Neal, Bill. "The Mass Lynching at Belton." REAL WEST [Derby, CT], Vol. 28, No. 203 (June 1985): 25.   Nine men were shot to death in a Texas jail, 1874.

3235. O'Neal, Bill. "The Medicine Lodge Bank Robbery." TRUE WEST [Iola, WI], Vol. 30, No. 8, Whole No. 191 (Aug. 1983): 51-56, 94.   Includes lynching of Henry Brown, John Wesley, Billy Smith, and Ben Wheeler at Medicine Lodge, Kansas, 1884.

3236. Ophus, John. "The Lake County War, 1874-75." THE COLORADO MAGAZINE, Vol. 47, No. 2 (Spring 1970): 119-35.   Vigilantism and violence in Colorado, 1874-1881.

3237. Ormes, Carl. "Blood at Bisbee." REAL WEST [Derby, CT], Vol. 2, No. 7 (May 1959): 23, 54-55.   Includes lynching of John Heath in Tombstone, Arizona, 1884.

3238. Ostrogorsky, Michael. "Night of the Vigilantes." FRONTIER TIMES [Iola, WI], Vol. 55, No. 3, New Series No. 131 (April-May 1981): 52-53.   Lynching of John Clark at Boise City, Idaho, April 7, 1866.

3239. Otero, Miguel Antonio. MY LIFE ON THE FRONTIER, 1864-1882 . . . 2 vols.; New York: The Press of the Pioneers, 1935, 1939.   Includes various accounts of vigilantism and lynchings.

3240. Outland, Chas. F. "The Saticoy Regulators." VENTURA COUNTY HISTORICAL SOCIETY QUARTERLY, Vol. 2, No. 4 (Aug. 1957): 13-16. Anti-horse-thief society in California, 1880s, probably did not commit lynchings ascribed to it. Mentions lynchings which occurred earlier.

3241. Owens, Kenneth N.   "Judge Lynch in Washington Territory." PACIFIC NORTHWEST QUARTERLY, Vol. 55, No. 4 (Oct. 1964): 177-78.   The letter from "Judge Lynch" in 1862 to governor of Washington Territory recommending action against a murderer is indicative of governmental problems.

3242. Pace, Dick. GOLDEN GULCH: THE STORY OF MONTANA'S FABULOUS ALDER GULCH. 2d ed.; Virginia City, MT: Virginia City Trading Co., 1970; originally published in 1962.   Chapter IV (pp. 23-38) is about the road agents and vigilantes. See pp. 49-51 for lynchings of Slade and Brady.

3243. Parish, John C. "White Beans for Hanging." THE PALIMPSEST, Vol. 1, No. 1 (July 1920): 9-28.   Citizens committee at Bellevue, Iowa Territory, battled criminals and then decided whether to hang or whip them.

3244. Parker, Bryan T. "Extra-Legal Law Enforcement on the Nebraska Frontier." M.A. thesis, Univ. of Nebraska, 1931.

3245. Parsons, Chuck. "Clay Allison--Vigilante?" REAL WEST [Derby, CT], Vol. 25, No. 186 (Aug. 1982): 15-17.   He was probably not involved in the lynching of Charles Kennedy in New Mexico Territory, 1870.

3246. Patterson, Richard. HISTORICAL ATLAS OF THE OUTLAW WEST. Boulder: Johnson Books, 1985.   Cover illustration of lynching is not in book and is not identified. See pp. 28, 96, 116.

3247. Paul, Almarin B. "The Vigilance Committee of 1856." OVERLAND

MONTHLY, Vol. 24 (Second Series), No. 142 (Oct. 1894): 433-41.

3248. Paul, Almarin B. "The Vigilance Committee of 1856." OVERLAND MONTHLY, Vol. 24 (Second Series), No. 143 (Nov. 1894): 529-42.

3249. Paul, Almarin B. "The Vigilance Committee of '56." OVERLAND MONTHLY, Vol. 24 (Second Series), No. 144 (Dec. 1894): 622-34.   Title is as here on p. 622, but most other pages have "The Vigilance Committee of 1856" at tops of pages.

3250. Pauley, Art. HENRY PLUMMER: LAWMAN AND OUTLAW. White Sulphur Springs, MT: The Meagher County News, 1980.   Montana [Idaho Territory], 1863-1864.

3251. Pearce, Bennett R. "No Grave for Big Nose George." THE WEST [Freeport, NY], Vol. 10, No. 6 (May 1969): 22-27, 55-56.   He was lynched in Wyoming, 1881.

3252. Perrigo, Lynn I. "Law and Order in Early Colorado Mining Camps." THE MISSISSIPPI VALLEY HISTORICAL REVIEW, Vol. 28, No. 1 (June 1941): 41-62.   Includes lynching, attempted lynching, and a riot.

3253. Pfalser, Ivan L. "Schoolhouse Lynching." TRUE WEST [Austin, TX], Vol. 16, No. 4, Whole No. 92 (March-April 1969): 37, 48.   Mob hanged Weaver brothers, Phillip, Henry, and Oliver, from schoolhouse rafters, town of Anthony, Harper County, Kansas, April 1886.

3254. A Philanthropist.   "A Tale of the Vigilance Committee at San Francisco."   THE ECLECTIC MAGAZINE OF FOREIGN LITERA-TURE, SCIENCE, AND ART [New York], Vol. 49 (New Series), No. 3 (March 1889): 357-69.   Originally published in Blackwood's Magazine. Can't tell which 1850s committee this is about; seems only semi-historical.

3255. Pires, Joe. "The Underground Hanging." TRUE WEST [Austin, TX], Vol. 8, No. 1, Whole No. 41 (Sept.-Oct. 1960): 17, 51-52.   Supposed-ly, vigilantes lynched two men in basement of courthouse at Belmont, Nevada, 1874--but experts dispute this.

3256. Pitt, Leonard. "Greasers In The Diggings: Californians And Sonorans Under Attack." In CHICANO: THE EVOLUTION OF A PEOPLE, pp. 92-101.   Ed. by Renato Rosaldo, Robert A. Calvert, and Gustav L. Seligmann. Minneapolis: Winston Press, 1973.

3257. Pitts, J. W. "Tales of the California Gold Trail." THE AMERICAN WEEKLY [Magazine Section--New York Journal-American], (July 16,

1939): 10-11, 16; (July 23, 1939): 10-11, 15-16; (July 30, 1939): 10-12, 15; (Aug. 6, 1939): 10-12, 14; (Aug. 13, 1939): 8-9, 13-14; (Aug. 20, 1939): 10-11, 15-16; (Aug. 27, 1939): 10-12, 15; (Sept. 3, 1939): 10-11, 15.   See Sept. 3, 1939, p. 10 (with illustration on p. 11) for lynching of Juanita at Downieville, California, 1851. See issues of July 23 and Aug. 13 for other lynchings.

3258. Pons, A. C. "The Lynching of Cattle Kate." THE WEST [New York], Vol. 1, No. 1 (March 1964): 34-36, 64-65.   Wyoming, 1889.

3259. Potter, Chester D. "Reminiscences of the Socorro Vigilantes." Paige W. Christiansen, ed. NEW MEXICO HISTORICAL REVIEW, Vol. 40, No. 1 (Jan. 1965): 23-54.   New Mexico in 1880s.

3260. Powers, Jacob Mathews. "Montana Episodes: Tracking Con Murphy." MONTANA, THE MAGAZINE OF WESTERN HISTORY, Vol. 30, No. 4 (Oct. 1980): 52-56.   Vigilante lynching, 1885.

3261. Praast, Vera Lund. "Historian of the Vigilantes." OLD WEST [Austin, TX], Vol. 4, No. 4, Whole No. 16 (Summer 1968): 28-29.   Thomas J. Dimsdale.

3262. Price, Eliphalet. "The Trial and Execution of Patrick O'Connor at the Dubuque Mines in the Summer of 1834." THE PALIMPSEST, Vol. 1, No. 3 (Sept. 1920): 86-97.   First trial for murder in what is now Iowa; not in a regular court of law but not really by vigilantes either.

3263. Price, Will. "A Pair of Dried Ears." TRUE WEST [Austin, TX], Vol. 7, No. 4, Whole No. 38 (March-April 1960): 18-19, 44-46.   Jack Slade, lynched by Montana [sic] vigilantes, 1864.

3264. Raffety, Robert O. "The History and Theory of Capital Punishment in Montana." M.A. thesis, Univ. of Montana, 1968.   See "Executions by Vigilantes and Early Settlers," pp. 27-47; included are four tables listing names, dates, and locations for men lynched (or legally executed).

3265. Ralph, Julian. "A Man from Another World." HARPER'S WEEKLY, Vol. 37, No. 1914 (Aug. 26, 1893): 815, 818.   Johnny Healey, ex-sheriff of Choteau County, Montana. (The other world was early Montana.) Includes vigilantes.

3266. Rasch, Philip J. "Joel A. Fowler 'The Human Hyena.'" In BRAND BOOK OF THE DENVER WESTERNERS, Vol. 21, pp. 38-51.   Ed. by Arthur L. Campa. Denver: The Denver Westerners, 1966. He was lynched at Socorro, New Mexico, Jan. 1885.

3267. Rasch, Philip J. "The Lake County (Colorado) War." REAL WEST [Derby, CT], Vol. 27, No. 195 (Feb. 1984): 10-13, 56.   Conflicts led to creation of Committee of Safety and rival Regulators and numerous murders, 1874-1881.

3268. Reimers, Henry. "Henry Plummer's Second in Command." FRON-TIER TIMES [Austin, TX], Vol. 46, No. 2, New Series No. 76 (Feb.-March 1972): 6-9, 45, 48-50.   Bill Bunton was lynched by Montana vigilantes.

3269. Remington, Frank L. "Mother lode 'justice.'" CORONET, Vol. 46, No. 8 [sic; should be No. 2] (June 1959): 58-59.   Floggings, tortures, and lynching in gold-rush California.

3270. Repp, Ed Earl. "Eighty Years of Violence." GOLDEN WEST [Freeport, NY], Vol. 5, No. 6 (Sept. 1969): 30-33, 65-66, 68.   Includes lynching of Pete Little at Buckeye, California, circa 1868 (p. 31), and of the Ruggles brothers at Shasta, California, 1892 (p. 68 and photo on p. 30). Same author, title, and article in The West [Rockville Centre, NY], Vol. 16, No. 5 (Dec. 1972): 28-31, 43-44.

3271. Repp, Ed Earl. "She Walked the Plank." REAL FRONTIER [Valley Stream, NY], Vol. 2, No. 1 (Feb. 1971): 29-31, 52, 54-55.   See last two pages for lynching of Juanita at Downieville, California, 1851.

3272. Rickards, Colin. "Boone Helm--Man Eater!" TRUE WEST [Austin, TX], Vol. 20, No. 4, Whole No. 116 (March-April 1973): 6-9, 18-21, 30-32, 46-47, 50-52, 54.   Lynched in Montana [Idaho Territory], 1864.

3273. Rickey, Don, Jr. FORTY MILES A DAY ON BEANS AND HAY, THE ENLISTED SOLDIER FIGHTING THE INDIAN WARS. Norman: Univ. of Oklahoma Press, 1963.   See p. 164 for Dec., 1877, lynching in Wyoming by men of Company A, 3d Cavalry, of one of their number who had murdered a sergeant.

3274. Riker, C. L. "Wild Old Days: The Downieville Affair." TRUE WEST [Austin, TX], Vol. 5, No. 1, Whole No. 23 (Sept.-Oct. 1957): 23.   Lynching of Juanita in California, 1851. Brief.

3275. Rister, C. C. "Outlaws and Vigilantes of the Southern Plains, 1865-1885." THE MISSISSIPPI VALLEY HISTORICAL REVIEW, Vol. 19, No. 4 (March 1933): 537-54.

3276. Rister, Carl Coke. SOUTHERN PLAINSMEN. Norman: Univ. of Oklahoma Press, 1938.   See Chapter 15, "Frontier Justice," for vigilance committees.

3277. Rivors, C. A FULL AND AUTHENTIC ACCOUNT OF THE MURDERS OF JAMES KING, OF WM., DR. RANDALL, DR. BALDWIN, WEST, AND MARION. THE EXECUTION OF JAMES P. CASEY, CHARLES CORA, PHILANDER BRACE, AND JOSEPH HEATHERINGTON, BY THE VIGILANCE COMMITTEE OF SAN FRANCISCO. . . . Rochester, NY: E. Darrow & Brother, 1857.

3278. Roberts, D. W. "The Mason County War." FRONTIER TIMES [Bandera, TX], Vol. 11, No. 4 (Jan. 1934): 183-86. From his book Rangers and Sovereignty. Conflict among cattlemen, 1875.

3279. Roberts, Dan W. "Hoo-Doo War' in Mason County." FRONTIER TIMES [Bandera, TX], Vol. 20, No. 10 (July 1943): 213-15. From Rangers and Sovereignty. Tim Williamson was killed by Texas mob. Another incident: mob broke into jail, took out five rustlers, hanged three, shot another dead, and one escaped. One of hanged men later recovered.

3280. Roberts, William. "The Administration of Justice in America." THE FORTNIGHTLY REVIEW, Vol. 57, Old Series, Vol. 51, New Series, No. 301 (Jan. 1, 1892): 91-108. Cases of lynch law in California and whitecapping elsewhere.

3281. Robeson, Geo. F. "Justice in Early Iowa." THE PALIMPSEST, Vol. 5, No. 3 (March 1924): 102-13. Citizens committees, trials, and punishments (pp. 105-06).

3282. Roensch, Dell. "Bisbee's Bath of Blood!" TRUE WESTERN ADVENTURES [Greenwich, CT]. No. 11 (Dec. 1959): 38-41, 72-74. Robbery and murder led to lynching of John Heath [sic] in Tombstone, Arizona, 1884.

3283. Rosenbaum, Robert. "Las Gorras Blancas of San Miguel County, 1889-1890." In CHICANO: THE EVOLUTION OF A PEOPLE, pp. 128-36. Ed. by Renato Rosaldo, Robert A. Calvert, and Gustav L. Seligmann. Minneapolis: Winston Press, 1973. Mexican-American vigilantes protected "native" rights to land in New Mexico.

3284. Rosenbaum, Robert J. MEXICANO RESISTANCE IN THE SOUTHWEST: "THE SACRED RIGHT OF SELF-PRESERVATION." Austin: Univ. of Texas Press, 1981. Includes Las Gorras Blancas. See "Vigilantes" in index.

3285. Rosenhouse, Leo. "When the Hangman Ruled San Francisco." TRUE FRONTIER [Valley Stream, NY], Vol. 1, No. 7 (Jan. 1969): 46-49, 64. Vigilance Committee, 1851.

3286. Rousseau, B. G. "Juanita." OVERLAND MONTHLY AND OUT WEST MAGAZINE, Vol. 82 (2nd Series), No. 6 (June 1924): 249-51. Hanging of a woman at Downieville, California, July [1851].

3287. Royce, Josiah. CALIFORNIA, FROM THE CONQUEST IN 1846 TO THE SECOND VIGILANCE COMMITTEE IN SAN FRANCISCO: A STUDY OF AMERICAN CHARACTER. Boston: Houghton Mifflin, 1886. See "Popular justice" and "Vigilance . . ." in index.

3288. Rummell, Helen. "When Eleven Were Lynched." FRONTIER TIMES [Bandera, TX], Vol. 7, No. 10 (July 1930): 449-51. People of McDade, Texas, hanged six outlaws on Christmas Eve, 1885, then hanged two more. On Christmas Day, three more were killed in a gun fight. [Compare articles by Luckett P. Bishop, Sr., Frontier Times (June-July 1965), G. K. Martin, Old West (Spring 1969), and T. U. Taylor, Frontier Times (May 1939).]

3289. Russailh, Albert Benard de. LAST ADVENTURE: SAN FRANCISCO IN 1851. Trans. by Clarkson Crane. San Francisco: Westgate Press, 1931.

3290. Russell, Sharman Apt. "Russian Bill: The True Story of an Outlaw." JOURNAL OF THE WEST, Vol. 23, No. 2 (April 1984): 91-93. Story of lynching in Shakespeare, New Mexico, Sept., 1881, of Russian Bill and Sandy King, the latter having been convicted of "being a damned nuisance."

3291. Sanders, Helen Fitzgerald. A HISTORY OF MONTANA. 3 vols.; Chicago and New York: Lewis, 1913. See Volume 1, Chapter XI, for road agents, flour riots in Virginia City in 1865, and vigilantes; see Chapters XII and XIII for outlaws and vigilantes. Volumes 2 and 3: short biographies.

3292. Schelle, Don. "Necktie Party, Arizona Style." REAL WEST [Derby, CT], Vol. 6, No. 28 (March 1963): 14-16, 44-45. Committee of Public Safety lynched four murderers in Tucson, Aug. 1873.

3293. Scherer, James A. B. "THE LION OF THE VIGILANTES": WILLIAM T. COLEMAN AND THE LIFE OF OLD SAN FRANCISCO. Indianapolis and New York: Bobbs-Merrill, 1939. In addition to committees of 1851 and 1856, includes revival of committee in 1877 and action against anti-Chinese rioters (see Chapter 8).

3294. Schlesinger, Andrew Bancroft. "Las Gorras Blancas, 1889-1891." THE JOURNAL OF MEXICAN AMERICAN HISTORY, Vol. 1, No. 2 (Spring 1971): 87-143. Mexican-American vigilantes protected "native" rights to certain land in New Mexico.

3295. Schuessler, Raymond. "Judge Rope: Vigilantes Of The Old West." REAL WEST [Derby, CT], Vol. 12, No. 75 (Oct. 1969): 32-34.   Various incidents. Includes photos of lynchings of John Heith [sic] at Tombstone, Arizona, and Miller, et al., at Ada, Oklahoma.

3296. Seagraves, Anne. "JUANITA, First Woman Lynched in California." In WOMEN OF THE SIERRA, pp. 29-33 (with illustration on p. 28). 3d (revised) printing; Hayden, ID: Wesanne Publications, 1992.

3297. Secrest, William. "39 Lashes for Stealing." TRUE FRONTIER [Valley Stream, NY], Vol. 4, No. 1 (Jan. 1971): 26-27, 49-50, 52, 54.   Corporal punishment and lynching in gold-rush California.

3298. Secrest, William B. "Fire-Eater: The Saga of Will Hicks Graham." TRUE WEST, Vol. 38, No. 5 (May 1991): 14-21.   Duel between Graham and William Walker (the filibusterer), San Francisco, Jan. 12, 1851. Also deals with San Francisco vigilantes.

3299. Secrest, William B. JUANITA: THE ONLY WOMAN LYNCHED IN THE GOLD RUSH DAYS. Fresno, CA: Saga-West, 1967.

3300. Secrest, William B. "The Mayor of Old Los Angeles." OLD WEST [Austin, TX], Vol. 2, No. 3, Whole No. 7 (Spring 1966): 30-32, 80-81. Mayor Foster resigned as mayor to help lynch Dave Brown, 1855 (p. 81).

3301. Secrest, William B. "Revenge of Rancheria." FRONTIER TIMES [Austin, TX], Vol. 42, No. 5, New Series No. 55 (Aug.-Sept. 1968): 16-19, 59-61.   After Mexicans attacked town of Rancheria, California, 1855, and killed several people, Anglos retaliated with lynching and destruction.

3302. Senkewicz, Robert M.   VIGILANTES IN GOLD RUSH SAN FRANCISCO. Stanford, CA: Stanford Univ. Press, 1985.   Both committees.

3303. Senkewicz, Robert M. "'The Inflation of an Overdone Business': The Economic Origins of San Francisco Vigilantes." THE PACIFIC HISTORIAN, Vol. 23, No. 3 (Fall 1979): 63-75.   Vigilantes of 1856.

3304. Senkewicz, Robert M. "Religion and Non-Partisan Politics in Gold Rush San Francisco." SOUTHERN CALIFORNIA QUARTERLY, Vol. 61, No. 4 (Winter 1979): 351-78.   Examines composition and strategies of 1856 Vigilance Committee.

3305. Senkewicz, Robert Michael. "Business and Politics in Gold Rush San Francisco, 1851-1856." Ph.D. diss., Stanford Univ., 1974.   See Diss. Ab.

Intl., Vol. 35, No. 3 (Sept. 1974): 1605A-1606A.   Analyzes vigilantism in San Francisco as part of an attack by economically hard-pressed businessmen on outside adversaries.

3306. Shannon, Dan [sic]. "When Lucky Bill Wasn't Lucky." REAL WEST [Derby, CT], Vol. 6, No. 28 (March 1963): 30-31, 45-47.   Lynching of William Jefferson Torrington, Carson City, Nevada, May 1859.

3307. Shannon, Don [sic]. "How Lanky Bill Joined the Vigilantes." THE WEST [New York], Vol. 1, No. 3 (July 1964): 37, 59-60.   He was lynched at Benton, Montana Territory, 1868.

3308. Shannon, Ed. "The Thirty-Ninth Hanging." WESTERN FRONTIER [Rockville Centre, NY], [no vol. # or issue #] (Aug. 1985): 32-33, 54-55. In 1862, 38 Indians were legally hanged at one time at Mankato, Minnesota. In 1865, John Campbell was lynched in Mankato.

3309. "Sherman and the San Francisco Vigilantes. Unpublished Letters of General W. T. Sherman." THE CENTURY MAGAZINE, Vol. 43 (New Series, Vol. XXI), No. 2 (Dec. 1891): 296-309.   Letters written in 1856.

3310. Shirley, Glenn.   THE FIGHTING MARLOWS: MEN WHO WOULDN'T BE LYNCHED. Fort Worth: Texas Christian Univ. Press, 1994.   Lynching attempt against brothers in jail, Graham, Texas, 1889. Two days later two brothers were killed in ambush near Graham while prisoners. Other brothers escaped but were later caught. Fictionalized in movie The Sons of Katie Elder.

3311. Shirley, Glenn. "Wild Willie and His Terrible Forty." OLD WEST [Stillwater, OK], Vol. 25, No. 2, Whole No. 98 (Winter 1988): 14-20. William Coe was lynched at Pueblo, Colorado, 1868.   Also mentions lynching of 11 members of Coe's gang in No Man's Land (present panhandle of Oklahoma) in 1868.

3312. Shull, Charles W., ed. "Minutes of Vigilance Committee, Florence, Nebraska, May 29-July 30, 1857." NEBRASKA HISTORY, Vol. 58, No. 1 (Spring 1977): 72-87.

3313. Shulsinger, Stephanie C. "Coleman of the Vigilantes." REAL WEST [Derby, CT], Vol. 15, No. 106 (Aug. 1972): 46-52, 80.

3314. Shulsinger, Stephanie C.   "The Spirit of the Vigilantes." REAL WEST [Derby, CT], Vol. 15, No. 107 (Sept. 1972): 46-49, 69, 71-74, 78. Deals with western U.S., 1850s-1870s, especially California and Montana. Traces American vigilantism back to the Mayflower Compact. Describes

George Washington as a "vigilante leader."

3315. Silliman, Lee.   "1870: To The Hangman's Tree: Helena's Last Vigilante Execution." MONTANA, THE MAGAZINE OF WESTERN HISTORY, Vol. 28, No. 4 (Autumn 1978): 50-57.

3316. Simmonds, A. J.   "Cause of Death--Lynching."   THE WEST [Rockville Centre, NY], Vol. 17, No. 6 (Jan. 1974): 26-27, 48.   Victim: Charles Benson. Logan, Utah Territory; Feb. 1873.

3317. Simmonds, A. J. "Chinaman's Chance." REAL WEST [Derby, CT], Vol. 15, No. 109 (Nov. 1972): 46-49.   Lynching of man named Ah Sing by mistake at Corinne, Utah Territory, 1874.

3318. Siringo, Charles.   RIATA AND SPURS: THE STORY OF A LIFETIME SPENT IN THE SADDLE AS COWBOY AND RANGER. Rev. ed.; Boston and New York: Houghton Mifflin, 1927.   See pp. 206-13 in Chapter XVI for Marlow brothers; Texas, 1889. See pp. 214-18 (Chapter XVII) for Jim Miller and his lynching; Ada, Oklahoma, 1909.

3319. Siwinski, Sherry A. "'The Devil's Best Doings Yet!'" OLD WEST [Stillwater, OK], Vol. 28, No. 3, Whole No. 111 (Spring 1992): 52-56. Includes lynching of Nicholas Foley; Nebraska, 1889.

3320. Slotkin, Richard. "Apotheosis of the Lynching: The Political Uses of Symbolic Violence." WESTERN LEGAL HISTORY: THE JOURNAL OF THE NINTH JUDICIAL CIRCUIT HISTORICAL SOCIETY, Vol. 6, No. 1 (Winter/Spring 1993), pp. 1-15.   Adapted from Slotkin's book Gunfighter Nation: The Myth of the Frontier in Twentieth Century America (1992).

3321. Smith, Frank Meriweather, ed. SAN FRANCISCO VIGILANCE COMMITTEE OF '56, WITH SOME INTERESTING SKETCHES OF EVENTS SUCCEEDING 1846. San Francisco: Barry, Baird & Co., 1883.

3322. Smith, Joe Heflin.   "Slade of the Overland."   GOLDEN WEST [Freeport, NY], Vol. 3, No. 5 (July 1967): 32-33, 48-50.   He was lynched at Virginia City, Montana [Idaho Territory].

3323. Smurr, J. W. "Afterthoughts on the Vigilantes." MONTANA, THE MAGAZINE OF WESTERN HISTORY, Vol. 8, No. 2 (April 1958): 8-20.

3324. Sonnichsen, C. L. "Justice After Dark." TRUE WEST [Austin, TX], Vol. 13, No. 3, Whole No. 73 (Jan.-Feb. 1966): 18-20, 57-58. Vigilantism, lynching, and a feud in Texas, 1878. From the author's book I'll Die Before I'll Run.

3325. Soulé, Frank; Gihon, John H.; and Nisbet, James. THE ANNALS OF SAN FRANCISCO; CONTAINING A SUMMARY OF THE HISTORY OF THE FIRST DISCOVERY, SETTLEMENT, PROGRESS, AND PRESENT CONDITION OF CALIFORNIA, AND A COMPLETE HISTORY OF ALL THE IMPORTANT EVENTS CONNECTED WITH ITS GREAT CITY: TO WHICH ARE ADDED, BIOGRAPHICAL MEMOIRS OF SOME PROMINENT CITIZENS. New York: D. Appleton & Co., 1855.   See pp. 308-10, 314-21, 339-40, 350-53, 390, 553-61 ("The Hounds"), and 562-87 ("The Vigilance Committee").

3326. Stevens, Herbert. VIGILANTES RIDE IN 1882. Fairfield, WA: Ye Galleon Press, 1975.   Lynching of Neil Oldie in Washington Territory.

3327. Stewart, George R. COMMITTEE OF VIGILANCE: REVOLUTION IN SAN FRANCISCO, 1851: AN ACCOUNT OF THE HUNDRED DAYS WHEN CERTAIN CITIZENS UNDERTOOK THE SUPPRESSION OF THE CRIMINAL ACTIVITIES OF THE SYDNEY DUCKS. Boston: Houghton Mifflin, 1964.

3328. Stimmel, Thomas. "The Miners Hanged Juanita." FRONTIER TIMES [Austin, TX], Vol. 38, No. 4, New Series No. 30 (June-July 1964): 23, 71-72.   Downieville, California, 1851.

3329. Strickler, Carolyn. "The Noose About Dave Brown." WESTWAYS, Vol. 69, No. 6 (June 1977): 28-31, 80.   An 1855 lynching in Los Angeles. Mayor Foster resigned so he could lead the lynch mob.

3330. Stuart, Granville. FORTY YEARS ON THE FRONTIER . . . Paul C. Phillips, ed. 2 vols.; Cleveland: Arthur H. Clark, 1925.   See chapter on "Cattle Rustlers and Vigilantes" in Vol. 2.

3331. Swan, Oliver, G., ed. FRONTIER DAYS. Philadelphia: Macrae Smith, 1928; New York: Grosset & Dunlap, 1928.

3332. Swanson, Budington. "The Lynching of a Lady." REAL WEST [Derby, CT], Vol. 19, No. 144 (March 1976): 8-11, 62.   Elizabeth Taylor and her brother Tom Jones, in Nebraska, 1885.

3333. Taylor, Nat M. "Story of the Marlow Boys." TRUE WEST [Austin, TX], Vol. 9, No. 3, Whole No. 49 (Jan.-Feb. 1962): 32-33, 68-69.   Subtitle: "Handcuffed and manacled, four brothers defied the mob intent upon their lynching . . ." Texas, 1889.

3334. Taylor, T. U. "In and Around Old McDade." FRONTIER TIMES [Bandera, TX], Vol. 16, No. 7 [sic; should be No. 8] (May 1939): 342-49.

Wade Alsup, John Kuykendall, Young Floyd, and Beck Scott were hanged in Lee County, Texas, June 1877. About 1880 stockmen shot two men (Turner and Crow) to death. On Dec. 24, 1883, members of league for law and order lynched Thad McLemore, Wright McLemore, and Henry Pfeiffer near McDade, Bastrop County. Christmas Day gun battle in McDade left two men dead.

3335. Terry, David S., defendant. TRIAL OF DAVID S. TERRY BY THE COMMITTEE OF VIGILANCE, SAN FRANCISCO. San Francisco: Whitten, Towne & Co., 1856.   Terry was charged with violence against some citizens and some members of the Committee of Vigilance.

3336. Thompson, Francis M. "Reminiscences of Four Score Years." THE MASSACHUSETTS MAGAZINE, Supplement to Vol. 5 (1912): 122-67; Vol. 6, No. 1 (Jan. 1913): 28-45; Vol. 6, No. 2 (April 1913): 63-81; Vol. 6, No. 3 (July 1913): 99-124; Vol. 6, No. 4 (Oct. 1913): 159-90; Vol. 7, No. 1 (Jan. 1914): 11-31; Vol. 7, No. 2 (April 1914): 85-94; Vol. 7, No. 3 (July 1914): 129-36; Vol. 8, No. 1 (Jan. 1915): 15-22.   See Vol. 6, p. 65, for lynching of C. W. Spillman near Deer Lodge [MT], 1862. See Vol. 6, pp. 116-17, for Henry Plummer and a sightseeing trip in 1863, and p. 118 for Plummer's marriage, and pp. 123, 124, for Plummer. See Vol. 6, pp. 159-61, for Plummer. See Vol. 6, pp. 162-90, for Chapter V, "The Vigilantes and the Road Agents", which is concluded in Vol. 7, pp. 11-13, about Plummer, etc., in Bannack, Virginia City area, 1863-1864.

3337. Thompson, George A. "Railroad Ride to a Hanging." FRONTIER TIMES [Austin, TX], Vol. 47, No. 6, New Series No. 86 (Oct.-Nov. 1973): 39-40.   "Black Jack" Murphy was lynched at Park City, Utah, 1883.

3338. "Throat Trouble." THE AMERICAN WEST, Vol. 7, No. 1 (Jan. 1970): 22-23.   Lynching text and two photos of the lynching of three men near Russell, Kansas, in 1894.

3339. Tibbets, Robin. "'Don't Cross That Line.'" FRONTIER TIMES [Austin, TX], Vol. 38, No. 6, New Series No. 32 (Oct.-Nov. 1964): 41, 64. Sheriff William Z. Cozens thwarted Colorado lynch mob, 1863.

3340. Tilford, Van W. "Print Olive's Special Ticket To Hell." FRONTIER TIMES [Austin, TX], Vol. 35, No. 1, New Series No. 13 (Winter 1960): 20-21, 40-41.   Includes Nebraska lynching of Ami Ketchum and Luther Mitchell, 1878.

3341. Timmons, Herbert M. "When Cooper Wright Met the Mob." OLD WEST [Austin, TX], Vol. 1, No. 1 (Fall 1964): 26-27, 54.   Texas sheriff prevented a lynching, (1880s?).

3342. Tinnemann, Ethel May. "The Opposition to the San Francisco Vigilance Committee of 1856." M.A. thesis, Univ. of California, Berkeley, 1941.

3343. Torrez, Robert J. "The Man Who Was Hanged Twice." TRUE WEST, Vol. 36, No. 11 (Nov. 1989): 24-27. Theodore Baker was hanged by a lynch mob in Springer, New Mexico, in 1885, but survived, only to be legally hanged in 1887.

3344. Towle, Virginia Rowe. VIGILANTE WOMAN. South Brunswick, NJ: A. S. Barnes and Co., 1966. Lives of seven women of Virginia City and Bannack, Montana [sic; Idaho Territory], 1863-1864, who make the composite vigilante woman.

3345. Towne, Charles Wayland. "Ghost Towns of the Vigilantes." TRAVEL, Vol. 85, No. 3 (July 1945): 26-28, 33-34. Bannack, Virginia City, and Montana vigilantes of 1860s.

3346. Townshend, R. B. "A Trial by Lynch Law." THE NINETEENTH CENTURY, Vol. 32, No. 186 (Aug. 1892): 243-53. Vigilante lynching in Colorado. True story but names have been changed. No date given.

3347. Traywick, Ben T. "Lynch Law of the Mother Lode." GOLDEN WEST [Freeport, NY], Vol. 1, No. 2 (Jan. 1965): 8, 44-45.

3348. Treece, Paul Robert. "Mr. Montana: The Life of Granville Stuart, 1834-1918." 2 vols; Ph.D. diss., Ohio State U., 1974. See Diss. Ab. Intl., Vol. 35, No. 8 (Feb. 1975): 5325A.

3349. "The Trial of Charles Cora for the Murder of William H. Richardson, San Francisco, California, 1856." In AMERICAN STATE TRIALS, Vol. 15, pp. 16-54. Ed. by John D. Lawson. 17 vols.; St. Louis: F. H. Thomas Law Book Co., 1914-1936 [this vol.: 1926].

3350. TRIAL OF DAVID S. TERRY BY THE COMMITTEE OF VIGILANCE, SAN FRANCISCO. San Francisco: R. C. Moore & Co., 1856. See also Terry, David S.

3351. "The Trial of James P. Casey for the Murder of James King of William, and the Trial of Charles Cora for the Murder of William H. Richardson by the Second Vigilance Committee, San Francisco, California, 1856." In AMERICAN STATE TRIALS, Vol. 15, pp. 97-124. Ed. by John D. Lawson. 17 vols.; St. Louis: F. H. Thomas Law Book Co., 1914-1936 [this vol.: 1926].

3352. "The Trial of Various Criminals by the First Vigilance Committee, San Francisco, California, 1851." In AMERICAN STATE TRIALS, Vol. 15, pp. 1-15. Ed. by John D. Lawson. 17 vols.; St. Louis: F. H. Thomas Law Book Co., 1914-1936 [this vol.: 1926].

3353. "The Trial of Various Criminals by the Second Vigilance Committee, San Francisco, California, 1856." In AMERICAN STATE TRIALS, Vol. 15, pp. 55-96. Ed. by John D. Lawson. 17 vols.; St. Louis: F. H. Thomas Law Book Co., 1914-1936 [this vol.: 1926].

3354. Tuolumne Courier, Sonora, Calif. FULL PARTICULARS OF THE WATER CELEBRATION, ORATION &C. -- ROBBERIES, MURDERS, TRIAL AND LYNCHING. Columbia [Courier print.?], 1858.   Yale Library Catalog. Two pages. Broadside.

3355. TWO ERAS IN THE LIFE OF THE FELON GROVENOR I. LAYTON. WHO WAS LYNCHED BY THE VIGILANCE COMMIT-TEE AT SONORA, . . . CALIFORNIA, JUNE 17TH, 1852 FOR ROB-BERY, MURDER, AND ARSON . . .   New Orleans; Philadelphia: A. R. Orton, 1853.

3356. Underwood, Larry. "Golden Justice." TRUE WEST, Vol. 37, No. 12 (Dec. 1990): 37-41.   Lynching of Sam Woodruff and Joe Seminole at Golden, Colorado, Dec. 27, 1879.

3357. U.S.   President.   MESSAGE OF THE PRESIDENT OF THE UNITED STATES, IN COMPLIANCE WITH A RESOLUTION OF THE SENATE OF THE 28TH ULTIMO, CALLING FOR INFORMATION RESPECTING ANY CORRESPONDENCE OR PROCEEDINGS IN RELATION TO THE SELF-STYLED VIGILANCE COMMITTEE IN CALIFORNIA. Sen. Ex. Doc. No. 101, 34th Cong., 1st Sess. (Aug. 6, 1856). Serial Set 824 (SENATE EXECUTIVE DOCUMENTS. Vol. 15).

3358. U.S. Secretary of War. REPORT OF THE SECRETARY OF WAR, COMMUNICATING, IN COMPLIANCE WITH A RESOLUTION OF THE SENATE, OF THE 2D INSTANT, CORRESPONDENCE IN RELATION TO THE PROCEEDINGS OF THE VIGILANCE COMMIT-TEE IN SAN FRANCISCO, CALIFORNIA. Sen. Ex. Doc. No. 43, 34th Cong., 3d Sess. (Feb. 10, 1857). Serial Set 881 (SENATE EXECUTIVE DOCUMENTS, Vol. 8).

3359. Valentine, Alan. VIGILANTE JUSTICE. New York: Reynal & Co., 1956. San Francisco committees, 1851 and 1856.

3360. Valentine, Alan. "Vigilante Justice." AMERICAN HERITAGE, Vol.

7, No. 2 (Feb. 1956): 72-95.   San Francisco, 1850s.   Condensed from Vigilante Justice.

3361. "The Vigilance Committee of 1856." THE OVERLAND MONTH- LY, Vol. 12, No. 2 (Feb. 1874): 105-16.   Largely consists of two letters (1868 and 1873) from William Tecumseh Sherman to Supreme Court Justice Stephen J. Field.

3362. "Vigilance in the Far West." ALL THE YEAR ROUND [London], Vol. 20, No. 479 (June 27, 1868): 60-65.   Bannack and Virginia City, Montana [sic; Idaho Territory].

3363. "The Vigilants in California." THE DIAL, Vol. 8, No. 89 (Sept. 1887): 101-02.   Review of H. H. Bancroft's writings in Popular Tribunals favoring vigilantism but criticizing lynch mobs.

3364. Walker, Jon Jeffrey.   "The Intellectual Grounding of the San Francisco Committee of Vigilance of 1851." M.A. thesis, Portland State Univ., 1993.   See Masters Abstracts Intl., Vol. 32, No. 1 (1994): 106.

3365. Walker, Wayne T. "Sand in His Craw." FRONTIER TIMES [Austin, TX], Vol. 37, No. 6, New Series No. 26 (Oct.-Nov. 1963): 13, 65.   Some information about John X. Beidler (Montana [sic] vigilante).

3366. Wallace, Alice Wright. "Eleven Limbs For Eleven Killers." OLD WEST [Austin, TX], Vol. 9, No. 1, Whole No. 33 (Fall 1972): 38-39, 45. Indians lynched 11 Mexicans near Pike's Peak, 1830s(?).

3367. Wallis, Mather C., and Wallis, Joan S., contributors. "The Court That Never Adjourned." In THE 1966 BRAND BOOK, pp. 256-76.   Ed. by William D. Powell. Denver: The Denver Westerners, 1967.   Lynching of John J. Hoover at Fairplay, Park County, Colorado, 1880.

3368. Warford, Sherrill. VERDICT, GUILTY AS CHARGED: LEAD- VILLE JUSTICE, 1879-1886. Leadville, CO: Warford, 1977.   Lynching.

3369. Warner, Frank W., ed. MONTANA TERRITORY. HISTORY AND BUSINESS DIRECTORY, 1879 . . . WITH A SKETCH OF THE VIGILANTES. Helena, MT: Fisk Bros., 1879.

3370. Watkins, George T., III. "Johnson County War." THE PACIFIC NORTHWESTERNER, Vol. 5, No. 2 (Spring 1961): 17-28.   Page 20: "It is hard to pick the first definitely related bit of violence . . . but most historians begin with the lynching of Ella Watson . . . and her paramour, Jim Averill."

3371. Weatherford, Anne. "Boone Helm." GREAT WEST [New York], Vol. 4, No. 4 (Dec. 1970): 12-15, 38-40.   Lynched at Virginia City, Montana [Idaho Territory], 1864.

3372. Webb, Grayce R. "Cow Country Vigilantes of 1884." THE WEST [Freeport, NY], Vol. 12, No. 5 (April 1970): 10-13, 50-54.   Montana.

3373. Webb, Grayce R. "X. Beidler--Man Without Fear." THE WEST [Rockville Centre, NY], Vol. 18, No. 1 (Aug. 1974): 32-33, 51-55. Montana [sic] vigilante.

3374. Webb, Harry E. "With a Noose Around Her Neck." WESTERNER [Encino, CA], Vol. 4, No. 3 (May-June 1972): 14-15, 58.   Revisionist information on Cattle Kate and Jim Averill, who were lynched in Wyoming, 1889.

3375. Webb, Stephen Palfrey. "A Sketch of the Causes, Operations and Results of the San Francisco Vigilance Committee in 1856." ESSEX INSTITUTE HISTORICAL COLLECTIONS, Vol. 84, No. 2 (April 1948): 96-130.   Written in 1874.

3376. West, Helen B. "Tragedy On the Teton: 1881. MONTANA, THE MAGAZINE OF WESTERN HISTORY, Vol. 12, No. 3 (July 1962): 21-33. Lynching of Brackett E. Stewart in Montana.

3377. "A Western View of Judge Lynch." THE AMERICAN, Vol. 3, No. 75 (Jan. 14, 1882): 215-16.   Necessity of vigilance committees in new mining towns.

3378. White, Nathan Longfellow. "The Hanging of Juanita." THE FAR-WESTERNER [Stockton Corral of Westerners], Vol. 1, No. 3 (July 1960): 1-12.   Woman lynched at Downieville, California, 1851.

3379. Wick, Julian Gerhard. "Lynch Law In North Dakota: An Impression." THE QUARTERLY JOURNAL OF THE UNIVERSITY OF NORTH DAKOTA, Vol. 22, No. 2 (Winter 1932): 117-22.   Reaction of some people to Bannon lynching (no date).

3380. Williams, Jean. THE LYNCHING OF ELIZABETH TAYLOR. Series of Western Americana, No. 11.   Santa Fe, NM: Press of the Territorian, 1966.   The hanging of Taylor and her brother Thomas Jones in Clay County, Nebraska, 1885.

3381. Williams, Mary Floyd. HISTORY OF THE SAN FRANCISCO COMMITTEE OF VIGILANCE OF 1851: A STUDY OF SOCIAL

CONTROL ON THE CALIFORNIA FRONTIER IN THE DAYS OF THE GOLD RUSH. Univ. of California Publications in History, Vol. 12. Berkeley: Univ. of California Press, 1921.

3382. Williams, Mary Floyd, ed. PAPERS OF THE SAN FRANCISCO COMMITTEE OF VIGILANCE OF 1851. III. MINUTES AND MISCEL-LANEOUS PAPERS FINANCIAL ACCOUNTS AND VOUCHERS. Publications of the Academy of Pacific Coast History, Vol. 4. Berkeley: Univ. of California, 1919.   See also Garnett, Porter.

3383. Williams, R. H. WITH THE BORDER RUFFIANS: MEMORIES OF THE FAR WEST, 1852-1868. Ed. by E. W. Williams. London: John Murray, 1907.   Lynching and vigilantism, passim (index is inadequate). For examples see pp. 180-82, 223-24, 297-98.

3384. Wilson, Paul E. "Law on the Frontier." THE TRAIL GUIDE, Vol. 5, No. 3 (Sept. 1960): 1-16.

3385. Wiltsey, Norman B. "Boone Helm, Man Beast Of The Frontier." REAL WEST [Derby, CT], Vol. 14, No. 99 (Dec. 1971): 32-34, 42-44. Lynched in Virginia City, Montana [Idaho Territory], 1864.

3386. Winslow, John J. "Hanging on the Teton." THE WEST [Freeport, NY], Vol. 4, No. 3 (Feb. 1966): 22-25, 57-58.   Brackett E. (Tom) Stewart was lynched near Choteau, Montana, 1881.

3387. Wolfe, George D. "Curtains for Big Nose George." TRUE WEST [Austin, TX], Vol. 8, No. 4, Whole No. 44 (March-April 1961): 18-19, 50-52. He was lynched at Rawlins, Wyoming, 1881.   Article also tells about lynching of Dutch Charlie Burris at Carbon, Wyoming, 1879.

3388. Wood, William P. "The Committee of Vigilance: Justice and the legal order." CALIFORNIA STATE BAR JOURNAL, Vol. 53, No. 3 (May/June 1978): 154-59.   San Francisco committee, 1851.

3389. Woolsey, Ronald C. "L.A. Law: 1856 Vigilante Wars." TRUE WEST [Stillwater, OK], Vol. 41, No. 12, Whole No. 320 (Dec. 1994): 19-25. Influence of San Francisco vigilantes and killing of Antonio Ruis led to ethnic clashes in Los Angeles and 1857 lynching of 13 Mexican bandits.

3390. Wooster, Robert. "'The Whole Company Have Done It': The U.S. Army and the Fort Davis Murder of 1860." JOURNAL OF THE WEST, Vol. 32, No. 2 (April 1993): 19-28.   Soldiers in Texas lynched a civilian.

3391. Wright, James A.   "The Last Frontier Vigilance Committee."

FRONTIER TIMES [Bandera, TX], Vol. 12, No. 9 (June 1935): 408-09. Just last one in Texas. Fairview, Wilson County, 1860s-1870s.

3392. X. BEIDLER: VIGILANTE. Ed. by Helen Fitzgerald Sanders in collaboration with William H. Bertsche, Jr. Norman: Univ. of Oklahoma Press, 1957.   Montana [sic; Idaho Territory], 1860s.

3393. Yost, Genevieve. "History of Lynchings in Kansas." THE KANSAS HISTORICAL QUARTERLY, Vol. 2, No. 2 (May 1933): 182-219.

3394. Yost, Nellie Snyder. "The Olive Story." TRUE WEST, Vol. 37, No. 5 (May 1990): 30-32, 37-39.   Print Olive and the lynching of Mitchell and Ketchum in Nebraska, 1878.

3395. Young, Jon. "Katie Was A Lady." REAL WEST [Derby, CT], Vol. 4, No. 18 (July 1961): 32-33, 61-63.   Ella Watson (also known as Cattle Kate) was lynched with Jim Averill in Wyoming, 1889.

3396. Zamonski, Stanley W. "When the Stranglers Ruled Denver." THE DENVER WESTERNERS MONTHLY ROUNDUP, Vol. 38, No. 5 (Sept.-Oct. 1982): 3-14. Reprinted in Wild West [Leesburg, VA], Vol. 4, No. 4 (Dec. 1991): 46-53.   Vigilance Committee, 1860. See p. 49 for photo of Sanford S. C. Dugan (or Dougan), lynched in 1868.

3397. Zarbin, Earl. "'The Whole Was Done So Quietly': The Phoenix Lynchings of 1879." THE JOURNAL OF ARIZONA HISTORY, Vol. 21, No. 4 (Winter, 1980): 353-62.

3398. Zincke, F. Barham. "Lynch Law." THE LEISURE HOUR [London], No. 913 (June 26, 1869 [sic; June 1, 1869]): 416.   Justifies lynching in Denver and other parts of the West.

VII

Anti-Lynching (Bills, Laws, Organizations, and Leaders)

3399. "Act Against Lynching." THE MISSIONARY REVIEW OF THE WORLD, Vol., 58, No. 6 (June 1935): 306. Mainly verbatim copy of recent statement of Commission on Interracial Cooperation in favor of a federal anti-lynching bill.

3400. Addams, Jane. "Respect for Law." THE INDEPENDENT, Vol. 53, No. 2718 (Jan. 3, 1901): 18-20. Anti-lynching.

3401. Addams, Jane, and Wells, Ida B. LYNCHING AND RAPE: AN EXCHANGE OF VIEWS. Ed. by Bettina Aptheker. Occasional Paper No. 25 [AIMS]. New York: Institute of Marxist Studies, 1977. Includes "Introduction" (pp. 1-21); Jane Addams, "Respect for Law" (pp. 22-27; from The Independent, Jan. 3, 1901); Ida B. Wells Barnett, "Lynching and the Excuse for It" (pp. 28-34; from The Independent, May 16, 1901); "Reference Notes" [to the "Introduction"] (pp. 35-39).

3402. "Address to the Nation: An Appeal against Mob Violence Signed by Hundreds of Well-Known Citizens." THE SURVEY, Vol. 42, No. 18 (Aug. 2, 1919): 675. Anti-lynching.

3403. "Again, Mr. Howard." THE CRISIS, Vol. 25, No. 4 (Feb. 1923): 154. Defeat of Dyer Bill.

3404. "Against Lynching." THE COMMONWEAL, Vol. 17, No. 25 (April 19, 1933): 675-76. Praise for Association of Southern Women for the Prevention of Lynching.

3405. "Against Lynching." THE COMMONWEAL, Vol. 26, No. 1 (April 30, 1937): 17. Duck Hill, Mississippi, double lynching gave boost to Gavagan anti-lynching bill.

3406. "All About the Dyer Bill." THE CRISIS, Vol. 23, No. 6 (April 1992): 276-77.

3407. "All Honor to the Women of Georgia!" THE CHRISTIAN CENTURY, Vol. 48, No. 4 (Jan. 28, 1931): 123.   Georgia Association of Women for the Prevention of Lynching.

3408. "Along the Color Line: America: Lynching." THE CRISIS, Vol. 40, No. 11 (Nov. 1933): 257.   One-sentence report of anti-lynching conference held in Birmingham, Alabama, in September.

3409. American Civil Liberties Union.   HOW GOES THE BILL OF RIGHTS? THE STORY OF THE FIGHT FOR CIVIL LIBERTY, 1935-36. New York: American Civil Liberties Union, 1936.   See "Mob Violence and Lynching," pp. 29-31.

3410. American Civil Liberties Union.   MOB VIOLENCE IN THE UNITED STATES: THE STRIKING FACTS IN BRIEF PRESENTED BY THE AMERICAN CIVIL LIBERTIES UNION.   New York: A.C.L.U., 1923.   Four pages.

3411. American Crusade to End Lynching.   SHALL THIS BE THE SYMBOL OF AMERICAN LIBERTY? JOIN, AMERICAN CRUSADE TO END LYNCHING, NATIONAL PILGRIMAGE TO WASHINGTON, D.C., MONDAY, SEPTEMBER 23. Washington, DC: The Crusade, 1946.

3412. Ames, Jessie Daniel.   ASSOCIATION OF SOUTHERN WOMEN FOR THE PREVENTION OF LYNCHING: BEGINNING OF THE MOVEMENT.   Atlanta: Commission on Interracial Cooperation, 1932.

3413. Ames, Jessie Daniel. DEMOCRATIC PROCESSES AT WORK IN THE SOUTH: REPORT OF THE COMMISSION ON INTERRACIAL COOPERATION, INC., 1939-1941.   Atlanta: Commission on Interracial Cooperation, 1941.

3414. Ames, Jessie Daniel.   "Southern Women Against Lynching." CHRISTIAN INDEX, Vol 131 (Nov. 5, 1931): 647.

3415. Ames, Jessie Daniel.   SOUTHERN WOMEN AND LYNCHING. Atlanta: Association of Southern Women for the Prevention of Lynching, 1935.   Originally published in Crime Survey, Vol. 1, No. 1 (April 1935): 22-25.

3416. Ames, Jessie Daniel, and Newell, Bertha Payne.   "REPAIRERS OF THE BREACH": A STORY OF INTERRACIAL COOPERATION

BETWEEN SOUTHERN WOMEN, 1935-1940. Atlanta: Commission on Interracial Cooperation, 1940.

3417. "Anti-Lynch Bill Again Before Senate." INTERNATIONAL JURIDICAL ASSOCIATION MONTHLY BULLETIN, Vol. 8, No. 8 (Feb. 1940): 88.

3418. "Anti-Lynch Bill Up Before Senate." THE CATHOLIC WORKER, Vol. 1, No. 9 (March 1, 1934): 1.

3419. "Anti-Lynch Bill: Wire Your Congressman." THE CRISIS, Vol. 41, No. 3 (March 1934): 66. Costigan-Wagner bill.

3420. "Anti-Lynch Fight: Filibuster Continues in Face of Closure [sic] Threats." NEWSWEEK, Vol. 11, No. 5 (Jan. 31, 1938): 13-14.

3421. "Anti-Lynch Law Is Effective Threat." THE CATHOLIC WORKER, Vol. 2, No. 10 (March 1935): 4.

3422. "Anti-Lynching." THE CONGRESSIONAL DIGEST, Vol. 16, No. 5 (May 1937): 131. In section titled "Major Legislation Moves Forward." House of Representatives passed Gavagan bill.

3423. "Anti-Lynching." THE CONGRESSIONAL DIGEST, Vol. 17, No. 2 (Feb. 1938): 35. Status and provisions of bill passed by House and now in Senate.

3424. "Anti-Lynching." THE CONGRESSIONAL DIGEST, Vol. 17, No. 4 (April 1938): 98.

3425. "The Anti-lynching bill." AMERICA, Vol. 58, No 14 (Jan. 8, 1938): 326.

3426. "The Anti-lynching bill." AMERICA, Vol. 58, No. 17 (Jan. 29, 1938): 398.

3427. "The Anti-Lynching Bill." THE CRISIS, Vol. 26, No. 2 (June 1923): 67-68. Representative Dyer's tour in support of his bill.

3428. "Anti-Lynching Bill." THE CRISIS, Vol. 31, No. 5 (March 1926): 230. Revised Dyer Bill.

3429. "Anti-Lynching Bill." THE CRISIS, Vol. 41, No. 9 (Sept. 1934): 276. Costigan-Wagner bill.

3430. "Anti-Lynching Bill." INTERRACIAL REVIEW, Vol. 8, No. 9 (Sept. 1935): 132-33.   Editorial in favor of the bill.

3431. "The Anti-Lynching Bill." INTERRACIAL REVIEW, Vol. 10, No. 3 (March 1937): 36-37.   Reprint of editorial in America, Feb. 20, 1937.

3432. "The Anti-Lynching Bill." INTERRACIAL REVIEW, Vol. 13, No. 4 (April 1940): 51-52.   Editorial.

3433. "The Anti-Lynching Bill." THE NATION, Vol. 114, No. 2970 (June 7, 1922): 664.   Examines arguments against the Dyer Bill.

3434. "The Anti-Lynching Bill Again Haunts Congress." THE UNITED STATES NEWS. [Later U.S. News & World Report.] [Washington, DC] Vol. 4, No. 20 (May 18, 1936): 5.

3435. "Anti-Lynching Bill Again Postponed." INTERNATIONAL JURIDI-CAL ASSOCIATION MONTHLY BULLETIN, Vol. 6, No. 3 (Sept. 1937): 32.

3436. "Anti-Lynching Bill Approved by House." SCHOLASTIC, Vol. 30, No. 12 (May 1, 1937): 33-34.

3437. "Anti-lynching Bill Endangered." THE CRISIS, Vol. 44, No. 4 (April 1937): 113.   Editorial.

3438. "Anti-Lynching Bill Goes to Senate." THE CRISIS, Vol. 44, No. 5 (May 1937): 138-40.

3439. "Anti-Lynching Bill in West Virginia." THE CRISIS, Vol. 22, No. 2 (June 1921): 67.   A two-paragraph item.   Bill passed in West Virginia legislature.

3440. "Anti-Lynching Bill Introduced Again In Senate." INTERRACIAL REVIEW, Vol. 10, No. 3 (March 1937): 47.

3441. "Anti-Lynching Bill Laid Aside." INTERNATIONAL JURIDICAL ASSOCIATION MONTHLY BULLETIN, Vol. 3, No. 12 (May 1935): 2.

3442. "Anti-Lynching Bill Likely To Be Passed."   INTERRACIAL REVIEW, Vol. 10, No. 9 (Sept. 1937): 143.   From New York Amsterdam News.

3443. "Anti-Lynching Bill on Senate Calendar Next Session." THE CRISIS, Vol. 44, No. 9 (Sept. 1937): 278-80.

3444. "Anti-Lynching Bill Reveals Sectional Differences." THE CHRISTIAN CENTURY, Vol. 54, No. 48 (Dec. 1, 1937): 1477.

3445. "Anti-Lynching Bill Shelved." INTERNATIONAL JURIDICAL ASSOCIATION MONTHLY BULLETIN, Vol. 7, No. 2 (Aug. 1938): 16-17. Includes lynching of Tom Green, black, at Rolling Fork, Mississippi, and John Dukes, black, in Arabi, Georgia.

3446. "Anti-Lynching Bill Still An Issue." THE CHRISTIAN CENTURY, Vol. 53, No. 32 (Aug. 5, 1936): 1052.

3447. "The Anti-Lynching Campaign." THE CHAUTAUQUAN, Vol. 38, No. 2 (Oct. 1903): 111-12.

3448. "The Anti-Lynching Conference." THE CRISIS, Vol. 18, No. 2 (June 1919): 92.

3449. "Anti-Lynching Conference, May 5-6." THE CRISIS, Vol. 18, No. 1 (May 1919): 23-24.

3450. "The Anti-Lynching Crusade." THE LITERARY DIGEST, Vol. 9, No. 19 (Sept. 8, 1894): 4-5 (544-45). Newspaper comments on activities of Ida B. Wells. Also, resolution for Congressional investigation.

3451. "An Anti-Lynching Crusade in America Begun." THE LITERARY DIGEST, Vol. 9, No. 15 (Aug. 11, 1894): 1-2 (421-22). Comments from Ida B. Wells and various newspapers.

3452. "The Anti-Lynching Crusaders." THE CRISIS, Vol. 25, No. 1 (Nov. 1922): 8. Effort to "unite a million women to stop lynching."

3453. "Anti-Lynching Crusaders." THE CRISIS, Vol. 42, No. 6 (June 1935): 176. Portraits and brief text on Senate Costigan and Representative Wagner.

3454. "Anti-Lynching Fund." THE CRISIS, Vol. 12, No. 4 (Aug. 1916): 202. An ad placed by the NAACP to solicit funds.

3455. "The Anti-Lynching Fund." THE CRISIS, Vol. 12, No. 5 (Sept. 1916): 215. Editorial.

3456. "An Anti-lynching law." THE SIGN, Vol. 16, No. 10 (May 1937): 580-81. Gavagan bill. Editorial.

3457. "Anti-Lynching Legislation." THE CRISIS, Vol. 22, No. 1 (May

1921): 8-9.   This is part of the regular "Opinion" department written by W. E. B. DuBois.

3458. "Anti Lynching Legislation and Labor." THE MESSENGER, Vol. 4, No. 4 (April 1922): 385.   Dyer Anti-Lynching bill.

3459. "The Anti-Lynching Membership Drive of 1922." THE CRISIS, Vol. 24, No. 1 (May 1922): 22-24.

3460. "Anti-Lynching Movement Stressed."   FEDERAL COUNCIL BULLETIN, Vol. 17, No. 9 and 10 (Nov.-Dec. 1934): 18.

3461. "Anti-Lynching Work." THE CRISIS, Vol. 10, No. 1 (Nov. 1918): 19. Efforts of NAACP.

3462. "An appeal from the National Afro-American Council to set aside a day of fasting as a protest against lynching."   In CHRONICLES OF NEGRO PROTEST: A BACKGROUND BOOK FOR YOUNG PEOPLE DOCUMENTING THE HISTORY OF BLACK POWER, pp. 178-81. Ed. by Bradford Chambers.   New York: Parents' Magazine Press, 1968. Newspaper article from New York Tribune, May 4, 1899.

3463. Aptheker, Bettina.   WOMAN'S LEGACY: ESSAYS ON RACE, SEX, AND CLASS IN AMERICAN HISTORY.   Amherst U. of Mass. Press, 1982.   See Chapter 3 (pp. 53-76), "Woman Suffrage and the Crusade against Lynching"; especially about Ida B. Wells.

3464. "Association Does Not Support Federal Anti-Lynching Bill." THE SOUTHERN FRONTIER, Vol. 1, No. 2 (Feb. 1940): [p. 4].   Association of Southern Women for the Prevention of Lynching.

3465. Association of Southern Women for the Prevention of Lynching. ANNUAL BULLETIN (Jan. 1933).

3466. ___. ARE THE COURTS TO BLAME? Bulletin No. 3. Atlanta: Association of Southern Women for the Prevention of Lynching, 1934. Especially about 1933 lynchings.

3467. ___. "DEATH BY PARTIES UNKNOWN." Bulletin No. 6. [Atlanta?]: Association of Southern Women for the Prevention of Lynching, 1936.   Deals especially with 1935.

3468. ___. "FEELING IS TENSE." Bulletin No. 8. Atlanta: Association of Southern Women for the Prevention of Lynching, 1938.   Deals especially with 1937; but includes statistics and charts for 1882-1936. The

Association published a one-page flyer with same title in March 1940 about sheriffs and lynching.

3469. ___. "LYNCHING IS WHOLESALE MURDER." Bulletin No. 7. Atlanta: Association of Southern Women for the Prevention of Lynching, 1937.   Deals especially with 1936.

3470. ___. A LYNCHING THREATENS.   Atlanta: Association of Southern Women for the Prevention of Lynching, 1936.   What sheriffs should do to prevent lynchings. One page.

3471. ___. A NEW PUBLIC OPINION ON LYNCHING, A DECLARATION AND A PLEDGE. Atlanta: Association of Southern Women for the Prevention of Lynching, 1932.

3472. ___. ORGANIZATIONS COMMITTED TO A PROGRAM OF EDUCATION TO PREVENT LYNCHING.   Atlanta: Association of Southern Women for the Prevention of Lynching, 1941.

3473. ___. SOUTHERN WOMEN LOOK AT LYNCHING. Rev. ed.; Atlanta: Association of Southern Women for the Prevention of Lynching, 1938.   Originally published in 1937; "A review of the work of the Association . . . presented to the Central Council of the Association" (p. 3).

3474. ___. THIS BUSINESS OF LYNCHING. Bulletin No. 4. Atlanta: Association of Southern Women for the Prevention of Lynching, 1935. Deals especially with 1934.

3475. ___. WHAT IS THE ASSOCIATION OF SOUTHERN WOMEN FOR THE PREVENTION OF LYNCHING? Atlanta: Association of Southern Women for the Prevention of Lynching, 1936.   Brief flyer.

3476. ___. WHAT ONE WOMAN CAN DO TO PREVENT LYNCHINGS. Atlanta: Association of Southern Women for the Prevention of Lynching, 1936; reprinted 1938.   Brief flyer.

3477. ___. WHAT WE KNOW ABOUT LYNCHING--AND MOBS (1931-1935). Atlanta: Association of Southern Women for the Prevention of Lynching, [1936].   Brief flyer; based on The Mob Still Rides by Commission on Interracial Cooperation.

3478. ___. WHERE WERE THE POLICE OFFICERS?   Atlanta: Association of Southern Women for the Prevention of Lynching, 1937.

3479. ___. WHY WE LYNCH. Atlanta: Association of Southern Women for the Prevention of Lynching, 1932.

3480. ___. "WITH QUIETNESS THEY WORK." REPORT OF THE ACTIVITIES OF SOUTHERN WOMEN IN EDUCATION AGAINST LYNCHING DURING 1937. Atlanta: Association of Southern Women for the Prevention of Lynching, 1938.

3481. Bagnall, R. W. "Fighters or Cowards." THE CRISIS, Vol. 24, No. 1 (May 1922): 8.   Dyer Bill.

3482. Balthrope, Robin Bernice. "Lawlessness and the New Deal: Congress and Antilynching Legislation, 1934-1938." Ph.D. diss., Ohio State Univ., 1995.   See Diss. Ab. Intl., Vol. 56, No. 4 (Oct. 1995): 1494A.

3483. Barber, Henry E.   "The Association of Southern Women for the Prevention of Lynching, 1930-1942." PHYLON, Vol. 34, No. 4 (Dec. 1973): 378-89.

3484. Barber, Henry Eugene. "The Association of Southern Women for the Prevention of Lynching, 1930-1942." M.A. thesis, Univ. of Georgia, 1967.

3485. Barnard, Amii Larkin. "The Application of Critical Race Feminism to the Anti-Lynching Movement: Black Women's Fight Against Race and Gender Ideology, 1892-1920." UCLA WOMEN'S LAW JOURNAL, Vol. 3, No. 1 (Spring 1993): 1-38.

3486. Bederman, Gail.   "'Civilization,' the Decline of Middle-Class Manliness, and Ida B. Wells's Antilynching Campaign (1892-94)." RADICAL HISTORY REVIEW, Vol. 52 (Winter 1992): 4-30.

3487. Berson, Robin Kadison. MARCHING TO A DIFFERENT DRUMMER: UNRECOGNIZED HEROES OF AMERICAN HISTORY. Westport, CT: Greenwood Press, 1994.   See sections on Mary White Ovington, 1865-1951, "Civil Rights Activist," (pp. 234-42); and George Henry White, 1852-1918, "Civil Rights and Anti-lynching Activist," (pp. 303-12).

3488. "The Best of the Anti-Lynching Fights." THE CRISIS, Vol. 42, No. 6 (June 1935): 177.   An editorial on the Costigan-Wagner crusade. See also next editorial (ibid.) criticizing Senator Borah's hypocrisy on this issue.

3489. "'Bill for Promotion of Rape.'" THE CRISIS, Vol. 42, No. 2 (Feb. 1935): 48.   Editorial about a reference to the anti-lynching bill.

3490. "Bill H.R. 1. The Dyer Anti-Lynching Bill." THE CRISIS, Vol. 27, No. 4 (Feb. 1924): 164-65.

"Black's White." See "The Congress: Black's White."

3491. Blair, John L. "A Time for Parting: the Negro during the Coolidge Years." JOURNAL OF AMERICAN STUDIES, Vol. 3, No. 2 (Dec. 1969): 177-99.   Includes efforts for anti-lynching legislation, pp. 180-82.

3492. "Block the Filibuster!" INTERRACIAL REVIEW, Vol. 11, No. 10 (Oct. 1938): 147.   Editorial favoring anti-lynching bill.

3493. Borah, William E.   "Anti-Lynching Bill."   REPRESENTATIVE AMERICAN SPEECHES: 1937-1938 (New York: H. W. Wilson Co., 1938): 17-38; Vol. 11, No. 10 of THE REFERENCE SHELF.   Speech in U.S. Senate, Jan. 7, 1938; also in Congressional Record, Vol. 85, No. 5 (Jan. 7, 1938): 186-91.

3494. "Brief Summary of Anti-Lynching Work." THE CRISIS, Vol. 17, No. 4 (Feb. 1919): 182-84.   Deals with 1919.

3495. Brisbane, Robert Hughes, Jr.   "The Rise of Protest Movements Among Negroes Since 1900." Ph.D. diss., Harvard Univ., 1949.

3496. Brown, Ina Corinne.   "Hearing on the Costigan-Wagner Bill." WORLD OUTLOOK [Nashville], Vol. 24, No. 4 (April 1934): 21 (129), 34 (142).

3497. Brundage, Fitzhugh. "'To Howl Loudly': John Mitchell Jr. and his Campaign against Lynching in Virginia." THE CANADIAN REVIEW OF AMERICAN STUDIES, Vol. 22, No. 3 (Winter 1991): 325-41.   Mitchell was black and was editor of the Richmond Planet from 1884 to 1929.

3498. Burroughs, Nannie. LYNCHERS. District One for the Suppression of Lynching and Mob Violence, n.d.

3499. Burrows, Edward Flud. "The Commission on Interracial Cooperation, 1919-1944; A Case Study in the History of the Interracial Movement in the South." Ph.D. diss., Univ. of Wisconsin, 1954.   Includes account about Association of Southern Women for the Prevention of Lynching.

3500. Calvin, Floyd. "Catholic Anti-Lynching Fight." INTERRACIAL REVIEW, Vol. 10, No. 6 (June 1937): 91.

3501. "Candidates Queried on Federal Anti-Lynching Bill." INTERRACIAL REVIEW, Vol. 11, No. 10 (Oct. 1938): 160-61.

3502. Carr, Robert K. FEDERAL PROTECTION OF CIVIL RIGHTS:

QUEST FOR A SWORD. Ithaca: Cornell Univ. Press, 1947.   See "Lynching" in index.

3503. "Catholic Writer Asks Anti-Lynching Bill."   INTERRACIAL REVIEW, Vol. 10, No. 6 (June 1937): 93.   Brief.

3504. "Catholics and the Anti-Lynching Bill." INTERRACIAL REVIEW, Vol. 9, No. 9 (Sept. 1936): 131-32.

3505. "Catholics and the Anti-Lynching Fight." INTERRACIAL REVIEW, Vol. 10, No. 5 (May 1937): 69.

3506. "CAW Announces Anti-Lynching Campaign."   A MONTHLY SUMMARY OF EVENTS AND TRENDS IN RACE RELATIONS, Vol. 4, No. 4 (Nov. 1946): 113-14.   CAW = Congress of American Women.

3507. Celler, Emanuel.   [Remarks on Proposed Anti-Lynching Law.] CONGRESSIONAL DIGEST, Vol. 29, No. 2 (Feb. 1950): 62, 64.

3508. Chadbourn, James. "Open Court: Plan for Survey of Lynching and the Judicial Process." THE NORTH CAROLINA LAW REVIEW, Vol. 9 (April 1931): 330-36.   Study financed by Commission on Interracial Cooperation. Laws passed and laws still needed.

3509. Chadbourn, James H. LYNCHING AND THE LAW. Chapel Hill: Univ. of North Carolina Press, 1933.

3510. Chadbourn, James H. "Lynching and the Law." AMERICAN BAR ASSOCIATION JOURNAL, Vol. 20, No. 2 (Feb. 1934): 71-76. Based on his book of the same title.

3511. Chadbourn, James Harmon. "Analysis of Anti-Lynching Laws Now Existing in the States." In "The Pro and Con Feature: Congress Considers the Costingan-Wagner Anti-Lynching Bill." CONGRESSIONAL DIGEST, Vol. 14, No. 6-7 (June-July 1935): 167-68.   From Chadbourn's Lynching and the Law.

3512. "Child Labor and Lynching Legislation Advance." THE CHRISTIAN CENTURY, Vol. 54, No. 27 (July 7, 1937): 859.

3513. "Christian Front Editorial Urges Anti-Lynching Law."   INTER-RACIAL REVIEW, Vol. 9, No. 11 (Nov. 1936): 174.

3514. Cobb, Andrew J. "The Right to Live: Will the State Protect It or Must We Rely Upon Federal Authority?" THE GEORGIA HISTORICAL

QUARTERLY, Vol. 6, No. 3 (Sept. 1922): 189-96.   Examines whether a federal anti-lynching law would be desirable.

3515. "A Colored Legislator." THE CRISIS, Vol. 2, No. 2 (June 1911): 55. Edward D. Green, Illinois. His "Anti-Mob-Law" has won court approval. Provides punishment for lynchers and "delinquent sheriffs."

3516. "Combating Mobs: Campaign Against Lynching Dramatized by Banner on Fifth Avenue." THE LITERARY DIGEST, Vol. 122, No. 5 (Aug. 1, 1936): 32.

3517. Commission on Interracial Cooperation.   ASSOCIATION OF SOUTHERN WOMEN FOR THE PREVENTION OF LYNCHING: BEGINNING OF THE MOVEMENT. Atlanta: Commission on Interracial Cooperation, 1932.   Two-page pamphlet.

3518. "Congress and Lynching." AMERICA, Vol. 50, No. 17 (Jan. 27, 1934): 390.   Opposes Wagner bill.

3519. "Congress and Lynching." AMERICA, Vol. 52, No. 5 (Nov. 10, 1934): 99.   Announcement of change in editorial policy to favor federal intervention in a state to punish lynchers. Reason: state officials sometimes do not oppose lynching.

3520. "Congress and Lynching." INTERRACIAL REVIEW, Vol. 7, No. 12 (Dec. 1934): 145-46.   Reprint.

3521. "The Congress: Black's White." TIME, Vol. 31, No. 4 (Jan. 24, 1938): 8-10.   Anti-lynching bill in the Senate; Walter F. White (on this issue's cover).

3522. "Congress May Legislate under the Fourteenth Amendment to Punish Lynching." In BRIEF DRAWING, pp. 197-214. By Ralph Curtis Ringwalt. New York: Longmans, Green and Co., 1923.   Sample legal brief.

3523. "Congressman Dyer." THE CRISIS, Vol. 26, No. 5 (Sept. 1923): 218. Anti-lynching bill.

3524. "Congressman White Introduces the first Antilynching Bill."   In EYEWITNESS: THE NEGRO IN AMERICAN HISTORY, pp. 362-63. William Loren Katz. New York: Pitman Pub. Corp., 1967.   Two selections from The Congressional Record give different versions of events leading to lynching of [Sam] Hose in Georgia.

3525. "Constitutional Basis for Federal Anti-Lynching Legislation."

LAWYERS GUILD REVIEW, Vol. 6, No. 5 (Nov.-Dec. 1946): 643-47.

3526. "Constitutionality vs. Common Sense." THE CRISIS, Vol. 23, No. 5 (March 1922): 228-29.   Dyer Bill.

3527. "Contagious Lynching." AMERICA, Vol. 55, No. 21 (Aug. 29, 1936): 493-94.   Enactment of federal anti-lynching laws would help create public opinion against lynching.

3528. "Contributions to the Anti-Lynching Fund." THE CRISIS, Vol. 13, No. 1 (Nov. 1916): 16.

3529. "Contributions to the $10,000 Anti-Lynching Fund." THE CRISIS, Vol. 12, No. 5 (Sept. 1916): 219-20.   And an appeal for more contributions.

3530. Costigan, Edward P.   "Open and Boastful Anarchy."   THE CRISIS, Vol. 42, No. 3 (March 1935): 77-78.   A speech by the Colorado Senator in favor of the federal anti-lynching bill.

3531. [Costigan, Edward P.] PUBLIC OWNERSHIP OF GOVERNMENT: COLLECTED PAPERS OF EDWARD P. COSTIGAN.   New York: Vanguard Press, 1940.

3532. Cothran, Ben. "Ousting Judge Lynch." FORUM AND CENTURY, Vol. 98, No. 4 (Oct. 1937): 158-63.   Argues that anti-lynching laws are not the way to end lynchings.

3533. Crites, Laura Hardy.   "A History of the Association of Southern Women for Prevention of Lynching, 1930-1942." M.A. thesis, The American Univ., 1965.   See Masters Abstracts, Vol. 3, No. 3 (Sept. 1965), p. 7.

3534. Culley, John Joel. "Muted Trumpets: Four Efforts to Better Southern Race Relations, 1900-1919." Ph.D. diss., Univ. of Virginia, 1967.   See Diss. Ab., Vol. 28, No. 9 (March 1968): 3585A-3586A.   Four organizations: Southern Society For The Promotion of The Study of Race Conditions and Problems in The South (the Montgomery conference), Southern Sociological Congress, University Commission on Southern Race Questions, and Southern Publicity Committee.

3535. Dabney, Virginius. "Dixie Rejects Lynching." THE NATION, Vol. 145, No. 22 (Nov. 27, 1937): 579-80.   South seems to be reaching an acceptance of a federal anti-lynching law.

3536. Darcy, Sam.   "Fight on Lynching Moves Forward."   LABOR DEFENDER, Vol. 5, No. 12 (Dec. 1930): 251.   Anti-lynching sentiment at meeting of American Negro Labor Congress. Brief.

3537. "Defeat of Congressmen." THE CRISIS, Vol. 24, No. 6 (Oct. 1922): 264-65. Efforts to defeat Representatives who voted against the Dyer Bill.

3538. "Defense Campaigns Conducted By the I.L.D." EQUAL JUSTICE, Vol. 15, No. 3 (Winter 1941): 24-28. Briefly includes support for anti-lynching bill.

3539. "A Diminishing Crime." THE SATURDAY EVENING POST, Vol. 207, No. 51 (June 22, 1935): 22. No federal duty to deal with lynch mobs.

3540. "Do We Need an Antilynch Law?" COLLIER'S, Vol. 105, No. 6 (Feb. 10, 1940): 58.

3541. Dubay, Robert W. "Mississippi and the Proposed Federal Anti-Lynching Bills of 1937-1938." THE SOUTHERN QUARTERLY, Vol. 7, No. 1 (Oct. 1968): 73-89.

3542. Ducey, Mitchell F. THE COMMISSION ON INTERRACIAL COOPERATION PAPERS, 1919-1944 [,] AND THE ASSOCIATION OF SOUTHERN WOMEN FOR THE PREVENTION OF LYNCHING PAPERS, 1930-1942: A GUIDE TO THE MICROFILM EDITIONS. Ann Arbor, MI: University Microfilms International, 1984.

3543. Dudley, Julius Wayne. "A History of the Association of Southern Women for the Prevention of Lynching, 1930-1942. Ph.D. diss., Univ. of Cincinnati, 1979. See <u>Diss. Ab. Intl.</u>, Vol. 41, No 1 (July 1980): 367A-368A.

3544. Duffus, Robert L. "Counter-Mining the Ku Klux Klan." THE WORLD'S WORK, Vol. 46, No. 3 (July 1923): 275-84. Early history of Commission on Inter-racial [<u>sic</u>] Cooperation. Includes lynching (pp. 276-77, 280-81).

3545. Duster, Alfreda M., ed. CRUSADE FOR JUSTICE: THE AUTO-BIOGRAPHY OF IDA B. WELLS. Chicago: Univ. of Chicago Press, 1970. See "Lynchings" in index. [Duster was youngest daughter of Ida B. Wells.]

3546. "Dyer Anti-Lynching Bill." THE CRISIS, Vol. 25, No. 1 (Nov. 1922): 23-26.

3547. "Dyer Anti-Lynching Bill." THE CRISIS, Vol. 29 No. 5 (March 1925): 209-10.

"The Dyer Bill." See "All About the Dyer Bill," "Early Vote . . .," and "The Shame of a Nation."

3548-3555. "The Dyer Bill." THE CRISIS, Vol. 22, No. 5 (Sept. 1921): 212. The expected federal anti-lynching law. Other items with same title in this journal: Vol. 23, No. 3 (Jan. 1922): 114; Vol. 23, No. 4 (Feb. 1922): 179-80; Vol. 23, No. 6 (April 1922): 262-63; Vol. 24, No. 5 (Sept. 1922): 215-16; Vol. 24, No. 6 (Oct. 1922): 261-62, 264; Vol. 25, No. 3 (Jan. 1923): 118-19; Vol. 27, No. 3 (Jan. 1924): 123.

3556. "The Dyer Bill in the Senate." THE CRISIS, Vol. 23, No. 6 (April 1922): 248.

3557. "The Dyer Bill Is Ready--Will Negroes Act?" THE CRUSADER, Vol. 5, No. 3 (Nov. 1921): 18.

3558. "The Dyer Bill Moves Toward Passage." THE CRISIS, Vol. 28, No. 1 (May 1924): 22-23.

3559. "The Dyer-Johnson-Howard Triangle." THE MESSENGER, Vol. 5, No. 1 (Jan. 1923): 562-63.   Dyer anti-lynching has been bill defeated.

3560. Dyer, L. C., and Dyer, George C. "The Constitutionality of a Federal Anti-Lynching Bill." ST. LOUIS LAW REVIEW, Vol. 13, No. 3 (May 1928): 186-99.

3561. "Early Vote Expected on Dyer Bill." THE CRISIS, Vol. 23, No. 4 (Feb. 1922): 167.

3562. "Editorial Notes." OUR DAY, Vol. 9, No. 54 (June 1892): 458-60. Report of meeting of black citizens at Columbus, Ohio, with copy of anti-lynching resolution adopted.

3563. "Editorial of the Month." THE CRISIS, Vol. 42, No. 1 (Jan. 1935): 19.   St. Augustine, Florida, Record supports Wagner-Costigan bill.

3564. "Editorial of the Month: The Anti-Lynching Bill." INTERRACIAL REVIEW, Vol. 11, No. 1 (Jan. 1938): 17.   From Baltimore Catholic Review.

3565. "Editorial of the Week." INTERRACIAL REVIEW, Vol. 10, No. 5 (May 1937): 79.   Danville, Virginia, Register reverses itself and favors federal anti-lynching law because of blow-torch lynchings at Duck Hill, Mississippi.

3566. "Either Federal Action or Continued Lynching." THE CRISIS, Vol. 44, No. 1 (Jan. 1937): 17.   Editorial.

3567. Eleazer, R. B. "Southern Women Against the Mob." THE SOUTHERN WORKMAN, Vol. 60, No. 3 (March 1931): 126-31.   Two dozen women from states of the Old South met in Atlanta. They proclaimed that lynching "is not a defense of womanhood or of anything else" (p. 127).

3568. Ellis, Ann Wells. "The Commission on Interracial Cooperation, 1919-1944; Its Activities and Results." Ph.D. diss., Georgia State Univ., 1975. See Diss. Ab. Intl., Vol. 37, No. 2 (Aug. 1976): 1143A.   An anti-lynching campaign was one effort of the Commission.

3569. Ellis, Mark.   "Joel Spingarn's 'Constructive Programme' and the Wartime Antilynching Bill of 1918." JOURNAL OF POLICY HISTORY, Vol. 4, No. 2 (1992): 134-61.

3570. "English Criticism of the English Anti-Lynching Committee." THE LITERARY DIGEST, Vol. 9, No. 26 (Oct. 27, 1894): 7 (757).

3571. Epstein, Miriam A.   "The Struggle to Pass a Federal Antilynching Law During the 1930's." A course research paper of 144 pages. Brandeis Univ., 1964. Archives 274395 (at Brandeis).

3572. Ethridge, Willie Snow. "Southern Women Attack Lynching." THE NATION, Vol. 131, No. 3414 (Dec. 10, 1930): 647, 650.

3573. "A Federal Anti-Lynching Bill." THE CRISIS, Vol. 23, No. 2 (Dec. 1921): 71.

3574. "The Federal Anti-Lynching Bill." COLUMBIA LAW REVIEW, Vol. 38, No. 1 (Jan. 1938): 199-207.

3575. "The Federal Anti-Lynching Bill." INTERNATIONAL JURIDICAL ASSOCIATION MONTHLY BULLETIN, Vol. 2, No. 8 (Jan. 1934): 9.

3576. "The Federal Anti-Lynching Bill." LAW NOTES [Northport, NY], Vol. 25 (Feb. 1922): 202-03.

3577. "Federal Anti-Lynching Bill Introduced in Congress." THE CRISIS, Vol. 16, No. 2 (June 1918): 76.

3578. "Federal Bill to Halt Lynching." IN NEGRO YEAR BOOK . . . 1921-1922, pp. 70-71. Ed. by Monroe N. Work. Tuskegee Institute, AL: Negro Year Book Pub. Co., 1922.

3579. "A Federal Bill to Halt Lynching." THE LITERARY DIGEST, Vol. 71, No. 14 (Dec. 31, 1921): 11-12.

3580. "Federal Cognizance of the Acts of Lynchers." COLUMBIA LAW REVIEW, Vol. 5, No. 6 (June 1905): 465-66.

3581. "A Federal Curb for Lynching." THE CHRISTIAN CENTURY, Vol. 52, No. 19 (May 8, 1935): 598-600.

3582. "Federal Law for Lynching." THE CRISIS, Vol. 18, No. 1 (May 1919): 30-31.

3583. "A Federal Law is Essential." INTERRACIAL REVIEW, Vol. 10, No. 2 (Feb. 1937): 19-20.   Anti-lynching.

3584. "Federal Power to Prosecute Violence Against Minority Groups." THE YALE LAW JOURNAL, Vol. 57, No. 5 (March 1948): 855-73.

3585. "Federal Step Urged To Stop Lynchings."   INTERRACIAL REVIEW, Vol. 9,, No. 4 (April 1936): 64.

3586. Ferrell, Claudine L.   NIGHTMARE AND DREAM: ANTI-LYNCHING IN CONGRESS 1917-1922. New York: Garland Publishing, 1986.

3587. Ferrell, Claudine L.   "Nightmare and Dream Antilynching in Congress, 1917-1922." Ph.D. diss., Rice Univ., 1983.   See Diss. Ab. Intl., Vol. 44, No. 2 (Aug. 1983): 556A.

3588. "The Fight Has Just Begun." THE CRISIS, Vol. 42, No. 6 (June 1935): 175, 183.   A report on the filibuster against the anti-lynching bill.

3589. "Filibuster Endangers Anti-Lynching Bill."   INTERRACIAL REVIEW, Vol. 10, No. 11 (Nov. 1937): 175-76.

3590. "FILIBUSTER in the Senate." LITERARY DIGEST, Vol. 1 [sic. Vol. 124 of original numbering], No. 21 (Dec. 4, 1937): 5-6. Opposition to anti-lynching bill.

3591. "The Final Drive To End Lynching." INTERRACIAL REVIEW, Vol. 10, No. 5 (May 1937): 68.

3592. "Financing the Fight Against Lynching." THE CRISIS, Vol. 27, No. 3 (Jan. 1924): 123-24.

3593. Findley, James Lee, Jr. "Lynching and the Texas Anti-Lynch Law of 1897." M.A. thesis, Baylor Univ., 1974.   Includes descriptions of some Texas lynchings.

3594. Fish, Hamilton, Jr.   SENATOR BORAH AND THE ANTI-LYNCHING BILL. Washington, DC: The author (U.S. House of Representatives), 1936. Four pages.

3595. FIVE LETTERS OF THE UNIVERSITY COMMISSION ON SOUTHERN RACE QUESTIONS. The Trustees of the John R. Slater Fund, Occasional Papers No. 24.   Charlottesville, VA: Michie Company, Printers, 1927.   See pp. 5-7 for "Lynching" (the first letter, Jan. 5, 1916).

3596. "Five States Pass Laws Against Lynching."   In NEGRO YEAR BOOK . . . 1921-1922, pp. 68-70.   Ed. by Monroe N. Work.   Tuskegee Institute, AL: Negro Year Book Pub. Co., 1922.

3597. "For a Federal Anti-Lynching Bill."   THE CRISIS, Vol. 44, No. 3 (March 1937): 76, 82.   Editorial from a Richmond, Virginia, newspaper.

3598. "For a Federal Anti-Lynching Bill."   THE SOUTHERN WORK-MAN, Vol. 66, No. 3 (March 1937): 83-85.   Editorial from Richmond Times-Dispatch, Feb. 2, 1937.

3599. "Force Bill: South Objects."   SPHERE, Vol. 21, No. 2 (Feb. 1938): 18-19.   Various anti-lynching bills.

3600. Ford, William D.   "Constitutionality of Proposed Federal Anti-Lynching Legislation."   VIRGINIA LAW REVIEW, Vol. 34, No. 8 (Nov. 1948): 944-53.

3601. Fraenkel, Osmond K.   "The Federal Civil Rights Laws."   MINNESOTA LAW REVIEW, Vol. 31, No. 4 (March 1947): 301-27.   For lynching see pp. 302, 318, 324.

3602. Fraenkel, Osmond K.   "The Lynch Bill--A Different View."   LAWYER'S GUILD REVIEW, Vol. 4, No. 2 (March-April 1944): 12-15.

3603. Friedman, Lawrence M.   "State Constitutions and Criminal Justice in the Late Nineteenth Century."   ALBANY LAW REVIEW, Vol. 53, No. 2 (Winter 1989): 265-81. See lynching and vigilantism on pp. 275-77.

3604. Friedman, Morris.   "New York Anti-Lynching Legislation."   ST. JOHN'S LAW REVIEW, Vol. 13, No. 1 (Nov. 1938): 209-14.

3605. "Frontal and Flank Attacks." STATE GOVERNMENT, Vol. 7, No. 3 (March 1934): 60-61.   Text and chart on the anti-lynching legislation in 36 states.

3606. Frost, Michael. "Borah the Lynch Bill-Buster." KEN, Vol. 1, No. 1 (April 7, 1938): 88, 90.   Analysis of how bill was defeated.

3607. Fry, Joseph A. "Rayon, Riot and Repression: The Covington Sit Down Strike of 1937." THE VIRGINIA MAGAZINE OF HISTORY AND BIOGRAPHY, Vol. 84, No. 1 (Jan. 1976): 3-18.   The violence was minor, but Virginia's anti-lynching law was used against the strikers.

3608. Fuller, Helen. "Section 52 Is News," THE NEW REPUBLIC, Vol. 108, No. 7 (Feb. 15, 1943): 204; condensed version: "Section 52 Is News," NEGRO DIGEST, Vol. I, No. 6 (April 1943): 64-65.   Use of Sections 51 and 52, Title 18, United States Code, against lynchers.

3609. "A Fund for the Suppression on Lynching." THE SURVEY, Vol. 40, No. 21 (Aug. 24, 1918): 593.

3610. "Further Debate in the House on the Dyer Anti-Lynching Bill." THE CONGRESSIONAL DIGEST, Vol. 1, No. 6 (March 1922): 14-15.   See "The House Debates . . ."

3611. Gardner, Katherine. "The Anti-Lynching Bill." THE CHRISTIAN CENTURY, Vol. 52, No. 5 (Jan. 30, 1935): 147-48.   Letter. Recounts events leading to lynching, Jan. 1935, of black man named Jerome.

3612. "Gavagan Anti-Lynching Bill." INTERNATIONAL JURIDICAL ASSOCIATION MONTHLY BULLETIN, Vol. 5, No. 11 (May 1937): 128-29.

3613. Gerber, David A. "Lynching and Law and Order: Origin and Passage of the Ohio Anti-Lynching Law of 1896." OHIO HISTORY, Vol. 83, No. 1 (Winter 1974): 33-50.

3614.. Giddings, Paula. "Ida Wells-Barnett." In PORTRAITS OF AMERICAN WOMEN: FROM SETTLEMENT TO THE PRESENT, pp. 366-85. Ed. by G. J. Barker-Benfield and Catherine Clinton. New York: St. Martin's Press, 1991.

3615. Giddings, Paula. "Woman Warrior." ESSENCE, Vol. 18, No. 10 (Feb. 1988): 75-76, 142, 146.   Ida B. Wells.

3616. "The Glorious Task of 'Lifting As We Climb.'" THE COMPETITOR,

Vol. 3, No. 1 (Jan.-Feb. 1921): 39-43. Page 42: Nannie Burroughs is head of Anti-Lynching Department of National Association of Colored Women.

3617. Grant, Donald L. THE ANTI-LYNCHING MOVEMENT, 1883-1932. San Francisco: R and E Research Associates, 1975.   Author's dissertation.

3618. Grant, Donald Lee. "The Development of the Anti-Lynching Reform Movement in the United States, 1883-1932." Ph.D. diss., Univ. of Missouri, Columbia, 1972. See Diss. Ab. Intl., Vol. 34, No. 3 (Sept. 1973): 1206A.

3619. Greenbaum, Fred. "The Anti-Lynching Bill of 1935.: The Irony of 'Equal Justice--Under Law.'" JOURNAL OF HUMAN RELATIONS, Vol. 15, No. 3 (Third Quarter 1967): 72-85.

3620. Greenbaum, Fred. FIGHTING PROGRESSIVE: A BIOGRAPHY OF EDWARD P. COSTIGAN. Washington, DC: Public Affairs Press, 1971. See Chapter X, "The Costigan-Wagner Anti-Lynching Bill" (pp. 160-78). Page 177, note 1: "Portions of this chapter appeared, in somewhat different form, as 'The Anti-lynching Bill of 1935: The Irony of "Equal Justice--under Law,"' Journal of Human Relations, XV (1967), 72-85. The volume was reissued as Daniel Walden, ed., American Reform: The Ambiguous Legacy (Ampersand Press, 1967)."

3621. "Growing Sentiment for Federal Anti-Lynch Law." THE CRISIS, Vol. 41, No. 12 (Dec. 1934): 368.

3622. Hall, Elizabeth Jane. "The Crusade Against Lynching." M.A. thesis, North Texas State Univ., 1975. See Masters Abstracts, Vol. 14, No. 2 (June 1976): 100.

3623. Hall, Jacquelyn. "Reminiscences of Jessie Daniel Ames: 'I Really Do Like a Good Fight.'" NEW SOUTH, Vol. 27, No. 2 (Spring 1972): 31-41.

3624. Hall, Jacquelyn. "Women & Lynching." SOUTHERN EXPOSURE, Vol. 4, No. 4 (Winter 1977): 52-54.

3625. Hall, Jacquelyn Dowd.   "'The Mind That Burns In Each Body': Women, Rape, and Racial Violence." SOUTHERN EXPOSURE, Vol. 12, No. 6 (Nov./Dec. 1984): 61-71.   On lynching and the Association of Southern Women for the Prevention of Lynching. Slightly different in Anne Snitow, Christine Stansell, and Sharon Thompson, eds., Powers of Desire: The Politics of Sexuality (New York: Monthly Review Press, 1983), pp. 328-49.

3626. Hall, Jacquelyn Dowd. "Revolt Against Chivalry: Jessie Daniel Ames and the Women's Campaign Against Lynching." Ph.D. diss., Columbia Univ., 1974.   See Diss. Ab. Intl., Vol. 37, No. 7 (Jan. 1977): 4560A-4561A.

3627. Hall, Jacquelyn Dowd. REVOLT AGAINST CHIVALRY: JESSIE DANIEL AMES AND THE WOMEN'S CAMPAIGN AGAINST LYNCH-ING.   New York: Columbia Univ. Press, 1979.   Rev. ed.; New York: Columbia Univ. Press, 1993.

3628. Hall, Jacquelyn Dowd. "'A Truly Subversive Affair': Women Against Lynching in the Twentieth-Century South." In WOMEN OF AMERICA: A HISTORY, pp. 360-83 [see "Documents," pp. 383-88]. Ed. by Carol Ruth Berkin and Mary Beth Norton. Boston: Houghton Mifflin, 1979.   Taken from Revolt Against Chivalry.

3629. Hamilton, Tullia Kay Brown. "The National Association of Colored Women, 1896-1920." Ph.D. diss., Emory Univ., 1978.   See Diss. Ab. Intl., Vol. 40, No. 1 (July 1979): 405A. Ida B. Wells Barnett was one of "major leaders." This organization fought lynching.

3630. Harris, Trudier, ed.   THE SELECTED WORKS OF IDA B. WELLS-BARNETT. Schomburg Library of Nineteenth-Century Black Women Writers. Ed. by Henry Louis Gates, Jr. New York: Oxford Univ. Press, 1991.   Has: Southern Horrors: Lynch Law in All Its Phases (1892); The Reason Why the Colored American Is Not in the World's Columbian Exposition (1893); A Red Record: Tabulated Statistics and Alleged Causes of Lynchings in the United States, 1892-1893-1894 (1895); Mob Rule in New Orleans: Robert Charles and His Fight to the Death (1900).

3631. Harvey, William B. "Constitutional Law--Anti-Lynching Legislation." MICHIGAN LAW REVIEW, Vol. 47, No. 3 (Jan. 1949): 369-77.

3632. Haynes, Richard M. IDA B. WELLS. See Books In Print 1993-94.

3633. "Help Crush Out Lynching." THE CRISIS, Vol. 17, No. 2 (Dec. 1918): 54.   NAACP advertisement.

3634. Hemphill, Robert W., and Woodward, J. Henry, Jr. "The Constitu-tionality of the Proposed 'Anti-Lynching' Bill." THE YEAR BOOK OF THE SELDEN SOCIETY [University of South Carolina School of Law], Vol. 2 (June 1938): 12-21.

3635. Hershey, O. F. "Lynch Law." THE GREEN BAG, Vol. 12, No. 9 (Sept. 1900): 466-69.   Sees cause as Americans' feeling that laws are local in origin, application, and breach; that elected law officers, especially if mediocre, command no respect for law; and that liberty and license are rights. Federal anti-lynching law is necessary.

3636. Hixson, William B., Jr. "Moorfield Storey and the Defense of the Dyer Anti-Lynching Bill." THE NEW ENGLAND QUARTERLY, Vol. 42, No. 1 (March 1969): 65-81. Bill was introduced in the House in 1918.

3637. Holmes, Michael Stephan. "The Costigan-Wagner and Wagner-Van Nuys Anti-Lynching Bills, 1933-1938." M.S. thesis, Univ. of Wisconsin, 1965.

3638. Holt, Thomas C. "The Lonely Warrior: Ida B. Wells-Barnett and the Struggle for Black Leadership." In BLACK LEADERS OF THE TWENTI-ETH CENTURY, pp. 36-61. Ed. by John Hope Franklin and August Meier. Urbana: Univ. of Illinois Press, 1982.

3639. "The House Debates the Dyer Anti-Lynching Bill." THE CON-GRESSIONAL DIGEST, Vol. 1, No. 6 (March 1922): 13. See also "Further Debate . . ."

3640. "House Passes Anti-Lynching Bill; Senate Will Block It." SCHO-LASTIC, Vol. 35, No. 16 (Jan. 22, 1940): 7.

3641. "How Miss Wells' Crusade is Regarded in America." THE LIT-ERARY DIGEST, Vol. 9, No. 13 (July 28, 1894): 6-7 (366-67). Press comments.

3642. "Huge Anti-Lynching Meeting January 6." THE CRISIS, Vol. 42, No. 1 (Jan. 1935): 26-27.

3643. Huthmacher, J. Joseph. SENATOR ROBERT F. WAGNER AND THE RISE OF URBAN LIBERALISM. New York: Atheneum, 1968. See "Anti-lynching bill" in index.

3644. Hutton, Mary Magdelene Boone. "The Rhetoric of Ida B. Wells: The Genesis of the Anti-lynch Movement." Ph.D. diss., Indiana Univ., 1975. See Diss. Ab. Intl., Vol. 36, No. 8 (Feb. 1976): 4850A.

3645. "If There Had Been An Anti-Lynching Law . . ." NEW SOUTH, Vol. 4, No. 7 (July 1949): 2-4. Compares provisions of three federal anti-lynching bills and new Texas law.

3646. "Interracial Activities." THE SOUTHERN WORKMAN, Vol. 59, No. 10 (Oct. 1930): 443-44. Commission on Interracial Cooperation is sponsoring a project to study each lynching in 1930.

3647. "Interracial Commission Endorses Federal Anti-Lynch Law." THE SOUTHERN WORKMAN, Vol. 64, No. 10 (Oct. 1935): 315. Resolution adopted by The Commission on Interracial Cooperation.

3648. "Interracial Cooperation: Constructive Measures Recommended by Southern White Woman." THE SOUTHERN WORKMAN, Vol. 50, No. 1 (Jan. 1921): 35-37.

3649. "Is the Anti-Lynching Law To Fail Again?" THE CHRISTIAN CENTURY, Vol. 55, No. 5 (Feb. 2, 1938): 134. One paragraph.

3650. "It Can Be Passed." THE CRISIS, Vol. 44, No. 6 (June 1937): 177. Recent poll: most U.S. Senators favor the Gavagan bill. Brief.

3651. Jack, Robert L. HISTORY OF THE NATIONAL ASSOCIATION FOR THE ADVANCEMENT OF COLORED PEOPLE. Boston: Meador Pub. Co., 1943. See page 13 and Chapter III, "Anti-Lynching Crusade" (pp. 26-46).

3652. Johnson, George W. "Hon. Harry C. Smith, Father of Ohio's Civil Rights and Anti-Lynching Laws." THE VOICE (formerly THE VOICE OF THE NEGRO), Vol. 4, No. 6 (June 1907): 265-66.

3653. Johnson, James Weldon. "The Achievements and Their Significance." THE CRISIS, Vol. 34, No. 7 (Sept. 1927): 222-24, 242, 244. Includes "The Aiken Lynching" [South Carolina] (pp. 222-23). The NAACP's fight against lynching.

3654. Kahn, E. J., Jr. "Mr. White Goes to a Lynching." NEGRO DIGEST, Vol. 7, No. 5 (March 1949): 52-64. Activities of Walter White. Orig. in The New Yorker, Vol. 24, No. 29 (Sept. 11, 1948): 38-40, 42-50, as "Profiles: The Frontal Attack--II" (2d of two articles on White); see lynching on p. 40.

3655. Kahn, E. J., Jr. "Profiles: The Frontal Attack--I." THE NEW YORKER, Vol. 24, No. 28 (Sept. 4, 1948): 28-32, 34-38. NAACP's Walter White. See his stance on anti-lynching bill, pp. 34, 36.

3656. Kaiser, Ernest. "The Federal Government and the Negro, 1865-1955." SCIENCE & SOCIETY, Vol. 20, No. 1 (Winter 1956): 27-58. A few brief references to lynching.

3657. Kellogg, Charles Flint. NAACP: A HISTORY OF THE NATIONAL ASSOCIATION FOR THE ADVANCEMENT OF COLORED PEOPLE. VOL. I: 1909-1920. Baltimore: Johns Hopkins Press, 1967. See "Lynching" in index and Chapter X, "Lynching and Mob Violence," pp. 209-46.

3658. "Kill the Filibuster!" NEW MASSES, Vol. 26, No. 6 (Feb. 1, 1938): 10. Anti-lynching bill. See illustration on p. 11.

3659. Konvitz, Milton R. THE CONSTITUTION AND CIVIL RIGHTS. New York: Columbia Univ. Press, 1947; reprint: New York: Octagon Books, 1977. See Chapter 4, "Lynching as a Federal Crime" (pp. 74-90), and Appendix 3, "Antilynching Bill: H.R. 51 (78th Congress, 1st Session)" (pp. 155-57).

3660. "The Last Round-Up." INTERRACIAL REVIEW, Vol. 10, No. 12 (Dec. 1937): 179-80. Supreme Court Justice and former Senator Hugo Black and anti-lynching bills.

3661. "Law and Lynching." AMERICA, Vol. 62, No. 19 (Feb. 17, 1940): 520. Federal anti-lynching bill would be good but real solution is increased civilization in lynching communities.

3662. "A Law Making Lynching a Federal Offense." THE CRISIS, Vol. 21, No. 3 (Jan. 1921): 119.

3663. [A law that ought to prevent lynching.] THE ALBANY LAW JOURNAL, Vol. 67, No. 6 (June 1905): 163. State law in Illinois. This note is untitled in the journal, but title is supplied here because it is thus given in U.S., Library of Congress, Division of Bibliography, List of References on Lynch Law (Washington, DC, 1921), #134.

3664. "Let Us Have Action." THE COMPETITOR, Vol. 2, No. 2 (Aug.-Sept. 1920): 87. Desires federal effort against lynching.

3665. "Letters to the Association of Southern Women for the Prevention of Lynching, Atlanta, Georgia." THE SOUTHERN FRONTIER, Vol. 1, No. 7 (July 1940): [2].

3666. Lloyd, R. Grann. "The States' Rights Myth and Southern Opposition to Federal Anti-Lynching Legislation." THE NEGRO EDUCATIONAL REVIEW, Vol. 1 (April 1950): 78-88.

3667. Logan, Shirley W. "Rhetorical Strategies in Ida B. Wells's 'Southern Horrors: Lynch Law in All Its Phases.'" SAGE, Vol. 8, No. 1 (Summer 1991): 3-9.

3668. "Lynch Law: Congress Toys with Wagner-Van Nuys Anti-Lynching Bill." THE LITERARY DIGEST, Vol. 123, No. 12 (March 20, 1937): 8-9.

3669. "Lynch Law Gained Headway in 1930." FEDERAL COUNCIL

BULLETIN, Vol. 14, No. 5 (May 1931): 14.

"Lynched." LABOR DEFENDER. See this entry in Chapter V for an anti-lynching conference.

3670. "The Lynchers." AMERICA, Vol. 53, No. 17 (Aug. 3, 1935): 386-87. Wagner-Costigan bill was defeated due to opposition "that commands votes, if not respect."

3671. "Lynchers on the Run." THE CRISIS, Vol. 42, No. 1 (Jan. 1935): 16. Editorial favoring anti-lynching bill.

3672. "Lynching." AMERICA, Vol. 58, No. 22 (March 5, 1938): 518. Demise of Wagner-Van Nuys bill.

3673. "Lynching." THE CRISIS, Vol. 18, No. 2 (June 1919): 59. Anti-Lynching conference.

3674. "Lynching." THE CRISIS, Vol. 25, No. 3 (Jan. 1923): 106. There will be a new anti-lynching bill in the next Congress.

3675. "Lynching." THE CRISIS, Vol. 26, No. 3 (July 1923): 127. More on Representative Dyer's tour and his anti-lynching bill.

3676. "Lynching." THE CRISIS, Vol. 32, No. 1 (May 1926): 10. Dyer Bill.

3677. "Lynching and Filibuster." AMERICA, Vol. 53, No. 4 (May 4, 1935): 76. Wagner-Costigan bill.

3678. "Lynching and legislation." THE CATHOLIC WORKER, Vol. 3, No. 10 (April 1936): 3. Recent lynching of Philip Baker, black, in Georgia shows need for passage of Van Nuys resolution (for investigation of lynching) and Costigan-Wagner bill.

3679. "Lynching and the Federal Government." AMERICA, Vol. 25, No. 5 (May 21, 1921): 113. Editorial. Avers that anti-lynching bill introduced in Congress by Representative Dallinger is "wildly unconstitutional."

3680. "Lynching and the States." AMERICA, Vol. 60, No. 18 (Feb. 4, 1939): 420. Wagner-Van Nuys-Capper anti-lynching bill. Editorial.

3681. "Lynching Before the United States Congress." THE CRISIS, Vol. 19, No. 6 (April 1920): 323-24.

3682. "The Lynching Bill." THE CRISIS, Vol. 23, No. 4 (Feb. 1922): 152.

3683. "The Lynching Fund." THE CRISIS, Vol. 12, No. 6 (Oct. 1916): 275. One sentence.

3684. "The Lynching Fund." THE CRISIS, Vol. 13, No. 2 (Dec. 1916): 61-62.   Proposes ways to eliminate lynchings.

3685. "Lynching in the North." AMERICA, Vol. 53, No. 6 (May 18, 1935): 123.   Filibuster killed Wagner-Costigan bill.

3686. "Lynching Must Go!" INTERRACIAL REVIEW, Vol. 11, No. 9 (Sept. 1938): 133.   Editorial supporting anti-lynching bill. Brief.

3687. "Lynching Must Go!" INTERRACIAL REVIEW, Vol. 12, No. 8 (Aug. 1939): 118.   Editorial supporting anti-lynching bill. Brief.

3688. "Lynching Must Go!" INTERRACIAL REVIEW, Vol. 12, No. 10 (Oct. 1939): 149.   Editorial supporting anti-lynching bill. Brief.

3689. "The Lynching Protest." THE CRISIS, Vol. 3, No. 3 (Jan. 1912): 105. Southern newspapers report on recent NAACP anti-lynching meeting.

3690. "Lynching: Southern Senators Filibuster in Name of Virtue." NEWS-WEEK [sic], Vol. 5, No. 18 (May 4, 1935): 10.   "Cotton Ed" Smith and others acted against federal anti-lynching bill. Includes three photos.

3691. "Lynchings and Legislation." THE CATHOLIC WORKER, Vol. 2, No. 5 (Oct. 1934): 7.   Lynching increase after Wagner-Costigan bill failed to pass.

3692. MacKenzie, Amy. "Walter White on Lynching." INTERRACIAL REVIEW, Vol. 9, No. 9 (Sept. 1936): 134-35.

"Major Legislation Moves Forward." CONGRESSIONAL DIGEST (May 1937). See "Anti-Lynching" in this chapter.

3693. Marans, Joel Eugene. "The Struggle for Federal Anti-Lynching Legislation, 1933-1945." Honors thesis, Harvard Univ., 1962.

3694. "'The Mark of the Beast.'" THE INDEPENDENT, Vol. 117, No. 3987 (Oct. 30, 1926): 489.   Opposition to Dyer anti-lynching bill despite recent increase in number of lynchings.

3695. "Mary White Ovington Sends Open Letter to President Roosevelt."

INTERRACIAL REVIEW, Vol. 8, No. 4 (April 1935): 64.   In support of Costigan-Wagner anti-lynching bill.

3696. Maslow, Will, and Robinson, Joseph B. "Civil Rights Legislation and the Fight for Equality, 1862-1952." THE UNIVERSITY OF CHICAGO LAW REVIEW, Vol. 20, No. 3 (Spring 1953): 363-413.   See pp. 380-84 for anti-lynching bills and laws.

3697. Mason, Karen Malinda. "Testing the Boundaries: Women, Politics, and Gender Roles in Chicago, 1890-1930 (Illinois)." Ph.D. diss., Univ. of Michigan, 1991.   See Diss. Ab. Intl., Vol. 52, No. 3 (Sept. 1991): 1053A. Focuses on four women, including Ida B. Wells-Barnett.

3698. McClellan, John L. [Remarks on Proposed Anti-Lynching Law.] CONGRESSIONAL DIGEST, Vol. 29, No. 2 (Feb. 1950): 63-64.

3699. McDonough, Julia Anne. "Men and Women of Good Will: A History of the Commission on Interracial Cooperation and the Southern Regional Council, 1919-1954." Ph.D. diss., Univ. of Virginia, 1993.   See Diss. Ab. Intl., Vol. 54, No. 8 (Feb. 1994): 3178A.

3700. McKissack, Patricia, and McKissack, Fredrick. IDA B. WELLS-BARNETT: A VOICE AGAINST VIOLENCE. Springfield, NJ: Enslow Publications, 1991.

3701. "A Memorial to the Senate of the United States." THE CRISIS, Vol. 24, No. 2 (June 1922): 69-72.   Support for the Dyer bill.

3702. "The Memorial to the Senate." THE CRISIS, Vol. 24, No. 3 (July 1992): 122-24.   Support for the Dyer Bill.

3703. "Mencken, Costigan, Wagner and Guffey Urge Anti-Lynching Law." INTERRACIAL REVIEW, Vol. 8, No. 3 (March 1935): 49.

3704. Merrill, Taylor. "Lynching the Anti-Lynching Bill." THE CHRISTIAN CENTURY, Vol. 55, No. 8 (Feb. 23, 1938): 238-40.   Includes account of Duck Hill horror [in Mississippi] printed in Congressional Record (from Senator Neely).

3705. Mertins, Leon Evans. "HAS THE UNITED STATES GOVERNMENT THE POWER TO PROSECUTE 'LYNCHING' AS A FEDERAL CRIME WITHOUT AN AMENDMENT TO THE CONSTITUTION?" New York: J. A. Quail, [1921].

3706. "A Military Anti-Lynching Measure." THE CRISIS, Vol. 16, No. 3

(July 1918): 124.   Substitute for Dyer Bill proposed by Military Intelligence Bureau.

3707. Miller, E. E. "What Southerners Think of the Dyer Bill." THE OUTLOOK, Vol. 132, No. 14 (Dec. 6, 1922): 598-99.

3708. Miller, Kathleen Atkinson. "The Ladies and the Lynchers: A Look at the Association of Southern Women for the Prevention of Lynching." SOUTHERN STUDIES, Vol. 17, No. 3 (Fall 1978): 221-40.

3709. Mims, Edwin. A HANDBOOK FOR INTER-RACIAL COMMITTEES CONTAINING OPINIONS OF REPRESENTATIVE SOUTHERNERS AND NOTEWORTHY ACHIEVEMENTS OF STATES AND COMMUNITIES. Atlanta: Inter-Racial Committee, 1920.   See antilynching sections, pp. 9-10.

3710. "Minnesota Anti-Lynching Bill." THE CRISIS, Vol. 22, No. 2 (June 1921): 67-68.   Includes copy of new law.

3711. "Mississippi Women in Anti-Lynching Campaign." THE CHRISTIAN ADVOCATE [New York], Vol. 101 (June 17, 1926): 754-55.

3712. "Mob Violence a Federal Offense." THE OUTLOOK, Vol. 130, No. 8 (Feb. 22, 1922): 285-86.   Dyer bill to make lynching a federal crime.

3713. Moncrief, Adiel J., Jr., ed. "Southern Women Fight Lynch Evil." THE CHRISTIAN CENTURY, Vol. 54, No. 18 (May 5, 1937): 593.

3714. "More Lynchings!" THE CATHOLIC WORKER, Vol. 3, No. 4 (Sept. 1935): 2.   Need for federal anti-lynching law.

3715. Morris, J. Frank. "The Costigan-Wagner Anti-Lynching Bill." INTERRACIAL REVIEW, Vol. 8, No. 4 (April 1935): 61.   Letter.

3716. Morse, Josiah.   "The University Commission on Southern Race Questions." THE SOUTH ATLANTIC QUARTERLY, Vol. 19, No. 4 (Oct. 1920): 302-10.   Page 305: two paragraphs on lynching from the Commission's "Open Letter to the College Men of the South," Jan. 5, 1916.

3717. "Mr. Dyer to Mr. Johnson." THE CRISIS, Vol. 23, No. 5 (March 1992): 202.   Anti-lynching bill.

3718. "Mrs. L. W. Alford, McComb, Miss. Completes A Decade's Work Against Lynching." THE SOUTHERN FRONTIER, Vol. 2, No. 7 (July 1941): [2, 4].

3719. National Association for the Advancement of Colored People. FIRST ANNUAL REPORT, JANUARY 1, 1911. New York: NAACP, 1911. Lynching references are in "Possibilities" section (working against lynching and for anti-lynching laws).

3720. ___. THIRD ANNUAL REPORT. New York: NAACP, 1913. See "Coatesville," pp. 9, 11.

3721. ___. FOURTH ANNUAL REPORT: 1913. New York: NAACP, 1914. See "Lynching," p. 24, and "Anti-Lynching Bill," pp. 24-25.

3722. ___. FREEING AMERICA: SEVENTH ANNUAL REPORT OF THE NATIONAL ASSOCIATION FOR THE ADVANCEMENT OF COLORED PEOPLE. New York: NAACP, 1917. See "Lynching" section, pp. 6-7.

3723. ___. REPORT OF THE NATIONAL ASSOCIATION FOR THE ADVANCEMENT OF COLORED PEOPLE FOR THE YEARS 1917 AND 1918: EIGHTH AND NINTH ANNUAL REPORTS: A SUMMARY OF WORK AND AN ACCOUNTING. New York: NAACP, 1919. In Eighth Annual Report see p. 10. In Ninth Annual Report see pp. 26-36, 76, 79, 89-92; the last section is individualized listings for 1917 and 1918.

3724. ___. TENTH ANNUAL REPORT OF THE NATIONAL ASSOCIATION FOR THE ADVANCEMENT OF COLORED PEOPLE FOR THE YEAR 1919: A SUMMARY OF WORK AND AN ACCOUNTING. New York: NAACP, 1920. See Chapter II, "Making Lynching a National Issue" (pp. 13-33), Appendix I, "Lynching Record for 1919" (pp. 92-93, and Appendix II, "Signers of the Call for the First National Conference on Lynching and of The Address to the Nation" (pp. 94-100).

3725. ___. ELEVENTH ANNUAL REPORT OF THE NATIONAL ASSOCIATION FOR THE ADVANCEMENT OF COLORED PEOPLE, FOR THE YEAR 1920: A SUMMARY OF WORK AND AN ACCOUNTING. New York: NAACP, 1921. See Chapter II, "Legal Defense" ("The Duluth Cases," p. 22); Chapter IV, "Lynching" (pp. 32-43); Chapter V, "Congressional Legislation" (pp. 44-45).

3726. ___. TWELFTH ANNUAL REPORT OF THE NATIONAL ASSOCIATION FOR THE ADVANCEMENT OF COLORED PEOPLE, FOR THE YEAR 1921: A SUMMARY OF WORK AND AN ACCOUNTING. New York: NAACP, 1922. See Chapter III, "Lynching" (pp. 40-53); Chapter VIII, "Investigations" (p. 68).

3727. ___. THIRTEENTH ANNUAL REPORT OF THE NATIONAL

ASSOCIATION FOR THE ADVANCEMENT OF COLORED PEOPLE, FOR THE YEAR 1922: A SUMMARY OF WORK AND AN ACCOUNTING. New York: NAACP, 1923.   See Chapter I, "The Dyer Anti-Lynching Bill" (pp. 9-24); Chapter III, "Lynching" (pp. 30-40).

3728. ___. FOURTEENTH ANNUAL REPORT OF THE NATIONAL ASSOCIATION FOR THE ADVANCEMENT OF COLORED PEOPLE, FOR THE YEAR 1923: A SUMMARY OF WORK AND AN ACCOUNTING. New York: NAACP, 1924.   See Chapter II, "The Dyer Anti-Lynching Bill" (pp. 14-15); Chapter III, "Lynching" (pp. 16-21).

3729. ___. FIFTEENTH ANNUAL REPORT OF THE NATIONAL ASSOCIATION FOR THE ADVANCEMENT OF COLORED PEOPLE, FOR THE YEAR 1924: A SUMMARY OF WORK AND AN ACCOUNTING. New York: NAACP, 1925.   See Chapter V, "Dyer Anti-Lynching Bill" (pp. 29-30); Chapter VI, "Anti-Lynching Campaign in England" (pp. 30-31); Chapter VII, "Lynching" (pp. 31-35).

3730. ___. SIXTEENTH ANNUAL REPORT OF THE NATIONAL ASSOCIATION FOR THE ADVANCEMENT OF COLORED PEOPLE, FOR THE YEAR 1925: A SUMMARY OF WORK AND AN ACCOUNTING. New York: NAACP, 1926.   See Chapter III "Lynching" (pp. 16-21).

3731. ___. EIGHTEENTH ANNUAL REPORT OF THE NATIONAL ASSOCIATION FOR THE ADVANCEMENT OF COLORED PEOPLE, FOR 1927: A SUMMARY OF WORK AND AN ACCOUNTING. New York: NAACP, 1928.   See "Legislation" (Dyer Bill, p. 18); lynchings, pp. 27-31.

3732. ___. NINETEENTH ANNUAL REPORT OF THE NATIONAL ASSOCIATION FOR THE ADVANCEMENT OF COLORED PEOPLE, FOR 1928: A SUMMARY OF WORK AND AN ACCOUNTING. New York: NAACP, 1929.   For lynching see pp. 22-25.

3733. ___. TWENTIETH ANNUAL REPORT OF THE NATIONAL ASSOCIATION FOR THE ADVANCEMENT OF COLORED PEOPLE, FOR 1929: A SUMMARY OF WORK AND AN ACCOUNTING. New York: NAACP, 1930.   For lynching see pp. 35-38.

3734. ___. TWENTY-FIRST ANNUAL REPORT OF THE NATIONAL ASSOCIATION FOR THE ADVANCEMENT OF COLORED PEOPLE, FOR 1930: A SUMMARY OF WORK AND AN ACCOUNTING. New York: NAACP, 1931.   For lynching see pp. 34-39.

3735. ___. TWENTY-SECOND ANNUAL REPORT OF THE NATIONAL ASSOCIATION FOR THE ADVANCEMENT OF COLORED PEOPLE, FOR 1931: A SUMMARY OF WORK AND AN ACCOUNTING. New York: NAACP, 1932.   See Chapter VI, "Lynching" (pp. 28-33).

3736. ___. TWENTY-THIRD ANNUAL REPORT OF THE NATIONAL ASSOCIATION FOR THE ADVANCEMENT OF COLORED PEOPLE, FOR 1932: A SUMMARY OF WORK AND AN ACCOUNTING. New York: NAACP, 1933.   See Chapter IV, "Lynching" (pp. 33-37).

3737. ___. TWENTY-FOURTH ANNUAL REPORT OF THE NATIONAL ASSOCIATION FOR THE ADVANCEMENT OF COLORED PEOPLE, FOR 1933: A SUMMARY OF WORK AND AN ACCOUNTING. New York: NAACP, 1934.   See Chapter 3, "Lynching" (pp. 20-26).

3738. ___. N.A.A.C.P. 25TH ANNUAL REPORT FOR 1934. New York: NAACP, [1935].   See Chapter 3, "Lynching" (pp. 23-29).

3739. ___. N.A.A.C.P. 26TH ANNUAL REPORT FOR 1935. New York: NAACP, [1936].   See Chapter 4, "Lynching" (pp. 19-31).

3740. ___. N.A.A.C.P. 27TH ANNUAL REPORT FOR 1936. New York: NAACP, [1937].   See Chapter 1, "Lynching" (pp. 4-9).

3741. ___. N.A.A.C.P. 28TH ANNUAL REPORT FOR 1937. New York: NAACP, [1938].   See Chapter 1, "Lynching" (pp. 4-8).

3742. ___. N.A.A.C.P. 29TH ANNUAL REPORT FOR 1938. New York: NAACP, [1939].   See Chapter 1, "Lynching" (pp. 4-10).

3743. ___. N.A.A.C.P. 30TH ANNUAL REPORT FOR 1939. New York: NAACP, [1940].   See Chapter 1, "Lynching" (pp. 4-5).

3744. ___. NAACP ANNUAL REPORT FOR 1940. New York: NAACP, [1941].   See Chapter 2 (pp. 11-15).

3745. ___. NAACP ANNUAL REPORT FOR 1941. New York: NAACP, [1942].   See Chapter V, "Lynching" (pp. 32-33).

3746. ___. NAACP ANNUAL REPORT FOR 1942. New York: NAACP, [1943].   See Chapter VI, "Lynching" (pp. 33-34).

3747. ___. NAACP ANNUAL REPORT FOR 1943. New York: NAACP, [1944].   See Chapter V, "Lynchings and Riots" (pp. 24-28).

3748. ___. ANNUAL REPORT FOR 1947. New York: NAACP, 1948. See pp. 35 ("Anti-Lynching Bill), 93 ("Lynching Record 1944-1947." No separate reports were issued for 1944, 1945, and 1946. The Annual Report for 1947 has "Summary Report for 1944" (pp. 62-73; see pp. 68-69 for "Lynching" [brief]; "Summary Report for 1945" (pp. 73-82; nothing on lynching); "Summary Report for 1946" (pp. 83-93; see pp. 86-87 for only references to lynching).

3749. ___. THE FORTIETH YEAR IN THE CRUSADE FOR CIVIL RIGHTS: NAACP ANNUAL REPORT FOR 1948. New York: NAACP, [1949].   See Chapter XII, "Lynchings in 1948" (p. 76).

3750. ___. AMERICAN RIGHTS FOR AMERICAN CITIZENS: ANNUAL NAACP REPORT FORTY-FIRST YEAR 1949. New York: NAACP, 1950.   See Chapter XV, "Lynchings in 1949" (p. 88).

3751. National Association for the Advancement of Colored People. THE FIGHT AGAINST LYNCHING: ANTI-LYNCHING WORK OF THE NATIONAL ASSOCIATION FOR THE ADVANCEMENT OF COL-ORED PEOPLE, FOR THE YEAR NINETEEN EIGHTEEN. New York: NAACP, 1919.

3752. National Association for the Advancement of Colored People. A TEN-YEAR FIGHT AGAINST LYNCHING. [New York: NAACP, n.d.].

3753. National Association for the Advancement of Colored People. THE WHY AND WHEREFORE OF THE NATIONAL ASSOCIATION FOR THE ADVANCEMENT OF COLORED PEOPLE. New York: NAACP, [1918]. Six-page flyer. Includes illustration and text on lynching.

3754. Nelson, Susan McGrath. "Association of Southern Women for the Prevention of Lynching and the Fellowship of the Concerned: Southern Churchwomen and Racial Politics." M.A. thesis, Emory Univ., 1982.

3755. "New Anti-Lynch Bill Introduced in Senate." INTERRACIAL REVIEW, Vol. 12, No. 2 (Feb. 1939): 32.

3756. "New Anti-Lynching Bill Now in Senate." NEW SOUTH, Vol. 2, No. 7 (July 1947): 6, 8.

3757. "The New Federal Anti-Lynching Bill." THE CRISIS, Vol. 44, No. 3 (March 1937): 72, 94.

3758. "New Phases of the Fight Against Lynching." CURRENT OPINION, Vol. 67, No. 1 (July 1919): 45.   Report on recent anti-lynching conference held in New York City.

3759. Nicholas, John Wallace. "Constitutional Problems Involved in An Anti-Lynching Bill." Masters thesis, State Univ. of Iowa, 1938.

3760. "1939 Saw Widest Support for Anti-Lynching Bill." INTERRACIAL REVIEW, Vol. 13, No. 7 (July 1940): 111.

3761. "The Ninth Crusade." THE CRISIS, Vol. 25, No. 5 (March 1923): 213-17.   Women's group called the Anti-Lynching Crusaders.

3762. [No author. No title; in section titled "The Week."] THE NEW REPUBLIC, Vol. 82, No. 1066 (May 8, 1935): 352.   Southern feeling against proposed federal anti-lynching law.

3763. [No author. No title.] AMERICA, Vol. 57, No. 9 (June 5, 1937): 195.   Gavagan bill.

3764. "No Check on Mobs." THE CRISIS, Vol. 43, No. 5 (May 1936): 145. Franklin Roosevelt administration will do nothing to obtain passage of anti-lynching law. Arthur W. Mitchell, black member of House of Representatives from Illinois, is a strong opponent of such a law.

3765. Ochiai, Akiko. "Ida B. Wells and Her Crusade for Justice: An African American Woman's Testimonial Autobiography." SOUNDINGS, Vol. 75, No. 2-3 (Summer/Fall 1992): 365-81.

3766. Olivier, Robert S.   "Civil Rights--Constitutionality of Federal Antilynching Legislation." NOTRE DAME LAWYER, Vol. 23, No. 4 (May 1948): 591-99.

3767. "Our Future Political Action." THE CRISIS, Vol. 25, No. 4 (Feb. 1923): 155-58.   Suggestions for action after defeat of Dyer Bill.

3768. "Outline of Dyer Anti-Lynching Act." THE CONGRESSIONAL DIGEST, Vol. 1, No. 6 (March 1922): 11.

3769. Ovington, Mary White.   "The Anti-Lynching Conference." THE SURVEY, Vol. 42, No. 7 (May 17, 1919): 292.

3770. Ovington, Mary White. THE WALLS CAME TUMBLING DOWN. New York: Harcourt, Brace and Co., 1947. Reprint ed.: New York: Arno Press and The New York Times, 1969.   See "Lynching" in index.

3771. Parrott, Lisbeth. "Seven Thousand Women Pledge to Eradicate Mob

Violence." WORLD OUTLOOK, Vol. 23 (Aug. 1933): 23, 31.

3772. "Pass Anti-Lynching Law Before Adjournment!" THE CHRISTIAN CENTURY, Vol. 63, No. 32 (Aug. 7, 1946): 956-57.

3773. Pelkey, David West. "Anti-Lynching Legislation." M.A. thesis, Univ. of Illinois, 1940.

3774. "The People Want It." THE COMPETITOR, Vol. 2, No. 4 (Dec. 1920): 239. Federal anti-lynching law.

3775. "Philadelphia Interracial Forum Adopts Anti-Lynching Resolution." INTERRACIAL REVIEW, Vol. 10, No. 6 (June 1937): 93. Brief.

3776. "Picket Crime Conference." THE CRISIS, Vol. 42, No. 1 (Jan. 1935): 26. District of Columbia branch of NAACP protested exclusion of lynching from program of National Crime Conference in December.

3777. Pillsbury, Albert E. "A Brief Inquiry into a Federal Remedy for Lynching." HARVARD LAW REVIEW, Vol. 15, No. 9 (May 1902): 707-13.

3778. Pillsbury, Albert E. "A Federal Remedy for Lynching." THE CRISIS, Vol. 3, No. 5 (March 1912): 205-08. Reprinted from Harvard Law Review [above]. Does federal power exist to protect citizens from lynching?

3779. "Point No. 3--Anti-Lynching Proposals." CONGRESSIONAL DIGEST, Vol. 29, No. 2 (Feb. 1950): 45.

3780. "Politics and Lynching." AMERICA, Vol. 57, No. 5 (May 8, 1937): 108. Gavagan bill.

3781. Portwood, Shirley J. "Videotape Review Essay: Ida B. Wells: A Passion For Justice." HAYES HISTORICAL JOURNAL, Vol. 11, No. 4 (Summer 1992): 46-49.

3782. Powell, Kimberly A. "The Association of Southern Women for the Prevention of Lynching: Strategies of a Movement in the Comic Frame." COMMUNICATION QUARTERLY, Vol. 43, No. 1 (Winter 1995): 86-99. Comic frame "makes people students of themselves" and of society so that faults can be corrected (p. 87).

3783. Powell, Ruth Gilliam. "History of the Southern Commission on Inter-Racial Cooperation." M.A. thesis, Univ. of South Carolina, 1935. See especially "Lynching," pp. 98-121; also many other references to lynching.

3784. "Press Comment on Anti-Lynching Bill." THE CRISIS, Vol. 44, No. 5 (May 1937): 143, 153.

3785. "President Would Send G-Men After Lynchers." THE CRISIS, Vol. 45, No. 4 (April 1938): 118.   Five paragraphs.

3786. "The Pro and Con Feature: Congress Considers the Costigan-Wagner Anti-Lynching Bill." CONGRESSIONAL DIGEST, Vol. 14, No. 6-7 (June-July 1935): 165-92.   Made up of "Introduction to Subject with Study Outline," and articles by James Harmon Chadbourn and David O. Walter, and "Anti-Lynching Legislation In Present Congress," and articles by Edward P. Costigan (pro), William E. Borah (con), Robert F. Wagner (pro), Millard F. Tydings (con), Arthur Capper (pro), Tom Connally (con), Senate Committee on the Judiciary (pro), Charles H. Tuttle (pro), James F. Byrnes (con), Hugo L. Black (con), Henry L. Mencken (pro), Charles H. Houston (pro), Hatton W. Sumners (con), John H. Bankhead (con), and Walter White (pro).

3787. "The Proposed Federal Anti-Lynching Bill."   VIRGINIA LAW REGISTER, Vol. 8, N.S., No. 12 (April 1923): 933-36.   No author; this article only refers to R. C. Ringwalt (under whom it is listed in Monroe Work's bibliography).

3788. Propst, Paul Nelson. "The History of the Commission on Interracial Cooperation to 1933." B.D. thesis, Candler School of Theology, Emory Univ., 1933.

3789. "Public Conduct Legislation: History of Anti-Lynching Legislation in Congress." THE CONGRESSIONAL DIGEST, Vol. 1, No. 6 (March 1922): 10.

3790. Rable, George C.   "The South and the Politics of Antilynching Legislation, 1920-1940."   THE JOURNAL OF SOUTHERN HISTORY, Vol. 51, No. 2 (May 1985): 201-220.

3791. "Recent State Anti-Lynching Acts."   INTERNATIONAL JURIDICAL ASSOCIATION MONTHLY BULLETIN, Vol. 6, No. 12 (June 1938): 149.

3792. Reed, John Shelton. "An Evaluation of an Anti-Lynching Organization." SOCIAL PROBLEMS, Vol. 16, No. 2 (Fall 1968): 172-82. Association of Southern Women for the Prevention of Lynching.

3793. Reeder, Jesse Woodland.   "Federal Efforts to Control Lynching." Ph.D. diss., Cornell Univ., 1952.

3794. ["Report of Committee appointed to present to the Conference of Commissioners on Uniform State Laws and to the American Bar Association the matter of framing and promulgating a model law against lynching."] PROCEEDINGS OF THE ILLINOIS STATE BAR ASSOCIATION, . . . 1915, pp. 211-13.   Chicago: Chicago Legal News Co., 1915.

3795. "Report of House Judiciary Committee on Dyer Anti-Lynching Bill (H.R. 13)." THE CONGRESSIONAL DIGEST, Vol. 1, No. 6 (March 1922): 12.

3796. "Report on Lynching by the Southern Commission on the Study of Lynching." THE EPWORTH HIGHROAD, Vol. 1, No. 7 (July 1932): 20, 54.

3797. "Revised Anti-Lynching Bill Is Introduced."   INTERRACIAL REVIEW, Vol. 10, No. 2 (Feb. 1937): 32.   Brief note.

3798. Ringwalt, Ralph Curtis. "Lynching Legislation." CENTRAL LAW JOURNAL, Vol. 96 (Feb. 20, 1923): 61-63.   On whether Congress may legislate against lynching.

3799. Robinson, N. T. N.   "Anti-Lynching."   THE CONGRESSIONAL DIGEST, Vol. 14, No. 5 (May 1935): 130-31.

3800. Ross, B. Joyce.   J. E. SPINGARN AND THE RISE OF THE NAACP, 1911-1939.   New York: Atheneum, 1972.   See "Lynching" in index.

3801. Rotnem, Victor W.   "The Federal Civil Right 'Not To Be Lynched.'" WASHINGTON UNIVERSITY LAW QUARTERLY, Vol. 28, No. 2 (Feb. 1943): 57-73.

3802. Royster, Jacqueline Jones, ed.   SOUTHERN HORRORS AND OTHER WRITINGS: THE ANTI-LYNCHING CAMPAIGN OF IDA B. WELLS, 1892-1900.   Boston: Bedford Books, 1997.

3803. Schechter, Patricia Ann. "'To Tell the Truth Freely': Ida B. Wells and the Politics of Race, Gender, and Reform in America, 1880-1913." Ph.D. diss., Princeton Univ., 1993.   See Diss. Ab. Intl., Vol. 54, No. 10 (April 1994): 3902A.

3804. Schipper, Martin Paul. A GUIDE TO THE MICROFILM EDITION OF PAPERS OF THE NAACP.   PART 7, THE ANTI-LYNCHING CAMPAIGN, 1912-1955. Editorial advisor, Robert L. Zangrando; associate editors, Randolph H. Boehm and Francine Cary. Frederick, MD: University

Publications of America, 1987.

3805. Seagle, William. "How Not to Stop Lynching." THE NATION, Vol. 140, No. 3647 (May 29, 1935): 626.   Wagner-Costigan anti-lynching bill was amended so as to make it a sham.

3806. "Senate Travesty." INTERRACIAL REVIEW, Vol. 11, No. 1 (Jan. 1938): 13-14.   Part of "As Youth Sees It" section.   Mrs. Dixie Graves, Senator from Alabama, on anti-lynching bill.

3807. "Senators Van Nuys and Wagner To Present Anti-Lynching Bill." INTERRACIAL REVIEW, Vol. 12, No. 1 (Jan. 1939): 16.   Brief.

3808. "Sentiment for Anti-Lynching Bill." THE CRISIS, Vol. 44, No. 3 (March 1937): 81.   Editorial.

3809. "Sentiment on Anti-Lynching Bill." THE CRISIS, Vol. 42, No. 1 (Jan. 1935): 14, 25.   Letters from members and members-elect of Congress.

3810. "Sentiment on Anti-Lynching Bill." THE CRISIS, Vol. 42, No. 2 (Feb. 1935): 42-43, 61-62.   More letters from members of Congress.

3811. "The Shame of a Nation." THE CRISIS, Vol. 25, No. 3 (Jan. 1923): 132-33.   Defeat of Dyer Bill.

3812. "The Shame of America." THE CRISIS, Vol. 25, No. 4 (Feb. 1923): 167-69.   Ad from NAACP against lynching and for Dyer Bill.   Also lynching photos and a map and statistics on lynchings in 1922.

3813. Shillady, John R.   SUMMARY OF LAW, RELATING TO LYNCHING, OF THE STATES (EXCEPT TEXAS) HAVING MORE THAN TWENTY-FIVE LYNCHINGS IN THE PAST THIRTY YEARS. Broadside, prepared for the National Conference on Lynching, New York, May 5-6, 1919. New York, 1919.

3814. "Should America have a federal anti-lynching law? Pro [and] Con." LITERARY DIGEST, Vol. 1 [sic. Vol. 124 of original journal], No. 21 (Dec. 4, 1937): 12.

3815. "Six Anti-Lynching Bills Introduced in Congress." THE SOUTHERN FRONTIER, Vol. 2, No. 2 (Feb. 1941): [1].

3816. Smith, Helena Huntington. "Mrs. Tilly's Crusade." COLLIER'S, Vol. 126, No. 27 (Dec. 30, 1950): 28-29, 66-67.   Southern women working against mob violence and for civil rights.

3817. Smith, J. Clifton. A DIGEST OF THE DYER ANTI-LYNCHING BILL, EXPOSING THE GREATEST FRAUD AGAINST NEGROES SINCE THE FREEDMAN'S BANK. Cambridge, MA: Classic Press, n.d.

3818. Snodderly, Daniel Ross. "The First Anti-Lynching Movement." Thesis (A.B., Honors), Harvard Univ., 1968.

3819. "Some Southern Papers Favor[,] Some Oppose[,] Federal Anti-Lynching Bills." In NEGRO YEAR BOOK . . . 1921-1922, P. 71. Ed. by Monroe N. Work, Tuskegee Institute, AL: Negro Year Book Pub. Co., 1922.

3820. Southern Sociological Congress. "DISTINGUISHED SERVICE" CITIZENSHIP. Ed. by J. E. McCulloch. Washington, DC: Southern Sociological Congress, [1919]. Includes "Resolution on Lynching. Adopted by the Southern Sociological Congress in Annual Session at Knoxville, Tenn., May 12, 1919" (p. 106); J. L. Kesler, "The Outlook" (pp. 112-22; see lynching, p. 121); Edwin Mims, "The Call of the South to Prevent Lynching" (pp 129-36).

3821. "Southern Women and Lynching." THE JOURNAL OF SOCIAL FORCES, Vol. 1, No. 4 (May 1923): 469-70. Anti-lynching resolutions of two groups. Very brief.

3822. "Southern Women Fight Lynching Evil." THE LITERARY DIGEST, Vol. 117, No. 4 (Jan. 27, 1934): 22. Anti-lynching resolution by Association of Southern Women for the Prevention of Lynching; Costigan-Wagner bill.

3823. Spurgeon, Anne M. "'Breaking the Silent Indifference': The Intellectual Development of Ida B. Wells and the Genesis of the Anti-lynching Crusade." M.A. thesis, Univ. of Wisconsin--Madison, 1988.

3824. "St. Louis Dailies Demand Federal Anti-Lynching Law." INTERRA-CIAL REVIEW, Vol. 15, No. 9 (Sept. 1942): 143.

3825. "The States: Texas Minds Its Own Business." TIME, Vol. 53, No. 12 (March 21, 1949): 24. Texas House of Representatives passed anti-lynch bill; Arkansas legislature blocked such a measure.

3826. "The Status of the Dyer Bill." THE CRISIS, Vol. 24, No. 1 (May 1922): 25.

3827. Sterling, Dorothy. BLACK FOREMOTHERS: THREE LIVES. 2d ed.; New York: Feminist Press, 1988. See pp. 61-117 for Ida B. Wells, and pp. 119-57 for Mary Church Terrell, and see "lynching and antilynching crusades" in index.

3828. Stone, Alfred H. "A Mississippian's View of Civil Rights, States Rights, and the Reconstruction Background." THE JOURNAL OF MISSISSIPPI HISTORY, Vol. 10, No. 3 (July 1948): 181-239. See section IV, "'Federal Protection Against Lynching': Senator William E. Borah in the Senate of the United States, January 7, 1938)" (pp. 199-212).

3829. Stone, Gertrude. "How Laws Are Passed--When, If, And Maybe." LABOR DEFENDER, Vol. 11, No. 6 (July 1937): 8-9, 12. Anti-lynching bill.

3830. Storey, Moorfield. BRIEF IN SUPPORT OF THE DYER ANTI-LYNCHING BILL SUBMITTED TO THE COMMITTEE ON THE JUDICIARY OF THE UNITED STATES SENATE. New York: National Assn. for the Advancement of Colored People, [192-].

3831. Straight, Michael. "Revolt in the South." NEW REPUBLIC, Vol. 118, No. 10 (March 8, 1948): 14-15. Includes information about new federal anti-lynching bill.

3832. "Strategy and the Dyer Bill." THE CRISIS, Vol. 28, No. 3 (July 1924): 134.

3833. Streitmatter, Rodger. RAISING HER VOICE: AFRICAN-AMERI-CAN WOMEN JOURNALISTS WHO CHANGED HISTORY. Lexington: University Press of Kentucky, 1994. See Chapter 4, "Ida B. Wells-Barnett: Militant Crusader Against Lynching" (pp. 49-60).

3834. Taft, William Howard. "Shall the Federal Government Protect Aliens in Their Treaty Rights?" THE INDEPENDENT, Vol. 77, No. 3400 (Feb. 2, 1914): 156-58. Federal government should pass laws to protect aliens from lynching and race riots.

3835. Taft, William Howard. "The Unprotected Alien and Our National Responsibility.: THE INDEPENDENT, Vol. 77, No. 3401 (Feb. 9, 1914): 204-08. Lists cases of riot and lynching against aliens. Quotations from Presidents B. Harrison, McKinley, T. Roosevelt, and Taft. Includes proposed federal law.

3836. "Talked Out." COLLIER'S, Vol. 101, No. 10 (March 5, 1938): 66. Time Congress spent on anti-lynching bill means less time for other issues.

3837. Taylor, Alva W. "Growing Support for Federal Anti-Lynching Law." THE CHRISTIAN CENTURY, Vol. 54, No. 51 (Dec. 22, 1937): 1603.

3838. Taylor, Alva W. "Pastors Support Lynching Bill." THE CHRISTIAN

CENTURY, Vol. 54, No. 32 (Aug. 11, 1937): 1003.

3839. Tedrol, Peter. 500 YEARS OF HATE. Dallas: Tol. Higginbotham & Co., 1952.   Only section on lynching is "A Law Against Lynching?" (pp. 100-01); it's unnecessary and "lynching is not merely a device for the control of the Negro" because 21 states lynched more whites than blacks.

3840. Teel, Leonard Ray. "The African-American Press and the Campaign for a Federal Antilynching Law, 1933-34: Using 'Race News' to Shape Public Opinion." AMERICAN JOURNALISM, [Vol. 8] (Spring-Summer 1991): 84-107.

3841. "Temple Board Urges Anti-Lynching Bill." INTERRACIAL REVIEW, Vol. 9, No. 3 (March 1936): 48-49.   Jewish women in National Federation of Temple Sisterhoods. Brief.

3842. "Tennessee Mobilizing for Law and Order." THE SURVEY, Vol. 39, No. 25 (March 23, 1918): 690-91.   Law and Order League organized by whites to combat lynching.

3843. Terborg-Penn, Rosalyn. "African-American Women's Networks in the Anti-Lynching Crusade." In GENDER, CLASS, RACE, AND REFORM IN THE PROGRESSIVE ERA, pp. 148-61 (Chap. 10). Ed. by Noralee Frankel and Nancy S. Dye. Lexington: Univ. Press of Kentucky, 1991.

3844. "Texas Anti-Lynch Law." NEW REPUBLIC, Vol. 120, No. 10 (March 7, 1949): 7.   Not in the special section of this issue, which also has a p. 7.

3845. "These Women and Lynching." HOLLAND'S, THE MAGAZINE OF THE SOUTH, Vol. 59, No. 2 (Feb. 1940): 3.   Editorial; praise for Association of Southern Women for the Prevention of Lynching and its activities.

3846. "The Thirteenth Annual Conference of the N.A.A.C.P." THE CRISIS, Vol. 24, No. 4 (Aug. 1922): 164-67.   Includes references to Dyer Bill.

3847. Thompson, Mildred. "Ida B. Wells-Barnett: An Exploratory Study of an American Black Woman, 1893-1930." Ph.D. diss., George Washington Univ., 1979.   See Diss. Ab. Intl., Vol. 40, No. 1 (July 1979): 404A.

3848. Thompson, Mildred I. IDA B. WELLS-BARNETT: AN EXPLORATORY STUDY OF AN AMERICAN BLACK WOMAN, 1893-1930. Brooklyn, NY: Carlson Pub., 1990. Black Women in United States History, Vol. 15.

3849. "Three Letters." THE CRISIS, Vol. 25, No. 4 (Feb. 1923): 170-72. Dyer Bill.

3850. Tillman, Nathaniel Patrick, Jr. "Walter Francis White: A Study in Interest Group Leadership." Ph.D. diss., Univ. of Wisconsin, 1961.   See Diss. Ab., Vol. 22, No. 6 (Dec. 1961): 2055-56.   Does not mention lynching (or other violent race conflicts). Is mainly about leadership.

3851. Tindall, George. THE EMERGENCE OF THE NEW SOUTH, 1913-1945. Baton Rouge: Louisiana State Univ. Press and the Littlefield Fund for Southern History of the Univ. of Texas, 1967.   Vol. 10 of A History of the South, ed. by Wendell Holmes Stephenson and E. Merton Coulter.   See pp. 550-56 for anti-lynching bills and response of Roosevelt administration; p. 554 for causes of reduced number of lynchings.

3852. "To Make Democracy Safe for America: Resolutions of the Conference on Mob Violence." THE SURVEY, Vol. 38, No. 20 (Aug. 18, 1917): 444.

3853. "'To Secure These Rights.'" RACE RELATIONS: A MONTHLY SUMMARY OF EVENTS AND TRENDS, Vol. 5, Nos. 3 and 4 (Dec. 1947-Jan. 1948): 63-65.   Report of the President's Committee on Civil Rights. Includes lynching. See "Recommendations of the Committee on Civil Rights," ibid., pp. 66-71. See "Press Reactions to the Report of the Committee on Civil Rights," ibid., pp. 72-74.

3854. Toedtman, John. "Federal Anti-lynching Legislation During the New Deal." Honors thesis, College of William and Mary, 1964.

3855. "Tours of the Secretary During the Drive." THE CRISIS, Vol. 16, No. 4 (Aug. 1918): 174-76.   See p. 174 for creation in March of Tennessee Law and Order League to work against lawlessness, especially lynching.

3856. Townes, Emilie M.   "Ida B. Wells-Barnett: An Afro-American Prophet." THE CHRISTIAN CENTURY, Vol. 106, No. 9 (March 15, 1989): 285-86.

3857. "The Un-democratic Filibuster." INTERRACIAL REVIEW, Vol. 11, No. 3 (March 1938): 37.   Anti-lynching bill.

3858. Underwood, R. S. "'I am opposed to lynching, but--.'" THE CRISIS, Vol. 25, No. 2 (Dec. 1922): 70-71.   Support for Dyer anti-lynching bill.

3859. University Commission on Southern Race Questions. AN OPEN LETTER FROM THE UNIVERSITY COMMISSION ON SOUTHERN

RACE QUESTIONS TO THE COLLEGE MEN OF THE SOUTH, ON LYNCHING. N.p.: 1916.   Broadside.

3860. University Commission on Southern Race Questions. MINUTES OF THE UNIVERSITY COMMISSION ON SOUTHERN RACE QUES-TIONS. [Lexington, VA: The Commission, 191-.]   For lynching see pp. 7, 16 [Mob Violence], 32, 39, 45-46 [open letter on lynching from the Commission to the college men of the South], 72-73 ["An Open Letter on Lynching to the Stuttgart (Ark.) Committee"].

3861. "Up To The President." INTERRACIAL REVIEW, Vol. 10, No. 6 (June 1937): 84.   Whether Wagner-Van Nuys bill will become law.

3862. U.S. Congress. House. Committee on the Judiciary. ANTILYNCH-ING BILL. . . . MINORITY REPORT. [To accompany H. R. 1.] House Report No. 71, 68th Cong., 1st Sess. [Jan. 19, 1924].   Serial Set 8226 (HOUSE REPORTS ON PUBLIC BILLS, ETC. Vol. 1).

3863. U.S. Congress. House. Committee on the Judiciary. ANTILYNCH-ING BILL. . . . MINORITY REPORT. [To accompany H. R. 14097.] House Report No. 1027, Part 2, 66th Cong., 2d Sess. [May 29, 1920]. Serial Set 7654 (HOUSE REPORTS. Vol. 3).

3864. U.S. Congress. House. Committee on the Judiciary. ANTI-LYNCHING BILL. . . . REPORT. [To accompany H. R. 13.] House Report No. 452, 67th Cong., 1st Sess. [Oct. 31, 1921] Corrected print. Serial Set 7921 (HOUSE REPORTS. Vol. 2).

3865. U.S. Congress. House. Committee on the Judiciary. ANTI-LYNCHING BILL. . . . REPORT. [To accompany H. R. 14097.] House Report No. 1027 [part 1], 66th Cong., 2d Sess. [May 22, 1920]. Serial Set 7654 (HOUSE REPORTS. Vol. 3).

3866. U.S. Congress. House. Committee on the Judiciary. ANTILYNCH-ING. . . . REPORT [To accompany H. R. 2251] House Report No. 563, 75th Cong., 1st Sess. Serial Set 10083 (HOUSE REPORTS ON PUBLIC BILLS, ETC. Vol. 1).

3867. U.S. Congress. House. Committee on the Judiciary. CIVIL RIGHTS. HEARINGS . . . EIGHTY-FIFTH CONGRESS FIRST SESSION . . . Washington, DC: USGPO, 1957.   Supt. of Doc. #: Y4.J89/1:85/1. Anti-lynching provisions of bills, part of Atty. General's statement, statements of members of Congress, and testimony of various people.

3868. U.S. Congress. House. Committee on the Judiciary. CIVIL RIGHTS. HEARINGS . . . EIGHTY-FOURTH CONGRESS SECOND SESSION . . . Washington, DC: USGPO, 1955. Supt. of Doc. #: Y4.J89/1:84/11/PT.1. Anti-lynching provisions of bills, Attorney General's statement on proposed Antilynching Act, and testimony of various people.

3869. U.S. Congress. House. Committee on the Judiciary. CIVIL RIGHTS. HEARINGS . . . EIGHTY-FOURTH CONGRESS SECOND SESSION . . . EXECUTIVE SESSION. APRIL 10, 1956. PART 2. Washington, DC: USGPO, 1956. Supt. of Doc. #: Y4.J89/1:84/11/PT.2. Includes anti-lynching provisions of proposed bill.

3870. U.S. Congress. House. Committee on the Judiciary. CIVIL RIGHTS. HEARINGS . . . EIGHTY-SIXTH CONGRESS FIRST SESSION . . . Washington, DC: USGPO, 1959. Supt. of Doc. #: Y4.J89/1:86/5

3871. U.S. Congress. House. Committee on the Judiciary. CONSTITU-TIONALITY OF A FEDERAL ANTILYNCHING LAW. HEARING . . . SIXTY-SEVENTH CONGRESS FIRST SESSION ON H. R. 13 . . . SERIAL 10--PART 1 . . . Washington, DC: GPO, 1921. Supt. of Doc. #: Y4.J89/1:L99/6-1

3872. U.S. Congress. House. Committee on the Judiciary. CONSTITU-TIONALITY OF A FEDERAL ANTILYNCHING LAW. HEARING . . . SIXTY-SEVENTH CONGRESS FIRST SESSION ON H. R. 13 . . . SERIAL 10--PART 2 . . . Washington, DC: GPO, 1921. (Pagination continues from Part 1 as pp. 33-55). Supt. of Doc. #: Y4.J89/1:L99/6-1, 2

3873. U.S. Congress. House. Committee on the Judiciary. CONSTITU-TIONALITY OF A FEDERAL ANTILYNCHING LAW. HEARING . . . SIXTY-SEVENTH CONGRESS FIRST SESSION ON H. R. 13 . . . SERIAL 10--PART 3 . . . Washington, DC: GPO, 1921. (Pagination continues from Part 2 as pp. 57-62). Supt. of Doc. #: Y4.J89/1:L99/6-2, 3

3874. U.S. Congress. House. Committee on the Judiciary. CONSTITU-TIONALITY OF FEDERAL ANTILYNCHING LAW, H. R. 13, CORRE-SPONDENCE FROM ATTORNEY GENERAL, AUG. 9, 1921. Reprint 1922. Serial 10, pt. 3. Supt. of Doc. #: Y4.J89/1:L99/6-3, 1922

3875. U.S. Congress. House. Committee on the Judiciary. MOB VIOLENCE AND LYNCHING . . . REPORT [To accompany H. R. 5673]. House Report No. 1597, 80th Cong., 2d Sess. [March 23, 1948]. Washing-ton, DC: USGPO, 1948. Serial Set 11210 (HOUSE MISCELLANEOUS REPORTS. Vol. 2).

3876. U.S. Congress. House. Committee on the Judiciary. PART I, SEGREGATION. PART II, ANTI-LYNCHING. HEARINGS . . . SIXTY-SIXTH CONGRESS, SECOND SESSION . . . JANUARY 15 AND 29, 1920. Washington, DC: GPO, 1920. Part I: pp. 3-12; Part II: pp. 13-75. Supt. of Doc. #: Y4.J89/1:L99/5

3877. U.S. Congress. House. Committee on the Judiciary. Subcommittee No. 3. ANTILYNCHING AND PROTECTION OF CIVIL RIGHTS. HEARINGS . . . EIGHTY-FIRST CONGRESS FIRST AND SECOND SESSIONS . . . Washington, DC: USGPO, 1950. Supt. of Doc. #: Y4.J89/1:81-2/18

3878. U.S. Congress. House. Committee on the Judiciary. Subcommittee No. 4. ANTILYNCHING. HEARINGS . . . EIGHTIETH CONGRESS SECOND SESSION . . . Washington, DC: USGPO, 1948. Supt. of Doc. #: Y4.J89/1:An8/9

3879. U.S. Congress. House. Committee on the Judiciary. TO PRO-TECT CITIZENS AGAINST LYNCHING. HEARINGS . . . SIXTY-FIFTH CONGRESS SECOND SESSION . . . Washington, DC: GPO, 1918. Serial 66, pt. 1. Supt. of Doc. #: Y4.J89/1:L99/2

3880. U.S. Congress. House. Committee on the Judiciary. TO PRO-TECT CITIZENS AGAINST LYNCHING, HEARING . . . SIXTY-FIFTH CONGRESS SECOND SESSION . . . PART 2 BRIEF OF GEORGE S. HORNBLOWER, JULY 12, 1918. Washington, DC: GPO, 1918. Serial 66, pt. 2. Supt. of Doc. #: Y4.J89/1:P94/7

3881. U.S. Congress. Senate. Committee on the Judiciary. ANTI-LYNCHING. . . . REPORT [To accompany S. 1978] Senate Report No. 710, 73d Cong., 2d Sess. [March 28 (calendar day, April 12), 1934]. Serial Set 9770 (SENATE REPORTS ON PUBLIC BILLS, ETC. Vol. 2).

3882. U.S. Congress. Senate. Committee on the Judiciary. ANTI-LYNCHING. . . . REPORT [To accompany S. 24] Senate Report No. 340, 74th Cong., 1st Sess. [March 13 (calendar day, March 18), 1935]. Serial Set 9878 (SENATE REPORTS ON PUBLIC BILLS, ETC. Vol. 1).

3883. U.S. Congress. Senate. Committee on the Judiciary. ANTILYNCH-ING. . . . REPORT [To accompany H. R. 1507] Senate Report No. 793, 75th Cong., 1st Sess. Serial Set 10077 (SENATE REPORTS ON PUBLIC BILLS, ETC. Vol. 2).

3884. U.S. Congress. Senate. Committee on the Judiciary. ANTI-LYNCHING. . . . REPORT [To accompany H. R. 801] Senate Report No.

1380, 76th Cong., 3d Sess. Serial Set 10429 (SENATE MISCELLANEOUS REPORTS. Vol. 2). Washington, DC: USGPO, 1940.

3885. U.S. Congress. Senate. Committee on the Judiciary. ANTI-LYNCHING. . . . REPORT [To accompany S. 2860]. Senate Report No. 1625, 80th Cong., 2d Sess. [June 14, 1948]. Washington, DC: USGPO, 1948. Serial Set 11208 (SENATE MISCELLANEOUS REPORTS. Vol. 4).

3886. U.S. Congress. Senate. Committee on the Judiciary. ANTI-LYNCHING. . . . REPORT [To accompany S. 230]. Senate Report No. 462, 81st Cong., 1st Sess. [June 6, 1949]. Washington, DC: USGPO, 1949. Serial Set 11292 (SENATE MISCELLANEOUS REPORTS. Vol. 2).

3887. U.S. Congress. Senate. Committee on the Judiciary. ANTI-LYNCHING BILL. . . . REPORT. [To accompany H. R. 13.] Senate Report No. 837, 67th Cong., 2d Sess. [April 20 (calendar day, July 28, 1922]. Serial Set 7951 (SENATE REPORTS. Vol. 2).

3888. U.S. Congress. Senate. Committee on the Judiciary. BRIEF OF HERBERT K. STOCKTON ON DYER ANTILYNCHING BILL. 1922. Supt. of Doc. #: Y4.J89/2:L99

3889. U.S. Congress. Senate. Committee on the Judiciary. CIVIL RIGHTS. HEARINGS . . . EIGHTY-SIXTH CONGRESS FIRST SESSION . . . Washington, DC: USGPO, 1959. Supt. of Doc. #: Y4.J89/2:C49/13/959/1-4

3890. U.S. Congress. Senate. Committee on the Judiciary. CRIME OF LYNCHING. HEARINGS . . . EIGHTIETH CONGRESS SECOND SESSION . . . Washington, DC: USGPO, 1948. Supt. of Doc. #: Y4.J89/2:L99/6

3891. U.S. Congress. Senate. Committee on the Judiciary. CRIME OF LYNCHING, HEARINGS . . . SEVENTY-SIXTH CONGRESS THIRD SESSION. . . . Washington, DC: GPO, 1940. Supt. of Doc. #: Y4.J89/2:L99/5

3892. U.S. Congress. Senate. Committee on the Judiciary. PUNISH-MENT FOR THE CRIME OF LYNCHING, HEARINGS . . . SEVENTY-FOURTH CONGRESS FIRST SESSION. Washington, DC: GPO, 1935. Supt. of Doc. #: Y4.J89/2:L99/4

3893. U.S. Congress. Senate. Committee on the Judiciary. PUNISH-MENT FOR CRIME OF LYNCHING, HEARINGS . . . SEVENTY-THIRD CONGRESS SECOND SESSION. Washington, DC: GPO, 1934.

Supt. of Doc. #: Y4.J89/2:L99/3/pt. 1

3894. U.S. Congress. Senate. Committee on the Judiciary. PUNISH-MENT FOR THE CRIME OF LYNCHING, HEARINGS . . . SEVENTY-THIRD CONGRESS SECOND SESSION. Washington, DC: GPO, 1934. Supt. of Doc. #: Y4.J89/2:L99/3/pt. 2

3895. U.S. Congress. Senate. Committee on the Judiciary. TO PRE-VENT AND PUNISH THE CRIME OF LYNCHING. HEARING . . . SIXTY-NINTH CONGRESS FIRST SESSION ON S. 121 . . . Washington, DC: GPO, 1926. Supt. of Doc. #: Y4.J89/2:L99/2

3896. "Value of Federal Action in Lynching." THE CRISIS, Vol. 42, No. 3 (March 1935): 81.

3897. Van Hecke, M. T. "Lynching or the Law?" STATE GOVERN-MENT, Vol. 7, No. 3 (March 1934): 58-59.   Mainly about proposed model anti-lynching law in Chadbourn's Lynching and the Law.

3898. Van Nuys, Frederick. "by U. S. Senator Frederick Van Nuys." THE CONGRESSIONAL DIGEST, Vol. 19, No. 8 and 9 (Aug.-Sept. 1940): 208-10. Report on anti-lynching bill. Part of "Pro: Should the Powers of the Federal Government Be Increased?"

3899. Van Steenwyk, Elizabeth. Ed. by Mary P. Rich. IDA B. WELLS-BARNETT: WOMAN OF COURAGE. Danbury, CT: Franklin Watts, Inc., 1992.

3900. Villard, Oswald Garrison. "Issues and Men." THE NATION, Vol. 143, No. 7 (Aug. 15, 1936): 185.   Victories by black Americans in Olympics should shame Congress into passing an anti-lynching bill.

3901. "Violence May Bring U.S. Lynch Law."   THE SATURDAY EVENING POST, Vol. 219, No. 8 (Aug. 24, 1946): 120.   Editorial.

3902. "Virginia's Anti-Lynching Law." THE LITERARY DIGEST, Vol. 96, No. 10 (March 10, 1928): 14.

3903. "Wagner To Continue Fight For Anti-Lynching Law." INTERRA-CIAL REVIEW, Vol. 11, No. 8 (Aug. 1938): 128.   Brief.

3904. Waldman, Jacob.   "The Constitutionality of the Wagner-Costigan Anti-Lynching Bill." THE GEORGE WASHINGTON LAW REVIEW, Vol. 2, No. 4 (May 1934): 498-504.

3905. Walker, Alice. "Advancing Luna--and Ida B. Wells." In YOU CAN'T KEEP A GOOD WOMAN DOWN, pp. 85-104. San Diego: Harcourt Brace Jovanovich, 1981.   Rape of a white civil rights worker (Luna) by black man in Georgia, 1965. Brief references to Ida B. Wells and lynching.

3906. Walter, David O. "Proposals for a Federal Anti-Lynching Law." THE AMERICAN POLITICAL SCIENCE REVIEW, Vol. 28, No. 3 (June 1934): 436-42.

3907. "Washington and Lynchers." AMERICA, Vol. 52, No. 8 (Dec. 1, 1934): 170-71.   Refusal of federal government to act against Florida lynchers who kidnapped victim in Alabama raises question of whether a federal anti-lynching law would be enforced.

3908. "Washington Vigilance." THE CRISIS, Vol. 10, No. 1 (May 1915): 30-31.   Washington, DC, branch of NAACP acts as vigilance committee regarding legislation in Congress.

3909. Watson, Charles H. "Need of Federal Legislation in Respect to Mob Violence in Cases of Lynching of Aliens." YALE LAW JOURNAL, Vol. 25, No. 7 (May 1916): 561-81.   Reprinted in Chicago Legal News, Vol. 48, No. 43 (May 25, 1916): 342-44; ibid., Vol. 48, No. 44 (June 1, 1916): 350-52.

3910. "We Lose, But We Win." THE CRISIS, Vol. 45, No. 3 (March 1938): 81.   Editorial on the demise of the anti-lynching bill.

Wells, Ida B. CRUSADE FOR JUSTICE: THE AUTOBIOGRAPHY OF IDA B. WELLS. See Duster, Alfreda M., in this chapter.

Wells, Ida B. "Lynch Law." See THE REASON WHY THE COLORED AMERICAN IS NOT IN THE WORLD'S COLUMBIAN EXPOSITION in Chapter IV of this bibliography.

3911. Wells, Ida B. IDA B. WELLS TELLS ABOUT LYNCHINGS. Introduction by Al I. Obaba.   African Islamic Mission Publications, n.d. See Books In Print 1993-94.

3912. Wells, Ida B. THE MEMPHIS DIARY OF IDA B. WELLS. Ed. by Miriam DeCosta-Willis. Boston: Beacon Press, 1995.

3913. Wells, Ida B. SOUTHERN HORRORS: LYNCH LAW IN ALL ITS PHASES. New York: New York Age Print, 1892.   Reprinted in Ida B. Wells-Barnett On Lynchings (1969).

3914. White, Walter. "The Costigan-Wagner Bill." THE CRISIS, Vol. 42,

No. 1 (Jan. 1935): 10-11, 29.

3915. White, Walter. "Rope and Fagot Detective." NEGRO DIGEST, Vol. 2, No. 9 (July 1944): 63-68.   Condensed from The American Mercury (Jan. 1929).

3916. White, Walter F.   "The Anti-Lynching Bill in the New Congress." THE CRISIS, Vol. 44, No. 1 (Jan. 1937): 15, 29.

3917. White, Walter F.   "The Costigan-Wagner Bill." THE CRISIS, Vol. 42, No. 1 (Jan. 1935): 10-11, 29.   Campaign to pass federal anti-lynching bill.

3918. Whittington, W. M.   "by U.S. Representative W. M. Whittington." THE CONGRESSIONAL DIGEST, Vol. 19, No. 8 and 9 (Aug.-Sept. 1940): 217-18.   Opposition to anti-lynching bill. Part of "Con: Should the Power of the Federal Government Be Increased?"

3919. "Who Checked Lynching." THE CRISIS, Vol. 29, No. 4 (Feb. 1925): 154, 156.   Statistics on lynching 1885-1924, and who and what are responsible for reduction in number of lynchings, e.g., NAACP, publicity, and fear of a federal anti-lynching law. Urges passage of Dyer Bill.

3920. WHY WE MARCH.   In EYEWITNESS: THE NEGRO IN AMERICAN HISTORY, p. 393. William Loren Katz. New York: Pitman Pub. Corp., 1967.   Leaflet about the Negro Silent Parade, July 28, 1917, in New York City to protest lynchings and discrimination.

3921. Wilkins, Roy. "Sweet Land of Liberty." LABOR DEFENDER, Vol. 11, No. 3 (April 1937): 4-5.   Anti-lynching struggle--with map, chart, and illustration.

3922. "Will Anti-Lynching Bill be Passed?" SOCIAL JUSTICE REVIEW, Vol. 42, No. 4 (July-Aug. 1949): 126.   Reprinted from What's Happening in Washington, published by Prentice-Hall.

3923. Winfrey, Annie Laura. "The Organized Activities of the Women of Southern Methodism in the Field of Negro-White Relationships, 1886-1937." M.A. thesis, Scarritt College for Christian Workers [Nashville, TN], 1938.

3924. "Women and Lynch Law." THE COMMONWEAL, Vol. 13, No. 7 (Dec. 17, 1930): 171-72.   Recent protests by Southern women.

3925. Woofter, T. J., Jr.   PROGRESS IN RACE RELATIONS IN GEORGIA: REPORT OF THE SECRETARY OF THE GEORGIA

COMMITTEE ON RACE RELATIONS FOR 1922. [Atlanta]: Georgia Committee on Race Relations [Commission on Interracial Cooperation], [1922].

3926. Woofter, T. J., Jr. "Southern Backfires against Lynch Law." THE SURVEY, Vol. 51, No. 2 (Oct. 15, 1923): 99-100. Federal, state, and local efforts against lynching, especially in the South.

3927. "Would the Dyer Bill Halt Lynching?" THE LITERARY DIGEST, Vol. 73, No. 11 (June 10, 1922): 14.

3928. Yandle, Carolyn Devore. "A Delicate Crusade: The Association of Southern Women for the Prevention of Lynching." M.A. thesis, Univ. of Virginia, 1969.

3929. "Yesterday in Negro History." JET, Vol. 17, No. 9 (Dec. 24, 1959): 9. Entire item: "December 20, 1893--The first anti-lynch statute in the U.S. was enacted by the state of Georgia as 'an act to prevent mob violence in this state.'"

3930. Zangrando. Robert L. "The Efforts of the National Association for the Advancement of Colored People to Secure Passage of a Federal Anti-Lynching Law, 1920-1940." Ph.D. diss., Univ. of Pennsylvania, 1963. See Diss. Ab., Vol. 24, No. 10 (April 1964): 4169.

3931. Zangrando. Robert L. "The NAACP and a Federal Antilynching Bill, 1934-40." THE JOURNAL OF NEGRO HISTORY, Vol. 50, No. 2 (April 1965): 106-17.

3932. Zangrando. Robert L. THE NAACP CRUSADE AGAINST LYNCHING, 1909-1950. Philadelphia: Temple Univ. Press, 1980.

3933. Zangrando. Robert L. "The 'Organized Negro': The National Association for the Advancement of Colored People and Civil Rights." In THE BLACK EXPERIENCE IN AMERICA: SELECTED ESSAYS, pp. 145-71. James C. Curtis and Lewis L. Gould, eds. Austin: Univ. of Texas Press, 1970.

VIII

Prose Fiction, Poems, Ballads, and Films

3934. Adams, E. C. L. "The Lynchers." In NIGGER TO NIGGER, pp. 110-13. New York: Scribner's, 1928. A poem.

3935. Alexander, David. "And On the Third Day." In MAIDEN MURDERS, pp. 174-89. Mystery Writers of America. New York: Harper & Brothers, 1952. Temporary "borrowing" of five-year-old white girl leads to lynching of three blacks.

3936. Alexander, Truman H. LOOT. Dallas: Southwest Press, 1932. Ends with an attempted lynching.

3937. Allan, Lewis. "Strange Fruit." Words and music of short song about lynching of Southern blacks. Printed copy in compact disc recording "lady in autumn: the best of the verve years," sung by Billie Holiday. New York: PolyGram Records, 1991.

3938. Andrews, Regina. Climbing Jacob's Ladder. In Schomburg Center for Research in Black Culture, New York. A 1931 play including a lynching. Source: Kathy A. Perkins, Black Female Playwrights: An Anthology of Plays before 1950 (Bloomington: Indiana Univ. Press, 1989, 1990), pp. 10, 281.

3939. "Anti-Lynching Film A Hit in New York." INTERRACIAL REVIEW, Vol. 9, No. 7 (July 1936): 112. One paragraph. Film: Fury.

3940. Arcudi, John. THE LYNCHING. Philadelphia: Dorrance & Co., 1965. Poem of 93-pages; locale unclear. Young man hanged by mob.

3941. Ashby, Rickie Zayne. "The Possum Hunters in the Oral Tradition." KENTUCKY FOLKLORE RECORD, Vol. 21, No. 2 (April-June 1975): 56-61. Two songs and a poem about a vigilante group in Muhlenberg and

Ohio counties in Kentucky after the Kentucky Tobacco War and before World War I.

3942. Ashmun, Margaret. "The Vigilantes." In SONGS OF THE CATTLE TRAIL AND COW CAMP, pp. 150-51. Ed. by John A. Lomax. New York: Macmillan, 1939.   Lyrics only.

3943. Baird, Keith E. "Poplarville II." FREEDOMWAYS, Vol. 2, No. 2 (Spring 1962): 172.   Poem about lynching of Mack Parker.

3944. Baker, Carlos. "Sinner." ARTS QUARTERLY, No. 1 (Jan. 1931): 37-42.   Lynching story.

3945. Baldwin, James. Blues for Mister Charlie. New York: Dial Press, 1964.   No lynching, but black man is murdered after false allegation that he made sexual advances to wife of white store owner. Baldwin wrote (p. 5) that the play "is based, very distantly indeed, on the case of Emmett Till."

3946. Baldwin, James. "Going to Meet the Man." In GOING TO MEET THE MAN, pp. 227-49. New York: Dial Press, 1965.   Short story. Impotent white man is aroused, in part by memory of black man's lynching he saw when a child. Analyzed in Harris, Exorcising Blackness, pp. 86-94.

3947. Bates, Arthenia J. "Lost Note." In SEEDS BENEATH THE SNOW, pp. 113-21. Washington, DC: Howard Univ. Press, 1975.   Woman's lesson to a black youth to avoid white women and whistling. [Influence of Till case?]

3948. Beecher, John. "Their Blood Cries Out." NEGRO DIGEST, Vol. 3, No. 3 (Jan. 1945): 13-15.   Poem. Partly about lynched black man.

3949. Bodenheim, Maxwell. "Lynched Negro." In THE POETRY OF THE NEGRO, pp. 273-74. Ed. by Langston Hughes and Arna Bontemps. Garden City, NY: Doubleday, 1949.   Also in Hughes and Bontemps, The Poetry of the Negro 1746-1970 (rev. ed.; Garden City, NY: Doubleday, 1970), pp. 509-10.

3950. Bradley, David. THE CHANEYSVILLE INCIDENT. New York: Harper & Row, 1981.   Includes attempted lynching of two black men. Analyzed in Harris, Exorcising Blackness, pp. 162-83.

3951. Brooks, Gwendolyn. "The Last Quatrain of the Ballad of Emmett Till." In SELECTED POEMS, p. 81. Gwendolyn Brooks. New York: Harper & Row, 1963. Also in The World of Gwendolyn Brooks, p. 324. Gwendolyn Brooks Blakely. New York: Harper & Row, 1971.   Brief poem.

3952. Brooks, Gwendolyn. "Southern Lynching." THE CRISIS, Vol. 44, No. 6 (June 1937): 189.   A poem.

3953. Brown, Sterling A. "Old Lem." In I AM THE DARKER BROTH-ER: AN ANTHOLOGY OF MODERN POEMS BY BLACK AMERI-CANS, pp. 68-69.   Ed. by Arnold Adoff.   Collier Books.   New York: Macmillan, 1970.   Includes lynching.

3954. Brown, William Wells.   The Escape; Or, a Leap for Freedom: a Drama in Five Acts. Philadelphia: Rhistoric [sic] Publications, 1969 (reprint courtesy of The Library Company of Philadelphia).   Judith L. Stephens, African American Review (Summer 1992): 338, calls it the 1858 play which introduced lynching in American drama.   See pp. 40-44: no actual lynching.

3955. Bryant, Ira Samuel. "'An Unfortunate Affair.' A Story Illustrative of How Accidents Sometimes Happen in the Sunny South." THE COLORED AMERICAN MAGAZINE, Vol. 4, No. 4 (March 1902): 373-76.   Lynching story.

3956. Buckland, Roscoe L. "Contrasting Views of Lynching in Two Wister Stories." WYOMING ANNALS, Vol. 65, No. 4 (Winter 1993): 36-46.   Ex-amines the book The Virginian and short story "The Gift Horse."

3957. Burbridge, Edward Dejoie. "'They Went About Their Business.'" THE CRISIS, Vol. 42, No. 3 (March 1935): 77.   A poem about the lynching of Jerome Wilson in Franklinton, Louisiana, Jan. 1935.

3958. Burdett, Samuel.   A TEST OF LYNCH LAW, AN EXPOSE OF MOB VIOLENCE AND THE COURTS OF HELL.   Seattle: Samuel Burdett, 1901.   Black author's 100-page booklet, most of which is a fictional account of a lynching and the trial of a white lyncher.

3959. Burrill, Mary.   Aftermath.   THE LIBERATOR, Vol. 2, No. 4 (April 1919): 10-14.   Anti-lynching play.   Black war hero comes home to South Carolina and learns his father was lynched while he was overseas.

3960. Burt, Olive W., ed.   AMERICAN MURDER BALLADS AND THEIR STORIES. New York: Oxford Univ. Press, 1958.   See pp. 57-60 ("The Ashland Tragedy"), 60-64 (Mary Phagan and Leo Frank), 110-11 (Joseph and Hyrum Smith), 163-65 (Bald Knobbers), 165-67 (David Hennessy and lynching of Italians), 167-68 (lynching of Reno brothers and C. Anderson, 1868), 168-69 ("Lay of the Vigilantes"), 170-72 (lynching of Ella Watson), 177-78 (lynching of Dr. J. B. Crane by California vigilantes, 1854).

3961. Caccavari, Peter Jerome. "Reconstructions of Race and Culture in America: Violence and Knowledge in Works by Albion Tourgee, Charles Chesnutt, and Thomas Dixon, Jr." Ph.D. diss., Rutgers Univ., 1993.   See Diss. Ab. Intl., Vol. 54, No. 11 (May 1994): 4090A.   Abstract has several references to lynching.

3962. Caldwell, Erskine. THE COMPLETE STORIES OF ERSKINE CALDWELL. New York: Duell, Sloan and Pearce; Boston: Little, Brown [1953?].   See "Saturday Afternoon" (pp. 28-33) and "Kneel to the Rising Sun" (pp. 641-64), which are lynching stories.

3963. Caldwell, Erskine. TROUBLE IN JULY. New York: Duell, Sloan & Pearce, 1940.   Rape charge leads to lynching of innocent black man. When supposed rape victim says nothing happened, mob stones her to death.

3964. Camp, Will. VIGILANTE JUSTICE. New York: HarperPaperbacks [sic], 1994.   A novel of the old West; conflict between large and small ranchers leads to several killings.

3965. Campbell, Bebe Moore. YOUR BLUES AIN'T LIKE MINE. New York: G. P. Putnam's Sons, 1992.   Novel which fictionalizes the Emmett Till case.

3966. Carby, Hazel V.   RECONSTRUCTING WOMANHOOD: THE EMERGENCE OF THE AFRO-AMERICAN WOMAN NOVELIST. New York: Oxford Univ. Press, 1987. See pp. 108-16 for Ida Wells and lynching. See pp. 136-41 for Pauline Hopkins and lynching.

3967. Carlyle, Sylvia J. INNOCENT, IGNORANT, AND BLACK. New York: Vantage Press, 1964.   Six whites lynch young black man. Some of the lynchers later meet violent deaths.

3968. Chapin, Katherine Garrison. "And They Lynched Him on a Tree." THE NATION, Vol. 150, No. 23 (June 8, 1940): 707-08.   A poem.

3969. Chesnutt, Charles. THE MARROW OF TRADITION. Boston and New York: Houghton Mifflin, 1901. Reprint: Ann Arbor: Univ. of Michigan Press, 1969.   See pp. 187-235 for threatened lynching of a black man for a murder committed by a white man in black-face.

3970. Clark, L. D. A BRIGHT TRAGIC THING: A TALE OF CIVIL WAR TEXAS. El Paso: Cinco Puntos Press, 1992.   Historical novel recreating mass hanging at Gainesville, Texas.

3971. Clark, Walter Van Tilburg. THE OX-BOW INCIDENT. New York: Signet Classic, New American Library, 1960. Innocent men lynched. This edition includes "Afterword" by Walter Prescott Webb (pp. 219-24).

3972. Coburn, Walt. "Vigilante Vengeance." LONG JOHN LATHAM'S WESTERN FICTION MAGAZINE [Conroe, TX], Vol. 1, No. 2 (Sept.-Oct. 1970), 4-17.

3973. Coe, Charles Francis. "Vigilante." SATURDAY EVENING POST, Vol. 205, No. 32 (Feb. 4, 1933): 3-5, 71-72, 76. First installment of fictional story. See also Vol. 205, No. 33 (Feb. 11, 1933): 18-19, 38-39; Vol. 205, No. 34 (Feb. 18, 1933): 16-17, 39, 42, 44-45; Vol. 205, No. 35 (Feb. 25, 1933): 18-19, 36, 40-41; Vol. 205, No. 36 (March 4, 1933): 20-21, 32, 34; Vol. 205, No. 37 (March 11, 1933): 20-21, 91-92, 96.

3974. Cooke, John Byrne. THE COMMITTEE OF VIGILANCE: A NOVEL OF GOLD RUSH SAN FRANCISCO. New York: Bantam Books, 1994.

3975. Cullen, Countee. "The Black Christ." In THE BLACK CHRIST & OTHER POEMS, pp. 67-110. New York: Harper & Brothers, 1929. Poem which includes lynching. Includes illustration by Charles Cullen. The poem is analyzed in Jean Wagner, Black Poets of the United States, trans. by Kenneth Douglas (Urbana: Univ. of Illinois Press, 1973), pp. 336, 341-43.

3976. Cullen, Countee P. "Christ Recrucified." KELLEY'S MAGAZINE (Oct. 1922): 13. Reprinted and analyzed in Jean Wagner, Black Poets of the United States, trans. by Kenneth Douglas (Urbana: Univ. of Illinois Press, 1973), pp. 335-36.

3977. Curran, J. J. "Lynching forecast." THE CATHOLIC WORKER, Vol. 4, No. 8 (Dec. 1936): 7. Fanciful description of lynching conducted in holiday mood.

3978. Cuthbert, Marion. "Mob Madness." THE CRISIS, Vol. 43, No. 4 (April 1936): 108, 114. "A stark story reminiscent of the Claude Neal lynching of 1934." Seems like fiction.

3979. Davis, Frank Marshall. "Lynched." In BLACK MAN'S VERSE, p. 25-29. Chicago: Black Cat Press, 1935. See comments in Jean Wagner, Black Poets of the United States, trans. by Kenneth Douglas (Urbana: Univ. of Illinois Press, 1973), p. 188.

3980. de la Roché, Francois. MISSISSIPPI MOOD. Chicago: Howard A. Burk & Co., 1937. Half-wit mulatto is lynched after false accusations.

3981. Dempsey, Al. WHAT LAW THERE WAS. A Tor Book. New York: Tom Doherty Associates, 1991.   Masons, vigilantes, and Henry Plummer in Bannack-Virginia City area, 1860s.

3982. Diggs, Clara Morris. THE CURSE AT THE DOOR. Boston: Cornhill Pub. Co., 1922.   Includes murder of white woman by two white men so they could incriminate a black man and get him lynched. Also, miscellaneous lynching references: pp. 26, 135, 156, 185-88.

3983. Dreiser, Theodore. "Nigger Jeff." In MAJOR WRITERS OF AMERICA, Vol. II, pp. 472-84.   From Free and Other Stories (1918). A black man is lynched for assaulting a white girl.

3984. Dresser, Davis. LYNCH-ROPE LAW. New York: William Morrow and Co., 1941.   Western fiction. Truth about old murder (made to look like suicide) comes out during attempted lynching.

3985. DuBois, W. E. B. "Jesus Christ in Georgia." In CREATIVE WRITINGS BY W.E.B. [sic] DU BOIS: A PAGEANT, POEMS, SHORT STORIES AND PLAYLETS, pp. 79-84. Ed. by Herbert Aptheker. White Plains, NY: Kraus-Thomson Organization, 1985.   Orig. in The Crisis, Vol. 3 (Dec. 1911): 70-74.   Revised and reprinted as "Jesus Christ in Texas" in Darkwater, pp. 123-33.   A black man is lynched in this short story.

3986. Dunbar, Paul Laurence. "The Haunted Oak." In THE LIFE AND WORKS OF PAUL LAURENCE DUNBAR, pp. 297-98. Ed. by Lida Keck Wiggins. Naperville, IL: J. L. Nichols & Co., n.d.; New York: Kraus Reprint Co., 1971.   Poem about lynching an innocent man.

3987. Dunbar, Paul Laurence. "The Lynching of Jube Benson." In THE PAUL LAURENCE DUNBAR READER, pp. 232-39. Ed. by Jay Martin and Gossie H. Hudson. New York: Dodd, Mead & Co., 1975.   Story about hanging an innocent black man for the crime of a white man in black-face.

3988. Edmonds, Randolph. Bad Man. In SIX PLAYS FOR A NEGRO THEATER, pp. 11-35. By Randolph Edmonds. Boston: Walter H. Baker Co., 1934.   Black man gives himself up to lynch mob and is burned to death.

3989. Edmonds, Randolph. The Land of Cotton. In THE LAND OF COTTON AND OTHER PLAYS, pp. 3-145. By Randolph Edmonds. Washington, DC: Associated Publishers, 1942.   Economic conflicts in 1930s cause lynching attempt which fails as lynchers and sharecroppers battle.

3990. Edmunds, Murrell. "Brothers." In RED, WHITE AND BLACK:

TWELVE STORIES OF THE SOUTH, pp. 24-41. New York: Bernard Ackerman, 1945.   Lynching of a black man in this short story.

3991. Edwards, Josh. SEARCHER: LYNCH LAW. New York: Charter/-Diamond Books (Berkley Publishing Group), 1990.   In this Western novel the hero is almost lynched; much violence follows.

3992. Elliott, Sarah Barnwell. "An Incident." HARPER'S NEW MONTH-LY MAGAZINE, Vol. 96, No. 573 (Feb. 1898): 458-72.   Sheriff saves black man from being lynched.

3993. Ellison, Ralph. "The Birthmark."   A short story. See Trudier Harris, Exorcising Blackness, p. 77.

3994. Emanuel, James A. "Emmett Till." In THE POETRY OF BLACK AMERICA: ANTHOLOGY OF THE 20TH CENTURY, p. 179. Ed. by Arnold Adoff. New York: Harper & Row, 1973.   Brief poem.

3995. Evans, Frank K.   A PLEA TO PRESIDENT ROOSEVELT. Eastland, TX: Weekly Record, 1935.   Letter to Franklin Roosevelt, Dec. 1934, enclosing anti-lynching poem "A Plea to President Roosevelt."

3996. Faulkner, William. "Dry September." In COLLECTED STORIES OF WILLIAM FAULKNER, pp. 169-83. New York: Random House, 1950. Rumor of white woman's rape leads to ('offstage') lynching.

3997. Faulkner, William. LIGHT IN AUGUST. New York: H. Smith & R. Haas, 1932.   A murder in this novel is sometimes referred to as a lynching--but it fits almost no definition of lynching.

3998. Fearing, Kenneth. "The Screen: 'Fury'--Anti-Lynch Film." NEW MASSES, Vol. 19, No. 12 (June 16, 1936): 28.   A review.

3999. Flannagan, Roy. AMBER SATYR. Garden City, NY: Doubleday, Doran & Co., 1932.   Mulatto man is lynched.

4000. Fletcher, T. Thomas Fortune. "That Other Golgotha." In NEGRO: AN ANTHOLOGY, p. 261. Ed. by Nancy Cunard and Hugh Ford. NY: Frederick Ungar Pub. Co., 1970.   A lynching poem.

4001. Frank, Doctor [pseud. of Henry F. Triplett]. NEGROLANA. Boston: Christopher Publishing House, 1924.   Numerous factual accounts of American slavery (pp. 24-51), lynching (pp. 143-228), and black American soldiers (pp. 259-65) are grafted onto fictional story of creation and existence of black republic named Negrolana.

4002. Frank, Waldo. HOLIDAY. New York: Boni and Liveright, 1923. Includes lynching.

4003. Freeman, Carol. "i saw them lynch." In THE POETRY OF BLACK AMERICA: ANTHOLOGY OF THE 20TH CENTURY, p. 397. Ed. by Arnold Adoff. New York: Harper & Row, 1973.   Brief poem. Lower case letters, as here.

4004. Garland, Hamlin.   "A Lynching in Mosinee."   In STRANGE HAPPENINGS, BEING STORIES, pp. 233-53. London: Methuen & Co., 1901.   Festive mood in town changes because of a murder. Lynching follows. Originally published in <u>Pocket Magazine</u> [New York], Vol. 2 (July 1896).

4005. Giovannitti, Arturo.   [From] "When the Cock Crows."   In AN ANTHOLOGY OF REVOLUTIONARY POETRY, pp. 192-94.   Ed. by Marcus Graham. New York: Active Press, 1929.   Segment of poem about Frank Little's lynching in Montana.

4006. Goldberg, Gerald J. THE LYNCHING OF ORIN NEWFIELD. New York: Dial Press, 1970.   Dairy farmer in Vermont is local bully. Townspeople turn against him. He writes letter about his own lynching and then commits suicide.

4007. Gordon, Arthur. REPRISAL. New York: Simon and Schuster, 1950. Fiction, but reminiscent of real Georgia lynching of four blacks (two men and two women) in 1946 (Malcolm case).

4008. Gores, Joe. "The Mob." NEGRO DIGEST, Vol. 11, No. 2 (Dec. 1961): 64-71.   Minnesota sheriff dies protecting Mississippi editor from lynch mob.

4009. Graham, Rudy Bee. "A Lynching   for Skip James." In BLACK FIRE: AN ANTHOLOGY OF AFRO-AMERICAN WRITING, pp. 374-76. Ed. by Leroi Jones and Larry Neal. New York: William Morrow & Co., 1968.   A poem. Title is spaced as given here. Author's name is Ruby at top of p. 375.

4010. Green, Paul. <u>In Abraham's Bosom</u>. In FIVE PLAYS OF THE SOUTH, pp. 105-77. A Mermaid Dramabook. New York: Hill and Wang, 1963.   Turn-of-the-century setting; play ends with black man killing white man and then being shot down by white mob.

4011. Green, Saul. "Lessons." NEW MASSES, Vol. 17, No. 2 (Oct. 8, 1935): 16-18.   Fiction? Lynching of black man named Richard.

4012. Greene, Ward. DEATH IN THE DEEP SOUTH. New York: American Mercury, 1938. Ends with lynching of white man--for murdering a white girl. Based on Leo Frank case.

4013. Gretlund, Jan Nordby. "'The Man in the Tree': Katherine Anne Porter's Unfinished Lynching Story." THE SOUTHERN QUARTERLY, Vol. 31, No. 3 (Spring 1993): 7-16.

4014. Griggs, Sutton. THE HINDERED HAND: OR, THE REIGN OF THE REPRESSIONIST. 3d ed.; Nashville: Orion Pub. Co., 1905. Includes lynching of a black couple (based on lynching of Luther Holbert and wife in Mississippi, 1904). See Harris, Exorcising Blackness, pp. 1-2, 79-80.

4015. Grimke, Angelina. Rachel. In BLACK THEATER, U.S.A.: FORTY-FIVE PLAYS BY BLACK AMERICANS 1847-1974, pp. 139-72, with introduction on pp. 137-38. Ed. by James V. Hatch; Ted Shine, consultant. New York: Free Press (Macmillan), 1974. Anti-lynching play.

4016. Gunning, Sandra, ed. RACE, RAPE, AND LYNCHING: THE RED RECORD OF AMERICAN LITERATURE, 1890-1912. New York: Oxford Univ. Press, 1996.

4017. Haldeman-Julius, Marcet, and Haldeman-Julius, E. VIOLENCE: A NOVEL OF LOVE AND JUSTICE IN THE CENTRAL SOUTH. New York: Simon and Schuster, 1929. In Book Three, Chapter IV, "The Lynching," black man is hanged, then body is shot. The body is dragged and burned in Chapter VII, "Rockworth's Orgy."

4018. Hansberry, Lorraine. "Lynchsong." MASSES & MAINSTREAM, Vol. 4, No. 7 (July 1951): 19-20. A poem.

4019. Harben, William Nathaniel. MAM' LINDA: A NOVEL. New York: Harper & Brothers, 1907. Plot includes effort to lynch black man (son of Mammy Linda) and actual lynching of another black.

4020. Harris, Trudier. "Ceremonial Fagots: Lynching and Burning Rituals in Black Literature." SOUTHERN HUMANITIES REVIEW, Vol. 10, No. 3 (Summer 1976): 235-47.

4021. Harris, Trudier. EXORCISING BLACKNESS: HISTORICAL AND LITERARY LYNCHING AND BURNING RITUALS. Bloomington, IN: Indiana Univ. Press, 1984. See Chapter 1: "Ritual and Ritual Violence in American Life and Culture" for historical aspects.

4022. Hart, Jerome. A VIGILANTE GIRL. 2d ed.; Chicago: A. C.

McClurg & Co., 1910.   Lynching and vigilantism; 1856 California. Transparent disguises of real places and people (see typed list of people pasted to free endpaper at front of book in University of Chicago Library).

4023. Hayden, Robert. "Night, Death, Mississippi." In COLLECTED POEMS, pp. 15-16. Ed. by Frederick Glaysher. New York: Liveright Pub. Corp., 1985.   Lynching poem. See also Pontheolla T. Williams, <u>Robert Hayden: A Critical Analysis of His Poetry</u> (Urbana: Univ. of Illinois Press, 1987), pp. 100-01; 228, n. 11.

4024. Henegan, L. Herbert. "A National Academy of Lynching." THE CRISIS, Vol. 42, No. 2 (Feb. 1935): 53.   A satire.

4025. Hickey, Daniel Whitehead. "Dark Justice." In THE CHANGING CHARACTER OF LYNCHING, p. vii. By Jessie Daniel Ames. Atlanta: Commission on Interracial Cooperation, 1942.   Lynching poem.

4026. Hill, Abram Barrington. <u>Hell's Half Acre; a Play in Three Acts and Six Scenes</u>. [New York?], 1938.   Listed in <u>Dictionary Catalog of the Schomburg Collection</u>, p. 4259, as typescript of a lynch law drama.

4027. Hill, Constance Valis. "Katherine Dunham's <u>Southland</u>: Protest in the Face of Repression." DANCE RESEARCH JOURNAL, Vol. 26, No. 2 (Fall 1994): 1-10.   Dunham's ballet about lynching caused hostile reaction in 1951 and was never performed in the U.S.

4028. Hill, Leslie Pinckney. "So Quietly." In I AM THE DARKER BROTHER: AN ANTHOLOGY OF MODERN POEMS BY BLACK AMERICANS, p. 65. Ed. by Arnold Adoff. Collier Books. New York: Macmillan, 1970.   Poem occasioned by a Georgia lynching, Dec. 21, 1919.

4029. Hill, Leslie Pinckney. "Vision of a Lyncher." THE CRISIS, Vol. 3, No. 3 (Jan. 1912): 122.   Poem about a lyncher being driven out of hell. Accompanied by two photos of lynching victims.

4030. Hirsch, David A. Hedrich. "Speaking Silences in Angelina Weld Grimke's 'The Closing Door' and 'Blackness.'" AFRICAN AMERICAN REVIEW, Vol. 26, No. 3 (Fall 1992): 459-74.   Both stories deal with lynching. Page 470: "The active violence of lynching is never directly represented in Grimke's work but is always recounted in retrospect." Page 471: "Blackness" was retitled "Goldie" when published.

4031. Hopkins, Pauline E. CONTENDING FORCES: A ROMANCE ILLUSTRATIVE OF NEGRO LIFE NORTH AND SOUTH. Boston: Colored Co-operative Pub. Co., 1900.   Main lynching references occur in

Chapters XIII-XV at church meeting in Boston about race and lynching--after news in Chapter XII about a quadruple lynching in the South. Clapp's speech in Chapter XIII was based on that of former Georgia governor Northen at Congregational Club, Boston, May 22, 1899. See analysis in Carby, Reconstructing Womanhood, Chapter 6.

4032. Horn, I. M. "Vigilantes of Nugget Gulch." OVERLAND MONTH-LY, Vol. 88, No. 9 (Sept. 1930): 266, 270, 276.

4033. House, Homer C. "Lynchers' Rally Song." THE CRISIS, Vol. 42, No. 1 (Jan. 1935): 29.   A poem from The Advance.

4034. Housman, Laurence. Judge Lynch. In 8 NEW ONE-ACT PLAYS OF 1935, pp. 37-48. Ed. by John Bourne. London: Lovat Dickson & Thompson Ltd., 1935.   James Lynch, Judge and Warden of Galway, hangs his own son for murder.

4035 Hughes, Langston. "The Bitter River." In THE COLLECTED POEMS OF LANGSTON HUGHES, pp. 242-44. Ed. by Arnold Rampersad and David Roessel. New York: Knopf, 1994.   Dedicated to 14-year-old blacks Charlie Lang and Ernest Green, who were lynched in Mississippi in 1942.

4036. Hughes, Langston. "Blue Bayou." In THE COLLECTED POEMS OF LANGSTON HUGHES, p. 292. Ed. by Arnold Rampersad and David Roessel. New York: Knopf, 1994.   Refers to lynching of black man who objects to a white man taking his woman.

4037. Hughes, Langston. "Flight." In THE COLLECTED POEMS OF LANGSTON HUGHES, p. 127. Ed. by Arnold Rampersad and David Roessel. New York: Knopf, 1994.   "Black boy" is running from whites who falsely claim he did something to a white female. Only eight lines.

4038. Hughes, Langston. "Freedom [2]." In THE COLLECTED POEMS OF LANGSTON HUGHES, p. 290. Ed. by Arnold Rampersad and David Roessel. New York: Knopf, 1994.   Mentions lynching.

4039. Hughes, Langston. "Georgia Dusk." In THE COLLECTED POEMS OF LANGSTON HUGHES, p. 448. Ed. by Arnold Rampersad and David Roessel. New York: Knopf, 1994.   Jean Wagner, Black Poets of the United States, trans. by Kenneth Douglas (Urbana: Univ. of Illinois Press, 1973), p. 458, says this has same message as "Lynching Song"; see below.

4040. Hughes, Langston. "Home." In THE WAYS OF WHITE FOLKS, pp. 32-48. New York: Knopf, 1969; originally published in 1934.   Short story. "Uppity" black man gets lynched for talking to a white woman. Analyzed in Trudier Harris, Exorcising Blackness, pp. 83-84.

4041. Hughes, Langston. "Lynching Song." In THE COLLECTED POEMS OF LANGSTON HUGHES, p. 214. Ed. by Arnold Rampersad and David Roessel. New York: Knopf, 1994. Whites will feel guilty after hanging an innocent "black boy." Jean Wagner, Black Poets of the United States, trans. by Kenneth Douglas (Urbana: Univ. of Illinois Press, 1973), p. 458: "The poem implies that such crimes endanger all our lives and, quite particularly, all our liberties."

4042. Hughes, Langston. "Magnolia Flowers." In THE COLLECTED POEMS OF LANGSTON HUGHES, p. 122. Ed. by Arnold Rampersad and David Roessel. New York: Knopf, 1994. Explained as poet "unexpectedly happens on a lynching party that is almost over" in Jean Wagner, Black Poets of the United States, trans. by Kenneth Douglas (Urbana: Univ. of Illinois Press, 1973), p. 457.

4043. Hughes, Langston. "Silhouette." In THE COLLECTED POEMS OF LANGSTON HUGHES, pp. 305-06. Ed. by Arnold Rampersad and David Roessel. New York: Knopf, 1994. A black man has been hanged from a tree as a way of protecting white women; asks Southern women to "be good."

4044. Hughes, Langston. "Southern Mammy Sings." In THE COLLECTED POEMS OF LANGSTON HUGHES, p. 227. Ed. by Arnold Rampersad and David Roessel. New York: Knopf, 1994. Whites lynched a "colored boy."

4045. Hughes, Langston. "Song for a Dark Girl." In I AM THE DARKER BROTHER: AN ANTHOLOGY OF MODERN POEMS BY BLACK AMERICANS, p. 67. Ed. by Arnold Adoff. Collier Books. New York: Macmillan, 1970. Also in THE COLLECTED POEMS OF LANGSTON HUGHES, p. 104. Ed. by Arnold Rampersad and David Roessel. New York: Knopf, 1994. Black lover is hanged by lynch mob.

4046. Huie, William Bradford. WOLF WHISTLE AND OTHER STORIES. New York: Signet, 1959.

4047. Hunt, William R. "Jack London's Lynching: A Murder on Lituya Bay in 1899." THE ALASKA JOURNAL, Vol. 15, No. 1 (Winter 1985): 20-23. Martin Severts killed one man, wounded one man, was subdued and later hung by a woman and her husband. Jack London wrote a partially fictionalized account of this as "The Unexpected" in McClure's Magazine (August 1906).

4048. Jannath, Heba. "Deep Dixie: A Short Story in Verse." THE CRISIS, Vol. 39 [sic, should be 38], No. 3 (March 1931): 87-89.   Fictional lynching.

4049. Jarrette, A. Q. BENEATH THE SKY. New York: Weinberg Book Supply Co., 1949.   "A novel of love and murder among the poor whites and Negroes of the deep South." See pp. 17, 87-90, for lynchings.

4050. Jasper, Bob (pseud. of Robert J. Hogan). FEUD AT SUNDOWN. Boston: Houghton Mifflin, 1951.   Innocent man lynched in Western mining town as part of scheme to remove business competitor.

4051. Jenkins, Welborn Victor. THE "INCIDENT" AT MONROE. Atlanta: United Negro Youth of America for the Malcolm-Dorsey Memorial Committee, 1948.   Free-verse poem of 39 pages as requiem for Rodger Malcomb [sic] and three other blacks slain in Walton County, Georgia, July 25, 1946. Little about the lynching. Includes several photos.

4052. Johnson, Alvin. "The Lynching in Bass County." THE NEW REPUBLIC, Vol. 12, No. 146 (Aug. 18, 1917): 75-77.   Fiction? A farmer's account of the proposed lynching of a white county official. The mob abandoned its purpose. No state mentioned. Coxville was county seat. There is no Bass County in any U.S. state nor any town named Coxville.

4053. Johnson, Dorothy. THE HANGING TREE. New York: Ballantine Books, 1957.   Nine short stories and a novelette. See "The Hanging Tree" (pp. 161-272); Western locale. Made into a 1959 movie of the same name.

4054. Johnson, Georgia Douglas. Blue Blood. In WINES IN THE WILDERNESS: PLAYS BY AFRICAN AMERICAN WOMEN FROM THE HARLEM RENAISSANCE TO THE PRESENT, pp. 17-25 (with "Synopsis and Analysis," pp. 12-13). Ed. by Elizabeth Brown-Guillory. Westport, CT: Greenwood Press, 1990.   Black lovers have the same white father. One mother never told of her rape by the white man for fear her black fiance would take action and be lynched.

4055. Johnson, Georgia Douglas. Blue-Eyed Black Boy. In WINES IN THE WILDERNESS: PLAYS BY AFRICAN AMERICAN WOMEN FROM THE HARLEM RENAISSANCE TO THE PRESENT, pp. 33-37 (with Synopsis and Analysis," pp. 14-15). Ed. by Elizabeth Brown-Guillory. Westport, CT: Greenwood Press, 1990.   Responding to plea of black youth's mother, the white governor sends soldiers to prevent the youth's lynching--because he's the unacknowledged father.

4056. Johnson, Georgia Douglas. Safe. In WINES IN THE WILDER-

NESS: PLAYS BY AFRICAN AMERICAN WOMEN FROM THE HARLEM RENAISSANCE TO THE PRESENT, pp. 26-32 (with "Synopsis and Analysis," pp. 13-14). Ed. by Elizabeth Brown-Guillory. Westport, CT: Greenwood Press, 1990.   Black woman gives birth to a son on same night she sees lynching of "Sam Hosea" (1893).   She strangles the baby so he will be "safe from the lynchers."

4057. Johnson, Georgia Douglas.   <u>A Sunday Morning in the South</u>.   In BLACK THEATER, U.S.A.: FORTY-FIVE PLAYS BY BLACK AMERI-CANS 1847-1974, pp. 213-17, with introduction on pp. 211-12. Ed. by James V. Hatch; Ted Shine, consultant.   New York: Free Press (Macmillan), 1974. Lynching of black teenager, 1924.

4058. Johnson, James Weldon.   THE AUTOBIOGRAPHY OF AN EX-COLORED MAN.   Reprint; New York: Hill and Wang, 1960; originally published in 1912.   Despite title, this is a novel (see p. vii, introduction by Arna Bontemps).   See pp. 184-90 for a black man burned alive.   Analyzed in Harris, <u>Exorcising Blackness</u>, pp. 72-73.

4059. Johnson, James Weldon.   "Brothers."   In THE BOOK OF AMERI-CAN NEGRO POETRY, pp. 127-30. James Weldon Johnson, ed.   Revised ed.; New York: Harcourt, Brace & World, 1958.   Also in FIFTY YEARS & OTHER POEMS, pp. 14-17. James Weldon Johnson.   Boston: Cornhill Co., 1917.   Graphic description of black man being burned alive.   Jean Wagner, <u>Black Poets of the United States</u>, trans. by Kenneth Douglas (Urbana: Univ. of Illinois Press, 1973), p. 368, says this "forceful, realistic description of the lynching . . . is the first of its kind in American poetry."

4060. Johnson, James Weldon.   "Brothers--American Drama."   A verse-drama published in 1935.   See Trudier Harris, <u>Exorcising Blackness</u>, pp. 73-75.   Identification of speakers makes this version easier to understand than shorter "Brothers."

4061. Johnson, Victor H.   THE HORNCASTERS.   New York: Greenberg, 1947.   Black man had sex with white woman and killed her.   Mob kidnapped and lynched him.   Set in southern Maryland.

4062. Kelley, William Melvin.   A DIFFERENT DRUMMER.   Garden City, NY: Doubleday, 1962.   Concludes with an undescribed lynching of a black man.

4063. Killens, John O.   YOUNGBLOOD.   New York: Dial Press, 1954. Pages 287-301: white man tried to rape white woman, who fell down injured. Black man found her and carried her home.   Her family decided the black man had tried to rape her.   Whites tried to find the black man and lynch him, but he got away. So whites burned the homes of some blacks and shot them as they ran out of the flaming houses.

4064. Klotman, Phyllis R. "'Tearing a Hole in History': Lynching as Theme and Motif." BLACK AMERICAN LITERATURE FORUM, Vol. 19, No. 2 (Summer 1985): 55-63. Deals with fiction.

4065. Knott, Will C. LYNCHER'S MOON. A Charter Book. New York: Berkley Publishing, 1984. Orig. pub. in 1980. Two lynchings (pp. 74-76, 158-59) in Western novel about conflicts between cattlemen and farmers.

4066. Lee, Harper. TO KILL A MOCKINGBIRD. Philadelphia: Lippincott, 1960. See Chapter 15 for attempted lynching of black man which is defused by a little girl.

4067. Leonard, William Ellery. "The Lynching Bee." THE NATION, Vol. 111, No. 2895 (Dec. 29, 1920): 778-81. A poem. From The Lynching Bee and Other Poems.

4068. Leonard, William Ellery. THE LYNCHING BEE AND OTHER POEMS. New York: B. W. Huebsch, 1920. Includes "The Lynching Bee" and "Leo Frank."

4069. Livingston, Myrtle A. Smith. For Unborn Children. THE CRISIS, Vol. 32, No. 3 (July 1926): 122-25. A play. Black man gives himself up to Southern lynch mob wanting to kill him for dating a white woman.

4070. Loggins, Vernon. "'--Neber Said a Mumblin' Word.'" In PRIMER FOR WHITE FOLKS, pp. 297-310. Ed. by Bucklin Moon. Garden City, NY: Doubleday, Doran and Co., 1945. Fiction. Lynching of an innocent black man. Originally published in Opportunity.

4071. Loughead, Flora Haines. "Counsel Must Hang Too: A Story of Frontier Justice." OVERLAND MONTHLY, Vol. 23 (Second Series), No. 138 (June 1894): 633-44. Fiction.

4072. Luce, Philip Abbott. "Mack Parker." FREEDOMWAYS, Vol. 2, No. 1 (Winter 1962): 95-96. Poem about black man lynched in April, 1959.

4073. "Lynch-Law." THE VOICE OF THE NEGRO, Vol. 1, No. 11 (Nov. 1904): 567. A poem. In a section titled "Wayside" by Silas X. Floyd. Otherwise no author listed.

4074. "Lynching As It Might Be." THE CRUSADER, Vol. 1, No. 1 (Sept. 1918): 10. Satire of how a lynching might be reported as a pleasant event "if the South is left alone."

4075. Madden, Osceola. "An Innocent Criminal." THE COLORED AMERICAN MAGAZINE, Vol. 10, No. 2 (Feb. 1906): 119-21.   Story about attempted lynching.

4076. Maier, Howard. UNDERTOW. Garden City, NY: Doubleday, Doran & Co., 1945.   Lynching of black soldier in Texas during World War II (pp. 118-21) triggers mental problems for white soldier who failed to save him.

4077. Mathews, Dorothea. "The Lynching." In SHADOWED DREAMS: WOMEN'S POETRY OF THE HARLEM RENAISSANCE, p. 92. Ed. by Maureen Honey. New Brunswick: Rutgers Univ. Press, 1989.   Brief poem.

4078. McKay, Claude. "If We Must Die." In I AM THE DARKER BROTHER: AN ANTHOLOGY OF MODERN POEMS BY BLACK AMERICANS, p. 63. Ed. by Arnold Adoff. Collier Books. New York: Macmillan, 1970.   Blacks "dying, but fighting back."

4079. McKay, Claude. "The Lynching." In SELECTED POEMS OF CLAUDE McKAY, p. 37. New York: Bookman Associates, 1953.

4080. McKay, Claude. "To the White Fiends." In SELECTED POEMS OF CLAUDE McKAY, p. 38. New York: Bookman Associates, 1953.   This poem touches on lynching.

4081. McKay, Claude. TRIAL BY LYNCHING: STORIES ABOUT NEGRO LIFE IN NORTH AMERICA. Trans. from the Russian by Robert Winter.   Ed. by A. L. McLeod.   Mysore: Centre for Commonwealth Literature and Research, Univ. of Mysore, 1977.   Translation of Sudam Lincha.

4082. McMillen, Neil R., and Polk, Noel. "Faulkner on Lynching." THE FAULKNER JOURNAL, Vol. 8, No. 1 (Fall 1992): 3-14.   Analysis of a 1931 letter, arguably written by William Faulkner, which excuses lynching and has errors.

4083. Meyer, Annie Nathan. "The Shoe Pinches Mr. Samuels." THE CRISIS, Vol. 42, No. 1 (Jan. 1935): 8-9, 24-25.   Story illustrating the danger of lynching spreading.

4084. Miller, May. Nails and Thorns. In THE ROOTS OF AFRICAN AMERICAN DRAMA: AN ANTHOLOGY OF EARLY PLAYS, 1858-1938. Ed. by Leo Hamalian and James V. Hatch. Detroit: Wayne State Univ. Press, 1991.   Mob lynched black man and killed sheriff's baby son.

4085. Millican, Arthenia Bates. "James Weldon Johnson: In Quest of an Afrocentric Tradition for Black American Literature." Ph.D. diss., The Louisiana State Univ. and Agricultural and Mechanical College, 1972. See Diss. Ab. Intl., Vol. 33, No. 5 (Nov. 1972): 2385A-2386A

4086. Mississippi Burning. A 1988 movie relating to Chaney, Goodman, & Schwerner, who were lynched in Mississippi in 1964.

4087. "The Mob Victim." THE MESSENGER, Vol. 2, No. 7 (July 1919): 4. Poem about a lynching victim.

4088. Monger, Miriam. TALES FROM TOUSSAINT. Boston: Bruce Humphries, 1945. See pp. 21-26 for lynching of three blacks.

4089. Moorer, Lizelia Augusta Jenkins. "Lynching." In COLLECTED BLACK WOMEN'S POETRY, Vol. 3, pp. 31-35. Ed. by Joan R. Sherman. New York: Oxford Univ. Press, 1988.

4090. Morris, Gilbert. THE VIGILANTE. Living Books. Wheaton, IL: Tyndale House Publishers, 1988. Set in Virginia City, Montana [sic], [1860s].

4091. Morrison, Toni. Dreaming Emmett. See Anne Sarah Rubin (in Chapter V in this bibliography), p. 61. In this play the murdered Emmett Till has dreams.

4092. Morrison, Toni. SONG OF SOLOMON. New York: Signet Books, 1977. See pp. 80-82 for use of Emmett Till case.

4093. "Munday, Billy" [pseud. of Wray, J. E.; see The New York Public Library, Dictionary Catalog of the Schomburg Collection of Negro Literature & History (9 vols.; Boston: G. K. Hall, 1962), vol. 5, p. 4259]. THE BLACK SHADOW AND THE RED DEATH. New York: Broadway Pub. Co., 1914. Extremely racist mixture of facts, preaching, and fictional story about rape and mass murder by a black man, ending in his lynching near "Cobbtown," "Tangerine County," Florida.

4094. The Murder of Mary Phagan. A 1988 TV movie about the Leo Frank case. Larry McMurtry wrote the story for this movie.

4095. Murray, Pauli. "For Mack C. Parker." In THE POETRY OF BLACK AMERICA: ANTHOLOGY OF THE 20TH CENTURY, p. 110. Ed. by Arnold Adoff. New York: Harper & Row, 1973. Brief poem.

4096. Mygatt, Tracy D. The Noose. THE DRAMA [Mount Morris, IL],

Vol. 20, No. 2 (Nov. 1929), pp. 42-48.   Play in which wife and mother-in-law recall a past lynching while new one takes place in a Georgia town. Husband comes home and has conflict with wife about his prominent role in new lynching. He will be named next governor--but his wife leaves him.

4097. Nelson, Alice Dunbar. Mine Eyes Have Seen. THE CRISIS, Vol. 15, No. 6 (April 1918): 271-75.   Described by Judith L. Stephens, African American Review, Vol. 26, No. 2 (Summer 1992), p. 330, as anti-lynching play; but lynching is only hinted at except for one sentence.

4098. Nemiroff, Robert. "From These Roots: Lorraine Hansberry and the South." SOUTHERN EXPOSURE, Vol. 12, No. 5 (Sept./Oct. 1984): 32-36. Mentions several lynchings and includes a poem about lynching.

4099. Newell, Catherine Parmenter. "The Lynching." THE CATHOLIC WORLD, Vol. 147 (June 1938): 332.   A poem.

4100. Nichols, Franklin O. "Sheriff Griffin." THE CRISIS, Vol. 13, No. 4 (Feb. 1917): 196-98.   Fictional (?) story of white sheriff who committed suicide because he had raped and murdered a white girl. Lynch mob burned three blacks for the crime.

4101. [No author. No title.] NEGRO DIGEST, Vol. 18, No. 9 (July 1969): 5.   Comment on William Bradford Huie's "Wolf Whistle" and the lynching of Emmett Till in Mississippi in 1955.

4102. Nordan, Lewis. WOLF WHISTLE. Chapel Hill: Algonquin Books of Chapel Hill, 1993.   Novel reminiscent of Emmett Till case.

4103. Ornstein, William. "The Crime of These Corners." In DEEP CURRENTS, pp. 20-30. Dallas: Story Book Press, 1953.   Lynching of a black man in this short story.

4104. Ostenso, Martha. "Jubilee." THE CRISIS, Vol. 42, No. 1 (Jan. 1935): 7.   Poem. Black man lynched for smiling at a white woman.

4105. Ovington, Mary White. The Awakening: A Play. New York: National Association for the Advancement of Colored People, 1923. This includes lynching and extradition.

4106. Ovington, Mary White. "Mary Phagan Speaks." THE NEW REPUBLIC, Vol. 4, No. 43 (Aug. 28, 1915): 101.   In this poem the murdered Mary Phagan asks why she was not treated better while she was alive.

4107. Owen, Guy. "Erskine Caldwell's Unpublished Poems." SOUTH ATLANTIC BULLETIN, Vol. 43, No. 2 (May 1978): 53-57. See pp. 55-56 on poem about a lynched black man--and lynching in other Caldwell works.

4108. Patchen, Kenneth. "Nice Day for a Lynching." In ALIENATION: MINORITY GROUPS, p. 51. Donald Rude, ed. New York: John Wiley and Sons, 1972. Short poem. Reprinted from Kenneth Patchen, Collected Poems (New Directions Pub. Corp., 1939).

4109. Patten, Lewis B. LYNCHING AT BROKEN BUTTE. Boston: G. K. Hall, 1983. U.S. marshal breaks journey. He learns of local lynching five months earlier by townsmen, who then try to kill him and three others.

4110. Peters, Paul, and Sklar, George. "Lynchtown--A Mass Chant. Two Theatre Union playwrights recount an incident of life in the Deep South." NEW MASSES, Vol. 21, No. 10 (Dec. 1, 1936): 7-8. Poem.

4111. Popel, Esther. "Flag Salute." THE CRISIS, Vol. 47, No. 11 (Nov. 1940): cover. A poem with lines about a lynching (in Princess Anne, Maryland, 1933) interspersed between the lines of the Pledge of Allegiance.

4112. Porteous, Clark. SOUTH WIND BLOWS. New York: Current Books, 1948. In Chapter I a black man is lynched in Mississippi--by hanging and shooting. See also Clark Porteous, "South Wind Blows," Negro Digest, Vol. 6, No. 12 (Oct. 1948): 81-92.

4113. Rascoe, Burton. "Caldwell Lynches Two Negroes." THE AMERI-CAN MERCURY, Vol. 49, No. 196 (April 1940): 493-98. This is largely a review of Erskine Caldwell's Trouble in July but it also includes some historical facts and interpretations.

4114. Reece, Byron Herbert. THE HAWK AND THE SUN. New York: Dutton, 1955. Includes lynching of black man named Dandelion.

4115. Robertson, Frank C. VIGILANTE WAR IN BUENA VISTA. New York: E. P. Dutton, 1942. Idaho Territory in frontier times.

4116. Rogers, John William, Jr. Judge Lynch: A Drama In One Act. New York: S. French [etc.], 1924.

4117. Sartre, Jean-Paul. The Respectful Prostitute. In THREE PLAYS, pp. 153-95. Trans. from the French by Lionel Abel. New York: Knopf, 1949. Whites in a Southern town in U.S. want to lynch black man and do lynch the wrong one.

4118. Schuyler, George. BLACK NO MORE. Reprint; New York: Negro Universities Press, 1969; originally published in 1931.   A satire. See pp. 224-44 for the threatened lynching of two white men in black-face, their reprieve upon showing white skin, and their lynching after news that they had some black ancestors. Another lynching is on p. 216.

4119. Schuyler, George S. "Scripture for Lynchers." THE CRISIS, Vol. 42, No. 1 (Jan. 1935): 12.   Parodies of a hymn and Biblical verses.

4120. Schwartz, Irving. EVERY MAN HIS SWORD. Garden City, NY: Doubleday, 1951.   The dragged-behind-car lynching of a black man in a Southern town after World War II is followed by the murders of several whites.

4121. Seymour, Ann. Lawd, Does Yo' Undahstan'? Atlanta: Association of Southern Women for the Prevention of Lynching, 1936.   Play.   Black woman whose son was lynched poisons her grandson to prevent his lynching.

4122. Shaw, [George] Bernard. The Shewing-up of Blanco Posnet. In TEN SHORT PLAYS, pp. 245-76. New York: Dodd, Mead & Co., 1960.   A 1913 play.   Vigilance Committee and people in U.S. town want to lynch Posnet.

4123. Sinclair, Bennie Lee. THE LYNCHING. New York: Walker and Co., 1992.   Young black man seeks information on death of his father years ago.

4124. Sinclair, Jo. "Noon Lynching." NEW MASSES, Vol. 20, No. 13 (Sept. 22, 1936): 16-18.   Threat by janitor and policeman to hang ten-year-old black youth at school.

4125. Smith, Lillian. STRANGE FRUIT. Athens: Univ. of Georgia Press, 1985.   Originally published in 1944.   This edition has foreword by Fred Hobson. Lynching of black man near end of book. Lynch victims were the "strange fruit" hanging on Southern trees.

4126. "Song of the Vigilantes." MOTHER EARTH, Vol. 8, No. 5 (July 1913): 129-30.   Satirical poem against anarchists.   Says they will lynch a woman [Emma Goldman?].

4127. Spearman, Walter. Country Sunday. ASWPL Papers.   Anti-lynching play set in South Carolina.   Author's foreword and the play set forth some lynching causes.

4128. St. Amant, Fred. 'Lynch Him'. THE EPWORTH HIGHROAD,

Vol. 1, No. 7 (July 1932): 16-19, 31-32.   A play. Whites burn courthouse to lynch black man. Mob then lynches his son for protesting.

4129. St. John, Primus. "Lynching and Burning." In THE POETRY OF BLACK AMERICA; ANTHOLOGY OF THE 20TH CENTURY, p. 349. Ed. by Arnold Adoff. New York: Harper & Row, 1973.

4130. Stephens, Judith L. "The Anti-Lynch Play: Toward an Interracial Feminist Dialogue in Theatre." JOURNAL OF AMERICAN DRAMA AND THEATRE, Vol. 2, No. 3 (Fall 1990): 59-69.   Discusses Rachel by Angelina Grimke (1916), A Sunday Morning in the South by Georgia Douglas Johnson (1925), and Trouble in Mind by Alice Childress (1952).

4131. Stephens, Judith L. "Anti-Lynch Plays by African American Women: Race, Gender, and Social Protest in American Drama." AFRICAN AMERICAN REVIEW, Vol. 26, No. 2 (Summer 1992): 329-39.

4132. Stevans, C. M. LUCKY TEN BAR. OF PARADISE VALLEY. HIS HUMOROUS, PATHETIC AND TRAGIC ADVENTURES.   Chicago: Rhodes & McClure Pub. Co., 1909.   See Chapter XVII for "An Interrupted Lynching" of a black man.

4133. Summerfield, Charles [pseud. of A. W. Arrington]. THE RANGERS AND REGULATORS OF THE TANAHA: OR, LIFE AMONG THE LAWLESS. A TALE OF THE REPUBLIC OF TEXAS. New York: Robert M. De Witt, 1856.   Includes lynching. Also published with title A Faithful Lover.

4134. Summers, Richard Aldrich. VIGILANTE. New York: Duell, Sloan and Pearce, 1949.   Novel about California and David C. Broderick, 1850s.

4135. Sutton, William A. BLACK LIKE IT IS/WAS: ERSKINE CALDWELL'S TREATMENT OF RACIAL THEMES. Metuchen, NJ: Scarecrow Press, 1974.   See "Lynching" in index.

4136. Thanet, Octave. "Beyond the Limit." COSMOPOLITAN, Vol. 34, No. 4 (Feb. 1903): 451-59.   Lynching for purpose of revenging rape-murder of white girl.

4137. They Won't Forget. Movie, 1937. Based on Ward Greene, Death in the Deep South (listed under Greene in this chapter).

4138. Thompson, Julius E. "Till." In BLACK SOUTHERN VOICES: AN ANTHOLOGY OF FICTION, POETRY, DRAMA, NONFICTION, AND CRITICAL ESSAYS, pp. 288-89. Ed. by John Oliver Killens and Jerry W.

Ward, Jr. A Meridian Book. New York: Penguin Books, 1992.   Poem about Emmett Till.

4139. "'The Thrill Murder.'" INTERRACIAL REVIEW, Vol. 9, No. 9 (Sept. 1936): 137.   Two poems (by Anonymous and by Maurice C. Fields). See "'What You Have Done to the Least . . .'" in Chapter IX.

4140. Toomer, Jean. CANE. New York: Boni & Liveright, 1923.   See Trudier Harris, Exorcising Blackness.

4141. Tracy, Don. HOW SLEEPS THE BEAST. London: Constable, 1937. Black man is nailed to wall of barn, but mob gives him a knife so he can cut himself loose when barn is burned.   Upon emerging, he is shotgunned to death.   National Guard unit arrives in town and clashes with mob.

4142. Trent, Lucia. "Black Men." In POEMS OF JUSTICE, p. 118. Ed. by Thomas Curtis Clark. Chicago: Willett, Clark & Colby, 1929.   Lynching victims.

4143. Trent, Lucia. "A White Woman Speaks." In POEMS OF JUSTICE, pp. 117-18. Ed. by Thomas Curtis Clark. Chicago: Willett, Clark & Colby, 1929.   Expresses white shame for lynching of a black man.

4144. Upshaw, Helen. DAY OF THE HARVEST. Indianapolis: Bobbs-Merrill, 1953.   Interracial love affair leads to attempted lynching of a black youth. Book ends as a black doctor is about to be lynched.

4145. Ward, Jerry W., Jr. "Don't Be Fourteen (In Mississippi)." In BLACK SOUTHERN VOICES: AN ANTHOLOGY OF FICTION, POETRY, DRAMA, NONFICTION, AND CRITICAL ESSAYS, pp. 296-97. Ed. by John Oliver Killens and Jerry W. Ward, Jr. A Meridian Book. New York: Penguin Books, 1992.   Poem; partly in reference to Emmett Till.

4146. Webb, Walter Prescott. "Afterword." In THE OX-BOX INCIDENT, pp. 219-24.   A Signet Classic. New York: New American Library, 1960. Includes Clark's explanation of what message he was trying to convey.

4147. Westbrook, Henry S. BURNED AT THE STAKE. Benton, AR: n.p., 1899.   Book of 116 pages meant to be condemnatory of lynching. Fictional story of murder and rape of six-year-old white girl and subsequent lynching of black man [slave?] in the South.

4148. White, Lillian Zellhoefer.   "Hangman's Tree."   In AMERICA FOREVER NEW: A BOOK OF POEMS, pp. 103-04. Ed. by Sara and John E. Brewton. New York: Thomas Y. Crowell Co., 1968.   Vigilantes hanged two bandits.

4149. White, Walter F. THE FIRE IN THE FLINT. New York: Knopf, 1924.   Good blacks being cheated, whipped, murdered, and lynched by mostly-bad whites.

4150. White, William Patterson. LYNCH LAWYERS. Boston: Little, Brown, 1920.   Western story with attempted lynching.

4151. Wideman, John Edgar. THE LYNCHERS. New York: Harcourt Brace Jovanovich, 1973.   Fiction, with some factual instances of lynching in "Matter Prefatory" (pp. 3-23).   Four black men plan to lynch white policeman. Analyzed in Harris, Exorcising Blackness, 129-47.

4152. Wiley, Stephen R. "Songs of the Gastonia Textile Strike of 1929: Models of and for Southern Working-Class Women's Militancy." NORTH CAROLINA FOLKLORE JOURNAL, Vol. 30, No. 2 (Fall-Winter 1982): 87-98.   See pp. 94-95 for references to song "Little Mary Phagan." Analysis based on assumption of Leo Frank's guilt.

4153. Williams, Melvin G. "Black Literature vs. Black Studies: Three Lynchings." BLACK AMERICAN LITERATURE FORUM, Vol. 11, No. 3 (Fall 1977): 104-07.   Considers Leslie Pinckney Hill's poem "So Quietly," Claude McKay's poem "The Lynching," and Richard Wright's short story "Big Boy Leaves Home."

4154. Wister, Owen. "The Gift Horse." THE SATURDAY EVENING POST. Vol. 181, No. 3 (July 18, 1908): 3-5, 27-29.   Man is almost lynched in Wyoming for horse theft.   Compare somewhat longer version that has some language changes in Owen Wister, Members of the Family (New York: Macmillan, 1911), pp. 159-206. See also Buckland, Roscoe L.

4155. Wister, Owen. THE VIRGINIAN: A HORSEMAN OF THE PLAINS. New York: Macmillan, 1911 [originally published in 1902].   Includes a double lynching (see pp. 334-43) and children playing lynching game (p. 366) but is more important for discussion (pp. 373-76) about rights and wrongs of burning Southern blacks vis-a-vis lynching Wyoming cattle thieves.

4156. Witherspoon, Mary-Elizabeth. SOMEBODY SPEAK FOR KATY. New York: Dodd, Mead & Co., 1950.   For lynching and related information see pp. 16, 21-22, 24, 27-34. McGovern, Anatomy of a Lynching, p. 35, says this novel is [partially] set in Marianna, Florida, 1930s, and that it depicts "the lynching of [Claude] Neal and the subsequent riot."

4157. Wright, Richard. "Between the World and Me." In EXORCISING

BLACKNESS: HISTORICAL AND LITERARY LYNCHING AND BURNING RITUALS, pp. 98-99. Trudier Harris. Bloomington: Indiana Univ. Press, 1984. Poem. Narrator comes across evidence of a black man's lynching. Analyzed in Harris, pp. 97, 99-105. Originally published in The Partisan Review, Vol. 2, No. 8 (July-Aug. 1935): 18-19.

4158. Wright, Richard. "Big Boy Leaves Home." In UNCLE TOM'S CHILDREN: FIVE LONG STORIES, pp. 1-70. Richard Wright. New York: Harper & Brothers, 1938. Black youths get into inadvertent trouble with whites. Bobo is burned alive; Big Boy gets away. Analyzed in Harris, Exorcising Blackness, pp. 105-09.

4159. Wright, Richard. "Bright and Morning Star." In UNCLE TOM'S CHILDREN: FIVE LONG STORIES, pp. 319-84. Richard Wright. New York: Harper & Brothers, 1938. Lynchings are not very "traditional."

4160. Wright, Richard. "Down by the Riverside." In UNCLE TOM'S CHILDREN: FIVE LONG STORIES, pp. 71-166. Richard Wright. New York: Harper & Brothers, 1938. Black man kills white man; whites want to lynch him, but soldiers shoot him dead. Analyzed as a figurative lynching in Trudier Harris, Exorcising Blackness, pp. 110-12.

4161. Wright, Richard. "Long Black Song." In UNCLE TOM'S CHILDREN: FIVE LONG STORIES, pp. 167-217. Richard Wright. New York: Harper & Brothers, 1938. Black man kills white man and dies in his house set afire by white mob. Analyzed as a figurative lynching in Trudier Harris, Exorcising Blackness, pp. 110, 112-13.

4162. Wright, Richard. THE LONG DREAM. Garden City, NY: Doubleday, 1958. Black male caught with white woman is lynched by Mississippi mob, and protagonist later views victim's body. Analyzed in Harris, Exorcising Blackness, pp. 45-49, 115-28.

4163. Wright, Scott. THE LYNCHING OF JOHN HANSON. Lawrenceville, VA: Brunswick, 1986.

4164. Wyman, Lillie Buffum Chace. ANGELINA W. GRIMKE'S DRAMA OF RACHEL AND THE LYNCHING EVIL. N.p.: n.p., n.d. Pamphlet giving some "historic background" of lynching to examine how Grimke's drama compares. Largely drawn from book review "Rachel," The Journal of Negro History, Vol. 6, No. 2 (April 1921): 248-54.

IX

Works of Art

4165. Alexander, Stephen. "Art." NEW MASSES, Vol. 14, No. 11 (March 19, 1935): 29. Explains differences between anti-lynching exhibitions: "An Art Commentary on Lynching" sponsored by NAACP, and "The Struggle for Negro Rights" at A.C.A. Gallery [sponsored by the John Reed Club, et al.].

4166. "An Art Exhibit Against Lynching." THE CRISIS, Vol. 42, No. 4 (April 1935): 106. Recent show in New York. Includes illustrations of "Dixie Holiday" by William Mosby and "A Lynching" by Thomas Hart Benton.

4167. "Art: Lynching Show Opens in Spite of Opposition 'Outburst.'" NEWS-WEEK, Vol. 5, No. 8 (Feb. 23, 1935): 19.

4168. "Artist Praises Lynching Exhibit." INTERRACIAL REVIEW, Vol. 8, No. 4 (April 1935): 64. Irwin D. Hoffman on exhibition Art Commentary on Lynching. Brief.

4169. "Background!" INTERRACIAL REVIEW, Vol. 11, No. 12 (Dec. 1938): 189. Cartoon. American lynching and Nazi activities.

4170. Bard, Phil. "By the way Sheriff, what did that nigger do?'" NEW MASSES, Vol. 7, No. 3 (Aug. 1931): 15. Cartoon showing black man hanging from a tree as lynch mob departs.

4171. Bearden, Romare. [An untitled cartoon about lynching.] THE CRISIS, Vol. 4, No. 9 (Sept. 1934): 257.

4172. "Behind the Filibuster." INTERRACIAL REVIEW, Vol. 11, No. 3 (March 1938): 45. Cartoon showing a U.S. Senator as a KKK member.

4173. Behrendt, Stephen C. "The Ambivalence of John Steuart Curry's Justice Defeating Mob Violence." GREAT PLAINS QUARTERLY, Vol. 12, No. 1 (Winter 1992): 3-18. Mural of "Justice" protecting a man from a lynch mob.

4174. Berg, R. O. "The Tree and Its Fruit." THE CRISIS, Vol. 41, No. 2 (Feb. 1934): 30. Cartoon about lynching.

4175. Berkeley, Stanley. "Judge Lynch: California Vigilantes, 1848." A copy of this illustration is in WILD WEST [Leesburg, VA], Vol. 4, No. 4 (Dec. 1991): 52.

4176. Berrick, Andrew. "The Vigilantes." FRONTIER TIMES, Vol. 52, No. 5, New Series No. 115 (Aug.-Sept. 1978): cover. Illustration showing Western lynchers riding away from man hanging from a tree. See contents page for artist, title, and source.

4177. "Black Determination." THE LITERARY DIGEST, Vol. 63, No. 3 (Oct. 18, 1919): 11. Anti-lynching cartoon.

4178. Bloch, Julius. [Untitled illustration of black man being lynched.] NEW MASSES, Vol. 17, No. 2 (Oct. 8, 1935): 17. Accompanies "Lessons" by Saul Green.

4179. Bracken, Lil. "The Lynching of Emmett Till." NEW ODYSSEY, Vol. 1, No. 1 (Spring 1992): 12. Brief note on why Till, who was murdered in Mississippi in 1955, is part of statue of Martin Luther King, Jr., in Denver's City Park.

4180. Burck [?]. [Untitled illustration on cover.] NEW MASSES, Vol. 7, No. 1 (June 1931). Shows black man from the neck upward; he has a noose around his neck. Seems like he has just been lynched.

4181. "Celebrities Jam Opening of Lynching Art Exhibit." INTERRACIAL REVIEW, Vol. 8, No. 3 (March 1935): 48. Brief.

4182. "Christmas in Georgia, A.D., 1916." THE CRISIS, Vol. 13, No. 2 (Dec. 1916): 78-79. Lynching cartoon.

4183. "The Circus Is Coming." THE CRISIS, Vol. 42, No. 1 (Jan. 1935): 9. Lynching cartoon.

4184. "Civilization in America, 1931: One of Our Major Sports." THE CRISIS, Vol. 39 [sic; should be 38], No. 3 (March 1931): 95. Lynching cartoon.

4185. "Congressional Blockade." INTERRACIAL REVIEW, Vol. 12, No. 2 (Feb. 1939): 29.   Cartoon on filibusterers blocking anti-lynching sentiment.

4186. Cullen, Charles. For illustration by him see Cullen, Countee, in Chapter VIII in this bibliography.

4187. Doherty, M. Stephen.   "Emerging Artist: James H. Hoston." AMERICAN ARTIST, Vol. 56, No. 594 (Jan. 1992): 14-15. Includes color reproduction of Universal Injustice, a painting about lynching.

4188. Doyle, Jerry. "The Challenge." THE CRISIS, Vol. 44, No. 6 (June 1937): 176. Cartoon. Subtitle: "Mississippi Sends a Message to Congress." Mob armed with blowtorch has just lynched a black man.

4189. Doyle, Jerry. "Th' Law." THE CRISIS, Vol. 42, No. 1 (Jan. 1935): 27.   Cartoon about the inaction of law enforcement officials when a lynching impends. Originally published in Philadelphia Record.

4190. Duffy, Edmund. "Remember Me Mister?" THE CRISIS, Vol. 44, No. 11 (Nov. 1937): 336.   Cartoon about the federal anti-lynching bill.

4191. Edwards, Melvin. "Lynch Fragments." In FREE SPIRITS: ANNALS OF THE INSURGENT IMAGINATION I, pp. 94-96. Ed. by Paul Buhle, et al. San Francisco: City Lights Books, 1982.   Nonrepresentational sculptures.

4192. "The Exodus from Dixie." A cartoon. See "Why Lynching Has Slumped" in Chapter V of this bibliography.

4193. "'A few days ago in Germany, events occurred which . . . made me . . . physically sick.'" THE CRISIS, Vol. 41, No. 9 (Sept. 1934): 257. Cartoon about hypocrisy because of U.S. lynching victims.

4194. Flemister, Frederick. The Mourners. ATLANTA HISTORY, Vol. 37, No. 1 (Spring 1993): cover and p. 40.   Lynching painting.

4195. Frenzeny and Tavernier [artists].   "Sketches in the Far West-- Vigilance Court in Session." HARPER'S WEEKLY, Vol. 18, No. 902 (April 11, 1874): 326.   An illustration. See brief explanatory text on p. 328; three horse thieves being tried on Texas-Indian Territory border as a telegraph pole is readied as a gallows.

4196. Gellart, Hugo. "Sheriff Shamblin: 'The I. L. D. is directly responsible.'" NEW MASSES, Vol. 8, No. 12 (Aug. 1933): 7.   Cartoon showing lynching of two black men. [Spacing in title is as given here.]

4197. Gropper, Bill. "In U. S. S. R. and U. S. A." LABOR DEFENDER, Vol. 5, No. 11 (Nov. 1930): 214.   Cartoons and cutlines make contrasts, one of which involves lynching. [Spacing in title is as given here.]

4198. Gropper, William. "The Lynching." NEW MASSES, Vol. 6, No. 5 (Oct. 1930): 10-11.   Series of four illustrations. Black victim.

4199. Harris, Lorenzo. "A Christmas in Georgia." THE CRISIS, Vol. 13, No. 2 (Dec. 1916): 78-79.   Cartoon of a lynching; cutline reads, "Inasmuch as ye did unto the least of these, My brethren, ye did it unto Me."

4200. "In 'Civilized' America: Fifteen Negro Workers Have Been Lynched This Year." NEW MASSES, Vol. 6, No. 4 (Sept. 1930): 8.   An illustration.

4201. "Is This The Symbol of the Lone Star State?" THE CRISIS, Vol. 42, No. 12 (Dec 1935): 360.   A cartoon about lynching. Originally published in the Milwaukee Journal. Unclear who the cartoonist is.

4202. "It would have been futile to call out the militia."   An illustration. See this title in Chapter V of this bibliography.

4203. Jackson, Jay. "The Circus Is Coming." THE CRISIS, Vol. 42, No. 1 (Jan. 1935): 9.   A cartoon about publicizing an upcoming lynching. Originally published in The Chicago Defender.

4204. Jakira, A. Cartoon listed with this author's entry in Chapter V.

4205. Lane, James W. "Lynching--As the Artist Sees It." INTERRACIAL REVIEW, Vol. 8, No. 3 (March 1935): 36.   Recent exhibition "An Art Commentary on Lynching" at the Newton Gallery.

4206. "The Law Gaining on Lynching." See entry in Chapter V for cartoon.

4207. "Lords of Lynching." THE CRISIS, Vol. 27, No. 4 (Feb. 1924): 169. Cartoon.

4208. "Lynched!" THE CATHOLIC WORKER, Vol. 1, No. 7 (Dec. 15, 1933): 7.   Cartoon of black man hanging from tree.

4209. "Lynching as a Japanese Sculptor Sees It."   THE CHRISTIAN CENTURY, Vol. 52, No. 7 (Feb. 13, 1935): 196-97.   Page 196: "Isamu Noguchi, is exhibiting . . . bronze figure of a Negro who was lynched at Sherman, Texas, four years ago."

4210. M. M. "Art Commentary on Lynching." THE ART NEWS, Vol. 33, No. 21 (Feb. 23, 1935): 13. Brief criticism of the current show at the Arthur U. Newton Galleries.

4211. MacKenzie, Amy. "Richmond Barthe--Sculptor." INTERRACIAL REVIEW, Vol. 12, No. 7 (July 1939): 107-09. Includes photo and text about "The Mother," depicting "agony of a Negro mother at the moment when she receives into her arms the body of her lynched son."

4212. Marsh, Reginald. "This is her first lynching." THE NEW YORKER, Vol. 10, No. 30 (Sept. 8, 1934): 27. A cartoon showing a mother holding up her little daughter for a better view. Also in THE NEW YORKER TWENTY-FIFTH ANNIVERSARY ALBUM. New York: Harper & Brothers, 1951. Pages in book are not numbered.

4213. Marshall, Elmer Grady. "The History of Brazos County, Texas." M.A. thesis, Univ. of Texas, 1937. Contains illustration of a lynching scene.

4214. "Maryland Has a Lynching." See entry in Chapter V for a cartoon.

4215. Miller, Kelly. "Art as a Cure for Lynching." THE CHRISTIAN CENTURY, Vol. 52, No. 16 (April 17, 1935): 516-17. Letter dealing with "Lynching as a Japanese Sculptor Sees It" [see above].

4216. Norem [artist]. [No title.] REAL WEST [Derby, CT], Vol. 28, No. 202 (April 1985): cover and inside back cover. Lynching illustration relating to Chuck Hornung, "The Lynching Of Gus Mentzer," ibid., pp. 10-16.

4217. "On Certain Advantages In Being a Large, Well-Developed Devil." THE CRISIS, Vol. 15, No. 6 (April 1918): 285. Lynching cartoon.

4218. Orban. NEW MASSES, Vol. 60, No. (Sept. 17, 1946): cover. Untitled illustration of man chopping down tree with limb from which hangs a [lynching?] noose.

4219. Orozco, Jose Clemente. "American Landscape." NEW MASSES, Vol. 10, No. 10 (March 6, 1934): 17. Illustration of blacks being burned alive.

4220. "O say, can you see . . ." THE CRISIS, Vol. 9, No. 4 (Feb. 1915): 197. Cartoon showing a burning lynch victim.

4221. Park, Marlene. "Lynching and Antilynching: Art and Politics in the 1930s." PROSPECTS: AN ANNUAL OF AMERICAN CULTURAL

STUDIES, Vol. 18 (1993): 311-65.   Scholarly study with several illustrations.

4222. Rapaport, Brooke Kamin. "Melvin Edwards: Lynch Fragments." ART IN AMERICA, Vol. 81, No. 3 (March 1993): 60-65.   See # 4191.

4223. Rea, Gardner. "Death by Filibuster." NEW MASSES, Vol. 26, No. 13 (March 22, 1938): 9.   Lynching cartoon.

4224. Rea, Gardner. "'Of course it's art, Honey, but as a dyed-in-the-wool, states-rights southerner, Ah miss the smell of burnin' flesh.'"   NEW MASSES, Vol. 24, No. 11 (Sept. 7, 1937): 14.   Lynching cartoon.

4225. Rehse. For a cartoon see O'Donnell, T. C., in Chapter V of this bibliography.

4226. Richter, Mischa. "'We are gathered here to protest the unconstitutionality of the anti-lynching bill.'" NEW MASSES, Vol. 26, No. 5 (Jan. 25, 1938): 5.   Cartoon.

4227. Rico, Dan. "Subject for a Senatorial Filibuster." NEW MASSES, Vol. 26, No. 6 (Feb. 1, 1938): 11.   Lynching illustration.

Rivers, Larry. See below SOME AMERICAN HISTORY.

4228. Robinson, Louie. "Charles White: Portrayer of Black Dignity." EBONY, Vol. 22, No. 9 (July 1967): 25-28, 30, 32, 34-36.   See reproduction of his mural with a lynching victim on pp. 26-27.

4229. Romero, Patricia W., ed. For two cartoons see entry in Chapter V of this bibliography.

4230. Rowe, Constance May. "The Vanguard of the Bloody Revolution." INTERRACIAL REVIEW, Vol. 9, No. 10 (Oct. 1936): 155.   Drawing in which radicals rejoice about another lynching; "illustrates the connection between mob violence and subversive movement."

4231. Russo, Michael. "The Lynching."   A 90-by-76 inch oil painting on display at America's Black Holocaust Museum, 2233 N. 4th St., Milwaukee, WI 53212. The museum's founder and director is James Cameron, a black man who was almost lynched in Marion, Indiana, 1930.

4232. Serrano. "'Well, Sheriff, think we can go back now? That lynching must be about over.'" NEW MASSES, Vol. 20, No. 10 (Sept. 1, 1936): 15. This is a cartoon.

4233. Smith, Albert A. "Lords of Lynching." THE CRISIS, Vol. 27, No. 4 (Feb. 1924): 169.   A cartoon.

4234. Smith, Albert A. "The Reason." THE CRISIS, Vol. 19, No. 5 (March 1920): 264.   This cartoon shows lynching as the reason blacks left the South to go to the North.

4235. Soglow, Otto. "Lynching, A Drawing." NEW MASSES, Vol. 3, No. 4 (Aug. 1927): 17.   Title is taken from Contents, page 3.

4236. SOME AMERICAN HISTORY. By Larry Rivers, et al. Introduced by Charles Childs. Houston: Institute for the Arts, Rice Univ., 1971.   Catalog of an exhibition of the same name. See illustrations of Rivers' works of art about lynching (numbers 23, 24, and 29). See also "Listing" in back of catalog for four lynching drawings not illustrated (numbers 25, 26, 27, and 28).

4237. Steinhilber, Walter. [Untitled.] NEW MASSES, Vol. 5, No. 6 (Nov. 1929): 4.   This cartoon shows several men in suits and ties flogging a man. Cutline: "Down South: 'The hell it ain't legal' I says, 'why we got the county prosecutor doin' the floggin'!'"

"This is her first lynching."   See above Marsh, Reginald.

"The Tree and Its Fruit."   See Berg, R. O.

4238. "Uncle Sam Is Tremendously Interested In Disarmament." THE CRISIS, Vol. 23, No. 3 (Jan. 1922): 124.   Cartoon by Lorenzo Harris contrasting U.S. interest in Europe with lack of interest about lynch law in the South.

4239. "The victim, lynched and lying dead, has no appeal."   A cartoon. See "The Invincible Power of Public Opinion" in Chapter V of this bibliography.

4240. Warsager, Hyman. ["The Law.] NEW MASSES, Vol. 10, No. 2 (Jan. 9, 1934): 7.   For title see Park, Marlene, in this bibliography. Lynching cartoon.

4241. Weisberger, Bernard A. "The Immigrant Within." AMERICAN HERITAGE, Vol. 22, No. 1 (Dec. 1970): 30-39, 104.   See p. 34 for painting of lynching as a cause of migration.

4242. "What you have done to the least of these you have done to me." Illustration. See "News Item" in Chapter V of this bibliography.

4243. "The Worm Turns." THE CRUSADER, Vol. 2, No. 3 (Nov. 1919): 5. Two cartoons, one on lynching. Accompanying "Congress, the Lusk Committee and the Radical Leaders," ibid., pp. 5-7 (race riots and lynching).

4244. Wunder, John R. "Law On the Great Plains: An Introduction." GREAT PLAINS QUARTERLY, Vol. 12, No. 2 (Spring 1992): 83-85. Includes illustration of a hanging by vigilantes.

Author Index

Unless otherwise indicated, all numbers refer to entry numbers.

Goldenweiser, A. A., 807
Goldin, Gullie B., 808
Goldman, Eric, 809
Goode, Stephen, 80
Goolrick, William K., 1881
Gordan, John D., III, 3072
Gordon, Arthur, 4007
Gordon, Edward C., 810
Gores, Joe, 4008
Goss, Helen Rocca, 3073
Gould, Benjamin, 1882
Gould, Lewis L., 3074
Governors' Conference, 1133
Gower, Calvin W., 3075
Graham, C. M., 3076
Graham, Marcus, 4005
Graham, Rudy Bee, 4009
Graham, Stephen, 813
Grahame, Orville F., 3077
Grant, Ben O., 3078
Grant, Donald L., 81, 3617
Grant, Donald Lee, 3618
Grant, John H., 815
Graves, John William, 410
Gray, Frank H., 1885
Gray, Henry Martin, 3129
Gray, R. L., 1886
Green, Fletcher Melvin, 82
Green, Paul, 4010
Green, Saul, 4011
Greenbaum, Fred, 3619-20
Greenberg, Jack, 83
Greene, Ward, 4012, 4137
Greenfield, Charles D., 3079
Gregg, Andrew, 3080
Gregg, James E., 1891
Gregg, Richard B., 1892
Gregory, Dick, 2139
Gretlund, Jan Nordby, 4013
Griffey, M. G., 793
Griffin, Farah Jasmine, 84
Griffin, H. L., 260
Griffin, John Howard, 2139
Griffin, Larry J., 1893
Griggs, Sutton, 4014
Grill, Johnpeter Horst, 1894
Grimke, Angelina, 4015, 4130, 4164
Grimke, Francis James, 816
Grimshaw, Allen D., 85

Groom, C. H., 1055
Gropper, Bill, 4197
Gropper, William, 4198
Grossman, James R., 86
Groves, Billy, 817
Gruening, Martha, 1897-98
Gunning, Sandra, 4016
Gunther, John, 1899
Gustafson, Carl Stanley, 3081
Gustafson, Stan, 3082
Gutfeld, Arnon, 1900
Guzman, Jessie P., 1901
Guzman, Jessie Parkhurst, 121, 1902

H., M. A., 819
H., S. E., 1914
Haas, Edward F., 820
Hackett, Chauncey, 1903
Haefele, Walter R., 3083
Hagedorn, H., 1904
Haines, Francis D., Jr., 3084
Hairston, Julie B., 1905
Haldeman-Julius, E., 4017
Haldeman-Julius, Marcet, 1906, 4017
Hale, Richard W., 821
Hall, Elizabeth Jane, 3622
Hall, Jacquelyn, 3623-24
Hall, Jacquelyn Dowd, 3625-28
Hallanan, Walter S., 1907
Hamalian, Leo, 4084
Hamilton, Tullia Kay Brown, 3629
Hamilton, Wade, 3085
Hansberry, Lorraine, 4018
Hansen, Baird, 3086
Hanson, James E., 3087
Harben, William Nathaniel, 4019
Hare, Nathan, 1908
Harman, Everett Radcliff, 1909
Harper, C. W., 3088
Harper, Robert L., 1308
Harper, Suzanne, 87
Harr, John L., 261
Harrington, Oliver W., 1910
Harris, J. William, 1911
Harris, Lorenzo, 4199, 4238
Harris, Mark, 822
Harris, Trudier, 3630, 4020-21,

Subject Index

Unless otherwise indicated, all numbers refer to entry numbers.

Additions

4245.   Bellows, George.   "'The law's too slow!'"   THE CENTURY MAGAZINE, Vol. 106, No. 1 (May 1923): 2.   Drawing of a mob burning a man alive.

4246.   Blight, David W.   "The Martyrdom of Elijah P. Lovejoy."   AMERICAN HISTORY ILLUSTRATED, Vol. 12, No. 7 (Nov. 1977): 20-27.   See p. 22 for reproduction of a page from the Anti-Slavery Almanac (1840) describing and illustrating the lynch burning of the black man named McIntosh in St. Louis in 1836.

4247.   Christmas, Alysa L.   "Lynching and the American Legal System." Senior thesis, History Dept., Princeton Univ., 1981.

4248.   Dixon, Thomas, Jr.   THE LEOPARD'S SPOTS: A ROMANCE OF THE WHITE MAN'S BURDEN--1865-1900.   New York: Doubleday, Page & Co., 1902.   Fiction which includes lynchings on pp. 149-50 and 379-80. See also p. 403.

4249.   Dye, R. Thomas.   "Rosewood, Florida: The Destruction of an African American Community."   THE HISTORIAN, Vol. 58 (Spring 1996): 605-22.

4250.   Froman, Robert.   RACISM.   New York: Delacorte Press, 1972; reprint edition: New York: Dell Pub. Co., 1973.   See pp. 83-86 for lynching.

4251.   Garfield, Michelle Nichole.   "The Anti-Lynching Movement: The National Association for Colored People [sic] and the ASWPL as Vehicles of Reform."   Senior thesis, History Dept., Princeton Univ., 1991.

4252.   Hougen, Harvey Richard,   "The Strange Career of the Kansas Hangman: A History of Capital Punishment in the Sunflower State to 1944." Ph.D. diss., Kansas State Univ., 1979 [sic].   See Diss. Ab. Intl., Vol. 55, No. 8 (Feb. 1995): 2540A. Kansas's 200-plus lynchings indicate values not shown by the few legal executions.

4253.   Hutchinson, Earl Ofari. BETRAYED: A HISTORY OF PRESI-DENTIAL FAILURE TO PROTECT BLACK LIVES.   Boulder, CO: Westview Press, A Division of HarperCollins, 1996.   Begins with the year 1920. Devotes much attention to lynching and anti-lynching legislation in sections on Harding, Coolidge, Hoover, FDR, Truman, and Eisenhower.

4254.   Jackson, Jesse.   LEGAL LYNCHING: RACISM, INJUSTICE AND THE DEATH PENALTY. Bethesda, MD: National Press Books, 1995; New York: Marlowe & Co., 1996. Almost nothing on illegal lynching.

4255.   Johnston, Mary. "Nemesis." THE CENTURY MAGAZINE, Vol. 106, No. 1 (May 1923): 3-22.   Short story about lynching.

4256.   A Lynching in Marion. Film about 1930 lynching of two black men and the near-lynching of James Cameron. Reviewed by Nicole Etcheson in The Journal of American History, Vol. 83, No. 3 (Dec. 1996): 1126-27.

4257.   Marshall, Suzanne. VIOLENCE IN THE BLACK PATCH OF KENTUCKY AND TENNESSEE.   Columbia: Univ. of Missouri Press, 1994.   Includes lynching and, especially, vigilantism.

4258.   Massey, James L. "The Ideology of Lynch Law: A Case Study of Southern Editorial Opinion." QUARTERLY JOURNAL OF IDEOLOGY, Vol. 18 (June 1995): 65-85.

4259.   Miller, Ericka Marie. "The Other Reconstruction: Where Violence and Womanhood Meet in the Writings of Ida B. Wells-Barnett, Angelina Weld Grimke, and Nella Larsen." Ph.D. diss., Stanford Univ., 1996.   See Diss. Ab. Intl., Vol. 56, No. 12 (June 1996): 4775A.   Focus is on lynching.

4260.   [No author. No title; in section titled "The Week."] THE NEW REPUBLIC, Vol. 79, No. 1020 (June 20, 1934): 139.   Protests weakening of the federal anti-lynching bill.

4261.   Ryan, Perry T. LEGAL LYNCHING: THE PLIGHT OF SAM JENNINGS. Breckwood, Hardinburg, KY: P. T. Ryan, 1989.

4262.   Samuels, Charles, and Samuels, Louise.   NIGHT FELL ON GEORGIA. New York: Dell Publishing, 1956.   Leo Frank case.

4263.   Seltzer, O. C.   <u>Vigilante Ways</u>.   Thomas Gilcrease Institute of American History and Art, Tulsa, Oklahoma.   A painting showing horsemen riding away from lynching victim hanging from a tree.   Reproduced on cover of Thomas J. Dimsdale, <u>The Vigilantes of Montana</u> (Norman: Univ. of Oklahoma Press, 1953).

4264.   "Straight from the Shoulder and the Heart."   THE INDEPENDENT, Vol. 46, No. 2392 (Oct. 4, 1894): 12-13 (1280-81).   Editorial on lynching. Several quotations from other sources, including part of George C. Holt's recent paper "Lynching and Mobs," which was read to the American Social Science Association.

4265.   Whipple, Dan. "To Die on Good Friday." WILD WEST [Leesburg, VA], Vol. 9, No. 3 (Oct. 1996): 36-41, 86.   Charlie Woodard [<u>sic</u>] was lynched at Casper, Wyoming, in 1902.

About the Compiler

NORTON H. MOSES is Professor of History at Montana State University–Billings. His fields of specialization include nineteenth-century United States history, the history of England, and the history of American presidential assassinations.

ISBN 0-313-30177-8

90000>

EAN

9 780313 301773

HARDCOVER BAR CODE